Byzantium and the Emergence of Muslim-Turkish Anatolia, ca. 1040–1130

The arrival of the Seljuk Turks in Anatolia forms an indispensable part of modern Turkish discourse on national identity, but Western scholars, by contrast, have rarely included the Anatolian Turks in their discussions about the formation of European nations or the transformation of the Near East. The Turkish penetration of Byzantine Asia Minor is primarily conceived of as a conflict among empires, sedentary and nomadic groups, and religious and ethnic entities. This book proposes a new narrative, which begins with the waning influence of Constantinople and Cairo over large parts of Anatolia and the Byzantine-Muslim borderlands, as well as the failure of the nascent Seljuk sultanate to supplant them as a leading supra-regional force. In both Byzantine Anatolia and regions of the Muslim heartlands, local elites and regional powers came to the fore as holders of political authority and rivals in incessant power struggles. Turkish warrior groups quickly assumed a leading role in this process, not because of their raids and conquests, but because of their intrusion into pre-existing social networks. They exploited administrative tools and local resources and thus gained the acceptance of local rulers and their subjects. Nuclei of lordships came into being, which could evolve into larger territorial units. There was no Byzantine decline or Turkish triumph, but rather, the driving force of change was the successful interaction between these two spheres.

Alexander Daniel Beihammer received his PhD from the University of Vienna and is a member of the Institut für Österreichische Geschichtsforschung. From 2001 to 2015, he taught at the University of Cyprus and is currently Associate Professor of Byzantine History at the University of Notre Dame. He has published widely on Byzantine official documents, diplomacy, and cross-cultural communication between Byzantium and the Muslim world, as well as on Byzantine-Latin contacts and mutual perception in the crusader states and the Eastern Mediterranean.

Birmingham Byzantine and Ottoman Studies

Birmingham Byzantine and Ottoman Studies is devoted to the history, culture and archaeology of the Byzantine and Ottoman worlds of the East Mediterranean region from the fifth to the twentieth century. It provides a forum for the publication of research completed by scholars from the Centre for Byzantine, Ottoman and Modern Greek Studies at the University of Birmingham, and those with similar research interests.

For a full list of titles in this series, please visit https://www.routledge.com/series/BBOS

The Emperor Theophilos and the East, 829–842
Court and frontier in Byzantium during the last phase of iconoclasm
Juan Signes Codoñer

Rebuilding Anatolia after the Mongol Conquest
Islamic architecture in the lands of rum, 1240–1330
Patricia Blessing

Imperial Lineages and Legacies in the Eastern Mediterranean
Recording the imprint of Roman, Byzantine and Ottoman rule
Edited by Rhoads Murphey

Byzantium and the Emergence of Muslim-Turkish Anatolia, ca. 1040–1130
Alexander Daniel Beihammer

Centre for Byzantine, Ottoman and Modern Greek Studies
University of Birmingham

Byzantium and the Emergence of Muslim-Turkish Anatolia, ca. 1040–1130

Alexander Daniel Beihammer

Routledge
Taylor & Francis Group
LONDON AND NEW YORK

First published 2017
by Routledge
2 Park Square, Milton Park, Abingdon, Oxon OX14 4RN

and by Routledge
711 Third Avenue, New York, NY 10017

Routledge is an imprint of the Taylor & Francis Group, an informa business

British Library Cataloguing-in-Publication Data
A catalogue record for this book is available from the British Library

Library of Congress Cataloging-in-Publication Data
A catalog record for this book has been requested

ISBN: 978-1-138-22959-4 (hbk)
ISBN: 978-1-315-27103-3 (ebk)

Typeset in Baskerville
by codeMantra

Birmingham Byzantine and Ottoman Studies Volume 20

Contents

List of maps

Acknowledgments

Tarih yazmak, tarih yapmak kadar mühimdir.
Yazan, yapana sadık kalmazsa
değişmeyen hakikat insanlığı şaşırtacak bir mahiyet alır
Mustafa Kemal Atatürk

Ο τελευταίος χρόνος είν' αυτός. Ο τελευταίος των Γραικών
αυτοκρατόρων είν' αυτός. Κι αλίμονον
τι θλιβερά που ομιλούν πλησίον του.
Εν τη απογνώσει του, εν τη οδύνη
ο Κυρ Θεόφιλος Παλαιολόγος
λέγει «Θέλω θανείν μάλλον ή ζην».

Α Κυρ Θεόφιλε Παλαιολόγο,
Πόσον καημό του γένους μας, και πόση εξάντλησι
Οι τραγικές σου πέντε λέξεις περιείχαν.
Constantine Kavafis

My interest in Byzantine-Turkish contacts and the political transformation of Anatolia from Byzantine territories into Muslim-Turkish principalities goes back to 2007 when I began working on a series of articles on the perception of the Seljuk Turks in Byzantine historiography. My student years at the Institut für Österreichische Geschichtsforschung (1992–1997) made me aware of the fact that the Anatolian Turks share many commonalities with all those entities lying at the core of the genesis of modern European nations, although these Turks have hardly ever been included in the relevant scholarly discussions. The current situation in Cyprus, where I had the privilege to teach over the past 15 years, bears a certain resemblance to what happened in medieval Anatolia on a much larger scale. Political and ideological discourses, however, tend to obfuscate the realities of ongoing transformative processes.

During my research, I had access to the resources of a number of excellent libraries. This book profited especially from the Turkish collection of the University of Cyprus, the library of the Institut für Byzantinistik und Neogräzistik at the University of Vienna, the Austrian National Library, and Hesburgh Library at the University of Notre Dame. Savvas Neocleous (Cyprus), Miriam

Salzmann (Mainz), and Christopher Schabel (Cyprus) read drafts of the introduction and chapters 1–5 and contributed numerous linguistic improvements. Charles Yost (Notre Dame) undertook a thorough linguistic revision of chapters 6–9. An anonymous reader kindly provided me with additional linguistic comments on chapters 1–6. Another anonymous reader called my attention to the value of archaeological evidence. Myrto Veikou (Uppsala) was extremely helpful in discussing issues of modern archaeology with me and provided me with numerous bibliographical references. Theodore Galanopoulos prepared the maps and Evgenia Chatziloizou created the index for this volume. I am deeply indebted to all of them, but, naturally, all errors of fact and interpretation are my own.

I also thank Gabriel Pappas, who offered manifold support in Cyprus and on trips in Turkey. My special gratitude goes to John Haldon (Princeton) and Rhoads Murphey (Birmingham) for accepting this book in the Birmingham Byzantine and Ottoman Studies series, as well as to Michael Greenwood at Taylor & Francis, Routledge, for his generous support during the production of this book. The final stage of my work on this project coincided with my move from Cyprus to the University of Notre Dame. I am extremely grateful to John van Engen, Daniel Hobbins, Hildegund Müller, and Thomas Noble, as well as Charles and Lauren Yost for their much appreciated encouragement and support during my first year in the American Midwest.

To my deepest regret, my friend Jean Schotz did not live to see the completion of this book. Those who know his work may assess how much I owe to him as a constant source of inspiration. This book is dedicated with love to Ibrahim, Süleyman, Roxelane, Danai, Wilhelm, and, above all, Christiana and Aristotelis.

Notre Dame and Nicosia,
May 2016

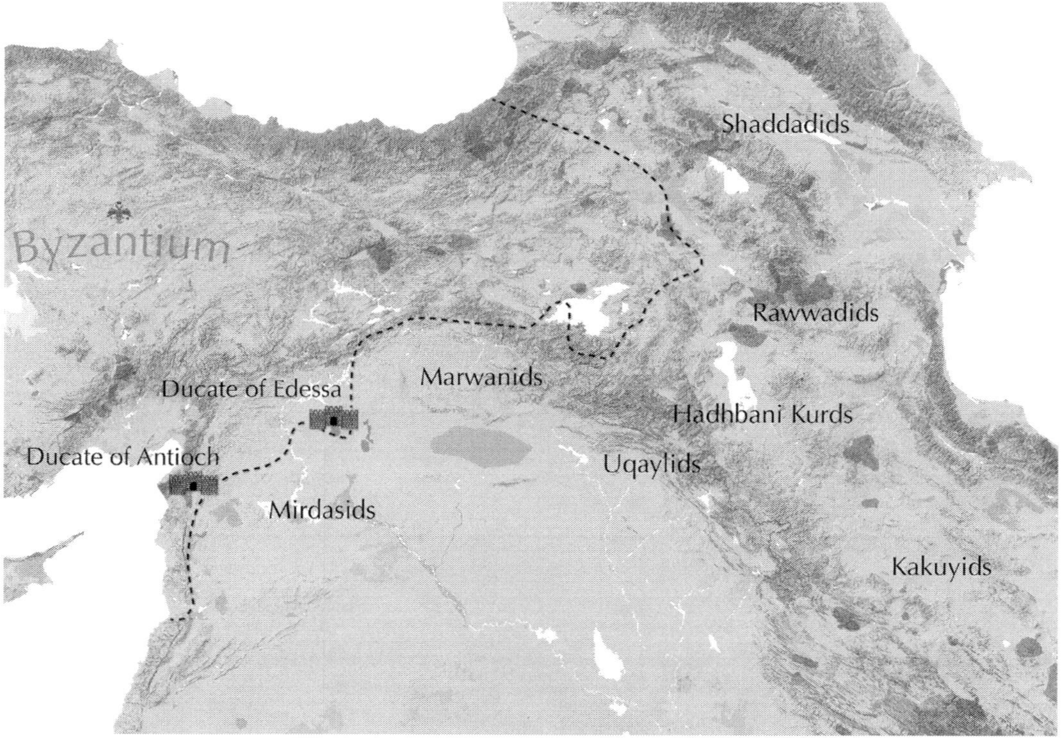

Map 1 Muslim emirates in the eastern borderland in the early eleventh century

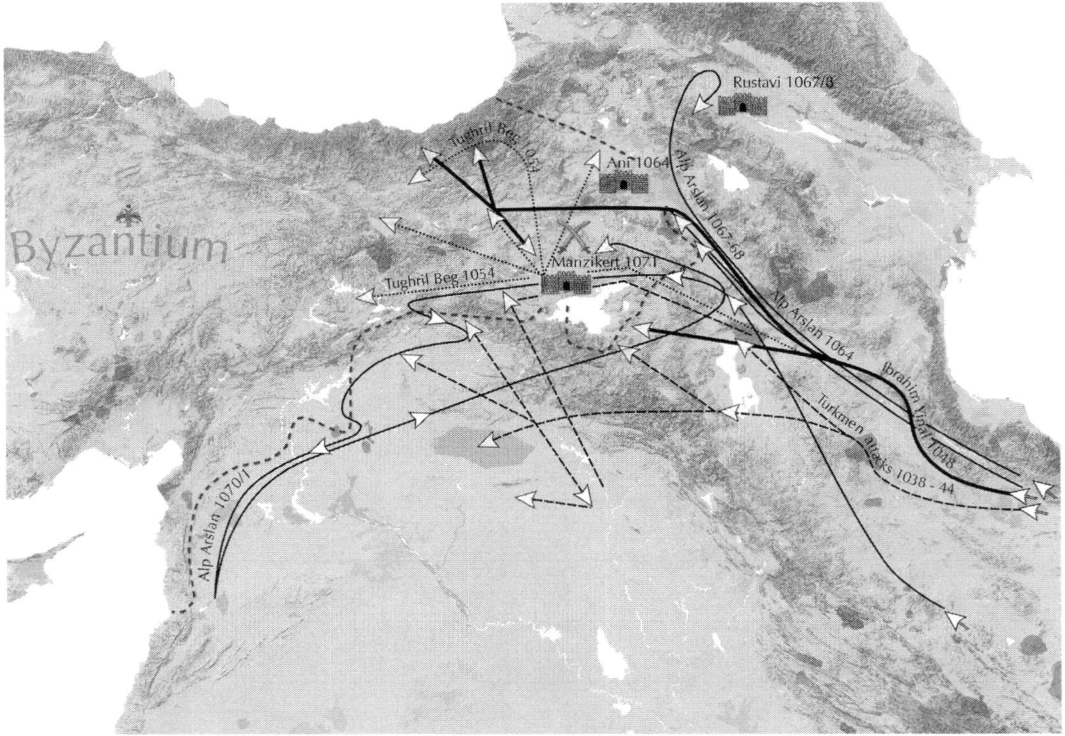

Map 2 Turkmen attacks and the Seljuk campaigns in the reign of Tughril Beg and Alp Arslān

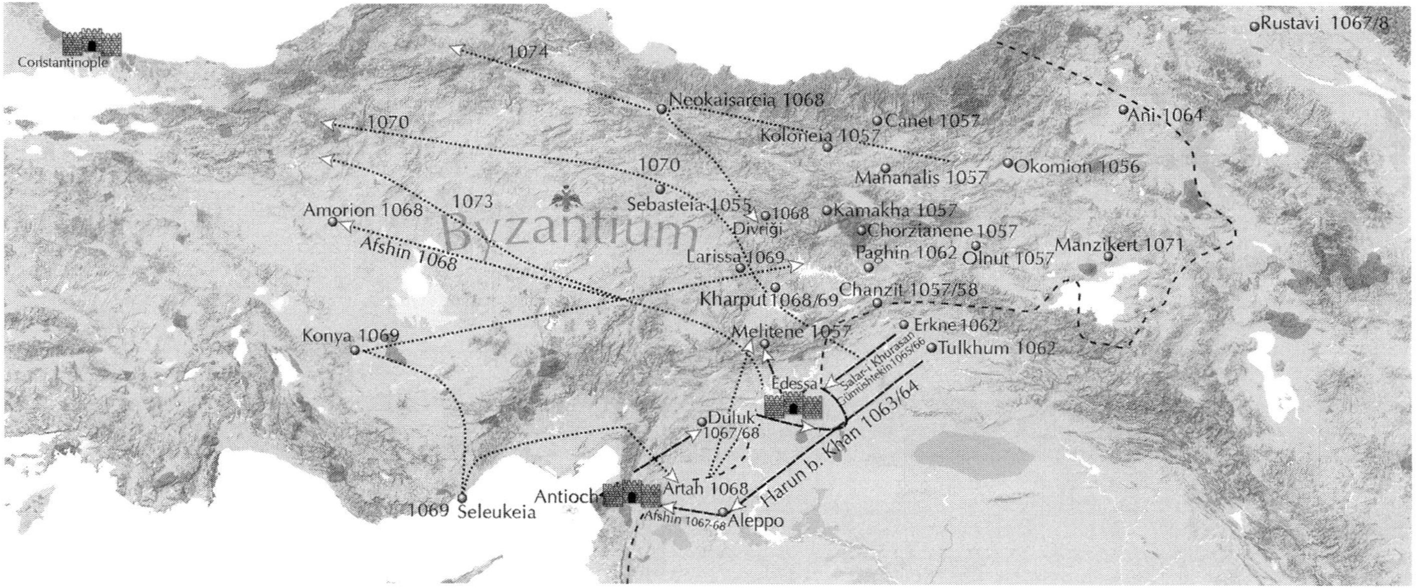

Map 3 Turkish raids on Byzantine territory during the 1050s and 1060s

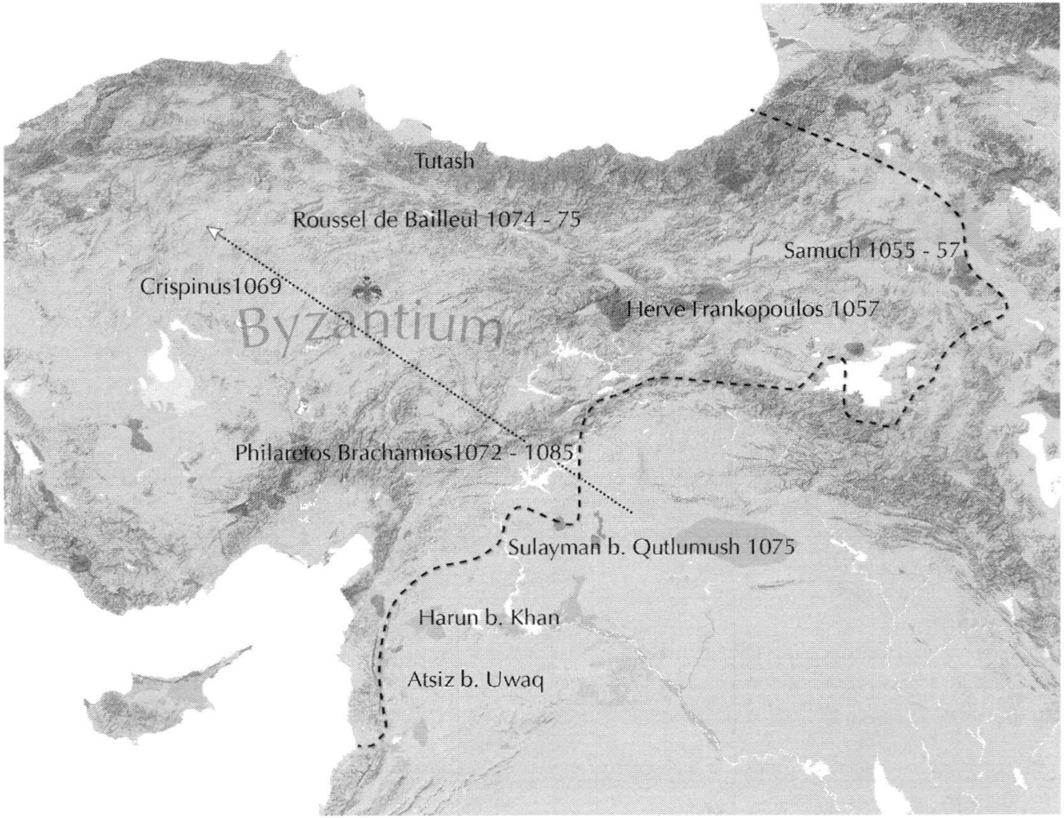

Map 4 Frankish mercenary commanders and Turkish warlords

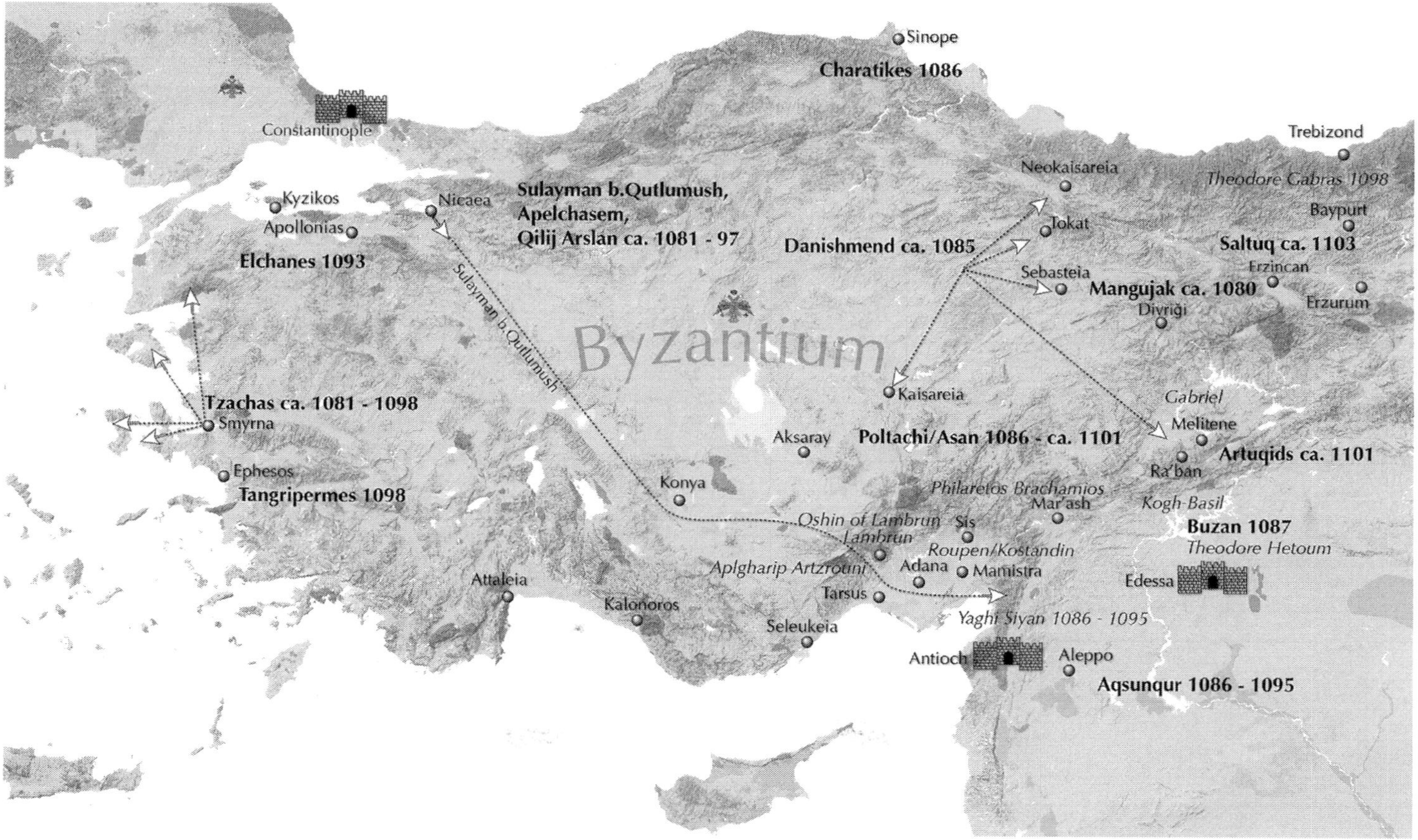

Map 5 Turkish lordships in Asia Minor in the 1080s and 1090s

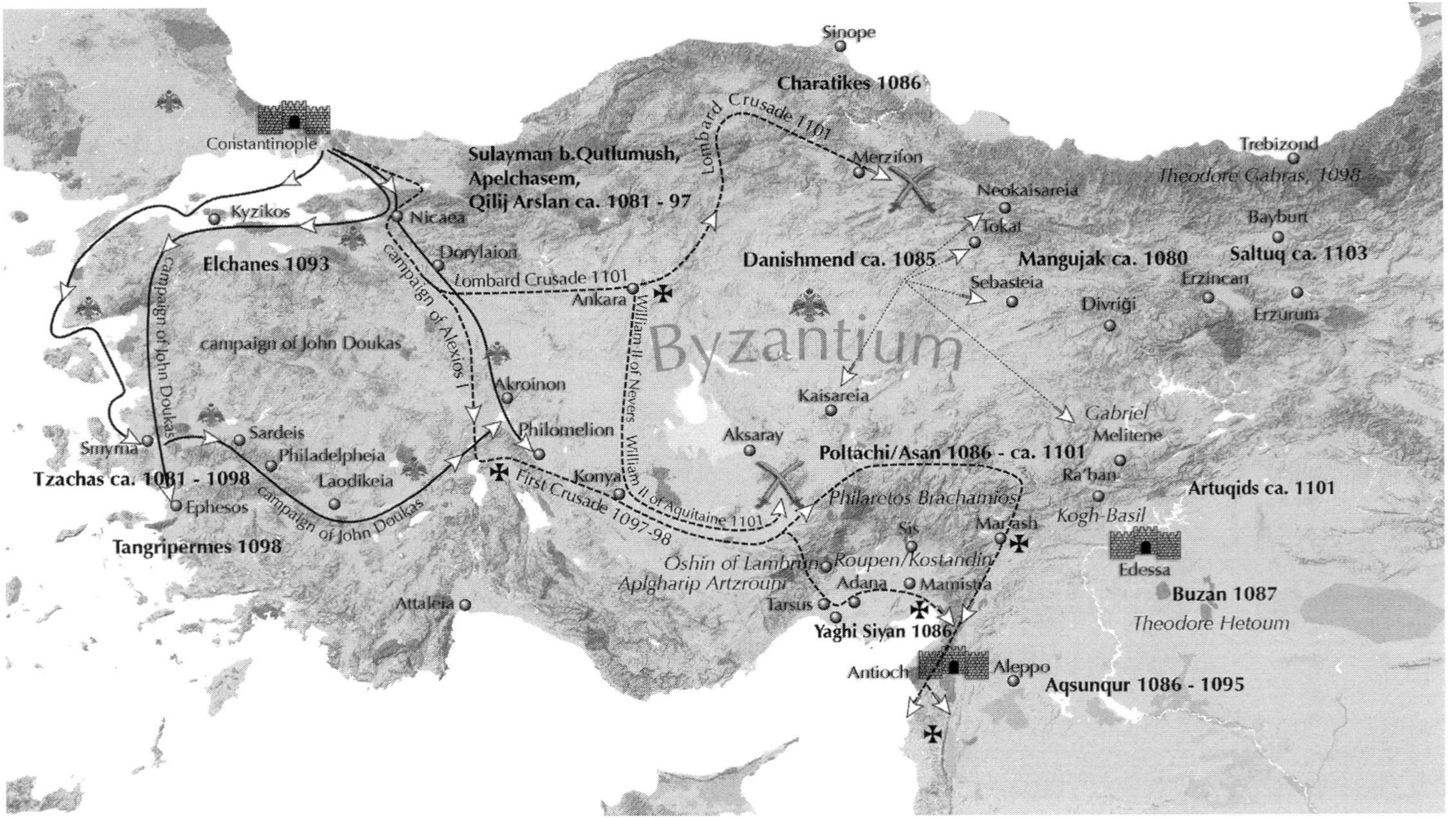

Map 6 Byzantium and the Muslim-Turkish emirates in Asia Minor in the time of the First Crusade

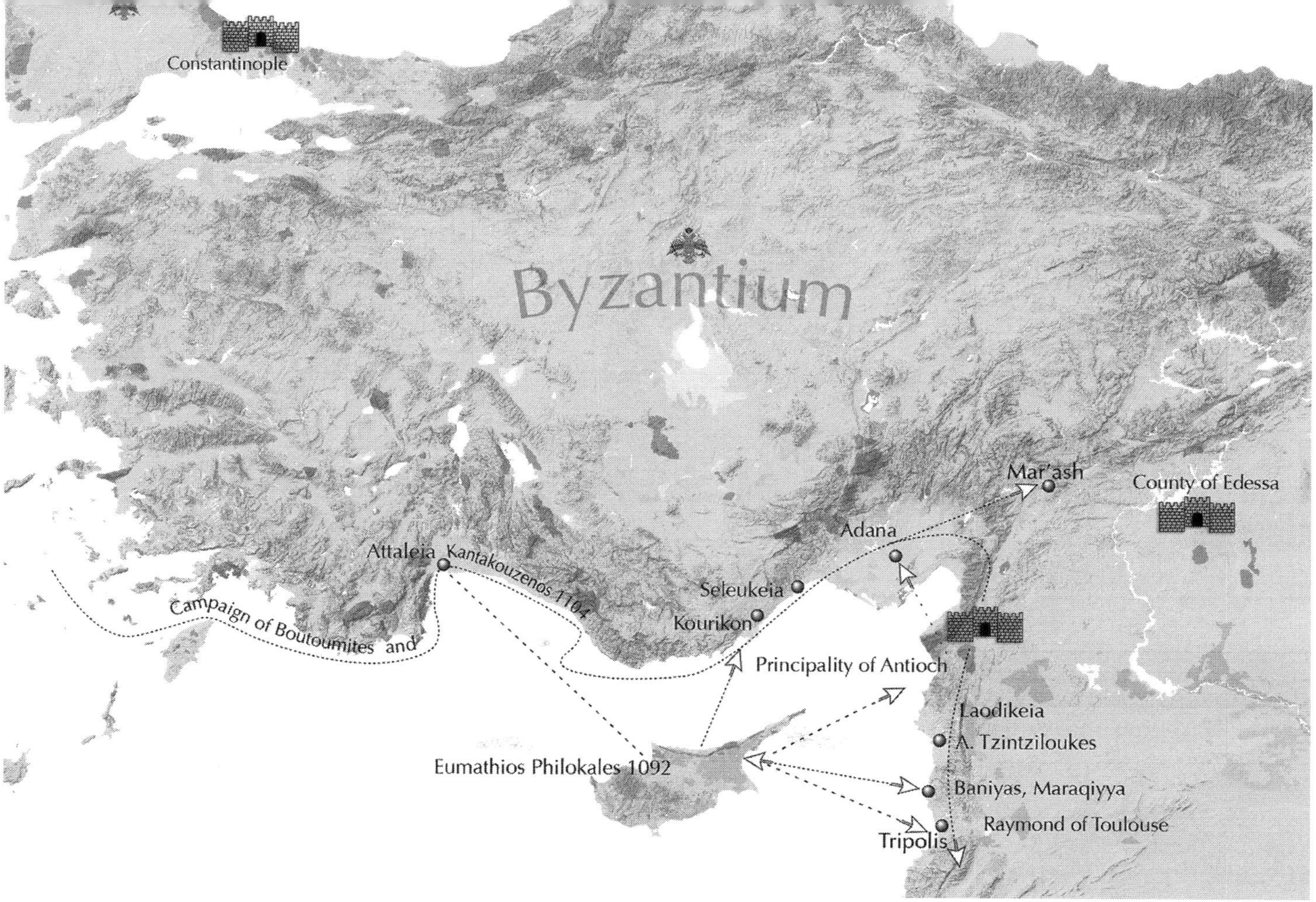

Map 7 The southern coastland of Asia Minor in the time after the First Crusade

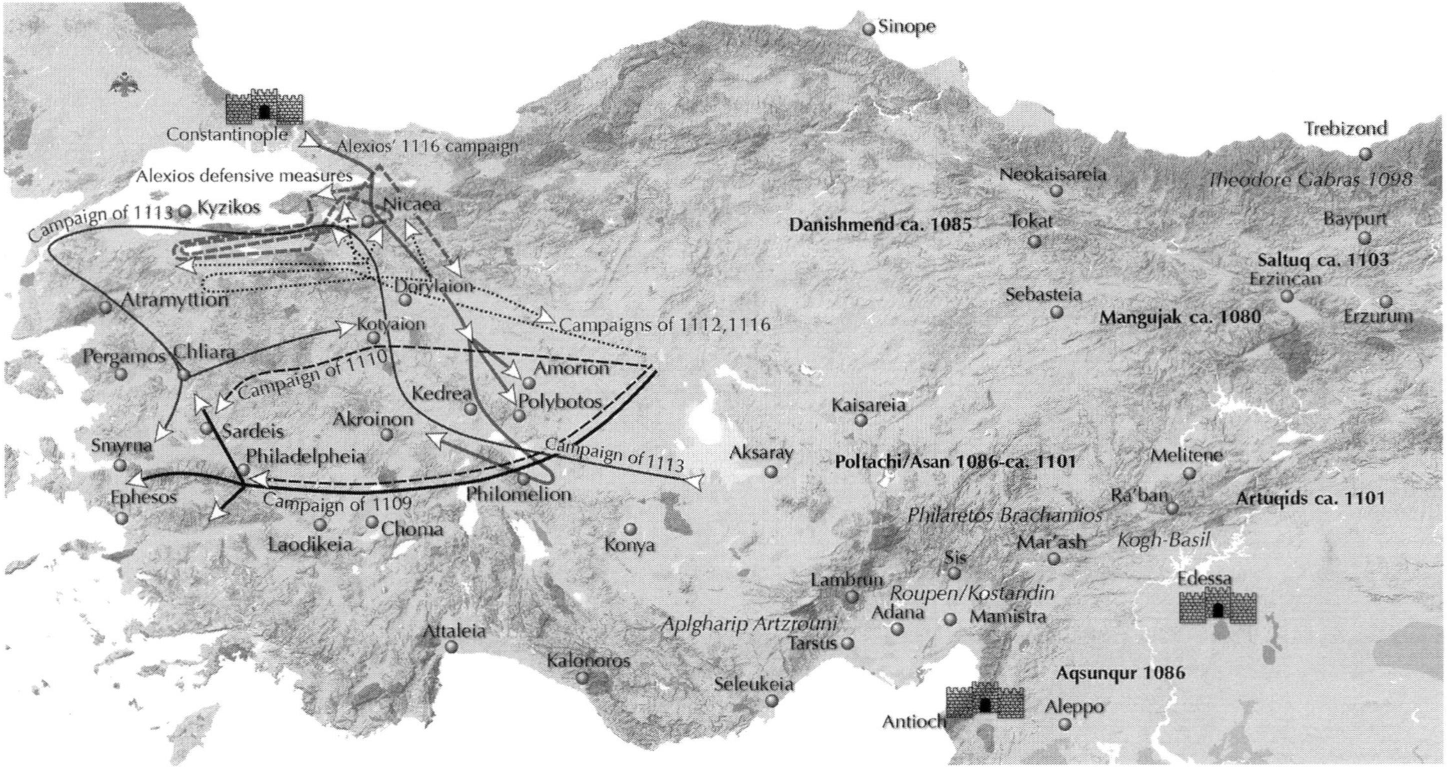

Map 8 Seljuk campaigns and Byzantine defensive measures in western Asia Minor in the years 1109–16

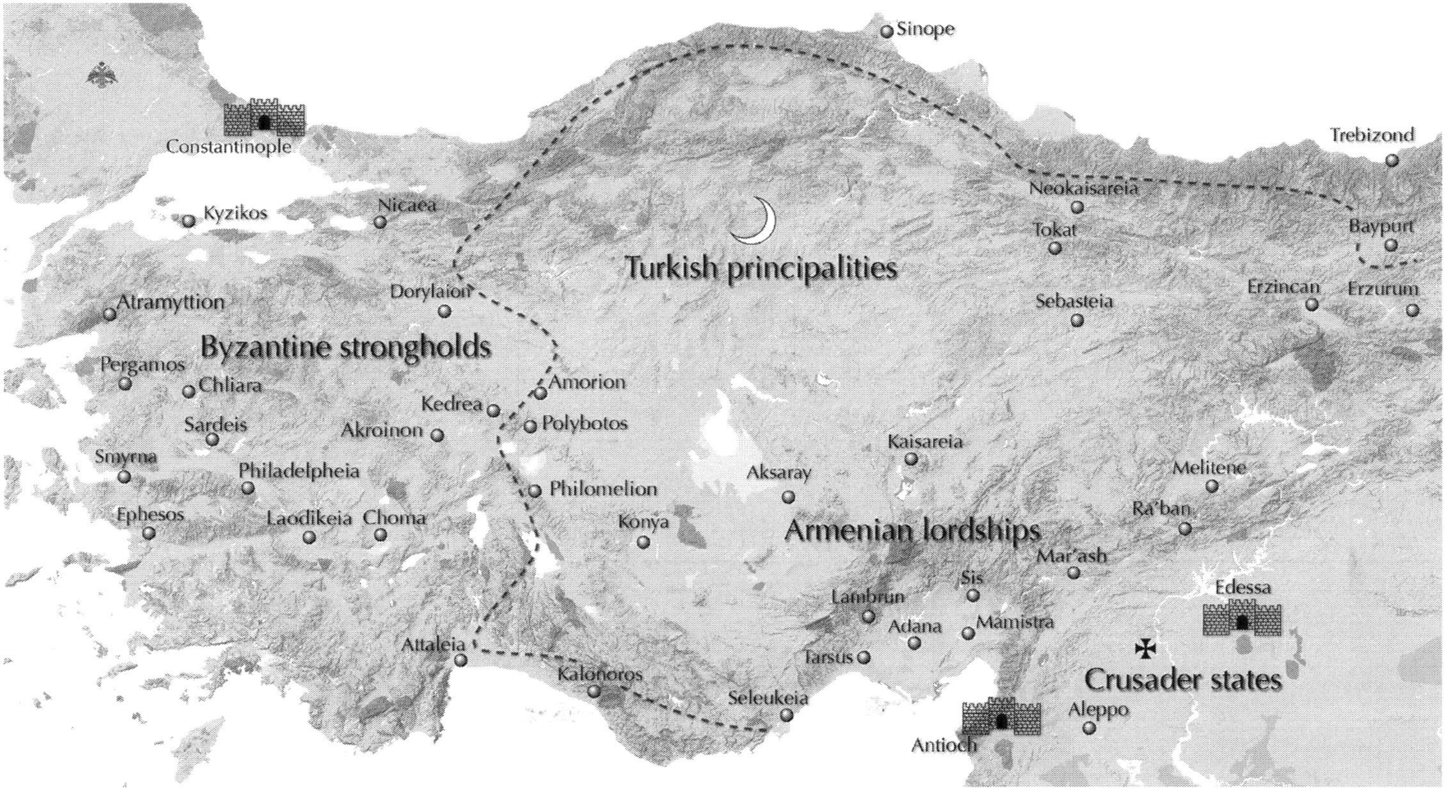

Map 9 Asia Minor in about 1120

Introduction

Conquests, modern nations, and lost fatherlands

The topic and its disciplinary perspectives

Anna Komnene, the well-educated and highly gifted daughter of Emperor Alexios I, describes a rather insignificant episode, which took place in Asia Minor among numerous other troublesome events during the early 1090s, in the following manner:

> When the message arrived from the East that the guardian of Nicaea, whom the Persians usually call *satrapes,* whereas the Turks, who nowadays think like the Persians, label him *ameras*, Apelchasem, was preparing his arms for a campaign against Nikomedeia, he [i.e., the emperor] sent these men [i.e., a newly arrived detachment of 500 horsemen under Robert of Flanders] in order to guard the region.[1]

The terminological and historical issues explicitly or implicitly raised in this passage pretty much summarize what this book will address. Anna, who wrote her father's encomiastic biography approximately 40 to 50 years after the aforementioned event, was one of the first Byzantine intellectuals to give us an account of how the elite of Constantinople perceived and handled the appearance of Turkish invaders in the Propontis coastland situated at an alarmingly small distance from the imperial city. No doubt, the emperor and his closest advisers and officers were on alert; a fierce clash was lying ahead. But who were these enemies, who were somehow associated with the cultural tradition of the Persians and used their language, although the title assigned to their chief was Arabic? It is not clear whether the author was aware of this fact, but what she actually alluded to in this passage is a highly complicated process of migration and acculturation, which through a long series of conflicts eventually resulted in the emergence of a new cultural and political entity. This entity was certainly not exclusively Turkish, nor Persian, nor Muslim, nor Greek, nor Byzantine, nor Christian, but included elements of all these substrates. Anna and her compatriots at some point had to admit that they had failed to expel these barbarians from their territories. Hence, they were forced to recognize them in their capacity as a considerable political factor and to seek for modes of co-existence.

This book concerns itself with the earliest stage in the penetration of Asia Minor by the so-called Seljuk Turks, their first encounter with the Byzantine-Christian sphere, and the beginnings of their gradual transformation from rather superficially Islamized warrior groups and nomadic shepherds to state founders and rulers of durable principalities based on distinct ideological and organizational patterns as well as a Muslim religious identity. With respect to the geographical space, this study alternately uses the terms "Asia Minor" and "Anatolia" as synonyms designating the peninsula of Asia Minor along with the adjacent regions of Upper Mesopotamia and Armenia, which in the time following the death of Emperor Basil II (1025) formed part of Byzantium's eastern provinces.[2] In comparison with the Republic of Turkey, the empire's borderline ran a little further north along the Anti-Taurus Mountains and in some parts of the Caucasus further east than that of the modern state, but as a whole, there is an amazing coincidence with the external boundaries of what is now called Güneydoğu and Doğu Anadolu, i.e., "Southeastern" and "Eastern Anatolia." Hence, geographical terms are largely employed in their modern sense but do not intend to suggest any ahistorical continuities. Chronologically, our analysis starts with the first incursions into the empire's eastern borderland in the middle of the eleventh century and traces the developments up to about 1130. By that time, the Seljuk sultanate of Konya, the Dānishmandid principality in Cappadocia, and a number of minor emirates in Upper Mesopotamia and the Armenian highlands had crystallized into consistent political powers. Likewise, a long strip of land stretching from the Taurus Mountains north of Attaleia across the fertile regions of the western river valleys and the fringes of the Anatolian plateau up to the mountainous areas of Paphlagonia had turned into a broad Byzantine-Turkish and/or Christian-Muslim contact and/or conflict zone, which proved to be of astonishing durability up to the time of Mongol rule in Anatolia in the second half of the thirteenth century. Two years before Alexios I's death in 1118, the Byzantine army successfully expelled the last major invading force, which was pushing as far as the Propontis coastland. At the same time, the emperor refrained from advancing towards Konya. The *status quo* reached on this occasion, some minor changes of local significance notwithstanding, by and large persisted until the rise of the Ottomans. In this sense, it can be said that the 1120s signify the end of the first Turkish expansion in Asia Minor. The transition process evolving over the preceding decades, no doubt, formed the most crucial turning point in the history of Byzantium's eastern territories since the Islamic conquests of the seventh century and had a deep and long-lasting impact on the entire Middle East.

Viewed in the broader context of the great migration movements between the Eurasian steppe and the Mediterranean basin from the fourth century onwards, it is important to note that the developments in Anatolia, though on a much smaller scale, have many things in common with the historical processes leading to the transformation of the Roman world, the creation of the so-called barbarian successor kingdoms in Europe, and the nomadic empires between the Danube and the Caspian Sea, as well as the emergence of the Arab-Muslim world. It is evident that the various aspects of the Byzantine-Seljuk encounter in Anatolia can and should be scrutinized with the aid of similar methodologies and analytical tools as have been applied to the aforementioned subject areas, which have adopted concepts and models originating from historical anthropology, ethnography, and acculturation theories. Especially since the 1970s, the barbarian migrations in early medieval Europe have internationally developed into a booming field with an increasing amount of scholarly production.[3] A number of groundbreaking studies published in the 1980s and 1990s stimulated a similar revision of views and source critical methods with respect to the emergence of Islam and the transformation of the Near East.[4] In contrast, the change from Byzantine-Christian to Turkish-Muslim Anatolia largely remained the domain of nationalistic historiographical discourses in the Turkish Republic.[5] Apart from a few important but rather isolated exceptions, this topic did not find much attention among European and American historians of Byzantium and the Muslim world. In part, this neglect may be due to the academic traditions of scholarly disciplines, which are still very much in line with the continuity concepts of modern nation states and the clear-cut divides set by cultural, religious, and linguistic barriers. For a long time, there was hardly any room for mixed and hybrid entities that fail to meet these criteria of classification. For modern scholarly discussions dealing with the medieval origins of the nation states, the roots of a common European identity, and the clash between Islam and Christendom, the Goths, Franks, and Muslim Arabs certainly offer many more points of reference than the Anatolian Turks. It is only in the past few years that European historians began to subject traditional views to critical scrutiny and to re-examine the linguistically highly diversified source material of medieval Anatolia under the light of new methodological approaches. Various thought-provoking studies pointing out new perspectives and trajectories of investigation have recently been published, but none of these works concerns itself with the early Turkish penetration of Asia Minor.

The co-existence, mutual permeation, and gradual merging of two previously distinct cultural and political spheres are characteristic features penetrating all levels of the historical development that began with the arrival of the Turks in the mid-eleventh century. It would be a serious over-simplification, however, if, as is often implied in the older scholarly literature, these entities were considered self-contained and homogenous blocks. Byzantine Asia Minor, no doubt, had a strong component of what may nowadays be called Orthodox Hellenism, which manifested itself in the widespread use of Greek as literary and administrative language, the persistence of Constantinopolitan institutions and administrative structures, a substrate of imperial traditions, a well-established ecclesiastical organization, and a Roman-Christian cultural identity.[6] On the other hand, there was a powerful aristocracy rooted in the provincial towns and domains of Anatolia, which possessed a marked local identity and up to the tenth and eleventh centuries set free strong centrifugal dynamics and autonomous tendencies. Moreover, the empire's eastern provinces always were the homeland of a variety of ethnic-religious minorities. With the empire's expansionist policy and the annexation of large strips of land in the tenth and eleventh century, the Armenians and the Syriac Christians became the strongest population groups in the East. In the late eleventh-century, remnants of the old Armenian nobility set about building up new semi-independent power bases and lordships.[7]

The Turkish groups, at the time of their arrival in Anatolia, combined cultural and linguistic features of the Turkic peoples of the central Asian steppes, a lifestyle of nomadic pastoralists, religious tenets ranging from Sunni Islam to syncretistic popular beliefs, and political, cultural, and ideological attitudes adopted in the time of their migrations from the Persian-Muslim milieu of Iran. The term "Seljuk Turks" has been commonly accepted as the collective name designating the Turkish-Muslim population of Pre-Ottoman Anatolia. Apart from misleadingly extending a clan's or dynasty's name to an entire ethnic group, this term implies a kind of political or ethnic homogeneity that never existed during the period in question. Just as all the other nomad groups and tribal confederations making their appearance in Southeast Europe, the Eurasian steppes, and the Middle East did, these people formed a conglomeration of very different ethnic and social elements. In their core, they were loosely connected groups of Islamized Oghuz Turks, frequently identified as "Turkmens," who under the leadership of the Seljuk clan, one of the chief lineages of the Oghuz tribes, had spread from Transoxania to Khurāsān and other regions of Iran as far as the central Muslim lands of Iraq and Syria.[8] Although the available data are rather scarce, it is quite evident that the Turkish warrior groups, in their structural and organizational patterns, must have adopted various characteristics of the Karakhanid and Ghaznawid armies, in the service of which they had been educated and fought for a long time. To a great extent, the Seljuk expansion was carried out and supported by confederations of subordinate or independent Turkmen warriors, at times with a certain tendency towards recalcitrant behavior. The first Seljuk chiefs, however, probably from an early stage onwards, combined their own Turkish tribal traditions with elements adopted from the eastern Iranian Muslim states. Thus, they included in their forces contingents of slave soldiers (*ghulām*), auxiliary troops provided by vassal lords, and voluntaries from various regions. It is a matter of debate when the Seljuk leaders began to build up regular troops of professional soldiers paid by "land grants" (*iqṭā'*), a system that is traditionally ascribed to Sultan Malikshāh's renowned vizier Niẓām al-Mulk.[9] Due to the loose structures of tribal coalitions and the manifold tensions among the leading members of the Seljuk clan, the internal cohesion among these forces could not have been very strong, and their bonds of allegiance with their commanders were rather unstable and short-lived. This manifested itself in frequent revolts, internal power struggles, and attempts of warrior groups to escape the centralizing control of the Seljuk sultanate.

The penetration of Anatolia started in the early 1040s with sporadic raids of independently operating Turkmen groups and some large-scale campaigns in the Armenian borderlands initiated by the leaders of the Seljuk clan. In the 1070s the Turkish warriors spread from the Upper Euphrates region and the valleys south of the Pontic Mountains over the rural areas of the central Anatolian plateau as far as the Bithynian coastland. Simultaneously, the disintegration of Byzantine military and administrative structures was progressing considerably as a result of internal power struggles and the Turkish incursions. A temporary strengthening of recalcitrant mercenary troops and a dangerous growth of various seditious movements aiming to gain the imperial throne characterized the political setting. Under these circumstances, the Turks turned from invaders into powerful players operating within a patchwork of numerous competing forces. From the early 1080s onwards, first signs of a permanent establishment in fortified places and urban centers can be perceived. The First Crusade and the ensuing deployment of Byzantine troops in 1097–1098 caused the violent displacement of Turkish groups from the western coastal areas to the central Anatolian plateau and the loss of territories in Cilicia, Antioch, and the Euphrates region. But already in 1101 a remarkable re-stabilization of Turkish lordships, which began to take the shape of firmly established principalities in a smaller but better-controlled region stretching from the western fringes of the Anatolian plateau up to the Armenian highlands, can be observed. In the following decades, these nascent state-like entities developed administrative structures, mechanisms of legitimization, and a distinct religious and ideological identity. As such, they did not supplant a preexisting Byzantine substrate but grew out of a conflation of various indigenous and newly imported structures.

Generally speaking, the scholarly literature treats the topics just outlined in a highly selective and one-sided manner, either giving preference to certain categories of primary sources or explicitly adopting a Byzantine or a Turkish point of view. This overall tendency by and large corresponds to the modern division of the scholarly disciplines of Byzantine studies *vs.* Turkish or Islamic studies. A further subdivision is due to the long-lasting impact of various discourses of national historiography and the collective memories, stereotypes, and interpretations associated with them. The Turkish scholarly tradition, which took shape in the years following the foundation of the Republic of Turkey and produced a great number of remarkable works up to the 1970s, stands in clear opposition to the seminal work of the Greek-American historian Spyros Vryonis on the *Decline of Medieval Hellenism in Asia Minor* published in 1971. On account of its references to nationalistic views, including the idea of a pureblooded Greek-Orthodox ethnic stratum in medieval Asia Minor, the latter became a sort of standard work expressing prevailing academic and popular opinions in Greece and nationalistically oriented philhellenic circles. In Europe, the works of the French historian Claude Cahen on the formation of pre-Ottoman Turkey remained a brilliant achievement, presenting a more balanced version of Turkish continuity concepts, but until recently did not find many successors further delving into the various topics treated in his studies. Western scholars have done further substantial work on the Great Seljuk dynasty and its branches and institutions in the Muslim central lands. For many decades, work on the Seljuk Turks in Asia Minor was completely outweighed by a strong trend towards crusader studies and, to a lesser degree, by an interest in the internal developments of Byzantium during the eleventh century and the Komnenian period. In this context, the Seljuks, in one way or another, were constantly touched upon but hardly formed a subject *per se*. In what follows, we attempt to present the theoretical assumptions and interpretations of the relevant scholarly traditions in more detail. We will draw conclusions regarding the challenges posed by them with respect to a thorough re-examination of the first Byzantine-Turkish encounter in Asia Minor and its aftermath.

The Byzantine viewpoint

Much of the twentieth-century scholarly discourse on Byzantium on the eve of the Seljuk expansion is dominated by the idea of a profound internal crisis in the decades following the death of Emperor Basil II in December 1025. Irrespective of the widely diverging views concerning the nature and extent of the alleged decline, Byzantinists usually resort to this explanation in order to elucidate the reasons for the successful penetration of Asia Minor by the Turkish invaders, a region that in the context of traditional confrontation models is frequently conceived of as a well-defended bulwark resisting the onslaught of Islam for more than four centuries.[10] Although starting from a diametrically opposed perspective, they paradoxically arrive at similar conclusions as modern Turkish scholars, namely that the eastern provinces with their crumbling socio-political and military structures were ripe for conquest. In the context of discussions about the internal situation of the empire, historians of Byzantium normally confine themselves to equating the Turks with all other hostile forces threatening the empire in the eleventh century, such as the Pechenegs in the Danube region and the Normans in southern Italy and the Adriatic coastland. Thus, the transition of Byzantine to Turkish Asia Minor is largely reduced to the classical binary opposition of indigenous defenders *vs.* aggressive foreign invaders, who because of the empire's political and military decay were simply too strong to be stopped. This mono-causal explanation does not leave much room for a more comprehensive analysis of the various manners of intrusion and integration, through which Turkish warriors and nomads became permanent inhabitants of Anatolia, founded states, and developed forms of co-existence with the indigenous population. Chapters 1 and 2 of the present study develop a different approach by focusing on the complex interplay of different factors, such as the changing administrative and military structures of the Byzantine state, the raiding activities of Turkmen groups, and the expansion of the Seljuk sultanate.

The sharp contrast between the Byzantine state at the height of its territorial expansion, as it appeared at the time of Emperor Basil II's death, and a dwindling empire threatened on all sides by invading forces, as was the case in the years after Alexios I's rise to power in April 1081, naturally evokes associations of a total breakdown. The basic features of this idea can already be found in Ferdinand Chalandon's monograph on Alexios I (1900) and in Joseph Laurent's study on Byzantium and the Seljuk Turks in western Asia Minor (1913):[11] The landowning military aristocracy in Asia Minor was in rivalry with the European aristocrats and, above all, with the elite civilian functionaries represented by the senate of Constantinople. This opposition resulted in an estrangement between the army, which several decades earlier had been the moving force of the expansion in the East, and the central government.[12] In addition, special emphasis is placed on the personal shortcomings of emperors and high-ranking dignitaries. In Laurent's view, for instance, all emperors between 1025 and 1057 were either of advanced age, of poor health, or dominated by women. Likewise, the military forces, though sufficient in number, due to personal ambitions and bonds of allegiance, were frequently entrusted to inept officers, eunuchs, and Armenian noblemen.[13] The strength of the armed forces, he further argues, was relatively stable until the abdication of Isaac I (1059), but with the accession of Constantine X Doukas a sudden collapse began, which was exacerbated by the fact that all important offices in the central government were in the hands of favorites of the court, bureaucrats, chamberlains, eunuchs, and men of letters, none of whom were acquainted with military matters. Recruitments, armaments, and payments were neglected, and thus when Romanos IV came to power in early 1068, the army was already in full decay.[14]

In George Ostrogorsky's view (1963), the shortcomings of Basil II's successors, the power struggle between civil and military aristocrats, the ensuing decline of the defensive structures and the thematic system in the provinces, the abolition of local military units, and the increasing dependency upon mercenary troops constitute symptoms of feudalization in the Byzantine social fabric. This process manifested itself in the increasing power of the landed aristocracy based on revenues from growing estates, imperial privileges, purchases of offices, and tax farming, while the influence of the central government weakened.[15] Consequently, Speros Vryonis (1971) combines his image of Anatolia as "the most heavily populated, important, and vital province of medieval Hellenism ... subject to the integrating power of church, state, and culture emanating from the heart of the empire"[16] with the aforementioned explanatory model of the eleventh-century decline as the long-term cause lying behind the disaster of Manzikert and the ensuing Turkish expansion.[17]

More recent studies by Alexander Kazhdan (1985) and Alan Harvey (1989), however, put the notions of downfall and decay into perspective by demonstrating that the period in question evinced conspicuous signs of economic and demographic growth, the greatest building activity in Constantinople since the sixth century, and plenty of changes and innovative tendencies in the social structure and thought world of the Byzantine elite as well as in the literary production of Byzantine intellectuals.[18] This upswing certainly brought about growing markets in the provincial towns and strengthened the great landowners, to the detriment of the centralizing structures that had prevailed under Basil II. Ostrogorsky's over-simplifying model of feudalization and Paul Lemerle's counter-argument (1977) presenting Alexios I and his family's rule as the root of all evil[19] were thus replaced by more differentiated approaches that took into account the multi-dimensional complexity of Byzantine society in the eleventh century. The overall scarcity of evidence still raises many questions as to the impact of the economic growth. A case in point is the debasement of the Byzantine coinage under Constantine IX Monomachos, which was alternatively connected with the increased circulation of money and the constantly growing expenditure of the state apparatus and the court.[20] Be that as it may, the whole concept of crisis seems to have given way to the image of a multifaceted and contradictory society in flux, as is reflected in recent titles like "The Empire in Crisis (?)" or "Belle Époque or Crisis?"[21]

Equally unsatisfying was the traditional categorization of the Byzantine elite into a military and a civil class. In this respect, Jean-Claude Cheynet (1996) provided the most profound analysis.[22] In his study on revolts and power struggles of the Byzantine aristocracy between the tenth and the early thirteenth century, he convincingly reconstructed the geographical distribution and social networking of aristocratic clans, pointing out the close interplay between material resources based on landed estates, titles, and functions in the civil and military apparatus, bonds of kinship and marriage, allegiances with groups of servants, clients, and military units, and personal proximity to the innermost circle of imperial rule.[23] As for Asia Minor in the time after 1025, Cheynet discerns a number of upcoming clans rooted in the eastern military forces, such as the Doukai, the Argyroi, the Diogenai, and the Komnenoi, which came to fill the vacuum left by the great Anatolian families dissolved as a result of the power struggle with Basil II. These families abstained from any intermingling with the "Macedonians of Adrianople" and other western clans but created alliances with members of the Bulgarian and Georgian nobility.[24] In the center of power in Constantinople all claimants and incumbents of the imperial office except for the Paphlagonians were in one way or another related by bonds of kinship focusing on either the Argyros or the Doukas clan. The predominant military character of these families is, according to Cheynet, clear proof against the thesis of a civil aristocracy prevailing in eleventh-century Constantinople.[25]

With respect to their political goals and ambitions, Cheynet discerns two opposing factions among the aristocracy of Asia Minor, one centered around the Diogenes clan in Cappadocia and aiming at a continuation of the expansionist policy on the basis of a "national army," and another gathering around the Komnenos and the Doukas families and supporting an efficient mercenary army of lower cost.[26] Of decisive significance for the further development was the rebellion of 1056–57, which appears as a conflict between families formerly favored by Romanos III and Constantine IX Monomachos and supported by troops from the Euphrates region and the northeastern borderland, on the one hand, and families attached to Leo Paraspondylos, head of Michael VI's government, and backed by units from central Asia Minor, on the other. The accession of Constantine X Doukas, resting upon the same coalition of forces, did not cause further changes in the existing factionalism. But Eudokia Makrembolitissa's marriage with Romanos IV Diogenes in January 1068 marked a clear shift in the empire's military policy towards more energetic attempts to restore central control over the eastern provinces. The Doukas clan and its supporters emerged victorious from the 1071–72 civil strife, maintaining its position until the outbreak of a whole series of revolts in western Asia Minor (Nikephoros Botaneiates) and the European provinces (Nikephoros Bryennios, Nikephoros Basilakios) in 1077. During the ensuing contest for powerful coalitions, Botaneiates ultimately was defeated by the Komnenoi-Doukai alliance.[27] But apart from the emergence of a new strong dynasty, the invasions of the Turks and Pechenegs primarily contributed to a profound change in the Byzantine aristocracy.[28]

The main virtue of Cheynet's reconstruction is his avoidance of over-simplifying concepts that would reduce the complexity of the situation to a few social, political, or economic factors and thus create the impression that eleventh-century Byzantium despite all internal tensions was still a homogenous bloc. The notion of a conglomerate of competing forces evolving around a network of coalitions in the imperial palace of Constantinople and in various provincial centers not only accurately reflects the reality of political competition among autonomously operating elite members. It also helps explain many of the developments observable during the period of the Turkish invasions, such as the striking absence of specific forms of central control, the high degree of liberty of action among local military units and mercenary groups, and the frequent outbreak of local seditious movements. Chapters 2 and 5 of the present study will discuss these issues in detail.

The existence of these opposing tendencies within the Byzantine elite also goes a long way towards explaining the contradictory and sometimes highly critical statements articulated by contemporary or near-contemporary historians about the bad performance of the armed forces. Certainly, they did not just register observable grievances and shortcomings but also put their rhetoric into the service of certain factions and their political ambitions. This is one of the most crucial problems in estimating the military power of the Byzantine Empire in the time of the Turkish invasions. Well-known authors like Michael Attaleiates, Michael Psellos, and Kekaumenos complain openly about an erroneous state policy of withholding payments, neglecting the army, and converting military service into cash. Furthermore, they refer to ineffective strategic decisions, incompetence of leadership, lack of reliability, low morale, and cowardice as reasons for and symptoms of military failures.[29] On the basis of these statements, Speros Vryonis supports the opinion that the eleventh-century military forces must have actually undergone a disastrous decay in comparison with the great successes of the expansionist period.[30]

Moreover, by analogy with previous experiences of warfare against nomadic steppe peoples, defeats of the Byzantine troops are commonly also ascribed to disadvantages in matters of fighting technique and tactical difficulties, which resulted from the Turks' skillful use of archery.[31] Though it is certainly true that these matters actually caused a lot of trouble to the empire, it is equally important to see them, as John Haldon suggests, in a larger historical context of military developments, changing geopolitical conditions, strategic reorientations, and ideological attitudes.[32] Already during the period of offensive wars in the tenth and early eleventh centuries there were deep-rooted structural changes that replaced the traditional thematic structures in the eastern borderland with a more fragmented and localized organization of military forces.[33] Given that the proportional ratio between successful and failed military actions in the years 1025–1081, despite some phases of serious setbacks, does not differ from that in previous periods in Byzantine history, Haldon concludes that the level of training and effectiveness in the Byzantine army did not show any significant decline. On the other hand, it cannot be denied that from time to time there actually were serious problems, such as tactical disadvantages, insufficient availability of troops, lack of discipline, collapse of morale, and a damaging parsimony on the part of the central government. These factors were partly due to or combined with a lack of competent leadership.[34] The peculiarity of eleventh-century developments, in Haldon's view, lies in the fact that the strategic arrangements introduced during the expansionist period and the ideological attitudes focusing on a peaceful consolidation of the imperial power through diplomacy could not match the challenges posed by highly flexible and quickly moving groups of Turkish nomadic warriors.[35] Chapter 3 of the present study re-examines many of these questions on the basis of a fresh analysis of the sources on the Byzantine defensive strategy in the reign of Romanos IV (1068–1071).

Another issue frequently mentioned in connection with the disintegration of eleventh-century Anatolia and the Turkish invasions is the highly heterogeneous character of the population living in the empire's eastern provinces. According to the prevailing views, the inhabitants of the eastern regions were not especially attached to Constantinople, nor had they strong feelings of allegiance towards the imperial elite, because their linguistic, cultural and ecclesiastical identities differed widely from the overwhelmingly Greek-speaking Chalcedonian population in the empire's core lands.[36] A multi-ethnic mixture consisting of Armenians, Syrians, Muslim and Christianized Arabs, Kurds, and other minor population groups formed a highly diverse and complex social fabric that was characterized, on the one hand, by strong dynamics of acculturation in various directions and, on the other, by manifold tensions both amongst the local elites and with the central government, which from an attitude of tolerant pragmatism gradually changed to increasingly coercive centralizing tendencies.

Although already a culturally diverse region in former periods, Asia Minor saw a growing influence of these minorities in the centuries in question. The massive influx of Syriac Christians from Muslim regions starting with the reign of Nikephoros II Phokas led to the establishment of a vital ecclesiastical organization with a constantly increasing number of bishoprics and monastic foundations in the regions between the Pyramos/Jayḥān Valley (Ceyhan Nehri) and the Arsanias River (Murat Nehri) and around the urban centers of Germanikeia/ Marʿash (Kahramanmaraş), Melitene (Eski Malatya), and Edessa (Şanlıurfa). Another positive effect was a flourishing economic life largely based on profitable trade routes and merchant activities, which in turn expressed itself in the expansion of church buildings and monastic foundations and the patronage of art.[37]

The Armenians, "the largest non-Greek unit" in Byzantine society, forming a strong component of the army,[38] the aristocracy, and at times even of the imperial circle, considerably increased in number with the progressive annexation of Armenian provinces from the reign of Nikephoros II Phokas onwards and, above all, with the cession of the Bagratid and Artsrunid kingdoms of Vaspurakan (1021–22), Ani (1044–45), and Kars (1064–65) to the Byzantine Empire. These events resulted partly from the Byzantine expansionism in this period and partly from the growing pressure of hostile Arab and Turkish raids from Azerbaijan. The ensuing immigration turned into a massive influx of Armenian elements, including the former royal families, a large portion of the nobility, and their followers of lower social strata. As the royal families were compensated with domains in Cappadocia, an important number of these people took residence in this province's urban centers stretching from Dokeia (Tokat), Sebasteia (Sivas) and Tephrike (Divriği) in the northeast to Kaisareia (Kayseri), Tzamandos, Gabadonia (Develi), and Lykandos in the southwest, and thence spread to the Jayḥān region, Cilicia, and the Upper Euphrates area.

These populations underwent varying degrees of cultural, religious, and political integration. Whereas a significant part of the Armenians were fully absorbed by the Byzantine elite through military careers, titles, intermarriages, and conversion to the Orthodox dogma, other groups resisted these forms of acculturation, maintaining their own institutions and ecclesiastical organization. The former rulers were especially excluded from high ranks within the imperial elite and thus contributed to a strengthening of the Armenian cultural and religious presence in the regions in which they came to be established.[39] In the time of the Turkish invasions local lords of Armenian origin started to become powerful factors as raiders and outlaws and, in some cases, governors or even semi-independent rulers.[40] Older studies interpret these phenomena as tendencies of disobedience and unrest, which were caused by religious discords with the Church of Constantinople and by the political aspirations of the Armenian nobility and were further enhanced by the Turkish invasions.[41] It is quite obvious, however, that these groups did not differ very much from other warlords and local aristocrats operating in the eastern borderlands at that time. Another important consequence of the incorporation of the Armenian lands into the empire is the loss of an important buffer zone between the Caucasus region and the Anti-Taurus Mountains. As a result of the establishment of the new themes of Taron, Vaspurakan, Iberia, and Greater Armenia, the Byzantine military administration had to take care of the defense of these vast areas and thus was fully exposed to the Turkish invasions.[42] Chapter 7 of the present study develops a new approach to the notion of waning central power by examining the formation of Turkish and Armenian lordships in Byzantine territories during the 1080s and 1090s under the light of a general shift of political authority from the center to the peripheries. Chapter 9 describes the outcome of this process in the time after the First Crusade, in which central and eastern Anatolia developed into largely autonomous politico-cultural spheres with new forms of interaction among local Frankish, Armenian, Greek, and Muslim-Turkish entities.

Speros Vryonis' monumental work, *Decline of Medieval Hellenism,* is certainly a masterpiece of scholarly comprehensiveness, covering an amazing amount of primary material from five centuries of Anatolian history. It is also a work full of value judgments, insisting on a sharp and conflict-ridden opposition between Christian and Muslim cultural spheres and presenting the transformation process that began in the eleventh century as a disruptive turn for the worse. This assumption is based on the view that Byzantine Asia Minor was a highly prosperous region with thriving urban centers based on local industries as well as trade and commercial activities. Showing demographic vitality and a strong presence of great landed families, according to Vryonis, the whole region was tightly connected with the central government of Constantinople through well-functioning administrative institutions. A firmly established ecclesiastical organization, flourishing monastic centers, sanctuaries, and local cults bear witness to the vitality of the Christian faith in Asia Minor, and the widespread use of the Greek language amply demonstrates a high degree of Hellenization in linguistic terms.[43] This vision of a flourishing and culturally homogenous society necessarily makes the subsequent conquest and Islamization appear to be "something more than a negative historical event," as the author puts it in a recent summary of the principle findings and underlying concepts of his book from a distance of almost 30 years after its publication.[44] Accordingly, the changes triggered by the arrival of the Turks are described in negative terms as "major dislocation and partial destruction" of Byzantine society, its structures, and ecclesiastical institutions and as the gradual decay of the Christian communities, which were drawn into a maelstrom of conversion and assimilation to the Muslim environment. Institutions of Sunni Orthodoxy and Muslim patronage, such as mosques, *madrasa*s, and *waqf* foundations, as well as forms of popular piety represented by the dervish orders, were the main factors promoting the Islamization of Anatolia. On the other hand, Vryonis argues, the Christian population continued to maintain its presence in both rural and urban areas, high-ranking individuals of Christian background formed part of the Seljuk ruling elite, and the Byzantine cultural substrate deeply influenced the emerging Turkish popular culture.[45] It is certainly true that the notion of decay is inherent in most Byzantine and Eastern Christian sources commenting on the political and ecclesiastical situation in Anatolia. But it should not be forgotten that these texts were primarily written by people belonging to the old pre-conquest elite and thus articulate the viewpoint of those who had suffered great damage, losing territories, privileges, and sources of income, or were in a state of political and ideological competition with the Muslim-Turkish rulers. Hence, their statements, rather than generalizable realities, reflect the experiences and thoughts of specific groups in conjunction with the perceptions and literary conventions molding the mindset of these people. As will be shown below in more detail, descriptions of the Turks usually form subtopics of various overarching themes referring to alarming developments in the empire, the moral decay of secular and ecclesiastical leaders, or God's interventions into the course of history. Using these accounts as mere mines of information without sufficiently taking into account the ideological horizon into which they are embedded, unavoidably leads to anachronistic interpretation patterns based on clear-cut cultural and religious boundaries and the juxtaposition of inferior and superior cultural entities. These concepts are hardly appropriate to explain complex transformation processes and phenomena of hybridity with their countless grey zones and intermediary stages.[46]

Perhaps the most remarkable progress that has been achieved since Vryonis' book with respect to the early Turkish expansion in Byzantine Asia Minor concerns our understanding of the administrative and military structures in the eastern provinces. To a large extent, this is due to a much better knowledge of the sigillographic evidence in conjunction with developments in the domain of Byzantine court titles. On this basis, Jean-Claude Cheynet argues in favor of a much stronger presence than has been hitherto assumed of high-ranking Byzantine functionaries in many parts of Asia Minor well into the early years of Emperor Alexios I.[47] A rich collection of material is provided by the recent monograph by Georgios Leveniotis (2007) on the *Political Collapse of Byzantium in the East*. He gives extensive prosopographical lists of military and civil dignitaries and presents a detailed analysis of the institutional developments in each administrative unit of the eastern borderlands until the final breakdown of imperial rule, which is seen in connection with the transfer of the last remaining forces to the Balkans because of the Norman threat in 1081.[48] This historico-geographical approach enables us to grasp the specific particularities of each region in the vast area straddling the Armenian highlands, Upper Mesopotamia, Cilicia, and Cappadocia. Largely in line with traditional interpretation patterns are Leveniotis' conclusions regarding the reasons for the collapse. He draws the image of a powerful, ethnically and religiously homogenous central state, which was facing heavy assaults of overwhelming enemy forces, internal revolts, and the disloyalty of non-Greek and non-Orthodox populations in the East. The empire's defense was further undermined by the inadequacies of the military structures established during the expansionist period and by considerable losses of manpower and fighting force because of civil strife and wrong decisions made by various men in power.[49]

None of these aspects should be ruled out. Both Haldon and Leveniotis are certainly right in explaining the failures of the Byzantine army with structural shortcomings in the defensive system. But were they really confronted with an overwhelmingly superior enemy? Was it primarily a problem of inadequate strategies and insufficient fighting techniques that caused the loss of Asia Minor? No doubt, these factors played a certain role as long as the fighting and pillaging went on. But how then did these Turkish warriors manage to take permanent hold of Byzantine territories and turn into rulers? In order to understand the mechanisms lying behind this transformation, it is indispensable to view the political behavioral patterns of that time more comprehensively. The political situation of Byzantine Asia Minor from 1056 onwards was marked by serious tensions between centralizing tendencies and the gradual strengthening of regional powers backed by military forces. These consisted of seditious Byzantine aristocrats, foreign mercenary troops, Armenian noblemen, Arab and Kurdish emirs, and many others. This process resulted in a fragmentation of state authority and the emergence of numerous, mostly short-lived, semi-independent local lordships of limited size. Political power, to a large extent, was regionalized. This is to say that we are dealing not necessarily with a conflict between the Byzantine central government and Turkish invaders but with struggles and contentions within a complicated patchwork of local powers, in which the Turks intruded and eventually managed to prevail for reasons that have to be explained in the following chapters. Hence, besides the aforementioned aspects, the analysis has to focus on the very nature of both these local powers and the Turkish warrior groups as well as the strategies and forms of interaction they developed with respect to the relations among themselves and with the central government of Constantinople.

The Turkish viewpoint

The foundations of the modern Turkish scholarly tradition of Seljuk historiography were laid by a series of outstanding historians of the early Republican period, who published the greatest part of their work between the 1930s and the 1970s. Perhaps the most important among them are Mehmet Fuad Köprülü (1890–1966), Mükrimin Halil Yinanç (1900–1961), Ibrahim Kafesoğlu (1914–1984), Osman Turan (1914–1978), Mehmet Altay Köymen (1915–1993), Faruk Sümer (1924–1995), Ali Sevim (1928–2013), Işın Demirkent (1938–2006), and Erdoğan Merçil (born 1938).[50] In one way or another, this school of thought is deeply influenced by a key concept of Turkish nationalism, presenting Anatolia as the Turks' natural homeland (*vatan*) and final destination after a centuries-long process of migration.[51] The idea of a Turkish nation closely related to the geographical and cultural environment of Asia Minor has to be seen against the background of an ideological discourse that rejected both the traditional dynastic historiography of the Ottoman Empire and the ideas of Panturkism or Ottomanism, placing special emphasis, instead, on the historical continuities between the Seljuk legacy and modern Turkey. According to this view, Asia Minor, after centuries of Arab invasions and decades of civil strife, in the eleventh century was a vast, empty, and devastated area, in which new political and cultural entities based on Turkic-nomadic traditions of Central Asia and on Muslim elements imported from the central lands of Islam could be swiftly established.[52] Thus, the process of a rapid and deep-rooted Turkification of the whole region was inaugurated. A constantly recurring motif is the idea of huge masses of migrants, who within a few decades after the outset of the Turkish raids swamped most parts of Anatolia "like a storm tide" (*sel gibi*) and in a fierce life-and-death struggle successfully withstood all attempts to expel them thanks to their political unity in the state founded by Sulaymān b. Qutlumush.[53] In Osman Turan's view, the actual driving force of the Oghuz Turks' expansion and establishment in Anatolia was their conversion to Islam, which, because of the moral and material superiority of its high culture, proved especially attractive for the Turks in Transoxania and became their "common national religion" (*umûmî ve millî din*). The new Turkish Muslims, with their inherent vigor and dynamic, rescued the Muslim civilization from the state of decay, in which it had been trapped since the tenth century, thus inaugurating a period of religious, cultural, and political revival.[54] Accordingly, Islam is considered an indispensable part of or even a precondition for the immigration and state building of Turkish nomad tribes in Asia Minor. This process resulted in the identification of Seljuk political entities with Anatolian territory, which within a short time came to be called "Turkey." Expressions like *Selçuklu Türkiyesi* (Seljuk Turkey), *Türkiye Selçukluları* (The Seljuks of Turkey), and *Türkiye Selçuklu devleti*, (the Seljuk state of Turkey)[55] promote the notion of a culturally and linguistically unified nation, which possessed a collective identity and a common homeland bearing this people's name. Accordingly, in Turan's view the Islamization of Anatolia did not result from a long-lasting process of co-existence and acculturation, but rather from sudden and massive displacements of indigenous populations in conjunction with the gradual absorption of the remaining elements by the numerically superior Turkish conquerors and settlers.[56]

Another approach, which seems to prevail in more recent publications and frequently contradicts older religiously oriented interpretations of the Seljuk period, combines anthropological models constructed on the basis of nomadic tribal societies with the idea of a clearly discernible Oghuz Turkish cultural legacy.[57] This concept underlines the existence of specific Turkish institutions, social structures, and identity markers engendering the transition from tribal coalitions to warrior groups and state-like entities. In this context, the role of Islam is often downplayed, and thus the Turkish warriors are presented as only superficially Islamized, using religion as nothing more than a legitimization strategy.[58] Likewise, the idea of ethnic and cultural continuity serves the construction of links with later Turkish states, such as the Anatolian emirates (*beyliks*) of the fourteenth century and the Ottoman Empire. An extreme version of this concept even claims that what had begun with Alp Arslān and the Seljuk commanders in Anatolia during the 1070s and 1080s was eventually brought to completion by Kemal Atatürk's victory in the War of Independence in 1922.[59]

Over the past three decades, the academic interest in the Seljuk period was largely superseded by Ottoman studies, a fact that is also reflected in the reduction of teaching hours of Seljuk history in the study programs of Turkish universities.[60] Nevertheless, though on a smaller scale and with varying quality, there still is an ongoing flow of publications on various aspects of the political, institutional, and cultural history of the Great Seljuks and the Seljuks of Anatolia. Some especially noteworthy monographs of the past years, for instance, concern themselves with the Seljuks in Khurāsān and their first leader Jaghrī Beg;[61] the Great Seljuks' attitudes towards Islam;[62] outstanding sultans of Konya of the twelfth and early thirteenth centuries, such as Masʿūd I, Giyāth al-Dīn Kaykhusraw I, and Sulaymān-shāh II;[63] the political relations of the Anatolian Seljuks with the Armenians of Cilicia and the Euphrates region;[64] the army and warfare techniques of the Anatolian Seljuks;[65] their ambassadors and diplomacy;[66] and Seljuk identity through the lens of Byzantine sources.[67] In addition, there are some collected studies volumes by well-established specialists of the Seljuk period and a number of new textbooks and general introductions addressing a broader readership.[68] Of direct concern for the topic of the present book is Muharrem Kesik's new study on the battle of Manzikert and its aftermath.[69] The author reaffirms the well-established views of this battle in both Turkish and European scholarly discourses as a decisive event in the history of Turkish Anatolia and a landmark in the transition from Byzantine to Seljuk rule. While discussing various military aspects of the battle itself as well as the ensuing Turkish penetration of Asia Minor in the 1070s, however, his analysis is in line with the approaches and concepts of the Turkish scholarly tradition. Generally speaking, the Turkish bibliography of the past few years evinces a growing interest in hitherto neglected or understudied aspects of Seljuk political, institutional, and intellectual history and re-examines certain prominent topics of Seljuk history under the light of a fresh reading of the primary sources. Yet, there is hardly any innovation in terms of methodology or with respect to the prevailing concepts presenting the Seljuk conquests as a starting point for the formation of a Turkish nation and homeland. In spite of these differing viewpoints, the works of the Turkish scholarly tradition are extremely valuable for their deep knowledge of the available primary material and their detailed discussions of many matters of political and institutional history. Chapters 4 and 5 of this study present a new interpretation of the political activities of Sulaymān b. Qutlumush and other Turkish warlords during the 1070s and 1080s by focusing on structural similarities of the conflicts in Syria and in Anatolia, as well as on comparable behavioral patterns of the principle players.

The perspective of western oriental studies

Despite the attempts by Speros Vryonis and other Byzantinists to elucidate the reasons and characteristics of the internal change in eleventh-century Asia Minor and the transformation initiated by the Turkish invasions, western historians until recently showed astonishingly little interest in the Anatolian Seljuks. There are important studies on the Great Seljuk Empire and the innovations it brought to the institutions of the Muslim central lands and the law schools of Sunni Islam by Clara L. Klausner, Heribert Horst, Clifford E. Bosworth, Ann K. S. Lambton, S.G. Agadshanow, and Taef Kamal El-Azhari, to mention just the most important.[70] More recently, Eric Hanne, Deborah G. Tor, David Durand-Guédy, and Andrew Peacock questioned traditional views and developed a number of new topics, such as the power relationship between the Seljuk sultanate and the Abbasid caliphate, the status and loyalty of slave soldiers, the role of local elites, the image of Seljuk sultans as Muslim model rulers, and crucial questions related to the formation and expansion of the Seljuk Empire.[71] Chapters 1 and 2 of the present study try to contribute to this discussion by examining the earliest military conflicts and diplomatic relations with Byzantium in relation to the consolidation process of the Great Seljuk sultanate. Chapter 6 examines the repercussions of the centralizing policy of Sultan Malikshāh and the ensuing civil strife on the Turkish emirs in Syria, Upper Mesopotamia, and Anatolia in the time before the First Crusade. The concluding section of chapter 8 focuses on Upper Mesopotamia at the time of the final contest for control between the Great Seljuk sultanate and the Anatolian Seljuks up to 1107.

Western views of the Seljuks in Pre-Ottoman Anatolia for a long time almost exclusively depended upon Claude Cahen's articles and monographs written between the 1940s and the 1970s.[72] Though avoiding nationalistic views and anachronistic interpretations, his approach still shares some of the premises and assumptions of the Turkish scholarly tradition: the penetration of Anatolia was the historical consequence of the Turkish migrations; the *ghāzī* ideology developed in the eastern Iranian borderland decisively supported the expansion; Asia Minor, due to its demographic and economic decay during the Byzantine period, "was incapable of offering a solid and united front."[73]

The early phase of the Turkish expansion in Anatolia and the formation of the first Turkish-Muslim principalities still remain widely neglected. This lack of interest is reflected, for instance, in the first volume of the *Cambridge History of Turkey* edited by Kate Fleet in 2009, in which the Turkish penetration, even though the battle of Manzikert in 1071 is chosen as the chronological starting point, is only very briefly treated within a very general overview of Byzantine history between the eleventh and the fifteenth century. A more accurate treatment of Asia Minor starts only with the Mongol period beginning with the battle of Kösedağ in 1243.[74] More illuminating is Dimitri Korobeinikov's chapter in Jonathan Shepard's new *Cambridge History of the Byzantine Empire* (2008), which despite its succinctness offers a number of new insights into the problems of primary sources and their interpretation.[75] Carole Hillenbrand's recent monograph on the battle of Manzikert is, in its main part, a commented collection of Muslim primary sources in chronological order.[76] The focus of analysis lies not so much on the battle itself but on the diachronic development of the historiographical discourse about the event from the earliest surviving reports up to modern Turkish perceptions. In this respect, the study constitutes a useful guide to a proper understanding of Muslim accounts on the Seljuk expansion and the campaigns in Anatolia in particular. Hillenbrand's source-critical approach can be fruitfully combined with a number of thought-provoking ideas and suggestions most recently produced by Andrew Peacock. In various articles and his monograph on the earliest phase of Seljuk history, from the Seljuks' first appearance in Transoxania and Eastern Iran up to the death of Sultan Alp Arslan in 1072, he re-examines some essential core issues, such as the historiographical tradition on the Seljuk origins, the dynasty's relations with the Turkmen tribes, patterns of warfare and conquest, and the Seljuk attitudes towards Sunni Islam and Shiism.[77] In this context, he also presents some stimulating thoughts on the nomadic character and the aims of the first invasions into Byzantine territory.[78]

A factor contributing to a certain interest in the Anatolian Seljuks among western historians is the fact that the early Turkish expansion chronologically coincided with the First Crusade of 1096–1099. Ever since the massacre of Peter the Hermit's People's Crusade in the autumn of 1096, all crusading armies taking the way through Asia Minor were confronted with the fierce resistance of the Seljuks and other Turkmen groups. Likewise, the crusader states of Antioch and Edessa were constantly engaged in conflicts with Turkish potentates in eastern Anatolia, Syria, and northern Iraq. In the mid-twelfth century, this trend eventually culminated in the big clashes with the *atabeg* ʿImād al-Dīn Zangī and his son Nūr al-Dīn. Hence, the co-existence and conflicts between Franks and Turkish-Muslim rulers was a major theme of the crusader states' early history.

Nevertheless, crusader historians usually treat the Turks in a quite undifferentiated and superficial manner as one of many Muslim powers constituting the hostile environment surrounding the Latin East. They are described as a disturbing factor and dangerous menace, stubbornly opposing the crusaders on their march to the Holy Land and, later on, playing a leading role in the Muslim jihad against the Franks. More sophisticated issues (such as the peculiarities of Seljuk attitudes towards the Franks or the perception of the Turks in crusader chronicles) have hardly been examined systematically.[79] The main part of chapter 8 of this study forms an attempt to fill this gap.

In contrast to this neglect of the Anatolian Seljuks in the past decades, there has been a strong revival of scholarly discussions about the controversial subject of the origins and nature of the early Ottoman state, which in many respects shows similarities and parallels with the problems posed by the first arrival of the Turks in Asia Minor. Paul Wittek's *ghāzī* thesis and other theories articulated by Herbert A. Gibbon and Mehmet Fuad Köprülü were repeatedly submitted to severe criticism based on a thorough re-examination of the epigraphic evidence provided by the well-known Bursa inscription of 1337, early Ottoman historiography, and, to a certain degree, contemporary Byzantine historiography.[80] Rudi P. Lindner has made the point that "Holy War played no role in early Ottoman history, despite the later claims of Muslim propagandists," thus strictly distinguishing between later *ex post facto* reconstructions by Muslim scholars providing ideological coverage and legitimacy, on the one hand, and contemporary evidence supported by the results of anthropological studies on tribal and nomadic societies, on the other.[81] He mentions several elements that form an explanatory model describing the gradual transition from a clan-like band of warriors to an empire: The notions of clan and pastoral nomadism with all their implications for social organizations, the formation of political groupings, and specific forms of political behavior in insecure frontier regions, which lack strict central control and are characterized by blurred boundaries between various social and ethnic components. Colin Imber, Cemal Kafadar, and, most recently, Heath W. Lowry pushed the discussion forward in various directions and with diverging results. According to Imber's approach, the genealogical and historical material referring to the first Ottomans is so strongly intermingled with legendary features that a further elucidation of the facts is basically impossible. Kafadar developed a modified version of Wittek's theories. Lowry's interpretation of the Ottoman *ghazā* is that the combination of the nomadic practice of pillaging with the Muslim concept of jihad resulted from the ideological re-orientation in the time of the civil war in the early fifteenth century. He also highlights the significance of manifold syncretistic elements in early Ottoman society and tries, on the basis of early Ottoman tax registers from the Greek island of Limnos, to demonstrate the paramount importance of the principle of *istimālet*, i.e., winning over someone by generous promises and concessions, in the relations between the central government and non-Muslim subjects, as has been defined by previous studies by Halil İnalcık.[82]

All these ideas, in one way or another, call for a comparison between the Ottoman expansion in the fourteenth and the first Turkish penetration of Asia

Minor in the eleventh century. Various facets of the early period show striking parallels: the lack of contemporary sources written from the viewpoint of the Turkish conquerors; the construction of a Seljuk dynastic identity combining Persian-Muslim, Oghuz-Turkish, and Byzantine elements; the employment of the jihad ideology in decisive conflicts with the Byzantine enemies, such as the campaigns in Armenia and the battle of Manzikert; and various forms of collaboration and alliances with Byzantine commanders, rebels, foreign mercenary groups, and segments of the indigenous population. Nevertheless, it should not be forgotten that, when the Ottomans made their appearance, the political, social, cultural, and ethnic structures of Anatolia during the preceding two centuries had already undergone a deep-rooted transformation. The emergence of various Turkish-Muslim principalities, the political unification of central and eastern Anatolia under the Seljuk sultanate of Konya, and the subsequent period of Mongol domination created an environment that strongly differed from what the first Turkish warrior groups had found when arriving in the eastern provinces of eleventh-century Byzantium. In short, in order to reach a better understanding of the historical conditions in which the Ottomans made their appearance, it is indispensable to further illuminate the nature and particularities of the preceding Seljuk period.

Most recently, a number of noteworthy publications have taken important steps in this direction by combining the re-examination of aspects of Seljuk history in the Muslim central lands with new approaches to the Seljuk sultanate of Rum during its heyday and decay in the thirteenth century. A special focus lies on Seljuk political culture, dynastic identity, ideology, and the relations with Sunni Islam, the Abbasid caliphate, and indigenous local elites.[83] David Durand-Guédy's case study on the city of Iṣfahān examines the particularities of Seljuk rule in the intersection between central authority and local institutions, thus offering a useful model for comparable processes in other regions, be they Muslim or Christian.[84] Songül Mecit's monograph investigates the dynastic ideology of the Seljuk sultanate of Rūm, including its relations with the Byzantine Empire.[85] The groundbreaking studies by Sara Nur Yıldız and Şevket Küçükhüseyin present new source-critical approaches to core texts of Seljuk historiography and other genres of local Anatolian writing from the Mongol period onwards.[86] By exploring the Muslim literary production of Anatolia, they give us a better understanding of the structures and peculiarities of Mongol rule in Anatolia and offer us new insights into the cross-cultural experiences, perceptions, and literary representations of Muslims, Christians, and Turks in these texts. A collective volume edited by Andrew Peacock and Sara Nur Yıldız on *The Seljuks of Anatolia* further illuminates aspects of the dynastic identity and the royal household of the sultanate of Rum and sheds new light on the social and political role of the Sufi orders as an intrinsic part of the Seljuk elites.[87] Dimitri Korobeinikov's monograph on *Byzantium and the Turks in the Thirteenth Century* is the first comprehensive analysis of the Byzantine Empire's political and institutional relations with the Seljuks of Konya and the early Anatolian *beyliks* from the Fourth Crusade (1204) to the sultanate's collapse during the reign of Andronikos II Palaiologos.[88] An ongoing stream of publications by Scott Redford examines the great wealth of information to be gained from the analysis of the archaeological, architectural, and epigraphic evidence surviving from thirteenth-century Anatolia with respect to Seljuk elites, patronage, cultural behavior, and economic activities.[89] As a whole, over the past years much substantial work has been done on the Great Seljuk Empire, the classical age of the Anatolian Seljuks, and the literary production of medieval Anatolia. The early period largely remains outside the scope of these innovative trends in Seljuk studies. Hence, it has to be one of the main tasks of this and future works on the Seljuks to point out new possibilities of examining the first period of Turkish presence in Anatolia, free from the one-sided and ideologically biased perspectives of modern Greek and Turkish scholarship and that take advantage of the various new approaches developed on the basis of Seljuk and early Ottoman material from later centuries.

Material remains

The archaeological evidence for the earliest stages of Turkish presence in Anatolia is extremely difficult to grasp.[90] Systematic excavations in sites like Amorion and Sagalassos and archaeological surveys in areas like the Amuq and Kahramanmaraş Plains; the Euphrates region, in Lycia; and in the provinces of Kırşehir, Ankara, Konya, and Aksaray in Central Anatolia provide us with numerous invaluable insights into environmental, climatic, agricultural, economic, and urban developments.[91] Yet the available evidence derives mostly from late antique and early medieval (= middle Byzantine) layers, whereas the material remains pertaining to the transition period from Byzantine rule to the heydays of the Seljuk sultanate in the thirteenth century are extremely rare and raise a number of intricate chronological and interpretive issues.[92]

Data of environmental history indicate a decay of rural agrarian activities on the central Anatolian plateau around 1100, something that is explained as resulting from an interplay between climatic factors and the expansion of Turkish nomads in the said region.[93] Our written sources, however, mostly present the Turkish invaders as warriors and raiders or, occasionally, even as skillful politicians and state builders. Hence, it is virtually impossible to reconstruct the extent and nature of nomadic activities on the basis of the available accounts and thus to gauge the role of intruding pastoralists in the desertion of agricultural areas. The first known copper coins minted in the Seljuk sultanate of Konya and in eastern Anatolian emirates date to the first half of the twelfth century.[94] The oldest surviving monuments of Seljuk art and inscriptions were produced in Konya in the 1150s. Yet the bulk of the surviving material hardly predates the thirteenth century, and it is mostly in the 1210s and 1220s that we observe large-scale building activities in the towns and citadels of Anatolia.[95] Studies on Byzantine fortifications shed some light on the re-organization of defensive structures in Asia Minor under Alexios I and his successors.[96] Conclusions drawn on the basis of stylistic features and brickwork, however, are not always reliable and need a more thorough investigation with the aid of refined methods. Pottery that has been identified as Turkish-Muslim is usually dated to the thirteenth century, when Seljuk urban culture with its palaces, religious institutions, and sacred buildings flourished to the full.[97]

The lack of material for the eleventh century is usually interpreted as a sign of devastation and/or desertion in the years after the battle of Manzikert in 1071 or of a shift from sedentary to nomadic settlement patterns in vast areas of Anatolia.[98] Yet archaeologists usually face difficulties in adducing positive evidence to corroborate these assumptions. The traditional concept of a profound cultural and demographic upheaval caused by the Turkish onslaught certainly is an easily adaptable explanatory model,[99] but it hardly appears appropriate as long as both written and material sources fail to provide convincing arguments. The highly fragmentary and in many respects insufficient basis of material evidence may partly be due to the current state of archaeological research on Byzantine sites in present-day Turkey. It is to be expected that future excavations and surveys will modify our current understanding, but it is hardly predictable how and to what extent. For the time being, it seems more appropriate to assume that the Muslim-Turkish population groups and politico-cultural entities in Anatolia grew out of a relatively slow process of gradual penetration and transformation, which took at least some decades to leave archaeologically palpable traces and even longer to develop into a distinct elite culture with its own morphological characteristics and identity markers.[100] This study, first and foremost, focuses on a re-examination and fresh interpretation of historiographical traditions, as will be explained in more detail in the following chapter. A comprehensive analysis of the material evidence would go far beyond both the competence of the present writer and the scope of this book. Yet a selection of important archaeological studies will be referred to wherever their findings shed additional light on or modify what we know from the written record.

Notes

1 Anna Komnene 7.7.4, p. 222, ll. 63–67.
2 For the geographical terminology, see EI[2], pp. 461–80 s. v. Anadolu (F. Taeschner), esp. pp. 461–62.
3 For useful surveys of the current state of research, see, for instance, Walter Pohl, *Die Völkerwanderung. Eroberung und Integration* (Cologne and Stuttgart, 2005); Guy Halsall, *Barbarian Migrations and the Roman West, 376–568* (Cambridge, 2007); Peter Heather, *The Fall of the Roman Empire: A New History* (London, 2005); idem, *Empires and Barbarians: The Fall of Rome and the Birth of Europe* (London, 2009); Walter Pohl, Clemens Gantner, and Richard Payne, eds., *Visions of Community in the Post-Roman World: The West, Byzantium and the Islamic World, 300–1100* (Farnham, 2012).
4 Some representative works: Patricia Crone, *Slaves and Horses: The Evolution of the Islamic Polity* (Cambridge, 1980); Fred M. Donner, *The Early Islamic Conquests* (Princeton, 1981); Albrecht Noth, *The Early Arabic Historical Tradition: A Source-Critical Study*, second edition, in collaboration with Lawrence I. Conrad, trans. Michael Bonner, Studies in Late Antiquity and Early Islam 3 (Princeton, 1994); Walter Kaegi, *Byzantium and the Early Islamic Conquests* (Cambridge, 1992); Fred Donner, *Narratives of Islamic Origins: The Beginnings of Islamic Historical Writing*, Studies in Late Antiquity

and Early Islam 14 (Princeton, 1998); Walter Kaegi, *Muslim Expansion and Byzantine Collapse in North Africa* (Cambridge, 2010).

5 For full bibliographical documentation, see below, pp. 14–16.

6 For many of these aspects, see the contributions collected in the volume of Stelios Lampakis, ed., *Byzantine Asia Minor (6th-12th cent.)*, National Hellenic Research Foundation, Institute for Byzantine Research, International Symposia 6 (Athens, 1998). The above-mentioned elements are strongly emphasized in Vryonis, *Decline*, pp. 1–68, see, for instance, p. 2 ("These institutions produced an element of homogeneity in the life of the inhabitants of this immense area and at the same time integrated them effectively into a Constantinopolitan-centered organism."), p. 6 ("there had developed a large number of thriving cities ... with a considerable commercial life and money economy."), p. 7 ("it is even more doubtful [i.e., without a money economy and towns] that the Greek language and Byzantine Christianity could have spread and penetrated to the extent they did in Anatolia").

7 For bibliographical references, see below, pp. 10–11.

8 For details, see Golden, *Turkic Peoples*, pp. 205–13, 219–23, esp. 212–13 for the etymology of "Turkmen" ("Türk" + suffix of strengthening "-men"); for the terms Oghuz and Turkmen or Türkmen, see also Peacock, *Great Seljuk Empire*, pp. 27–28.

9 For details, see Göksu, *Türkiye Selçuklularında Ordu*, pp. 13–24, 79–94; on Niẓām al-Mulk's role in the transformation of the Seljuk Empire, see also Peacock, *Great Seljuk Empire*, pp. 68–71, esp. 69–70 for the *iqṭā'* system. I adopt his translation of the Arabic technical term.

10 Haldon and Kennedy, "Byzantine-Arab Frontier," pp. 79–116.

11 Chalandon, *Comnène* 1; Laurent, *Turcs*.

12 Chalandon, *Comnène*, 1:14–18.

13 Laurent, *Turcs*, pp. 45–48, 55.

14 Laurent, *Turcs*, pp. 50–59.

15 Ostrogorsky, *Geschichte*, pp. 262–89.

16 Vryonis, *Decline*, p. 68.

17 Vryonis, *Decline*, pp. 70–80.

18 Kazhdan and Epstein, *Change*; Harvey, *Expansion*.

19 Lemerle, *Cinq études*, pp. 251–312.

20 Harvey, "Competition," p. 176; Angold, "Belle Époque," pp. 590–91.

21 Vlyssidou, ed., *Empire in Crisis*; Angold, "Belle Époque," p. 583.

22 Cheynet, *Pouvoir*, pp. 337–57.

23 Ibid., pp. 207, 262, 287.

24 Ibid., pp. 272–73.

25 Ibid., pp. 273–80.

26 Ibid., p. 337.

27 Ibid., pp. 339–57.

28 Ibid., p. 280.

29 Vryonis, "Crisis," pp. 22–42.

30 Ibid., pp. 17–43.

31 Kaegi, "Archery," pp. 96–108.

32 Haldon, "Approaches," pp. 45–74.

33 Ibid., pp. 60–70.

34 Ibid., pp. 45–60.

35 Ibid., pp. 71–74.

36 Dagron, "Minorités," pp. 198–204; Garsoïan, "Integration," pp. 68–86.

37 Dagron, "Minorités," pp. 186–98.

38 Garsoïan, "Integration," p. 53.

39 Dédéyan, "Arméniens," pp. 75–95; Thierry, "Données," pp. 119–72; Garsoïan, "Integration," pp. 87–124.

40 Garsoïan, "Integration," pp. 61–66.

41 Laurent, *Turcs*, pp. 67–80.
42 Arutjunova-Fidanjan, "Administration," pp. 309–20.
43 Vryonis, *Decline*, pp. 1–68.
44 Vryonis, "Book," p. 1.
45 Vryonis, *Decline*, passim; Vryonis, "Book," pp. 1–2.
46 For source critical problems, see Beihammer, "Ethnogenese," pp. 589–614; idem, "Feindbilder," pp. 48–98, and the discussion below, pp. 26–44.
47 Cheynet, "Résistance aux Turcs," pp. 131–47.
48 Leveniotis, *Collapse*, pp. 1–6.
49 Leveniotis, *Collapse*, pp. 663–78.
50 For Turkish approaches to the Seljuk Turks in the late Ottoman and Republican period, see Strohmeier, *Geschichte*; Başan, *Seljuqs*, pp. 1–20; for an overview of more recent bibliography, see Ocak, "Bakış," pp. 15–16. Some of the most important monographs and manuals written by the said scholars: Köprülü, *Kaynakları*; Yinanç, *Anadolu'nun Fethi*; idem, *Türkiye Tarihi Selçuklular Devri*; Kafesoğlu, *Melikşah*; Turan, *Selçuklular Tarihi*; idem, *Türkiye*; idem, *Doğu Anadolu*, idem, *Selçuklular ve İslâmiyet*; Sümer, *Oğuzlar*; Köymen, *Selçuklu Imparatorluğu*, 3 vols.; Sevim, *Suriye*; idem, *Anadolu'nun Fethi*; idem, *Süleymanşâh*; idem, *Selçuklular Dönemi*; Sevim and Yücel, *Türkiye Tarihi*; Demirkent, *Kılıç Arslan*; Merçil, *Hükümdarlık Alâmetleri*; idem, *Büyük Selçuklu Devleti*; idem, *Müslüman Türk Devletleri*; a collection of articles are reprinted in idem, *Selçuklular, Makaleler* (Istanbul, 2011).
51 Turan, *Türkiye*, pp. 1–44, talks about the *Büyük Türk muhacereti*, i.e., the "great Turkish migration."
52 Strohmeier, *Geschichte*, pp. 91–101 (concerning the concept of *Anadoluculuk* in the work of Mükrimin Halil Yinanç). For further details, see Yinanç, *Anadolu'nun Fethi*, pp. 161–87.
53 Turan, *Türkiye*, pp. 37–44.
54 Turan, *Türkiye*, pp. xviii–xxii.
55 Turan, *Türkiye*, pp. xxiv–xxx, Ocak, "Bakış," pp. 15–16.
56 Turan, *Türkiye*, pp. 37–44.
57 Sümer, *Oğuzlar*; Divitçioğlu, *Oğuz'dan*.
58 Divitçioğlu, *Oğuz'dan*, pp. 85–95.
59 Kafali, "Conquest," p. 416.
60 Merçil, *Büyük Selçuklu Devleti*, iii–iv (ön söz).
61 Piyadeoğlu, *Çağrı Bey*; idem, *Güneş Ülkesi Horasan*.
62 Şeker, *Selçuklu Türklerinin İslam Tasavvuru*.
63 Baykara, I. *Gıyaseddin Keyhusrev*; Kesik, *Sultan I. Mesud Dönemi*; Kaya, *I. Gıyâseddin Keyhüsrev ve II. Süleymanşah Dönemi*.
64 Ersan, *Selçuklular Zamanında Anadolu'da Ermeniler*.
65 Göksu, *Türkiye Selçuklularında Ordu*; Kesik, *At üstünde Selçuklular*.
66 Uyumaz, *Elçiler*.
67 Tülüce, *Selçuklu Kimliği*.
68 Salim Koca, *Selçuklu Devri Türk Tarihinin Temel Meseleleri* (Ankara, 2011). Merçil, *Selçuklular: Makaleler*; Özgüdenli, *Selçuklular*; Mehmet Ersan and Mustafa Alican, *Selçukluları Yeniden Keşfetmek: Büyük Selçuklular* (Istanbul, 2012).
69 Kesik, *1071 Malazgirt*.
70 Klausner, *Seljuk Vizierate*; Horst, *Staatsverwaltung*; Bosworth, *Ghaznavids*; idem, "Political History," pp. 1–202; Lambton, "Structure," pp. 203–302; eadem, *Continuity*; Agadshanow, *Staat*; El-Azhari, *Saljūqs of Syria*.
71 Hanne, *Caliph*; Tor, "Mamlūk Loyalty," pp. 213–25; eadem, "Tale of two Murders," pp. 279–97; eadem, "Islamization," pp. 279–99; eadem, "Sovereign and Pious," pp. 39–62; for Durand-Guédy, see below, n. 84; for Peacock, see below, n. 77.
72 Cahen, *Pre-Ottoman Turkey*; idem, *Turcobyzantina*; idem, "Historiography," pp. 37–63; idem, *Formation*.
73 Cahen, *Pre-Ottoman Turkey*, pp. 1–8, 64–66.

74 Chrysostomides, "Byzantium," pp. 6–50; Melville, "Anatolia," pp. 51–101.
75 Korobeinikov, "Raiders," pp. 692–719.
76 Hillenbrand, *Turkish Myth.*
77 Peacock, *Early Seljūq History*; Peacock, "Nomadic Society," pp. 205–30; idem, "Balkan-Kuhiyan," pp. 60–85; for a summary of his views and findings in the context of a broader survey of Seljuk history, see now idem, *Great Seljuk Empire.*
78 Peacock, *Early Seljūq History*, pp. 128–63.
79 See, for instance, Mayer, *Kreuzzüge*, pp. 48–55, 65–68, 83–87, 94–99, 128–29; Asbridge, *First Crusade*, pp. 113–240; idem, *Kreuzzüge*, pp. 65–97, 154–58, 170–85, 210–16, 238–60, 453–55; Tyerman, *God's War*, pp. 124–47, 317–29, 417–30; Phillips, *Second Crusade*, pp. 168–206. Important thoughts and observations on the image of the Turks can be found in Völkl, *Muslime.*
80 Gibbon, *Foundation*; Köprülü, *Origines*; Wittek, *Rise.*
81 Lindner, *Nomads*, the quotation at p. 6.
82 Imber, "Myth," pp. 7–27; Kafadar, *Worlds*; Lowry, *Nature*; İnalcık, "Methods," pp. 112–22.
83 A broad variety of topics can be found in Lange and Mecit, eds., *The Seljuqs.*
84 Durand-Guédy, *Iranian Elites.*
85 Mecit, *Rum Seljuqs.*
86 Küçükhüseyin, *Selbst- und Fremdwahrnehnung*; Yıldız, *Mongol Rule.*
87 Peacock and Yıldız, eds., *The Seljuks of Anatolia.*
88 Korobeinikov, Dimitri, *Byzantium and the Turks in the Thirteenth Century*, Oxford Studies in Byzantium (Oxford, 2014).
89 See, for instance, S. Redford, "City Building in Seljuq Rum," in *The Seljuks*, ed. Lange and Mecit, pp. 256–76; S. Redford, "Paper, Stone, Scissors: 'Alā' al-Dīn Kayqubād, 'Iṣmat al-Dunyā wa-l-Dīn and the Writing of Seljuk History," in *The Seljuks of Anatolia*, ed. Peacock and Yıldız, pp. 151–70; Redford and Leiser, *Victory Inscribed.*
90 For early Muslim inscriptions in Anatolia, see Bakırer, "Kitâbeler," pp. 9–13; Duran, "Konya," pp. 23–29.
91 For Amorion, see the excavation reports by Lightfood et al., listed in the bibliography; for Sagalassos, see Vionis et al., "Pottery Assemblage," pp. 423–64; for archaeological surveys, Eger, *Islamic-Byzantine Frontier*; Pellegrino, "Céramiques," pp. 215–21; Anderson, "Settlement Change," pp. 233–39.
92 For central Anatolia, see Anderson, "Settlement Change," pp. 233–40.
93 Haldon et al., "Climate and Environment," p. 151.
94 Copper coins minted by the Anatolian Seljuks survive from the reign of Mas'ūd I (1116–1155) onwards; other twelfth-century coinage came down to us from the Turkmen emirates in eastern Anatolia (Dānishmandids, Mangūjakids, Artuqids, and Saltukids): Shukurov, "Self-identity," pp. 259–76; Aykut, *Sikkeleri*; Özme, "Sikke," pp. 565–73.
95 For architecture, see Peker, "Evrenin Binası," pp. 31–40; Tekinalp, "Yerel Geleneğin," pp. 45–53; Peker, "Anadolu Bazilika Geleneği," pp. 55–65; Eser, "Anadolu-Suriye," pp. 67–73; Aslanapa and Altun, "Anadolu Dışı," pp. 75–79; Kuban, "Mimarî Tasarım," pp. 83–109; İpekoğlu, "Yapılar," pp. 111–25; Sönmez, "Yapı Faaliyetlerinin Organizasyonu," pp. 127–35; Durukan, "Banîler," pp. 137–71; for the epigraphic and decorative programs of Seljuk citadels, see Redford, "Mamālik," pp. 305–46; for a fresh analysis of Islamic architecture in the time after the Mongol conquest, see now Blessing, *Rebuilding Anatolia.*
96 For fortifications, see the studies by Foss listed in the bibliography.
97 For samples of thirteenth-century Seljuk ceramics and their decorative features, which show a "common artistic and architectural vocabulary" with Byzantine and Muslim artifacts and palatial spaces, see Redford, "Portable Palaces," pp. 382–412;

Armstrong, "Nomadic Seljuks," identified a type of ceramic ware found in the region of Balboura and Xanthos in Lycia as products of Turkish nomads dating to the thirteenth century. See also Pellegrino, "Céramiques," pp. 215–16.

98 See numerous references in the Amorion excavations reports by Lightfood and others.

99 See, for instance, Armstrong, "Nomadic Seljuks," p. 329: "Such was their lifestyle that they not only brought about the depopulation of areas with their aggressive and bloodthirsty warrior culture, but they also undermined and destroyed longstanding agricultural practices."

100 For a typological analysis of urban layouts in Anatolia on the basis of quantitative descriptions of space syntax, see Kubat, A. S., "The Morphological Characteristics of Anatolian Fortified Towns," *Environment and Planning B: Planning and Design* 24 (1997), 95–123; for the transformation of fortifications from Byzantine to Seljuk times, see Redford, "Medieval Anatolian Arsenals," pp. 543–52; for the use and function of Byzantine churches, which were integrated into Seljuk citadel and palace complexes, see Tekinalp, "Palace Churches," 148–67; for issues of cultural transfer between Ayyūbid Syria and Seljuk Anatolia with respect to inscriptions and decorations of citadels, see Redford, "Mamālik," pp. 305–46.

Sources, images, perceptions

Memories and narratives

The Turkish expansion in Asia Minor has to be studied on the basis of a broad range of narrative sources written between the late eleventh and the fifteenth century in a geographical area stretching from Constantinople to Egypt and Baghdad, and, as far as the crusaders' viewpoint is concerned, even to Western Europe. Unavoidably, a reassessment of the available data has to begin with scrutinizing texts and juxtaposing historiographical traditions. In other words, whatever we know about our topic has been imparted to us through the imagination, perception, and interpretation of contemporary and later-born authors, who selected, re-constructed, and described the events and subject matters of their choice within the ideological context and collective memory of the socio-cultural environment to which they belonged. The focus of analysis necessarily shifts from the historical facts to modes of perception and manners of talking about historical events.[1] This also helps us reveal the tools and methods by which modern historians constructed their views of the Turkish expansion in Asia Minor.

A particular feature the early Seljuk period has in common with the first stages of the Ottoman emirate is the fact that the surviving source material written from the perspective of outside observers, mostly victims or enemies of the invaders, predates Muslim-Turkish narratives. This is to say that the various traditions reflect not only diverging perspectives but also different points in time in the creation process of historical memory. It is very important, therefore, to disentangle the chronological strata of the extant accounts and thus distinguish between primary material and subsequent additions and elaborations.

Each historiographical tradition is based on a set of well-established patterns of thought, literary conventions, and rhetorical rules shaping prejudices, topoi, and motifs in the presentation of the encounter between Turks and Byzantines. Conceptions of history, attitudes towards current issues, and authorial intentions are likewise important factors shaping the representation of conflicts and enemy images in the available narratives. The result is a broad range of images and modes of perception existing side by side. Byzantine or Armenian descriptions of Turkish invaders strongly differ from those in Persian and Arabic texts, but the distinction between Christian and Muslim sources is certainly not sufficient to grasp the multi-layered complexity of these phenomena. In what follows, an attempt is made to separately present the main characteristics of Byzantine, Eastern Christian, Muslim, and Frankish crusader historians in their treatment of the Turkish expansion in Asia Minor.

Byzantine historiography

Given that the primary focus of all Byzantine chronicles of the period in question lies on the imperial policy and the ruling elite of Constantinople, the Turkish invasions never form an independent topic but are always presented in conjunction with developments at the imperial court, military expeditions under the command of the emperor or his generals, and insurrections in the provinces threatening the central government. The oldest extant work of eleventh-century Byzantine historiography, Michael Psellos' *Chronographia,* written most probably shortly after 1075, with its introvert view on the leading figures of the imperial court and their character traits, provides very little information about the eastern provinces and the Turks. Even the account of Romanos IV's expeditions concentrates much more on the protagonist's psychological reactions to the challenges and menaces of warfare than on the enemies in Asia Minor.[2]

Michael Attaleiates' slightly younger *Historia,* written in about 1079/80, and the *Synopsis historion* by John Skylitzes, most likely to be dated to the late eleventh century, contain the most detailed descriptions of the first stages of the Turkish expansion from the invasions in the 1040s until Nikephoros III Botaneiates' rise to power and the commander Samouch's activities in the Armenian borderland during the years 1055–57 respectively. John Skylitzes is the only Byzantine author to collect reports concerning the origin and identity of the Seljuk Turks and to find information that, despite a considerable amount of alterations and simplifications, in its core still shares some common features with the material transmitted in the extant Arabic and Persian accounts on the Seljuk origins. The Byzantine version relates the story of the Seljuk chiefs from the crossing of the Oxus River until Ṭughril Beg's conflicts with the Būyid general al-Basāsīrī in Iraq and various inner-dynastic rivals and is conflated with some widespread motifs and stereotypes concerning the character and customs of barbarian nomad peoples.[3] Jonathan Shepard convincingly attributed extensive reports of the Seljuk attacks on the Armenian provinces in 1048 and the local Byzantine defenders' reactions to a laudatory biography of the Byzantine general Katakalon Kekaumenos, who in late 1045 seems to have been appointed *doux* of Iberia and Ani.[4]

Eudoxos Tsolakis supposes that Michael Attaleiates' text was used by John Skylitzes to produce a continuation of his narrative from 1057 up to 1079/80.[5] Attaleiates himself is quite succinct about the early Seljuk attacks but becomes fuller with the reign of Constantine X Doukas (1059–1067) and the conquest of Ani by Sultan Alp Arslan in 1064.[6] Having participated in all three campaigns of Romanos IV Diogenes in the capacity of a military judge, Attaleiates is able to give a very vivid and detailed description of what happened from the Byzantine army's first departure to the east in the spring of 1068 up to the disaster of Manzikert in August 1071. The range of his sometimes highly critical observations comprises the itinerary and strategic concerns of the imperial troops, short-sighted decisions by the emperor, cases of incompetence of commanders in charge and lack of discipline among the soldiers, the strains of marches and battles, the devastation caused by the Turkish raids, and, finally, the exemplary behavior of Sultan Alp Arslān towards the imprisoned emperor after the battle of Manzikert. The reign of Attaleiates' anti-hero Michael VII Doukas is primarily presented as a period of civil strife, decay, and upheavals, thus providing the justification for the revolt of Nikephoros Botaneiates. In this context, the author repeatedly refers to bands of Turkish warriors in central Anatolia and Bithynia inasmuch as these were involved in the inner-Byzantine conflicts of the years 1071–1078 as adversaries or allies of mercenary groups or rebels. The point of culmination was the coalition between Botaneiates and the sons of Qutlumush.[7]

Nikephoros Bryennios' *Hyle historias* also covers the conflict-ridden years 1070–1079, though from a different point of view. It was written about half a century after Attaleiates at the request of Alexios I's wife Empress Eirene Doukaina, most probably in the years before the author's death in 1137/38.[8] Drawing on a core of information transmitted by older historical works, Bryennios' narrative revolved around an encomiastic presentation of the young Alexios Komnenos and his family. His second focus was the positive portrayal of his father's or grandfather's failed insurrection. In his work, he made use of a distinct narrative technique based on extensive descriptions of individual scenes, romance-like anecdotes, and direct speeches. As far as the Turks and the situation in Asia Minor are concerned, he adopts Skylitzes' account of the origin of the Seljuk Turks but describes the battle of Manzikert very differently than Attaleiates does. As for the subsequent events, he adds interesting and otherwise unknown material and gives alternative interpretations. His account of the revolt of Nikephoros Melissenos, who appears as a kind of scapegoat blamed for handing over towns in Anatolia to the Turks,[9] is of special importance for understanding the transition period from Botaneiates to Alexios I.

John Zonaras' *Epitome historion* written most probably after 1142 is too succinct in its treatment of the period from the 1040s to 1118 to make substantial additions to the knowledge concerning the Turks.[10] At certain points, however, Zonaras makes some noteworthy observations, such as, for instance, his interesting definition of the relationship between the Seljuk sultanate and the Abbasid caliphate.[11] Given that neither Bryennios nor Zonaras provides much supplementary evidence to what Attaleiates had to say about the situation in Asia Minor in the years 1078–1081, Byzantine historiography has a remarkable lacuna with respect to this decisive turning point that brought about the establishment of Turkish warriors in urban centers of Bithynia and central Anatolia.

Anna Komnene's *Alexias*, which for the greatest part seems to have been written during the 1140s, continues the narrative where Bryennios and other predecessors left it. Nevertheless, the text represents a clear break with respect to the eleventh-century historians and fully reflects the attitudes and ideological tendencies of the Komnenian period.[12] While Alexios' early years are treated on the basis of extracts from her husband's account, the Turks appear in a completely new light. They are no longer marauding raiders but lords of firmly established principalities residing in cities like Nicaea, Smyrna, Sinope, Apollonias, and Ephesos and exerting political authority over the surrounding areas. Sulaymān b. Qutlumush and his successors at times are even ascribed the title of sultan.[13] Despite modern scholars' tendencies to take this information at face value, it would be misleading to suppose that these changes suddenly occurred around 1081. What the author actually did was to project the structure and outward appearance of the Muslim-Turkish principalities, as they gradually emerged between the 1080s and the 1140s, back to the first years of her father's reign. This applies not only to the emirates' institutional organization but also to ideological aspects of the Byzantine-Turkish encounter and the goals of Alexios' imperial policy. Anna is the first historian to allude to a sort of religious conflict and the Anatolian Turks' Muslim identity, while Alexios is styled as champion of the Christian faith rescuing his co-religionists from slavery and leading the barbarians to baptism. All of these ideas certainly reflect the imperial program promoted by Alexios' successors John II and Manuel I, as can be seen in the extant products of Komnenian court poets and rhetoricians. The earliest examples are the texts composed by Theodore Prodromos on the occasion of John II's campaigns against the Dānishmandid strongholds of Kastamon (Kastamonu) and Gangra (Çankırı) in 1133–34 and the ensuing triumphal entrances in Constantinople.[14] Anna Komnene concludes her report on the situation in Asia Minor with the peace treaty of Alexios I with Sultan Shāhinshāh (1110–1116) and the subsequent murder of the latter by his brother Masʿūd (1116–1155).

John Kinnamos and Niketas Choniates, the chief witnesses of twelfth-century Byzantium writing in 1180/82 and between 1185 and 1210 respectively, produced two historical works with the same starting point—John II's accession to the throne—and a set of common sources but based on very different concepts and literary approaches. Kinnamos' encomiastic presentation of the emperors John II and Manuel I primarily concentrates on diplomacy and wars, which the author in part seems to have witnessed in person in his capacity as imperial secretary.[15] Detailed descriptions of sieges and battles in the southwestern parts of the central Anatolian plateau and the Pontic region, the Byzantine ambitions towards Cilicia and the princedom of Antioch, the passage of the French and German contingents of the Second Crusade in 1147, and the Byzantine disaster at Myriokephalon in September 1176 dominate the narrative concerning the developments in the East. Despite the author's efforts to emphasize the successes of the imperial troops, it becomes clear that the Byzantines were facing powerful rivals determined to maintain the territories once conquered and possessing a strong network of coalitions and well-organized armed forces.[16] Choniates deals with the same topics but adopts more differentiated views regarding the emperors' policy and the Constantinopolitan elite and relates more details regarding the internal affairs of the Turkish principalities.[17] Choniates, too, supports the idea promoted by the imperial government that the provinces of Asia Minor are still Roman territory and the Turkish rulers are nothing but illegal usurpers, and he expresses the hope that with God's help righteous rule one day will be restored. This does not prevent him, however, from mentioning the deficiencies of the Byzantine men in power, such as the defection of John's brother Isaac and his son John to the Turks or Manuel I's tactical mistakes and cowardice before and during the battle of Myriokephalon. The emperor's diplomatic efforts had some positive results in outplaying rivaling emirs against each other but, on the other hand, Choniates also admits that the attempts to establish a durable peace agreement with Sultan Qilij Arslān II failed. The period after Manuel's death coincides with the apogee of Qilij Arslān II's power and the civil strife among his sons following the sultan's death in August 1192. Against this background, Choniates develops his increasingly negative image of the Byzantine Empire's decay. Accordingly, he places special emphasis on the chaos and disintegration of the provinces in Asia Minor, which fell victim to the attacks of Turkmen nomads living in the border zone and prepared the ground for the emergence of numerous local rebels, who readily took refuge at and collaborated with the Seljuk rulers.[18]

The Muslim-Turkish principalities' gradual consolidation is also reflected in the changing ethnic designations used by Byzantine historians. The eleventh-century authors had a clear preference for "Turks" and "Huns," thus pointing to the uncivilized and unstable character of the steppe nomads, whereas the term "Persians" was primarily used for the Seljuk elite in Iraq and Iran. Anna Komnene used the same terms, but later Komnenian authors started to employ the word "Persians" consistently for the Turks of Asia Minor. This was appropriate for the language and cultural features prevailing in the Seljuk environment of Anatolia. It is also to be seen in the context of the Byzantine historical memory, according to which the term "Persians" serves as an umbrella word for high-ranking non-Christian rivals in the East.[19] With the establishment of the Turks in Asia Minor, the Byzantine thought world transferred this exotic Persian sphere to the new boundaries along the western fringes of the Anatolian plateau and the regions of the Pontic Mountains. One may also speak of a geographical narrowing of the eastern world, which corresponded to the increasing territorial losses. Accordingly, encomiastic texts propagating the successes of imperial warfare in the East refer to the strongholds of Bithynia and western Phrygia as the empire's extreme outposts, and the imperial troops' crossing the Halys River (Kızıl Irmak) in the reign of John II is celebrated as an awe-inspiring advance.[20]

Eastern Christian (non-Chalcedonian) historiography

The authors belonging to the non-Chalcedonian Christian communities in the eastern provinces of the empire articulate the viewpoint of the victims suffering the disastrous consequences of the Turkish raids. Their descriptions are frequently combined with harsh critique against the negligence, incompetence, and maladministration of the Byzantine government. Geographically, their accounts mainly focus on the provinces characterized by a strong presence of Armenian and Syrian population, such as Cilicia, the Pyramos/Jayḥān region, Cappadocia, Antioch and its environs, the Upper Euphrates and Anti-Taurus region with Edessa and Melitene as principle urban centers, and the Armenian lands from Vaspurakan up to Transcaucasia, the Araxes Valley, and the Pontus region. Events and developments in the central Anatolian plateau and western Asia Minor are mostly beyond their scope while the imperial government of Constantinople appears as an oppressive but remote factor.

A contemporary witness of the first attacks in the Araxes and Upper Euphrates regions is the Armenian *vardapet* Aristakes of Lastivert (near Arcn), who in the years after 1072 wrote a chronicle covering the history of the Armenian kings from the death of David of Taykh in 1000 up to the death of Sultan Alp Arslan after his triumph at Manzikert in 1071.[21] A certain Matthew, a monk born in Edessa, who spent his life in the city's monastic circles and in Kaysūn (Keyşun) and probably died during the siege of his hometown in 1144, left us a chronicle covering the years 951–1136. In Matthew's historical thought, the Turks play a central role as an instrument of God's wrath caused by the moral decay of the political and spiritual leaders of the Armenian people and as characteristic feature of a new era.[22] In the introductory paragraph of the second part of his chronicle dealing with the period 502/1053-54-550/1101-2, the main subject of the narrative is defined by the author as "the horrible punishment, which the Armenian nation endured at the hands of … the nation of the Turks, and their brothers the Romans."[23] Accordingly, his report of Sultan Ṭughril Beg's 1054 campaign against Manzikert is preceded by that of the sacrilegious destruction of Syriac Gospels at the instigation of the Greek Patriarch of Antioch.[24] Likewise, the chronicle's last entry concerning the year 585/1136–37 combines an attack of Dānishmandid forces against Marʿash and Kaysūn with the removal of the Rubenid lord Leo of Cilicia by Emperor John II.[25] It has been convincingly argued that Matthew's views were not so much informed by an anti-Turkish or anti-Byzantine bias but rather by the conviction of an imminent apocalypse.[26] A continuation by Gregory the Priest, perhaps Matthews' pupil, pursues the narrative up to 611/1162–63.[27]

Michael the Syrian, monk in the Jacobite monastery of Mār Bar Ṣawmā near Melitene and patriarch of the Syriac Church from 1166–99,[28] shares with the Armenian historians the resentments against the Chalcedonian Byzantines as well as the idea that the emergence of the Turks marked the beginning of a new era. Yet, his narrative draws on different sources and reveals a much more differentiated view of the Turks' historical role. According to Michael, "the empire of the Turks," which persists until his own days, began with the proclamation of Ṭughril Beg, the first ruler of the Turks in Khurāsān. As is to be expected, the first event to be related in detail is the attack on Melitene in the winter 1057–58.[29] The hiatus caused by the Turkish expansion is further accentuated by an extensive historic-ethnographical digression, which forms Book XIV of Michael's chronicle.[30] It claims that the Turks are the instrument of God's wrath, identifying them with the Old-Testament people of Gog and Magog in Ezekiel's prophecies. This propagation is embedded in a survey referring to the original homeland of the Turks in the extreme northeast, the Gök-Turkic empire of the sixth century, the Turkish migration and diffusion into the Arab world, their nomadic manners and customs, and their religious beliefs before adopting one of the monotheistic faiths.[31] In addition, because of his exalted position as representative of the Syriac Monophysite Christians and his deep acquaintance with his Turkish overlords, Michael had the opportunity to gain many first-hand insights into the Seljuk sultanate of Konya and the eastern Anatolian emirates, as is documented, for instance, by his personal relations with Sultan Qilij Arslān II and the high esteem in which the latter held the Syriac hierarch.[32]

Gregory Abū l-Faraj Bar Hebraeus (1225–1286), a well-known Syriac cleric and man of letters, who after holding several bishoprics in 1264 was appointed Maphrian of Takrīt and the East, eventually managed to combine the Syriac historiographical tradition represented by excerpts from Michael's chronicle and some additional material with the earliest Seljuk sources starting with the *Malik-nāma*.[33] Since he had access to the original version of this work, he preserved for us the name of a certain Inanj Beg, who is referred to as the chief authority for the origins of the Seljuk family. As for the political history of the region in the twelfth century, Bar Hebraeus in large parts summarizes Michael's narrative, so that Chabot in his translation filled certain lacunas in the only surviving manuscript with excerpts from Bar Hebraeus' chronicle.[34]

All in all, the reactions of non-Chalcedonian authors to the first appearance of the Turks are dominated by keened lamentations about the invaders' merciless pillaging and killing and the unrestrained devastation of cultivated areas and wealthy urban centers. The Armenians further express their deep regret for the irrevocable loss of the glorious past of their powerful aristocracy and the independent kingdoms of the Artsruni and Bagratid dynasties. Another serious concern was the preservation of their religious identity and the traditions inherited from their forefathers, for with the increasing pressure of the Turkish invaders, representatives of the local elites sought to come to terms with the new strong men. As time went on, a tendency towards Islamization made its appearance, menacing the continued existence of the indigenous communities.[35]

Things changed in the decades following the first invasions, when the Turkish warlords not only pillaged as before, but also started more-systematic attempts to permanently occupy urban centers and to build up administrative structures and a flourishing economic life in the newly acquired territories. During this second stage, it became obvious that there actually were perspectives for a prosperous future. Accordingly, authors, who, writing in the middle or second half of the twelfth century, were able to give an overview of long-term developments after the end of the Byzantine presence in eastern Anatolia, gradually became more optimistic and adopted the attitude of loyal and in certain respects even grateful subjects of Turkish-Muslim powers.[36] Moreover, the incessant conflicts resulting from the establishment of the crusader states in Antioch and Edessa were perceived as a factor of instability, frequently causing new calamities to the eastern Christians.[37] It turned out that the rule of Latin Christians was no better than that of Muslim rulers. The overwhelmingly negative impressions prevailing in the descriptions of the Turkish raids came to be merged with feelings of respect and gratitude for leading figures of the Turkish-Muslim elite, who cared for the security and economic sustainability of the local Christian population, its ecclesiastical organization, and their monasteries.

Muslim historiography

The Muslim sources concerning the rise of the Seljuk Empire provide rich information about the origins of the dynasty and the activities of the warrior groups associated with its members but are always rather elusive and inaccurate with respect to the penetration of Byzantine territories beyond northern Syria and Upper Mesopotamia. Hence, they tell us a great deal about the large-scale campaigns initiated by the Seljuk sultans Ṭughril Beg and Alp Arslān and, later on, about the expansionist attempts of Sulaymān b. Qutlumush and Qilij Arslān I towards Antioch, Aleppo, and Mosul. But the situation in the interior of Asia Minor, the gradual formation of the Muslim principalities there, and the co-existence between the indigenous population and the conquerors largely remain beyond their scope.[38] Generally, the early Islamic *futūḥ* (conquest) narratives treat the process of political expansion and Islamization in Christian territories on the basis of retrospectively developed legal concepts and a set of recurring topoi and motifs.[39] In contrast, Muslim authors did not develop any comparable systematic treatment of the Turkish invasions of Byzantine Asia Minor. This certainly has to do with the nature and contents of the historiographical sub-genres that included narratives about the Seljuks into their account. Dynastic histories are mainly concerned with the rise of the Seljuk family from Oghuz tribal chiefs in Transoxania and Khurāsān to a supreme power in the Muslim world and leaders of Sunni Islam. Muslim universal histories consider the activities of the Seljuks and the Turkmen tribes subject to them as part of the broader political developments shaping the historical fate of the lands stretching between Syria and eastern Iran. Local histories refer to the Seljuk Turks only insofar as they directly affected the region on which they are focusing. The scope of all these sources, therefore, is largely confined to the Muslim core lands and the major urban centers. To a certain degree, they include the old Byzantine-Arab marches in Cilicia, the Upper Euphrates region, the Taurus Mountains, and Armenia. But the Anatolian plateau, let alone the regions of the Aegean and Black Sea shores, was simply too far off to be of any immediate relevance to these historians.[40]

Another issue is the highly complicated textual history of these works, which in most cases are traceable to contemporary witnesses and drafts but came down to us in the form of much later versions. These, in turn, evince several stages of re-working, in which original tendencies and perspectives were altered and material was added or removed. Since the relevant studies of Claude Cahen, it has been generally accepted that the oldest layer of the Seljuk historical tradition is a Persian *Malik-nāma*, i.e., "King's Book," which included material up to the death of Sultan Ṭughril Beg and was dedicated to his successor Alp Arslān.[41] Between the middle of the twelfth and the early fourteenth century this core piece, most likely on the basis of various versions and Arabic translations, was further elaborated and integrated into other works. A leading position in this process of textual transmission is held by Ẓahīr al-Dīn al-Nīshāpūrī, the author of a *Saljūq-nāma* datable to about 1177. One version of this work, which is quite close to the original, though enriched with various later additions, is transmitted in the *Jāmi' al-tawārīkh* by the early fourteenth-century Ilkhānid writer Rashīd al-Dīn Faḍlallāh.[42] On the basis of Anūshirwān b. Khālid's memoirs (ca. 1133), ʿImād al-Dīn al-Iṣfahānī in 579/1183–84 wrote a history of the Iraqi Seljuks, which has been abridged in a thirteenth-century version entitled *Zubdat al-Nuṣra* by al-Bundārī.[43] Muḥammad al-Rāwandī, who had previously served at the Great Seljuk court of Hamadhān, between 599/1202–1203 and 1210 composed the compendium *Rāḥat al-ṣudūr wa-āyat al-surūr* dedicated to Sultan Ghiyāth al-Dīn Kaykhusraw I of Konya. In its historical section, the work largely relies on Ẓahīr al-Dīn al-Nīshāpūrī's history.[44] The only surviving manuscript of an Arabic dynastic chronicle entitled *Akhbār al-dawlat al-Saljūqiyya* written after 622/1225 most probably erroneously mentions a certain Ṣadr al-Dīn al-Ḥusaynī as author.[45] Furthermore, extensive parts of the *Malik-nāma* and other material referring to the Seljuks in Asia Minor and the Islamic central lands are transmitted in the universal chronicle of Ibn al-Athīr (ca. 1231) and, as mentioned before, in that of Bar Hebraeus. The two authors in all likelihood used as their sources two different versions with strongly diverging tendencies.[46] These discrepancies illustrate the particularities of each version, but it is very difficult to say when and under what circumstances these changes occurred. As a result, the question as to whether certain reports reflect immediate knowledge of contemporary events or later interpretations still needs further clarification.

The second important universal chronicle for the early Seljuk expansion in Anatolia and adjacent regions is *Mir'āt al-zamān* by Sibṭ b. al-Jawzī (d. 1257), who included extensive excerpts from the eleventh-century work of Ghars al-Niʿma (d. 1080/1088), which concerned the policy of the first Seljuk sultans Ṭughril Beg, Alp Arslān, and Malik-Shāh.[47] Especially valuable are the reports about the activities of Turkish commanders and warrior groups in Syria, Alp Arslān's campaign of 1070–71, and the battle of Manzikert.[48] Rich additional material concerning the effects of the Seljuk expansion on specific regions can be found in the Aleppo chronicles written by al-ʿAẓīmī (d. shortly after 1160/61) and Kamāl al-Dīn b. al-ʿAdīm (d. 1262),[49] the Damascus chronicle by Ibn al-Qalānisī (d. 1160), who continued the narrative of older works from 448/1056–57 up to the year of his death,[50] and the chronicle of Mayyāfāriqīn (Silvan) in Diyār Bakr by Ibn al-Azraq al-Fāriqī (d. after 1181), who gives a noteworthy account of the Marwānid and Artuqid rulers of the region up to 572/1176.[51]

While the historical narratives of the various branches of the Seljuk dynasty were further elaborated in Persian chronicles of the fourteenth and fifteenth century, the local Anatolian historiography about the sultanate of Rūm began only in 680/1281–82 with Ibn Bībī's *al-Awāmir al-'alā'iyya fī l-umūr al-'alā'iyya* covering the period from Ghiyāth al-Dīn Kaykhusraw I's rise to power in 1192 up to 1280.[52] Lacking reliable sources, the author explains, he was not able to treat the history prior to this date. Hence, there is no elaborate presentation of the foundation period written from the Anatolian Seljuk viewpoint. At least, Ibn Bībī's statement sufficiently clarifies that, apart from the aforementioned texts, there was hardly any other near-contemporary and reliable material circulating in the twelfth and thirteenth centuries. This is also confirmed by Karīm al-Dīn Maḥmūd-i Aqsarā'ī, the author of *Musāmarat al-akhbār wa-musāyarat al-aḥyār* written in 723/1323. This work mainly concerns itself with the events after the end of Ibn Bībī's chronicle up to the first quarter of the fourteenth century, adding an extensive introduction based on the older *Saljūq-nāma* tradition.[53] An anonymous fourteenth-century *Saljūq-nāma* with a special focus on the sultanate of Rūm provides some additional material not known from other sources, but given the succinct character of the chronicle and the late date of its composition, it remains open to what degree these pieces of information can be considered trustworthy.[54] The problem of authenticity notwithstanding, the text clearly illustrates the potential of the Anatolian Seljuks in the time after the dynasty's collapse to serve as a point of reference for the construction of collective memories and continuances going back to the arrival of the sons of Qutlumush.[55] Consequently, when during the reign of Sultan Murād II (1421–51) increasing efforts were made to strengthen the foundations of an Ottoman dynastic ideology, Yazıcızāde ʿAlī translated Ibn Bībī's chronicle and other Persian works into Turkish. Thus, he wanted to create the historiographical basis for establishing close links among the Oghuz migrations, the Seljuk sultanate, and the emergence of Osman Beg.[56] The *Jihānnümā* of Meḥmed Neshrī written in the years of Sultan Bāyezīd II (1481–1512) once again presents the Seljuk period as a preparatory stage of the Ottoman Empire.[57] Henceforth, substantial chapters on the Seljuk sultanate of Rūm continued to be included in works of Ottoman universal history, as can be seen, for instance, in the late sixteenth century work of Cenābī (d. 1590).[58]

A particular case is the so-called *Dānishmend-nāme*, a Turkish epic romance dealing with the deeds of Malik Dānishmand, the conqueror of the northeastern parts of the Anatolian plateau around the basin of the Halys River (Kızıl Irmak) and founder of a homonymous local dynasty. In later Turkish collective memory, he came to be a legendary champion of *jihad*, carrying on the tradition of the Arab hero Sayyid Baṭṭāl of Malatya.[59] Some of the hero's most noteworthy characteristics are his zeal to draw Christian opponents to his side and to convert them to Islam as well as his readiness to use unrestricted violence against all those stubbornly insisting on their faith. The circle of his closest companions, thus, largely consisted of Christian converts to Islam, who by no means fell short of their lord in fulfilling the tasks of jihad warriors.[60] Central protagonists fighting on the side of Malik Dānishmand are Artukhī, the converted son of the Christian lord of Amaseia, a character combining epic features with memories related to Emir Artuk, and Efromiya (< Greek Εὐμορφία), the converted daughter of a Christian lord and Artukhī's wife, who combines elements of Amazon women in the Turkish epical tradition with the historical memory of Morphia, the daughter of Gabriel, the last Christian lord of Melitene. Furthermore, the text refers to faithful companions of Christian origin, such as the spy Yaḥyā bin

ʿĪsā, and former enemies who converted to Islam, such as Aḥmed-i Serkīs, the brothers of Toqat, and Pānīc, the nephew of Mikhāʾīl.[61]

This romance with its morale-boosting content and religious frame of reference apparently addresses an audience imbued with a fully developed concept of Muslim *ghāzī* fighters. It served to dignify the memories of the conquest period and to legitimize Turkish-Muslim rulers as heirs of an age-old *jihad* tradition in Anatolia going back to the time of the early caliphate. The earliest version of the romance is ascribed to a certain Mawlānā Ibn ʿAlā, who in 642/1245 or somewhat later put the oral tradition about Malik Dānishmand in writing and dedicated his work to Sultan ʿIzz al-Dīn Kaykāʾūs II, thus linking the legendary hero of the conquest period with the Seljuk dynasty. In 762/1360–61 this text was thoroughly revised by ʿĀrif ʿAlī, governor of Tokat, who reworked it stylistically, rearranged its contents, and adorned it with descriptions and poems reflecting the atmosphere of Turkmen-nomadic lifestyle and Islamic mysticism in fourteenth-century Anatolia. In the year 997/1586 the Ottoman bureaucrat and historian ʿAlī (Muṣṭafā b. Aḥmad) of Gelibolu (1541–1599) composed a paraphrase of this work, thus inserting the narrative into the Ottoman historiographical tradition.[62] Various characters and historical and geographical details echo realities of the conquest period or later chronological layers. They point to the conflation of a factual core with epic features, narrative patterns, and literary conventions of the Arabic heroic cycle and the Turkish-Persian poetic tradition. One should be extremely cautious in accepting the spirit and atmosphere expressed therein as reflecting genuine attitudes prevailing in the conquest period.

In summary, there is a great variety of texts in the Muslim historiographical tradition referring to the early Turkish penetration of Asia Minor, but these reports are usually embedded in the idealized presentations of Seljuk sultans in dynastic and universal chronicles or in locally colored narratives focusing on regions of the former Byzantine-Arab marches in Syria and Upper Mesopotamia. Developments taking place in central and western Anatolia are only off-handedly mentioned, whenever they are of direct relevance for the Muslim central lands. Later on, when the Seljuk sultanate of Rūm had become a dominant power with its own ideology and dynastic identity, the time of the Turkish expansion was re-interpreted as a glorious formative stage, in which loyal subjects of the Seljuk Empire extended their sway over Christian lands and champions of *jihad* brought Islam to Anatolia. In this way, the legendary beginnings turned into a point of reference for concepts of legitimacy and continuity. They established imaginary links between heroes of Muslim faith, Turkish tribal traditions, a branch of the Seljuk dynasty, and the founders of the Ottoman Empire.

The Turkish principalities as seen in crusader sources

Important information on the early establishment of Turkish lordships in Asia Minor can be gained from Latin eyewitness accounts and later narratives of the First Crusade, especially with respect to the period between the arrival of the so-called People's Crusade under Peter the Hermit in Bithynia in August 1096 and the defeat of Karbūqā outside the gates of Antioch on 28 June 1098.[63] These accounts certainly underwent various stages of literary elaboration and thus reflect retrospective interpretations and later perceptions, but they also include a considerable amount of (near-)contemporary material.[64] A part of the crusader narratives, especially the *Gesta Francorum* and its derivatives, presents the Turks of Anatolia in line with the Arab Muslims of Syria and Palestine as the embodiment of an evil and infidel force opposing the Christian pilgrims, who were conceived of as the chosen people fulfilling God's plan.[65] According to the strong propagandistic agenda of these texts, which intended to portray the crusaders' armed pilgrimage as an exemplary act of penitence pleasing to God and leading to salvation, they strongly emphasize the Turks' ferocity, moral inferiority, and aggressive attitude towards all adherents of the Christian faith.[66] The Turks are, as the anonymous author of the *Gesta Francorum* asserts, an accursed folk, misbelieving and abominable people, enemies of God and Christianity; they have the habit of looting churches, houses, and other places; they are innumerable and howl and shout like demons in battle.[67] Nevertheless, even in the context of such ill-disposed and emotionally charged descriptions it is admitted that the Turkish warriors were highly dangerous adversaries disposing of an effective battle technique and an amazing fighting force. The Turks had defeated Arabs, Saracens, Armenians, Syrians, and Greeks; they even claim to be of common stock with the Franks, and indeed, if they were good Christians, one would not find braver, stronger, or more skillful soldiers.[68] The Turks' military strength was a common experience shared by all participants in this expedition and a recurring motif highlighting the invincibility of the God-protected Christian army. Describing the Turks' flight after their defeat in the battle of Dorylaion, for instance, the *Gesta Francorum* have the Seljuk ruler deliver a speech to his troops. Reportedly, he referred to his army as being terror-stricken because of the innumerable host of crusaders filling mountains, hills, and valleys.[69] Despite the Turks' awe-inspiring strength, the passage leaves no doubt that the Christian knights will prevail.

Other crusader authors of the early twelfth century like Fulcher of Chartres (writing between 1100/01 and 1127) and Albert of Aachen (writing between 1102 and the 1130s) and later on William of Tyre (writing between 1170 and 1184) express more differentiated views of the Turkish enemy. These historians certainly regard the Seljuk ruler, the military chiefs, and their warriors in Nicaea, Antioch, and other places dangerous enemies of the pilgrims and the Christian faith, but they also respect them for the extent of their realm, the size and strength of their troops, and their military skills.[70] Moreover, they also refer to aspects of the internal organization of the Turkish principalities in Asia Minor and comment on the broader historical framework within which these political entities came into being. In the second half of the twelfth century, William of Tyre, for the first time in Latin historiography, offered his own original explanation of the emergence of the Turks and their rise to a leading political power in the Near East.[71]

Despite ample opportunities to gain direct insights into the situation of Anatolia during their march, the crusaders do not seem to have been especially interested in the internal structures of the Turkish-Muslim elites and warrior groups they were facing. Unlike the keen eye of Anna Komnene and other Byzantine observers for the constellations of power among the Turkish emirates, which under certain circumstances could be exploited for the purpose of favorable alliances and diplomatic contacts, the crusaders regarded the Turks of Asia Minor as a homogeneous group of enemies and conquerors, who had managed to extend their sway over the whole of *Romania*, i.e., the eastern provinces of the empire stretching from the Euphrates River to the shores of the Propontis. Indicative of this perception are Fulcher of Chartres' words referring to the advance of the crusading army towards Nicaea after the defeat of Peter the Hermit's forces:

> At that time, this city [Nicaea] was in the possession of the eastern Turks, highly skillful archers. Already fifty years ago, these people coming from Persia had crossed the Euphrates River and had subjugated the entire land of Romania as far as the city of Nikomedeia.[72]

Fulcher is quite accurate in terms of chronology: 50 years prior to 1097 is the time of the first Turkish raids in the Armenian marches. As regards the origin and identity of the Turks, however, he did not go deeper into the issue, but was content with identifying them as "pagans from Persia."[73] As to qualities and characteristics of the Turks, a central feature is the use of the bow, the basic weapon of their fighting technique, by which they were able to cover the Frankish armies with veritable clouds of harassing arrows resulting in high losses even before close combat began.[74]

As regards the extent of the Turkish realm, Fulcher's report gives us the impression that the crusader troops were confronted with Turkish enemies along the entire route from Bithynia to Antioch, but the author hardly distinguishes individual potentates and their respective positions in the conquered regions. As a result, he sees the supreme authority over the Turks in Anatolia concentrated in the hands of one man, Soliman, the emir and lord of the Turks, who held sway over Nicaea and Romania.[75] Likewise, the *Gesta Francorum* refer to "Solimanus their leader, the son of old Solimanus," and Albert of Aachen talks about "the territory of the city of Nicaea and the kingdom of Solimannus," "a magnificent man, the lord and prince of the Turks," and "Solimannus, one of the princes of the Turks, a very noble man but also a heathen."[76]

The crusader chroniclers' image of the Turkish ruler results from a confusion between Sulaymān b. Qutlumush and the actual Seljuk chief from 1093 onwards, his son and successor Qilij Arslān I. Given that these statements reproduce contemporary first-hand knowledge, it may be assumed that the name of the father, founder of the principality, had completely overshadowed that of his son. The distinction made by the *Gesta Francorum* between an elder and a younger Sulaymān reminds us of the Muslim practice of designating the son by his father's name, i.e., as *Ibn Sulaymān*. Despite the interlude of Apelchasem in the years 1086–93, the historical memory of Sulaymān's deeds was still alive among foreign and Turkish observers and helped Qilij Arslān assert his own claims to the father's realm, thus creating a sort of dynastic continuity among the Turks of Asia Minor. Another remarkable aspect of crusader conceptions of Seljuk rule in Asia Minor is the equation between Sulaymān's realm and *Romania*, one of the traditional Greek designations of the Byzantine Empire. In this way, Sulaymān and his successors appear as heirs of a country inhabited by Roman people and deeply permeated by a Roman cultural and political identity. In the collective memory of Frankish observers, the notions of Turkish dominion and Roman lands began to merge. This reminds us of the observations that can be made with respect to the new rulers' styles of self-representation combining Byzantine and Muslim elements. Contemporary observers noticed a process at the level of structural changes similar to what was transpiring in the case of those individual potentates. Territories and ruling elites gradually developed into new entities characterized by a mixed identity drawing on pre-existing substructures and newly imported institutional patterns.[77]

The most circumstantial description of Sulaymān's authority can be found in the chronicle of William of Tyre. He presents the picture of a well-established principality based on firmly controlled territories and a well-functioning administration and that derived its legitimacy from the conferral of rights of sovereignty by "the greatest sultan of the Persians" Belfetoh (= Abū l-Fatḥ, i.e., Alp Arslān). In the time of Romanos Diogenes, the latter had conquered all provinces between the Hellespont and Syria and had conceded them to Sulaymān, who ruled over them on the basis of rights of sovereignty. Hence, his officials within the sight of Constantinople imposed tolls on transients and collected taxes from the entire region.[78] The late twelfth-century crusader historian thus adopts the idea of Sulaymān's appointment by Alp Arslān, as is expressed in works of Seljuk court historiography and the chronicle of Michael the Syrian.[79] The fact that this detail does not appear in older Frankish narratives shows that it was not borrowed from the historical tradition of the First Crusade and that we are dealing with a later construction most likely originating from the sultanate of Konya in the time when its political ideology had achieved a high state of development. The same applies to the image of Sulaymān's dominion straddling the whole of Asia Minor, as is also expressed by Anna Komnene. In this way, the Turkish ruler is portrayed as a lawful successor to Byzantine rights of sovereignty over the empire's eastern provinces. Furthermore, William characterizes Sulaymān as "an extremely powerful commander of the Turks [...] who was also called *Ssa*, which in the language of the Persians means 'king.'"[80] Apparently, the author was acquainted with the Persian title *shāh*, which Seljuk sources sometimes add to Sulaymān's name, i.e., *Sulaymān-shāh*. The use of this specific Persian term suggests that William had access to an informant or a written source closely associated with the environment of the Seljuk court. In another passage, William comes back to the issue of the distribution of territories among the sultan's commanders.[81] Reportedly, the sultan of the Persians, Belfetoh (the author does not distinguish between Alp Arslan and Malikshāh), conferred all the provinces he had conquered to his nephews and companions. Besides Sulaymān, he explicitly mentions Yaghī Siyān of Antioch (*Acxianus*), Duqāq of Damascus (*Ducac*), and Aqsunqur of Aleppo (*Assungur*). The relationship between the sultan and his subordinate commanders is explained by bonds of loyalty, which the latter were obliged to maintain in remembrance of the sultan's benefits.[82] The centralizing tendencies of the Seljuk sultanate in 1087 thus are interpreted in terms of feudal relations between a seigneur and his vassals. Moreover, William refers to Malikshāh's awarding of the title of sultan (*soldanatus et nomen et dignitatem*) to Sulaymān and Duqāq as a special distinction due to his acknowledgment of the exposed position of their realm next to dangerous neighbors, i.e., the Greeks of the Empire of Constantinople and the Egyptians. In this sense, the rank of sultan is connected with especially demanding military tasks in border regions and is not conceived of as a title expressing political independence.

William of Tyre is the only crusader historian to offer this comprehensive view of Seljuk hierarchical relations, which despite all inaccuracies still reflects some knowledge of Muslim political structures. The early twelfth-century chroniclers of the First Crusade are rather inconsistent in their presentation of the Turkish chiefs with which the Frankish troops were dealing. Yaghī Siyān is *Aoxianus* or *Darsianus*, the "lord and emir" or even "the king of Antioch." Karbūqā is *Curbaram*, *Corbagath*, or *Corbahan*, "the leader and satrap," or in Albert of Aachen's account "a friend and favorite at the royal court and second to the king in the kingdom of Khurasan."[83] In a list of combatants fighting in the battle of Antioch on 28 June 1098, Fulcher mentions a number of Turkish officers by name, but they can hardly be identified with individuals known from other sources.[84]

Like William of Tyre, earlier crusader narratives too refer to a supreme authority of all Turks located in Persia or Khurāsān. The author of the *Gesta Francorum* speaks of the "sultan of Persia" and, in a fictitious letter ascribed to Karbūqā, he has the Seljuk overlord be addressed as "our king, the lord sultan, that most valiant warrior." Fulcher describes the sultan as "emperor of Persia" or "king of the Persians." Albert of Aachen characterizes Khurāsān (*Corruzan*) in a speech put into the mouth of Yaghī Siyān of Antioch as "the land and kingdom of our [the Turks'] birth" and regards the sultan or king of Khurāsān as "the head and prince of the Turks."[85] According to these descriptions, the sultan is both the ruler of a vast realm in the Muslim lands beyond Romania, i.e., Asia Minor, and a powerful military leader who is able to muster huge armies from among the Turks and other nations living in the Muslim world. In some sources the sultan figures along with a *calipha apostolicus* who is a supreme spiritual authority of all Muslims endowed with special competences, such as the right to issue licenses to kill all Christians.[86] Most intriguingly, the idea that the land of Khurāsān is a sort of homeland of all Turks, in which their supreme sovereign resides, is also shared by Anna Komnene.[87] Christian authors commonly believed that it was a land situated east of Syria and the Euphrates River, but no source gives an exact definition of its geographical position. Thus, it came to be tantamount to the original homeland of the Turks, from which an endless stream of immigrants was to be expected and that was the source of the Turks' political power.

As regards the character of Turkish rule in Anatolia, crusader texts sometimes stress the illegitimate nature of the conquests and distinguish between the rights of the Byzantine emperor and the unjust violence by which the Turks took possession of these territories. In Albert of Aachen's opinion, a heathen force of Turks unjustly snatched Nicaea from the emperor, for originally the city was subject to the emperor by hereditary law.[88] As opposed to the Byzantine historians, who at least in practice if not in theory recognize the *status quo* created by the Turkish expansion in Asia Minor from 1081 onwards, these texts support the Frankish claims based on the agreements between Emperor Alexios I and the leaders of the crusade and thus present the emperor as the only legitimate lord of Romania. Consequently, they evoke the violence by which the Turks had overthrown the emperor's lawful rule in order to justify the war the crusaders waged upon the newly established lordships.[89]

But the cities and provinces of Anatolia were labeled Romania not just by virtue of being part of the Byzantine Empire but also because of their overwhelmingly Christian and Greek-speaking population. This is another aspect frequently emphasized by crusader narratives referring to the people living under Turkish rule. Albert of Aachen, for instance, explicitly states that the followers of Peter the Hermit while wandering about the environs of Nicaea "plundered the herds of cattle, oxen, and sheep, [and] flocks of goats that belonged to Greek subjects of the Turks."[90] Likewise, the regions of Philomelion, Konya, and Herakleia, through which the crusader army passed on its march to the East, were inhabited by Christian citizens subject to the Turkish forces of Sulaymān.[91] Accordingly, with respect to Cilicia and northern Syria, there are references to the local Armenian and Syrian populations living in the cities attacked by the Franks. A case in point is the city of Samosata at the Euphrates, which was in the hands of the Turkish potentate Balduk.[92] William of Tyre describes him as an "infidel man, a Turk by nation, strong in arms, but devious and worthless," who oppressed the citizens with various harassments, imposed tributes, taxes, and compulsory labor upon them and kept their children as hostages. As a result, the inhabitants called upon Baldwin, following his takeover of Edessa, to help them against their lord. Eventually, Balduk sold the city to Baldwin for the sum of 10,000 gold coins.[93] Likewise, William describes Balak of Sarūj as a "satrap of the Turks," who did injustice to the inhabitants and oppressed them. Therefore, they asked Baldwin for peace and accepted a governor appointed by him and the payment of annual tribute to him in exchange for guarantees for their security.[94] Another example is the fortress of Artāḥ near Antioch, in which, according to Albert of Aachen, Armenian Christians lived under the yoke of the Turks. When the crusader army was approaching, these people, in revenge for the oppression they had endured, attacked and killed the Turks, cut off their heads, and threw them out of windows and from the walls, thus inviting the Franks to enter the town.[95]

As a result of their general tendency to perceive the historical context of the crusader movement as a bilateral Christian-Muslim antagonism, these reports underline the frictions between Christian subjects and Turkish conquerors in order to present the crusading forces as saviors liberating the local population from evil tyrants. The Christians are depicted as rising up against the severe oppression of their Turkish lords as soon as the Franks arrive. As will be shown below, however, the sources also talk about instances of collaboration between indigenous Christians and Turks against the Franks. Even crusader chroniclers admitted that despite all hostility there were numerous contacts and interactions between the two sides. Moreover, most accounts emphasize that most Christians continued to pursue their crafts and professions in urban centers and rural areas. The establishment of a new ruling class, apparently, did not bring about any major changes in the pre-existing social fabric.

Due to the outstanding significance of its siege and conquest for the course of the First Crusade, by far the most detailed reports that have come down to us are related to the city of Antioch. William of Tyre describes this city as a bulwark of the Christian faith surrounded by Muslim foes.[96] Less than 14 years ago, William relates, it had been handed over to the enemies of Christendom. Therefore, when the crusading army arrived, almost all inhabitants were still Christians but had no power in the city. They were free to engage in trade and crafts, but only Turks and Muslims were allowed to become soldiers and hold high offices. The Christians were prohibited from bearing weapons, and during the siege of Antioch their freedom of movement within the city was limited to several hours a day. The way William presents the relationship between Christians and Turks in Antioch in the years after the conquest most likely applies to most towns subjugated to Turkish rule at that time. The new potentates did not interfere in the local social and economic structures. Deep-rooted changes affected the ruling elite, which was replaced by Turkish commanders, although, in view of the manifold alliances with Christian military chiefs, it may be assumed that the division was not as strict as William's report may suggest. Most likely, the new rulers developed mechanisms to subsume Christian allies quite smoothly into the ranks of their fighting forces. Moreover, there were numerous local people forming a kind of connecting link between rulers and subjects. William mentions the Beni Zerra family (Banū Darrāʿ, i.e., "sons of the cuirass-smith"), who were allocated a tower near the Gate of St. George in order to pursue their craft. Bohemond's liaison Emirfeirus gained a powerful position due to his close relations with Yaghī Siyān and worked as notary in the emir's palace.[97] This did not prevent him from secretly informing Bohemond about the state of affairs in the city and the plans of Yaghī Siyān.[98]

As is to be expected, the Christian inhabitants of Antioch, Greeks, Armenians, and Syrians alike, greatly suffered during the siege, and with the increasing pressure of the besieging army, their situation deteriorated. Poor people, who could not be sustained by their relatives, were ousted. People of higher standing, who could afford enough food, were allowed to stay but endured other forms of mistreatment like heavy payments and compulsory labor. They were forced to construct catapults and carry heavy beams and boulders, were beaten and insulted. Allegedly, the commanders ultimately decided to kill all Christians in the city, but the execution of the plan was postponed because of an eight-day armistice.[99] These details, however, reflect living conditions under the deadly threat of a protracted siege. Most likely, the hostile attitudes of the Turkish defenders were further exacerbated by the fear of potential agreements between the Christian inhabitants and the Frankish besiegers.

In fact, the Greeks, Syrians, and Armenians opened the city gates to Bohemond and his troops. Nevertheless, William of Tyre claims that many Christians also lost their lives in the ensuing massacres. Partly, this was due to Turkish soldiers who continued to fight on the towers and hit many non-combatants with their arrows. At the same time, the Franks killed Christians along with Muslims as the dark of the night prevented the crusaders from properly discriminating between the two, while many Turks pretended to be Christians by using the language of one of the Christian communities or by proffering a cross.[100] According to William of Tyre it was difficult for the Franks to identify clearly recognizable markers distinguishing Turks from Christians. In a similar vein, he mentions a great number of spies (*exploratores*) sent by the Turks to the Frankish camp outside Antioch to gather intelligence about the habits, virtues, and goals of such a large army. Through their skill in language and adoption of the proper appearance, behavior, and manner of speaking, they impersonated Greeks, Syrians, or Armenians convincingly and apparently mingled with the people in the camp with great ease. It was so difficult for the Franks to discover these spies that their leaders took measures to prevent the dissemination of sensitive information among their enemies. For instance, Bohemond ordered some Turkish prisoners to be slain, roasted, and prepared as a meal, in order to intimidate and so deter potential spies by means of an extremely frightening form of punishment.[101] But there were also Armenians and Syrians collaborating with the Turks. By pretending to be refugees, they conveyed information about the state of affairs in the Frankish camp to the Turkish commanders in Antioch.[102] If we believe the *Gesta Francorum*, Armenians and Syrians not only spied on the Franks but also benefited from their lack of supplies. When the crusaders began to face increasing shortages, indigenous Christians were still able to buy grain and provisions because of their acquaintance with the local conditions and sold them at excessively high prices, thus causing the death of poor people who could not afford them.[103]

These details clearly illustrate that within a few years after the conquest strong tendencies towards assimilation between the local population and the Turkish ruling class with respect to clothing, habits, and language made their appearance. As a result, distinguishing markers were not always visible at first sight, and the Franks, who came as foreigners to both Turks and Eastern Christians, discriminated between them with difficulty. In spite of institutional and religious divisions, there was a broad zone of contact between Turks and local Christians in everyday life, administrative matters, and commercial transactions. The Turks swiftly adopted elements from the socio-cultural milieu in which they had come to live, and for their part, members of the local Christian communities were ready to collaborate with their new lords at various levels. Despite the oppressive measures taken by the Turks during the eight-month siege of Antioch, Christian townspeople supported their Turkish lords against the Frankish invaders and did not shrink from exploiting the crusaders' plight. The markets and agricultural produce in the environs of Antioch could hardly provide the tremendous amounts of supplies required to meet the needs of the crusading army during the siege. Hence, local traders were given the opportunity to make great profits. Under these circumstances, ethnic and religious identities were of secondary importance. What mattered to all groups involved was establishing a *modus vivendi* regulating the co-existence of subjects and rulers and a strategy of survival amidst the perils of the war against the Franks. No doubt, the crusaders' siege and conquest of Antioch in 1097/98 had much more devastating effects on local structures and the city's populace than its unspectacular takeover by Sulaymān b. Qutlumush in late 1084 or its conquest by the troops of Malikshāh in late 1086.

Notes

1 For theoretical approaches of this kind, see Goetz, *Geschichtsschreibung*, pp. 13–39; Küçükhüseyin, *Selbst- und Fremdwahrnehmung*, pp. 11–43.
2 Psellos 7.131-64, pp. 266–84; for the author, see Karpozilos, *Ιστορικοί*, 3:98–154.
3 Skylitzes, pp. 442–500; for the author, see Karpozilos, *Ιστορικοί*, 3:239–258; for more details concerning the image of the Seljuks in Skylitzes' work, see Beihammer, "Ethnogenese," pp. 597–98, 600–602, 606–608.
4 Shepard, "Armenia," pp. 269–83; idem, "Suspected Source," pp. 171–81.
5 Skylitzes Continuatus, ed. Tsolakis.
6 For the author, see Karpozilos, *Ιστορικοί*, 3:187–202, and now Krallis, *Attaleiates*.
7 Attaleiates, pp. 33–36, 59–195, 198–99, 206–207.
8 For the author, see Karpozilos, *Ιστορικοί*, 3:357–70.
9 Bryennios 1.7-21, 2.3-29, 3.15-23, 4.4-17, 4.31-40, pp. 88–129, 144–206, 236–50, 264–83, 300–311; for Melissenos, see Frankopan, "Fall of Nicaea," pp. 153–84.
10 For the author, see Karpozilos, *Ιστορικοί*, 3:465–89.
11 Zonaras 17.25.1-43, 18.10.3-18.19.25, 18.27.1-19, pp. 634–41, 683–724, 756–58.
12 For the author, see Karpozilos, *Ιστορικοί*, 3:397–425.
13 Anna Komnene 1.1.2-4.5, 1.6.1-9, 2.3.1, 2.4.2, 3.8.7, 3.9.3, 3.11.1-5, 5.6.4-7.2, 6.9.1-13.4, 7.7.4-8.10, 8.9.1-7, 9.1.2-3.4, 10.2.2, 10.2.6, 10.5.1-7, 10.6.1-6, 10.10.7, 10.11.8-10, 11.1.1-9.4, 12.1.1-2.6., 12.7.1-4, 14.1.2-2.2, 14.3.1-9, 14.5.1-6.6, 15.1.1-6.10, pp. 11–19, 24–27, 60, 62, 107, 110, 114–16, 159–160, 186–99, 222–26, 255–57, 258–65, 283–84, 286–87, 295–98, 299–301, 316–17, 320–21, 322–50, 359–63, 376–78, 424–28, 434–38, 443–49, 461–80.
14 Theodore Prodromos, no. 3–6, 8, pp. 191–228, 233–43; for details, see Beihammer, "Orthodoxy," pp. 23–26.
15 For the author, see Karpozilos, *Ιστορικοί*, 3:625–38.
16 Kinnamos 1.2-3, 1.5-10, 2.1, 2.4, 2.5-9, 2.11, 2.14-18, 4.17-18, 4.21-24, 5.3, 5.13, 6.1, 6.6, 6.7, 6.12, 7.1-3, pp. 5–7, 13–22, 30–31, 36, 38–56, 66–67, 72–86, 179–83, 188–202, 204–208, 238, 250–51, 265–68, 271, 288–90, 291–300.
17 For the author, see Karpozilos, *Ιστορικοί*, 3:699–728, and now Simpson, *Choniates*.
18 Choniates, ed. van Dieten, pp. 12–13, 18–21, 25, 32–38, 50, 52–53, 60–71, 116–25, 150, 176–98, 226, 286, 288–89, 367–68, 384, 400–401, 411–17, 420–22, 461–64, 474–75, 493–95, 504, 520–22, 528–29, 626, 638–39.
19 Beihammer, "Ethnogenese," pp. 608–609, and idem, "Der harte Sturz des Bardas Skleros: Eine Fallstudie zu zwischenstaatlicher Kommunikation und Konfliktführung in der byzantinisch-arabischen Diplomatie des 10. Jahrhunderts," *Römische Historische Mitteilungen* 45 (2003), 21–57, at pp. 33–34.
20 Beihammer, "Orthodoxy," pp. 21–25.
21 Aristakes 11–25, pp. 57–128.

22 Matthew of Edessa 1.64, 1.88, 2.1-137, pp. 56–60, 74, 83–179.
23 Matthew of Edessa 2.1, p. 83.
24 Matthew of Edessa 2.2-3, pp. 84–88.
25 Matthew of Edessa 3.109, pp. 238–239.
26 MacEvitt, "Chronicle of Matthew of Edessa," pp. 157–71.
27 Matthew of Edessa, Cont. 1, pp. 241–80.
28 For the author and his work, see Weltecke, *Beschreibung der Zeiten*.
29 Michael the Syrian 15.1, 3:158–59 (trans.), 4:571–73 (Syriac text); see also Beihammer, "Feindbilder," pp. 63–65.
30 Beihammer, "Ethnogenese," pp. 596–97, 599–600, 602–604.
31 Michael the Syrian 14.1-5, 3:149–57 (trans.), 4:566–70 (Syriac text).
32 Weltecke, "Beschreibung der Zeiten," pp. 107–109.
33 Bar Hebraeus, pp. 217–408, trans. Budge, pp. 195–352; for more details concerning the *Malik-nāma* tradition and its various versions, see Peacock, *Early Seljūq History*, pp. 27–46, who investigates the surviving material with respect to the origins and early migrations of the Seljuks.
34 Michael the Syrian 18.1-8, 18.10-19.5, 3:309–320, 324–336 (trans.).
35 See, for instance, Matthew of Edessa 1.47-49, 64, 66–70, 85, 2.1, 12–13, 22–23, 43, 55, pp. 44–46, 56–60, 61–64, 72–73, 83–84, 94–97, 102–105, 121–23, 129–30.
36 Beihammer, "Feindbilder," pp. 85–86.
37 Beihammer, "Feindbilder," pp. 82–84.
38 The following remarks are confined to Muslim sources that are of direct relevance for Anatolia and the adjacent regions of Syria and Mesopotamia. For sources on the Seljuks' activities in Iran like Bayhaqī's *Tārīkh-i Mas'ūdī*, see Cahen, "Historiography of the Seljuqid Period," pp. 44–47, 60–61; Peacock, *Early Seljūq* History, pp. 6–8. For Bayhaqī in particular, see now the full English translation of the surviving parts in *The History of Beyhaqi (The History of Sulta Mas'ud of Ghazna, 1030–1040) by Abu'l-Fazl Beyhaqi*, trans. C. E. Bosworth, fully revised and with further commentary by Mohsen Ashtiany, 3 vols. (Cambridge, MA, and London, 2011). Also beyond the scope of this study are the sources concerning the Seljuks' relations with the Abbasid caliphate and the court of Baghdad; see Hanne, *Putting the Caliph in his Place*, pp. 46–51.
39 For details, see Noth, *Historical Tradition*.
40 For a general overview of Muslim historiography in the Seljuk period, see Cahen, "Historiography of the Seljuqid Period," pp. 37–63; for various texts of the earliest Seljuk tradition, see Peacock, *Early Seljūq History*, pp. 6–12.
41 Cahen, "Malik-nameh," pp. 35–65; Peacock, *Early Seljūq History*, pp. 8–9, 27–35.
42 Nīshāpūrī/Rashīd al-Dīn, ed. Ateş, trans. Luther; the original text has been published recently: A. H. Morton, *The Saljuqnama of Zahir al-Din Nishapuri* (Chippenham, 2004); see also Peacock, *Great Seljuk Empire*, p. 14.
43 Al-Bundārī/ʿImād al-Dīn, ed. Houtsma; for more details concerning this work and its outstanding significance, see Peacock, *Early Seljūq History*, pp. 10–12, and idem, *Great Seljuk Empire*, p. 15 (the original text of *Nusrat al-Fatra* survives in a unique manuscript and is still largely unpublished).
44 Al-Rāwandī, ed. Iqbal; for this work, see now Sara Nur Yıldız, "A Nadīm for the Sultan: Rāwandī and the Anatolian Seljuks," in Peacock and Yıdız, eds., *The Seljuks of Anatolia*, pp. 91–111.
45 Al-Ḥusaynī, ed. Iqbal; see also the recent English translation *The History of the Seljuq State: A Translation with Commentary of the Akhbār al-dawla al-saljūqiyya*, trans. C. E. Bosworth, Routledge Studies in the History of Iran and Turkey (London, 2010).
46 *Annals of the Saljuq Turks*, trans. Richards, introduction, pp. 1–10; Bar Hebraeus, trans. Budge, introduction, pp. xxxvii–xli; Peacock, *Early Saljūq History*, pp. 29–33.
47 Sibṭ b. al-Jawzī, ed. Sevim; see also Peacock, *Great Seljuk Empire*, pp. 15–16.
48 Sibṭ b. al-Jawzī, pp. 122, 132–33, 136–38, 139, 142–58, 169–86, 191, 195–98, 201–205, 207–23, 226, 229–30, 234–48.

49 ʿAẓīmī, ed. Sevim; Ibn al-ʿAdīm, *Bughyat*, ed. Zakkar; Ibn al-ʿAdīm, *Bughyat*, trans. Sevim; Ibn al-ʿAdīm, *Zubdat*, ed. Zakkar.
50 Ibn al-Qalānisī, ed. Amedroz.
51 Ibn al-Azraq, ed. Awad, concerning the Marwānid and early Artuqid period up to 512/1118; the second part of the chronicle has been edited and translated by Hillenbrand, *Muslim Principality*. For the work and its author, see Chase F. Robinson, "Ibn al-Azraq, his Ta'rīkh Mayyāfāriqīn, and Early Islam," *Journal of the Royal Asiatic Society*, 3rd series, 6 (1996), 7–27.
52 Ibn Bībī, ed. Erzi (facsimile edition of MS Aya Sofya 2985); Ibn Bībī, ed. Houtsma (edition of the abridged version [*Mukhtaṣar*]); Ibn Bībī, trans. Duda (translation of the abridged version); Ibn Bībī, ed. Lugal and Erzi (first part of the full version); Ibn Bībī/Yazıcıoğlu, ed. Houtsma (partial edition of the Turkish translation), Yazıcızâde Ali, ed. Bakır (full edition).
53 Aksarāyī, ed. Turan; Aksarāyī, trans. Mürsel.
54 *Tārīkh-i Āl-i Saljūq*, ed. Uzluk.
55 For the use of the Anatolian Seljuks as legitimizing element in later historiographical traditions in general, see Peacock, "Seljuq legitimacy," pp. 79–95.
56 Yazıcızāde ʿAlī, ed. Bakır.
57 Neşrî, ed. Öztürk, pp. 13–29 (Chapter on the Seljuk rulers and the sultans of Rūm), pp. 33–34 (Ertugrul enters the service of Sultan ʿAlāʾ al-Dīn, receiving Söğüt and Tomalic as winter and summer pastures).
58 Kesik, "Cenâbî," pp. 213–59.
59 For details, see *Dānishmend-nāme*, ed. and trans. Mélikoff, introduction, pp. 71–170; Turan, *Türkiye*, pp. 123–28; *Dânişmend-nâme*, ed. Demir, introduction, pp. 15–56. The text (*Dānishmend-nāme*, 1:191 [translation], 2:9–10 [text]) creates imaginary bonds of kinship between the Arab and the Turkish hero: *ve dahı Emîr Ömerün bir kızı vardı, Mizrâb oğlı 'Aliye vermişlerdi, anun bir 'ayâli vucûda geldi, adını Melik Ahmed kodılar, katı 'âkıl u kâmil kopdı, lakabın Melik Dânişmend kodılar*, "et l'emir ʿÖmer [the brother of Sayyid Baṭṭāl] avait aussi une fille qui fut donnée en mariage au fils de Miẓrāb [a famous commander of troops from Khwarizm], ʿAlī; elle mit au monde un enfant qui fut appelé Melik Aḥmed, mais comme il devint fort intelligent et fort sage on le surnomma Melik Dānişmend."
60 Mélikoff, *Dānishmend-nāme*, introduction, p. 141: "Chez ces farouches conquérants animés par l'esprit de prosélytisme, on ne trouve aucun sentiment de discrimination ou de haine raciale: toute distinction entre vainqueurs et vaincus s'efface dès que le Mécréant est devenu musulman."
61 For these personalities, see ibid., 122–26, 126–27, 128–29, 129–31.
62 For details, see ibid., pp. 53–70; for ʿAlī's paraphrase, see Babinger, *Geschichtsschreiber*, no. 110, pp. 126–34, esp. 131.
63 For details concerning the historical background, see below, chapter 8.
64 For the problem of first-hand knowledge in crusader sources, see Lapina, "Eyewitnesses," pp. 117–39.
65 For the image of Muslims in crusader sources in general, see Tolan, "Pagan Idolaters," pp. 97–117; Jaspert, "Wahrnehmung der Muslime," pp. 307–40; Völkl, *Muslime*, pp. 161–214.
66 For theoretical approaches to the construction of enemy images, see Völkl, *Muslime*, pp. 161–66, esp. 164: "Anhand dieser negativen Attribuierungen zeigt sich die intendierte Wirkung des Feindbildes und damit die Hauptzielsetzung der Feindbildproduktion im Rahmen jeder Kriegspropaganda: Durch die dem Gegner unterstellte existentielle Bedrohung der Eigengruppe sollen Angst und vor allem Hass gegenüber dem identifizierten Feind hervorgerufen werden."
67 Gesta Francorum 3.9, p. 18: *videns innumerabiles Turcos procul, stridentes et clamantes demoniaca voce*; p. 19: *illa excommunicata generatione*, p. 20: *incredulos Turcos*; 4.10, p. 22:

iniquissimi Turci; 6.14, p. 32: *Turci denique, inimici Dei et sanctae christianitatis*; 4.10, p. 23: *spoliabant ecclesias et domos et alia omnia*. For the broader context of these stereotypes, see Völkl, *Muslime*, pp. 178–214.

68 Gesta Francorum 3.9, p. 21.

69 Gesta Francorum 4.10, p. 22: *vidi tam innumerabilem gentem eorum [...] timentes tam mirabiliter, ut vix evaserimus de illorum manibus, unde adhuc in nimio terrore sumus.*

70 For the ideological context of these ideas, see Völkl, *Muslime*, pp. 245–53.

71 On the image of the Turks in William of Tyre's chronicle, see Murray, "William of Tyre," pp. 217–29.

72 Fulcher 1.9.4, pp. 179–180: *quam urbem Turci Orientales tunc possidebant, acres nimis et arcubus sagittarii. Hi quidem de Perside iam a L annis, Euphrate fluvio transito, terram Romaniae totam usque Nicomediam urbem sibi subiugarant.*

73 Fulcher 1.11.4, p. 193: *congregatis sibi Turcis, scilicet paganis Persicis.*

74 See also Völkl, *Muslime*, pp. 247–48.

75 Fulcher 1.11.4, pp. 192–93: *Turci, quorum et admiratus et princeps erat Soliman, qui Nicaeam urbem et Romaniam in potestate sua tenebat, congregatis sibi Turcis, scilicet paganis Persicis.*

76 Gesta Francorum 4.10, p. 22: *Solimanus dux illorum, filius Solimani veteris*; Albert of Aachen 1.16, p. 32: *in terram Nicee urbis et regni Solimanni ducis Turcorum [...] castellum quoddam Solimanni viri magnifici, ducis ac principum Turcorum*; 2.21, p. 94: *Solimannus unus de principibus Turcorum, vir nobilissimus sed gentilis*. In addition, see William of Tyre 1.24, p. 150: *Solimannus Turcorum princeps [...] Solimannus vero illius regionis dux et moderator.* For the designations used for Muslim-Turkish rulers in crusader sources, see Völkl, *Muslime*, pp. 227–30.

77 For comparison, see the thoughtful observations on Byzantine-Turkish title making in eastern Anatolia in Shukurov, "Turkoman and Byzantine Self-Identity," pp. 265–75.

78 William of Tyre 3.2, p. 198: *predicti Solimanni patruus Belfetoh nomine, maximus Persarum soldanus, tempore Romani [...]occupaverat violenter et easdem predicto ex plurima parte tradiderat Solimanno. Possidebat ergo et iure proprietatis vendicabat sibi universas provincias a Tarso Cilicie usque ad Ellespontum.*

79 See below, pp. 204–07.

80 William of Tyre 3.2, p. 198: *quidam Turcorum potentissimus satrapa [...] cognomento Ssa quod Persarum lingua "rex" interpretatur.*

81 William of Tyre 4.11, pp. 248–49.

82 William of Tyre 4.11, p. 249: *ut tantorum beneficiorum memores perpetuo sibi fidelitatis nexu tenerentur obligati.*

83 Gesta Francorum, 9.21, p. 49: *Curbaram princeps militiae soldani Persiae*; Fulcher 1.15.7, p. 220: *misit Aoxianus, Antiochiae princeps et admiratus, filium suum, nomine Sanxadonem, ad Soltanum, scilicet imperatorem Persidis*; 1.19.1, p. 242: *cuius gentis* (the army sent by the sultan) *Corbagath dux fuit et satrapa*. Albert of Aachen 3.34, p. 194: *Darsianus princeps et caput civitatis*; 3.34, p. 196: *regis Darsiani*; 4.26 p. 286: *Darsianus vero rex Antiochie*; 4.5, p. 254: *Corbahan vero familiaris et primus in aula regis et secundus a rege in regno Corruzana.*

84 Fulcher 1.21.5, pp. 249–50: *principes Turcorum multi erant, quos admiratos praenominabant. Hi sunt: Corbagath, Maleducat, Amisoliman et multi alii, quos nominare perlongum est.* The edition enumerates a long list of variants in the manuscripts adding additional names. The identifications proposed by Hagenmeyer in most cases are rather doubtful. For the battle, see Asbridge, *First Crusade*, pp. 232–40.

85 Gesta Francorum 9.21, p. 49: *militiae soldani Persiae*; 9.21, p. 52: *ac nostri regi domino Soldano militia fortissimo*; Fulcher 1.19.1, p. 242: *Soltanus, rex scilicet Persarum*; Albert of Aachen 4.2, p. 248: *Corruzan in terram et regnum nativitatis nostre [...] de Corruzan soltano, qui caput et princeps est Turcorum*; 4.4, p. 252: *rex de Corruzana.*

86 Gesta Francorum 9.21, pp. 49, 52. For the identification of the caliph with the pope, see Völkl, *Muslime*, p. 230.

87 Anna Komnene 6.12.4, p. 195, l. 94 (πρέσβεις τὸν Χοροσὰν κατέλαβον), 6.12.8, p. 197, l. 38 (τὸν τοῦ Χοροσὰν σουλτάν), 11.4.3, p. 332, l. 23 (τῷ τοῦ Χοροσὰν σουλτάν).

88 Albert of Aachen 2.20, pp. 90–92: *civitatem Niceam, quam gentilis virtus Turcorum imperatori iniuste ereptam suo subiugavit dominio*; 2.37, p. 124: *in manus imperatoris Constantinopolis, sub cuius conditione urbs primitus hereditario iure serviens habebatur.*

89 For the theoretical basis of this propagandistic elements, see Völkl, *Muslime*, p. 179: "Die funktionale Umsetzung dieses Hasses in militärisch nutzbare Aggressivität und damit in die Bereitschaft, sich selbst an kriegerischen Auseinandersetzungen mit dem propagierten Feind zu beteiligen, ist ebenfalls eines der Hauptziele jeglicher Kriegspropaganda."

90 Albert of Aachen 1.16, p. 32: *depredati armenta, boves et oves, hyrcos, greges Grecorum Turcis famulantium.*

91 Albert of Aachen 3.2, p. 140: *ad urbes Finiminis, Reclei et Stancona descendit, in quibus Christiani cives habitabant Turcis viris Solimanni subiugati.*

92 See below, pp. 178, 256.

93 William of Tyre 4.4, p. 237 and 4.5, p. 239.

94 William of Tyre 4.6, p. 239: *Turcorum satrapa Balac nomine.*

95 Albert of Aachen 3.28, pp. 182–84: *Turci manentes Armenicos Christianos servili iugo subegerant.* For Artāḥ, see Asbridge, *Antioch*, pp. 25–26.

96 William of Tyre 5.11, pp. 285–86; for the siege of the city, see Asbridge, *Antioch*, pp. 25–33; idem, *First Crusade*, pp. 153–211. Eger, "(Re)Mapping Medieval Antioch," pp. 95–134, gives a comprehensive overview of the urban development of postclassical Antioch in the Islamic and middle Byzantine period. Against the traditional view of Antioch's decline, the author re-examines the city's religious, residential, commercial, industrial, and agricultural zones "as a process of continued abandonment and renewal" on the basis of material provided by the Princeton excavation of the 1930s and recent surveys. This concept tallies with much of the evidence provided by narrative sources.

97 There are various versions in the crusader sources concerning the identity of this figure. See Asbridge, *First Crusade*, pp. 200–201.

98 William of Tyre 5.11, pp. 286–87.

99 William of Tyre 5.19, pp. 296–97.

100 Albert of Aachen 4.23, pp. 282–84: *Greci, Syri, Armenici, cives et viri Christiane professionis* [...] *corporibus Christianorum tam Gallorum quam Grecorum, Syrorum et Armenicorum admixtis* [...] *nam voce et signo Christiane professionis Turci et Sarraceni timore mortis plurimi acclamantes.*

101 William of Tyre 4.23, pp. 265–66: *Nec erat difficile huiusmodi hominibus inter nostros latere, cum linguarum habentes commercium alii Grecos, alii Surianos, alii Armenios se esse confingerent et verborum idiomate et moribus et habitu talium personas exprimerent* [...] *non facile erat a castris expellere, quoniam a predictis nationibus lingua, moribus et habitu penitus erant indifferentes.*

102 Gesta Francorum 5.12, p. 29: *Hermenii et Suriani qui erant intus in urbe exeuntes et ostendentes se fugere.*

103 Gesta Francorum 6.14, p. 33.

Part I

First encounters in Byzantium's eastern marches, ca. 1040–71

1 The eastern provinces, Turkish migrations, and the Seljuk imperial project

Byzantine administrative and military structures in the East

The social, demographic, administrative, and military structures in Byzantium's eastern borderland, as they appeared on the eve of the first Turkish invasions, were the result of long-term developments, which in some respects had already begun in the late ninth century and culminated in the Byzantine eastward expansion between the 930s and the 1020s. Scholars concerned with the military and administrative history of the eastern frontier and with Byzantine-Arab relations have discussed the manifold aspects of this process repeatedly.[1] A much more recent strand of analysis concentrates on patterns of frontier settlement, agricultural production, farming, animal husbandry, and trade and exchange between peripheral communities, as well as relations between settled populations and nomadic elements in the centuries after the first Muslim conquests. Excavations, remains of material culture, and geomorphological studies yield a broad range of archaeological data. Yet survey methodologies are widely disparate, and the available evidence is still too sparse and unevenly dispersed to allow the reconstruction of chronological layers and to connect specific finds with written evidence of the tenth and eleventh centuries.[2] Hence, we have a fairly clear image of the structural changes that occurred during the period in question, though admittedly some crucial issues related to the social and economic background remain hypothetical or cannot be elucidated in a satisfactory way.

It is crucial for our understanding of the period that over the past decades the traditional notion of the Byzantine-Islamic frontier as a contested zone of Muslim-Christian warfare and cultural clash or as a depopulated and devastated no man's land gave way to new concepts, which focus on the particularities of borderlands, shared spheres, and plots of interaction. Medieval notions of border and territory differ largely from our modern understanding. We are dealing with complex zones, in which peripheral societies were closely interconnected and underwent dynamic processes of cultural change. There certainly were instances of decline and violent displacement of population groups as a result of military conflicts, but the available data also point to a high degree of unbroken continuance and economic prosperity based on fertile agricultural zones, irrigation systems, and road networks.[3]

Likewise, the traditional way of examining Byzantine institutions under the light of modern bureaucratic systems and their standards of efficiency was refined by increasingly accurate interpretations of medieval administrative structures. These are based on the presumption of less rigorously organized mechanisms and leave room for many grey zones and inconsistencies, as they reckon with much more limited possibilities for exerting centralizing control.[4] A basic issue, which needs to be addressed with respect to the early Turkish penetration of Asia Minor and the ensuing collapse of the Byzantine imperial administration, is the nature of the relationship among the central government, the eastern peripheries, and the military aristocracy in the provinces. As has been shown in the introductory chapter, the studies by Cheynet and others have widely rebutted the traditional views of antagonisms between a Constantinopolitan civil bureaucracy and provincial military magnates. Instead, they stress personal networks based on parentage, intermarriages, allegiances, and profitable collaborations as the main vehicles of political interaction and decision-making in eleventh-century Byzantium.[5] With respect to the gradual expansion of the Turkish invaders in Asia Minor, it is of primary importance to reach a better understanding of the mechanisms and behavioral patterns, through which the centralizing forces of the imperial government came to be superseded by semi-independent regional powers and by new coalitions between indigenous elements and the invading Turks. After a first phase of violent clashes, Byzantine, Armenian, and Syrian aristocrats, Muslim vassals in the borderland and foreign mercenary groups soon developed forms of collaboration and concluded alliances with the Turkish invaders. These processes allowed the gradual crystallization of new political structures based on a fusion of local and immigrating forces in Asia Minor, as the following sections will show in more detail. This development was further accelerated by serious internal conflicts that began with the civil war between the faction supporting Michael VI and the aristocratic coalition led by Isaac I Komnenos in 1057 and went on with the takeover of the Doukas clan in 1059 and its clashes with the followers of Romanos IV Diogenes in 1071/72. Even then, stability could not be restored, and thus a new series of rebellions ultimately brought about the downfall of the Doukas regime in 1078. These conflicts doubtlessly entailed the removal of military units from the eastern frontier, serious losses of manpower, and a general decline of power and cohesion among the leading clans of the military aristocracy and political elite. It may be safely assumed that they contributed to the disintegration of the imperial administration just as much as the disastrous campaigns of Seljuk sultans and Turkish warrior groups. It is certainly no coincidence that the Turkish attacks started to become a permanent and geographically more extensive threat in about 1057 while in the early 1070s the Turks started advancing without obstacles through the central Anatolian plateau as far as the western coastland. The battle of Manzikert in 1071, which is constantly referred to as the decisive turning point for the Turkish intrusion into Asia Minor, resulted from various coincidental movements and decisions made by commanders on both sides, who pursued different strategic plans and had no desire to fight with each other. It was a military setback for the empire and a humiliation for the imperial office at the hands of a Turkish newcomer, but for the fate of Asia Minor it was just one in a whole series of factors, events, and developments. In this sense, we may say that the civil strife of 1057 in conjunction with the Turkish invasions constituted a more decisive watershed.

In the first three decades of the Byzantine-Turkish encounter, the political and military developments in question mostly affected the recently acquired territories east of the Anatolian plateau stretching from the Caucasus and the Pontus region over the Armenian highlands and the Upper Euphrates provinces to Cilicia and northern Syria. Only few expeditions advanced further west to the districts of Koloneia and Sebasteia in northeastern Cappadocia and to Cilicia. Apart from the regions under direct Byzantine control, there was a broad sphere of imperial influence encompassing a network of Muslim vassal potentates in Azerbaijan, the Diyār Bakr province, the Syrian desert, and Aleppo. According to the political constellations, each of these emirates pursued its own strategy in facing the Turkish threat, but, all in all, there were many parallels and similarities in the developments in Christian-Byzantine and Muslim frontier regions with respect to forms of collaboration and mechanisms of integration.

In what follows the reader will find a brief survey of the administrative structures in the eastern Byzantine provinces on the eve of the Seljuk invasions. Despite all simplification, this endeavors to outline the institutional framework in which the first Turkish penetration of Byzantine territories occurred. As a general characteristic, it is important to note that we are not dealing with well-defined territorial units, but with a highly permeable border zone held together by a network of cities and fortresses "as primary nodes of political control."[6]

With its new edition and analysis by Nikos Oikonomides (1972), the so-called *Escorial Taktikon* written in 971–975 has been recognized as the most important source for the administrative organization of the eastern borderland in the second half of the tenth century. The structures in question, according to prevailing scholarly opinions, resulted from a reorganization, which most probably has to be associated with the Phokas clan and Emperor Nikephoros II (963–69).[7] This assumption draws on the fact that many of the data provided by the *Taktikon*'s hierarchically arranged catalogue of military officials harmonize with the data provided by near-contemporary narrative sources regarding Byzantine territorial gains in the eastern marches, that resulted from the campaigns of Nikephoros II and his successor John I Tzimiskes (969–76). The essence of their reform, according to this interpretation, lies in the emergence of an array of new *themata* in the newly conquered Byzantine provinces, while older *kleisourai* were upgraded to *themata*. Both formed a kind of buffer zone protecting the old thematic units on the Anatolian plateau. They differed from the latter in that they constituted small districts based around strongholds of *strategoi* manned with local garrisons. These small-size units were originally attached to three overarching administrative areas placed under the command of a *doux* or *katepano*.[8]

Byzantium's remarkable territorial gains in the years following the conquest of Melitene/Malaṭya (Eskimalatya) in 934 were mainly achieved through successful campaigns carried out in the 940s and 950s by generals from the Kourkouas and Phokas families and other members of the eastern military aristocracy. As the most important frontier city in the eastern parts of the borderlands, Melitene occupied a central position in the "mountain-ringed lowlands" of the Karababa, Tohma, and Elazığ Basins.[9] Its control allowed access to a large number of districts and fortresses situated in the area between the upper course of the Euphrates River and the Mouzouron Mountains (Munzur Dağları) and north of the Arsanias River (Murat Nehri). The Byzantine troops thus annexed strongholds like Charpezikion (near modern Amutka), Chozanon (Hozat), Asmosaton/Shimshāṭ,[10] and Romanoupolis (Bingöl). Conquests were also carried out in the areas south of the Anti-Taurus Mountains (Güneydoğu Torosları) and east of the Euphrates, such as Samosata/Sumaysāṭ (Samsat), the second largest town in the area after Melitene,[11] Chasanara/Severak/al-Suwaydā' (Siverek), Zermiou (Çermik), and Erkne (Ergani), as well as in districts further west, like Larissa (Mancılık) and Adata/al-Ḥadath west of the Pyramos/Jayḥān River (Ceyhan Nehri). In the 960s, under the reign of Nikephoros II, cities in the ancient province of Commagene east of the Pyramos Valley, such as Germanikeia/Marʿash (Kahramanmaraş) and Telouch/Dulūk (Dülük), the main cities of the fertile Cilician plain like Tarsus, Mopsuestia/Mamistra, and Anazarba, as well as Artāḥ east of Antioch, were likewise incorporated into the Byzantine territories.[12] At about the same time, the expansion continued in an easterly direction along the Arsanias River with the annexation of the Armenian province of Taron in 966, including strongholds like Melte (Ziyaret), Mous (Muş), and Khouet (Huyut) near the western shores of Lake Van. The gradual strengthening of the Byzantine military presence in northern Syria culminated in the surrender of Antioch in October 969 and the establishment of a kind of protectorate over the emirate of Aleppo a few months later.

The ducates of Chaldia and Mesopotamia situated in the northeastern and central sections of the borderland respectively were created by upgrading and expanding former *themata* known already from the first half of the ninth century. The region of Chaldia stretched from the Black Sea shores with the ports of Trebizond (Trabzon) and Kerasous (Giresun) across the Pontic Alps as far as the districts of Keltzene/Ekełeacʿ and Derzene/Tercan, touching the *thema* of Koloneia (Şebinkarahisar) in the west and the Akampsis Valley (Çoruh Nehri) in the east.[13] The ducate of Mesopotamia, which made its first appearance in about 970 or, according to other opinions, with the appointment of Bardas Skleros in 976, roughly comprised the districts along the Upper Euphrates Valley as far as Daranalis/Daranałikʿ and Kamākh (Kemah) north of the Mouzouron Mountains, as well as districts situated along the Anti-Taurus Mountains.[14] The western Arsanias Valley, the province of Taron, and the so-called *Armenika themata* seem to have been temporarily attached to this ducate but were reorganized later on into different administrative units.[15] A similar development can be observed with respect to the *thema* of Melitene, which in the decades between 934 and 970 became residence of a *strategos* and formed an especially profitable center of imperial domains (*kouratoria*). Moreover, the city enjoyed an outstanding position as religious and ecclesiastical center for the local population consisting of Greeks,

Christianized Arabs, Armenians, and Syrians. In the second half of the eleventh century, the city appears under the command of an independent *doux*.[16]

The ducate of Antioch established after the conquest of 969 encompassed the region of the Amanos Mountains, a narrow strip between the Mediterranean shores and the Orontes Valley (Asi Nehri) as far as Tripoli in the south, the districts east of the Pyramos River like Telouch/Dulūk and Germanikeia/Marʿash in the north, and Cilicia in the northwest.[17] The region of the ducate largely corresponds to the two fertile lowland rift valleys of the Amuq Plain and the Kahramanmaraş Plain, which are connected through the corridor of the Kara Su Valley and communicate with the western coastland and Cilicia via the passes of the Amanos Mountains.[18]

With the expansion into the Armenian and Georgian provinces of the Caucasus region during the reign of Basil II, Byzantium acquired the land of Taykh east of the Akampsis River in 1000/1001 from the Georgian prince David. The Artsruni principality of Vaspurakan south and east of Lake Van were taken from King Senekʿerim Yovanēs in 1019 or 1021/22, and a part of the Bagratid kingdom of Iberia was conquered in 1022/23.[19] Thus, in the first quarter of the eleventh century the new ducates of Vaspurakan and Iberia came into being beside the older ducate of Chaldia. While the former was mainly centered in the well-fortified strongholds around Lake Van, such as Ivan (Van), Manzikert (Malazgirt), and Perkri/Barkirī (Muradiye), the latter two covered a vast region straddling the province of Taykh/Iberia, Bassiane/Basean and Theodosioupolis/Karin (Erzurum), as well as the districts of Bagrewand, Apachounes/Apahunikʿ, and Taron in the eastern section of the Arsanias Valley.[20]

As for the Euphrates region south of Mesopotamia, the last important acquisition was the conquest of Edessa/al-Ruhā (Şanlıurfa) in October 1031 during the reign of Emperor Romanos III Argyros.[21] The newly established ducate seems to have exerted control over the entire Euphrates region opposite the Marwānid territories in the Diyār Bakr province with a circle of fortresses covering the frontier zone as far as Chasanara.[22] Moreover, the *doux* of Edessa closely collaborated with garrisons stationed in fortresses north of the Euphrates, such as Gerger, Ḥiṣn Manṣūr (Adıyaman), and Samosata/Sumaysāṭ.[23] Geographically, the territory of the ducate comprised the Harran Plain and the Balikh River Valley, a fertile lowland area, which in the south is bounded by the dry steppe land of northern Syria.[24]

The annexation in 1045 of the kingdom of Shirak/Ani from Gagik II Bagratuni (1042–45) and in 1064/65 of the kingdom of Vanand/Kars from Gagik Abas (1029–1064/65) were the imperial government's last expansionist acts in the Caucasus region.[25] Administratively, the former was incorporated into the ducate of Iberia and the latter became a *katepanato*, but in practice these measures had very limited results for the defensive structures in the East. As early as 1064, Ani was conquered by Sultan Alp Arslān, and during the 1070s Kars fell under the influence of local Turkish-Muslim emirates that had established themselves in the region.

Due to the annexation of new territories in the Armenian highlands, western Caucasia, and the Euphrates region and the frequent changes in the distribution of responsibilities and the organization of administrative units, the whole system evinces a high degree of fluctuation and instability. Most decisions were made *ad hoc* and in response to specific strategic considerations and requirements, the exact nature of which is no longer tangible for modern observers. As Catherine Holmes has recently pointed out, none of these ducates or *katepanata* should be imagined as a fully developed administrative mechanism with clearly defined responsibilities, territorial boundaries, or an unbroken sequence of office holders appointed by the central government. Most arrangements and appointments had a temporary character and were driven by specific military and political constellations and pressures. The appointment of certain outstanding personalities, such as Bardas Phokas in Chaldia, Eustathios Maleinos and Michael Bourtzes in Antioch, or Mumahhid al-Dawla b. Marwān as a kind of high commander in the central section of the borderland, were *ad personam* arrangements, which took into account the personal networks and abilities of these people.[26] Frequently, suprathematic supreme commanders holding the title of *doux* or *katepano* made their appearance during the decades of Basil II's long reign, but their positions were rarely permanently occupied. In various cases, it seems that *themata* and their respective *strategoi* continued to exist alongside the newly established ducates, and thus there was a certain overlap of old and new institutions.[27]

All in all, in the years after Basil II, the Byzantine marches east of the Anatolian plateau appear as a highly diversified conglomeration of disparate areas and populations with different historical experiences, religious denominations, and institutional traditions. It would have been virtually impossible for eleventh-century governmental mechanisms to unify this vast, mountainous, and deeply fissured region under the umbrella of a strong central power. Thus, among the more or less unavoidable consequences of this state of affairs we can count deficiencies in the communication between the center and the eastern peripheries, an unequal and unsatisfactory distribution of military forces and a lack of coordination among them, discontinuities in command structures, a disintegration of local defensive structures due to the removal of the indigenous aristocracy in the Armenian provinces, as well as other forms of migration and demographic change. All these phenomena account for an overall unpreparedness for massive hostile attacks occurring simultaneously on many different points. It would be misleading, however, to assume that what in view of the subsequent events appeared as shortcomings of the military and administrative structures could have been easily avoided by a better-organized governmental system. It is extremely hard to judge to what extent eleventh-century institutions, according to the criteria and possibilities of their time, were actually able to improve their efficiency. Even more inaccurate appear all those explanations that, with the benefit of hindsight, blame individual rulers and decision makers for their shortsighted policy regarding the eastern military forces and for their inability to diagnose imminent dangers in time. Most symptoms of weakness that might be held responsible for the Byzantine government's inability to react aptly to the Turkish invasions were either the result of long-term developments and changes in the broader geo-political constellations or were connected with the periods of civil strife from 1057 onwards. Byzantine rulers merely thought and acted in accordance with long-established models and practices based on centuries of governmental experience. They simply had no suitable response in store for the twofold threat emanating from the gradual strengthening of centrifugal local forces and the sudden emergence of Turkish warrior groups with their aggressive raiding activities and effective strategies of intrusion and infiltration.

A network of Muslim vassals

The expansionist policy of tenth-century Byzantium resulted not only in substantial territorial gains but also in a significant increase of influence in the adjacent Muslim regions. This brought about a further tightening of relations between the imperial government and Arab nomadic tribes and Muslim emirs in the borderland and led to the creation of numerous coalitions based on payments of tribute and, if need be, on military support by auxiliary troops in exchange for high-ranking honorary titles and access to the court of Constantinople. With the enfeeblement of the Buwayhid dynasty after the death of the Great Emir ʿAḍud al-Dawla in March 983, Byzantium's chief rival in its efforts to extend its influence over the political powers in the border zone was the Fatimid caliphate of Egypt.[28] From its base in Damascus and other urban centers of Syria, the caliphate was trying either to impose direct rule over the emirate of Aleppo and adjacent regions through military interventions or to strengthen its influence through bonds of allegiance and claims to formal supremacy.[29] All the same, the political affairs in post-Ḥamdānid Syria were characterized by a fierce antagonism of numerous competing forces, such as Arab nomad chiefs, town militias (*aḥdāth*), and local military commanders.[30] The increasing intrusion of nomad tribes since the early tenth century formed an additional source of conflict between sedentary and (semi-)pastoral groups. The territories around Mosul, Ḥarrān, and Edessa in Upper Mesopotamia, Palestine, and the Syrian Desert were deeply permeated by powerful tribal groups.[31] In this situation, both Constantinople and Cairo were taking pains to gain predominance in the region. But especially after the defeat of the eastern military aristocracy in 989, Basil II managed to build up a network of Muslim vassal principalities forming a protective screen along the boundaries of the eastern provinces.[32] At the same time, Byzantium turned towards a policy of equilibrium vis-à-vis the Fatimid caliphate, showing respect to spheres of influence and forestalling open conflicts. In the year 1000, Basil concluded a treaty with Caliph al-Ḥākim (996–1021), which was more or less regularly renewed over the following decades. Thus, the emperor initiated a period of peaceful relations with Cairo, which was interrupted only by local clashes from time to time.[33] Large-scale attacks on Muslim territories by Byzantine troops were extremely rare, the only exceptions being Romanos III's inglorious attempt to seize Aleppo in the summer of 1030, George Maniakes' conquest of Edessa in 1031, and much later, Romanos IV's Syrian campaign in 1068, which was already a reaction to Seljuk infiltration.[34] The Byzantine government maintained its influence over the local powers in Syria and Upper Mesopotamia until the outset of the Turkish raids. These forced many Muslim potentates to formally recognize the sultan's overlordship even before the actual conquest of their realm by paying tribute and proclaiming the Friday prayer in his name.

The most powerful emirate beyond the empire's northeastern marches and the Araxes River was that of the Shaddādids, which held sway over the province of Arrān with its main centers Ganja and Dvin. From the second half of the tenth century onwards, Muḥammad b. Shaddād and his sons gradually achieved substantial territorial gains in this region. While Byzantine pressure on the adjacent Armenian and Georgian lordships was growing, the Shaddādid principality reached the apogee of its power under the reign of Faḍl's two sons: ʿAlī b. Lashkarī (1034–49) in Ganja and Abū l-Aswār Shāwur in Dvin (1022–67). The Seljuk campaign of 1054 into the Caucasus region forced Abū l-Aswār to recognize the suzerainty of Sultan Ṭughril Beg.[35] At the same time, we know of treaties between Abū l-Aswār and the imperial government under Constantine IX. According to John Skylitzes, they were violated by raids into Byzantine territory in about 1055. A Byzantine counter-attack on Dvin by the *stratopedarches* Nikephoros compelled the Shaddādid emirs to renew their agreements with the empire, sending ʿAlī's son Ardashīr (Artaseiras) as hostage to Constantinople.[36] We have no further information about this treaty and the reasons for the Shaddādid hostilities, but it seems that the assaults were due to the emirate's dependency on the Seljuk sultanate and the ensuing changes in the balance of power in the region.

In the late 980s, the major cities in the Diyār Bakr district, such as Mayyāfāriqīn (Silvan), Āmid (Diyarbakır), and Niṣībīn (Nusaybin), as well as Khilāṭ (Ahlat) at the western shore of Lake Van, fell into the hands of the Kurdish chief Bādh. He was killed in 990 and was succeeded by his sister's husband, the founder of the Marwānid dynasty. His sons Abū ʿAlī l-Ḥasan b. Marwān (990–997) and Mumahhid al-Dawla (997–1011) consolidated the emirate's position in the region and established a durable alliance with the Byzantine Empire. The close relation with the imperial government is expressed in the fact that in the year 1000, Mumahhid al-Dawla, besides being granted the high rank of *magistros*, was appointed *doux tes anatoles*, a position exclusively created for this ruler. Holmes explains this function as the empire's military representative in the east replacing David of Tao, and Ripper underlines the crucial significance of this agreement for the protection of the central section of the borderland, especially against the Rawwādids of Azerbaijan.[37] During the reign of the aforementioned emirs' brother Naṣr al-Dawla Aḥmad (1011–1061) the Marwānid court in Mayyāfāriqīn became a flourishing political, commercial, and cultural center. The emirate secured its survival by maintaining friendly relations with all major powers in the region. It recognized Seljuk suzerainty in 1056–57.[38]

In the region south of Vaspurakan, Armenian and Byzantine potentates were facing the Arabic dynasty of the ʿUqayl tribe founded by Abū l-Dhawwād Muḥammad b. al-Musayyab. Around 990, he had managed to take hold of the cities of Jazīrat b. ʿUmar (Cizre), Niṣībīn, Balad, and Mosul, thereby defeating the Kurdish chief Bādh. The most important representatives of the dynasty were al-Dhawwād's nephew, Muʿtamid al-Dawla Qirwāsh b. Muqallad (1001–1050), who in the 1040s became engaged in fierce conflicts with invading Turkmen groups,[39] and the latter's grandnephew Sharaf al-Dawla Muslim b. Quraysh (1061–1085). The latter managed to consolidate his emirate and even to extend his sway towards the Euphrates region and northern Syria through a successful policy of accommodation with the Seljuk sultanate. In 1079, he eventually took possession of Aleppo. This drove him into a major clash with Sulaymān b. Qutlumush in 1085. For the Byzantine imperial government, the ʿUqaylids were certainly too far off to integrate them into its network of Muslim vassals in the east, but, due to their position as major players in the northern Jazira and adjacent regions, Constantinople must have been eager to maintain friendly relations with them.[40]

In the Diyār Muḍar district, a clan of the Numayr Arabs appeared as heirs to the Ḥamdānid dynasty. Their chief Waththāb b. Sābiq, then governor of Ḥarrān, conquered Sarūj (Sürüç), al-Raqqa, and Edessa/al-Ruhā, which was subsequently governed by Waththāb's cousin ʿUṭayr.[41] When internal conflicts developed among various claimants to the rule over Edessa, both the Marwānids of Diyār Bakr and the Byzantine general George Maniakes residing in Samosata actively intervened in the fights, and thus the latter in October 1031 managed to take possession of the city. Although the state of war lingered on until 1038, the Byzantines succeeded in maintaining control over Edessa.[42] Over the following decades until the Seljuk conquest by Malikshāh in 1086/87, the city was in the hands of numerous governors, who repeatedly fended off Turkish attacks.[43]

Byzantium's most important ally in northern Syria was the emirate of Aleppo, since late 969 a sort of imperial protectorate, which on the basis of a treaty committed itself to annual tributes, military obligations, and exemptions from customs duties and conceded the emperor a say in matters of succession to the emirate's throne.[44] The city's position in the sensitive area between Antioch and the Euphrates River made the maintenance of this dependency a matter of high priority. In pursuing this aim, the Byzantine representatives were facing internal struggles within the Ḥamdānid elite, incessant threats by the Fatimid caliphate, and changing attitudes of local potentates in central Syria. Therefore, the imperial government applied a careful strategy based on sheltering and bestowing ranks upon ex-rulers who had been expelled from the city and on avoiding direct interventions into the emirate's internal affairs.

Still, an eight-year period of direct Fatimid administration in Aleppo (1017–25) caused a temporary breakdown of the balance of power established by Basil II. Likewise, the conflict-ridden second reign of the Arab chief Ṣāliḥ b. Mirdās (1025–29), who had expelled the last representatives of the old Ḥamdānid regime but eventually fell victim to local antagonisms in Syria, could not result in any viable re-stabilization.[45] In this sense, Romanos III's campaign against Aleppo in the summer of 1030, despite its unsuccessful outcome, formed a decisive turning point initiating a new phase of close cooperation and diplomatic relations between Constantinople and Aleppo. Henceforth, every ruler of Aleppo became a high-ranking dignitary at the imperial court, and many rulers visited the

Byzantine emperor in person. The practice of conferring titles was extended from ousted ex-rulers to the actual men in power. Through a treaty concluded in May 1031, Naṣr b. Ṣāliḥ restored peaceful relations with the Byzantine government. Accordingly, in a summit meeting of Arab delegations at the imperial court in September 1032, the emir of Aleppo was granted the rank of *patrikios anthypatos vestes*, a distinction that put him on the side of important military officials, just below the rank of *magistros*.[46]

When Michael IV signed the peace treaty with the regency council of Caliph al-Mustanṣir (1036–1094) in 1036, the Aleppo issue, which previously had led the Byzantine-Fatimid negotiations to failure, was resolved on the basis of a double investiture of the Mirdāsid emir by both the emperor and the caliph. The imperial government, thus, was forced to share its claims to suzerainty with the second major power in the region. After a new series of violent upheavals in Aleppo and another interlude of direct Fatimid rule under Anūshtakīn al-Dizbirī (July 1038–February 1042), Naṣr's brother and successor Thimāl b. Ṣāliḥ in April/May 1042 sent an embassy to the empress sisters Zoe and Theodora, asking for military support against his opponents in the citadel of Aleppo and confirming his obedience to the imperial government. On this occasion, the leading members of the Mirdāsid clan were further promoted in the Byzantine court hierarchy by gaining the titles *magistros*, *vestarches*, and *patrikios*.[47] A new struggle between Aleppo and Cairo, in which Byzantium supported Fatimid interests for a certain period, ended with the promotion of the Mirdāsids to even higher ranks. Perhaps in response to the claims of the Fatimid caliphate, in 1052 Constantinople reaffirmed its overlordship of Aleppo by bestowing the title of *proedros* upon the emir, so far the highest title a Muslim ruler had ever been granted by the emperor.

The 1050s, however, were marked by growing Fatimid influence over Aleppo and a general shift in the balance of power in the Muslim world due to the ongoing Seljuk expansion. As will be shown below in greater detail, Constantinople's first official contacts with Sultan Ṭughril Beg resulted in a symbolic demonstration of Sunni-Abbasid predominance articulated in restoration works and Abbasid Friday prayers in the mosque of Constantinople.[48] This episode gave rise to a serious estrangement between Constantinople and Cairo and unavoidably reduced Byzantine influence on the Fatimid government's Syrian allies. After a last mission to Empress Theodora (1055–56), it became increasingly clear that by the mid-1050s Byzantine suzerainty over Aleppo had lost its substance, so that Emir Thimāl retreated to the Fatimid capital after his resignation in January 1058.[49] A few years later, Turkish warrior groups coming from the Marwānid territories in the Diyār Bakr province actively interfered with the power struggle among Thimāl's successors and gained a foothold in the emirate. At that time, the Byzantine administration in Antioch, being increasingly pushed into the defensive by attacks on the ducate's territories, was no longer able to exert any influence over Aleppo.[50]

Another ally in Syria was Ḥassān b. al-Mufarrij—the Byzantines called him *Pinzarach*—, the head of the Jarrāḥ clan and chief of the Ṭayyi' Arabs.[51] The

Jarrāḥīds had a long tradition of seditious behavior towards the Fatimid caliphate, going back to Ḥassān's father Mufarrij b. Daghfal, who in 981–82 rose up against Caliph al-ʿAzīz (975–96) in his Palestinian territories around al-Ramla. After his defeat, he fled via Ḥimṣ to Antioch, where he asked for the emperor's protection. In 1024, Ḥassān participated in an anti-Fatimid alliance of Arab tribal chiefs who were aiming to gain control over the whole of Syria and to divide the provinces among themselves. The battle of Uqḥuwāna in May 1029, in which the Fatimid governor of Damascus, Anūshtakīn al-Dizbirī, defeated Ḥassān and his allies, weakened the latter's position decisively. Romanos III's campaign against Aleppo, therefore, occasioned an alliance between Ḥassān and the emperor. The former hoped thus to recover his lost territories in Palestine.[52] Despite another defeat against the Fatimid forces, the imperial government insisted on keeping up its alliance with the Jarrāḥ clan, calling Ḥassān to settle with his tribe on Byzantine soil near Antioch and bestowing the title of *patrikios* upon the emir's son ʿAllāf. The emir's future status and his claims to his domains in Palestine in 1032 even formed part of the peace negotiations with the Fatimid government. In the following years, Ḥassān appears fighting together with Byzantines forces outside Apameia and Edessa and thus fulfilling an important task in the Byzantine defense system in Syria, but eventually he seems to have fallen into disgrace and was imprisoned in Constantinople for a certain period.

The above details clearly show how important a factor this network of Muslim vassals was for the imperial policy in the lands beyond the eastern borderland between the 990s and the 1050s. It significantly reduced the outside menaces originating from the Caucasus region and Azerbaijan to the Armenian provinces, which had been acquired during the first half of the eleventh century, and re-strained the Fatimid caliphate's expansionism in northern Syria. Furthermore, it created a kind of buffer zone in Upper Mesopotamia south of the Anti-Taurus Mountains, allowing a certain amount of control over the Arab nomad tribes moving between Mosul and the Diyār Muḍar. The undermining of this network as a result of the progressive subjugation of all these local potentates by Turkmen warriors and the Seljuk sultanate was the first decisive step towards the intrusion of the Turks into the Byzantine borderland and the interior of Anatolia. The recognition of Seljuk supremacy by the Shaddādids of Arran and the Rawwādids of Azerbaijan allowed the seizure of strongholds in Armenia and thus opened the way to the Araxes and Arsanias Valleys. The submission of the Marwānids and the ʿUqaylids enabled Turkish forces to proceed from the province of Vaspurakan to the Diyār Bakr and thence in a southwesterly direction across the Euphrates to northern Syria, where they eventually reached Aleppo and the Byzantine territories of Antioch. The involvement of Turkmen warriors in the internal matters of Aleppo also opened the way for other Turkish groups to invade central and southern Syria. Besides the shortcomings in the administrative and military structures within the Byzantine territories, the gradual disintegration of the network of allies outside the borderland goes a long way towards explaining the Turkish invasions' eventual resulting in the establishment of new political entities.

The raids of the Iraqi Turkmens, 1038–44

The first Turkish attacks on Byzantine territory in the years 1038–44 were no more than side effects of the penetration of Azerbaijan and Upper Mesopotamia by independently operating groups of Turkmen warriors, who are characterized by Ibn al-Athīr as "Oghuz Turkmens" (*al-Atrāk al-Ghuzzīya*), "Iraqi Oghuz" (*al-Ghuzz al-'Irāqīya*) (because of their association with the western Iranian region of 'Irāq-i 'Ajam), or "followers" (*aṣḥāb*) of Arslān b. Saljūq al-Turkī.[53] Under the year 420/20 January 1029–28 January 1030, the chronicler gives a detailed overview of their activities from their first clash with the Ghaznawids in Khurāsān to their fights with local forces in the region of Mosul in 1044.[54] This is the most accurate source, though some additional information regarding their presence in the borderlands can be gained from Byzantine and Armenian reports. As regards the collective identity of these Turkmen groups, which despite a great number of commanders and separate itineraries still seem to have maintained a certain sense of cohesion, Ibn al-Athīr classifies them as the "tribe" (*'ashīra*) of Arslān b. Saljūq, thus clearly distinguishing them from the *Saljūqīya*, i.e., the Turkmen warriors under the command of Mikā'īl's sons Ṭughril Beg and Jaghrī Beg.[55] Combining these details with Nīshāpūrī's idealized presentation of the invincible manpower at Arslān Isrā'īl's disposal,[56] one gets the impression that in the earliest stage of Seljuk history this prominent figure was a focus for coalitions and solidarity among broad sections of the Oghuz tribal society in Transoxania.[57] When Maḥmūd of Ghazna arrested their leader, they split up and went in two main directions.[58] One group moved from Khurāsān in a southwesterly direction to Iṣfahān and thence westwards to Azerbaijan. The other moved to the Balkhān Mountains near the eastern shores of the Caspian Sea and to the northeastern Iranian provinces between Nīshāpūr and Dihistān. From there the Turks following this route proceeded further westward to Jurjān and the region of Rayy. These migrations were accompanied by incessant raiding and pillaging and heavy military clashes with various local lords, the Ghaznawid sultan, and his governors.[59]

The analysis of the patterns of action of these Turkmen groups is highly illuminating for the interpretation of similar behavior recurring during the early invasions of Asia Minor. In contrast to the Byzantine sources, which because of their imperial viewpoint are mostly silent about the Turkmen strategies, the Muslim accounts give much more detailed descriptions of the Turkish movements and attacks and the forms of interaction between Turkish chiefs and the local elites. By juxtaposing the data available for Byzantine and Muslim territories one easily detects numerous common patterns, which give us a fairly clear image of the basic characteristics of Turkish warfare in both spheres.

As for the size and composition of these groups, Ibn al-Athīr mentions several figures that, in spite of their vagueness, may give us an approximate idea of the situation: the group fleeing towards Iṣfahān reportedly comprised 2,000 tents (*kharkāt*), but the greater part of the Turkmens moved to the region of the Balkhān Mountains.[60] The number of Turkmen warriors fighting in Rayy amounted to

5,000 men.[61] It is also explicitly stated that the Turkmens were moving with their womenfolk, their belongings, and the booty they took during their raids.[62] This is to say that they were usually accompanied by large baggage trains and herds of livestock. On the basis of a broader collection of data including material from later centuries and modern nomadic societies, Andrew Peacock has recently argued that figures of several thousand warriors meant a number four to six times greater for non-combatant household members and even greater numbers of beasts and sheep. Although it is not possible to assess the proportional ratio between these migrants and the sedentary population in the rural areas and urban centers of the Iranian provinces with any certainty, it is quite obvious that the presence of Turkmen groups, due to their size and needs for supplies, was a heavy economic burden for the inhabitants of regions affected by their movements.[63] Climatic conditions and the availability of foodstuff presumably determined their itinerary to a high degree. Although the chronological details in Ibn al-Athīr's account are confused and events stretching over longer periods are frequently summarized in a few lines, it becomes clear that the Turkmens traveled intermittently with long interruptions, during which the warriors swarmed out for raids or established contacts with local rulers. At all events, it took them several years to cover the distance from eastern Iran to Azerbaijan. The Turkmen attacks in the region of Nīshāpūr lasted until 1033, the first raids in the region of Rayy are dated to 427/5 November 1035–23 October 1036, and the first assaults in Azerbaijan took place in 429/14 October 1037–2 October 1038.[64] Thus, they reached the Byzantine borderlands after almost a decade of wandering.

It is hardly possible to give an accurate description of the internal structure and organization of eleventh-century Turkmen groups. Both Muslim and Christian narrative sources insist on traditional semantic fields and literary conventions related to nomadic tribes. It is clearly discernible, however, that the Oghuz society of Transoxania was constantly exposed to various forms of sedentary and urban life and that the boundaries between nomadic and settled spheres were largely blurred.[65] This goes a long way towards explaining the ease with which many Turkmen groups in the course of their migrations were able to adapt themselves to the urban environment of the city-based principalities in Muslim and Christian territories. With respect to the tribal structures of the Oghuz Turks, the sources make use of some rather elusive terms and mention a few names, but there are no recognizable organizational patterns based on firmly established tribal traditions and commonly accepted genealogical concepts.[66] As has already been pointed out, the most important integrative force and the nucleus of political authority among the Turkmen warriors was the personality of a strong leader. As a result, the Turkish groups during their migrations never appeared as self-contained combat forces relying on common parentage and tribal solidarity but always demonstrated an amazing readiness to establish contacts with the local population and to refresh their strength by including new elements of different ethnic and social origin into their ranks. When Turkmen chieftains formed coalitions and marriage alliances with local rulers, people with military skills were given the opportunity to join the Turkish warriors, provided that they submitted to the authority of their commanders. The incorporation of Daylamite troops from the region of Rayy, for instance, is explicitly mentioned.[67] Over time, this process must have caused remarkable changes in the composition and character of the original groups.

The fact that Ibn al-Athīr transmits the names of some of the most renowned leaders (*umarā'*)—Kūktāsh (Göktaş), Būqā (Boğa), Qizil (Kızıl), Yaghmur (Yağmur), a sister's son (*ibn ukht*) of Yaghmur, Nāṣoghlī (Nasoğlı), Dānā and Manṣūr b. Ghuzzoghlī[68]—clearly shows that the bands subject to their command were perceived as largely autonomous groups that at times collaborated with other groups on common targets. Successful coalitions with local elites and the accumulation of wealth enabled these warriors to form the nucleus of new hegemonic groups that passed from a semi-nomadic lifestyle to that of sedentary territorial lords. The Iraqi Turkmens, however, did not make much headway in this process and were frequently routed or otherwise compelled to move on before they managed to settle permanently in regions they came to pillage.

When in 429/1037–38 the first wave of Turkmen warriors arrived in Azerbaijan, they entered the service of the Rawwādid ruler of Tabriz Wahsūdhān b. Mamlān but soon came into conflict with him and were driven out by a coalition of Kurdish forces. As a result, they withdrew towards the western Iranian provinces, launching attacks on Rayy and Hamadhān.[69] In 432/11 September 1040–20 August 1041, the remaining groups fell victim to an attack of Wahsūdān in Tabriz or were killed during an unlucky campaign starting from Urmiya against the Kurds in the Hakkārīya Mountains.[70] When the Emir of Rayy, Qizil, died in 433/31 August 1041–20 July 1042 and Ibrāhīm Yināl conquered the city in the following year, the Turkmens there had to flee from the Seljuk troops to Azerbaijan. From there they advanced across the highlands to Jazīrat b. ʿUmar and launched assaults into the Diyār Bakr province and the region between Niṣībīn, Sinjār, and Mosul.[71] These activities mainly affected the ʿUqaylid and Marwānid principalities as well as a number of petty Kurdish lords in the region, but there are also explicit mentions of at least two raids into Armenian or Byzantine territory.

First, a detachment of Turkmens residing in Urmiya in 1038 or 1039 is said to have set off for the "land of the Armenians" (*balad al-Arman*), where they inflicted heavy damage by killing, pillaging, and making prisoners. Thereafter, they returned to Urmiya and the territories of the Kurdish chief Abū l-Hayjā' b. Rabīb al-Dawla al-Hadhbānī. The situation escalated into a new series of heavy clashes, in the course of which a great number of both Turks and Kurds perished.[72] Given the geographical position of the expedition's point of departure it can be safely assumed that the target of the attacks was the region of Vaspurakan. The second raid on Byzantine territory started farther west and has to be viewed in connection with the Turkmen invasion into the ʿUqaylid principality of Mosul ruled at that time by Qirwāsh b. al-Muqallad. The assaults culminated in a temporary seizure of Mosul and the sack of the city in late February 1044 due to the townspeople's resistance.[73] This prompted local potentates in the region like Naṣr al-Dawla b. Marwān and the Buwayhid emir Jalāl al-Dawla b. Būyah of Baghdad to ally against them and to send letters of complaint to Ṭughril Beg. During their brief and turbulent rule in the area, the Turkmen warriors undertook new raids into Armenian territory, acquiring booty and captives in such a great number, as Ibn al-Athīr states, that the prices of slave girls sank to five dinars and boys had no demand at all.[74] Given that these attacks must have started from the region of Jazīrat b. ʿUmar, it can be assumed that the Turkmens invaded either the western parts of Vaspurakan or certain targets along the Anti-Taurus Mountains. Additional information provided by the chronicle of al-ʿAẓīmī allows us to get a more comprehensive picture of the situation. *Sub anno* 434/21 August 1042–9 August 1043 he notes that during the raids in Armenian territory, Byzantine troops made their appearance in the region. In the course of the hostilities in Jazīrat b. ʿUmar and the Diyār Bakr province, the Marwānids requested help from Emperor Constantine IX, who supported them with troops from the *katepano* of Charpete/Kharput (*qaṭbān Harbuṭ*),[75] the administrative center of the ducate of Mesopotamia situated near the confluence of the Arsanias and Euphrates Rivers. This city, along with Romanoupolis further east, controlled the access routes to the Marwānid territories.[76] We are dealing with one of the first known military involvements of Byzantine frontier units with Turkish invaders. One may think of activities in the region of the fortresses Erkne and Tulkhum, which in 1044 were a transit area for marauding Turkmens and later in 1051 became centers of local Armenian rebel movements.[77]

A crucial issue is the relationship of the Iraqi Turkmens with the sons of Mīkāʾīl and their companions. According to Ibn al-Athīr, the Seljuk leaders vehemently laid claim to suzerainty over these warriors whereas the latter were reluctant to submit. These attitudes are illustrated by the Turkmens fleeing from Rayy before the advancing forces of Ibrāhīm Yināl and, even more explicitly, by the reply put into the mouth of Ṭughril Beg in response to the complaints of Jalāl al-Dawla b. Būya:

> These Turkmens were slaves, servants, subjects, and dependents of ours, who obeyed our command and served the princely state [...] they withdrew to Rayy and caused damages and destructions there. Then we marched with our troops from Khurāsān against them, reckoning that they would take refuge to a guarantee of safety (*amān*) and seek asylum in pardon and forgiveness. But they were overwhelmed with awe and fear drove them away. Inevitably we will make them again subject to our banners and in our might we will let them taste the punishment of rebels (*jazāʾ al-mutamarridīn*), be they near or distant, in the lowlands or the heights.[78]

From the Seljuk point of view, the Iraqi Turkmens appear as rebels who have escaped their overlords' control and therefore will be forced back to obedience and punished by the dynasty's superior military power. Thus, Ṭughril Beg claims a sort of universal authority over all Turkmen warriors and at the same time presents himself as powerful protector of minor Muslim lords seeking his support and acknowledging his supremacy.

Most recently, Andrew Peacock has pointed out that this statement most probably reflects a later state of affairs, in which the concept of Seljuk universal rule was fully developed and propagated as such in historical writing.[79] This may be the case as far as the wording of the letter and the rigidity of the argument are concerned. On the other hand, especially in the years following the Seljuk advance to the western Iranian provinces in the early 1040s, it seems highly plausible that Ṭughril Beg made efforts to increase his influence over Turkmen groups operating in Azerbaijan and northern Iraq. He would have tried to take political advantage of the difficulties local rulers in these regions were facing because of hostile attacks. It is also remarkable that the salient sense of antagonism between the Iraqi Turkmens and the Seljuk leaders did not prevent the former from performing acts of obedience whenever they considered it useful in order to strengthen their position. After the sack of Mosul in February 1044, for example, the Friday prayer was spoken in the name of the caliph and Sultan Ṭughril Beg.[80] If we accept this piece of information, it can be seen as a Turkmen attempt to legitimize their rule over the city against the claims of the 'Uqaylid Arabs by referring themselves to the caliph and the Seljuk chief as supreme religious and political authorities. This is one of the earliest examples for this specific demeanor, which later on evolved into a widely used practice among the Turks in Syria and Asia Minor. Equally noteworthy is the case of the commander Qizil, who obviously managed to establish bonds of marriage with the Mīkā'īl lineage in order to secure his rule over the city of Rayy between the years 1038 and 1042.[81]

The decisive turning point in the early fate of the Iraqi Turkmens was their defeat in a battle fought on 22 April 1044 near the city of Mosul against Qirwāsh b. Muqallad and his Arab and Kurdish allies.[82] The surviving Turkmens fled via Niṣībīn to Tulkhum, where according to Matthew of Edessa a heavy massacre of the Christian population took place. Given that their enemies dominated the regions to the south, they decided to return to Azerbaijan through Byzantine territories north of Lake Van, reaching thus the city of Arjīsh (Erciş).[83] With respect to the ensuing clash between the Turkmens and the Byzantine provincial forces of Vaspurakan, Matthew's account largely agrees with that of John Skylitzes. Both versions refer to the *katepano* Stephen, who may be identified with a nephew of Constantine Leichoudes, the well-known chief minister in the early years of Constantine IX Monomachos.[84] Weakened by their defeat near Mosul, the Turkmens sought for an agreement, asking for safe conduct in exchange for gifts and promises not to cause any damage to the districts they were going to pass through. A haphazard attack on the Turkmen warriors ended with Stephen's defeat and capture. According to Skylitzes he was handed over to the ruler of Tabriz, while Matthew has him tortured to death in the city of Khoy.[85]

The political context of the Iraqi Turkmens' migrations and raids was characterized by the absence of a centralizing authority and the inability of supra-regional powers to exert effective control and to establish durable coalitions with local rulers. A case in point is 'Alā' al-Dawla b. Kākūya, head of a dynasty based in the regions of Iṣfahān and Hamadhān, who after the first Turkmen raid of Rayy in 1036 managed to take hold of the city by presenting himself as subject of Sultan Masʿūd of Ghazna. Abū Sahl al-Ḥamdūnī, the Ghaznawid governor of the province of Rayy, however, refused to recognize his authority, and so ʿAlāʾ al-Dawla concluded an alliance with a group of 1,500 Turkmen warriors under the command of Qizil. Shortly afterwards, relations with the Turkmens deteriorated, but ʿAlāʾ al-Dawla reached an agreement with Abū Sahl, who retreated to Nīshāpūr. Thus, the former maintained his control over the city until April 1038, when Rayy was attacked by a strong coalition of Turkmen and Daylamite forces. In the meantime, Sultan Masʿūd took no measures to restore direct rule over the city.[86] Several years later, in early 1044, when Qirwāsh sought allies in order to drive the Turkmens out of Mosul, the Buwayhid *amīr al-umarāʾ* of Baghdad Jalāl al-Dawla had lost the loyalty of his Turkish troops in the months before his death and thus was unable to support him in his campaign.[87]

These examples clearly demonstrate that in the 1030s and 1040s, previously powerful potentates, who in the past had laid claim to suzerainty over provinces in western Iran and Iraq, had serious difficulties making themselves recognized as the supreme authority and exerting influence on the local dynasties of the region. A vacuum of power ensued. This was partly filled by regional forces but could not be translated into new forms of stability because of the incessant rivalries among these rulers. On entering this political setting, the Turkmen warrior groups, on the one hand, precipitated the overall destabilization as a result of their devastating raids and, on the other, were given the opportunity to infiltrate the pre-existing network of political players by interfering with the constantly changing coalitions and conflicts amongst the competing potentates. Most characteristically, the appeal addressed by the local lords of Upper Mesopotamia to Ṭughril Beg in view of the increasing pressure exerted by the Turkmens in Mosul and Diyār Bakr reflects the overall desire to find a new regulatory power, which would be able to put an end to this disastrous state of affairs.

In the available reports, the Turkmens primarily appear as undisciplined brigands and ruthless robbers lacking moral principles or ideological incentives. The burning of the mosque of Marāgha is supposed to show that they did not even respect the most basic rules of Muslim piety.[88] On the other hand, they are depicted as skillful negotiators in their contacts with the local elites, through which they gained access to the urban centers. The local potentates frequently reacted positively to these attempts by creating personal ties and employing them as mercenaries. Wahsūdhān b. Mamlān established bonds of marriage with the first Turkmen chiefs arriving in Azerbaijan, and ʿAlāʾ al-Dawla of Hamadhān did the same with Kūktāsh.[89] Similarly, the Marwānid ruler of Jazīrat b. ʿUmar, Sulaymān b. Naṣr al-Dawla, offered a peace agreement (*al-muṣālaḥa*) to the Turkmen chief Manṣūr b. Ghuzzoghlī providing that he stay in the district of the town until the end of the winter and thereafter march to Syria with the rest of the Turkmens.[90]

These understandings were usually short lived and not able to create durable and peaceful relations. It seems that at the slightest pretext, the Turkmens returned to their customary habit of gaining incomes through pillaging, while their allies frequently violated the agreements by luring the Turkmen chiefs into traps. The aforementioned Sulaymān, for instance, "secretly thought of treachery," inviting Manṣūr to a banquet in the town and arresting him while his followers scattered in all directions. Instead of calming the situation, this act caused a dangerous escalation of hostilities in the entire area between Sinjār and Diyār Bakr.[91] Another round of talks initiated by Sulaymān's father Naṣr al-Dawla, who offered payments and the release of Manṣūr in exchange for the Turkmens' withdrawal from his territories, ended with treachery on the part of the Turkmen warriors, who intensified their raids.[92] Qirwāsh b. Muqallad's attempts from Mosul to arrive at a peaceful solution were also without success. He first offered them 3,000 and then 15,000 dinars, but the Turkmens would not stop advancing. After the conquest of the city, they imposed excessive demands on the townspeople exacting a sum of 24,000 dinars and eventually caused an upheaval after killing one of the city's dignitaries. The town was seized by force. Despite a heavy plundering for 12 days, the Turkmen chiefs respected an agreement with the inhabitants of the Abū Najīḥ quarter who had shown good treatment to one of their leaders.[93]

It is obvious that neither the local elites nor the Turkmen warriors were able or willing to keep their agreements and to make them a working basis for new forms of cooperation. This stands in contrast to later developments in Syria, where in the 1060s and 1070s these kinds of coalitions quite quickly led to a permanent settlement of Turkmen warriors in urban centers and the adoption of administrative practices. There were no long-term strategies or clearly defined plans of conquest and territorial expansion. Temporary control over cities like Rayy, Hamadhān, and Mosul first and foremost served the exploitation of the local population through pillaging and punitive tax levies. The Turkmen chiefs were not yet able to integrate themselves into the framework of sedentary rule, which the local Arab and Kurdish lords represented. Agreements, therefore, hardly encouraged the development of stabilizing forces and were mainly viewed as an additional means of gaining money. In a situation where supra-regional powers were hardly able to make their presence felt, while local elites and warrior groups exhausted themselves in constant conflicts about the accumulation of wealth, it is hardly surprising that treachery was part of the day-to-day business. The behavior of the Byzantine *katepano* Stephen, who in spite of an initial agreement launched an attack on the Turkmen warriors passing through his territory, was nothing unusual and completely in line with the practices observable in the Muslim regions as well.

The Byzantine perception of the first Turkish raids

Michael Attaleiates, so important an observer of the developments in the East from the 1060s onwards, has little to say about the first emergence of the Turks. Very elusively and with the usual ethnographic anachronism of the Byzantine literary tradition, he refers to the "Hephthalite Huns, neighbors of the Persians," who managed to cross the "Ganges River," obviously a confusion with the Oxus River of Central Asia, under the command of a leader who, although of humble and servile origin, managed to take possession of Persia after the death of its sovereign. Thus the Huns, showing invincible force to all people in the East, approached the borderland of Iberia, i.e., the Caucasus region, and, launching as many assaults as they could, took captive "the commander of the Romans who was entrusted with the command of Syria and was called Leichoudes."[94] These few lines epitomize some basic knowledge of the Turks' first emergence in the eastern borderland up to the defeat of the *katepano* of Vaspurakan in 1044. The brief account also exhibits all fundamental characteristics of Byzantine perceptions of the Seljuk Turks, combining ethnographic traditions of the steppe peoples identified as Huns with some vague ideas about the merging of Persians and Turks and first invasions into the Armenian highlands.

Much more detailed is the report by John Skylitzes.[95] While speaking about the origin of the Turks and their expansion in the eastern Islamic lands, he also refers to the aforementioned events of 1044.[96] His account shows some chronological confusion: he puts Ṭughril Beg's victory against the Buwayhid commander Arslān al-Basāsīrī (*Pissasirios*) on 18 January 1060 and the beginning of Qutlumush's rebellion (which actually broke out in about 1061)[97] in one sequence with the first raids on Byzantine territory.[98] Accordingly, in this version the commander who had been sent against Qirwāsh of Mosul (*Karbeses*) is Qutlumush (*Koutloumous*) himself, who thus appears as officially appointed leader of an expedition ordered by the sultan. Claude Cahen sees the reason for this confusion in the fact that Qutlumush had actually fought in the region more than 12 years later.[99] On 9 January 1057, however, he was an ally of Qirwāsh's successor Quraysh b. Badrān (1052–61), in a fierce battle near Sinjār against al-Basāsīrī and his allies. The former suffered a heavy defeat and was forced to recognize Fatimid suzerainty in Mosul, but within a short time Ṭughril Beg arrived in person, restoring the previous state of affairs.[100] It does not seem very probable that this rather insignificant event in Qutlumush's career would have influenced the knowledge of Byzantine informants. More important for the intrinsic logic of the Byzantine narrative is that after his father Arslān's death, the Turkmen raiders of 1044 considered Qutlumush their supreme leader, so that the warriors in question came to be identified with the person who laid the groundwork for their cohesion as a military group. The new feature the Byzantine historical tradition added to this authentic core of information was the assumption that the forefather of the lineage, which later on was to establish the Seljuk sultanate in Asia Minor, must have played a crucial role in the Turkish conquest of the region from the very first moment. As a result, Qutlumush appears as the man who, after winning the first battle against the Byzantines, persuaded Sultan Ṭughril Beg to undertake new campaigns against Vaspurakan (*Baasprakan*), which is "a fertile land in the hands of women."[101]

Another element of purely Byzantine origin is the idea of the empire's fame resulting from the glorious deeds of the three military emperors Nikephoros II Phokas, John Tzimiskes, and Basil II. They inspired awe and respect in all potential enemies and the Seljuk sultan in particular, for "he assumed that the Romans still possessed the same virtue and power."[102] Accordingly, Ṭughril Beg is described as a barbarian potentate ruled by passion. He felt anger and shame about his commander's defeat and, knowing about the empire's strength, "he was afraid from launching war against the Romans."[103] Instead, he was mainly concerned with the war against the Arabs, in which he suffered another unidentifiable defeat, and with the rebellious Qutlumush, whom he besieged in a fortress of Khwārizm called Pasar.[104] The mention of this otherwise unknown place seems to reflect distorted knowledge about the fortress of Girdkūh north of Damghān in the Elburz Mountains, where Qutlumush is said to have found refuge along with a strong contingent of Turkmen warriors between May 1061 and early 1064.[105] All in all, Skylitzes' account conflates events from the 1040s and the last years of Ṭughril Beg's reign so as to place special emphasis on Qutlumush as forefather of the Turkish conquerors of Asia Minor and his conflicts with the sultan. Moreover, the text, by referring to the legacy of the tenth-century soldier emperors, uses historical memory as a means to project the empire's image as an invincible power intimidating all barbarian forces surrounding it. Implicitly, this also involves a critique of Basil II's successors, who did not meet the same high standards of successful military leadership.

The emergence of the Seljuk imperial project

Most of the Turkish migrations and military activities on Byzantine soil took place without any direct involvement of the Great Seljuk dynasty. Most warlords who in the decades after 1040 came to invade Anatolia did so outside the sultanate's centralizing control, and Qutlumush's descendants proceeded to Bithynia in the late 1070s as disobedient rebels. Yet it would be misleading to view the developments in Asia Minor independently of the ideological and political framework provided by the Seljuk Empire. Apart from various campaigns and attempts by the sultans to exert direct influence over the Turks in Anatolia, both the sons of Qutlumush and other Turkish warlords were in one way or another imbued with the dynastic and political concepts of the Seljuk Empire, and the events in Anatolia have to be interpreted in light of and in connection with the latter.

The conquest of Nīshāpūr in May 1038 and a series of successes against Ghaznawid forces culminating in Sultan Mas'ūd's defeat in the battle of Dandānqān on 21 May 1040 laid the foundations of independent Seljuk rule in Khurāsān.[106] Henceforth Ṭughril Beg, his younger brother Jaghrī Beg, and other chiefs of the Seljuk clan formed a powerful confederation emancipated from Ghaznawid or Karakhanid influence and embarked on their own imperial project, which within a few years encompassed not only the eastern Iranian provinces but also the greatest part of the Muslim central lands as far as Syria. The period 1038–40, thus, can be considered the initial step in the gradual transformation from a Turkic clan rooted in semi-nomadic tribal traditions into a Muslim dynasty drawing on the principles of Sunni Islam, the caliphate, and Arab-Persian kingship.[107] With the increasing penetration of the Iranian provinces by Turkmen warrior groups and the occupation of urban centers, the Seljuk leaders established links with the local elites and adopted institutions and administrative structures in order to exert political authority over the indigenous population.[108] Moreover, their victory over the Ghaznawids enabled them to adopt the conceptions of lordship from their defeated predecessors and to present themselves as legitimate heirs of the latter. This required the formal recognition by the Abbasid caliph in his capacity as the supreme authority conferring legitimacy in the Muslim lands. The customary appointment procedure required a ceremonial act of investiture consisting of the bestowal of titles (*alqāb*), honorary robes, and insignia of authority. Subsequently, the incumbent's name was mentioned along with that of the caliph in the Friday prayer and on coins.[109] The surviving narrative sources want to make us believe that in about 1040 the first important steps towards this goal were taken. As they describe this procedure with the benefit of hindsight and under the light of the final outcome of the Seljuk expansion, they project the main features of the Seljuk dynastic ideology back to the early days. They depict Ṭughril Beg and his companions as already possessing a fully developed Sunni identity, a clear concept of allegiance to the Abbasid caliph, a catalogue of royal virtues exemplifying the qualities of a model Muslim ruler, and ideas of shared rule within the clan.[110] The latter are based on a hierarchical differentiation between the family members, who were allocated various Iranian provinces to be conquered in the near future.[111] Moreover, the Seljuk chiefs are said to have developed arguments in their contacts with the Abbasid court, which underpinned the righteousness of their rebellion against the Ghaznawid sultans and the legitimacy of their claims to supersede them by declaring themselves subjects of the caliphate and by evoking traditional Muslim virtues of lordship for purposes of self-justification.[112] As a result, according to the image projected by our narrative sources, the Seljuk expansion from eastern Iran to the Byzantine-Muslim frontier appears to have been a carefully planned and ideologically well-founded enterprise. It goes without saying that many details mentioned in this context actually reflect various levels of idealized literary reconstructions, but, on the other hand, both contemporary coins and independent statements of non-Muslim sources make sufficiently clear that a specific Seljuk imperial ideology began to emerge in the years around 1040 and henceforth exerted some influence on the attitudes of Turkish commanders and raiders invading the Armenian highlands and Anatolia.

Jaghrī Beg adopted the title of *malik al-mulūk* (king of kings) on the occasion of the Friday prayer held in Marw on 22 April 1037, and Ṭughril Beg sat on Sultan Masʿūd's throne after his first entrance into the city of Nīshāpūr in May 1038 and was proclaimed *al-sulṭān al-muʿaẓẓam* (the highly exalted sultan).[113] The adoption of these titles was a visualization of the successful negotiations with the local nobility who had given their consent to the replacement of Ghaznawid authority with an upcoming power from outside. As the conflicts with Sultan Masʿūd lingered on until 1040, this act can also be seen as an attempt of the Seljuk chiefs to consolidate their newly acquired rule over the lands of Khurāsān by embedding themselves in a pre-existing institutional and ideological framework. A remarkable piece of evidence for this process is a letter addressed to Caliph al-Qāʾim bi-Amr Allāh, which has come down to us in two different versions quoted by Nīshāpūrī and Bar Hebraeus. According to the former it was dispatched along with an embassy sent to Baghdad shortly after the battle of Dandānqān whereas the latter dates it a little later to 435/10 August 1043–28 July 1044. Neither of the two versions should be considered a faithful rendering of the original document, but they seem to give a rough impression of the ideas brought forward at that time by the Seljuk leaders. Most probably, we are dealing with disparate memories of the discussions about the relationship that was to be implemented between the Seljuk ruling house and the Abbasid caliphate. In this way, representatives of the encomiastic court historiography tried to explain the ideological constituents of the Seljuk imperial project.

In Nīshāpūrī's version, Ṭughril Beg presents the Seljuk family (*āl-i Saljūq*) as an obedient subject of the Abbasid dynasty (*dawlat-i 'Abbāsī*), abiding by all obligations and norms of the Muslim faith (*farā'iḍ wa sunan*) and preoccupied with the duty of Holy War (*ghazw wa jihād*). Maḥmūd and Mas'ūd of Ghazna represent the antipode of this exemplary conduct. They had imprisoned the Seljuk leader Arslān-Isrā'īl and other chiefs and, being committed to indecent amusements, had neglected the affairs of kingship and justice (*bi-maṣāliḥ-i mulk wa ma'dalat*). Hence, the notables and renowned men of Khurāsān (*a'yān wa mashāhīr-i Khurāsān*) summoned the Seljuk commanders to afford them support and protection. With God's help they were granted victory (*nuṣrat wa ẓafar*) over their enemies. As regards the future, they wish to secure prosperity and justice for the people, and they are striving on the path of Islamic religion and law under the caliph's command (*bar nahj-i dīn wa qānūn-i Islām bi-farmān-i khalīfa*).[114] The much briefer version by Bar Hebraeus likewise refers to the Seljuk rulers' obedience towards the caliph and the Ghaznawids' oppressive policy, but adds a new element not mentioned in the Muslim sources: In contrast to the Ghaznawids, who are the caliph's slaves, he, Ṭughril Beg, is "the son of freeborn men belonging to the royal stock of the Huns" (*w-enā bar ḥērē men shāqā dh-malkūthā dh-Hūnāyē*).[115] Whereas the Muslim accounts mainly focus on the religious and royal virtues of the Seljuk rulers, Bar Hebraeus places much stronger emphasis on their ethnic identity by identifying the Turks with the Huns in the same way as the Byzantine historian Michael Attaleiates had in the early 1080s.[116] This idea can be traced back to late antique ethnographical models, which perceived the Turks as a subgroup of the Huns ever since the emergence of the Gök-Turkic Empire of Central Asia in the sixth century.[117] The view that a man of noble descent suits the royal office much better than a slave-born potentate, however powerful he may be, reflects Christian-Roman concepts of kingship rather than Muslim ones, where nobility of birth is of importance only inasmuch as the family of the prophet and ancient Arabic tribal traditions are concerned.[118] Hence, the argument Bar Hebraeus put into Ṭughril Beg's mouth most likely is a secondary Christian interpretation of Seljuk claims to ascendancy within the Muslim world, not an element that formed part of the Seljuk-Abbasid discussions on legitimate rule in the mid-eleventh century.

The Syriac version of the letter appears within a longer passage outlining the nature of Ṭughril Beg's rule and military power in the time after 1040. Apart from a number of well-known elements pertaining to the Muslim ideals of just kingship, such as the ruler's obligation to protect Muslim pilgrims traveling to Mekka and his commitment to the religious practices of fasting and the daily prayers,[119] there are some noteworthy features pointing to specific Turkish ideas of lordship. Bar Hebraeus mentions the bow and arrow figure used by Ṭughril Beg for his monogram (*tamgha* or *ṭughra*) on the top of his letters.[120] Surviving numismatic evidence attests that this symbol, the meaning of which is most probably closely related to the political and legal traditions of the Oghuz tribes, was broadly used on coins both by members of the Seljuk dynasty and by their vassals from the early 1040s onwards.[121] According to the same report, Ṭughril Beg used to present himself in official ceremonies seated on the throne with a magnificent bow placed in front of it and holding two arrows in his hands.[122] This symbolism recalls the overall significance of the bow among the Turks and the Eurasian steppe peoples in general as the most important weapon of the nomad warriors fighting on horseback.[123] Bar Hebraeus also underlines Ṭughril Beg's endeavor to present himself as an all-mighty military commander holding sway over a fully devoted fighting force. Collective gestures of deference regularly performed by companies of 2,000 men, who at a certain distance from the ruler dismounted and kissed the ground, served to visualize the sultan's absolute power and uncontested authority.[124]

The universalist pretension of the Seljuk imperial project is expressed in a letter Ibrāhīm Yināl is said to have sent to the caliph, informing him about the intention of "the great Shāhinshāh, which means 'king of kings', and ruler of Khurāsān and Khwārizm" to send his troops to Baghdad so as to protect the route of pilgrimage from marauding nomads. The caliph is called to make peace with him "to reign over the whole world."[125] The ancient Persian royal title appears here along with the idea of an alliance with the caliphate, putting claims to universal rule commonly exerted by both sides. These thoughts have a much earlier parallel in the Byzantine chronicle of John Skylitzes,[126] who in his chapter about the origins and early expansion of the Turks offers a very similar explanation of the title of sultan: *Tangrolipex*, as Ṭughril Beg is called by the Byzantine author, after his final victory against *Mouchoumet*, a personality combining features pertaining to the historical memory of the Ghaznawid sultans Maḥmūd and Mas'ūd, was proclaimed by all his companions "king of Persia." Subsequently, his compatriots beyond the *Araxis* River—apparently an erroneous location of what in the Muslims accounts of the Seljuks' origin is the land of Transoxania and the Oxus River—destroyed the ramparts protecting the bridge over the river to intrude massively into the provinces of Persia. The Turks thus routed the Persians and Saracens and became themselves lords of the land, granting Tangrolipex the title of *soultanos*, "which means the almighty one and king of kings." A typical feature of late antique *origo gentis* narratives, i.e., the overcoming of an obstacle as a sort of primordial deed, is combined here with the idea of a Turkish conquest of lands previously possessed by Persians and Arabs, so that the chieftain of the Turks became the heir of the Persian royal tradition and was exalted to the position of a universal ruler of all these nations. The Byzantine version certainly favors a negative view of this process by underlining the hostile character of the invasion rather than the conquerors' successful integration, but still recognizes the extraordinary power and expansionist dynamics of the Seljuk sultanate.[127] Taken together, we arrive at the conclusion that much of the material transmitted in Bar Hebraeus' thirteenth-century chronicle shows striking similarities and comparable patterns of thought with Byzantine accounts from the late eleventh century and thus reflects a near-contemporary Christian perception of the emergence of the Seljuk sultanate. As has been pointed out, Bar Hebraeus also included into his account rich information originating from the Seljuk court historiography reaching back to the *Malik-nāma*.[128] This explains the numerous congruities with Nīshāpūrī and other Muslim works referring to the early Seljuk period. Both Muslim dynastic and Christian ethnographic elements obviously draw on a very early substrate of written material and therefore can claim a high degree of authenticity regarding the ideological dimensions of the Seljuk expansion, although literary conventions and encomiastic embellishments certainly contributed to a further exaltation and refinement of the original messages. Nevertheless, in the time when the raids of the Iraqi Turkmens began to affect the outermost extremities of the Byzantine borderland, the expansionist movement of Ṭughril Beg and his companions was increasingly undergirded by ideas of Muslim universal rule. This, in turn, affected Ṭughril Beg's attitudes towards the seditious Turkmens and the Muslim local lords in the Byzantine-Arab frontier zone and gave rise to a Seljuk variant of the Muslim jihad tradition. Several years later, these ideas crystallized into large-scale invasions initiated by the sultan and his entourage in Armenian and Byzantine territories. Thus, the Turkmen warriors' practice of political entrepreneurship based on raiding and profitable coalitions was supplemented by the Seljuk imperial project focusing on Muslim kingship and jihad. The combination of these factors resulted in the explosion that blew up the foundations of Byzantine rule in the East.

The first Seljuk invasions, 1046–48

In comparison to the activities of the Turkmen groups in the Armenian frontier zones close to southern Azerbaijan and northern Iraq, the Seljuk campaigns of the years 1046–48 were of a very different character. Instead of spontaneous attacks and coincidental forays we are now dealing with centrally organized expeditions of the Seljuk military elite aiming at the acquisition of booty and captives from the land of the infidels, which took place under the umbrella of the Muslim *jihad* tradition. In this way, the sultan and his entourage gained additional income and strengthened their prestige vis-à-vis the caliphate, the religious authorities and the nobility of the recently acquired urban centers, and the military forces under their command.[129] Modern Turkish scholarship is correct in sharply distinguishing between these expeditions and the earlier raids as well as in stressing their relevance for the relationship between the Seljuk elite and their army. On the other hand, Turkish scholars from Yinanç's time onwards unanimously exaggerate their significance by presenting them as efforts resulting from a fully developed long-term strategy of conquest and laying the foundations for a new homeland for migrating Turkmen tribes. Andrew Peacock in his recent study on the first Seljuk campaigns mainly focused on the nomadic character of the Turkmen military forces, thus trying to connect the itineraries and targets of these campaigns with nomad movements between winter and summer pastures.[130] The pastoralist point of view certainly should not be discarded in analyzing military operations of this kind of troops. Nevertheless, perhaps even more than the Iraqi Turkmens, Ṭughril Beg's forces in the 1040s must have already included large contingents of Iranian, Kurdish, and Arab warriors and slave soldiers. Hence, it is questionable to what extent the early invaders of the Byzantine provinces still had the character of preponderantly Turkmen nomadic fighters. Moreover, although there may well be a certain overlapping with pasture zones, the available accounts clearly indicate that the main targets of the individual operations were insufficiently fortified towns and trade centers and, in the campaign of 1054 under Ṭughril Beg's personal command, some crucial strongholds controlling the main routes between Azerbaijan and the Arsanias Valley.[131] Taking into account the perspicuous tendency of the Muslim narratives to present these expeditions as exploits of *jihad*, one arrives at the conclusion that gaining booty and projecting a spirit of Holy War were more urgent for Ṭughril Beg's policy than acquiring pasturelands for nomads.

The main architects of these enterprises were Ṭughril Beg and his brother Ibrāhīm Yināl, who apparently started to pay attention to the eastern provinces of the Byzantine Empire after advancing from Khurāsān via Jurjān and Ṭabaristān to western Iran and subduing various local dynasties and urban centers like Rayy and Hamadhān in 1042/43.[132] The immediate motives and reasons are presented quite disparately in the surviving narratives. Ibn al-Athīr under the year 440/16 June 1048–4 June 1049 ascribes the incursions to the arrival of "a great number of Oghuz Turks from Transoxania," to whom Ibrāhīm is said to have made the following statement:

> My territories are too narrow to offer you space to settle and to provide you with what you need. My opinion is that you should go to raid the Romans (*al-Rūm*) and to strive on the path of God (*tujāhidū fī sabīl Allāh*) and to make booty, and I will follow behind you and aid you in your enterprise.[133]

Although these words doubtlessly constitute a later reconstruction of what the Seljuk commander might have said to his soldiers, the passage is extremely valuable in that it summarizes two crucial factors giving rise to the idea of military expeditions on Byzantine territories. On the one hand, there was a massive influx of Oghuz Turks in the newly conquered territories. These people formed a considerable fighting force and had to be provided with new sources of income and areas of military activities. On the other hand, for the first time in the context of the Seljuk expansion, there is a clear reference to the *jihad* concept, which the Seljuk elite could easily adopt from well-established ideological patterns living on in the legal and political discourse about Muslim-Christian relations. Although the first half of the eleventh century was a relatively quiet period in terms of military conflicts between Byzantium and its Muslim neighbors, it can be safely assumed that the ideals of *jihad* and the historical memories of the Ḥamdānid rulers of

Aleppo and previous times were still circulating among the representatives of Sunni Orthodoxy and encomiastic court poetry. Hence, the Seljuk commanders had plenty of opportunities to become acquainted with the tradition of Muslim warfare against Byzantium.

As has already been explained,[134] in his report on the origins of the Seljuk dynasty and the rise of Ṭughril Beg (*Tangrolipex*), John Skylitzes refers to the intra-dynastic conflict with Ṭughril's cousin Qutlumush and the latter's campaign against *Karbeses*, "the chief of the Arabs," i.e., Qirwāsh of Mosul. In this context Qutlumush was presented as the instigator of the Seljuk attacks on Vaspurakan (*Baasprakan*).[135] The Byzantine narrative conflates knowledge about the quarrels between the two Seljuk lords, Qutlumush's reputation as ancestor of the future conquerors of Asia Minor, and the outside perception of the sultan as a barbarian potentate vacillating between the anger against his internal opponent and the fear of the Roman might. Consequently, the dispatch of Seljuk troops against Byzantine territory appears as the outcome of greed, irrational decisions, and chaos. From the perspective of the later developments in the second half of the eleventh century, when the Turks had already overrun the greatest part of Asia Minor and the Byzantine aristocracy was wearing itself out in incessant civil strife, this account can be read as an admonition supporting a revival of the empire's traditional values and military virtues so as to regain its superiority against the invading barbarian tribes.

Despite all discrepancies, both versions agree that the prospect of easy prey was an important incentive for these campaigns and that the first incursions of the Iraqi Turkmens had given rise to an increasing interest in the Christian territories. Skylitzes explicitly refers to the annexation of *Media*, i.e., Vaspurakan, as one of the targets of the expedition,[136] but most probably we are dealing here with an *ex eventu* explanation. It would be anachronistic to assume that at the time, the Seljuk leadership was already able to have a clear strategy regarding future conquests and directions of further expansion beyond the western Iranian regions. Neither Armenian nor Muslim sources speak about conquests or successful sieges prior to 1054. Yet there is another aspect in which Skylitzes agrees with the Armenian historian Matthew of Edessa: The Seljuk chiefs are said to have been confident that the Byzantine borderland was largely unprotected at the time of their first invasion.[137] From the Armenian point of view, this weakness is closely related to the removal of the Bagratid royal house from Ani and the Byzantine occupation of the city in 1045.[138] Byzantine "eunuch generals" were not able to secure the same degree of safety as the "brave and mighty men" of the indigenous aristocracy.[139] It is striking that the Byzantine author expresses an equally critical stance towards the decay of the empire's military power in the east, but in his or his informants' eyes, the source of these problems is located in the personal flaws of Emperor Constantine IX Monomachos, who is contrasted with outstanding commanders like Katakalon Kekaumenos.[140] The latter, a general of Armenian descent, who played an important role in Byzantine political affairs up to the revolt of Isaac Komnenos (1057), has been recognized as protagonist of one of the main sources used by Skylitzes for the period in question.[141] All in all, though for different reasons, there was a consensus that the Byzantine central government was not able to react aptly to military threats from the East. But this does not have much to do with insufficient defensive measures or inadequate fortifications, as has been brought forward from time to time.[142] Our narrative sources rather emphasize a lack of coordination and serious dissents between the imperial court and the military leaders in the East.

According to Skylitzes, the commander of the first expedition was one of Ṭughril Beg's nephews called Asan (= Ḥasan) "the Deaf," who is perhaps erroneously identified by modern scholars with a son of Mūsā Yabgu.[143] This first invasion was successfully fought off by the two highest commanders in the north-eastern part of the Byzantine frontier, the *katepano* of Vaspurakan Aaron and the *katepano* of Ani and Iberia Katakalon Kekaumenos.[144] Ḥasan obviously did not manage to penetrate deeply into Byzantine territory, for the place where the decisive battle took place is described as situated on the bank of the Stragna River (Zāb al-Aʿlā) east of Lake Van. According to the only available account, the Seljuk forces were outmaneuvered by a stratagem. The Byzantine troops seemed to have left their camp, thus prompting the enemy to undertake an assault to pillage the place. The Byzantine soldiers all of a sudden attacked the Turks from their ambush, killing a great number of them along with their commander. Only a few survivors managed to escape through the mountains and returned to their base in Azerbaijan.[145]

The second campaign, this time under the command of Ṭughril's brother Ibrāhīm Yināl, was crowned by success. Because of the detailed account of the near contemporary Armenian author Aristakes of Lastivert, we are able to reconstruct exactly the geographic reach of this expedition. Aristakes and Matthew of Edessa reflect the viewpoint of the local population, which was directly affected by this incursion.[146] Skylitzes adds the perspective of the Byzantine military leadership in the East, especially stressing Katakalon Kekaumenos' exploits.[147] Given that in this expedition, too, the Seljuk troops headed towards Vaspurakan, most probably starting from Tabriz, they seem to have followed the course of the Araxes River until they reached Byzantine territory.[148] Thence individual detachments spread in a fan-shaped manner into various districts north and south of the Araxes. The detachments reached Chaldia and the fortresses along the Akampsis River (Çoruh Nehri) in the north, as well as the province of Taron and other districts along the Arsanias in the south as far as Chorzianene near the Peri River. The main burden of the attack struck the province of Basean as well as the region between Theodosioupolis/Karin (Erzurum), Artze/Arcn, and the Mananalis district near the Tuzla River.[149] According to Skylitzes, the Seljuk forces were five times larger than those under Ḥasan's command, although the figures given—20,000 and 100,000 respectively—are certainly exaggerated.[150] Apart from Turkmen warriors, they also comprised detachments of *Kabeiroi* and *Dilimnites*[151] terms, which in all likelihood refer to Iranian (perhaps Khurāsānī?) and Daylamī soldiers. This is a remarkable piece of evidence pointing to the heterogeneous and composite character of the Seljuk troops at a very early stage. Just like the Iraqi Turkmens who in the course of their westward advance were joined by various local elements, Ibrāhīm Yināl's army of 1048, too, consisted of Turkish and Persian contingents originating from the recently conquered territories.

Ibrāhīm was another of Mūsā Yabgu's grandsons. After his father's death, he had invaded Khurāsān along with the forces of Ṭughril and Jaghrī as the leader of the *Yinālīyān*, another large confederation of Turkmen warriors. In 1038, he had seized Nīshāpūr for the first time. After serving as the city's governor for a while, Ibrāhīm advanced as far as Azerbaijan in several campaigns in the years 1045–48.[152] As he was one of the most powerful Seljuk warlords and was staunchly devoted to Ṭughril Beg, his appointment to the command of the Armenian expedition ensured that the sultan kept control over these large forces. In addition, Skylitzes mentions two subordinate officers, a certain *Chorosantes* (Khurāsānī), who may have commanded the Iranian contingents, and a half-brother of Ibrāhīm called *Aspan Salarios*, apparently a Greek transliteration of the Persian military rank of *sipāh-sālār* (cavalry commander).[153] In this expedition, Byzantine witnesses had the first opportunity to gain first-hand information on the command structures and the family relationships of the Seljuk leaders. They noted that they were dealing with a clan of closely related Turkish warriors bearing Persian titles and supported by Iranian forces. Although it is hardly possible to identify these men, it is clear that the two chief commanders represented two ethnically distinct groups in the invading army. In comparison to the preceding *origo gentis* narrative, which primarily emphasizes the Turks' nature as nomadic steppe people, the Katakalon report already shows a clear awareness of the process of Turkish-Iranian acculturation.

As regards the military aspects, Skylitzes mainly concentrates on the Byzantine commanders' inability to counter the Seljuk attack with an effective strategy. Kekaumenos, instead, is presented as a prudent general who would have been able to resolve the situation, had the other commanders only been willing to follow his advice. Kekaumenos was in favor of an offensive strategy aiming at a counter-attack on the Seljuk army as long as the Turks were exhausted from their march and not prepared to fight. In contrast, Aaron supported a defensive plan, giving priority to the fortification of towns and fortresses while granting shelter to the population and expecting orders from the imperial government.[154] The Byzantine troops pitched camp in the plain of Ourtrou, approximately half way between Theodosioupolis and Basean. Emperor Constantine IX Monomachos thought it best to rely on his alliance with the kingdom of Georgia under Bagrat IV and in particular with one of the most powerful Iberian noblemen, Liparit IV (*Liparites*), duke of Trialeti, inviting him to lend support to the imperial troops.[155] While the Byzantine contingents in compliance with the emperor's orders—and of course against Kekaumenos' advice—stayed in their camp awaiting the arrival of their allies, the Seljuk forces circumvented them, assaulting the market town of Arcn/Artze, which was laid to ashes, because the invaders could not overcome the barricades that had been hastily piled up by the inhabitants. The siege ended in a horrible massacre.[156] On the arrival of Liparit's forces, the Byzantine troops transferred their position from Ourtrou to the plain below the fortress of Kapetron (Hasankale) situated on the foothills of a mountain range nowadays called Palandöken Dağları.[157] Again Kekaumenos could not convince his fellow officers to attack the dispersedly arriving detachments. On 18 September 1048, the battle of Kapetron took place. Kekaumenos and Aaron, who fought in the right and left wings of the allied Christian forces, managed to repel the enemies, whereas Liparites, who commanded the center, fell from his horse and was captured by the Seljuk soldiers. When the latter withdrew in a northeasterly direction to Okomion/Okomi (near modern Pasinler), the remaining Byzantine forces, decisively weakened by the Georgians' defeat and no longer able to put up resistance, fled to their respective bases in Ani and Ivan. Thus, the Turks retreated unhindered to Azerbaijan.[158] Ibrāhīm Yināl reportedly reached Ṭughril Beg's residence in Rayy within five days, announcing the success of his expedition and the capture of his prominent prisoner.[159] Once again, Skylitzes uses this scene to present the sultan as a tyrant nurturing envy for Ibrāhīm's success, and to give a sound explanation for the subsequent civil strife between the two Seljuk leaders.[160]

While the Byzantine historian mainly stressed the idea of the Turkish barbarian's moral inferiority vis-à-vis Byzantine-Christian virtues, Muslim sources underline the Seljuk ruler's efforts to project the military success against the Christian Empire as a symbol of the sultanate's power and invincibility. Ibrāhīm Yināl's campaign thus served as a means to support the dynasty's claims to be the new leading force in the Muslim world. This was of crucial importance in view of the complex challenges posed by the developments within the Islamic sphere. As has been shown on the basis of the aforementioned examples of Seljuk-Abbasid correspondence,[161] the gradually crystallizing alliance with Caliph al-Qā'im required an ideological framework firmly rooted in the concepts of Muslim kingship. Commitment to the war against the infidels formed a central aspect therein.[162] Moreover, the sultan was called to highlight his commitment to supreme leadership of Muslim *jihad* vis-à-vis the pre-eminence of the Fatimid caliphate of Cairo and Sunni-Shiite antagonism. At the same time, the Seljuk leaders became more and more involved in the contentions among Sunni law schools (*madhāhib*), which over the eleventh century gained a more institutionalized character.[163]

Over time, the tendency of Seljuk *jihad* narratives to present the sultan and his followers as champions of Islam increased, eventually culminating in the depiction of Alp Arslān as a virtuous and pious hero, who successfully opposed Emperor Romanos IV in the battle of Manzikert.[164] The reports about the 1048 campaign reflect the first traces of these idealizing tendencies.[165] The clashes with the Byzantine troops including the not explicitly mentioned battle of Kapetron[166] appear as a confrontation between "Romans" (*Rūm*) or "Abkhazians" (*al-Abkhāz*), on the one hand, and "Muslims" (*al-muslimūn*), on the other. A designation referring to the warriors' religious identity replaces the terms *al-Ghuzz* and *al-Turkumān*, which dominate in the descriptions of the Iraqi Turkmens. In order to further highlight the Muslim exploits, special emphasis is placed on the Christians' outstanding military power: "There were numerous engagements between them in which one time prevailed this and the next time the other side [...] they killed a great many of the Romans and put them to flight and captured a great number of their patricians."[167] Moreover, the text refers to Constantinople (*al-Qusṭanṭīnīya*) as another strong element of *jihad* propaganda. The westernmost point the Muslims forces reached in their expedition is said to have been only 15 days' march from the Byzantine capital.[168] Finally, unlike Byzantine and Armenian texts, which refer to the tremendous damage the local population suffered by the Turks, Muslim authors describe the campaign's booty so as to extoll the immense profit gained: more than 100,000 captives, an uncountable number of horses, mules, spoils, and goods, among them 19,000 coats of mail, transported on 10,000 carts.[169] No doubt, these figures are exaggerated, but the important thing is to stress the wealth of the Christian regions and the high profitability of these raids in order to inspire enthusiasm for new expeditions.

Ṭughril Beg's 1054 campaign

Ṭughril Beg's second large-scale campaign of 1054 was preceded by an attack on Kars in the district of Vanand, the residence of a collateral branch of the Bagratid dynasty at that time represented by King Gagik-Abas II (1029–65).[170] It is useful to have a closer look at this preparatory expedition in order to elucidate Ṭughril's strategy and the state of affairs among leading members of the Seljuk military elite. We have only meager information about the circumstances of this assault, which according to Aristakes took place on the feast day of Epiphany of 502 (= 6 January 1054).[171] According to Skylitzes, Kars was besieged and, except for the citadel, conquered by Qutlumush's forces, who upon getting involved in Ibrāhīm Yināl's revolt fled to *Persarmenia*. From there he sent a message to the Byzantine imperial court asking for sanctuary. Muslim sources attest to an estrangement between Ibrāhīm Yināl and the sultan in 441/1049–50, caused by Ṭughril's demand to Ibrāhīm to hand over the city of Hamadhān and his castles in the Uplands.[172] Yet it is not possible to establish a link with Qutlumush, who revolted much later towards the end of Ṭughril Beg's reign.[173] Skylitzes apparently conflates events of the early and late 1050s, and thus the possibility of any causal relation between seditious activities and the attack on Kars can be excluded. Nevertheless, Qutlumush most likely was the commander of this expedition, as is corroborated by the chronicle of al-ʿAẓīmī.[174]

If we believe Aristakes, the inhabitants were completely surprised by the assault because it was on the feast day and they could not prevent the enemies from ravaging and looting their town. The invaders left after setting the city on fire.[175] At about the same time, Ṭughril Beg led his troops to Azerbaijan so as to impose his suzerainty upon the local potentates before advancing to Byzantine territory.[176] Thus, we may assume that the besiegers of Kars were a vanguard of the sultan's army. Both Wahsūdhān b. Muḥammad of Tabriz and Abū l-Aswār of Ganja paid allegiance to Ṭughril Beg, putting his name in the Friday prayer. Likewise, the Marwānid ruler of Diyār Bakr, Naṣr al-Dawla, declared his obedience to the sultan, sending many gifts and soldiers in support of the imminent

Seljuk expedition.[177] Muslim sources even claim that Ṭughril Beg passed through Marwānid territories near Jazīrat b. ʿUmar on his way to the Byzantine borderland. He is supposed to have intervened with Naṣr al-Dawla's son Sulaymān in favor of a Kurdish chieftain, who had been imprisoned by the former.[178] In this way, the Seljuk sultan inaugurated a new strategy, which aimed at the formal subjugation of the local Muslim lords along the frontier, thus undermining the Byzantine network of vassal potentates in the borderlands.[179] This strategy paralleled the incursions into the Byzantine provinces. Ṭughril Beg's successors Alp Arslān and Malikshāh systematically continued these attempts until they managed to build up a network of Seljuk allies stretching from the Caucasus region and Azerbaijan to northern Syria. For the time being, Ṭughril Beg was mainly interested in securing free access to the Araxes Valley and the Lake Van region in order to control the radius of action that had been achieved in 1048.

The 1054 campaign mostly affected the same area as the first expedition but concentrated its power slightly further south in the territories stretching from the shores of Lake Van along the Anti-Taurus Mountains as far as the northernmost section of the Euphrates Valley between Charpete/Kharput and Erzinkan/Erznka (Erzincan) in the Byzantine province of Mesopotamia.[180] This expedition also differed from the first by attempting the conquest of certain key points, namely the fortresses of Berkri (Muradiye), Arjīsh (Erciş), and Manzikert (Malazgirt). These covered the northern shores of Lake Van and controlled the routes leading to the Arsanias Valley.[181] Manzikert was an especially important administrative center in the province of Vaspurakan and residence of a *strategos*.[182] The objective apparently was to establish a kind of bridgehead opening the way from Azerbaijan to the Byzantine territories north and northwest of the Arsanias River. As regards the individual movements of the Seljuk forces, the most detailed accounts are provided by Aristakes and Matthew of Edessa, who in some points can be supplemented by Skylitzes and the Muslim sources.[183] In particular, the Seljuk invaders, upon taking the city of Berkri by assault, laid siege to Arjīsh, whose inhabitants surrendered in exchange for a peace agreement after eight days. The next target was Manzikert, where the army pitched camp and occupied the entire river valley.[184] From there, detachments spread in different directions, with one group heading northwards to the district of Taykh and the Akampsis River as far as the Parkhar Mountains (Parhal Dağları) in Abkhazia and thence following the river valley westward to the city of Baberd/Paipert (Bayburt) in the Chaldia district.[185] Some troops are said to have proceeded eastward to the kingdom of Vanand, where they met the fierce resistance of King Gagik-Abas of Kars.[186] This piece of information clearly indicates that the attack on Kars earlier this year did not affect the kingdom's military forces as a whole. Other units advanced along the Armenian Anti-Taurus Mountains in Taron as far as the district of Chorzianene, from where they undertook forays in a southwesterly direction along the Peri River to Chanzit, the district around the city of Charpete/Kharput, and northwestward to the districts of Derzene and Keltzene on the Euphrates and Kara Rivers around Erzincan.[187] The sultan personally undertook a foray through the province of Turuberan, passing Awnik, Basean, and

Du (Büyük Tuya) as far as Theodosioupolis/Karin, which could not be assaulted because of its formidable fortifications.[188]

The failed siege of Manzikert occupies a central place in the Byzantine and Armenian accounts, giving a vivid description of the heavy assaults against the ramparts with catapults throwing rocks and sappers undermining the foundations.[189] This is one of the very few instances in which Seljuk troops operating in Byzantine territories possessed the necessary equipment for full-scale sieges and the destruction of fortifications. The two traditions agree that the champion of the city's resistance was the Byzantine *strategos* Basileios Apokapes, a man of Georgian origin, who obviously enjoyed the support and respect of the local population.[190]

A common feature of our accounts is the tendency to stress the sultan's humiliation as a result of his fruitless efforts to take possession of the city. A high-ranking commander in the Seljuk army, alternatively called "the sultan's father-in-law, whose name was Osketsam" (Matthew) or "Alkan, the commander of the Khwārizmian forces" (Skylitzes) was captured and killed by the townspeople.[191] A Frankish soldier burned down an enormous catapult and insulted the sultan by refusing to accept his gifts as a reward for bravery.[192] The defenders kept on insulting Ṭughril Beg by shouting from the walls and throwing a pig into his camp.[193] These details obviously intend to underline the spirit of resistance prevailing among the people of Manzikert. In addition, they illustrate the close relationship between a leader's personal honor and his military success. The conquest of Manzikert would have meant a tremendous increase of the sultan's prestige as conqueror and *jihad* warrior. His failure, instead, entailed mockery and scorn on the part of his opponents and doubtlessly weakened his position among his companions. The Muslim sources respond to this critique by stressing the amounts of booty gained and the sultan's intention to resume the siege in the next spring, but it is apparent that the descriptions are much less laudatory than those of the 1048 campaign, and there are no allusions to the *jihad* ideology, which would have certainly been overwhelming in the case of a successful outcome.[194] A similar motif appears in Skylitzes' report: The sultan is said to have avoided a clash with the *akolouthos* Michael, for a defeat at the hands of the emperor's servant would have been a great shame, whereas a victory in this case would have brought no glory.[195] Again, it is the idea of the sultan's personal honor, which is viewed in close connection with military setbacks or indecisive results. All in all, the Seljuk troops may have acquired huge amounts of booty and captives, but the target of gaining the main route connecting Azerbaijan with the Arsanias Valley could not be achieved.

As regards the Byzantine defensive strategy, both the central government and the local authorities after the 1048 campaign and the first diplomatic contacts with the new enemies in the east were certainly much better prepared for new incursions, as is explicitly stated by John Skylitzes.[196] The transfer of a considerable force of Pecheneg soldiers to the eastern frontier failed,[197] but various measures were taken for a more efficient protection of the local population and the fortification of strongholds. With respect to the district of Basean, Skylitzes relates that the Turks could not cause much harm to the inhabitants because they managed to take refuge to a great number of well-fortified places in time.[198] Likewise, in Okomion the sultan decided not to proceed further because of messages announcing that Roman forces had been gathered in Cappadocia.[199] This may suggest a concentration of troops west of the Euphrates, perhaps in the region between Sebasteia and Tephrike. Apart from this, the local forces seemingly continued to follow the passive defense strategy so harshly criticized by Katakalon Kekaumenos.[200] According to the available accounts, the raiding units of the Seljuk army moved over long distances without meeting any serious resistance. The soldiers in Cappadocia seem to have guarded the crossings over the Euphrates but did not proceed to any attacks. An additional strengthening of the local defensive structures seems to have been achieved through the stationing of mercenary troops. Aristakes mentions a battle between Turkish raiders and Varangians in the region of Baberd/Paipert, in which the former were routed, losing their booty and captives. In fear of stronger Turkish forces coming from the east, however, the Varangians did not pursue them.[201] Likewise, the imperial government dispatched the *akolouthos* Michael to the East, where he gathered a force of Frankish and Varangian mercenaries in the provinces of Chaldia and Iberia.[202] Neither Michael nor the sultan seems to have proceeded to hostile actions. Thus, the mercenaries, too, were mainly concerned with the protection of certain areas, being attuned to the overall wait-and-see attitude of the Byzantine chief commanders. The same applies to the Armenian forces in Kars that fended off local attacks but did not collaborate with the Byzantine troops in the adjacent regions.[203]

In sum, the first emergence of Turkish warriors in the Byzantine-Muslim borderlands in the years 1038–54 did not result in major conquests or in a massive influx of nomads into the empire's eastern provinces. Nevertheless, these invaders in several respects prepared the ground for the ensuing breakdown: Recalcitrant warrior groups infiltrated the Muslim elites in the borderlands and thus undermined the empire's screen of allies in Upper Mesopotamia and Syria. The nascent Seljuk sultanate quickly grew into a supra-regional centralizing power, which posed a serious challenge to the dominant position of both Byzantium and the Fatimid caliphate and channeled much of its driving force into a revival of the Muslim *jihad* spirit. Byzantine defensive structures, fortifications, and provincial units occasionally reinforced by the troops of Armenian and Georgian marcher lords, were certainly in place and the local commanders made concerted attempts to repel both Turkmen incursions and large-scale Seljuk invasions. Yet there seems to have been a lack of coordination between the central government and the peripheral units and disagreements on tactical issues among the provincial chiefs. The recurring motif of excessive caution and sluggishness in taking adequate military measures most likely reflects *ex eventu* assessments or biased views favoring individual protagonists, such as Katakalon Kekaumenos. But it cannot be denied that in the decades following the last expansionist phase of the 1030s the Byzantine military structures in the East were not prepared to adequately cope with this new type of aggressive invasions. Most probably, this happened not because of specific shortcomings in comparison to the previous period, but because of an unprecedented situation resulting from a combination of unruly Turkmen groups, powerful armies of Turkish and non-Turkish Muslim warriors, and a highly determined Seljuk ruling elite on the verge of becoming a leading power in Iran and the center of the Abbasid caliphate.

Notes

1 For the most recent discussions with extensive bibliographical references, see Holmes, *Basil II*, pp. 299–391 (for the period of Basil II); Leveniotis, *Collapse*, passim (for the development up to the downfall of the Byzantine administration under the pressure of the Turkish invasions). For political and military events in the expansionist period and the first half of the eleventh century, we still largely depend upon Vasiliev and Canard, *Byzance et les Arabes*, 2.1; Canard, *H'amdanids*; Felix, *Byzanz*. Additional information on the situation in Syria and the relations with the Fatimid caliphate can be found in Bianquis, *Damas*.
2 From among the most recent bibliography, see, for instance, Decker, "Frontier Settlement and Economy," pp. 217–22; Eger, "Ḥiṣn al-Tīnāt," pp. 49–76; idem, "(Re) Mapping Medieval Antioch," pp. 95–134; idem, *Islamic-Byzantine Frontier*.
3 Eger, *Islamic-Byzantine Frontier*, pp. 1–21.
4 See, for instance, the remarks of Brubaker and Haldon, *Iconoclast Era*, pp. 723–71 (for an earlier period), and Holmes, *Basil II*, pp. 302–303.
5 See, for instance, Cheynet, *Contestations*, pp. 207–29, 261–301, 337–57, in contrast to Vryonis, *Decline*, pp. 70–80.
6 Decker, "Frontier Settlement and Economy," p. 220.
7 Oikonomidès, *Listes*, pp. 255–77; idem, "Organisation," pp. 285–302, esp. 299–300.
8 Oikonomidès, "Organisation," pp. 287–95.
9 Eger, *Islamic-Byzantine Frontier*, pp. 102–21, 123–24.
10 Eger, *Islamic-Byzantine Frontier*, pp. 124–25.
11 Decker, "Frontier Settlement and Economy," pp. 232–34, emphasizes the city's significance as an agricultural center in the Karababa Basin and as a hub on the crossing between Melitene and Manbij and the route from Anatolia to Edessa; see also Eger, *Islamic-Byzantine Frontier*, pp. 102, 122–23.
12 For the chronological sequence of the conquests, see Oikonomidès, "Organisation," pp. 287–94; for the significance of Cilicia and its towns, rivers, and the road systems connecting Syria and Anatolia, see Decker, "Frontier settlement and Economy," pp. 246–49; Eger, *Islamic-Byzantine Frontier*, pp. 158–81.
13 Holmes, *Basil II*, pp. 313–22; Leveniotis, *Collapse*, pp. 240–45. For the surviving Byzantine circuit walls of Koloneia, see Foss and Winfield, *Byzantine Fortifications*, p. 20.
14 For Kamākh as "the town closest to the source of the Euphrates," see Eger, *Islamo-Byzantine Frontier*, p. 125.
15 Holmes, *Basil II*, pp. 322–30 (who supports the opinion of an *ad hoc* appointment of Bardas Skleros in view of increasing military threats in the region); Leveniotis, *Collapse*, pp. 196–202.
16 Leveniotis, *Collapse*, pp. 255–62; for archaeological evidence in Melitene and its environs, see Decker, "Frontier Settlement and Economy," p. 246.
17 Holmes, *Basil*, pp. 330–60; Leveniotis, *Collapse*, pp. 322–35 (Antioch).
18 Eger, *Islamic-Byzantine Frontier*, pp. 33–39; for archaeological surveys in these areas and their results with respect to settlement patterns, agricultural systems, and urban centers, see ibidem, pp. 39–68; see also Decker, "Frontier Settlement and Economy," pp. 234–38.
19 For details with further bibliographical references, see Holmes, *Basil*, pp. 360–67.
20 Yuzbashian, "Administration," pp. 148–68; Holmes, *Basil*, pp. 360–67; Leveniotis, *Collapse*, pp. 55–65 (Iberia), pp. 126–47 (Vaspurakan).
21 Felix, *Byzanz*, pp. 100, 143–44; Beihammer, "Rulers," pp. 174–75.

22 Leveniotis, *Collapse*, pp. 274–78.
23 For details, see below, pp. 115–117; see also Decker, "Frontier Settlement and Economy," p. 233: "The plains south and east of the modern town of Adıyaman ... formed part of the hinterland of Samsosata." A survey in the region discovered 73 medieval sites.
24 Eger, *Islamo-Byzantine frontier*, pp. 128–31; for the Harran Plain Survey and its results, see ibidem, pp. 132–36, 140–48. Eger, ibidem, pp. 156–57, highlights the differences of the Jazīra in demographic and agricultural developments during the early Abbasid period from the western frontier zone; for settlement patterns, see also Decker, "Frontier Settlement and Economy," pp. 224–29.
25 Yuzbashian, "Administration," pp. 159–60; Leveniotis, *Collapse*, pp. 74–79 (Ani), 116–17 (Kars).
26 Holmes, *Basil II*, pp. 315, 321, 333–35, 339.
27 Holmes, *Basil II*, pp. 313–67, esp. 315–19, 328–31, 342–54.
28 Donohue, *Buwayhid Dynasty*, pp. 65–92, esp. 89: "In short, under Ṣamṣām al-Dawla the vision of ʿAḍud al-Dawla's Baghdad centered Empire collapsed."
29 For the Fatimid policy in Syria, see Bianquis, *Damas*, esp. 1:135–248.
30 For the buffer function of the Ḥamdānids of Aleppo, see Cappel, "Response," pp. 117–18.
31 Cappel, "Response," pp. 114–15.
32 The first study to analyze the significance of this network of allies for the Byzantine defensive system in the borderland with a special emphasis on the role of the nomadic tribes in Syria and Byzantine methods of nomad control is Cappel, "Response," pp. 113–32; other works focus on the relations with the Buwayhids, the Fatimids, and the Ḥamdānids: Farag, "Aleppo Question," pp. 44–60; Beihammer, "Rulers," pp. 164–77.
33 Lev, "Fatimids," pp. 204–208 and pp. 273–74; for the negotiations with Caliph al-Ḥākim, see Müller and Beihammer, *Regesten*, no. 788, 789e, 792b, 798f.
34 For these campaigns, see Bianquis, *Damas*, 2:472–75, 487–90, 588.
35 Ibn al-Athīr, 6:172, trans. Richards, *Annals*, p. 93; EI[2] 9:169–170 s. v. Shaddādids (C. E. Bosworth); Özgüdenli, *Selçuklular*, p. 100.
36 Skylitzes, p. 464.
37 Müller and Beihammer, *Regesten*, no. 790c; Holmes, *Basil*, pp. 320–21, 329; Ripper, *Marwāniden*, pp. 140–41.
38 EI[2] 6:626–27 s. v. Marwānids (Carole Hillenbrand); Ripper, *Marwāniden*, esp. 109–91.
39 Ripper, *Marwāniden*, pp. 66–72.
40 EI[2] 10:786–87 s. v. ʿUḳaylids (C. E. Bosworth); Ripper, *Marwāniden*, pp. 59–62, 128–35; a possible contact between Emperor Basil II and the ʿUqaylids: Müller and Beihammer, *Regesten*, no. 792.
41 For details, see Heidemann, *Renaissance*, pp. 60–67, 80–82, 86–88.
42 For details, see Heidemann, *Renaissance*, pp. 89–97.
43 EI[2] 8:589–91, at p. 590, s. v. al-Ruhā (E. Honigmann and C. E. Bosworth).
44 For the situation of Aleppo in general, see Felix, *Byzanz*, pp. 46–47, 49–50, 54–56, 63–70, 76–79, 81–90, 93–94, 100–103, 105, 108–14, 116–17, 120–23; Cappel, "Response," pp. 120–24; Beihammer, "Rulers," pp. 164–71.
45 Felix, *Byzanz*, pp. 63–70, 76–82.
46 Felix, *Byzanz*, pp. 82–90, 99–102; Beihammer, "Rulers," pp. 167–70.
47 Felix, *Byzanz*, pp. 110–14; Beihammer, "Rulers," pp. 170.
48 See below, pp. 92–94.
49 Felix, *Byzanz*, pp. 116–22; Beihammer, "Rulers," pp. 170–71.
50 For the political situation in Aleppo after 1058, see Heidemann, *Renaissance*, pp. 109–10, 117–21, 122–23; for further details, see below, pp. 117–24.
51 Felix, *Byzanz*, pp. 95–96; Cappel, "Response," pp. 124–26; Beihammer, "Rulers," pp. 172–73.
52 Felix, *Byzanz*, pp. 81–82; Cappel, "Response," p. 125.

53 Ibn al-Athīr, 6:38–39, trans. Richards, *Annals*, pp. 13–15; for the identity and activities of these Turkmen groups in general, see Yinanç, *Anadolu'nun Fethi*, pp. 37–38; Turan, *Selçuklular Târihi*, pp. 119–21; Sümer, *Oğuzlar*, pp. 67–73, 80–84, 93–95; Cahen, "Pénétration," pp. 8–9; idem, *Pre-Ottoman Turkey*, p. 68; Sevim, *Anadolu'nun Fethi*, pp. 23–24; Sevim and Yücel, *Türkiye Tarihi*, pp. 35–36; Divitçioğlu, *Oğuz'dan*, pp. 69–70; Sevim and Merçil, *Selçuklu Devletleri*, pp. 39–43; Öngül, *Selçuklular*, 1:19–21; Başan, *Great Seljuqs*, pp. 64–65; Peacock, *Early Seljūq History*, pp. 68–71; idem, *Great Seljuk Empire*, pp. 29–32.

54 Ibn al-Athīr, 6:38–46, trans. Richards, *Annals*, pp. 13–25.

55 Ibn al-Athīr, 6:39, 46, trans. Richards, *Annals*, pp. 14, 25.

56 Nīshāpūrī/Rashīd al-Dīn, p. 7, trans. Luther, p. 31.

57 For his position as head of the Seljuk clan, see Sümer, *Oğuzlar*, pp. 62–63, 65–67.

58 Ibn al-Athīr, 6:38, trans. Richards, *Annals*, p. 13; an elaborated version of Arslān Isrā'īl's imprisonment can be found in Nīshāpūrī/Rashīd al-Dīn, pp. 7–10, trans. Luther, pp. 30–32; for the historical background, see Peacock, *Great Seljuk Empire*, pp. 28–32.

59 Ibn al-Athīr 6:38–40, trans. Richards, *Annals*, pp. 13–16.

60 Ibn al-Athīr, 6:38, trans. Richards, *Annals*, p. 13.

61 Ibn al-Athīr, 6:39, trans. Richards, *Annals*, p. 15.

62 Ibn al-Athīr, 6:39, trans. Richards, *Annals*, p. 15. For further evidence regarding the presence of women and children during Turkmen campaigns, see Peacock, *Early Seljūq History*, pp. 83–84.

63 Peacock, *Early Seljūq History*, pp. 83–89; idem, *Great Seljuk Empire*, pp. 45–46.

64 Ibn al-Athīr, 6:38–40, trans. Richards, *Annals*, pp. 14–18.

65 Peacok, *Early Seljūq History*, pp. 53–55.

66 Peacok, *Early Seljūq History*, pp. 57–60; this view is at variance with the prevailing opinions of Turkish scholars, who very much emphasize the persistence of Oghuz-Turkic traditions as a driving force of Seljuk state building. See, for instance, Sümer, *Oğuzlar*, pp. 1–90; Divitçioğlu, *Oğuz'dan*, pp. 53–109.

67 Ibn al-Athīr, 6:41, trans. Richards, *Annals*, p. 17.

68 Ibn al-Athīr 6:39, 40, 43, trans. Richards, *Annals*, pp. 15, 17, 18, 20; see also Peacock, *Seljūq History*, pp. 69–70, who tries to draw a terminological distinction between *amīr* and *muqaddam*.

69 Ibn al-Athīr 6:38, 40–42, trans. Richards, *Annals*, pp. 13, 16–19.

70 Ibn al-Athīr, 6:42, trans. Richards, *Annals*, p. 19.

71 Ibn al-Athīr, 6:42–43, trans. Richards, *Annals*, pp. 20–21.

72 Ibn al-Athīr, 6:41, trans. Richards, *Annals*, p. 18.

73 Ibn al-Athīr, 6:45, trans. Richards, *Annals*, pp. 21–22; 'Aẓīmī, p. 4 (Arabic text), p. 6 (trans.) (*sub anno* 435/10 August 1043–28 July 1044).

74 Ibn al-Athīr 6:43–45, trans. Richards, *Annals*, pp. 21–23: *wa-kānū yaqṣudūna bilād al-Arman wa-yanhabūna wa-yasbūna*.

75 'Aẓīmī, p. 3 (Arabic text), p. 6 (trans.).

76 For the ducate of Mesopotamia, see Leveniotis, *Collapse*, pp. 196–202.

77 Leveniotis, *Collapse*, pp. 211–12.

78 Ibn al-Athīr, 6:45, trans. Richards, *Annals*, p. 23: *hā'ulā'i l-Turkumān kānū lanā 'abīdan wa-khadaman wa-ra'āyā wa-taba'an yamtathilūna l-amr wa-yakhdimūna l-bāb*; see also Peacock, *Great Seljuk Empire*, pp. 44–45, whose translation of this passage differs in some points.

79 Peacock, *Early Seljūq History*, p. 70.

80 Ibn al-Athīr, 6:44, trans. Richards, *Annals*, p. 23.

81 Bar Hebraeus, p. 222, trans. Budge, p. 198: *wa-khthabh tūbh Qezel ḥathnhōn āwbeth b'el ḥāthhōn* "Qezel, their brother-in-law, that means the husband of their sister, also wrote [a letter to the caliph]." See also Divitçioğlu, *Oğuz'dan*, p. 74; Peacock, *Early Seljūq History*, p. 71.

82 Ibn al-Athīr, 6:45, trans. Richards, *Annals*, pp. 23–24.

83 Matthew of Edessa 1.88, p. 74. The report also refers to the battle with Qirwāsh, presenting the Turkish commanders Pōghi, Puki and Anazughli (the distorted forms of Būqā and Nāṣoghlī are clearly recognizable) erroneously as men of Ṭughril's court.

84 Skylitzes, p. 446, ll. 81–82: Στέφανος πατρίκιος ὁ Κωνσταντίνου τοῦ παραδυναστεύοντος τῷ βασιλεῖ τῆς Λειχουδίας υἱός. For Stephen' identity, see the translation of Flusin and Cheynet, p. 371, n. 120; the same person is also mentioned in a brief note of ʿAẓīmī, p. 4 (Arabic text), p. 6 (trans.): *wālī Asrahān al-qaṭbān Iṣṭifān*; for Leichoudes, see Angold, *Empire*, 42, 67, 69.

85 For these events, see Ripper, *Marwāniden*, pp. 98, 315; Leventiotis, *Collapse*, pp. 147–50.

86 Ibn al-Athīr, 6:39–40, 41, 42, trans. Richards, *Annals*, pp. 16, 17, 19.

87 Ibn al-Athīr, 6:45, trans. Richards, *Annals*, p. 23.

88 Ibn al-Athīr, 6:40, trans. Richards, *Annals*, p. 17.

89 Ibn al-Athīr, 6:40–41, trans. Richards, *Annals*, pp. 16–17: *ṣāharahum*; *rāsala Kūktāsh wa-ṣālaḥahū wa-ṣāharahū*.

90 Ibn al-Athīr, 6:43, trans. Richards, *Annals*, p. 20: *fa-taṣālaḥā wa-taḥālafā*.

91 Ibn al-Athīr, 6:43, trans. Richards, *Annals*, p. 20: *wa-aḍmara Sulaymān al-ghadr bihī*.

92 Ibn al-Athīr, 6:43, trans. Richards, *Annals*, p. 21.

93 Ibn al-Athīr, 6:43–44, trans. Richards, *Annals*, pp. 21–23.

94 Attaleiates, p. 33, ll. 16–25.

95 For other aspects of this interesting text, especially with regard to the Byzantine version of the origins of the Seljuk sultanate, see Beihammer, "Ethnogenese," pp. 597–98, 600–602, 605–608.

96 See above, p. 66.

97 Cahen, "Qutlumush," pp. 18–19; İA 10:366–67 s. v. Selçuklular (I. Kafesoğlu); Turan, *Selçuklular Târihi*, pp. 138–41.

98 Skylitzes, pp. 445–47.

99 Cahen, "Qutlumush," p. 19.

100 Ibn al-Athīr, 6:189–90, 192, trans. Richards, *Annals*, pp. 106, 110–11.

101 Skylitzes, p. 446, ll. 1–3.

102 Skylitzes, pp. 446–47, esp. 447, ll. 6–8.

103 Skylitzes, p. 446, ll. 3–5.

104 Skylitzes, p. 447, ll. 9–19.

105 Sibṭ b. al-Jawzī, p. 77, ll. 10–12 (in Rabīʿ II 453/25 April-23 May 1061 Ṭughril Beg sent troops against Girdkūh), p. 82, ll. 10–12 (in Rajab 453/22 July-20 August 1061 the sultan came to Rayy where he decided to take up the siege of Girdkūh in person), p. 85, l. 20 (the sultan besieged the fortress in Shaʿbān/21 August-18 September 1061); p. 101, ll. 9–11 (in Jumādā II 463/1–30 June 1063 Qutlumush is still in Girdkūh with 10,000 soldiers), p. 110, ll. 17–18 (in Muḥarram 456/25 December 1063–23 January 1064, a few months after Ṭughril Beg's death, Qutlumush left Girdkūh and collected a strong army).

106 For the Seljuk conquest of Nīshāpūr, especially with respect to the reaction of the local aristocracy, see Paul, "Nishapur," pp. 575–85. For further details concerning the Iranian response to the Seljuk expansion, see Durand-Guédy, "Iranians at War," pp. 587–606, and idem, *Iranian Elites*. For the Seljuk conquest of Khurāsān in the years 1038–40, see Bosworth, Ghaznavids, pp. 241–68; idem, "Political History," pp. 11–23; Köymen, *Kuruluş Devri*, pp. 161–351; Agacanov, *Selçuklular*, pp. 74–97; Merçil, *Gazneliler*, pp. 62–76; idem, *Müslüman Türk Devletleri*, pp. 54–56; Sevim and Merçil, *Selçuklu Devletleri*, pp. 30–35; Piyadeoğlu, *Çağrı Bey*, pp. 47–103; idem, *Horasan*, pp. 33–43; Öngül, *Selçuklular*, 1:10–15; Özgüdenli, *Selçuklular*, pp. 67–89; Peacock, *Great Seljuk Empire*, p. 36–40.

107 İA 10:361–62 s. v. Selçuklular (I. Kafesoğlu); Turan, *Selçuklular Târihi*, pp. 98–109; Başan, *Great Seljuqs*, pp. 61–62; Sevim and Merçil, *Selçuklu Devletleri*, pp. 34–35; Öngül,

Selçuklular, 1:15; Özgüdenli, *Selçuklular*, pp. 87–89; Divitçioğlu, *Oğuz'dan*, pp. 79–83, describes this process according to socio-historical models as a transition from 'tribe' (*boy*) to 'state' (*devlet*); Peacock, *Great Seljuk Empire*, pp. 39–41, emphasizes the tendency of later chronicles, which "aim to legitimize the Seljuks by portraying them as rulers in the Sunni Perso-Islamic tradition," but he still agrees with other scholars that there was "an ideological change … with dreams of conquest and empire."

108 For details of this process, see Paul, "Nishapur," pp. 575–85; Durand-Guédy, "Iranians at War," pp. 587–606.

109 For eleventh-century theoretical thought on the caliph-sultan relationship, see Lambton, "Internal Structure," pp. 205–12; for insignia and symbols of sovereignty in Ghaznawid and Seljuk Iran, see EI^2 6:521–24 s. v. Marāsim (A. Lambton); for *khuṭba* and *sikka* as insignia of caliphal authority, see Tyan, *Institutions*, pp. 395–403; for honorifics, see EI^2 5:618–31, esp. 622–23 s. v. Laḳab (C. E. Bosworth); for a systematic study of Seljuk insignia of sovereignty, see Merçil, *Hükümdarlık Alâmetleri*, pp. 30–34, 37–40 (titles, *alqāb*), pp. 44–54 (*khuṭba*), pp. 89–93 (coins), pp. 123–26 (banners), pp. 142–53 (honorary robes [*khil'a*]).

110 For the religious Sunni Muslim aspects in Seljuk ideology, see Tor, "Sovereign and Pious," pp. 39–62, who argues in favor of a mixture of actual attitudes of pious behavior, fervent Sunni beliefs, and idealized literary descriptions in response to overstated revisionist views rejecting the Seljuk Sunni identity as later constructions.

111 Modern Turkish scholarship interprets the institutional basis regulating this distribution of power as "great assembly" (*büyük kurultay*) of the leading clan members according to Turkish tribal traditions. See, for instance, Köymen, *Kuruluş Devri*, pp. 356–66; Merçil, *Müslüman Türk Devletleri*, p. 56; Sevim and Merçil, *Selçuklu Devletleri*, pp. 34; Öngül, *Selçuklular*, 1:15; Özgüdenli, *Selçuklular*, p. 87.

112 See the examples cited below, pp. 72–73, as well as Tor, "Sovereign and Pious," pp. 39–40.

113 al-Ḥusaynī, pp. 8–9; Ibn al-Athīr, 6:99–100, trans. Richards, *Annals*, pp. 37–38; for a thorough analysis of these events, see Bosworth, *Ghaznavids*, pp. 252–68; Merçil, *Hükümdarlık Alâmetleri*, pp. 30–31, 73–74, asserts that on coins the title of *al-sulṭān al-mu'aẓẓam* first appears in the year 438/1046–47 after the official recognition of Ṭughril Beg's rule in Khurāsān on the part of the caliphate whereas the titles on his earliest coins are *al-amīr al-ajall* and *al-amīr al-sayyid*; for Jaghrī's title, see also Peacock, *Great Seljuk Empire*, p. 42.

114 Nīshāpūrī/Rashīd al-Dīn, pp. 18–19, trans. Luther, pp. 39–40.

115 Bar Hebraeus, p. 225, trans. Budge, p. 201.

116 See above, p. 68.

117 Beihammer, "Ethnogenese," pp. 598–99.

118 For these matters, see, for instance, Drews, *Karolinger*, pp. 102–46.

119 Bar Hebraeus, p. 225, trans. Budge, p. 201.

120 Bar Hebraeus, p. 224, trans. Budge, p. 200: *rsham-(h)wāth dēn b-rēshāh d-eggarthā ṭūpsā dh-qeshtā w-ghērā*. For the bow and arrow symbol in general, see Merçil, *Hükümdarlık alâmetleri*, pp. 193–95; Peacock, *Great Seljuk Empire*, pp. 41–42.

121 Özgüdenli, "Yeni Paraların Işığında," pp. 548–62.

122 Bar Hebraeus, p. 225, trans. Budge, p. 201: *wa-qddāmāy(hy) qeshtā myattarthā w-bh-īdhēh trēn ghērē*.

123 Heather, *Untergang*, pp. 187–91 (with further details concerning archaeological finds of gold-plated bows and late antique reports about the efficiency of this weapon).

124 Bar Hebraeus, p. 225, trans. Budge, p. 202; see also Beihammer, "Ethnogenese," pp. 605–606.

125 Bar Hebraeus, p. 224, trans. Budge, p. 200: *d-shāhēnshāh rabbā āwbēth mlekh malkē Ṭūghrel Bāgh Salgūqāyā amlekh 'al Kōrāsān wa-Khwārazm*.

126 Skylitzes, pp. 442–45, esp. 445, ll. 62–71.

127 For details, see Beihammer, "Ethnogenese," pp. 600–608.

128 Peacock, *Early Seljūq History*, pp. 27–32.

129 For the early Anatolian campaigns under the reign of Ṭughril Beg, see Cahen, "Première Pénétration," pp. 13–17; idem, *Pre-Ottoman Turkey*, pp. 66–69; Yinanç, *Anadolu'nun Fethi*, pp. 44–50, idem, *Türkiye Tarihi*, pp. 40–44; Vryonis, *Decline*, pp. 85–87; Turan, *Selçuklular Târihi*, pp. 119–23, 129–31; Shepard, "Scylitzes on Armenia," pp. 270–83; Köymen, *Selçuklu Devri*, pp. 242–51; Felix, *Byzanz*, pp. 164–70, 173–79; Sevim, *Anadolu'nun Fethi*, pp. 29–34; Sevim, *Süleymanşah*, pp. 3–5; Turan, *Türkiye*, pp. 17–18; Leveniotis, *Collapse*, pp. 90–96, 147–57; Merçil, *Müslüman Türk Devletleri*, pp. 57–58; Peacock, *Early Seljūq History*, 128–39, 144–51; Sevim and Merçil, *Selçuklu Devletleri*, pp. 43–48; Öngül, *Selçuklular*, 1:22–25, 26–27; Özgüdenli, *Selçuklular*, pp. 97–101.
130 Peacock, *Early Seljūq History*, 128–39, 144–51.
131 For more details and sources, see the extensive discussion below, pp. 80–84.
132 Sevim and Merçil, *Selçuklu Devletleri*, pp. 43–44; Öngül, *Selçuklular*, 1:22; Özgüdenli, *Selçuklular*, pp. 91–94.
133 Ibn al-Athīr, 6:138–39, trans. Richards, *Annals*, pp. 67–68: *khalqan kathīran min al-Ghuzz bi-Mā warā' al-Nahr*.
134 See above, pp. 69–70.
135 Skylitzes, pp. 446–47.
136 Skylitzes, p. 447: καὶ εἰ προσχωροίη, προσκτήσασθαι αὐτῷ τὴν Μηδίαν.
137 Matthew of Edessa 1.92, p. 76: [...] because they knew that, being in the hands of the Romans, the entire country was abandoned and unprotected. John Skylitzes, p. 446: [...] περὶ τοῦ Βαασπρακᾶν, ὡς εἴη μὲν χώρα πάμφορος, κατέχεται δὲ ὑπὸ γυναικῶν, τοὺς πεπολεμηκότας πρὸς αὐτὸν στρατιώτας ὑπαινιττόμενος.
138 Matthew of Edessa 1.85, pp. 72–73.
139 Matthew of Edessa 1.92, p. 76.
140 See, for instance, Skylitzes, p. 476, where the dissolution of the Byzantine troops in Iberia (Ἰβηρικὸς στρατός) is ascribed to the wasteful financial policy of the emperor.
141 Shepard, "Scylitzes on Armenia," pp. 269–311.
142 For a recent discussion, see Peacock, *Early Seljūq History*, pp. 129–39, who summarizes the main arguments of older scholarship and brings together written and archaeological evidence for fortifications in the northeastern and southeastern sections of the frontier. He concludes that, although there were some fortified places, the available evidence also points to neglect, inadequate investment, or to fortifications oriented toward other directions than the east.
143 Skylitzes, p. 447: στρατηγὸν ἐπιστήσας αὐτῇ ἀδελφόπαιδα Ἀσὰν τὸν λεγόμενον κωφόν. For Asan's identity, see Felix, *Byzanz*, p. 164, n. 94; Özgüdenli, *Selçuklular*, p. 98, n. 31, rejects this assumption on the basis of numismatic evidence from Herat.
144 Skylitzes, p. 448: ὁ δὲ τῆς χώρας ἄρχων Ἀαρὼν βέστης, ὁ τοῦ Βλαδισθλάβου υἱὸς καὶ τοῦ Προυσιάνου ἀδελφός, [...] γράμματα ἐκπέμπει πρὸς τὸν βέστην Κατακαλὼν τὸν Κεκαυμένον τοῦ Ἀνίου καὶ τῆς Ἰβηρίας κατάρχοντα.
145 Skylitzes, p. 449.
146 Aristakes 11–13, pp. 57–72; Matthew of Edessa 1.92, pp. 76–77.
147 Shepard, "Scylitzes on Armenia," pp. 270–83.
148 Skylitzes, p. 448: παρελθὼν τὸ Ταβρέζιον καὶ τὸ λεγόμενον Τεφλὶς ἦλθεν εἰς Βαασπρακανίαν (in the first expedition), p. 450: ὁ Ἀβράμιος τὴν Βαασπρακανίαν καταλαβών (in the second expedition).
149 Aristakes 11, pp. 57–61, speaks of three different expeditions before, during, and after the Armenian year 497 (= 9 March 1048–8 March 1049). While it is no problem to identify them with the invasions of Ḥasan (1047) and Ibrāhīm Yināl (1048), there seems to be a geographic confusion, for the first is said to have reached the "*gawaṙ* de Basean, jusqu'au grand *dastakert* appelé Vałaršawan" (Eleşkirt), and 24 other provinces, but the Turks failed to reach Karin. These details most probably duplicate the description of the second raid, which is more extensive, in particular mentioning the plain of Basean and Karin, the province of Chaldia/Xałtikʻ and the fortress of Sper

(İspir), as well as the districts of Taykh, Aršarunik', Tarawn, Hašteank', Xorjean, Sisak, and Mananaɫi. A separate chapter (ibidem 12, pp. 63–68) describes the attack on Arcn.

150 Skylitzes, p. 447 (ἀμφὶ τὰς εἴκοσι χιλιάδας), p. 449 (περὶ τὰς ἑκατὸν χιλιάδας).

151 Skylitzes, p. 449: συστησάμενος ἔκ τε Τούρκων καὶ Καβείρων καὶ Διλιμνιτῶν. The exact meaning of *Kabeiroi*, which in the ancient tradition denotes a variety of real and mythical peoples, is unclear.

152 Sevim and Merçil, *Selçuklu Devletleri*, pp. 34, 36, 38; Öngül, *Selçuklular*, 1:12, 15, 18–19, 20, 22; Özgüdenli, *Selçuklular*, p. 57, n. 168, p. 62, n. 3, pp. 76, 88–89, 93.

153 Skylitzes, p. 453: Χωροσάντης ἅτερος στρατηγός, [...] Ἀσπὰν Σαλάριος ὁ τοῦ Ἀβραμίου ἑτεροθαλὴς ἀδελφός.

154 Skylitzes, p. 450.

155 Skylitzes, p. 450; see also Dölger and Wirth, *Regesten*, no. 890a and 890b; for Ourtrou and the identity of Liparites, see Leveniotis, *Collapse*, p. 91.

156 Skylitzes, pp. 450–52; see also MacEvitt, "Chronicle of Matthew," p. 163.

157 Skylitzes, p. 452; for Kapetron, see Felix, *Byzanz*, map, and Leveniotis, *Collapse*, p. 93.

158 Skylitzes, pp. 452–53; for details, see Leveniotis, *Collapse*, pp. 94–96.

159 Skylitzes, p. 453.

160 Skylitzes, p. 454: ἐφθόνησε δὲ τῷ ἀδελφῷ τοιτούτου καταξιωθέντι τοῦ εὐτυχήματος.

161 See above, pp. 71–73.

162 For the initial phase of Seljuk-Abbasid contacts, see Hanne, *Caliph*, pp. 87–91.

163 For Byzantine-Fatimid relations in this period, see Felix, *Byzanz*, pp. 117–21, 170–71, 177–78, and the details below, pp. 94–102; for the Seljuk sultanate and Sunni Islam, see Peacock, *Early Seljūq History*, pp. 99–127.

164 See below, pp. 155–161.

165 'Aẓīmī, p. 6 (Arabic text), pp. 8–9 (trans.); Ibn al-Athīr, 6:138–39, trans. Richards, *Annals*, pp. 67–68.

166 Ibn al-Athīr, 6:139, trans. Richards, *Annals*, p. 67: *wa-kāna ākhir al-amr al-ẓafar li-l-muslimīn*, "ultimately victory went to the Muslims."

167 Ibn al-Athīr, 6:139, trans. Richards, *Annals*, p. 67. Liparit is called *Qārīṭ malik al-Abkhāz* ("the king of the Abkhazians"). *qāf* may be a misreading of the Arabic letter *fā'* rendering the consonant 'p'.

168 Ibn al-Athīr, 6:139, trans. Richards, *Annals*, p. 68: *ilā an baqiya baynahū wa-bayna l-Qusṭanṭīnīya khamsata 'ashara yawman*, "until there was between him and Constantinople [a distance] of fifteen days."

169 Ibn al-Athīr, 6:139, trans. Richards, *Annals*, p. 68.

170 Aristakes 15, pp. 74–75; Skylitzes, p. 474, ll. 93–95; for the political situation in Kars, see Felix, *Byzanz*, p. 173 with n. 117; *Oxford Dictionary of Byzantium* 2, p. 1108 s. v. Kars; Leveniotis, *Collapse*, pp. 116–17.

171 Aristakes 15, p. 74: "Au jour de la grande Fête de l'Épiphanie de Notre Seigneur." The date is corroborated by 'Aẓīmī, pp. 9–10 (Arabic text), p. 12 (trans.), *sub anno* 445/23 April 1053–11 April 1054: *wa-hajama Quṭlumush ṣāḥib Ṭughril-bak madīnat al-Qarṣ wa-qatala kull man kāna bihā*, "Qutlumush, the companion of Ṭughril Beg, attacked the city of Kars and killed everybody who was there."

172 Ibn al-Athīr, 6:145–46, trans. Richards, *Annals*, p. 73 (*sub anno* 441/5 June 1049–25 May 1050); for this revolt, see Özgüdenli, *Selçuklular*, pp. 119–20.

173 Sevim and Merçil, *Selçuklu Devletleri*, pp. 59–60; Öngül, *Selçuklular*, 1:35–36; Özgüdenli, *Selçuklular*, pp. 132–33, 138 (1061–64).

174 See above, n. 171.

175 Aristakes 15, pp. 74–75.

176 Aristakes 16, pp. 75–87; Matthew of Edessa 2.3, pp. 86–88; Skylitzes, pp. 462–64, 474; Ibn al-Athīr, 6:172, trans. Richards, *Annals*, p. 93.

177 Ibn al-Athīr, 6:172, trans. Richards, *Annals*, p. 93.

178 Ibn al-Athīr, 6:177, trans. Richards, *Annals*, p. 97.

179 For this system, see above, pp. 57–61.
180 For the scholarly literature on this campaign, see the references above, n. 129.
181 For the geographic details, see the discussion below, pp. 81–83.
182 For the significance of Manzikert, see Leveniotis, *Collapse*, p. 142.
183 Aristakes 16, pp. 75–87; Matthew of Edessa 2.3, pp. 86–88; Skylitzes, pp. 462–64; Ibn al-Athīr, 6:172, trans. Richards, *Annals*, p. 93; ʿAẓīmī, p. 12 (Arabic text), p. 13 (trans.); for an analysis of the sources, which in some points differs from the reconstruction below, see Leveniotis, *Collapse*, pp. 152–57.
184 Aristakes 16, p. 75; Matthew of Edessa 2.3, p. 86.
185 Aristakes 16, p. 76: au nord jusqu'aux forteresses des Apʿxaz, jusqu'à la montagne de Parxar et jusqu'au pied du Kovkas (Caucase), p. 79: Ayant pénétré dans le Taykʿ [...] parvinrent jusqu'au grand fleuve appelé Čorox [...] et descendirent dans le pays de Xałtikʿ [...] ils revinrent en arrière et arrivèrent à la ville forteresse (*berdakʿalakʿ*) appelée Baberd.
186 Aristakes 16, p. 80: Ils parvinrent jsuqu'au Vanand et là, furent attaqués par les braves *išxan* de Gagik, fils d'Abas.
187 Aristakes 16, p. 78: Quand je me rapelle le Xorjean et le Hanjetʿ, p. 79: les massacres qui eurent lieu sans le Derjan et l'Ekełeacʿ.
188 Aristakes 16, pp. 81–82: le sultan [...] se dirigea vers le Tuaracatapʿ [...] dans la large vallée de Basean [...] à la forteresse inaccessible appelée Awnik [...] au village de Du à la place admirablement défendue de Karin.
189 Aristakes 16, pp. 82–87: Le sultan recommença le siège de Manazkert avec une fureur terrible; Matthew of Edessa 2.3, pp. 86–88; Skylitzes, pp. 462–64.
190 Aristakes 16, p. 82: L'*išxan* qui avait la charge de veiller sur la ville était un homme pieux qui soumettait humblement à Dieu par l'abstinence et les prières, p. 87: L'*ixšan* de la ville, Vasil; Skylitzes, 462, ll. 60–62: εὐρώστως δὲ τῶν ἔνδον ἀποκρουομένων τὰς προσβολὰς ἐμπειρίᾳ καὶ συνέσει τοῦ στρατηγοῦ (ἦν δὲ Βασίλειος πατρίκιος ὁ Ἀποκάπης).
191 Skylitzes, p. 462, l. 64: Ἀλκάν ὁ τῶν Χωρασμίων ἡγεμών; Matthew of Edessa 2.3, p. 87.
192 Matthew of Edessa 2.3, p. 88.
193 Matthew of Edessa 2.3, p. 88; se also Aristakes 16, p. 87.
194 Ibn al-Athīr, 6:172, trans. Richards, *Annals*, p. 93.
195 Skylitzes, p. 475.
196 Skylitzes, p. 454, ll. 27–29: καὶ ὁ βασιλεὺς τὸ ἀπ' ἐκείνου ἐκδεχόμενος πόλεμον ἀπὸ τοῦ σουλτάνου, καθ' ὅσον οἷόν τε ἦν, τὰ ὁμοροῦντα τῇ Περσῶν γῇ πέμψας κατησφαλίσατο.
197 Skylitzes, pp. 460–61.
198 Skylitzes, p. 462, ll. 47–49: ἔφθασαν γὰρ οἱ τῆς χώρας προασφαλίσασθαι ἑαυτούς τε καὶ τὰ αὐτοῖς ἀναγκαιότατα ἐν τῆς φρουρίοις· γέμει δὲ ἡ Ἰβηρία φρουρίων ἐρυμνοτάτων.
199 Skylitzes, p. 462.
200 Skylitzes, p. 450.
201 Aristakes 16, p. 80.
202 Skylitzes, pp. 472, 474–75.
203 Aristakes 16, p. 80, also relates the capture and execution of the nobleman Tʿatʿul, who was killed because of the death of a son of the Persian emir Arsuban.

2 Byzantine-Seljuk diplomacy and the first Turkish footholds

The Seljuk sultanate as a new factor in Byzantine-Muslim diplomacy, 1049–55

An exchange of embassies in 1049/50 inaugurated diplomatic relations between Byzantium and the Great Seljuk sultanate.[1] This step, although primarily aimed at a political settlement of issues resulting from the 1048 campaign, significantly affected the relationship between Constantinople and the Fatimid caliphate of Cairo, as had been reaffirmed by the treaty of 1046.[2] The objectives of the negotiations were the conclusion of a peace treaty and the release of prisoners, especially the Georgian prince Liparit, who had been captured in the battle of Kapetron.[3] From an ideological point of view, most noteworthy is the fact that Ṭughril Beg, already on the occasion of this first official encounter, underlined his leading position in Sunni Islam by choosing a *sharīf*, i.e., a member of the Prophet's family, who can perhaps be identified with a certain Nāghiya b. Ismāʿīl al-Ḥasanī, as ambassador to the Byzantine capital. Moreover, he laid claims to the mosque of Constantinople, which was to be repaired at his own expense and in which the Friday prayer was to be held in his and the Abbasid caliph's name.[4] This was tantamount to a direct affront to Fatimid rights on this mosque conceded first in 988 to Caliph al-ʿAzīz.[5] Although Skylitzes' report takes great pains to depict the imperial government as being in a position of strength in these negotiations, it is quite obvious that the military pressure of the Seljuk invaders on the eastern provinces made Constantine IX comply with the demands of the treaty partners, thus opting for a restriction of Fatimid influence in favor of a retightening of relations with the Abbasid caliphate of Baghdad and its new powerful protectors.

The fact that Emir Naṣr al-Dawla b. Marwān had recently recognized Seljuk suzerainty clearly indicated that Ṭughril Beg's presence in the region was more than a short-term harassment or a temporary disruption of the pre-existing balance of power.[6] Constantine IX made use of the new state of affairs, asking Naṣr al-Dawla to mediate negotiations with the Seljuk sultan. While George Drosos, a secretary (*hypogrammateus*) of Aaron and thus a man well acquainted with the situation in the Armenian borderland, represented the imperial government at Ṭughril Beg's court, the Marwānid dignitary Shaykh al-Islām Abū ʿAbdallāh b.

Marwān lent additional support to the emperor's cause.[7] The available accounts at first sight convey the impression that the main issue discussed in these contacts was the release of Liparit, but in view of the manifold results it seems that they envisaged more far-reaching ends, aiming at a comprehensive settlement of relations with the Seljuk sultanate with the mediation of the Muslim allies in the borderland. At about the same time, Ṭughril Beg was granted by Caliph al-Qā'im a number of honorifics extolling him as a lawful ruler and protector of Islam. This was a further step in the process of the Seljuk lord's gradual transformation from a Turkmen chief and conqueror to a legitimate holder of supreme power within the legal and ideological context of Muslim conceptions of public authority. It thus decisively contributed to the foundation of a clearly defined relationship between the Seljuk sultanate and the Abbasid dynasty.[8] Ṭughril Beg's intra-dynastic position was further consolidated by the submission of Ibrāhīm Yināl.[9] Accordingly, Ṭughril Beg's recognition as the supreme representative of Islam by the Byzantine emperor has to be interpreted as both an important complementary feature in the overall endeavor of the Seljuk sultan to become established as one of the leading authorities in the Muslim world and as another substantial gain in prestige, which enhanced his position vis-à-vis his Muslim, mainly Shiite, adversaries.

In the years after 1050, Ṭughril Beg once more turned his attention to the Kākūyid dominions in the western Uplands of Iran, ultimately seizing Iṣfahān in May/June 1051 after a siege of one year and transferring his residence from Rayy to this newly acquired city. In addition, he further forged bonds with the Abbasid caliphate through the exchange of embassies and lavish gifts.[10] A letter of Constantine IX addressed to Caliph al-Qā'im, which according to Bar Hebraeus, our only source, reached Baghdad in the Muslim year 443/15 May 1051–2 May 1052,[11] bears testimony to a remarkable revival of diplomatic contacts between Constantinople and the Abbasid court after decades of silence. After Bardas Skleros in late 986/early 987 had come to an agreement with the Buwayhid *amīr al-umarā'* in order to stage his coup against Basil II,[12] Baghdad became completely overshadowed by the Fatimid court of Cairo and henceforth was considered a place of secondary significance by Constantinople. The new Sunni prospects and the shifting of the center of gravity in the Muslim world from Egypt to western Iran in the wake of Ṭughril Beg's expansionist movement resulted in a re-opening of the old lines of communication with the court of Baghdad. Unfortunately, apart from quoting the letter's address and giving a short description of its splendid outward appearance, Bar Hebraeus fails to tell us anything about the political purposes of this contact. But it can be assumed that there must have been a causal relationship with the new situation in the Armenian and Upper Mesopotamian borderland and the constellations resulting from the growing influence of the young Seljuk sultanate. The proclamation of the prayer in Constantinople in the name of the Abbasid caliph meant that the latter was explicitly involved in the Byzantine-Seljuk negotiations and was considered an indispensable party to the agreements in his capacity as the uncontested legal and spiritual authority among Sunni Muslims.

A few years later, most probably in the months before Ṭughril Beg's triumphal entrance into Baghdad in Ramaḍān 447/December 1055, the sultan re-affirmed his claims to formal control over the mosque of Constantinople by sending an embassy to Empress Theodora.[13] Eastern Christian sources mainly emphasize the tribute the empress was forced to pay as a token of submission to the sultan's overwhelming power, thus implicitly criticizing the weakness of the supreme head of Orthodox Christianity.[14] From the viewpoint of the Fatimid caliphate, the issue at stake was the antagonism between Sunni and Shiite doctrine. The renowned Egyptian jurist and man of letters Abū ʿAbdallāh Muḥammad b. Salāma al-Quḍāʿī, who had served as a judge of the Sunni population in Egypt under Caliph al-Ḥākim and thereafter worked as a high-ranking official in the Fatimid chancery,[15] had been dispatched at about the same time as ambassador of Caliph al-Mustanṣir to Constantinople and was thus able to follow the negotiations between the Seljuk representative and the imperial government. When with the latter's permission the rival ambassador held the Friday prayer in the name of Caliph al-Qā'im bi-Amr Allāh, al-Quḍāʿī swiftly informed his lord of this event. The Fatimid caliph reacted by confiscating the property of the Church of the Holy Sepulcher in Jerusalem and by other repressive measures against the Greek patriarch and the Christians in Syria and Egypt.[16] In this way, Cairo basically suspended all previous concessions regarding the emperor's control over the said church and the patriarchal see of Jerusalem,[17] thus taking vengeance on its Christian subjects for their spiritual leader's breach of allegiance and rejecting the Abbasid and Seljuk claims.

In the context of the intra-Muslim conflict between the Shiite elite of Egypt and the upcoming Seljuk power representing the Sunni caliphate, both sides sought to make their influence felt in Constantinople through the pressure they were able to exert, the former by oppressing the Christians living under Fatimid rule and the latter by threatening with new invasions and demanding sums of tribute. The Muslim place of worship in Constantinople, which, perhaps along with Rome, was considered the most awe-inspiring center of Christianity and the Roman imperial tradition,[18] served as a reference point for ambitions to exercise a patronage reaching beyond the boundaries of *dār al-Islām*, i.e., the Muslim realm, in favor of co-religionists living under infidel rule. The Byzantine equivalent of this idea is the emperor's claim to authority over the patriarchal sees living under Muslim rule. The imperial government's decision to confer the formal suzerainty over the mosque to Cairo's rival power seriously disturbed the pre-existing equilibrium of mutual respect for the other side's authority over its co-religionists and institutions in one's own realm. Thus, Constantinople unavoidably became an intrinsic part of the struggle between Shiite and Sunni claims to the Muslim caliphate.

The factors leading the empress and her advisers to side with Ṭughril Beg by conceding him pre-eminence in Constantinople most probably have to be sought in the unprecedented military power the Seljuk commanders and their Turkmen soldiers were able to deploy in the eastern provinces. Although further developments were not yet foreseeable in 1055, only several months after the second large-scale Seljuk expedition, it was clear that this new enemy with his newly acquired strongholds in Transcaucasia, Azerbaijan, and western Iran and his alliances with local lords in Upper Mesopotamia was able to provoke serious harassment in the northern and central section of the eastern borderland.[19] In contrast, the Fatimid caliphate, while a dangerous rival for control over northern Syria and the emirate of Aleppo, was hardly able to mount attacks into the interior of Byzantine Asia Minor.

Another incident of Fatimid-Seljuk antagonism occurring in these years bears witness to the fact that, despite the concessions made to the Seljuk sultanate with respect to the mosque of Constantinople, the imperial government by no means abandoned its obligations towards Cairo and even intervened on behalf of the Fatimid caliphate when the existing order was jeopardized by seditious internal enemies. The conflict was triggered by al-Muʿizz b. Bādīs (1016–62), head of the Zīrid dynasty of al-Qayrawān in the province of Ifrīqiya, who from the late 1040s onwards felt secure enough to renounce his allegiance to Cairo, submitting instead to Abbasid suzerainty.[20] At some point before 443/13 May 1051–2 May 1052, al-Muʿizz sent an ambassador to Baghdad, declaring his readiness to proclaim the Friday prayer in the Abbasid caliph's name (*al-daʿwa al-ʿAbbāsīya*) and asking for a formal investiture.[21] Both the Abbasid caliph and Ṭughril Beg must have been highly pleased at the prospect of gaining an ally in the rear of the Fatimid state as strong as the Zīrid emir. In July 1051, Baghdad was afflicted by heavy riots between the Sunni and the Shiite quarters because of certain inscriptions that had stirred up Sunni sentiments. The caliph and his officials were unable to restore order in the city, and a number of tombs of Shiite imams and Buwayhid emirs were seriously damaged.[22] At the time following the conquest of Iṣfahān in May/June 1051, Ṭughril Beg decisively strengthened his bonds with the Abbasid caliphate by receiving robes of honor and titles, while a few months after these riots in January 1052 his ambassadors were received with huge amounts of gifts in Baghdad.[23] Hence the sultan came into conflict with various Shiite or pro-Fatimid factions in Iraq.[24]

The Buwayhid emir al-Malik al-Raḥīm and his Turkish military commander Arslān al-Basāsīrī in Baghdad still controlled substantial territories in the region. In December 1052 the two potentates seized Baṣra and received the allegiance of Daylamī soldiers from the Iranian province of Khūzistān.[25] Likewise, the lord of Ḥilla and central Iraq, Nūr al-Dawla Mazyad b. Dubays, who was Shiite along with the majority of his subjects, refused to perform the prayer in the caliph's name.[26] Ṭughril Beg, therefore, was eager to undermine the Shiite opposition by gaining allies from among their ranks. A case in point is al-Malik al-Raḥīm's brother Abū ʿAlī b. Abī Kālījār, who after the conquest of Baṣra took refuge with Ṭughril Beg. The latter received him honorably in Iṣfahān, married him to a relative of his, and gave him important domains as land grant (*iqṭāʿ*).[27] The emirs Abū Manṣūr and Hazārasb in al-Ahwāz, instead, had initially submitted to Ṭughril Beg, but then they arrived at a new agreement with the Buwayhid lord.[28] These examples clearly demonstrate how unstable the situation in 1051–52 was and how easily Ṭughril Beg's newly acquired predominance in Iraq could collapse.

In response to al-Muʿizz b. Bādīs' query, the Abbasid caliph readily sent a certain Abū Ghālib al-Shayzarī as emissary to al-Qayrawān, carrying with him a letter of appointment (*al-'ahd*), the black banner (*al-liwā' al-aswad*) of the Abbasid dynasty, and robes of honor. On his trip through Byzantine territory, Abū Ghālib was arrested at the emperor's behest and handed over to the emissaries of Caliph al-Mustanṣir. In Cairo a public act of humiliation was staged, in which the ambassador was paraded through the city sitting back-to-front on a camel and carrying the letter of appointment around his neck. In Bayna l-Qaṣrayn, the heart of the Fatimid palace city, the Abbasid symbols of authority destined for al-Muʿizz were put in a hole and burned.[29] By destroying these objects and by deriding the Abbasid representative, the Fatimid government expressed its defiance of Sunni claims to provinces under its sway and denounced the lawlessness of the Zīrid-Abbasid coalition.

Baghdad harshly reacted to the Fatimid affront by organizing a propagandistic campaign supported by all leading jurists and authorities of *fiqh*, who composed treatises condemning the Ismāʿīliyya doctrine.[30] At about the same time al-Muʿizz b. Bādīs dispatched a certain Abū l-Qāsim b. ʿAbd al-Raḥmān as ambassador to Baghdad and Constantinople in order to discuss the issue with both the Abbasid court and the imperial government.[31] The Zīrid ruler most probably tried to take advantage of this diplomatic episode and gain official recognition as an independent ruler by Constantinople, should the latter have been willing to enter negotiations with his representative. The sources fail to give us more details about the talks in Baghdad, but in all likelihood, emissaries of Sultan Ṭughril Beg were present in the caliphal palace and participated in these discussions, so that a certain Abū ʿAlī b. Kabīr was dispatched on behalf of the sultan and set off along with Abū l-Qāsim for Constantinople.[32] In his baggage, he had a very carefully couched letter full of allusions to the political ambitions and ideological claims of the Seljuk sultan, thus illustrating the discursive strategies that underpinned Ṭughril Beg's political program of Sunni leadership.

On this occasion, the Byzantine emperor was primarily interested in displaying his loyalty towards the Fatimid caliphate. Accordingly, he did not receive the emissary of al-Muʿizz b. Bādīs,[33] thus refusing to recognize the latter as an independent potentate and stressing his commitment to the treaty concluded with al-Mustanṣir in 1046. During the discussions with the Seljuk ambassador, Constantine IX stressed his friendship (*al-mawadda*) with the Fatimid caliph, stating that he would not consent to an action detrimental to his ally.[34] Despite its change of course in 1049/50 towards a revival of relations with the Abbasid caliphate, the imperial government still abided by the treaty with Cairo and avoided interfering with the internal affairs of the Fatimid caliphate and its relations with subordinate rulers. The mosque of Constantinople was a place of ideological significance within the empire's realm. No doubt, the emperor considered it his own business to decide which foreign power should have access to this place of worship. Supporting the aspirations of a powerful rebel, who sought collaboration with Cairo's most dangerous rival, would have been a flagrant breach of the existing treaty. On the other hand, with the agreements of 1049/50 a new state of affairs had come into being. Constantinople could by no means afford to ignore the claims of the Seljuk sultan and the Abbasid caliphate. Indicative of the emperor's appeasing attitude is his treatment of the Abbasid ambassador, who after his humiliation in Cairo was safely brought back to Constantinople, receiving the emperor's apologies for the mistreatment he had had to endure.[35] The imperial government seems to have been fully aware of the heavy insult, which the Abbasid caliph had to bear on account of the public denigration of his ambassador. Being interested in maintaining good relations with the Abbasid court and the Seljuk sultan, the emperor had to avoid giving the impression that he would have consented to the behavior of his Fatimid allies.

As regards the content of Ṭughril Beg's letter, it is worth having a closer look at the address formula and the summary that came down to us in order to see the allusions and propagandistic devices employed by the Seljuk chancery.

> From the pillar of religion and the aid of the Muslims, the splendor of the religion of God and the sultan of the lands of God, and the helper of the servants of God, Abū Ṭālib, the right hand of the caliph, the commander of the faithful, to the lord of the Romans (*min Rukn al-dīn wa-ghiyāth al-muslimīn, bahā' al-dīn Allāh wa-sulṭān bilād Allāh, wa-mughīth 'ibād Allāh, Abī Ṭālib, yamīn al-khalīfa amīr al-mu'minīn ilā 'aẓīm al-Rūm*). And its content after the *basmala* was as follows: Praise be to God, whose dominion is mighty and whose demonstration is brilliant, whose position is sublime and whose benevolence is generous. The letter continued in this way until it stated: Many years ago a man of deception (*nājim al-ḍalāla*) made his appearance in Egypt. He invites the people to follow him; he is deceived by those of his companionship whom he has deceived; in doctrinal matters, he believes what no one of the men of knowledge—be it at the time of the first imams or nowadays—considers lawful and what no reasonable man of the people of Islam and the infidels (*ahl al-islām wa-l-kufr*) considers correct. Thereafter the letter referred to the emissary Abū Ghālib, uttered criticism on this issue, and demanded that he should be sent under guard to al-Mu'izz b. Bādīs.[36]

As in the case of the mosque of Constantinople, this was a favorable opportunity for Ṭughril Beg to project himself as the defender and supreme political representative of Sunni Islam to the outside world. A list of six compound honorifics (*alqāb*) designates the Seljuk sultan as the holder of a central position in *dār al-Islām*, which consisted of three essential components, i.e., the orthodox Sunni faith (*dīn*), the territories under Muslim rule (*bilād Allāh*), and the faithful Muslim subjects (*al-muslimūn,'ibād Allāh*). At these levels, Ṭughril Beg appears as supporter and protector (*rukn, ghiyāth, mughīth*), as brightly shining example (*bahā'*), or as sovereign (*sulṭān*) respectively. After the sultan's *kunya* "Abū Ṭālib" signaling the end of the list of *laqab*s, there is a specific reference to the relationship between sultan and caliph. Ṭughril Beg is presented as the caliph's "right hand," i.e., the most powerful authority in Islam second only to the incumbent of the Abbasid throne. The title of sultan, which the Seljuk chief had been using since the first conquest of Nīshāpūr in 1038 on coins and elsewhere in the form *al-sulṭān al-mu'aẓẓam* (the highly exalted sultan),[37] is here embroidered with the specification "of the lands of God" and thus points to concepts of Muslim universal rule.

Historical accounts first mention the honorifics *Rukn al-Dīn* and *Ghiyāth al-Muslimīn,* in the context of Ṭughril Beg's solemn entrance in Baghdad in 1055 or in the course of the preceding diplomatic contacts with the Abbasid court. Hence, they illustrate the ideological elevation, which the Seljuk chief achieved in return for his shows of respect and obedience to the caliphate.[38] A case in point is the reception of the renowned chief *qāḍī* al-Māwardī, who in 1043/ early 1044 was sent as Caliph al-Qā'im's envoy to Ṭughril Beg in order to mediate a peace treaty with the Buwayhid rulers. In honor to the caliph, the sultan escorted the emissary four leagues and declared his readiness to be the caliph's loyal servant.[39]

The message conveyed by the aforementioned titles is also in line with a statement Bar Hebraeus put into the mouth of a Seljuk envoy at the caliph's court several months before the sultan's entry into Baghdad: Ṭughril Beg expressed his desire to be honored and blessed by serving the Prophet. He would perform the pilgrimage to Mecca, provide for the safety of the pilgrims' routes, and wage war against all rebels.[40] According to the itinerary presented by the sources, Ṭughril Beg announced his plan to perform the pilgrimage to Mecca in Hamadhān, where he had arrived in April 1055 after spending the winter of 1054/55 in Rayy. Subsequently, however, having proceeded further west to Ḥulwān, the sultan became involved in the internal affairs of Baghdad and entered negotiations with Caliph al-Qā'im and other factions. These endeavors culminated in his personal entrance in the city in December 1055.[41]

The letter to the Byzantine emperor, thus, clearly draws on aspects of the caliph-sultan relationship, as it was defined in the course of the negotiations between the court of Baghdad and the Seljuk leadership in the years before 1055. A diplomatic affair in which both the Fatimid court of Egypt and the imperial government of Constantinople were immediately involved offered the ideal setting for the promotion of these ideas. Consequently, Fatimid doctrines had to be presented as being in contradiction not only with the teachings of the first imams and contemporary theologians but also with the opinions of all reasonable men, both Muslims and infidels. Hence, the Byzantine emperor is summoned to distance himself from his allies in Cairo and to support the Abbasids as the representatives of the true Islamic faith.

From the Byzantine point of view, the Sunni-Shiite antagonism for predominance in Iraq and the Seljuk-Fatimid conflict for control over the Zīrid emirate in particular forced Constantinople to become entangled with intra-Muslim disputes and to reconsider its one-sided reliance upon peaceful relations with the caliphate of Cairo. This resulted in the appearance of a twofold allegiance, in which the Byzantine government, on the one hand, acknowledged the formal supremacy of the Abbasid caliphate and Sunni Islam by allowing the proclamation of the Friday prayer in its name according to older traditions, and, on the other hand, abided by commitments emanating from the treaties with Cairo, as regards the integrity of the Fatimid realm and its protection from rebels and hostile threats.

The further development of the diplomatic network between Constantinople, Cairo, and Baghdad was to a large extent determined by the political situation in Syria and the degree of Fatimid influence on Iraqi affairs. The temporary replacement of the Mirdāsid emir Thimāl b. Ṣāliḥ by direct Fatimid rule over Aleppo between January/February 1057 and September 1060, as well as the collaboration with the Turkish commander Arslān al-Basāsīrī during his activities between early 1056 and January 1060 in Iraq led to a significant strengthening of Fatimid influence in the entire region. Expectations of an imminent collapse of Seljuk predominance may have arisen.[42]

Heavy riots among the townspeople, Ṭughril Beg's Turkmen warriors, and the Buwayhid soldiery in December 1055 forced al-Basāsīrī along with a great part of the Baghdadi Turks to flee to al-Raḥba, from where he communicated with the Fatimid government, offering his allegiance. Thereupon al-Basāsīrī concluded an alliance with the Shiite Mazyadids and attacked Quraysh b. Badrān of Mosul, whom he defeated in a battle outside Sinjār on 9 January 1057. As a result of this victory, the Friday prayer in Mosul was proclaimed in the name of the Fatimid caliph, while al-Basāsīrī and his companions were invested with robes of honor sent by al-Mustanṣir.

At that time, Ṭughril Beg took action against this dangerous threat, leaving Baghdad for a large-scale campaign in the northern Jazīra between Takrīt, Ḥarrān, and the Marwānid territories around Jazīrat b. ʿUmar. Several local rulers and some of al-Basāsīrī's allies returned to Seljuk obedience and Ibrāhīm Yināl took control of Mosul. Yet in early 1058, the latter launched his rebellion, departing for the Uplands to gain Hamadhān. Therefore, al-Basāsīrī and Quraysh swiftly retook Mosul and in late December 1058 entered Baghdad, abducting the Abbasid caliph and his entourage and proclaiming the Friday prayer in the name of his Fatimid rival. Both the local Shiites and—because of their bad experiences with Turkmen soldiers—a large section of the Sunni populace sided with the new potentates while other Iraqi urban centers like Baṣra and Wāsiṭ also submitted to their authority. Being preoccupied with the rebellion of Ibrāhīm Yināl, Ṭughril Beg was unable to react immediately to this threat. It was only with the support of his nephews Alp Arslān, Yāqūtī, and Qāwurt Beg that he managed to eliminate his recalcitrant half-brother in July 1059, whereupon he invaded Iraq, took possession of Baghdad, and restored the caliph to his position, whereas al-Basāsīrī was killed in a battle near Kūfa in January 1060.[43]

This brief digression on the developments in Iraq should underline the significant gain of prestige the Fatimid caliphate achieved in these years until the supremacy of the Seljuk sultanate was ultimately re-established. It is also noteworthy that the sudden expansion of Fatimid suzerainty into the heartlands of the Abbasid caliphate materialized on the basis of diplomatic contacts with the Shiite elements of Iraq and without direct involvement in military affairs. The Fatimid caliphate served as a counterweight and legitimizing authority for the political ambitions of all those discontent with the perspective of an Abbasid

Sunni revival under the aegis of the Seljuk sultanate. Hence, the Fatimid decision makers' sudden mid-1050s alteration in behavior towards Byzantium and increased aggressive attitude in terms of military operations in Syria and pretentious demands put forward by means of diplomacy becomes understandable. Unfortunately, the available accounts are contradictory and quite deficient in historical and chronological details. Yet it is still possible to perceive the increasing amount of pressure the Fatimid government was able to exert at that time.

More specifically, the commander Makīn al-Dawla al-Ḥasan b. ʿAlī b. Mulhim was dispatched from Cairo to lead a campaign against the Byzantine port of Laodikeia, which he put under siege. A second expedition under the emir al-Saʿīd Layth al-Dawla resulted in the conquest of the city. A third contingent invaded Byzantine territory, pillaging, killing, and taking captives.[44] Besides Laodikeia, Ibn Mulhim is recorded to have attacked the city of Apameia/Afāmiya, the environs of Antioch, and the fortress of Qasṭūl/Qasṭūn, which surrendered in exchange for a guarantee of safety (*amān*).[45] The Byzantine military presence in the region was eventually enhanced by a naval force of 80 ships, arriving in Laodikeia and fending off the troops of Ibn Mulhim.[46] On the whole, we are dealing with a serious disturbance of the previously peaceful relations. The reasons for this clash have to be sought in a diplomatic dispute between the two sides, which erupted during the negotiations that took place during the hostilities. Hence, the military operations were not an end in itself, but they aimed at forcing the Byzantine government to make concessions in matters pertaining to the bilateral relations at that time.

A tricky issue is the exact dating of these events. An important *terminus ad quem* is provided by the years 446/12 April 1054-1 April 1055 and 447/2 April 1055-20 March 1056, in which Egypt was afflicted by famine and plague due to an irregularity in the inundation of the Nile.[47] All accounts agree that the estrangement between Cairo and Constantinople began on account of a considerable load of wheat—the sources mention 100,000 *qafīz* or 400,000 *irdabb*, respectively. In an exchange of embassies, it was agreed that the load would be sent to Cairo in support of the starving population, but, after the accession of a new emperor to the imperial throne, it was eventually withheld.[48] As for the actual incumbent of the throne, the details provided by our accounts are conflicting. According to one version, the "ruler of the Romans in Constantinople" (*mutamallik al-Rūm bi-Qusṭanṭīniyya*) died and was succeeded by a woman (*imra'a*), who asked Caliph al-Mustanṣir in a letter whether he would be willing to support her with his troops in case she were attacked by a rebel. When the caliph refused, she was angered and impeded the transport of the grain.[49] The change of government mentioned in this report can only refer to Empress Theodora's succession to Constantine IX in January 1055. This chronology is in accordance with the aforementioned presence of al-Quḍāʿī as Fatimid ambassador at the court of Theodora in 1055 and fits well with the date of the surrender of Qasṭūl on 8. Rabīʿ I 447/27 June 1055.[50]

The same report also mentions Mīkhā'īl, i.e., Michael VI (31 August 1056-31 August 1057), as successor of Theodora.[51] According to the second version, a certain Michael described as *ṣāḥib ḥarb* (man of war) *stratiotikos*, in the days of the vizier Abū Naṣr al-Falāḥī (1045–48)[52] had participated in an embassy to Cairo, where he was especially enticed by the attractions of the Fatimid court. After his accession to the throne, he wished to send a load of grain and gifts to the caliph, but the Romans suspected him of sympathy for Islam, killed him, and replaced him with a certain Ibn Saqlārūs.[53] There are fictitious elements drawing on recurring motifs in idealized narratives of Byzantine-Muslim relations, and the chronology is jumbled. Yet the violent overthrow of Michael VI and the takeover of the throne by Isaac Komnenos (1 September 1057-22 November 1059) are still recognizable. Although most chronological indications support a dating of the whole incident to the spring/early summer of 1055, it seems that the year 1057 fits better with the historical circumstances. The decline of Byzantine military power in the civil war preceding Isaac's rise to power in conjunction with the general increase of Fatimid influence in Iraq created very favorable conditions for military intervention in Syria. One version claims that the leading head of the whole enterprise was the Fatimid vizier and supreme *qāḍī* al-Yāzūrī, a Palestinian from al-Ramla, who owed his rise to power to the caliph's mother. He dominated the political scene in these years until he was executed in March 1058 under the pretext of treacherous contacts with the Seljuk sultan.[54]

The available reports point to Theodora's anger or Ibn Saqlārūs' maliciousness and cruelty as the reasons for the imperial government's change of mind, but if the identification with Isaac I is correct, the civil war of 1057 provides a good explanation as to why the load of grain never reached Egypt. During the conflict, various parts of the eastern provinces were heavily ravaged and the military units of Asia Minor suffered serious losses of manpower.[55] It was at the same time that Turkmen warrior groups, who had come to Armenia in the wake of Ṭughril Beg's 1054 campaign in the region, managed to stay for a longer period in the eastern territories without being expelled by local units.[56] The administrative and military structures in the region, no doubt, had suffered serious damage. In 1057, the overall situation may simply have been too chaotic to allow the transport of such a load.

As regards the diplomatic contacts, the Fatimid accounts provide a number of details regarding the arguments put forward by the two sides to support their viewpoints and political objectives. The issues in question concerned both ideological and practical aspects. The Fatimid government very much insisted on the delivery of the gifts,[57] which formed an indispensable part of the diplomatic protocol and were of major significance for the public visualization of the mutual relations between the two powers.[58] Matters of political importance were the release of Muslim prisoners detained in Byzantine territory and the restoration of former Muslim strongholds, which had come under imperial control.[59] Constantinople was willing to comply with the first demand but requested the release of Byzantine prisoners and the restoration of Byzantine fortresses in return for the other two issues.[60] The Greek prisoners, according to the Fatimid counter-arguments, were widely dispersed in various Muslim countries, where the caliph had no authority. Furthermore, the Muslim inhabitants had acquired gardens and real estates in former Byzantine towns and thus would have to receive compensations should the possessions have been restored to their original owners.[61]

The Fatimid government obviously felt itself in a position of strength, being able to dictate its conditions for an armistice. Practical problems of political authority and geographical distance within the Muslim orbit and the property rights of Muslim landowners were regarded as important enough to reject an agreement with the Byzantine side. Evidently, the Fatimid caliphate primarily aimed at a demonstration of superiority. This attitude can be explained as a reaction to preceding setbacks, as were the affairs of al-Muʿizz b. Bādīs and the mosque of Constantinople. It also manifested the new self-awareness that resulted from the alliance with al-Basāsīrī and other powerful Syrian and Iraqi potentates. Furthermore, Cairo sought to degrade the Byzantine court in matters of diplomatic etiquette, requiring that the gifts the caliph was to give in return for the imperial presents should have only half the value of the latter instead of the customary two thirds.[62] The symbolic language of Byzantine-Fatimid gift exchange is used to project the strengthening of the Fatimid position in the Muslim world in the years after 1055. The imperial government of Constantinople was forced to accept a sort of ceremonial devaluation in its relationship with the court of Cairo.

Internal developments in Constantinople and Asia Minor, 1055–57

While Ṭughril was still in his winter residence in Hamadhān, in January 1055 Empress Theodora succeeded her brother-in-law Constantine IX to the imperial throne, doing away with a number of opponents and promoting her partisans to the highest ranks. This 'regime change' also had its impact on the Byzantine policy regarding the eastern frontier. Certain allusions in the extant narratives suggest that there were discussions in Constantinople on how to cope with the Turkish threat. Aristakes refers to a speech of Theodora held before an assembly of dignitaries to the effect that the man who feels himself capable to set out for the east with an army to put an end to the Persian attacks and restore peace in those regions is worthy of becoming emperor.[63] According to Skylitzes, on removing Isaac Komnenos from the office of *stratopedarches*, i.e., high commander in the East, Theodora appointed a certain Theodore, a leading member of the faction supporting her accession, to the post of *domestikos ton scholon* of the East and sent him to stop the attacks of the Turks, for Constantine IX while still alive had transferred "Macedonian forces" to Asia Minor.[64] These details, though very fragmentary, certainly indicate that the political leadership in Constantinople in the months following Ṭughril Beg's 1054 campaign was fully aware of the precarious situation in the East and was taking pains to decisively handle the problem. Likewise, at the diplomatic level, the new government wished to maintain the relations established by Constantine IX, sending "generous gifts," i.e., the tribute requested by the sultan.[65] Apparently, it was hoped that buying time in this way would allow a further strengthening of the defensive structures.

Irrespective of what measures Empress Theodora actually took during her short reign, the results of her policy were undone by the subsequent developments in both the Byzantine capital and the eastern provinces. The discord, which in Easter 1057 broke out between Emperor Michael VI and some of the most influential army chiefs in the East, such as Isaac Komnenos, Katakalon Kekaumenos, Michael Bourtzes, and the brothers Constantine and John Doukas, not only led to a new civil strife but also precipitated the disintegration of the defensive system in the eastern provinces.[66] The clique in power that had imposed its rule over Constantinople after the end of the Macedonian dynasty gave rise to deep discontent among the leading generals, mercenary chiefs, and aristocratic families in the East by constantly rejecting these people's demands for promotion. Komnenos and Kekaumenos were denied the rank of *proedros*; Bryennios, upon being appointed high commander (*strategos autokrator*) of Cappadocia, did not obtain the restitution of his money, which Empress Theodora had confiscated; the Frankish mercenary leader Erbebios Frangopoulos (Hervé) was disgracefully chased away when he came to ask for the rank of *magistros*.[67] All these individuals were in one way or another involved in the conflicts with the Turks and closely connected with a number of other important military commanders in the East. Kekaumenos was transferred from the ducate of Ani to that of Antioch; Bryennios on being appointed in Cappadocia was immediately sent against the Turks along with the Macedonian *tagmata*; smarting from this humiliation Frangopoulos retired to his domains in an otherwise unknown place called *Dagarabe* in the Armeniakon region and made contact with the Turkmen chieftain Samouch.[68]

When Isaac Komnenos was proclaimed emperor on 8 June 1057 in his residence in Kastamona, a group of commanders residing in the theme of Anatolikon, such as Romanos Skleros, Nikephoros Botaneiates, and the sons of Basileios Argyros, joined the rebels.[69] While collecting forces for his march to Constantinople, Isaac, supported by the close circle of his relatives, servants, and clients, set up his headquarters in Nikopolis (Suşehri) in the Koloneia district, gathering the local troops and those of adjacent Chaldia as well as auxiliary units of Frankish and Varangian soldiers. Interestingly, Isaac managed to win over these units by presenting forged imperial documents to the effect that he was ordered to march with them against the Turks of Samouch.[70]

Thereupon, *archontes* and soldiers from the northeastern and central frontier section, namely Sebasteia, Melitene, Tephrike, and the rest of the Armeniakon further reinforced Isaac's army.[71] His rebellion attracted an ever-increasing number of people consisting of "close companions," "regular troops" (*tagmata*), and "foreign mercenaries." Their leadership was made up by "the commanders of the East" (οἱ ἑῷοι ἄρχοντες) and the "chiefs of the themes" (οἱ τοῦ θέματος κορυφαῖοι). All in all, this power appeared as "the entire Roman force of the East except for a few," the latter being mainly units from the themes of Anatolikon and Charsianon.[72]

With Isaac's march on the Byzantine capital, a significant portion of the military forces entrusted with the protection of the borderlands came in conflict with the central government. This certainly undermined the spirit of cohesion among the troops in Asia Minor. The rebel forces for some time abandoned the frontier, neglecting their tasks and turning their whole power against the internal rivals. Moreover, a considerable number of them perished on the battlefield near Nicaea with both sides suffering heavy losses.[73] No doubt, the events between June and September 1057 largely dismantled the Byzantine defense system in the East. At the same time, an estrangement occurred between the central government and the Anatolian peripheries, which neither Isaac I nor his successors with their weak hold on power were able to overcome. This situation unavoidably gave rise to a phenomenon that had already been perceivable as a result of the time of the civil strife under Basil II (976–989) and loomed large from the late 1050s onwards. Lacking of a strong central authority, Byzantine aristocrats and commanders of mercenary troops began to build up their own centers of power based on family bonds and coalitions with military forces irrespective of whether they were Byzantines, Franks, Turks, or belonged to other ethnic groups.[74] Even more than the blows caused by outside attacks, it was the emergence of these semi-independent local powers exerting military control and state-like functions that seriously undermined the authority of the central government, thus contributing to the breakdown of the empire's administrative system. From a structural point of view, the provinces of Anatolia began to lose their internal cohesion and came to resemble the political groupings in the adjacent Muslim lands of Syria, northern Iraq, and Azerbaijan with their complicated patchworks of rivaling petty rulers. The Turkish warrior groups, which started to spend increasingly longer periods on Anatolian soil, imported many of the practices they had adopted in the Muslim lands to the Byzantine territories. The interactions between local potentates and newly arrived invaders gave rise to a gradual transformation.

The Upper Euphrates Valley and Northeastern Cappadocia, 1055–59

According to John Skylitzes, it was in the wake of Ṭughril Beg's campaign of 1054 that the chieftain Samouch, a man "not of noble descent, but brave and energetic in warfare," came to Byzantine territory and stayed there along with a band of 3,000 men, wandering about the plains of Armenia, launching assaults, and pillaging the country.[75] This development inaugurated a new phase of Turkmen activities, which in the years 1055–59 gradually spread from the western Armenian highlands to the central section of the borderland along the Anti-Taurus Mountains, the Euphrates Valley, and the eastern parts of Cappadocia.[76] Unlike previous invasions, which were either small-scale raids in the margins of the borderland or large but temporary limited expeditions, these new raids had a much more permanent and pervasive character. For the first time, warrior groups were able to penetrate larger sections of the eastern provinces, thus causing an erosion of economic and administrative structures in certain regions and urban centers without conquering them. A decisive factor contributing to this development was the civil strife of 1057, which, because of its disintegrative effects on Byzantine military units and defensive structures in the borderlands, gave marauding warrior groups the opportunity to significantly extend their radius of action. Another feature, which began to gain significance as a vehicle of structural change, was the emergence of various forms of collaboration between Turkish invaders and local groups.

Michael Attaleiates' brief description of the state of affairs shortly after Constantine X Doukas' ascent to the imperial throne (1059) is indicative of how the Turkish incursions began to be conceived of as a major threat for the survival of Byzantine rule in Asia Minor.

> In the East everything was pillaged and destroyed by the assault and predominance of the Hephthalite Huns, i.e., the Turks, as well as the hasty withdrawal and fear of the neglected soldiers of the Roman army. The incursions were incessant, and the rich land of Iberia was completely devastated, for it had already been attacked, as we have said before. All the adjacent regions, Mesopotamia and Chaldia, Melitene and Koloneia, and the districts along the Euphrates River were likewise affected by this evil. Had the barbarian forces and one of their chiefs called Chorosalaris or a certain Zamouches not been fended off from time to time by troops or rather by rumors of forces and had they not been defeated in battle by some favorable coincidence, the enemy would have invaded Galatia, Honorias, and even Phrygia.[77]

Modern scholars frequently identify Samouch as an emir subject to Jaghrī Beg's son Yāqūtī, reading his name alternatively as Sabuk, Sunduk, or Saltuk.[78] In lack of further evidence, the identity of this person and his relationship with the Seljuk dynasty remain a matter of speculation. In any case, the available sources present him, just like the commanders of the Iraqi Turkmens in the early 1040s, as operating largely independently from any supreme authority, although there may have been relations with the Seljuk dynasty. Aristakes mentions a murderous attack on the city of Okomion, which can be dated to early January 1056 and resulted in a horrible massacre of the inhabitants.[79] Moreover, Skylitzes relates that the Frankish commander Hervé Frangopoulos, after having broken with the emperor, allied with Samouch, who seems to have had his base camp somewhere in the province of Vaspurakan.[80] They obviously wished to combine their forces in order to lend support to each other and to undertake joint operations. The Turkmen warlords' well-established practice of collaborating with local potentates so as to strengthen their position and to infiltrate the local structures appears here for the first time in the context of a Christian-Muslim coalition on Byzantine soil. The common ground for this agreement was the fact that both sides were in urgent need of backing against the provincial elites and military units loyal to the imperial government. If we believe Skylitzes, however, this alliance did not last for long: discord quickly developed between the two sides, resulting in a battle in which many Turks were killed while the survivors managed to escape to Khilāṭ on Marwānid territory.[81]

Interestingly, in view of the threats emanating from the simultaneous activities of unruly Frankish and Turkish warriors in Vaspurakan, Emir Abū Naṣr sought to create a counter-weight by resorting to his bonds of allegiance with both the Seljuk sultan and the Byzantine emperor. It was most probably due to his dependence upon Ṭughril Beg that he opted for siding with Samouch against the Franks of Hervé. When the Frankish warriors, on approaching Khilāṭ, decided against their leader's advice to take a rest in the town, Abū Naṣr attacked them, took Hervé captive, and informed the emperor of the rebel's imprisonment. The traditionally close relations of the Marwānid emirate with Constantinople prompted Abū Naṣr to hand the rebel over to the imperial government. "Supposedly," Skylitzes explained, "he was well-disposed towards him [i.e., the emperor] and destroyed those who were doing harm to his affairs and captured their chief."[82] Despite the chronicler's distrustful tone, it becomes evident that there was an ongoing tension between centralizing and centrifugal tendencies. In spite of some setbacks, however, Byzantine imperial authority still made its presence felt in the borderlands. At the same time, the Seljuk sultanate, especially after its tremendous gain of prestige in late 1055, increasingly emerged as a new regulating power in the region, raising hopes for a future stabilization.

Besides Frankish mercenaries, members of the remaining Armenian and Georgian aristocracy took advantage of the situation by forging military coalitions with Turkish warlords. Aristakes gives a detailed account of the Georgian potentate Iwanē, son of Liparit IV, duke of Trialeti, who in 1048 had been taken captive by the forces of Ibrāhīm Yināl. During the chaotic days of the civil war, this man, from his residence in Erēz in the district of Asthianene (Hašteank') north of the Arsanias River, undertook raids into the adjacent towns of Olnoutin/Ełnut (Gönük), Hawačič, and Theodosioupolis/Karin. Because of the fierce resistance of the local governor, who was supported by the Byzantine commander of Ani (Aaron?),[83] Iwanē's father Liparit sent emissaries "to Persia," i.e., to Turkmen warlords in Azerbaijan, proposing a joint incursion into Byzantine territory.[84] Aristakes does not further elucidate the background of these events, but the absence of most of the Byzantine troops during Isaac's march to Constantinople seems to have been a great opportunity to take rich booty. The author stresses the great number of warriors, stating that Iwanē was horrified by the enormous gathering, and explicitly refers to the "state of weakness of the land deprived of its defenders."[85] The territories afflicted by these raids were largely the same as those attacked in 1048: one group of invaders advanced as far as the forest of Kharton/Xrt'i in the district of Čanet' between Chaldia and the Akampsis River;[86] another one reached the province of Mananalis/Mananałi, from where another one proceeded to Olnoutin/Ełnut and the village of Blur west of Theodosioupolis. Since many inhabitants of the villages and monasteries east of the Euphrates and the district of Artze/Arcn had taken refuge to this place, this assault had especially disastrous consequences.[87] A second group headed to Khorzianene/Xorjean and thence in a southwesterly direction to Khanzit/Hanjēt' near the Euphrates Valley.[88] As a whole, these extensive military activities were the result of collaboration of Armenian-Georgian noblemen and Turkish warriors and were favored by the temporary withdrawal of Byzantine military units. It is important to note how unstable and fluctuating the lines of conflict were in this period. The ruling house of Trialeti, which previously had been one of the main supporters of the imperial army resisting the 1048 invasion, a decade later undertook raids on its own account and allied with Turkish invaders to further extend their activities.

These attacks seem to have prepared the ground for a campaign against Melitene, one of the key cities in the Upper Euphrates region, in October of the same year, 1057.[89] The invaders apparently belonged to the same group of warriors who had come at the call of Liparit to Byzantine territory, for Matthew of Edessa explicitly refers to Liparit's son Iwanē as "commander of the infidel forces," distinguishing him from the otherwise unknown Turkmen chief Dinar, "a great and mighty emir."[90] Aristakes tells us that the Turkish forces managed to proceed unnoticed as far as Kamākh (Kemah) on the Euphrates southwest of Erzincan, from where one part of the warriors headed to Koloneia and the other, probably a force of 3,000 men, to Melitene.[91]

Apart from the decay of Byzantine defensive structures due to the civil war, this expedition was further favored by the fact that the fortifications of the city had been dismantled in the tenth century.[92] Apparently, the local garrison was not able to sufficiently protect the townspeople against the raiders or to regain the booty and free the prisoners.[93] All sources agree that the attack resulted in horrible depredation and bloodshed lasting about 10 days and afflicting also places in the vicinity, such as the monastery of Bar Gaga'ī.[94]

It was a combination of harsh weather conditions and ambushes of local forces that eventually led to the annihilation of the Turkmen invaders. Masses of snow and archers controlling the main routes trapped them over the whole winter season in the mountains of Khanzit/Hanjētʿ. Upon retreating via Khorzianene/Xorjean and Olnoutin to the province of Taron, in the autumn of 1058 they were eliminated by the so-called Sanasunites, a group of Armenian warriors inhabiting the Sim Mountains in the Anti-Taurus, under the command of Tʿornik, the son of Mushegh.[95] Before this battle, the Turks managed to attack the renowned Armenian monastery of Saint Karapet (Prodromos) near Mush, a foundation going back to the fourth century, destroying the church and a number of other buildings.[96]

As a result of this campaign, the entire region between Melitene and Taron had turned into a war zone exposed to Turkish incursions, as is indicated by Attaleiates' statement quoted above. Apart from the devastation caused by warfare, the supply situation and living conditions of the urban and rural population further deteriorated because of an extremely harsh winter in 1058/59.[97] The noteworthy example of the Sanasunites Armenians illustrates that local groups at times were able to put up fierce resistance against the invaders irrespective of the military performance of the imperial troops, such as the garrison of Melitene. Another consequence of the overall disintegration of the Byzantine central government was that state-organized defense came to be replaced by initiatives of autonomous regional forces, which under certain circumstances proved more effective than the former.

With the Turkmen attacks having proceeded westward as far as Kamākh and perhaps Koloneia, it comes as no surprise that Sebasteia on the Halys River, an Armenian bishopric and since 1021/22 the residence of the royal family of Senekʿerim Artsruni of Vaspurakan, was the next target of a Turkmen raid in August 1059.[98] Along with the fortresses of Tephrike and Koloneia, this town formed one of the most important administrative and military centers in north-eastern Cappadocia and attracted large numbers of Armenian settlers in the course of the eleventh-century migrations. Militarily, Sebasteia stood in close contact with both the thematic troops of Koloneia and the *Armenika themata* centered in Tephrike, and all of them were actively involved in the civil war of 1057 as supporters of Isaac Komnenos.[99]

Matthew, the only source for the 1059 assault, mentions three commanders, Samuk, Amr-Kāfūr and Kijaziz, "who had come forth from the court of Sultan Tughrul."[100] Given that the first one can undoubtedly be identified with the chieftain Samouch, who after his conflict with Hervé was operating in Vaspurakan as an ally of the Marwānids in Khilāṭ, we may assume that this was an independent group of Turkmen warriors only loosely attached to the Seljuk army.[101] As in the case of Melitene and other places in the Armenian highlands, the invaders were mainly interested in taking booty and captives. The political and religious pre-eminence of Sebasteia and the wealth of the Armenian aristocracy undoubtedly made the city an especially enticing target as soon as the Turks were able to extend their activities to eastern Cappadocia. This is clearly reflected in the Armenian chronicler's gloomy picture of the eight-day pillaging, stressing the profanation of the city's sacred areas and the humiliation of the Armenian clergy and nobility. Sebasteia also offered the opportunity to take numerous high-ranking captives, although Senekʿerim's sons Atom and Abusahl managed with other noblemen to escape to Gabadonia (Develi) south of Kaisareia.

In summary, the period between 1055 and 1059 witnessed a decisive extension and diversification of Turkish raiding activities in the eastern provinces. From regions that had been penetrated in previous expeditions, such as the province of Vaspurakan around Lake Van and the Araxes Valley, groups of invaders advanced along the northernmost bends of the Euphrates and the Lykos Valley (Kelkit Nehri) to eastern Cappadocia or, further south, along the Arsanias Valley as far as Melitene. The collapse of the defensive structures due to the events of 1057 and the coalitions among local lords, mercenary groups, and Turkish warriors were the main factors favoring the unhindered expansion of these incursions. The collaboration with independent regional forces enabled the invaders to stay for longer periods in Byzantine territory, at times being reinforced by newly arrived warrior groups.

These attacks did not yet cause any substantial changes to the existing structures nor did they lead to conquests of towns or a permanent occupation of larger territorial units. Nevertheless, they must have caused considerable damage, a high degree of insecurity for the local population, and, unavoidably, a decay in agricultural production and trade. It is hard to say to what extent the overall demographic situation of the region was affected by these developments. Most probably, a certain percentage of the population moved to safer places and the westward movements of Armenian migrants may have further increased, but it is impossible to express these assumptions in concrete figures. Undoubtedly, the Turkish raiders continued to be attracted by the prospect of new gains, invading regions that had hitherto remained untouched by their attacks. Likewise, in the late 1050s, with its successive victories over Turkish rebels and Shiite opponents, the Seljuk sultanate further strengthened its supremacy in Iraq and the Muslim frontier regions. Hence, the influx of fresh groups of invaders went on undiminished. Irreversibly, an inexorable mechanism of political and military infiltration was set into motion.

Upper Mesopotamia and the Anti-Taurus Region, 1062–66

A few years later, in about 1062, the center of gravity of the Turkish raids shifted to the Anti-Taurus region, namely the marches situated between the Byzantine district of Taron, the ducate of Mesopotamia, and the Marwānid territories in the Diyār Bakr province.[102] With respect to the political setting, the situation there resembled the developments in the Armenian highlands insofar as the invaders became directly involved in various local rivalries. Alliances with the Marwānid lords of Āmid and defeats of Byzantine garrisons enabled Turkish warrior groups to gain a permanent foothold in the region and thus pave the way for further advances towards the Euphrates River and northern Syria.

Matthew of Edessa mentions three chieftains coming forth "from the court of the sultan Tughrul" called Slar-Khorasan, Chmchm and Isuly, i.e., the commander of Khurāsān (*sālār-i Khurāsān*), who most probably can be identified with the *'amīd Khurāsān* mentioned by Ibn al-Athīr as one of the commanders in Alp Arslān's Caucasian campaign of 1064,[103] and two otherwise unknown leaders whose original names may have been Cemcem and İsulu/Anasıoğlu.[104] The fact that these commanders do not appear earlier may suggest that they were new warriors coming from Azerbaijan to the Armenian highlands. Obviously, following the southern invasion route along the Arsanias Valley, they reached the area of the Byzantine administrative centers of Romanoupolis and Asmosaton/Shimshāṭ, where they attacked the strongholds of Pałin/Bagin, Erkne, and Tulkhum situated on the slopes of the Anti-Taurus Mountains not far from the Marwānid residence of Āmid.[105]

Most intriguingly, despite the assaults of the Iraqi Turkmens in the early 1040s and the incursions into Taron and the Euphrates region during the 1050s, Matthew describes the entire area as "unprepared" and "unfortified" but "prosperous and filled with men and animals."[106] It is not possible to say whether this alleged lack of military protection reflects consequences of the 1057 crisis or subsequent measures of dismantlement taken by the Byzantine central government under Constantine X Doukas, as is often assumed. We have no information about the situation of the military units in nearby Charpete/Kharput, one of the main strongholds in the ducate of Mesopotamia. Subsequent reactions, however, show that there was a concentration of forces in Edessa, which soon became involved in the hostilities around Āmid.[107] This seems to indicate that, perhaps as a result of the increasing pressure of Turkish raiders, Romanoupolis and other fortresses guarding the Arsanias Valley and the routes leading to Taron have been largely neglected in favor of an enhanced military presence in the Euphrates region. On the other hand, the reported persistence of economic prosperity in the Anti-Taurus Mountains implies that the destructions caused by the Iraqi Turkmens had been repaired. Moreover, the vicinity to the Marwānid principality with its agreements with both Sultan Ṭughril Beg and the Byzantine emperor seems to have resulted in regional stability, seemingly with favorable results for the local agriculture and trade.

Shortly before the outset of the aforementioned raids, in 1061, after an incredibly long reign of 52 years, Naṣr al-Dawla Aḥmad b. Marwān, the senior head of the dynasty, passed away.[108] In exchange for a high sum of tribute, Ṭughril Beg acknowledged the succession of the late emir's sons. But an intra-dynastic discord between the rulers of Āmid and Mayyāfāriqīn seems to have caused a political upheaval that favored Turkish incursions.[109] Upon the Turks' arrival, the ruler of Āmid, a certain Saʿd/Saʿīd, made an agreement with Sālār-i Khurāsān, providing that all captives were to be sold to people in Āmid. This may have been understood as a gesture of good will and mercy towards the Christians, thus at least ensuring that captives would not have been completely uprooted from their homeland and could more easily be ransomed. The Byzantines reacted resolutely by concentrating forces in the region of Tulkhum. One of their chief commanders was Hervé Frangopoulos, who obviously had managed to survive the turmoil of 1057 and 1059, regaining imperial favor after the Doukas clan's rise to the imperial throne. The bulk of the Byzantine forces came from the ducate of Edessa. Their commander, a certain Dabatenos, had assembled troops from his place of residence as well as Gargar (Gerger) and Ḥiṣn Manṣūr (Adıyaman).[110]

The death of Saʿd, who had been poisoned by his internal opponents, and probably the existing agreements between the Marwānids and the Turkish commanders served as a pretext for an attack on Āmid. After Saʿd's death, the *qāḍī* Abū ʿAlī b. al-Baghl exercised the regency for the deceased ruler's minor son and invited the Turkmen chief Hārūn b. Khān to come to protect the city against their opponent Naṣr b. Marwān of Mayyāfāriqīn.[111] The arrival of this new warrior group may have prompted the Byzantines to take up arms against the Marwānid allies. The inhabitants, however, successfully fended off their attack, playing off the two commanders against each other by means of bribery. While Hervé entered a secret agreement with the townspeople, Dabatenos died in battle. Thereafter Hervé reportedly pursued and defeated the Turkmen warriors near Theodosioupolis, but his feats of war did not save him from being executed on the emperor's order after his return to Constantinople.[112] At about the same time, a certain Hehnuk, most likely a local Armenian chief, mounted another assault on Marwānid territories, but he was fended off in a battle fought near al-Suwaydāʾ (Siverek).[113] These hostilities point to a serious estrangement between the Byzantines and the Marwānid principality in the period following the old emir's death in 1061, something that enabled Sālār-i Khurāsān, Hārūn b. Khān, and other Turkish chiefs to gain a firm foothold in the Diyār Bakr province in the years 1062–63.

The presence of Turkmen warriors in Āmid turned out to have long-term effects. On reaching an agreement with Sa'd's widow, Naṣr b. Marwān arrested the *qāḍī* and took possession of the city, and thus Ibn Khān and his companions were forced to flee. An account transmitted by Sibṭ b. al-Jawzī claims that the Banū Tamīm Arabs captured the Turkish chief and thereafter executed him in Mārdīn. But it is preferable to give credence to another version corroborated by a number of sources, according to which in about 1064 Ibn Khān al-Turkumānī and his 500 warriors were invited by Emir 'Aṭiyya of Aleppo and thus became involved in the dynastic quarrels of the Mirdāsid emirate.[114] In this way, Turkmen troops began to infiltrate the political structures of northern Syria and the southwestern section of the Byzantine borderland.

Simultaneously, in 1065–66 Turkmen activities expanded from the district of Tulkhum into the ducate of Edessa.[115] This development clearly illustrates the negative results caused by the collapse of the Byzantine network of Muslim vassals in the borderland. As soon as the alliance with the Marwānid emirate broke down and internal unrest occurred, the Diyār Bakr province became vulnerable to Turkmen penetration, while the ducate's troops proved too weak to put a halt to Turkish forays and raids. Again, the political setting was further complicated by activities of unruly local lords, as is attested by the attack of Hehnuk. The Turkish invaders seem to have gained a foothold in the region of Tulkhum, from where they gained access to the routes leading across the Anti-Taurus Mountains to the Arsanias Valley and to those leading in a southwesterly direction to the Euphrates. The Turkish warlords chose the Muslim provincial capitals of Āmid and Aleppo as focal points of their infiltration strategy, thus gaining permanent footholds and, in the time span between 1065 and Romanos IV's first eastern campaign in the summer of 1068, gradually increasing their pressure on the Byzantine centers of Edessa and Antioch.

Sultan Alp Arslān's Caucasus campaign of 1064

The developments in the borderlands' northeastern section in 1064 brought about a revival of the Seljuk policy of conducting large-scale campaigns into Armenia and the Caucasus region. On Ṭughril Beg's death on 5 September 1063 in Rayy, Alp Arslān succeeded his uncle to the sultanate, being immediately confronted with various centrifugal forces threatening the very existence of the newly established empire, among them the rebellion of Qutlumush, one of his most powerful intra-dynastic opponents. This troublesome period came to an end in April 1064 with the proclamation by Caliph al-Qā'im of the Friday prayer in Baghdad in the new sultan's name.[116] Nevertheless, Alp Arslān was in urgent need of a clear political success stemming from a victorious strike against an external enemy in order to strengthen his image as an energetic ruler and to foster the spirit of cohesion among the dynasty members, his subordinate commanders, and warriors. It was most probably thoughts of this sort that induced the sultan to resume his uncle's aggressive attacks against the Christians.

In his recent studies on the Caucasian campaigns, Andrew Peacock shifts the emphasis to Alp Arslān's Turkish-nomadic background and his need to prove himself a capable chief for his Turkmen followers in view of his conflict with Qutlumush. Accordingly, the main purpose of his expedition must have been the acquisition of suitable pastureland in the southern Caucasus.[117] It should not be ignored, however, that dynastic and imperial concerns reaching beyond the mindset of nomadic warriors had already been important during the reign of Ṭughril Beg and became a central issue under his successors. The Muslim sources' focus on *jihad*, therefore, should not be seen as superficial rhetorical flourish but as an essential expression of hegemonic self-awareness. The main objectives of the new campaign seem to have been to advance the Seljuk sultanate's claims to supreme leadership articulated through a fervent commitment to the Muslim idea of Holy War, at an ideological level, and to seize a key point situated on the routes between Azerbaijan and the Byzantine territories, at a military level. The acquisition of pasturelands certainly was a welcome side effect.[118]

The documentation in the narrative sources is especially rich, including detailed accounts transmitted by Ibn al-Athīr and the Seljuk court historiography and reports reflecting Byzantine, Armenian, and Georgian viewpoints about the conquest of the royal city of Ani.[119] Armenian and Georgian accounts primarily focus on the calamities the indigenous population had to endure and the agreements between local rulers and the sultan. The Byzantine historian Michael Attaleiates blames the fall of Ani on Emperor Constantine X's greed and the blatant incompetence of the local governors. The Muslim narratives, instead, portray the whole expedition in a highly idealized way as an ambitious endeavor of Holy War crowned by a brilliant victory of Islam. This tendency has already been perceivable in the reports on Ṭughril Beg's campaigns and will finally culminate in the exalted presentation of Alp Arslān as victorious Muslim model-ruler in the battle of Manzikert in 1071.

As regards the itinerary of this campaign, it is noteworthy that it represented the northernmost advance of Seljuk troops in Christian territories, sharply deviating from the routes along the Araxes and Arsanias Valleys, which earlier invasions had followed. Ani was the only major stronghold on Byzantine soil to be affected by this expedition. In this respect, the campaign was more an attempt to subjugate the Christian population of the Caucasus region than a strike against the Byzantine Empire. Another innovative feature lies in the fact that Alp Arslān not only led his troops in person but was also accompanied by his heir apparent Malikshāh and his vizier Niẓām al-Mulk. The presence of some of the sultanate's most outstanding associates further underlined the expedition's significance as a dynastic project, resembling the early ninth-century campaigns of the Abbasid caliphs on Byzantine territory. It may well be that, perhaps on the advice of his historically well-informed vizier, Alp Arslān consciously aimed to encourage associations of this kind.[120]

For its greatest part, the course of events presents no problems of interpretation. On 22 February 1064, the sultan set off from Rayy for Azerbaijan. In the city of Marand northwest of Tabriz he met the Turkmen emir Ṭughtikīn,[121] a man well acquainted with the *jihad* in these regions, who guided him over mountain paths to Nakhchawān north of the Araxes. During this first stage, the sultan obviously sought to strengthen or to re-establish Seljuk authority over the Muslim potentates in Azerbaijan. The inhabitants of Khoy and Salmās north of Lake Urmia were forced into obedience.[122] In Nakhchawān, which served as a gathering point for troops joining the expedition, the army was divided in two parts, one placed under the command of Alp Arslān and the other under that of Malikshāh and Niẓām al-Mulk. The latter followed the Araxes River in a northwesterly direction as far as Surmari (Qalʿat Surmārā) and thence alongside the river Akhurean to the monastery of Marmashen (Marīm Nishīn) near Ani.[123] Thereupon the two parts reunited, continuing their march northwards as far as the city of Akhalkʿalak on the Kyros River (Kura Nehri). Having seized this city in June/July 1064, the army turned back in a southerly direction towards Kars and Ani.[124] During these weeks it seems that diplomatic contacts with the Bagratid king Gurgēn II of Lori (1046/8–1081/9) took place, while Ani was seized and plundered in August.[125]

As do the reports on the 1048 and 1054 campaigns, these narratives especially elaborate upon the confrontation between faithful Muslims and infidel Christians/Romans. Al-Ḥusaynī and Ibn al-Athīr strongly emphasize the unrestrained use of violence in the Muslim attacks, the huge amounts of booty, and the complete subjugation of the Christian population. Instead of dismantled and largely unprotected places, the targets of this campaign were mostly well-fortified strongholds situated near riverbanks and steep rocks, so that the attacks unavoidably involved much bloodshed and heavy losses on both sides.[126] After the conquest of Surmari, Malikshāh at first wished to destroy the town, but then Niẓām al-Mulk convinced him to use it as a frontier fortress (*thaghr*) manned by a garrison under the command of the emir of Nakhchawān.[127] In Marmashen many churches were destroyed and inhabitants were killed, the only possibility to escape death being conversion to Islam.[128] Likewise, the population in certain districts around Ani and Kars accepted Islam, destroyed their churches, and erected mosques.[129] In this framework, the narratives make frequent use of specific notions connected to *jihad*: Muslims die as martyrs[130] and attack the infidels, shouting "God is great."[131] In the midst of heavy fighting, the sultan did not interrupt his prayer until he finished.[132] The sudden collapse of a large section of the walls of Ani is viewed as something that happened through God's grace.[133] When the campaign was over, a letter of conquest (*kitāb al-fatḥ*) was sent to Baghdad and read aloud in the palace of the caliph, who issued a reply praising Alp Arslān.[134] It becomes clear thus that the sultan himself was anxious to cultivate his image as a glorious champion of the Holy War in the Muslim world. In all likelihood, these messages of conquest and victory formed the core of the surviving Muslim narratives on the 1064 campaign.

In the eyes of Matthew of Edessa, Alp Arslān's expedition marked the beginning of the Armenian nation's slavery with a homeland destroyed and filled with blood and without hope of deliverance.[135] Besides the tragic events in Ani and the rest of the country, the chronicler's pessimistic outlook was mainly the result of the surrender of the kings Gurgēn II of Lori and Gagik-Abas of Kars, who both recognized the sultan's suzerainty over their respective kingdoms; the former by giving his daughter in marriage to the sultan; the latter by demonstrating his grief about Ṭughril Beg's death and inviting the sultan to a banquet of friendship.[136]

The *doux* of Ani mentioned by both Attaleiates and Matthew has been identified with the Armenian nobleman Bagrat Vxkacʿi, who also appears as commander of Vaspurakan and *katepano* of the East bearing the title of *magistros*. Attaleiates harshly criticizes both him and Emperor Constantine X. In particular, he accused the emperor of having conferred the ducate to the former in exchange for waiving the customary payments connected with this office and blamed Bagrat for having failed to take the necessary military and administrative measures for the town's defense.[137] Moreover, he reportedly provoked the sultan's assault by attacking and pillaging the rearguard and some isolated detachments of the Seljuk army. It is certainly correct that the sultan, while proceeding east of the border, hardly caused any damage to Byzantine fortresses, but the assumption that the siege of Ani was not planned beforehand is rather questionable. The subjugation of a number of Christian and Muslim lordships situated along the Araxes and Kyros Rivers points to a clearly defined strategy of undermining the Byzantine network of alliances in the Caucasus region and thus making the frontier zone permeable to future invasions. Attaleiates' statement, according to which Ani "was for us an extremely important stronghold and an obstacle for the barbarians who wished to invade from there into the Iberian land" illustrates the immense strategic significance of this place, as is perceived by people acquainted with the contemporary state of affairs in the Byzantine marches.[138] In all likelihood, the Seljuk invaders were fully aware of these considerations. Accordingly, in Ibn al-Athīr's report Ani is characterized as "a well-fortified city, very defensible, offering no chance of an assault [...] a large, flourishing and populous city with more than 500 churches."[139] Accusing the local commanders of wrong military decisions is a motif that also appears in Skylitzes' account on campaigns of the 1040s, but in this case it seems more likely that Bagrat, instead of provoking a major attack, sought to weaken the enemy forces before they laid siege to the city. All in all, one gains the impression that Attaleiates' critique mainly reflects tensions among competing factions of the military aristocracy rather than an objective assessment of the situation in 1064.

Taken together, the Caucasus campaign certainly was a great success for the Seljuk military elite. Apart from fostering the internal cohesion and bonds of loyalty among the emirs and their troops, the sultan decisively strengthened his presence among the Christian and Muslim potentates in the Caucasus region and Azerbaijan and gave a demonstration of his military power by seizing one of the most impregnable frontier strongholds. This did not inaugurate a series of territorial gains on Byzantine soil, nor was there an intensification of Seljuk raids in the Armenian highlands. Summer and winter pastures may have had some importance for Turkmen nomad groups, but the greatest advantage was that the entire hinterland of the Byzantine borderland between the ducate of Iberia and

Vaspurakan ceased to be under the empire's sphere of influence. Former vassals of Constantinople henceforth oriented themselves towards the Seljuk sultanate. This policy was to be further pursued in a southwesterly direction by Alp Arslān's Syrian campaign of 1070.

The ducate of Edessa, 1065–67

The city of Edessa and a group of fortified places north and south of the Euphrates, such as Chasanara/al-Suwaydā', Gargar, Samosata/Sumaysāṭ, and Ḥiṣn Manṣūr, formed an advanced outpost of the Byzantine defensive system stretching from the banks of the river deep into the Diyār Muḍar province and covering the whole area from the northwestern part of the Anti-Taurus Mountains as far as the district of Telouch/Dulūk and the Pyramos/Jayḥān Valley around Germanikeia/Mar'ah.[140] We have already discussed the significance of this area for the protection of the borderland further east opposite the Marwānid territories around Āmid and the Tigris River. On the other hand, from the viewpoint of the Turkish invaders it was only natural to extend their activities into the region of the Byzantine ducate.

The detailed account of Matthew of Edessa gives the impression of rather strong local forces. At times, troops were removed from this province in order to be employed elsewhere. The Armenian forces of Basil, the son of Abukap, and the former tent guard of David of Taykh, who at that time was residing in Edessa, were transferred to the Balkan frontier to be used against Turkic nomadic tribes and never came back.[141] The region, however, was by no means deprived of its manpower. Matthew speaks of 4,000 infantry and cavalrymen in Edessa itself, forces, that consisted of Greek, Armenian, and Frankish units.[142] The local troops, however, were widely dispersed over various places. Two hundred Frankish horsemen were stationed in Chasanara/al-Suwaydā', which is described as a "heavily populated" region.[143] Considerable garrisons seem to have been based in Gargar and Hiṣn Manṣūr.[144] The surroundings of Edessa were protected by a number of minor strongholds that formed a screen of forts covering the approaches to the main city. In particular, Matthew mentions the fortresses of T'orich, Nshenek, Dzulman, Gullāb, Tēp, K'sōs/Aksās, T'lak, and Kupin, which must have been located in a half circle between Chasanara and Ḥarrān from the northeast to the southeast of Edessa.[145] On the basis of their geographic distribution, it is obvious that these castles mainly served defensive purposes against the Muslim regions in the ducate's vicinity. From an organizational point of view, there was a close collaboration with the units of Antioch, as is illustrated by the presence of the *doux* of Antioch in Edessa.[146] Matthew, however, ascribes the failure of a Byzantine attack on a group of Turkish invaders to a sharp rivalry between the two Byzantine commanders.[147] Personal discords would be another factor seriously undermining the effectiveness of the Byzantine defensive system. Yet it is quite probable that the historian elaborates upon the motif of Byzantine treachery, for the *doux* of Antioch Pext was a "brave Armenian soldier," who on discovering his rival's deceitful behavior is said to have complained about the "usual treacherous acts of the apostate Romans." The *doux* of Edessa, a certain Pegonites, supposedly ordered his *proximus* to kill Pext, and thus the latter warned the enemies with the sound of trumpets during a night attack on the Turks outside Nshenek.[148] Hence, the episode may also be read as an edifying story explaining the antagonism between virtuous Armenians and wily Byzantines. According to the same source, on the orders of Emperor Constantine X, Pegonites was replaced by a certain Aruandanos, who is also described as having strong troops under his command.[149] Despite the heavy attacks of the years 1065–1066, the local military power seems to have been kept at a high level.

The commanders of the Turkish incursions were, once again, men belonging to the Seljuk military elite. Apart from the aforementioned Sālār-i Khurāsān, who had been active in the Diyār Bakr province, we come across the "Persian emir" Afshīn, an especially energetic chief, who in the following years was to play a crucial role in the operations in Asia Minor, and "a very illustrious and mighty emir" called Gümüshtekīn, who held the office of *ḥājib* (chamberlain).[150] They were closely connected to Sultan Alp Arslān but were largely operating on their own. This can be concluded from the fact that, from the time of his departure to Iṣfahān in August 1064 until his second Caucasian campaign in early 1068, the sultan was constantly on the move in the eastern parts of his empire. He traveled to Marw via Kirmān and to the residence and last resting place of his ancestor Seljuk in Jand of Transoxania, whence he returned to Kirmān and to the province of Fārs suppressing various insurrections of Seljuk commanders. In 1065 in Rāykān north of Nīshāpūr he officially nominated his son Malikshāh as successor to the sultanate and assigned the Iranian provinces to his brothers, sons, and relatives.[151] It is highly unlikely that Alp Arslān in the course of these activities in the East would have been personally engaged in the affairs of the Euphrates region.

As regards the chronological details, Matthew *sub anno* 514/1065–66 mentions three attacks under the command of Sālār-i Khurāsān against various fortresses and the surrounding districts of Edessa.[152] In the following year, 515/1066–67, the commander Gümüshtekīn, following the same route, unsuccessfully besieged Niṣībīn al-Rūm/Sibar[153] and thence crossed the Euphrates, invading the district of Ḥiṣn Manṣūr.[154] The incursions concentrated on ravaging rural areas and taking booty and captives. The invaders entered some fortified places, such as Nshenek, Gullāb, Tēp, Kupin, and T'lēt'ut', and slaughtered the local population but made no attempts to entrench themselves therein. The Turkish camp at Nshenek, for instance, is explicitly described as being outside the fortress. Attacks on stronger fortifications like those of Niṣībīn al-Rūm failed whereas a siege of Edessa was apparently outside the scope of these raids. The invaders usually followed the route via Tulkhum and Chasanara/al-Suwaydā', from where they spread out in various directions. A major battle between Gümüshtekīn and the *doux* of Edessa reportedly took place near a fortress called Ōshēn. The Byzantines suffered heavy losses and were forced to retreat. The Byzantine *doux* and his officers were captured and ransomed outside the walls of Edessa.[155]

All these activities were fully in line with the behavioral patterns known from previous raids and other regions. There was no far-reaching strategy of permanently occupying towns or taking advantage of high-ranking captives beyond extorting huge amounts of money. The relatively strong defensive structures in the region prevented the Turks from further intruding into the network of the local military elite. Hence, they continued their way in a southwesterly direction across the Euphrates, penetrating the territories of Aleppo and Antioch. As a result, in the winter of 1066/67 Afshīn eventually advanced as far as the Black Mountains (Amanos Dağları) north of Antioch, destroying many monasteries and villages.[156] Henceforth, the ducate of Antioch was within the reach of Turkish raiding activities, and it was only a matter of time before they would become a serious threat for one of the most sensitive zones of the Byzantine administrative and military structures in the East.

Northern Syria and Aleppo

In the early 1060s, the ducate of Antioch lost its dominant position in the Syrian borderland west of the Euphrates while the Mirdāsid emirate of Aleppo continued to vacillate between Byzantine and Fatimid spheres of influence.[157] The local Arab aristocracy, bolstered by Fatimid and subsequently Turkmen support, gradually freed itself from Byzantine influence and became strong enough to impose its will on the local Byzantine commanders. In May/June 1062, Emir Thimāl mounted a successful attack on the frontier stronghold of Artāḥ, thereupon being able to dictate his conditions for a peace agreement. He demanded the demolition of recently restored castles, the cession of certain territories, and payments to the emirate. A Byzantine counter-attack in October of the same year was repelled.[158] Nor was Byzantium able to intervene in the intra-dynastic strife that broke out in the emirate after Thimāl's death on 30 November 1062. A decisive factor, instead, proved to be the Turkmen chief Hārūn b. Khān, who appeared on the scene in late 1064 after two years of almost incessant hostilities between the late emir's brother ʿAṭiyya and his nephew Maḥmūd, who was not willing to recognize his uncle's rise to power. While Maḥmūd and his allies put Aleppo under siege, ʿAṭiyya established contact with the Turkish warlord, who at that time tried to gain a foothold in Marwānid territory, being in rebellion against Sultan Alp Arslān.[159] Ibn al-ʿAdīm describes his arrival and the Arabs' reactions as follows:

> The Romans bestowed upon Asad al-Dawla ʿAṭiyya robes and gold coins in order to honor him, for he had concluded a peace treaty with them. When Ibn Khān came to ʿAṭiyya with 1.000 archers, he received them honorably and treated them well. When Ibn Khān arrived at the gate of Aleppo—this was the first time the Turks entered Syria—the Banū Kilāb gathered around Maḥmūd b. Naṣr b. Ṣāliḥ and they set off for Aleppo. But Maḥmūd saw that they were not strong enough to fight against the Turks, and thus he fled.[160]

As had been the case in the Diyār Bakr region a few years earlier, the first Turkmen warriors in Syria came as mercenary forces at the invitation of one of the local rival factions. This was to be a characteristic feature of the expansion of Turkmen groups in the entire region until Atsiz b. Uwaq's conquests in the early 1070s. ʿAṭiyya had the advantage of having free access to the revenues of Aleppo and, after restoring peaceful relations with the Byzantine neighbors, he obtained additional income from imperial pensions, as Ibn al-ʿAdīm explicitly states. These were most probably connected with high-ranking court titles, as had been granted to his predecessors, and served as a means of reasserting the lost Byzantine influence in the emirate. With this money, ʿAṭiyya was able to offer generous payments to his Turkish allies in addition to the prospect of rich booty. The fact that the Banū Kilāb withdrew without becoming engaged in a battle suggests that the Arab nomad fighters regarded the Turkmens as militarily superior. This goes a long way towards explaining the decisive role they henceforth played in many of the internal conflicts of the Syrian ruling elite. Nevertheless, the outstanding fighting skills of these mercenaries also entailed the risk of quickly losing control over them. Many instances show that the slightest cause of discontent was enough for them to break off their alliances, switch sides, and turn against their former employers. It is also noteworthy that Ibn Khān's companions, like most other Turkish warrior groups, were not homogeneous Turkmen troops (*al-Turk*) but also included Daylamīs and Kurds (*al-Kurd*), who most probably had joined them on their way through western Iran and Upper Mesopotamia. Moreover, there was a group referred to as *al-ūj* (frontier people), a term that in all likelihood means nomad warriors living in the border zones.[161] This implies that Ibn Khān's troops included all kinds of local elements in their ranks.

Additional information on the situation in Syria can be drawn from Michael Attaleiates, who refers to "one of their noblemen called Amertikes."[162] The fact that the Byzantine narrative, too, refers to his taking refuge with the lord of Aleppo led many scholars to identify the person in question with Hārūn b. Khān in spite of the different name.[163] Several years before his arrival in Syria, this version goes, he had come to the imperial court of Constantinople, entering the service of Emperor Michael VI. Terms like "agreements" (ὁμολογίαι) and "great honors" (μεγάλαι δεξιώσεις) point to a formal recognition of the emperor's authority in exchange for the bestowal of imperial titles upon him. In this way, Amertikes, following the example of numerous Muslim potentates in the borderland, was the first Turkmen commander to establish this kind of vassal relationship with the imperial government. The alliance, however, did not last long, for Constantine X Doukas reportedly accused him of planning an attempt against his life and therefore sent him into exile. The rest of Attaleiates' report is somewhat confused and contradictory, for in spite of this alleged breach of allegiance the author asserts that the emperor sent him against the invading Turks, refusing, however, to pay him and his soldiers their salaries, which, in turn, caused Amertikes to defect to Aleppo. Although Ibn Khān's appearance in the Diyār Bakr province actually coincides chronologically with the beginning of the Turkmen raids in Syria, it is still questionable whether the two Turkish chiefs were one and the same person. It may well be that they were two different individuals, one of whom defected to Aleppo because of outstanding payments on the part of the emperor and the other going there as a result of ʿAṭiyya's invitation. Being in general highly critical of the measures taken by the imperial government against the Turkish raids, Attaleiates obviously intends to blame Constantine X Doukas for Amertikes' defection, but the whole story is not very sound, and the Byzantine historian seems to conflate contradictory pieces of information.

From 1064 onwards Ibn Khān and his soldiers became involved in the warfare against the Byzantines of Antioch and gradually inserted themselves into the ruling elite of the Mirdāsid emirate. When ʿAṭiyya and Maḥmūd in December 1064/January 1065 achieved a temporary reconciliation on the basis of an agreement of shared rule, the emir of Aleppo along with the Turks and the town militia (*al-aḥdāth*) undertook a raid on Byzantine territory,[164] probably to recompense the warriors with booty from foreign territories. Thereafter, for unclear reasons that may have been related to the Turks' growing influence, the militia of Aleppo one night in January/February 1065 mounted an assault, killing a number of Ibn Khān's followers and robbing them of their horses and weapons.[165] Trying to escape to the East, they were attacked by the Banū Numayr Arabs and, subsequently, fell upon a large detachment of Byzantine forces, probably the troops of Antioch, which in 1065 were operating in the region of Edessa. Ibn Khān managed to slip away unharmed, taking refuge with Maḥmūd, who at that time had pitched camp at Sarmīn, southwest of Aleppo.[166] A guarantee of safety issued by Maḥmūd formed the basis of a new alliance with the Turkish chieftain, who this time threw in his lot with the opposite faction in the Mirdāsid civil strife. The emir, in turn, was given the opportunity to launch a new initiative against his uncle, sending Ibn Khān to Maʿarrāt al-Nuʿmān. At the same time, he restored peaceful relations with the Byzantines, sending his son as a hostage to Antioch.

After a new series of hostilities—a battle near Marj Dābiq (20 May 1065) and a heavy siege of Aleppo leading to famine—ʿAṭiyya eventually surrendered, and on 20 August 1065 Maḥmūd took possession of the city. According to the peace treaty agreed upon on this occasion, Maḥmūd was recognized as emir while ʿAṭiyya took the cities of al-Raḥba, A'zāz, Manbij, and Bālis, as well as several domains north and east of Aleppo.[167] Maḥmūd also took measures to consolidate his position. During the siege of Aleppo, the Fatimid caliph through an emissary bestowed a number of honorifics upon Maḥmūd, thus reaffirming Cairo's suzerainty over the emirate. By re-establishing the formal dependency upon both Byzantium and the Fatimid caliphate, Maḥmūd minimized the possibility of future attempts by his uncle to gain power. Moreover, the emir appears to have been interested in setting the alliance with the Turkmen warriors on a more solid basis. He gave Maʿarrat al-Nuʿmān as land grant (*iqṭāʿ*) to Ibn Khān, who entered the city on 11 September 1065. The mercenary leader turned into a high-ranking dignitary and governor, being obliged to take effective administrative measures in the territories granted to him in order to maximize his profit. Accordingly, Ibn al-ʿAdīm points to a remarkable change in the Turkmen warriors' behavior. They were no longer depicted as lawless brigands but as disciplined soldiers showing respect for the rights and properties of the inhabitants: "They did not do any harm to the orchards and vineyards and did not take anything from anybody if not at its price and they gave water to their animals at its price."[168] Moreover, Ibn Khān remained loyal to Maḥmūd in political and military matters, helping him establish his authority in the territory of Ḥamāh. This was very important for the stability of Maḥmūd's rule as the local Arab leaders sided with him only in part, while others sought for opportunities to trigger a new intra-dynastic conflict with ʿAṭiyya. Others readily submitted to the Fatimid governors because of ongoing Turkish assaults. The situation further deteriorated because of a plague epidemic, which in Aleppo alone cost the lives of more than 4,000 people until May/June 1067.[169]

The overall instability in the emirate of Aleppo and the simultaneous penetration of the ducate of Edessa by Turkish raiders made Upper Mesopotamia, the Euphrates region, and northern Syria increasingly permeable for the newly arriving warrior groups, as is illustrated by a new series of attacks conducted by Afshīn b. Bakjī.[170] An emir of Alp Arslān's retinue, he had fallen in disgrace after killing one of the sultan's officers and thereupon fled with his followers across the Euphrates to the emirate of Aleppo. It is not quite clear what kind of relationship he established with the Mirdāsid emirs and Ibn Khān, but the fact that he sold the booty and the captives he made in the territory of Antioch on the markets of Aleppo suggests a kind of agreement.[171] He also seems to have coordinated his raids with Ibn Khān, for the latter undertook a five-month siege of Artāḥ when Afshīn carried out his attacks. Ibn al-ʿAdīm's detailed report refers to attacks in the region of Antioch and to an advance in a northerly direction as far as Dulūk. As attested to in other cases, the Byzantine defense strategy was rather passive, concentrating on the population's safety but neglecting the people's livestock and belongings and avoiding open battles. In spite of the extensive raiding activities in the neighboring regions, it seems that neither the military units nor the peasantry in the ducate were prepared for a Turkish attack.

> The land of the Romans was destroyed to such an extent as it was never heard before. The harvest remained in the threshing floors; there was no one who would have transported it away from them. Even people of the peasants and the rest of the common folk could go and take whatever they wanted, for they met no one to prevent them from that. The reason was that the Romans entrenched themselves in castles, mountains, and caves and left their houses as they were without taking anything from there, for the Turks attacked them all of a sudden.[172]

According to Ibn al-ʿAdīm the raids lasted from August/September 1067 until the spring of 1068,[173] while Matthew reports that Afshīn wintered at the foot of the Black Mountains, where he burned and looted many monasteries and villages.[174] The same author gives detailed figures concerning the booty brought to Aleppo: more than 40,000 buffalos, an uncountable number of cows, sheep, goats, mules, and wheat, about 70,000 male and female slaves, 100,000 dinars in cash and about the same amount in brocade cloths and precious objects. This unexpected surplus supply caused a temporary price decline on the local markets. One buffalo was sold for one dinar, a slave maid for two, two *qafīz* of wheat—being equivalent to approximately 100 kg[175]—for two dinars. No matter to what extent the above numbers are exaggerated, the raiders' profit in any case must have been remarkable. The fact that Afshīn in the same year was able to return to Iraq and to regain the favor of Sultan Alp Arslān suggests that the successful outcome of his invasion into Byzantine territory had strengthened his position both practically and ideologically. It therefore comes as no surprise that in the course of the events culminating in Alp Arslān's Syrian campaign of 1070/71 and the battle of Manzikert Afshīn served as one of the sultan's leading commanders, operating mostly on Byzantine territory and being the first Turkish chief to invade regions of western Asia Minor.[176]

One side effect of Afshīn's raid was the conquest of Artāḥ accomplished by Ibn Khān on 1 July 1068 after more than five months of siege. Ibn al-ʿAdīm presents this as a great strategic advantage achieved by the Muslim side, for the fortress was a major strongpoint in the frontier region, controlling large parts of northern Syria from the banks of the Euphrates as far as the Orontes River and the cities of Apameia, Antioch, and al-Athārib.[177] After having been conquered by the Byzantines in 966, Artāḥ became residence of a *strategos* and along with the nearby castle of ʿImm was endowed with a number of important imperial domains,[178] which may have further increased the place's attractiveness to the Turkish raiders. The fact that a large portion of the local population had taken refuge therein resulted in a cruel massacre—about 3,000 were reportedly killed—and an extremely rich booty for the conquerors.[179] Ibn Khān obviously grasped the opportunity offered by Afshīn's activities to launch a campaign on his own account, whereas the Byzantine troops, distracted by other assaults, were unable to offer sufficient support to the garrison of Artāḥ. Indicative of the overall situation is a piece of information referring to the arrival of a strong detachment of Byzantine forces, which tried to force Ibn Khān to consent to a peace agreement regarding the surrender of Artāḥ and other territories but failed to do so. Ibn al-ʿAdīm believes that the real objective of this overture was to transport foodstuff that had arrived by sea to the city of Antioch. If this is true, the Byzantines seemed to already perceive the Turks as a serious threat to Antioch.[180] The same source asserts that about 300,000 of the Byzantines who were on the road to Apameia were either captured or killed by the month of Ramaḍān 461/4 July-August 2 1068.[181] This number is no doubt extremely exaggerated, but it bears witness to the chaos the Turkish raids caused in the ducate. The local defense system was obviously no longer able to meet these challenges.

It is difficult to reconcile the information transmitted by the Armenian and Muslim sources with the details provided by Michael Attaleiates. Though highly illuminating with respect to the Byzantine viewpoint and the state of affairs of the imperial troops, Attaleiates' narrative can hardly be spliced into the sequence of events presented by non-Byzantine accounts. In particular, Attaleiates mentions a Turkish attack across the Euphrates on the territory of Melitene, dated in the time after Constantine X's death and his widow Eudokia's accession to the throne in June 1067.[182] On putting the Roman troops stationed in Melitene to flight, the invaders proceeded westward into the heartland of Cappadocia and attacked Kaisareia, an important center of pilgrimage and commerce and an imperial field camp, which was looted and devastated. Among other things, the Turkmen warriors pillaged the church of Saint Basil, removing the door leafs of the chamber in which the saint's relics were kept.[183] From Cappadocia the raiders passed unhindered the passes of the Taurus Mountains into Cilicia, where they caused a great panic among the population.[184]

If Attaleiates' description is correct, this was the westernmost advance achieved so far by Turkish warriors in the southwestern section of the borderland. It cannot be ruled out, however, that the historian merely conflated a number of isolated events into one chronological string. The crossing of the Euphrates may have related to Gümüshtekin's advance to Ḥiṣn Manṣūr in the year 1066, and it may well be that the raid in Cappadocia and Cilicia, instead of beginning in the region of Melitene, as Attaleiates asserts, followed, in fact, Afshīn's raids in the ducate of Antioch in 1067. Otherwise it is not possible to identify the leaders of this/these successful expedition(s). A definite answer to this question cannot be given, but it seems to be beyond doubt that the Turkmen activities in Upper Mesopotamia and northern Syria in the years 1066/67 for the first time extended to the southern part of the central Anatolian highlands.

Other details refer to the Byzantine military forces in the area. Attaleiates mentions the state of poverty and moral decay caused by outstanding salary payments and the lack of coordination between the individual units. The *Romaika tagmata* in Melitene, for instance, were unable to cross the Euphrates and join the troops of Mesopotamia,[185] i.e., the units stationed in Charpete/Kharput and adjacent regions. As a result, the far-reaching arrows of Turkmen bowmen easily defeated the garrisons guarding the fords of the Euphrates.[186] Likewise, the troops of the ducate of Antioch proved to be completely incapable of repelling Afshīn's attacks. Because of the emperor's unwillingness to pay satisfactory salaries, the troops were highly reluctant to fight, and a great part of them quickly withdrew from the territories exposed to the assaults.[187] Another force of young and inexperienced soldiers was insufficiently equipped and lacked an effective cavalry to fend off the invading raiders.[188]

A problem posed by Attaleiates' narrative lays in his unabashed partiality in favor of the future rebel and emperor Nikephoros Botaneiates, who after holding various crucial posts on the Danube frontier and in Thessalonica, was appointed *doux* of Antioch in 1067.[189] By contrasting the short-sighted and greedy emperor with the prudent and virtuous general Botaneiates, the historian paints the picture of a decaying central government putting at risk the very existence of the empire, which expected its savior in the person of Botaneiates. The general, Attaleiates asserts, effectively resisted the Turkish raids even under the most difficult circumstances but nevertheless was removed from his post.[190] Attaleiates also implies that Botaneiates had been considered a highly suitable candidate for the imperial throne before the choice fell on Romanos Diogenes, but envy prevented this plan from materializing.[191] In light of this strong encomiastic tendency, one may assume that the author's black-and-white painting of the situation unavoidably entails oversimplifications and exaggerations. Problems in coordinating forces and organizing efficient resistance are also mentioned in non-Byzantine sources, but it seems misleading to ascribe all these shortcomings to the imperial government's inability to take the required measures. It may well be that the Byzantine military units on the banks of the Euphrates were actually facing supply problems, fatigue, and decreasing fighting moral, but in 1067 Botaneiates was in no position to halt the process of disintegration. As a high-ranking officer with some remarkable successes at the Balkan front, he was perhaps a distinguished member of the military aristocracy, but it was only very recently that he had been appointed *doux* of Antioch, and he had hardly had enough time to build up a network of loyal supporters in the East. By presenting Diogenes' election as a second choice, which eventually led the empire to a disastrous defeat and civil strife, Attaleiates explained developments in the Byzantine Empire in this period in light of the coup d'état of 1078, linking his hero's claims to the throne with the deficiencies of the Doukas regime. As a result, the tumults and troubles of the reigns of Constantine X and Michael VII had to be depicted in the worst possible way. Attaleiates' attitudes towards Romanos IV Diogenes differed because the latter also eventually fell victim to the conspiracies of the Doukas faction; thus, he is described in the historian's account as an unsuccessful predecessor.

The events of 1067 certainly represented a decisive turning point in that for the first time it became clear that the Turkish threat would not remain an issue of the frontier zone, but was on the point of spreading into the interior of Asia Minor. As Attaleiates explicitly states, as long as the hostile attacks were directed against the overwhelmingly non-Greek and non-Chalcedonian population in the eastern provinces, they could be viewed as a sign of God's anger and an instrument of divine punishment against heretics. With their westward expansion they became increasingly perceived as a threat to the whole of the Byzantine Empire.[192] The justification pointing to religious apostates no longer applied; the root of the evil and the deeper reasons for God's wrath had to be sought in the very heart of the imperial government, the holder of the imperial office and his closest circle. The Turks came to be a symbol of divine resistance against a lawless ruler and could be used as a means to justify Botaneiates' revolt.

In summary, the Seljuk attacks of the years 1064–68, whether organized by the sultan himself, his supreme commanders, or independently operating Turkmen warriors, brought about a decisive expansion of military activities in the Caucasus region, culminating in the submission of the last independent Georgian rulers and the conquest of Ani, and in the central and southern sections of the frontier zone from the Anti-Taurus Mountains to the ducate of Antioch. Certainly, one cannot speak of conquests of major urban centers or substantial territorial gains. A large-scale annexation of Christian territories or the foundation of lordships on Byzantine soil was outside the scope of Seljuk and Turkmen policies, but the Seljuk sultanate, especially as a result of its Caucasian campaign, had made decisive steps in opening routes from Azerbaijan to Armenia and central Anatolia and in projecting itself as supreme leader of the *jihad* movement in the Muslim world. At the same time, by ravaging rural areas and fortresses, killing people, making captives of members of the local population, and accumulating considerable amounts of booty in cash, livestock, and movable goods, the Turkmen raiders had destroyed existing administrative and military structures, caused supply problems, and spread chaos and insecurity in the regions within their reach. Moreover, the income gained from the booty decisively increased their economic and financial power, allowing them to strengthen their influence over the Kurdish and Arab tribal emirates in the Diyār Bakr province and northern Syria by establishing alliances with the local potentates and inserting themselves into the pre-existing elites. These developments resulted in a strengthening of the military power within the Muslim emirates, which contrasted with the simultaneous dismemberment of the armed forces and structures of centralizing control in the Byzantine frontier region. The balance of power shifted to the detriment of Byzantium and thus increased the permeability of the eastern frontier. Romanos IV Diogenes' campaigns of the years 1068–71 should be viewed as an attempt to put a halt to or, if possible, reverse these developments.

Notes

1 Skylitzes, p. 454; Ibn al-Athīr, 6:146, trans. Richards, *Annals*, pp. 73–74 (*sub anno* 441/5 June 1049–25 May 1050); Bar Hebraeus, p. 230, trans. Budge, p. 206; Turan, *Selçuklular Târihi*, pp. 123–24; Felix, *Byzanz*, pp. 170–71; Dölger and Wirth, *Regesten*, no. 890d; Ripper, *Marwāniden*, pp. 157–60; Sevim and Merçil, *Selçuklu Devletleri*, p. 46; Öngül, *Selçuklular*, 1:24–25; Özgüdenli, *Selçuklular*, pp. 98–99.

2 Ibn al-Athīr, 6:136, trans. Richards, *Annals*, p. 66 (erroneously *sub anno* 439/28 June 1047–15 June 1048); al-Maqrīzī, *Itti'āẓ*, 2:194 (the emperor's gifts arrived in Cairo on 8 Dhū l-Ḥijja 437/16 June 1046). For details, see Felix, *Byzanz*, pp. 114–15; Halm, *Kalifen*, pp. 360–61.

3 Skylitzes, p. 454: ἐξῃτεῖτο τὴν ἐλευθερίαν καὶ σπονδὰς εἰρήνης. Ibn Athīr, 6:146, trans. Richards, *Annals*, p. 73: *rāsala malik al-Rūm Ṭughril Beg wa-arsala ilayhi hadiyyatan 'aẓīmatan wa-ṭalaba minhu l-mu'āhada* ("the king of the Romans sent a message to Ṭughril Beg, sending him precious gifts and asking him for a peace treaty"). Ṭughril Beg's itinerary in 1049/50 was largely determined by the incipient conflict with his half-brother Ibrāhīm Yināl, who, after refusing to hand over Hamadhān and other strongholds in the Uplands of western Iran, resisted his brother for a certain period in the fortress of Sarmāj (in the vicinity of Dīnawar?). At about the same time Ṭughril Beg was in contact with the Marwānid ruler Naṣr al-Dawla in the province of Diyār Bakr, requesting the latter's submission: Ibn al-Athīr, 6:146, trans. Richards, *Annals*, p. 73; Bar Hebraeus, p. 230, trans. Budge, p. 206.

4 Ibn al-Athīr, 6:146, trans. Richards, *Annals*, pp. 73–74: *wa-'ammarū masjid al-Qusṭanṭīnīya wa-aqāmū l-ṣalāt wa-l-khuṭba li-Ṭughril Beg* ("they repaired the mosque of Constantinople and established the prayer and the Friday sermon in the name of Ṭughril Beg"). For the identity of the emissary, who is known from another Seljuk embassy to Constantinople sent some years later, see Felix, *Byzanz*, p. 171, n. 114.

5 Dölger and Müller, *Regesten*, no. 770: Emperor Basil II conceded this privilege to the Fatimid caliph in exchange for a seven-year peace treaty during the blockade of Constantinople by Bardas Phokas in early 988.

6 See above, n. 3.

7 Ibn al-Athīr, 6:146, trans. Richards, *Annals*, p. 73.

8 Bar Hebraeus, p. 231, trans. Budge, p. 206: *malkā nāmūsāyā, bēth gāwsā dh-mashlmānē, Rūkn al-Dīn Sūlṭān Ṭūghrel Bāg* ("lawful king, house of refuge for the Muslims, pillar of religion, Ṭughril Beg"). For the Seljuk use of *sulṭān* as regular title for the holder of supreme rule, see EI^2, 9:850 s. v. sulṭān (J. H. Kramer and C. E. Bosworth); for the sultan-caliph relationship, see Lambton, "Internal Structure," pp. 205–208; for the Seljuk dynasty's relations with Sunni Islam in general, see Peacock, *Early Seljūq History*, pp. 99–127.

9 Ibn al-Athīr, 6:146, trans. Richards, *Annals*, p. 74: *wa-dāna ḥīna'idhin an-nās kulluhum lahū wa-'aẓuma sha'nuhū wa-tamakkana mulkuhū wa-thabata* ("at that time all people submitted to him, his prestige was great and his rule was strong and firmly consolidated").

10 Ibn al-Athīr 6:149–50, 160–61, trans. Richards, *Annals*, pp. 76–77, 82.

11 Bar Hebraeus, p. 231, trans. Budge, pp. 206–207; Turan, *Selçuklular Târihi*, p. 124.

12 Dölger and Müller, *Regesten*, no. 769a.

13 Dölger and Wirth, *Regesten*, no. 929; Turan, *Selçuklular Târihi*, p. 125; Theodora ruled from the death of Constantine IX Monomachos on 8 January 1055 until her own death on 27 August 1056. A more exact dating is possible on the basis of the Armenian chronicle of Aristakes 18, pp. 88–89, who places this diplomatic contact *sub anno* 504 of the Armenian era (8 March 1055–7 March 1056). Bar Hebraeus, p. 231, trans. Budge, p. 207, dates it a year earlier, i.e., to 1365 of the Seleucid era (1053–54), but immediately afterwards relates Ṭughril Beg's entrance into Baghdad. On the basis of these details it may be assumed that the Seljuk embassy arrived in Constantinople in about spring/early summer 1055, while the empress's response was dispatched in the subsequent months.

14 Aristakes 18, p. 88; Bar Hebraeus, p. 231, trans. Budge, p. 207 (who does not refer explicitly to the Seljuk embassy but mentions the tribute sent by the empress to the caliph of Baghdad).

15 Halm, *Kalifen*, p. 297.

16 Maqrīzī, *Itti'āẓ*, 2:230: "In this year [447/2 April 1055–20 March 1056] al-Mustanṣir sent troops to the Kanīsa Qumāma [i.e., Church of the Holy Sepulcher] and confiscated all its belongings. This happened because the *qāḍī* Abū 'Abdallāh al-Quḍā'ī had been dispatched by the caliph with a message to the ruler of the Romans (*mutamallik al-Rūm*). While he was in Constantinople, a messenger of Sultan Ṭughril Beg b. Saljūq arrived, who asked the queen Theodora (*al-malika Tiyūdūrā*) to allow his messenger to perform the prayer in the mosque of Constantinople. She gave him the permission to do so, and thus he entered the mosque and prayed there and spoke the Friday sermon in the name of Caliph al-Qā'im b. Amr Allāh al-'Abbāsī. Al-Quḍā'ī informed al-Mustanṣir about that, and therefore the latter confiscated everything that was in the Qumāma and took it away. He expelled the patriarch from there to a remote monastery, closed the gates of the churches in Egypt and Syria, demanded the *jizya* (poll tax) of four years from the monks and increased the *jizya* to be paid by the Christians. This was the beginning of the deterioration of the relations between the Romans and the Egyptians."

17 Turan, *Selçuklular Târihi*, pp. 124–25; Felix, *Byzanz*, p. 102 with n. 176; Dölger and Wirth, *Regesten*, no. 843.

18 El Cheikh, *Byzantium*, pp. 139–62.

19 For details, see Peacock, *Early Seljūq History*, pp. 128–63.

20 Felix, *Byzanz*, pp. 117–18; EI^2, 7:481, 483, s. v. al-Mu'izz b. Bādīs (M. Talbi); Brett, "Near East," p. 128/294; Halm, *Kalifen*, pp. 370–71.

21 Maqrīzī, *Itti'āẓ*, 2:214. Halm, *Kalifen*, p. 466, n. 66, dates the whole episode back to 1047/48, for in 1051/52 the Zīrid provinces were already affected by the invasions of the Hilāl and Sulaym Arabs. From other sources we know that the rejection of the Fatimid dogma was officially announced in al-Manṣūrīya on 9 March 1049: ibid., p. 371. It would be difficult, however, to reconcile an earlier date with the details

concerning the Seljuk involvement in this incident and thus I prefer to keep the year 443, as indicated in the sources.

22 Ibn al-Athīr, 6:158–59, trans. Richards, *Annals*, pp. 79–81.

23 Ibn al-Athīr, 6:160–61, trans. Richards, *Annals*, p. 82.

24 Turan, *Selçuklular Târihi*, pp. 126–34; Sevim and Merçil, *Selçuklu Devletleri*, pp. 51–52; Öngül, *Selçuklular*, 1:28–29; Özgüdenli, *Selçuklular*, pp. 104–105.

25 Ibn al-Athīr, 6:165–66, trans. Richards, *Annals*, pp. 86–87.

26 Ibn al-Athīr, 6:159, trans. Richards, *Annals*, p. 81.

27 Ibn al-Athīr, 6:166, trans. Richards, *Annals*, p. 87.

28 Ibn al-Athīr, 6:157, 166, trans. Richards, *Annals*, p. 87.

29 Maqrīzī, *Itti'āẓ*, 2:214.

30 Maqrīzī, *Itti'āẓ*, 2:223.

31 Maqrīzī, *Itti'āẓ*, 2:214, 223.

32 Maqrīzī, *Itti'āẓ*, 2:223.

33 Maqrīzī, *Itti'āẓ*, 2:214: "When al-Mu'izz b. Bādīs was informed of this [i.e., the ambassador's arrest], he sent a message to Constantine [IX Monomachos], the emperor of the Romans, on this matter, but he did not reply."

34 Maqrīzī, *Itti'āẓ*, 2:214: "He pointed out that there was friendship between him and al-Mustanṣir and that he would not allow any harm to be done to him."

35 Maqrīzī, *Itti'āẓ*, 2:223: "The emissary was sent back to the king of the Romans (*malik al-Rūm*). He was repentant for what had happened to him and he apologized to him. For he had given him guarantees that he would be brought back safely from Egypt, when he had been asked to hand him over. Subsequently, the king of the Romans sent him back to Baghdad where he arrived in the year 44 [3 May 1052–22 April 1053]."

36 Maqrīzī, *Itti'āẓ*, 2:223.

37 Ibn al-Athīr, 6:100, trans. Richards, Annals, p. 38; Özgüdenli, "Kuruluş devri," pp. 559–60.

38 See, for instance, Bar Hebraeus, pp. 231–32, trans. Budge, p. 207; Nīshāpūrī/Rashīd al-Dīn, p. 41.

39 Ibn al-Athīr, 6:124, trans. Richards, *Annals*, pp. 56–57.

40 Bar Hebraeus, pp. 231–32, trans. Budge, p. 207.

41 Ibn al-Athīr, 6:172, 179–80, trans. Richards, *Annals*, pp. 93, 99–100; Turan, *Selçuklular Târihi*, pp. 132–33; Bosworth, "Political History," p. 46; Sevim and Merçil, *Selçuklu Devletleri*, pp. 51–52; Öngül, *Selçuklular*, 1:28–29; Özgüdenli, *Selçuklular*, pp. 104–105.

42 For the situation in Aleppo, see Bianquis, *Damas*, 2:565–66, 569–71.

43 Sibṭ b. al-Jawzī, pp. 11–16, 24–26, 28–58, 64–68; Ibn al-Athīr, 6:181, 189–90, 191–93, 198–206, trans. Richards, *Annals*, pp. 102, 106, 108–13, 118–27; for Ṭughril Beg's relations with the Abbasid caliphate after 1055, the revolt of Ibrāhīm Yināl, al-Basāsīrī's role in the years 1055–60, and Fatimid interventions in Iraqi affairs during that period, see Turan, *Selçuklular Târihi*, pp. 132–39; Bosworth, "Political History," pp. 46–47; Halm, *Kalifen*, pp. 385–95; Sevim and Merçil, *Selçuklu Devletleri*, pp. 53–58; Hanne, *Caliph*, pp. 91–96; Öngül, *Selçuklular*, 1:29–34; Özgüdenli, *Selçuklular*, pp. 104–10, 121–23.

44 Maqrīzī, *Itti'āẓ*, 2:227–28.

45 Maqrīzī, *Itti'āẓ*, 2:228, 230–31.

46 Maqrīzī, *Itti'āẓ*, 2:229, 230; Maqrīzī, *Khiṭaṭ*, 1:335; for further details, see Bianquis, *Damas*, 2:566–68; Halm, *Kalifen*, pp. 382–83.

47 Halm, *Kalifen*, p. 382.

48 Maqrīzī, *Itti'āẓ*, 2:227; Maqrīzī, *Khiṭaṭ*, 1:335.

49 Maqrīzī, *Khiṭaṭ*, 1:335.

50 Maqrīzī, *Itti'āẓ* 2:230, 231.

51 Maqrīzī, *Itti'āẓ*, 2:231.

52 Bianquis, *Damas*, 2:548–49.
53 Maqrīzī, *Itti'āẓ*, 2:227.
54 Maqrīzī, *Itti'āẓ*, 2:227; Bianquis, *Damas*, 2:550–51; Halm, *Kalifen*, pp. 356–59, 390–91.
55 Cheynet, *Pouvoir*, pp. 68–70, 339–44.
56 Skylitzes, pp. 484–84: Τοῦρκος γάρ τις τὴν κλῆσιν Σαμούχ, τὸ γένος οὐκ ἐπίσημος, πρὸς δὲ τὰ πολεμικὰ γενναῖος καὶ ἐνεργός [...] αὐτὸς τῷ τόπῳ παρέμεινε μετὰ τρισχιλίων ἀνδρῶν, καὶ περιπλανώμενος ἐν ταῖς πεδιάσι καὶ τοῖς ὑπτίοις τόποις τῆς μεγάλης Ἀρμενίας.
57 Maqrīzī, *Itti'āẓ*, 2:227: "They replied that what made this [i.e., the attack on Laodikeia] necessary was his breach of the peace treaty (*al-hudna*), which had been agreed with his predecessor, and the detention of the gift and the [other] gift, which was not from his own belongings."
58 For the significance of gift exchange in Byzantine diplomacy, see for instance Cutler, "Gifts," pp. 247–48; Schreiner, "Geschenke," pp. 251–82.
59 Maqrīzī, *Itti'āẓ*, 2:227: "The condition was imposed upon him to release all prisoners in the land of the Romans (*bilād al-Rūm*)." Ibid., 2:228: "The condition was imposed upon him to hand over the Muslim fortresses which had come in the possession of the Romans."
60 Maqrīzī, *Itti'āẓ*, 2:227–28.
61 Maqrīzī, *Itti'āẓ*, 2:227–28.
62 Maqrīzī, *Itti'āẓ*, 2:227: "It was customary practice that when presents from the Romans arrived at the caliphal court, their value was estimated and presents of a value equal to two thirds of the former were sent to them. In this way, Islam had a profit of one third in comparison to them. Hence, the condition was imposed that the value of the presents which were to be sent to them in return for the value of their presents would be the half."
63 Aristakes 18, p. 92.
64 Skylitzes, p. 479.
65 Aristakes 18, p. 93; Bar Hebraeus, p. 231, trans. Budge, p. 207; Dölger and Wirth, *Regesten*, no. 929.
66 Skylitzes, p. 483; other important sources are Attaleiates, pp. 40–42; Psellos 7.4-43, pp. 208–28; for a detailed analysis of this conflict, see Cheynet, *Pouvoir*, pp. 68–69, 339–44.
67 Skylitzes, pp. 482–84; for Hervé, see Cheynet, *Pouvoir*, pp. 67–68.
68 Skylitzes, pp. 484–85, 487–88; Psellos 7.3 (on Kekaumenos); Attaleiates, p. 41 (on Bryennios); for the identity and the activites of Samouch, see below, pp. 104–108.
69 Skylitzes, pp. 488–89.
70 Skylitzes, pp. 490–91, esp. p. 491, ll. 26–29: γράμματα γὰρ πλασάμενος βασιλικά, ὡς εἴη προστεταγμένον αὐτῷ ἀνηλειφότι τὰ τῶν συμμάχων τρία τάγματα καὶ τὰ δύο τῶν Κολωνειατῶν καὶ τῶν Χαλδαίων ἀνελθεῖν κατὰ τοῦ Σαμούχ.
71 Skylitzes, p. 491, ll. 39–42.
72 Skylitzes, p. 486, l. 96 (οἱ δὲ τῆς ἕω στρατηγοί), p. 491, ll. 36–37 (τὰ δύο Ῥωμαϊκὰ τάγματα, μετ' ἐκεῖνα δὲ καὶ τοὺς οἰκείους, καὶ τοῖς ἐξ ἐθνῶν). p. 492, l. 69, p. 493, ll. 77–79 (πρὸς τὰ μὴ συναπαχθέντα ἑῷα τάγματα τῷ Κομνηνῷ, ἤτοι τοὺς Ἀνατολικοὺς καὶ τοὺς ἐκ τοῦ Χαρσιανοῦ).
73 Attaleiates, p. 42, ll. 6–12 (καὶ πίπτουσιν ἐξ ἑκατέρου μέρους συχνοί, τὸ δὲ πλεῖστον οἱ τὴν φυγὴν ἑλόμενοι κατεκόπησαν ...); Skylitzes, pp. 494–95.
74 For the composition of seditious movements and aristocratic coalitions in Byzantium from the late tenth century onwards, see Cheynet, *Pouvoir*, pp. 20–78, 261–301, 321–77; Angold, "Byzantine State," pp. 9–34, esp. 16–32, strongly insists on the characteristics of Byzantine central power in the period of Constantine IX and his successors but ignores the developments in the provinces.

75 Skylitzes, p. 484.
76 For these attacks in general, see Yinanç, *Anadolu'nun Fethi*, pp. 51–53, Cahen, *Pre-Ottoman Turkey*, pp. 69–70; Vryonis, *Decline*, pp. 87–88; Sevim, *Anadolu'nun Fethi*, pp. 35–37; Leveniotis, *Collapse*, pp. 102–105 (Armenia), 262–65 (Melitene and environs).
77 Attaleiates, pp. 59–60.
78 Yinanç, *Anadolu'nun Fethi*, p. 51; Sevim, *Anadolu'nun Fethi*, p. 35; Leveniotis, *Collapse*, p. 102.
79 Aristakes 18, pp. 93–94; Leveniotis, *Collapse*, p. 103.
80 Skylitzes, p. 485, ll. 55–56: καὶ ἀνελθὼν ἐν Μηδίᾳ κοινοπραγεῖ τῷ Σαμοὺχ ἐκεῖσε ἐνδιατρίβοντι, ὥστε πολεμεῖν Ῥωμαίοις.
81 Skylitzes, p. 485.
82 Skylitzes, pp. 485–86.
83 For details concerning the commander of Ani, see Leveniotis, *Collapse*, p. 538.
84 Aristakes 18, pp. 96–99. For the Liparit family, see ODB, 2:1232 s. v. Liparites; Leveniotis, *Collapse*, pp. 92, n. 437, 99, n. 480 (concerning the conflict of Liparit with the Georgian king Bagrat IV), 104.
85 Aristakes 18, p. 99: "Ils avaient vu l'état d'impuissance où se trouvait le pays privé de défenseurs."
86 Aristakes 18, p. 99.
87 Aristakes 18, pp. 99–101.
88 Aristakes 19, pp. 102–104.
89 Aristakes 21, pp. 104–105; Matthew of Edessa 2.8, pp. 92–93; Michael the Syrian 15.1, 3:158–60 (trans.), 4:572 (Syriac text); Bar Hebraeus, p. 238, trans. Budge, pp. 212–13. The exact dates given by Aristakes 21, pp. 105–106 (the Turkmen army arrived "au début du mois de areg [3 October-2 November 1057]," the Turkmens were trapped in the mountains "jusqu'à l'arrive du mois de nawasard [7 March 1058]") are more reliable than the rather arbitrary indication of Matthew of Edessa 2.8, p. 92 ("it was the winter season at the beginning of Lent"); for the details of this event, see also Leveniotis, *Collapse*, pp. 262–65.
90 Matthew of Edessa 2.8, p. 92; Aristakes 21, p. 105, refers to a new army, but "je ne sais si elle était composée de troupes anciennes ou de troupes nouvelles."
91 Aristakes 21, p. 105; the number is mentioned by Michael the Syrian 15.1, 3:158 (trans.), 4:572 (Syriac text).
92 Matthew of Edessa 2.8, p. 92; Michael the Syrian 15.1, 3:158 (trans.), 4:572 (Syriac text).
93 Aristakes 21, p. 105: "La garnison de la ville consistait en un corps de cavalerie romaine"; Matthew of Edessa 2.8, p. 93: "the Roman forces pursued the Turks but [...] did not dare give battle."
94 Michael the Syrian 15.1, 3:159 (trans.), 4:572 (Syriac text).
95 Aristakes 21, pp. 106–107; Matthew of Edessa 2.9, p. 93, who mentions the name of the Armenian commander.
96 Aristakes 21, pp. 107–108.
97 Matthew of Edessa 2.9-10, pp. 93–94, who speaks of many dying birds and animals and a severe famine due to the bad harvest.
98 Matthew of Edessa 2.12, pp. 94–96. The day on which the city was encircled by the enemy was "the day of the barekendan of Vardavar" (= feast of the Transfiguration of Christ on 6 August). For Sebasteia, see ODB 3:1861–62 s. v. Sebasteia.
99 For details, see Leveniotis, *Collapse*, pp. 230–38.
100 Matthew of Edessa 2.12, p. 95; for interpretations concerning these names, see Leveniotis, *Collapse*, pp. 104–105.
101 Sevim, *Anadolu'nun Fethi*, p. 36, taking Matthew's account at face value, argues that new Seljuk raids were conducted in 1059 on Sultan Ṭughril's order.
102 Yinanç, *Anadolu'nun Fethi*, pp. 55–57; Sevim, *Anadolu'nun Fethi*, pp. 36–38; Ripper, *Marwāniden*, pp. 187–94; Leveniotis, *Collapse*, pp. 181–86, 196–201.

103 Ibn al-Athīr, 6:229, trans. Richards, *Annals*, p. 152; Ibn al-Azraq, pp. 182–84, mentions Salār Khurāsān as commander of 5,000 horsemen dispatched by Alp Arslān in Rabī' I 458/31 January-1 March 1066 to Mayyāfāriqīn. Sālār-i Khurāsān is also mentioned by Attaleiates, p. 59, l. 24, as Χωροσάλαρις.

104 For these names, see Yinanç, *Anadolu'nun Fethi*, p. 55 (who points to the existence of a tomb ascribed to a certain Cemceme Sultan in Erzurum); Sevim, *Anadolu'nun Fethi*, p. 37.

105 For details, see Leveniotis, *Collapse*, pp. 105, 212.

106 Matthew of Edessa 2.15, pp. 97–98.

107 See below, pp. 115–117.

108 Ibn al-Azraq, pp. 176–77 (Naṣr al-Dawla's death is dated to 29 Shawwāl 453/16 November 1061); Ibn al-Athīr, 6:215, trans. Richards, pp. 135–36.

109 Ibn al-Azraq, pp. 180–81, speaks of a detachment of 5,000 horsemen that allegedly accompanied Sa'īd on Ṭughril Beg's order from the sultan's court back to Mayyāfāriqīn; for details and contradictory source reports, see Ripper, *Marwāniden*, pp. 189, 191–92.

110 Matthew of Edessa 2.17, pp. 99–100.

111 Sibṭ b. al-Jawzī, pp. 100–101: *wa-stadnā amīran min al-Ghuzz kāna bi-tilka l-diyār wa-ma'ahū jamā'a ilā Āmid*, "he summoned an emir of the Ghuzz, who was in this region and had troops under his command, to Āmid."

112 Matthew of Edessa 2.19, pp. 100–101; see also Ripper, *Marwāniden*, pp. 321–23.

113 Matthew of Edessa 2.18, p. 100.

114 Sibṭ b. al-Jawzī, p. 101; Ibn al-'Adīm, p. 250.

115 Matthew of Edessa 2.27-29, pp. 107–109.

116 Turan, *Selçuklular Târihi*, pp. 147–50; Sevim and Merçil, *Selçuklu Devletleri*, pp. 61–63; Öngül, *Selçuklular*, 1:37–39; Özgüdenli, *Selçuklular*, 135–40.

117 Peacock, "Nomadic Society," pp. 214–17, 219–26; Peacock, *Early Seljūq History*, pp. 146–50.

118 For this campaign in general, see Yinanç, *Anadolu'nun Fethi*, pp. 57–59; Turan, *Selçuklular Târihi*, pp. 154–57; Canard, "Campagne," 239–59; Vryonis, *Decline*, pp. 94–95; Cahen, *Pre-Ottoman Turkey*, pp. 70–71; Sevim, *Anadolu'nun Fethi*, pp. 39–42; Leveniotis, *Collapse*, pp. 109–13; Sevim and Merçil, *Selçuklu Devletleri*, pp. 63–65; Öngül, *Selçuklular*, 1:39–42; Özgüdenli, *Selçuklular*, pp. 140–42.

119 Aristakes 24, pp. 120–24; Attaleiates, pp. 60–62; Matthew of Edessa 2.20-23, pp. 101–105; Georgian Chronicles, pp. 297–301; Ibn al-Athīr, 6:228–31, trans. Richards, *Annals*, pp. 152–55; al-Ḥusaynī, pp. 34–38; For details, see the comprehensive survey in Canard, "Campagne," 239–59.

120 Incidents referring to Caliph al-Mu'taṣim's role as champion of jihad against the Byzantine Empire are included in Niẓām al-Mulk's *Siyāsat-nāma* 7.22, p. 53, trans. Darke, p. 58.

121 Ibn al-Athīr, 6:229, trans. Richards, *Annals*, p. 152; al-Ḥusaynī, p. 35.

122 Ibn al-Athīr, 6:229, trans. Richards, *Annals*, pp. 152–53.

123 Al-Ḥusaynī, pp. 35–36; Ibn al-Athīr, 6:229, trans. Richards, *Annals*, p. 153.

124 Al-Ḥusaynī, pp. 36–37; Ibn al-Athīr, 6:229–31, trans. Richards, *Annals*, pp. 153–54.

125 Al-Ḥusaynī, p. 38.

126 See for example the description of Akhalk'alak in Ibn al-Athīr, 6:230, trans. Richards, *Annals*, pp. 153–54: "a strong place with a high wall and beetling buildings. To the east and the west it stands on a high cliff, on which are several forts, and on the other two sides there is a large unfordable river."

127 Al-Ḥusaynī, pp. 35–36; Ibn al-Athīr, 6:229, trans. Richards, *Annals*, p. 153.

128 Al-Ḥusaynī, p. 36; Ibn al-Athīr, 6:230; trans. Richards, *Annals*, p. 153.

129 Ibn al-Athīr, 6:231, trans. Richards, *Annals*, p. 154.

130 Ibn al-Athīr, 6:230, trans. Richards, *Annals*, p. 153: *ḥurūb shadīd ustushhida fīhā kathīr min al-muslimīn* ("fierce fights in which many of the Muslims died as martyrs").

131 Al-Ḥusaynī, p. 36; Ibn al-Athīr, 6:230, trans. Richards, *Annals*, p. 153: *kabbara l-muslimūn 'alayhim.*
132 Al-Husaynī, p. 37; Ibn al-Athīr, 6:230, trans. Richards, *Annals*, p. 154: *fa-lam yabraḥ ḥattā faragha min ṣalātihī.*
133 Ibn al-Athīr, 6:231, trans. Richards, *Annals*, p. 155.
134 Ibn al-Athīr, 6:231, trans. Richards, *Annals*, p. 155.
135 Matthew of Edessa 2.23, pp. 104–105.
136 Matthew of Edessa 2.20, p. 101, and 2.23, p. 104. See also al-Ḥusaynī, p. 38, who refers to the Georgian king's (*malik al-Kurj*) asking for peace and the sultan's letter stating that the king either has to convert to Islam or to pay *jizya*. The example provided by the accounts about the early Muslim model conquerors is clearly recognizable.
137 For other details and sources about Bagrat, see Leveniotis, *Collapse*, pp. 113–15, who supports that he was only *doux/katepano* of Ani while Iberia had become an independent *ducate.*
138 Leveniotis, *Collapse*, p. 110, sees in the conquest of Ani a crucial turning point initiating a new phase of expansion of the Turks on Byzantine territory. Given that none of the regions affected by the 1064 attacks remained under permanent Seljuk control, this view is certainly exaggerated. See also Peacock, "Nomadic Society," p. 217.
139 Ibn al-Athīr, 6:231, trans. Richards, *Annals*, pp. 154–55.
140 Leveniotis, *Collapse*, pp. 274–78.
141 Matthew of Edessa 2.24, p. 105.
142 Matthew of Edessa 2.28, p. 109: "The Roman troops who were in the city, both infantry and cavalry forces consisting of four thousand men [...] two brothers from the Armenian infantry [...] the Roman troops fled [...] a Frank turned around."
143 Matthew of Edessa 2.27, p. 108.
144 Matthew of Edessa 2.17, p. 99.
145 For the identification of various places, see Dostourian, Commentary to Matthew of Edessa, p. 313. For further details and bibliographical references, see Leveniotis, *Collapse*, pp. 279–80.
146 Matthew of Edessa 2.28, p. 108.
147 Matthew of Edessa 2.27, p. 108.
148 Matthew of Edessa 2.28, p. 108. "Pext" is alternatively interpreted as corrupted form of *vestes* or *Pektes*, see Leveniotis, *Collapse*, pp. 278–79, n. 1619; for the title of *proximos* see ODB 3:1751 s. v. proximos (while used for both military and civil officials, here it seems to designate a sort of subordinate officer or adjutant).
149 Matthew of Edessa 2.49, p. 126: "one thousand five hundred horsemen and twenty thousand infantry" is certainly a strong exaggeration.
150 Matthew of Edessa 2.48-49, p. 125. For Afshīn, see Sevim, *Selçuklu Komutanları*, pp. 18–32. For these raids in general, see Yinanç, *Anadolu'nun Fethi*, pp. 59–61; Sevim, *Anadolu'nun Fethi*, pp. 42–44; Sevim, *Selçuklu Komutanları*, p. 19; Leveniotis, *Collapse*, pp. 278–81.
151 For details, see Sevim and Merçil, *Selçuklu Devletleri*, pp. 65–66; Öngül, *Selçuklular*, 1:43–44; Özgüdenli, *Selçuklular*, pp. 143–46.
152 Matthew of Edessa 2.27-29, pp. 107–109.
153 A town situated at the Euphrates River between Chasanara/al-Suwaydā' and Ḥiṣn Manṣūr, not to be confused with Nisibis (Nusaybin) southeast of Mārdīn.
154 Matthew of Edessa 2.49, pp. 125–27; for these attacks, see also Heidemann, *Renaissance*, pp. 123–24.
155 Matthew of Edessa 2.49, pp. 126–27.
156 Matthew of Edessa 2.47, pp. 124–25; for further details, see below, pp. 120–121; for the chronicler's presentation, see MacEvitt, "Chronicle of Matthew," pp. 157–58.
157 For the ducate of Antioch before the Turkish incursions, see Todt, *Antiocheia*, pp. 226–43 (political development 1025–62), pp. 267–428 (civil and military administrative

structures, prosopographical data, administrative regions); Leveniotis, *Collapse*, pp. 322–35.

158 Ibn al-ʿAdīm, p. 254. For the political situation in general, see Sevim, *Suriye*, pp. 30–31; Felix, *Byzanz*, p. 122; Todt, *Antiocheia*, pp. 243–44, esp. p. 244: "Jetzt hatte Byzanz nicht nur jeden Einfluß auf das völlig in die fāṭimidische Einflußsphäre übergegangene Emirat verloren, sondern es sah auch seine eigene Herrschaft am Orontes von den bescheidenen militärischen Kräften Aleppos bedroht."

159 Ibn al-ʿAdīm, p. 250. For further details, see Sevim, *Suriye*, pp. 35–38; Todt, *Antiocheia*, p. 246; Leveniotis, *Collapse*, pp. 335–36; Ripper, *Marwāniden*, p. 101.

160 Ibn al-ʿAdīm, p. 250.

161 Ibn al-ʿAdīm, p. 254. Peacock, "Turkmen of the Byzantine Frontier," pp. 267–87, proposes a new interpretation of the term as signifying primarily Turkmen people instead of frontier provinces. Although his observation refers to the thirteenth century, it would also fit in this case, for it is hardly possible to connect Ibn Khān's *ūj* with a specific region.

162 Attaleiates, pp. 71–72: τοῦ κατ' αὐτοὺς ἐπιφανοῦς Ἀμερτικῆ λεγομένου.

163 Sevim, *Suriye*, p. 37; Beihammer, "Defection," p. 607.

164 Ibn al-ʿAdīm, p. 251.

165 Ibn al-ʿAdīm, p. 251.

166 Ibn al-ʿAdīm, pp. 251–52.

167 Ibn al-ʿAdīm, pp. 252–53.

168 Ibn al-ʿAdīm, p. 254.

169 Ibn al-ʿAdīm, pp. 254–55.

170 For this Turkish warlord, see also above, p. 116.

171 Ibn al-ʿAdīm, p. 256.

172 Ibn al-ʿAdīm, p. 255.

173 Ibn al-ʿAdīm, pp. 255–56: the first attack is dated to Shawwāl 460/15 August-12 September 1067, Afshīn left for Iraq in Jumādā II/7 April-5 May 1068.

174 Matthew of Edessa 2.47, pp. 124–125: dated to 515 (1066–67), but the chronological details provided by Ibn al-ʿAdīm are more reliable, and it is reasonable to assume two different raids, of which only the second one would have been recorded by the Arabic source.

175 For *qafīz*, see EI^2 6:117–21, at p. 119, s. v. makāyil (E. Ashtor).

176 See below, pp. 150–151, 155.

177 Ibn al-ʿAdīm, pp. 256–57.

178 Todt, *Antiocheia*, pp. 407–10.

179 Ibn al-ʿAdīm, p. 256.

180 Ibn al-ʿAdīm, p. 256.

181 Ibn al-ʿAdīm, p. 257.

182 Attaleiates, p. 70–71: Μετὰ δὲ τὸ τὸν βασιλέα τεθνάναι πάλιν οἱ τὴν ἑῴαν κατατρέχοντες Οὖννοι περὶ Μεσοποταμίαν γενόμενοι.

183 Attaleiates, p. 71, ll. 5–16; for the significance of Kaisareia, see Decker, "Frontier Settlement and Economy," p. 240.

184 Attaleiates, p. 71, ll. 17–21.

185 Attaleiates, p. 70, ll. 18–20.

186 Attaleiates, pp. 70–71.

187 Attaleiates, p. 72, ll. 8–20: Ἡ δὲ φειδωλία ἄπρακτα πάλιν καὶ ἀκλεῆ κατειργάσατο, οὐ γὰρ ὁλοκληρίαν ἠθέλησαν οἱ κρατοῦντες τοῦ ὀψωνιασμοῦ παρασχεῖν ἀνθρώποις πολεμίοις καὶ μάχαις κακοπαθήσειν ὀφείλουσιν [...] κατὰ δὲ τῶν ἐναντίων πορευθῆναι οὐ κατεδέξαντο [...] εἰς τὰ οἰκεῖα διεσκεδάσθησαν. Καὶ πάλιν ἦσαν οἱ βάρβαροι τὴν ῥωμαϊκὴν χώραν ἀδεῶς κατατρέχοντες.

188 Attaleiates, p. 72, ll. 20–24: [...] οἱ δρᾶσαι μέν τι μὴ δυνηθέντες γενναῖον, ἀπειροπόλεμοι τινὲς καὶ δύσιπποι και ἄνοπλοι σχεδὸν καθεστῶτες.

189 Attaleiates, p. 72, ll. 24–25: Τοῦ παραλαβόντος αὐτοὺς δουκὸς, ἦν δὲ ὁ μάγιστρος Νικηφόρος ὁ Βοτανειάτης. For Botaneiates career, see Todt, *Antiocheia*, pp. 306–15.

190 Attaleiates, pp. 72–73: τὴν τῶν βαρβάρων δι' οἰκείας ἀρετῆς καὶ γενναιότητος καὶ φρονήσεως ἀνατρέποντος καὶ καταβάλλοντος ἔφοδον, κἀκείνου δὲ τῆς ἀρχῆς παραλυθέντος, ἔκτοτε τὰ τῶν βαρβάρων ἐθρασύνετο πλέον [...].

191 Attaleiates, p. 73, ll. 6–19: ὁ δὲ φθόνος καὶ ἡ ἄδικος κρίσις ἀνεβάλετο μὲν τότε τὸ δέον.

192 Attaleiates, p. 73, ll. 11–17: ἐπὰν δὲ καὶ τῶν ὀρθοδόξων ἥψατο τὸ δεινόν, εἰς ἀμηχανίαν ἦσαν πάντες οἱ τὰ Ῥωμαίων θρησκεύοντες.

3 Emperor Romanos IV and Sultan Alp Arslān, 1068–71

Manzikert a historical turning point?

It is commonly held that the three campaigns of Romanos IV Diogenes, which culminated in the battle of Manzikert in August 1071, sealed the failure of the Byzantine defense policy against the Turkish invasions. Despite objections and doubts occasionally voiced as to the significance of the Byzantine defeat in terms of casualties, military disadvantages, and political concessions imposed on the emperor during his brief captivity in the sultan's camp, this battle is still regarded a Byzantine "Stalingrad" and a crucial turning point in the historical development of Asia Minor.[1] Unsurprisingly, the 900-year anniversary of the battle in 1971 occasioned the publication of a Manzikert commemorative volume by the *Türk Tarih Kurumu*, while Osman Turan dedicated his scholarly work to the memory of the foundation of a Turkish homeland in Anatolia, which in his opinion began on the battlefield of Manzikert.[2] The nationalistic viewpoint of Turkish scholars supporting the official version of history in the Turkish Republic is epitomized in a statement of Mükrimin Halil Yinanç:

> The battle of Manzikert is one of the important events, which form a turning point in universal history. This victory was the reason that shortly afterwards the Turkmens took possession of the whole of Anatolia and settled there.[3]

In the context of the recent surge of scholarly interest in the Seljuk period, younger Turkish scholars have criticized the stereotypical and unsubstantial character of the public commemorative discourse on Manzikert, even though they have largely remained in line with traditional approaches of Turkish historiography.[4] Watered-down versions of this interpretation have also found their way into European scholarship. Thus, most modern textbooks on the history of Turkey and the Ottoman Empire in one way or another emphasize the significance of the battle of Manzikert as a starting point of Turkish dominion in Anatolia.[5]

No doubt, these views are supported by a great number of primary sources stressing the overall momentous importance of this battle, but in evaluating these texts it should not be ignored that they ascribe this significance to reasons very different from what modern observers would like to emphasize. The vivid and circumstantial eyewitness report of Michael Attaleiates is due to the author's personal involvement in the campaign.[6] He certainly blames the emperor and other military commanders for a number of wrong decisions causing fatal results, but the real tragedy in his eyes was the deplorable fate of Romanos IV Diogenes in conjunction with the loss of prestige of the imperial office reflected in the emperor's downfall rather than the setback of the armed forces. Most characteristically, Attaleiates interrupts his narrative with a literary sigh of desperation exactly at that point where he switches from the immediate outcome of the battle to the emperor's demise, thus highlighting the very apex of the calamities he is going to expose.[7] Armenian and Syriac sources mainly underline the moral lessons to be gained from the Byzantine emperor's humiliation and the treacherous behavior of his officials and courtiers.[8] Muslim authors refer to the battle of Manzikert in order to promote the Seljuk sultan's image as a champion of *jihad*, portraying the events as a major confrontation between the supreme representatives of two opposing politico-religious spheres.[9] Their main concern was religion and Seljuk dynastic legitimacy based on the virtues of Muslim rulership, not the actual political and military consequences of the battle.

The broad range of ideologically biased views and retrospective interpretations articulated in the primary sources and the over-emphasis placed by a great part of the scholarly literature on the historical significance of this battle make it difficult to achieve an appropriate understanding of the event and its context. It would be misleading to single out the battle as the most decisive turning point conditioning the fate of Byzantine Asia Minor. Instead, the military encounter has to be embedded in a broader framework of crucial events and upheavals occurring between the years 1068 and 1072, such as the flight of the Seljuk dignitary Arīsghī to the imperial court, the invasion of Afshīn into Byzantine territory, the Syrian campaign of Sultan Alp Arslān, the three eastern campaigns of Romanos IV, and the Byzantine civil strife in Asia Minor following the battle. All these developments, in one way or another, further intensified the tendencies that had emerged during the 1050s and 1060s and help to explain why the post-1072 situation in the eastern provinces differed so sharply from the previous state of affairs.

The rise of Romanos IV Diogenes in 1068

Byzantine historians establish a direct causal link between Romanos Diogenes' marriage to Empress Eudokia and his accession to the imperial throne on 1 January 1068 and the precarious situation in the East caused by the Turkish raids. Michael Psellos, who as a fervent supporter of the Doukas clan and the claims of the imperial children to the throne was naturally ill-disposed towards the empress's new husband, reported Eudokia as saying: "Don't you know that the affairs of our empire are fading away and collapsing while wars are frequently sparked off and masses of barbarians are pillaging the entire east?"[10] Likewise, according to Michael Attaleiates, "great distress and confusion resulting from the extremely cruel invasion of foreign nations pressed the state of the Romans."[11]

Hence, the *augousta*, the senior officials, and Patriarch John Xiphilinos are presented as having no other alternative but to place the common good above Eudokia's vow not to marry again and to choose the most capable man to avert the dangers threatening the empire.

Both Psellos and Attaleiates in principle reject the empress's choice. The former considers Michael old enough to assume responsibilities in conducting state affairs and stresses the young man's obedience to his mother.[12] Attaleiates, instead, underlines the qualities of his hero Nikephoros Botaneiates, who at that time had already distinguished himself as *doux* of Antioch in conflicts with Arabs and Turks in northern Syria.[13] Accordingly, the empress's and her advisors' preference for Diogenes is described as resulting from the evil force of "envy" and an "unjust decision" made "for reasons hidden from men."[14] Most remarkably, as a practiced encomiast, Attaleiates connects this statement with an allusion to the idea of divine wrath, which through the instrument of the barbarian raids initially struck the Armenian and Syrian Christians in the eastern provinces but thereupon afflicted the Orthodox people.[15] The same motif reappears in the context of Botaneiates' revolt, thus serving as a means of depicting the future rebel as a man who according to God's plan had been sent to restore law and order and to suppress the barbarian attacks. Attaleiates' account certainly contains numerous noteworthy details reflecting an eyewitness's point of view, but it has to be read against the background of the overarching tendency to present his champion as a savior from great misfortunes caused by the immorality and shortsightedness of incompetent men in power.

Despite all skepticism expressed by our historians, it seems that the government of Constantinople had a fairly clear picture of what was going on in the eastern borderlands in early 1068. This is well documented by Attaleiates himself, who not only gives a detailed account of the Turkish attacks in the southwestern section of the frontier zone between Antioch and Melitene but also refers to the sultan's expedition into the Caucasus region and the dangers of an ensuing invasion into Byzantine territory.[16]

In fact, both Muslim and Georgian sources fully corroborate the assessment made by the Byzantine historian. In the months between the autumn of 1067 and the spring of 1068, Alp Arslān along with his vizier Niẓām al-Mulk and the commander Sawtakīn led a second campaign into the Caucasian provinces so as to consolidate Seljuk supremacy among the Christian and Muslim rulers in the lands of Georgia north of the Kyros River (Kura). In particular, the expedition was directed against the provinces of K'art'li, Kakhet'i, and Heret'i, which at that time were for the greatest part unified under the rule of King Bagrat IV (1018–72). For decades, this potentate maintained especially close ties with the imperial government of Constantinople by bearing the title of *kouropalates* and having married his daughter Martha/Maria to the future emperor Michael Doukas. At the same time, he had succeeded in subjecting the greatest part of the Georgian nobility to his authority. Other powerful rulers like King Aghsart'an I of Kakhet'i (1054–84) and Kwirike I of Lori in the province of Tashir had been reduced to a status of impotence. Bagrat also achieved some temporary success against the Shaddādid emirs of Ganja, who already in 1054 had for the first time recognized a status of vassalage.[17]

The gains made by Alp Arslān in this campaign were, no doubt, impressive: huge amounts of booty and captives taken from the territories in question; the submission of King Aghsart'an I, who not only entered the service of the sultan but also converted to Islam; the conquest of Tp'ilisi (Tiflis) and Rust'avi, which were handed over to the sultan's vassal and lord of Ganja and Dvin, al-Faḍl/Faḍlūn II b. Abī l-Aswār Shāwur, in replacement for the emir Ibn Ja'far; peace negotiations with King Bagrat IV, who wedded the daughter of his sister and Kwirike I of Lori to the sultan; after consummating the marriage in Hamadhān, Alp Arslān passed the woman on to Faḍlūn. In this way, the Seljuk sultan extended his sphere of influence from the Araxes River and the provinces of Taykh and Apkhazeti, which had formed the main targets of the 1064 campaign and ever since stood under the control of Seljuk garrisons or vassals, to the Georgian lands beyond the Kyros River. It is noteworthy that Bagrat IV at that time was not only the most powerful local potentate in the region but also a key figure in the web of coalitions of Constantinople, the local aristocracy, and the Muslim lordships in the region. The newly established relations by marriage of the Seljuk dynasty with the family of Bagrat and the Shaddādids in conjunction with the subjugation of Aghsart'an further undermined the Byzantine presence in the region and deprived the imperial government of the possibility to regain its lost grounds through its former allies.[18]

> As for the northern regions, the sultan came there in person with his whole army, leading irresistible forces, and reached the frontier of the Romans in the autumn, intending to spend the winter there and with the beginning of the spring to invade and fully destroy and devastate Roman territory.[19]

Attaleiates' words accurately reveal at least one of the reasons the inner circle of Empress Eudokia looked for an energetic military man to be placed at the head of the state. In contrast to the previous years, when the Seljuk attacks were geographically limited, in early 1068 it became for the first time perceivable that the threat was expanding over the entire eastern borderland and turning out to be a serious problem for the interior of Anatolia as well. Romanos Diogenes seems to have been a reasonable choice. He was an experienced commander originating from the military aristocracy of Cappadocia, whose name must have been on everybody's lips at that time as he had been sentenced to exile in a spectacular case of high treason only to be later pardoned by Empress Eudokia. Moreover, the fact that his immediate homeland had only recently become the target of Turkish attacks may have been an additional incentive for Romanos to dedicate himself with great zeal to military expeditions and defensive measures in order to re-stabilize centralized control over the eastern borderlands.[20]

As a result of Turkish military activities up to the late 1060s, a number of strongholds in the Armenian provinces had come under direct Seljuk rule, several local potentates had accepted a status of vassalage vis-à-vis the sultan, parts of the towns and rural areas in the borderland had been ravaged and depopulated, and the Byzantine administrative and military apparatus in the eastern marches could hardly recover from the losses of manpower and financial resources it had suffered due to internal conflicts and hostile attacks. Henceforth, the invaders met less resolute resistance and were able to maintain lines of retreat linking them with their bases east of the border. Thus, by 1068 the Turks were able to penetrate central and western Anatolia deeper than ever before. The recruitment of large mercenary troops could hardly compensate for the overall disintegration of the local military units and the former Muslim allies' passing over to the Seljuk camp. The system of well-trained local garrisons attached to individual commanders certainly had disadvantages due to their uncoordinated dispersion along the borderline but countered attacks in geographically limited areas by means of effective measures of defense.[21] Once these units had been dissolved and the frontier zone remained unprotected, Romanos IV's new forces could hardly cope with incursions carried out simultaneously at different and frequently very distant points in the borderland. Operations of the main army or individual detachments at certain key points in the border zone brought some relief to areas heavily afflicted by hostile raids or allowed the empire to recover lost positions but were no substitute for a comprehensive defensive screen covering the entire frontier zone. It comes as no surprise therefore that in spite of some partial successes achieved by Romanos IV's expeditions, Turkish warrior groups at the same time made their most far-reaching advances into the interior of Asia Minor.[22]

The Byzantine campaign of 1068

Unlike Michael Psellos, who totally rejects the emperor's military endeavors as being ill-prepared and condemned to failure,[23] Michael Attaleiates, despite his critical stance towards Romanos' election, expresses a positive view of his attempts to reorganize the armed forces. The author especially underlines the firm determination of the emperor, who within two months of his accession to the throne crossed over to the Anatolian coast and within another three months made all necessary preparations for a large-scale expedition to the East.[24] The units that reportedly formed the core of the new army were the palace guard, "western troops," i.e., soldiers transferred from the Balkan provinces, "Scythians," i.e., Pechenegs or other Turkic nomadic groups settling in the Danube region, Frankish and Armenian mercenaries, troops from Cappadocia, i.e., soldiers from Romanos' homeland who were thus perhaps especially devoted to the new emperor, and the *tagmata*, a term that at the time in question seems to have designated the regular core units of the eastern districts. The latter are said to have joined the imperial army during its march through Bithynia and Phrygia.[25] It is virtually impossible to arrive at safe conclusions regarding the size of the newly mustered troops or their numerical relation with pre-existing units. John Haldon estimates the size of the field army marching to Manzikert at 30,000–40,000 soldiers, but these figures depend on numerous unknown variables and thus may have to be adjusted considerably downwards or upwards.[26]

A crucial problem in Attaleiates' view was the deplorable condition of the *tagmata*, which as a result of the incessant Turkish attacks and the lack of regular salary payments were worn out, impoverished, and deprived of equipment and horses.[27] Serious efforts were made to remedy these deficiencies through the enrollment of "young people from all provinces and towns," but the situation was insufficiently improved by new recruits who lacked the necessary training and experience to face strong enemy forces well-versed in battles. The imperial army, therefore, unfolded only a part of its potential and manifested signs of weakness and lack of cohesion in precarious situations. As will be shown below, however, serious problems putting at risk the objectives of the campaigns or the military strength of the army in most cases occurred not because of the soldiers' failure to fulfill their tasks but because of tensions within the imperial headquarters. In spite of all disdainful comments, Attaleiates readily admits that the emperor actually did assemble combat-capable forces and even inspired fear in the enemies, who noticed the fresh fighting spirit of the new man in power.[28]

Thanks to Attaleiates' detailed report, which can be complemented with additional evidence from Muslim and Eastern Christian sources, the strategy and itinerary of the imperial army during Romanos IV's campaigns can be accurately re-constructed.[29] The first expedition between March and late December 1068 falls into two distinct stages, namely the re-organization of the troops in the Anatolian provinces followed by a number of defensive operations in the hinterland of the frontier's central section between the Halys basin and the Euphrates and from early October onwards the invasion into northern Syria culminating in the conquests of Manbij and Artāḥ. Attaleiates' description of the military situation clearly implies that at that time the empire's eastern territories were mainly threatened by two invasion routes: northern from Azerbaijan and the Armenian highlands through the Araxes and Arsanias Valleys to the Upper Euphrates region and southern leading through the Diyār Bakr province, Edessa, and the emirate of Aleppo to the ducate of Antioch and Cilicia. The reference to "the sultan's withdrawal" apparently has to be understood as the departure of the Seljuk army from the Caucasus region, which chronologically coincided with the advance of the Byzantine army. Accordingly, the sultan's leaving behind a large detachment divided into a northern and a southern unit in all likelihood means that troops were stationed in the territories close to the northern part of the frontier zone while other Turkish warlords continued their activities in the region between Edessa and the Amanus Mountains. Although the situation in the northern section was still highly precarious, as later attempts of the Byzantines to regain strongholds in the Arsanias Valley clearly demonstrate, the main focus of the Seljuk attacks in 1068 obviously shifted to the southern section. This explains why the imperial army at a rather early stage deviated from its original route towards Sebasteia and Koloneia, marching to Lykandos west of Melitene in order to spend the hot summer months there before invading Syria.[30]

At this juncture, the weakness of the imperial government's defensive strategy became palpable: the Turks while retreating before the main body of the army chose new targets, bypassing the enemy forces. Thus, an unexpected attack on the city of Neokaisareia (Niksar) took place, which at that time formed the westernmost advance of Turkish warriors in the region of the Lykos River (Kelkit Nehri).[31] The emperor reacted by marching back to Sebasteia, where he left the baggage train and infantry forces under the command of Andronikos Doukas, whilst he himself along with the cavalry troops headed through the mountains towards Tephrike (Divriği). There he managed to trap the raiders returning from Neokaisareia, killing a great number of them, taking their booty, and releasing the captives.[32] Although the incident ended with a successful strike of the imperial troops, it must have been highly alarming to have hostile forces intrude so deeply into the Byzantine *thema* of Koloneia while the imperial army was deployed in central Cappadocia.

Another problematic issue was the personal incompetence of commanders charged with the defense of crucial positions. A case in point is a considerable detachment of troops including Frankish mercenaries that was left by the emperor in Melitene to watch over the frontier districts and fend off Afshīn's (Ausinalios') forces while he continued his march southward. According to Attaleiates, serious troubles arose from the "faint-heartedness," "fear," and "unwillingness to fight" of an anonymous commander (*syntagmatarches*), who despite the support of "belligerent and bloodthirsty" Frankish soldiers and his subordinates' summons to take action was not willing to check the enemies' activities. In this way he further weakened the advancing imperial troops instead of covering their rear. The garrison's passive stance enabled the Turks to pursue the Byzantine army through hidden places and attack a detachment that had left the camp to buy grain. Once again it was only the immediate reaction of the emperor that saved these soldiers from heavy losses.[33]

Even more disastrous were the results of a new expedition, which took place under the command of Afshīn in the late autumn of 1068, while the imperial army was returning from their Syrian campaign. In an unprecedented move, the Turkish raiders proceeded along the southern invasion route as far as Amorion (Hisar near Emirdağ), the old capital of the Anatolikon theme in Phrygia south of the Sangarios Valley (Sakarya Nehri). At that time, the troops stationed in Melitene had occupied a new position in a stronghold near Tzamandos east of Kaisareia, obviously in order to provide better protection to this important urban center in Cappadocia. Once again the aforementioned commander refused to take action against the enemies, thus allowing them to invade Phrygia and to return unhindered, forcing local Byzantine units to retreat.[34] Interestingly, this expedition seems to have made a deep impression on Muslim contemporaries as well, for it is also recorded in a number of eastern sources. In particular, Sibṭ b. al-Jawzī relates the case of a Byzantine dignitary who helped Afshīn seize the city of Amorion in revenge for the imprisonment of his brother called "the patrician" (*al-biṭrīq*). Another legendary account cited by Bar Hebraeus even mentions an advance as far as the Propontis and a crossing over to Macedonia.[35] Studies based on the finds of the Amorion excavation campaigns of the 1990s and early 2000s repeatedly emphasize that the city in the later part of the eleventh century seems to have been largely abandoned by its former inhabitants. This development is usually ascribed to the 1068 campaign or to the subsequent influx of Turks resulting from the battle of Manzikert in 1071.[36] The image thus evoked is in line with the classical notion of decay from a flourishing urban center to a deserted place, which in contrast to other central Anatolian cities did not develop into a new Turkish-Muslim center. In contrast to the Abbasid conquest of 838, however, there are no archaeological traces of destruction that can be related to this period, and finds of coins of Romanos IV and Michael VII and a lead seal of Nikephoros Melissenos make plain that 1068 brought no immediate disruption to local administrative structures.[37]

All in all, Romanos IV's army during its 1068 campaign was obviously unable to sufficiently safeguard the eastern access routes to Cappadocia and the Anatolian plateau from invaders coming from the Armenian highlands or the Euphrates frontier. This is partly due to strategic decisions giving preference to the Lykandos district and the southern section of the borderland and partly to the personal failure of certain commanders. As the officer responsible for the disasters in the Melitene region remains anonymous, it is not possible to elucidate the background of this curious behavior. Probably, Attaleiates exaggerated or deliberately concealed certain facts by putting the blame on one specific person. Nevertheless, the forbearance of the emperor, who refrained from removing the commander from his post, may point to close personal ties or problems resulting from his antagonism with the Doukas clan.

The encampment of the emperor's main forces in Lykandos until the end of the summer period was certainly dictated by logistical considerations. The disaster of his namesake Romanos III's summer attack on Aleppo in 1030 must have been a lesson on subsequent expeditions in hot and waterless regions.[38] In order to avoid famine and diseases, tolerable temperatures and sufficient water supply were indispensable pre-conditions for campaigning in such areas. This is to say that for several months the emperor's forces were assembled in the region between the Upper Pyramos/Jayḥān Valley and the Euphrates, thus putting a halt to attacks against Antioch and Cilicia but at the same time neglecting the defense of the northern districts around Sebasteia and Koloneia. The forced march to Sebasteia in late September was occasioned by the retreat of the enemies coming back from Neokaisareia but did not form part of a consistent defensive strategy.[39] In other words, the highly dispersed nature of the Turkish raids conducted by small and mobile groups operating simultaneously and independently from each other in different regions was decisive in facilitating the Turkish penetration of the heartlands of Byzantine Asia Minor. Expeditions of a single army, however large it may have been, could bring temporary relief, but they were unable to restore the empire's dominant position in the region.

As regards the sequence of events during the Syrian campaign, the imperial forces on 4 October 1068 set off from Sebasteia heading via Koukousos (Göksun), Germanikeia/Marʿash, and Telouch/Dulūk to Aleppo. Instead of besieging the capital of the Mirdāsid emirate, however, the emperor chose to pillage the rural environs of the city with the aid of his Scythian forces and proceeded after a three-day march to Hierapolis/Manbij.[40] By gaining this stronghold near the western bank of the Euphrates, Romanos IV apparently intended to cut the lines of communication between the emirate and the forces of Ibn Khān, on the one hand, and Turkish warriors in the Marwānid territories of the Diyār Bakr province and the Armenian lands, on the other. Having control over Manbij thus brought great advantages, which in turn explain why the imperial forces, the local Arab garrison, and the emir of Aleppo fought so fiercely for possession of this place. The Byzantines first seized the town and several towers of the ramparts kept by isolated detachments and, after bombarding the acropolis from all sides with catapults, achieved the citadel's surrender in exchange for guarantees of safety for the defenders.[41]

A joint attack of Emir Maḥmūd of Aleppo and the Turkmen warriors of Ibn Khān resulted in a defeat of the Byzantine units defending the area between the army's camp and the town. In view of an imminent assault against the camp, the emperor on 20 November made a sortie, putting the enemy forces to flight. On establishing a strong garrison under the command of an Armenian officer in Manbij, the imperial army marched to Aʿzāz. Unable to besiege the town because of its strong ramparts and the lack of water supplies, the troops continued their march in a southwesterly direction along the Nahr ʿAfrīn Valley towards Byzantine territory, burning down the village of Katma (Qatma) and fending off another attack of Muslim troops at a place near the Terchalas River.[42]

Crossing the border to the ducate of Antioch, the emperor expelled the Arab garrison from the fortress of Artāḥ, which as recently as 1 July 1068 had been conquered by Ibn Khān on behalf of the emir of Aleppo. The sources stress the importance of this place as it offered protection to a great number of people living in the surroundings and was situated on vital routes connecting the Euphrates and the Orontes Valleys as well as Apameia and Antioch.[43] Despite the cold weather in December 1068, the imperial army would not spend the winter near Antioch, the rural areas of which were heavily destroyed because of the Turkish raids and thus unable to provide sufficient foodstuff for such a great number of people. Therefore, the army went forth to Alexandrona (Iskenderun) in Cilicia and crossed the defiles of the Taurus Mountains, reaching the *kleisoura* of Podandos in late December. In January 1069 Romanos IV and the palace guard arrived in Constantinople.[44]

Attaleiates both praises and criticizes the emperor's actions during this second part of the 1068 campaign and, in his capacity as an eyewitness, is able to make valuable remarks on the overall situation in the areas affected by the Turkish raids. His judgments give the impression that the area around Antioch and the borderland vis-à-vis Aleppo had suffered serious devastations, leading to a disastrous decay of agricultural production and a dislocation of the rural population.[45] The image of an exhausted area deprived of its inhabitants and food supplies in conjunction with an administrative system reduced to some small and isolated garrisons can certainly be accepted as reflecting the immediate outcome of the 1067 and 1068 raids. Nevertheless, the description should not be generalized as depicting the overall situation of the eastern borderlands at the time of the Seljuk invasions. Because of their small size and fighting techniques based on quick surprise attacks, Turkish warrior groups unfolded their destructive force only within a limited range of action in the vicinity of main roads, agricultural zones, and urban centers. Likewise, it should be kept in mind that these descriptions constitute snapshots of the situation immediately after the raids and do not necessarily reflect long-term conditions. At the time of its conquest by Sulaymān b. Qutlumush in late 1084, Antioch still appears as a thriving and densely populated urban center.[46] The same applies to many other towns and territories in Asia Minor, which are repeatedly referred to as targets of raids, such as Sebasteia, Melitene, and Edessa. The destructions do not appear to have been of such a scale as to result in irreparable damage to the economic life of the regions in question. Views on the excessive exploitation of territories affected by the conflicts in northern Syria are articulated in the chronicle of Bar Hebraeus, who refers to the severe famine the Turks and the indigenous Arab population had to endure because food supplies had been completely consumed by the imperial troops. Most tellingly, he has an Arab of the Kalb tribe say that undigested grains of barley were found in the stomach of a slain Byzantine soldier.[47] Irrespective of the authenticity of this report, it can be ṣafely assumed that the presence of such a great number of troops unavoidably had more devastating effects than the attacks of small bands of Turkish raiders. The combination of both factors must have had disastrous consequences for both the local population and all parties involved in the conflict.

Attaleiates' criticism regarding the military operations in Syria is directed partly against the conduct and discipline of individual units and partly against certain attitudes and decisions of the emperor. Most of the problems in question occurred during the siege of Manbij, where the imperial army had to face precarious situations resulting from the arrival of relief forces from Aleppo. When the two companies of troops defending the plain between the imperial camp and the ramparts of the city were hard-pressed by attacks, the elite unit of the *scholai* did not intervene in the battle and was eventually itself attacked by the enemy, suffering heavy losses.[48] The Armenian infantry soldiers guarding the front-line trench of the camp during the night were considering desertion, disobeying the orders of their commanders, and thus forced the emperor with his Cappadocian soldiers to leave the city to support the defense of the camp.[49] These phenomena in Attaleiates' view were signs of cowardice, lack of experience, faintness, and deliberate passivity.[50] Interestingly they were not limited to foreign and loosely attached mercenary units but also affected some of the best-trained bodies of the imperial guard like the *scholai*. As it seems unlikely that the latter all of a sudden would be unable to adequately react to an enemy attack, the evidence, in fact, points not only to deficiencies in the army's fighting trim but also to symptoms of insufficient coordination between the emperor and his elite troops and perhaps even to disloyal behavior due to the hidden opposition of the Doukas clan in Constantinople. As in the case of the commander appointed to Melitene, a unit of outstanding importance for the army's military strength refused to take action at a crucial juncture. In this respect, it is highly indicative of the situation that the emperor placed all his confidence in his Cappadocian soldiers,[51] who obviously formed part of his Anatolian network of clients and supporters and were not influenced by the powerful Constantinopolitan circles.

Another aspect of Attaleiates' criticism refers to the emperor's decision not to pursue the Arabs fleeing to Aleppo after their defeat on 20 November. This point is in line with a number of similar judgments by the author, who in general tends to favor a more aggressive attitude towards the Turks. In his opinion, an immediate counter-attack exploiting the advantages gained on the battlefield of Manbij could have resulted in the conquest of Aleppo and thus a major blow against the Turkish and Arab enemies in the emirate.[52] It is impossible to verify the probability of these estimations made with the benefit of hindsight. Romanos IV's reluctance to continue to fight with the fleeing enemies far away from the main army's baggage train and camp could also be accounted for by previous experience concerning the Turkish strategy of feint retreats drawing the pursuing troops into dangerous ambushes. From this point of view, the emperor's judgment, just as the decision to wait in Cappadocia until the end of the hot summer period, shows great caution and tactical prudence. While Attaleiates refers to information gathered later on about the actual weakness of Aleppo's defense after the defeat at Manbij, it would have meant putting at risk the whole army had the emperor ordered the attack on Aleppo without having previously gathered reliable intelligence on the enemies' situation.

Apart from strategic considerations, the precarious supply situation should also be taken into account. Attaleiates mentions the "scarcity of grain" caused by previous raids in the region of Antioch as the reason that despite the imminent winter season the army continued its march over the Taurus Mountains back to Asia Minor. The overall picture of "severe famine" or "famine and pestilence" is further confirmed by a number of reports transmitted by eastern authors like Ibn al-Athīr, Ibn al-ʿAdīm, and, as mentioned before, Bar Hebraeus, although it is doubtlessly exaggerated to speak of "3,000 dead horses a day apart from the soldiers," as asserted by the report of an Egyptian ambassador.[53] Apparently, the severe cold of the Taurus Mountains in late December was considered less a strain than the fatal consequences, which would have befallen inhabitants and soldiers alike had the army decided to spend the winter in the already exhausted regions of the ducate of Antioch. Attaleiates' criticism, thus, may have been reasonable from a purely military point of view, but it was not fully justified in light of the overall circumstances.

Northern Syria after the emperor's retreat, 1069–70

After the departure of the imperial army from northern Syria, the conflicts continued at a local level. This becomes apparent from a report of Ibn al-ʿAdīm, who refers to the conquest of the fortress Asfūnā situated in the vicinity of Maʿarrat al-Nuʿmān by troops under the command of the *doux* of Antioch Khatatourios on 26 May 1069. This assault approximately coincides with Romanos IV's march towards Cappadocia in the early stage of his second campaign in the Euphrates region, but there was hardly any connection between the two events. It is most likely due to the increasing pressure of Turkish warriors marauding in the region that the fortress in the years 1067–68 had changed masters twice. First, the local lord Ḥusayn b. Kāmil b. al-Dawḥ handed it over to Fatimid officials because of Turkish raids ravaging his domains and, subsequently, when the attacks of Afshīn began, the Fatimid commander passed it on to Emir Maḥmūd, who in turn appointed a member of the Munqidh clan as governor.[54] This certainly points to the stronghold's strategic significance, and it may well be that after the conquest of Artāḥ and Manbij the local Byzantine commanders sought to strengthen their military presence within the territories of the emirate of Aleppo. According to our Muslim source, however, it was in retaliation for harassments afflicted upon the *doux* by a group of Banū Rabīʿ Arabs that he seized the fortress, killed about 80 men of the garrison commanded by a Turk called Nādir, and took the rest of the inhabitants captive.[55] Emir Maḥmūd of Aleppo, the same account reports, immediately launched a counter-strike with a great number of Turkish and Arab soldiers, re-taking the fortress and killing 2,700 men in revenge. Subsequently, it seems that neither side was interested in a further escalation of the conflict, thus arriving at a peace agreement providing that in exchange for a sum of 14,000 dinars to be paid by the Byzantines the emir would give his son Naṣr as a hostage and destroy Asfūnā. This was carried out with the help of the people from the nearby towns of Maʿarrat al-Nuʿmān and Kafarṭāb.[56]

Despite this agreement the region showed no signs of stabilization, for in the same year 1069 Aleppo witnessed a violent confrontation between the inhabitants of the city and a band of Turkish allies, and in late October/November a new group of Turkish invaders under the command of a certain Ṣunduq al-Turkī arriving from Byzantine territory made their appearance.[57] We do not know any further details on the identity and origin of these warriors, but they appear to have formed an especially strong force. For within a few weeks they managed to proceed from Aleppo in a southerly direction via Maʿarrat al-Nuʿmān and Kafarṭāb as far as the central Syrian towns of Ḥamāh, Ḥimṣ, and Rafaniyya, where they spent the winter pillaging domains, taking captives, and plundering grain storehouses. According to Ibn al-ʿAdīm, they were the first Turks to raid (central) Syria, and the people suffered great damage from them. Although they were obviously unable to threaten fortified urban centers, Emir Maḥmūd was anxious to avoid an open conflict with them, appeasing them and demonstrating his respect by bestowing gifts upon them before they returned to Byzantine territory.[58] Unfortunately, the source fails to record where exactly Ṣunduq's Turks were heading for, but it is in any case noteworthy that only a few months after the imperial army had left northern Syria there seems to have been no serious barrier preventing Turkish warriors from passing through Cilicia or the Euphrates region into the Byzantine frontier zone. The conquest of Manbij and other strongholds in the region in all likelihood did not lead to any strengthening of the Byzantine defense system.

Within a short period of time, Emir Maḥmūd was to face a much greater threat posed by the arrival of the army of the Seljuk sultan Alp Arslān and his claims to sovereignty over the whole emirate. According to an account transmitted by Sibṭ

b. al-Jawzī, it was the Byzantine conquest of Manbij that prompted the sultan to set off from Hamadhān, launching a new campaign into the Byzantine borderlands.[59] This is certainly an over-simplified presentation of Alp Arslān's political ambitions, but at least it shows that putting an end to the Byzantine presence in the Muslim territories of Syria and placing the entire frontier zone under immediate Seljuk control, no doubt, was a goal of high priority in the sultan's strategy. It is remarkable that in the framework of the tactical considerations brought forward in favor of a breaking off of the 1069 campaign, Attaleiates refers to a major attack of the sultan that was to take place in the following year.[60] This demonstrates that the imperial government had a rather clear idea of the situation in the Seljuk camp. The emperor and his advisers were aware of the pending threat of a large-scale military intervention of the Seljuk army.

Romanos IV's second eastern campaign, 1069

The following years, 1069 and 1070, despite a number of expeditions led by either the emperor in person or his leading commanders, brought about the definitive breakdown of the Byzantine defense system in the Upper Euphrates region and the Anti-Taurus Mountains. The failure of the detachments stationed in the region between Melitene and Tzamandos to put a halt to the Turkish incursions gave rise to a significant increase of hostile activities. The collapse of the Byzantine military structures was further accelerated by the revolt of Crispin (Krispinos), a mercenary commander from Italy, who like Frangopoulos in the 1050s felt insufficiently rewarded by the imperial government for his services. Hence, his soldiers, who prior to the main army's departure in early 1069 had been sent to secure sections of the *Armenika themata*, i.e., the districts of Koloneia, Sebasteia, and Amaseia, began to rob tax collectors and other officials. The local military units and even five western *tagmata* under the command of the *vestarches* Samuel Alousianos failed to suppress their riots. When Emperor Romanos IV shortly after Easter (12 April) 1069 came with his troops to Dorylaion, Crispin eventually gave in, sending emissaries asking for forgiveness and declaring his submission in a personal meeting with the emperor. Crispin's collaboration with the imperial troops, however, did not last for long and, as soon as new accusations of treason were leveled against him, he withdrew to his soldiers in Koloneia, where he resumed his raids into the Euphrates region.[61] Besides the internal tensions among the opposing factions in the imperial high command, which in turn may have influenced the demeanor of certain commanders in the frontier zone, Crispin's recalcitrant soldiers stand for another element of unrest within the imperial army. Like Frankopoulos, Crispin, too, swiftly turned into a marauding troublemaker, who on the basis of his military force defied the central government, extracted revenue, and established rudimentary forms of regional authority within a certain radius of action. No doubt, these activities contributed to a further weakening of the imperial forces and the remnants of the central administration. A few years later, these developments were to be continued by people like Roussel de Bailleul and Philaretos Brachamios.[62]

Considering the various operations of this second campaign, one gets the impression that the emperor was certainly taking pains to re-stabilize sections of the frontier zone, but in contrast to the Syrian expedition of the previous autumn, he was no longer able to take the initiative for an offensive strike against the enemies. The troops spent the greatest part of the expedition pursuing invading enemies or warding off their attacks in the area between Melitene and the northernmost branch of the Euphrates Valley. Romanos IV once more chose Cappadocia as the starting point of his expedition, proceeding from Kaisareia to Larissa. There he encountered a strong gathering of Turkmen forces pillaging the countryside. Attacks on the imperial camp could be successfully fended off and the Turks were put to flight. The Byzantine army chased them as far as the banks of the Euphrates near Melitene, where the emperor first decided to leave a detachment guarding the river valley and to break off the pursuit in order to gather additional forces to face a new invasion of the sultan's army expected for the following year.[63] Attaleiates credits the speech he made to an assembly of the army judges to the emperor's change of plan in favor of an eastward advance towards Chleat/Khilāṭ (Ahlat) situated on the northern shore of Lake Van. Being a key stronghold controlling access to the Arsanias Valley and the land of Taron, the city was to be seized in order to prevent the Turks from launching their invasions along this route towards the Euphrates region and Melitene.[64] For reasons not sufficiently clarified by Attaleiates, the emperor again changed his mind while proceeding towards Romanoupolis (Bingöl). He divided his army, leaving the stronger part on the spot under the command of the Armenian officer Philaretos, whereas the remaining troops headed northwestward via the district of Khanzit and the Mouzouron Mountains (Munzur Dağları) to the province of Keltzene/Ekełeacʻ around Erzincan.[65]

This move proved to be a major mistake, for the Turks immediately grasped the opportunity to attack the isolated troops of Philaretos, inflicting a heavy defeat upon them. Pursued by the Turks as far as Khanzit, the survivors fled in panic towards the imperial camp in Keltzene. On account of the difficult conditions in the Taurus Mountains, the Turks refrained from further pursuing the defeated Byzantines and continued their march westward, crossing the Euphrates north of Melitene and advancing through Cappadocia as far as Konya, the provincial center of Lycaonia.[66] When news about this dangerous attack reached the Byzantine army marching along the northern route to Koloneia and Sebasteia, the emperor, accompanied only by the quickest units of his cavalry forces, made a breath-taking advance through Cappadocia to Herakleia (Ereğli) situated west of the Cilician Gates. By the time he arrived, the Turks had already destroyed Konya and in fear of the approaching Byzantine forces had retreated to the Taurus Mountains, hoping to escape through the plains of Cilicia to the Muslim territories of Aleppo. In the defiles around Seleukeia (Silifke) they were trapped by Armenian soldiers, thus losing all their booty. Simultaneously, the emperor dispatched a detachment of the *tagmata* in support of the *doux* Khatatourios of Antioch in order to ambush the returning Turks in the region of Mamistra in Cilicia. The Byzantine forces, however, once more failed to fulfill their task, and thus the surviving raiders escaped unharmed. According to Attaleiates, this was another lost opportunity for a great victory causing much disappointment to the emperor, who because of the approaching winter season decided to return to Constantinople.[67]

As a whole, Romanos IV's second expedition did not reverse the situation prevailing in the late 1060s. Despite some minor successes of the Byzantine army, such as the victory in the region of Larissa and the seizure of the baggage train of the warriors returning from Konya, the Turks continued to dominate the main invasion routes and, above all, managed to strengthen their control over the Arsanias Valley and the Upper Euphrates region around Melitene. Although there were still no signs of an actual occupation of the area, the presence of Turkish groups moving freely between the Armenian provinces of Vaspurakan and Taron, the Diyār Bakr province south of the Anti-Taurus Mountains, and the Euphrates Valley becomes increasingly stronger. The rumor according to which "a gathering of Turks larger than ever before was pillaging the region" of eastern Cappadocia[68] is indicative of the precarious situation and can be taken literally, given the fact that the defensive measures of the previous year at the banks of the Euphrates had completely failed.

As indicated above, Attaleiates does not explain why the advance to Chleat/Khilāṭ was broken off. He ascribes the defeat of Philaretos' units implicitly to the personal deficiencies of this officer, who is presented as experienced but unsuccessful in major battles and highly ambitious, and to the demoralized condition of the Byzantine soldiers exhausted by the enemy's assaults and deceptive maneuvers.[69] The greater part of the higher officers' reluctance to take action and the emperor's sudden change of course seem to suggest that the situation east of the Euphrates was actually out of control, and thus a further advance would have entailed too great a risk for the army's security. If this is the case, it may be safely assumed that the forces left behind were simply too weak to resist the Turks' superior military power. Philaretos' future career as semi-independent potentate from the time of the Byzantine civil strife in the 1070s onwards requires us to be cautious in accepting Attaleiates' negative comments on this man's military abilities.[70] The imperial army, thus, was forced to evacuate the region of Khanzit, which is described as especially fertile, well watered, and therefore suitable for the encampment of large military units.[71] The region of Keltzene, instead, because of its well-protected position north of the Mouzouron Mountains and the banks of the Euphrates,[72] could easily be defended against the Turks coming from the south and thus served as a rallying point and temporary base of the imperial army. The same applied to the region of Melitene before the army's eastward advance,[73] but once the Byzantine forces withdrew in a northerly direction, the Turks bypassed it without meeting any obstacles.

Crispin's revolt certainly caused a further weakening of the defensive structures in the East. Despite the stereotype of the vile and unfaithful Frank, which figures prominently in this text as well,[74] Attaleiates primarily blames the emperor for not exerting every effort to win over the Frankish commander "who had accomplished great exploits when he encountered a large crowd of Turks," rather than expelling him merely on the grounds of unproven accusations. Thus, he not only lost a capable commander but also provoked Crispin's soldiers to make raids in the Upper Euphrates region south of Koloneia.[75]

It cannot be verified whether Attaleiates' speech in the assembly of the military judges actually renders the words spoken on this occasion or is a retrospective assessment of the situation and the steps that could have been taken at that time. His criticism of the emperor's decision not to immediately pursue the Turks fleeing from Cappadocia across the Euphrates[76] is in line with his judgments during the 1068 campaign and generally reflects Attaleiates' preference for a more aggressive attitude towards the enemies. Proceeding to Chleat/Khilāṭ and conquering it along with other towns in its vicinity, he argued, would have raised the fighting spirit of the imperial troops because of the rich booty to be gained there and would have prevented the enemy from undertaking further raids through Mesopotamia. His reasoning, no doubt, is convincing, but in view of the serious pressure the invaders exerted on the Byzantine troops west of the Euphrates, it seems overly optimistic to assume that the imperial army would have been able to proceed so far.[77]

Equally remarkable are his reflections on the psychological dimension of warfare: not pursuing the enemy makes the latter lose his fear and encourages him to continue his attacks. Slight setbacks do not seriously harm the enemy, and thus he easily recovers. This, in turn, may have negative results for the morale of the Byzantine troops stationed in the borderland, far away from the main body of the army.

> The more cowardice has overcome the Romans, the more boldness will dominate those people [i.e., the enemies] and they will easily be superior to us, because the Romans are already terrified and thus they are able to bear the vision of the enemy only when they see the bravery of the ruler being on their side. And if they [i.e., the Turks] put them to flight, an inescapable danger will threaten us, for the Turks certainly will not omit to attack us and win a glorious victory, finding us isolated and dispersed because of our eagerness to return home.[78]

In this passage, the author summarizes the basic principles of his belief in an offensive strategy against the Turkish threat. An aggressive attitude based on incessant counter-attacks and decisive victories over the enemy forces in the long run weakens the adversary's belligerent spirit. In contrast, a passive stance limited to the fending off of invasions and the protection of the local population fails to inflict serious blows on the enemy and, as a result, prompts him to intensify his destructive raids on Byzantine soil, bringing about an ever-increasing threat to the very foundations of the Byzantine Empire.

This assessment in short explains the reasons for the Byzantine army's failure to meet the challenges posed by the Turkish raids during the 1050s and 1060s, as seen through the eyes of a contemporary eyewitness. The question is whether the conditions of the frontier zone and the imperial army under Romanos IV would have actually permitted to adopt a more aggressive strategy than that followed by the emperor. Inadequate control over the main invasion routes in the eastern provinces and a serious lack of cohesion among the commanders, be they members of the ruling elite or foreign mercenaries, seriously restricted the emperor's freedom of action and the army's ability as a fighting force, rendering Attaleiates' advice nothing but a pious hope. The frequent references to the Byzantine soldiers' fear and their leaders' disappointment at the outcome of individual operations are highly indicative of a loss of morale. The emperor failed to build up an effective defensive line along the upper course of the Euphrates between Melitene and Keltzene. The troops of Antioch did not prevent Turkish invaders from crossing the Taurus Mountains and the plain of Cilicia. As a result, the Turks were able to successfully continue their new strategy of long-distant raids, deeply penetrating the interior of the central Anatolian plateau. With the attacks on Amorion in 1068 and Konya in 1069 the Turks for the first time had the opportunity to explore the western fringes of the Anatolian plateau south of the Sangarios River and east of Lake Busguse (Beyşehir Gölü), territories that in the decades after the First Crusade were to become sensitive contact and conflict zones between Byzantium and the Seljuk Sultanate of Konya.

Intra-dynastic conflicts and Byzantine-Seljuk diplomacy around 1070

In about 1070, the Seljuk sultan, for the first time, was in a position not only to negotiate with the Byzantine emperor about territorial concessions and tributes but also to lay claims to the control of Turkish warrior groups operating in the interior of Asia Minor. In this way, attacks on Byzantine territory could be justified on the basis of the sultan's legitimate rights to exert authority over his subjects. This brought about a significant change of Seljuk attitudes towards Byzantium, for henceforth the eastern provinces of the empire were to be conceived of as territories over which the sultan aspired to exert more substantial control. It is this change of attitude that later on formed the basis for legitimation strategies referring to the Seljuk sultanate as supreme authority conferring rights of sovereignty to subordinate governors in its realm. Seditious members of the Seljuk dynasty and Turkish warlords, who in the decades after Manzikert made their appearance in the eastern borderlands, were frequently presented in later historiographical works as being officially appointed by the sultan or even the caliph of Baghdad.[79] These are obviously fictitious reconstructions offering a kind of raison d'être for political entities of obscure and doubtful origin, but they also stand for a gradual intensification of claims to territories, which originally were outside the Muslim world and the Seljuk sphere of influence. The point of departure for this development was an encounter between the Byzantine supreme commander in the East and a rebellious brother-in-law of the sultan, an event that, in turn, caused the violent reaction of Alp Arslān.

In the spring of 1070, Emperor Romanos IV bestowed the title of *kouropalates* upon the *protoproedros* Manuel Komnenos, appointing him general commander of the army.[80] In this way, the future emperor Alexios' elder brother gained the most influential position in the imperial army after the emperor, and, after 10 years of marginalization since the overthrow of Isaac I in 1059, the Komnenoi clan once again entered the innermost circle of power.[81] With this decision, Romanos IV seemingly intended to create a counter-weight to the almighty Doukas clan and their allies, who had repeatedly tried to undermine his authority by causing troubles during the emperor's previous campaigns in the East. Romanos was in urgent need of a capable and staunch commander, who differed from the hesitant and feeble officers he had previously appointed to command posts in the Euphrates region. We should be cautious in accepting Attaleiates' assertion that the emperor was seized by envy at the first positive results of Manuel's activities in Kaisareia and for this reason deliberately weakened the general's forces by sending a strong detachment to Hierapolis in Syria.[82] In fact, as has been shown in the previous section,[83] the entire region of the emirate of Aleppo faced various threats, and it was only a matter of time before the sultan's army would reach the banks of the Euphrates River. In August/September 1070, it had begun its campaign with the conquest of Arjīsh and Manzikert north of Lake Van. In view of this attack, which had been expected by the imperial headquarters since the previous year, it was certainly a wise decision to transfer a part of the forces from Cappadocia to this exposed stronghold not far from the river's left bank.[84]

As regards the Seljuk ruling house, there was a serious intra-dynastic problem that came to the fore in the early stage of the sultan's Syrian campaign. This was the revolt of Alp Arslān's brother-in-law Arīsghī, who in Byzantine texts appears as Chrysoskoulos and according to modern Turkish scholars was originally called El-basan/Erbasgan. We have no information about the background of this discord, but as husband of the sultan's sister Jawhar Khātūn, he certainly represented a threat to the dynasty's internal stability. As a result of Alp Arslān's operations in the frontier zone, the rebel had no choice but to retreat with his Turkmen warriors to the interior of Anatolia towards Cappadocia, where he bumped into the forces of Manuel Komnenos in the vicinity of Sebasteia. Byzantine and Muslim sources give detailed reports of this encounter, Manuel's defeat and capture, and the subsequent alliance between the two commanders.[85] In the Muslim version, Arīsghī appears as unwilling to fight and primarily interested in finding a place of refuge from his pursuers. To this effect, he reportedly sent a message to Manuel and even took an oath of fidelity, but the Byzantine general refused to believe him and thus a battle was fought.[86] The Byzantine accounts agree with the Muslim historians in that at first Arīsghī offered his captive for ransom against a huge amount of money. But in view of the approaching troops of Afshīn, who had been sent by the sultan to pursue him, he came to an agreement with his prisoner, setting off with him for Constantinople. There he was accommodated in the house of the Komnenos family until he was granted an audience in the imperial palace, which took place in the Chrysotriklinos in the presence of the emperor and the senate. Most probably because of the refugee's close relation to the sultan, the emperor bestowed the outstanding title of *proedros* upon him. As it was the first time that the imperial government was directly involved in an intra-dynastic conflict of the Seljuk sultanate, this meeting provided a good occasion to celebrate Byzantium's superiority by including a high-ranking Seljuk nobleman into the ranks of the imperial court officials. Thus, he was transformed from a barbarian Scythian to a Roman dignitary.[87] Drawing on the same motif, Bryennios underlined the persuasiveness of Manuel Komnenos, who convinced Chrysoskoulos/Arīsghī that only with the emperor's support would he be able to succeed in his enterprise against the sultan. Moreover, he emphasized the close friendship between Manuel and the Seljuk refugee, who henceforth served as a loyal commander in the Byzantine army.[88]

The presence of Afshīn and his soldiers on Byzantine soil allows us to assume that the rumors of Arīsghī's transformation into a Byzantine dignitary were quickly spread among his Seljuk kinsmen. According to Sibṭ b. al-Jawzī, on reaching the littoral of the Propontis, Afshīn sent emissaries to the emperor, demanding the extradition of Arīsghī. On this occasion, a Muslim report introduces a new argument into the discourse of Byzantine-Seljuk diplomacy: The Seljuk troops are recorded entering Byzantine territory in search of an enemy of the sultan. Military interventions and a certain degree of influence in Byzantine territory are justified by the sultan's claim to secure seditious subjects, who were granted sanctuary by the imperial government. The emperor allegedly refused to hand over the refugee on the grounds of old Roman custom providing for the protection of people who were granted shelter in the empire.[89] In response, Afshīn looted the country before returning to Chleat/Khilāṭ with huge amounts of booty. Sibṭ b. al-Jawzī's source refers to an advance as far as the Gulf of Constantinople,[90] but this is certainly an exaggeration intended to highlight the *jihad* spirit of the Seljuk warriors. It was on this occasion, however, that the Turkish invaders reached the westernmost point of their incursions in Asia Minor, namely the city of Chonai (Honaz) in the Upper Meander Valley, where the famous church of the Archangel Michael was pillaged and partly destroyed.[91] It seems to be no coincidence that inscription fragments dated to 1070 attest to fortification work in Eumenia (on Lake Işıklı 12 miles south of Çivril) and Sozopolis (Uluborlu) in the southern part of Phrygia. Both fortresses, the latter of which in the twelfth century developed into a major frontier bastion, safeguarded access routes to the Upper Maeander Valley.[92] Apparently, the invasions of 1068 and 1070 for the first time prompted the Byzantine government to strengthen the defensive structures along the western fringes of the Anatolian plateau. Eventually, Arīsghī/Chrysoskoulos remained a capable Byzantine commander and court dignitary, thus strengthening the imperial court's prestige as a pole of attraction for Turkish rebels and apostates. The Seljuk sultan, however, made an impressive demonstration of power from both a military and an ideological point of view.

Seljuk supremacy in the Syrian and Mesopotamian borderland

Sultan Alp Arslān's Syrian campaign of 1070/71, no doubt, brought about profound changes in the political allegiances along the Byzantine-Muslim frontier.[93]

The expedition evidently aimed at extending Seljuk control from the Caucasus region and Azerbaijan to the central and southern section of the borderland in Upper Mesopotamia and northern Syria. During the 1060s, these territories were repeatedly afflicted by raids of Seljuk commanders and Turkish warrior groups. As a result, many of the local potentates had already entered alliances with Turkish chieftains and acknowledged the sultanate's suzerainty, but the overall situation was characterized by incessant conflicts among the local potentates and ongoing raids carried out by uncoordinated bands, which could hardly be subjected to any form of central authority.[94] Hence, the sultan was determined to put an end to this unstable state of affairs by imposing his authority upon these recalcitrant forces and uniting them into a single block dominated by the political and spiritual leadership of the Seljuk sultanate and the Abbasid caliphate.

The prevailing opinion in the secondary literature is that Alp Arslān with this campaign prepared the ground for a major invasion in Fatimid Egypt. From 1062 onwards, the Shiite rival caliphate of Cairo had been trapped in a deep political crisis, which was caused by conflicts between Turkish and Berber army units and was further aggravated by famine and epidemic diseases.[95] Caliph al-Mustanṣir and the officials of the central government were too weak to impose their authority and thus the power in the state passed to the military commanders, among them Nāṣir al-Dawla b. Ḥamdān, a descendant of the renowned Arab dynasty of Aleppo, who had served as governor of Alexandria and Damascus and during the years of unrest became the leader of the Turkish troops and for some time the most powerful man in Egypt.[96] According to an account transmitted by Ibn al-ʿAdīm, it was this man who sent an emissary to Alp Arslān, asking him to send his troops to take possession of Egypt and to re-establish the Abbasid prayer.[97] Although there is no reason to doubt the accuracy of this piece of information, other sources mention other motives for the sultan's Syrian campaign, which were directly related to the situation in the borderlands irrespective of any plans concerning Egypt. The sultan's strategy combined the demonstration of military power with skillful negotiations that sought to reassure the local potentates of the region and draw them into the hierarchy of the Seljuk state.

Before the beginning of the campaign, there were already diplomatic contacts that sought to regulate the status of the emirate of Aleppo.[98] Most probably in view of the principality's internal weakness and the various external threats, in June/July 1070 Emir Maḥmūd sent an embassy to Alp Arslān, announcing his intention to accept Seljuk suzerainty and to establish the Abbasid prayer in his city. Ibn al-ʿAdīm's report has the emir explain to the townspeople that the Seljuk sultanate represented a new powerful dynasty, which the emirate had to come to terms with, otherwise it ran the risk of being forced into complete subjugation.[99] After securing the consent of the local sheikhs (*mashāyikh al-balad*), he staged a public ceremony on 31 July 1070, celebrating the introduction of the Abbasid Friday prayer with the muezzins and the imam dressed in the Abbasids' black color and a formula referring to the caliph, the sultan, and the emir. This change of allegiance was obviously rejected by the common people, who protested against the abolition of the Shiite prayer. The emir was ready to use violence against his opponents, but the notables fearing an open revolt dissuaded him from doing so.[100] It becomes clear that from the outset there was serious dissent on the issue of switching allegiance from Fatimid to Abbasid-Seljuk suzerainty.

Despite these tensions, however, at first everything seemed to run smoothly. Caliph al-Qā'im's chief registrar (*naqīb al-nuqabā'*), Abū l-Fawāris Ṭirād b. Muḥammad al-Zaynabī, had been dispatched to Aleppo to make arrangements for the establishment of the prayer and to bestow honorifics, robes of honor, and other insignia upon the emir.[101] Hence, symbols of Abbasid supremacy and legitimation provided a formal framework for incorporating the emirate of Aleppo into the system of Seljuk vassalage. As regards the emir's personal status, Alp Arslān was ready to show the utmost respect to his new ally by exempting him in a letter from all ceremonial acts of submission.[102] In the course of the ensuing campaign, however, the situation changed. While the sultan's army was approaching Aleppo, for reasons not explicitly stated in the sources, a serious estrangement occurred between the emir and the sultan. Apart from the status of Aleppo, however, there were other issues that required settlement in northern Syria. According to one report, the sultan set off for his expedition because the people of Manbij had informed him about the Byzantine conquest of their town.[103] This version most likely over-emphasizes the significance of this fortress, but the danger posed by a further consolidation of the Byzantine position in northern Syria must have been a major concern for the sultan. The conquest of Egypt may have been on Alp Arslān's agenda, but the status of Aleppo, Byzantine influence in the region, and other issues concerning the situation in Upper Mesopotamia were no less important.

As regards the expedition's itinerary, in August/early September 1070 the sultan set off with his army from Hamadhān for the territories north of Lake Van, where he conquered the cities of Arjīsh and Manzikert.[104] From there he headed in a southwesterly direction towards the province of Diyār Bakr and the Marwānid lordship of Mayyāfāriqīn. On securing the submission of Naṣr b. Marwān with the aid of Niẓām al-Mulk, Alp Arslān invaded Byzantine territory, seizing al-Suwaydā', Tulkhum, and other fortresses in the region and pitching camp outside the city of Edessa while detachments of his slave soldiers (*ghilmān*) pillaged the nearby region of Ḥarrān. As the most important outpost of the Byzantine defense system east of the Euphrates, Edessa had to endure especially heavy attacks on its ramparts, but the local *doux* Basil, the son of Alousianos, successfully warded them off. Eventually it was agreed that the siege would be lifted in exchange for a tribute of 50,000 dinars.[105] The Seljuk ruler concluded another agreement on payments with the people of Ḥarrān and moved on to the Euphrates, where on 19 January 1071 the army set up camp in a fertile plain, remaining there until the end of March.[106] This two-month break seems to have been necessitated by both strategic considerations and internal problems in the sultan's army. According to our sources, Alp Arslān expected news from his commander, Afshīn, who in the previous summer had been dispatched on an expedition to Byzantine territory.[107] It may well be that before advancing further west the sultan wanted to ensure that he would be safe from potential Byzantine counter-attacks. In addition, he was faced with the unrest of Iraqi troops, who refused to fight unless they received their overdue salaries.[108] Despite the sums of money extracted from Edessa and Ḥarrān and the huge amounts of booty that must have been collected,[109] Alp Arslān, after four months of campaigning, seems to have faced financial difficulties, which produced expressions of discontent from some of his troops.

The final stage of the expedition, as mentioned above, was marked by an open clash between Alp Arslān and Maḥmūd b. Naṣr of Aleppo. In an attempt to implement the agreements made in the preceding year, the sultan sought to publicly assert his newly gained suzerainty over Aleppo by advancing with his army to the city and summoning the emir to pay him homage. Despite earlier concessions, however, the sultan now insisted that a personal act of submission be performed by the emir in the sultan's camp. This was not acceptable to Maḥmūd b. Naṣr, who along with the local elite had declared allegiance to Abbasid-Seljuk rule but was unwilling to reduce himself to the position of a subordinate governor of the sultan. As neither side was willing to give in, the discord had to be resolved by means of military pressure. In response to the emir's refusal, the Seljuk troops looted the areas around Aleppo and attacked a group of Kilāb Arabs in al-Qaryatayn near Ḥimṣ.[110] After this demonstration of power, the sultan resumed negotiations with Aleppo, but the disobedient emir insisted on his defiant attitude, sending a sum of money as well as his mother and son but being still unwilling to perform a personal submission. Abū Jaʿfar Muḥammad b. Aḥmad al-Bukhārī, an expert in Islamic law who had been appointed judge of Aleppo and had been sent by the sultan as an emissary to the city, unavailingly tried to mediate an agreement between the two sides.[111] As a result, on 3 April 1071 the sultan's army encamped outside the walls of Aleppo and mounted a full-scale attack on the city.[112] Being eventually forced to comply with the sultan's demand,[113] perhaps on 4 May 1071 the emir and his mother al-Sayyida ʿAlawiyya presented themselves at the Seljuk camp. The representatives of Aleppo performed a public act of submission, prostrating themselves before the sultan and handing him the keys of the city. One account even refers to a ritual act of humiliation, the emir's mother taking her son by the hand and presenting him to be judged at the sultan's discretion. In return, the latter treated them with favor and confirmed the emir in his position as ruler of Aleppo on his behalf by handing him robes of honor, gifts, and a decree of appointment. Thereafter the emir was ordered to march along with one of the Seljuk commanders called Ītakīn al-Sulaymānī against Damascus.[114]

Alp Arslān was not interested in replacing the local dynasty with direct Seljuk rule through one of his own commanders, as Malikshāh would do 15 years later in 1086. By that time, the local emirs had largely eliminated each other in internecine struggles, and Seljuk rule was firmly established over most parts of Syria. In 1071, the sultan obviously was not yet in a position to wield power over large urban centers and territorial units in northern Syria and thus had to maintain existing political configurations, as he had done in Armenia and Upper Mesopotamia. The emir's public self-humiliation was a necessary precondition for any compromise and reconciliation. For reasons of public prestige and further consolidation of his authority, Alp Arslān had to appear in the eyes of all parties involved as supreme ruler who deigned to show his favor to the repentant scion of the Mirdāsid family and thus kept the ruling elite of Aleppo in its place. This ritual submission also addressed other Turkish warrior groups who began at that time to penetrate the Syrian provinces. It is clear that from the outset the sultan was determined to claim overlordship over all military powers operating in the region. Soon, this claim was to be extended to the Turks intruding Byzantine territory as well.

The recognition of Seljuk suzerainty by the Mirdāsid dynasty decisively reduced Fatimid influence in northern Syria, while equally importantly Alp Arslān, as a result of this campaign, basically dissolved the Byzantine web of Muslim vassals at the outer range of the frontier zone. The entire defensive system, which during the 1060s had been seriously undermined in various respects, in the months before the battle of Manzikert suffered yet another fatal blow. Alp Arslān had managed to expand his sphere of influence as far as the Orontes River and thus to exert immediate control over the entire southwestern section of the borderlands, while the remaining Byzantine strongholds of Antioch and Edessa were driven into a dangerous state of isolation. The fact that Afshīn in the previous year was able to pillage the city of Chonai in the Meander Valley and to spend the winter season unharmed on Byzantine territory[115] demonstrates that the empire's defensive structures had become more permeable than ever before. Likewise, the fact that Afshīn returned along with his booty straight to Khilāṭ[116] indicates that in about 1070 Turkish invaders were already able to move freely along the entire Arsanias Valley between the crossings of the Euphrates River and Lake Van. Romanos IV's 1071 campaign obviously intended to reverse this situation by cutting the access to the Arsanias Valley through the fortresses north of Lake Van. The battle of Manzikert did not seal the fate of Asia Minor, but it certainly precipitated the definite breakdown of Byzantine control over the southern section of the Armenian highlands.

The battle of Manzikert (26 August 1071) and its aftermath

Three weeks before Alp Arslān and his army reached the outskirts of Aleppo, on 13 March 1071, the feast of Orthodoxy, Romanos IV crossed the straights for his last expedition to the East.[117] The imperial army followed the northern route leading via Dorylaion across the Sangarios River at the bridge *tou Zombou* and across the Halys River into the district of Charsianon. After pitching camp at a fertile place called *Krya Pege* (Cold Spring), the army went forth to Sebasteia and passing the battlefield, where Manuel Komnenos' soldiers slain in the previous year were still lying, reached Koloneia and Theodosioupolis. This town, which had been refortified after the Turkish campaign of 1048, served as a launching point for an attack on Khilāṭ and Manzikert conquered by the Seljuk army in the autumn of 1070.[118] The Muslim accounts largely agree that Alp Arslān on receiving the message of the imperial troops' new campaign accelerated his departure from Aleppo, heading in forced marches across the Euphrates back to Azerbaijan.[119] According to some accounts, he was already in Khoy when he was informed of the emperor's advance towards Khilāṭ.[120]

Given that as a result of his campaign Alp Arslān controlled the entire southern flank of the borderlands between the Diyār Bakr province and Aleppo, the route through Melitene and the Arsanias Valley, which already in 1069 had been hardly accessible, in 1071 must have been totally impassable to the Byzantine troops. This explains why the emperor after reaching Sebasteia decided to proceed on the northern route eastwards, thus evading possible attacks of detachments of the Seljuk army. As explained by Attaleiates in his alleged speech to the emperor during the 1069 campaign, the objective of this expedition was to restore Byzantine control over the main invasion route north of the Anti-Taurus Mountains to the Upper Euphrates Valley through the re-conquest of two places of crucial strategic significance on the northern shore of Lake Van and the eastern bank of the Arsanias River.[121] Had this plan succeeded, the imperial army would have cut communication with Azerbaijan and at the same time prepared the ground for wielding power over the whole region between the Arsanias and the Araxes River west of the cities of Arjīsh, Ani, and Kars, which had already passed under direct Seljuk domination. In the summer of 1071 this area is described as a "land uninhabited and ravaged by the barbarians,"[122] a phrase that points to serious devastation and the permanent presence of Turkish warrior groups moving forward from Azerbaijan.

The Byzantine defeat of Manzikert is ascribed partly to the overall decay of the Byzantine defense system and partly to an act of treason resulting from the internal tensions between the emperor and the Doukas clan. Attaleiates refers to the withdrawal of the *magistros* Joseph Tarchaniotes, commander of the greater part of the imperial army that had been dispatched along with Scythian and Frankish mercenary troops to the siege of Khilāṭ.[123] In first skirmishes with the vanguard of the Seljuk army outside Manzikert, Nikephoros Bryennios was put to flight and Basilakes, *katepano* of Theodosioupolis, was taken captive after pursuing the Turks to their camp. Thereafter, Tarchaniotes reportedly ordered his troops to retreat towards Mesopotamia.[124] In this way, he certainly rescued the greater part of the imperial army from peril but also sealed the defeat of Romanos IV's troops. The motivation for this decision may well have been the commander's concern about the safety of a considerable number of armed forces, for at that moment some 30 miles away from the spot near Manzikert it was not yet foreseeable that so great a section of the imperial army was to be completely routed or that the emperor, instead of retreating or coming to terms with the enemy, would seek a decision in open battle. Thus, from a strategic point of view, Tarchaniotes' withdrawal may well be interpreted as a sign of caution.

An undeniable act of treachery, however, was the rumor about the emperor's death spread by Andronikos Doukas, son of John Doukas and cousin of the future emperor Michael. At the most crucial moment of the battle, when the main body of the army was not aware of the emperor and the vanguard pursuing fleeing Turkish units, this rumor triggered an uncontrollable panic and chaotic flight, during which the greatest part of the soldiers were either slain or captured and the imperial camp together with the entire baggage train seized. Towards evening, after hours of fierce fights, Romanos IV, exhausted, wounded, and deprived of his horse that had been killed by arrows, eventually gave up and surrendered to the enemies.[125]

Andronikos' treachery was made possible by a series of wrong decisions on the part of the emperor, which were due to bad timing and a fatal underestimation of the Seljuk forces. From this point of view, the disaster of Manzikert is to a great extent to be explained as the result of unfortunate coincidences and personal miscalculations. Romanos' decision to divide his army in order to secure control over the fertile areas around Khilāṭ while Manzikert was put under siege was, as Attaleiates himself admits, correct in view of intelligence reports referring to the Seljuk army as being far off, heading to Persia.[126]

The Muslim sources confirm that the greatest part of Alp Arslān's troops together with the sultan's wife, his vizier Niẓām al-Mulk, and the baggage train were sent to Hamadhān, whereas Alp Arslān stayed behind with a force of 4.000 slave soldiers, ordering the vizier to send him reinforcements as soon as possible. In addition, an auxiliary force of Kurdish soldiers from the adjacent emirates gathered in the sultan's camp.[127] Had he continued his way back, the Byzantine army would have achieved its goals, as explicitly noted in Sibṭ b. al-Jawzī's report.[128] Despite the inferior forces being at his disposal, Alp Arslān had no choice but to put up resistance against the emperor's attack in order to prevent him from gaining a firm foothold in the region. Romanos IV's first serious mistake was to assume that the sultan would not dare to attack him or at least would not be able to reach him before his own departure from Manzikert towards his troops in Khilāṭ. Fortuitously for the Seljuk side, Alp Arslān managed to come within reach of Manzikert immediately after the town's surrender, before any efficient coordination with the troops in Khilāṭ could be arranged.[129] Another mistake of Romanos IV was to underestimate the Turks' fighting force and put excessive confidence in his own troops. This attitude led him to reject the peace proposal submitted by the Seljuk emissaries. From a military point of view, his decision is understandable, for in case of an agreement the sultan would have gained an advantageous position, whereas the imperial army would have been forced to give up all the achievements gained during the summer campaign of 1071.[130] Seeking a decision in open battle was the only way to secure and consolidate the recent conquest of Manzikert and the other targets of the campaign. Nevertheless, the haphazard persecution of the feignedly retreating enemy troops in conjunction with the deceitfully spread rumor about the emperor's death brought about the army's ruin.[131]

The eight-day captivity of Romanos IV in the camp of Sultan Alp Arslān, the reconciliation of the two rulers, and the ensuing peace treaty most likely would have put the relations between the Byzantine Empire and the Seljuk sultanate on a new basis of mutual recognition, had the outcome of this encounter been given enough time to yield results. Byzantine and Muslim accounts agree on the main points of this noteworthy event, which is generally imagined as an idealized encounter between a defeated and a victorious ruler.[132] Both figures stand as symbols of outstanding royal virtues, namely repentance and respect for God's almighty power in the case of the emperor and modesty and mercy in the case of the sultan. From the Byzantine point of view, the main focus lies on the fact that the barbarian ruler, although an infidel, demonstrates strong faith in God and therefore is more righteous and merciful than the emperor's internal opponents. Michael Attaleiates portrays the sultan as a symbolic foil to the moral decay of the imperial government before Botaneiates' rise to power. Muslim historians, instead, concentrate on the paradigmatic behavior of Alp Arslān as a champion of *jihad* and model victor, who in spite of his success is fully aware of God's power as the only source of all victories. In striving for the triumph of Islam, he uses his high-ranking captive to stage various symbolic acts and gestures signaling Muslim superiority, but refrains from any kind of personal retaliation or humiliation of his enemy. The Muslim historiographical tradition first and foremost portrays Manzikert as a clash of religions, not as a political conflict of empires and their supreme representatives. It is hard to gauge to what extent these descriptions accurately reflect what happened during the emperor's captivity, but the strong parallels between the Byzantine and Muslim narratives strongly suggest that the original spirit of this encounter with its ritual and ideological aspects must have been quite close to what later historians wrote about it. As regards the terms of the peace treaty, the emperor agreed to pay a considerable amount of money for his release as well as an annual tribute as a token of his recognition of the sultan's supremacy. The sultan, in exchange, contented himself with the restitution of a few important cities that had previously been in Muslim hands; apart from that, he respected the territorial boundaries as they had been before the war. In addition, he undertook the obligation to prevent his subjects, be they soldiers of the regular Seljuk army or Turkmen warriors, from raids into the Byzantine provinces.[133]

For the ruling elite in Constantinople Romanos IV's defeat was the signal for an internal *coup d'état*, in the course of which Empress Eudokia declared her husband dethroned before she herself fell victim to the intrigues of the *kaisar* John Doukas. He forced her to leave the imperial palace and to become a nun in one of her monastic foundations while he proclaimed her son Michael emperor.[134] As a result, the highly fragile unity among the imperial troops, which Romanos IV with much difficulty had managed to preserve during his reign, immediately fell to pieces. The troops abiding by their allegiance to Romanos after his departure from the Seljuk camp consisted of various groups: soldiers who had escaped the battlefield or had been released along with the emperor; newly recruited troops from the villages and towns in the region between Theodosioupolis, Koloneia, and Dokeia (Tokat), where Romanos temporarily established his headquarters; the greatest part of the Frankish mercenaries; a large number of Cappadocian soldiers, who stood under the command of the *proedros* Theodore Halyates and nourished especially strong sentiments of loyalty to Romanos; soldiers from the region of Tyropoion/Trypia, a fortress west of Melitene; the units of the ducate of Antioch under their *doux* Khatatourios, who had been appointed by Romanos; eventually, units from Cilicia. It appears that a considerable part of the eastern forces still sided with Romanos.[135] It is also noteworthy that Turkish warriors never harassed Romanos during the months of civil strife from September 1071 to late June 1072. Seljuk troops actually honored the agreement with the emperor while the latter was putting up resistance against his opponents. If we are to believe Psellos and Attaleiates, he even hoped for support from Turkish auxiliary forces.[136] The places he chose as strongholds were all situated in regions that had already been afflicted by Turkish attacks and were easily accessible to Turkmen warriors. Thus, on abandoning Dokeia he marched to Tyropoion, which was very close to one of the main invasion routes near Melitene.[137] With the aid of the soldiers of Antioch, he moved to Cilicia in order to obtain further reinforcements and to spend the winter there.[138] Romanos IV's last base was the city of Adana,[139] where he eventually decided to surrender.

This itinerary is all the more remarkable in that it was the last time in Byzantine history that an emperor, overthrown and persecuted by a large part of the imperial troops, could move so freely in the eastern territories. None of these regions had come yet under direct Turkish control, and Romanos IV was able to exert his authority, sending out orders, gathering troops, and being well received by the local garrisons. Another new element resulting from the treaty with the sultan was the notion of military support by Turkish forces. Romanos may have never included large numbers of Turkish warriors into his troops, yet it is still significant that the Turkish practice of entering coalitions with local potentates was transferred here to the highest level of bilateral agreements between the Byzantine emperor and the Seljuk sultan. Over the following years, this practice was to become an important tool for establishing collaborations between the imperial government, Byzantine rebels, and Turkish invaders, who eventually came into a position to present themselves as auxiliary troops of the empire.

The new strong men in Constantinople led by John Doukas and his two sons Constantine and Andronikos, who on being appointed to the posts of *strategos autokrator* and *domestikos tes anatoles*, respectively, took over the supreme command of the imperial forces in the east,[140] were supported by troops from the capital, soldiers recruited during their march through the eastern provinces, and the troops of the Norman mercenary leader Crispin, who because of his personal feud with Romanos IV and his dismissal in 1069 sided with his opponents.[141] Attaleiates, however, emphasizes the fact that the new regime had not yet achieved undisputed superiority in the provinces, for the western forces observing their oath taken to the dethroned emperor still kept their loyalty to him. In the historian's eyes, Romanos' failure once again was mainly due to his proclivity for defensive attitudes. Had he opted for an advance through Asia Minor towards Constantinople instead of retreating to Cappadocia and Cilicia, he would have drawn many eastern units to his side, while the western troops would have refused to support the Doukas faction. His withdrawal instead enabled his opponents to strengthen their power by gathering new forces.[142] Yet, even then, had he at least occupied the defiles of the Taurus Mountains giving access to Cilicia, the enemy would not have been able to enter the region through the *kleisoura* of Podandos. "By neglecting this," the author concludes, "the affairs of Diogenes were exposed to great danger."[143]

In this way, Attaleiates completes his portrayal of an emperor, who was credited with military skills and a brave character, making every effort to safeguard his empire, but eventually failing because of wrong assessments and inadequate strategic decisions. In this context, Michael VII's malicious order to blind his opponent appears to result from the overall moral decay permeating the imperial court and the ecclesiastical leadership. This punishment was all the more remissible insofar as Romanos Diogenes had already resigned from any claim to the throne by presenting himself dressed in a monk's habit on a humble mule and by delivering himself into the hands of Andronikos Doukas in exchange for a guarantee of safe-conduct.[144] By juxtaposing Romanos' humble submission with Michael's sacrilegious deed, the author especially highlights the incumbent emperor's moral deficiency. Accordingly, God punished his subjects with the intention of leading them back to the path of righteousness through the aid of a savior capable of restoring the previous order. In Attaleiates' narrative, the Turkish invaders form a part of this process of purification as a divine instrument of punishment, while Sultan Alp Arslān's indulgent behavior towards the defeated emperor is a model case of royal virtues, which Byzantine statesmen no longer possess.[145] Michael VII and his followers are thus condemned to succumb to the barbarian forces sent for their punishment.

> What do you have to say, emperor, and those who made this impious decision with you? The eyes of a man who has committed no crime, but has given his soul for the prosperity of the whole empire of the Romans and has offered resistance to the excessively belligerent nations with a strong army, while it was possible to stay in safety in the imperial palace and not to sustain any pains or fears of the military life? [The eyes of] a man, whose virtue even an enemy respected; he embraced him honestly, spoke to him like to a brother, and offered the captive a seat beside him; like a good doctor he gave a soothing remedy, these consolations, to this man afflicted by grief, so that the sultan, one may assume, rightfully took the victory from God, the arbiter, for he proved to be such a man who demonstrated so great a measure of wisdom and patience.[146]

The description of the dethroned emperor's blinding in Kotyaion gains expressiveness through a highly emotional presentation of Romanos "wriggling in supplications before the feet of the archbishops and with painful and unbearable contrition fervently calling them to help him as much as they can." The metropolitans of Chalkedon, Herakleia, and Koloneia, however, although willing, were too weak to effect anything in the supplicant's favor.[147] High-ranking representatives of the church who were expected to safeguard the norms of Christian ethics are thus described as being fully enmeshed in the demotion of the imperial office. The empire's decay up to the catastrophe of 1071 was not only a military one, but also, or even more importantly, a moral one. Naturally, Michael Psellos, as a spokesman of the Doukas clan, supports the opposite view: The act was certainly to be deplored, he argues, from a moral point of view, but absolutely necessary under these circumstances, for refraining from it would have entailed the risk of another attempt of Diogenes to gain the throne. Moreover, Psellos is quick to point out that Michael VII himself was not aware of his predecessor's deplorable fate.[148] Be that as it may, all parties agree that Diogenes' blinding was the symptom of a deep crisis of the ruling class of Constantinople, which was to last almost a decade until Alexios I Komnenos' rise to power. The Seljuk sultan because of his impressive military success became coincidentally involved in this conflict as a treaty partner and ally of Romanos Diogenes. With the civil strife of 1071–72 and the ensuing rebellions of mercenary commanders and military aristocrats, Byzantium lost the last opportunity to restore its rule over the Armenian highlands and the eastern fringes of the Anatolian plateau. Alp Arslān never intended to annex Byzantine regions on a large scale and soon after Manzikert retreated to the East, where he himself fell victim to an assassination in November 1072, only a few months after his respected Byzantine adversary.[149] But the Byzantine civil strife strengthened the Seljuk role in Asia Minor from an ideological point of view. The sultan after his encounter with the emperor could present himself as the protector of the legitimate incumbent of the throne and thus became directly involved in the internal affairs of the Byzantine imperial sphere. This is reflected in statements of Armenian, Syriac, and Muslim authors condemning the mutilation of the dethroned emperor and linking new Turkish invasions into the empire with the moral failure of the Byzantine ruling class.[150] Manzikert was certainly not the decisive event leading to the Turkish conquest of Asia Minor, but the Seljuk sultanate's involvement in Byzantine imperial affairs prepared the ground for more powerful interventions in the interior of Asia Minor, a tightening of diplomatic relations with Constantinople in the years of Sultan Malikshāh, and a gradual strengthening of claims to control over Turkish warrior groups operating on Byzantine soil.

Notes

1 On the expeditions of Romanos IV and the battle of Manzikert in general, see Cahen, "Campagne," pp. 628–42; Vryonis, *Decline*, pp. 95–103; idem, "Battle," pp. 125–40; idem, "Captivity," pp. 439–50; Cheynet, "Mantzikert," pp. 411–38 (who modifies older views concerning the military consequences of the battle); Hillenbrand, *Myth*, esp. 3–25; Leveniotis, *Collapse*, pp. 157–80 (with an extensive list of primary sources on pp. 159–61, n. 863); Korobeinikov, "Raiders," pp. 701–703. For modern Turkish presentations of the battle, which are mostly based on Muslim accounts, see Yinanç, *Anadolu'nun Fethi*, pp. 69–82; Turan, *Selçuklular Târihi*, pp. 168–88; Turan, *Türkiye*, pp. 21–37; Sevim "Malazgirt," pp. 219–29; Dirimtekin, "İki Zafer," pp. 231–58; Kaymaz, "Malazgirt Savaşı," pp. 259–68; Köymen, *Alp Arslan*, pp. 26–40; Sevim, *Suriye*, pp. 44–49, 56–62; idem, *Anadolu'nun Fethi*, pp. 51–76; Sevim and Yücel, *Türkiye Tarihi*, pp. 65–81; Sevim and Merçil, *Selçuklu Devletleri*, pp. 76–93; Merçil, *Büyük Selçuklu Devleti*, pp. 62–70; Öngül, *Selçuklular Tarihi*, 1:55–68; Özgüdenli, *Selçuklular*, pp. 147–59; the most recent Turkish monograph on the topic

is Kesik, *1071 Malazgirt*, esp. pp. 71–127 for the battle and its consequences. For a collection of the Arabic and Persian sources along with a Turkish translation, see Sümer and Sevim, *Malazgirt Savaşı*. Hillenbrand, *Myth*, pp. 26–110, provides an English translation with comments of all major sources, gives an analysis of the motifs and literary *topoi* figuring in the Manzikert narratives (ibid., pp. 111–43) and outlines the legacy of the battle in subsequent historical discourse on Muslim-Christian confrontation (ibid., pp. 147–225).

2 *Malazgirt Armağanı*; Turan, *Türkiye*, p. vi.

3 Yinanç, *Anadolu'nun Fethi*, p. 78; for further details concerning modern Turkish viewpoints, see Hillenbrand, *Myth*, pp. 196–225, esp. pp. 210–20, with illustrations of an equestrian statue of Alp Arslān as well as stamps and coins commemorating the battle.

4 Kesik, *1071 Malazgirt*, pp. 13–16; see also Özgüdenli, *Selçuklular*, p. 158: "Malazgirt Savaşı, uzun vadeli sonuçları itibariyle, dünya tarihinin en önmeli hadiselerinden biridir [...] bu zafer [...] Anadolu kapılarını Türkler'e sonuna kadar açarak [...] ve Anadolu'nun Türk yurdu haline gelmesine zemin hazırlamıştır." ("The battle of Manzikert, with respect to its long-term results, was one of the most important events in world history [...] this victory [...] eventually opened the gates of Anatolia to the Turks and prepared the grounds for transforming Anatolia into a Turkish homeland.").

5 See, for instance, Matuz, *Reich*, pp. 15–16: "Alp Arslān [...] schlug 1071 bei Manzikert die byzantinischen Streitkräfte. Kleinasien wurde in den folgenden Jahren von den Türkmenen überflutet." Kreiser, *Staat*, p. 4: "Der Sieg des Seldschuken Alp Arslān über die byzantinische Streitmacht bei Manzikert/Malazgirt (Armenien) im Jahr 1071 gilt als das entscheidende Ereignis bei der Turkisierung und Islamisierung Anatoliens." Much more careful is Kreiser and Neumann, *Türkei*, p. 44: "Die Schlacht zwischen Alp Arslān und Romanos IV. im August 1071 bei der Festung Malazgirt [...] war das Ende des dritten Feldzugs, den der oströmische Kaiser offensiv gegen die Seldschuken anführte."

6 Attaleiates, pp. 77–124, esp. 107–22 (Romanos IV's third campaign and the battle of Manzikert).

7 Attaleiates, p. 124.

8 See below, p. 205.

9 See below, pp. 157–158, 200–202.

10 Psellos 7.123–24, pp. 263–64.

11 Attaleiates, p. 75, ll. 17–18.

12 Psellos 7.127, p. 265, ll. 6–9.

13 Attaleiates, pp. 72–73.

14 Attaleiates, p. 73, ll. 9–11: ὁ δὲ φθόνος καὶ ἡ ἄδικος κρίσις ἀνεβάλετο μὲν τότε τὸ δέον [...] δι' αἰτίας ἴσως ἀπορρήτους ἀνθρώποις. Other sources for the accession of Romanos IV: Matthew of Edessa 2.51, p. 127; Michael the Syrian 15.3, ed. Chabot, 3:168 (trans.), 4:577 (Syriac text).

15 Attaleiates, p. 73, ll. 11–17.

16 Attaleiates, pp. 70–73, esp. p. 70, ll. 15–16: Μετὰ δὲ τὸ τὸν βασιλέα τεθνάναι πάλιν οἱ τὴν ἑῴαν κατατρέχοντες Οὖννοι περὶ Μεσοποταμίαν γενόμενοι [...] and p. 75, ll. 20–24.

17 For King Bagrat IV and the kingdom of Georgia in his time, see Suny, *Georgian Nation*, pp. 33–34.

18 For Alp Arslān's second Caucasian campaign, see Yinanç, *Anadolu'nun Fethi*, pp. 62–64; Cahen, "Campagne," pp. 17–20 (with a detailed discussion of Muslim sources); Turan, *Selçuklular Târihi*, pp. 163–65; Sevim, *Anadolu'nun Fethi*, pp. 46–47; Sevim and Yücel, *Türkiye*, pp. 55–56; Köymen, *Alp Arslan*, pp. 20–22; Sevim and Merçil, *Selçuklu Devletleri*, pp. 70–71; Öngül, *Selçuklular*, 1:47–48; Peacock, "Nomadic

Society," pp. 205–30. The main sources: Georgian Chronicles, pp. 300–302; al-Ḥusaynī, pp. 43–46, trans. Lügal, pp. 30–32; 'Imād al-Dīn/al-Bundārī, p. 31; Sibṭ b. al-Jawzī, p. 136.

19 Attaleiates, p. 75: ἐν δὲ τοῖς βορειοτέροις αὐτὸς ὁ σουλτάνος πανστρατιᾷ ἐξελήλυθε δυνάμεις ἄγων ἀνυποίστους καὶ τοῖς ὁρίοις ἐν τῷ φθινοπώρῳ τῶν Ῥωμαίων προσήνωτο [...].

20 Attaleiates, pp. 73–75.

21 Haldon, "Approaches," pp. 63–64.

22 For details, see below, pp. 139–140, 146–147, 150–151.

23 Psellos 7.133–34, pp. 267–68.

24 Attaleiates, pp. 77–78.

25 Attaleiates, p. 78, ll. 4–6: στρατιωτικὸν ἐκ τῆς ἑσπέρας καὶ τῆς τῶν Καππαδοκῶν [...] καὶ Σκύθας συνεκαλέσατο [...] μετὰ τῶν ἐν τῇ βασιλείῳ μόνων, p. 78, l. 13: οἱ τῶν ταγμάτων ἐξάρχοντες, p. 81, l. 17: τοὺς ἅπαντας Φράγγους, ἄνδρας αἱμοχαρεῖς καὶ πολεμικούς, p. 83, ll. 1–2: ὅσοι τῆς ὑπηρεσίας ὑπῆρχον καὶ τῆς τῶν Ἀρμενίων συντάξεως. For the interpretation of *tagmata*, see Haldon, *Warfare*, p. 78, and idem, "Approaches," p. 48. Matthew of Edessa 2.53, pp. 128, speaks of "a great number of troops from the whole empire of the Greeks, right up to the borders of Rome and from all parts of the east."

26 Haldon et al., "Marching across Anatolia," pp. 212–13.

27 Attaleiates, p. 78.

28 Attaleiates, p. 79.

29 For the sequence of events and the itinerary of the imperial troops during the first two campaigns of Romanos IV, see Hild and Restle, *Kappadokien*, pp. 100–102; Yinanç, *Anadolu'nun Fethi*, pp. 65–67; Sevim, *Anadolu'nun Fethi*, pp. 47–49; Kesik, *1071 Malazgirt*, pp. 50–61.

30 Attaleiates, p. 79, ll. 10–12: ὁ μὲν σουλτάνος ὀπισθόρμητος γέγονε, μοῖραν δέ τινα μεγάλην ἀποτεμόμενος καὶ ταύτην διχῇ διελὼν εἰς τὴν ἄνω Ἀσίαν στρατοπεδεύειν πεποίηται, τὴν μὲν βορειοτέραν, τὴν δὲ περὶ τὰ νότια θέμενος, and ibidem, p. 79, ll. 20–25. For the situation in the southern section, see above, pp. 117–24.

31 For the citadel walls and the Byzantine types of masonry used therein, see Foss and Winfield, *Byzantine Fortifications*, p. 20.

32 Attaleiates, pp. 80–81.

33 Attaleiates, pp. 81–82: τὸ γλίσχρον αὐτοῦ καὶ περιδεὲς καὶ ἀπόλεμον.

34 Attaleiates, p. 92.

35 Sibṭ b. al-Jawzī, p. 139; 'Aẓīmī, p. 14 (Arabic text), p. 18 (trans.); Bar Hebraeus, p. 245 (*kabhshāhā l-Āmōrīn mdhī[n]tā*), p. 247 (*'al sphār yammā dh-'ābhar 'al shūrāh d-Qūsṭanṭīnāpōlīs* [...] *wa-nphaq l-Māqēdōnyā*).

36 Lightfood and Ivison, "1995 Excavation Season," p. 330: "This period of peace and prosperity was brought to a rapid close in 1068 with the first Turkish incursion into central Anatolia." Lightfood and Ivison, "1998 Excavation Season," p. 392: "The Byzantine disaster at Manzikert in 1071, however, heralded a long period of unsettled and insecure conditions." Lightfood, Arbel, Ivison, Roberts, Ioannidou, "Excavation in 2002," 250: "Recent study has proposed that Byzantine control of Amorium ended by the late eleventh century, and that the city may have been partially or completely abandoned thereafter."

37 Lightfoot, "1996 Excavation Season," p. 331: "signed follis of Romanus IV;" Lightfood et al., "1997 Study Season," p. 339: a lead seal ascribed to the *vestarches*, *magistros*, and *katepano* Nikephoros Melissenos and datable to the period 1067–78; two signed folles of Constantine X; Lightfood, Mergen, Olcay, Witte-Orr, "Excavation in 2000," p. 288: one follis of Michael VII. Lightfood and Ivison, "1998 Excavation Season," p. 392: "There is no sign that the abandonment was unduly precipitate or accompanied by violent destruction [...] the inhabitants made an orderly withdrawal from the site."

38 Felix, *Byzanz*, pp. 84–86.

39 Attaleiates, p. 80, ll. 12–13, p. 81, l. 8.

40 Attaleiates, p. 81, ll. 10–12, p. 82, ll. 8–15.
41 Attaleiates, pp. 82–84.
42 Attaleiates, pp. 84–90. Other sources referring to these events, even though much more succinctly: Matthew of Edessa 2.53, pp. 128–29 (confirming the surrender of the inhabitants who presented themselves "with improvised crosses in their hands"); Bar Hebraeus, pp. 244–45, trans. Budge, p. 218 (providing an otherwise unknown account, according to which the fights outside *Mabbūgh* [= Manbij] were especially violent, leading to a great slaughter among the inhabitants, the destruction of the city walls, and a famine among the Turks due to the great number of Byzantine soldiers who had consumed all supplies in the region; the author also mentions the conquest of Artāḥ and *'Ēm* [= 'Imm]); Ibn al-Qalānisī, pp. 95, 98 (noting the departure of the "king of the Romans" [*mutamallik al-Rūm*] to the *thughūr sub anno* 460/11 November 1067–30 October 1068 and the conquest of Manbij *sub anno* 462/20 October 1069–8 October 1070, which is combined with the subsequent march of the imperial army to Manzikert); Ibn al-Athīr, 6:242–43, trans. Richards, *Annals*, p. 166 (likewise *sub anno* 462, especially emphasizing the defeat of Emir Maḥmūd and his allies); Sibṭ b. al-Jawzī, pp. 139, 142; Ibn al-'Adīm, p. 257 (*sub anno* 461/31 October 1068–19 October 1069, besides Manbij, this source also mentions the failed siege of A'zāz in accordance with Attaleiates); 'Aẓīmī, pp. 14–15 (Arabic text), 18–19 (trans.) (*sub anno* 461, this source also mentions the conquest of Artāḥ and erroneously refers to a conquest of A'zāz).
43 Attaleiates, pp. 90, ll. 4–11; for the previous conquest of Artāḥ and the importance of the place, see Ibn al-'Adīm, pp. 256–57 (27. Sha'bān 460, allegedly 3,000 Christian men were killed during Ibn Khān's conquest).
44 Attaleiates, pp. 90–92. Haldon et al., "Marching across Anatolia," pp. 215–22, arrives at surprisingly high amounts of provisions and fodder requirements for the 1071 army marching to Manzikert. The environs of Antioch in the Amuq Plain are normally considered a very fertile agricultural zone and the troops of the 1068 campaign most probably were numerically inferior, but the raids of the previous years apparently caused a serious shortage of available provisions.
45 Attaleiates, pp. 89–90.
46 Ibn al-Athīr, 6:293, trans. Richards, *Annals*, pp. 217–18.
47 Bar Hebraeus, p. 245, trans. Budge, p. 218.
48 Attaleiates, p. 85.
49 Attaleiates, p. 86.
50 Attaleiates, p. 85, ll. 20–25: τὴν τῶν Ῥωμαίων κατέγνων δειλίαν ἢ ἀπειροκαλίαν ἢ ταπεινότητα [...] ἀλλὰ πάντες ἔνδον καθήμενοι [...] καὶ κίνησις ψυχῆς οὐδ' ἀγωνία τούτους τὸ παράπαν ἐξώρμησεν.
51 Attaleiates, p. 86, ll. 2–3.
52 Attaleiates, p. 87.
53 Attaleiates, p. 91, ll. 1–5; Ibn al-Athīr, 6:243, trans. Richards, *Annals*, p. 166; Ibn al-'Adīm, p. 257 (the ambassador is the *qāḍī* al-Quḍā'ī, who allegedly quotes the emperor's own words).
54 Ibn al-'Adīm, pp. 254, 256.
55 Ibn al-'Adīm, p. 257.
56 Ibn al-Adīm, p. 258.
57 Ibn al-'Adīm, p. 258 (the events are dated before and after the beginning of the year 462 = 20 October 1069).
58 Ibn al-'Adīm, pp. 258–59: *wa-laqiya ahl al-Shām min 'askarihī shiddatan 'aẓīmatan wa-huwa awwal nahb wa-fasād jarā bi-l-Shām min al-Atrāk.*
59 Sibṭ b. al-Jawzī, p. 142.
60 Attaleiates, p. 97, ll. 7–8.
61 Attaleiates, pp. 93–95.

62 For these persons, see below, pp. 208–214 and pp. 201, 285–290.
63 Attaleiates, pp. 95–97.
64 Attaleiates, pp. 97–99.
65 Attaleiates, pp. 99–100.
66 Attaleiates, pp. 100–101.
67 Attaleiates, pp. 102–104.
68 Attaleiates, p. 95, ll. 5–6: Τούρκων πλῆθος ὅσον οὔπω ποτὲ [...] λεηλατεῖ καὶ κατατρέχει τὴν χώραν.
69 Attaleiates, p. 99, ll. 16–20, 100, ll. 21–23: Προκατειργασμένοι γὰρ ὄντες τὰς ψυχὰς οἱ Ῥωμαῖοι τῷ φόβῳ τῶν Τούρκων [...] καὶ εἰς ὁρμὰς τῶν ἐναντίων καὶ φενακισμοὺς ἐξ ἐπιδείξεων πολεμικῶν περιέστησαν.
70 Attaleiates, p. 99: "He [i.e., the emperor] entrusted the stronger part [i.e., of the army] to Philaretos, a man proud of his military rank, but leading an abominable and disgraceful life, who had variously fought the barbarians, but had been defeated in the greatest battles and thus, as a consequence, drawn disdain upon him. In spite of this, he did not stay away from these affairs, but continued to run after command posts because of the possibilities they offered to his greed and ambition."
71 Attaleiates, p. 100, ll.4–8.
72 Attaleiates, p. 100, ll. 10–12: εἰς τὴν Κελεσίνην χώραν κατήντησε, διαβὰς τὸ δεύτερον τὸν Εὐφράτην ποταμόν, κατὰ τοὺς ἀρκτῴους πρόποδας τοῦ Ταύρου παρὰ τὸ μέρος ἐκεῖνο παραρρέοντα [...].
73 Attaleiates, p. 96, ll. 23–24: ὁ δέ, ὡς ἀπὸ διαστήματος μιᾶς ἡμέρας ἢ καὶ πλείονος τῆς Μελιτηνῆς στρατοπεδευσάμενος.
74 Attaleiates, p. 94, ll. 21–22: φύσει γὰρ ἄπιστον τὸ γένος τῶν Φράγγων.
75 Attaleiates, pp. 94–95, esp. 95, l. 2: τὴν Μεσοποταμίαν κατέλαβον.
76 Attaleiates, pp. 97–98.
77 Attaleiates, p. 98, ll. 21–28.
78 Attaleiates, p. 98, ll.11–17.
79 For details, see below, pp. 201–202, 205–206.
80 Attaleiates, p. 104, ll. 10–11: στρατηγὸν τοῦ πολέμου καὶ ἀρχηγὸν τοῦ στρατεύματος ἀποδείκνυσι.
81 Angold, *Empire*, p. 115.
82 Attaleiates, p. 104, ll. 15–25.
83 See above, pp. 143–145.
84 For previous knowledge of the imminent campaign, see above, p. 147.
85 Attaleiates, pp. 105–107 (ὁ τῶν Τούρκων ἡγούμενος); Bryennios 1.11, pp. 100–103 (πλῆθος Τούρκων στρατηγὸν ἔχοντες τὸν Χρυσόσκουλον, ὃς ἐκ σουλτάνων σειρᾶς ὥρμητο); Sibṭ b. al-Jawzī, pp. 144, 146–47 (*wa-kāna Arīsghī zawj ukht al-sulṭān ma'ahū jamā'a min al-Nāwakiyya*); for the Turkish variants of the name, see Turan, *Türkiye*, p. 20; Sevim, *Suriye*, pp. 49–50.
86 Sibṭ b. al-Jawzī, pp. 146–47: "On receiving news from Arīsghī, the emperor (*al-malik*) sent Mīkhā'īl [= Manuel] to fight against him, because he believed him to be an enemy. When Mīkhā'īl approached him, he [= Arīsghī] sent a message to him: 'I did not come to wage war on you, but I came in order to take refuge with you from the sultan.' He [= Mīkhā'īl] replied: 'You are telling lies.' He [= Arīsghī] said: 'Had this been true, I would not have destroyed our land by pillaging and killing.' He [= Arīsghī] took an oath before him, but he [= Mīkhā'īl] did not believe him. Thus they fought a battle and Arīsghī defeated the Romans."
87 Beihammer, "Defection," p. 608.
88 Bryennios 2.11, pp. 100–103.
89 Sibṭ b. al-Jawzī, p. 146: "al-Afshīn [...] sent a message to the emperor (*al-malik*) saying: 'There is a peace treaty between us. When I entered your land, I did not attack anyone, but these Turkmen warriors (*al-nāwakiyya*) are enemies of the sultan.

They have looted and destroyed your country. Therefore, you should hand them over to us, otherwise I will destroy your land and there will be no treaty between us.' The emperor replied: 'All you said is true, but it is our custom not to hand over those who have taken refuge with us.'"

90 Sibṭ b. al-Jawzī, p. 147.

91 Attaleiates, *Historia*, pp. 105–106.

92 Foss, "Defenses," pp. 153–57; Foss and Winfield, *Byzantine Fortifications*, pp. 139–40.

93 For Alp Arslān's Syrian campaign in general, see Yinanç, *Anadolu'nun Fethi*, pp. 69–70; Turan, *Selçuklular Târihi*, pp. 168–71; Sevim, *Suriye*, pp. 56–61; Sevim, *Anadolu'nun Fethi*, pp. 51–54; Sevim and Merçil, *Selçuklu Devletleri*, pp. 74–76; Öngül, *Selçuklular*, 1:53–55; Heidemann, *Renaissance*, pp. 124–25; Özgüdenli, *Selçuklular*, pp. 150–51.

94 In contrast to my interpretation, Turkish scholars tend to present these events as centrally organized operations of regular Seljuk troops and Turkmen chieftains obedient to the sultan's rule: Sevim and Merçil, *Selçuklu Devletleri*, pp. 72–73 (Romanos Diogenes'in İstanbul'a dönmesinden bir süre sonra 1069 yılında, Afşin, Sunduk, Ahmetşah, Türkman, Demleçoğlu Mehmet, Duduoğlu, Serhenkoğlu, ve Arslantaş komutasındaki Selçuklu kuvvetleri, doğu, güney-doğu ve güney bölgelerinde Anadolu'ya akınlara başladılar); Öngül, *Selçuklular*, 1:45–47 (Sultan Alp Arslan'ın doğuda bazı hâdiseleri yatıştırmakla veya fütûhat yapmakla meşgul olduğu sıralarda Selçuklu emîrleri ve Türkmen beyleri Anadolu'da akınlara devam ettiler); Özgüdenli, *Selçuklular*, pp. 147–50.

95 Yinanç, *Anadolu'nun Fethi*, p. 69; Turan, *Selçuklular*, p. 169; Sevim, *Suriye*, pp. 56–57; Sevim, *Anadolu'nun Fethi*, p. 51; Sevim and Merçil, *Selçuklu Devletleri*, pp. 74; Öngül, *Selçuklular*, 1:53; Özgüdenli, *Selçuklular*, pp. 150 (Bu esnada Fâtımî Devleti içerisinde vuku bulan bazı gelişmeler, Sultan Alparslan'ın dikkatini Mısır'a çevirmesine sebep oldu); for the situation in Egypt in detail, see Halm, *Kalifen*, pp. 400–18.

96 Halm, *Kalifen*, p. 403.

97 Ibn al-ʿAdīm, pp. 260–61.

98 Ibn al-ʿAdīm, pp. 259–61.

99 Ibn al-ʿAdīm, p. 260; Ibn al-Athīr, 6:245, trans. Richards, *Annals*, p. 168.

100 Ibn al-ʿAdīm, pp. 259–6; Ibn al-Athīr, 6:245, trans. Richards, *Annals*, p. 168.

101 Sibṭ b. al-Jawzī, p. 145, ll. 6–8; Ibn al-ʿAdīm, p. 261; Ibn al-Athīr, 6:245, trans. Richards, *Annals*, p. 168.

102 Sibṭ b. al-Jawzī, p. 145, ll. 13–14 and ll. 18–19.

103 Sibṭ b. al-Jawzī, p. 142, ll. 8–9.

104 Sibṭ b. al-Jawzī, pp. 143–44 (Dhū l-Qaʿda 463 = 11 August-9 September 1070); Matthew of Edessa 2.56, p. 130, states that the Byzantine garrison had fled before the arrival of the Seljuk army; Bar Hebraeus, p. 246, trans. Budge, p. 219.

105 Ibn al-Athīr, 6:245, trans. Richards, *Annals*, p. 169; al-Iṣfahānī/Bundārī, p. 37, ll. 11–17; Sibṭ b. al-Jawzī, p. 144: Matthew of Edessa 2.56, pp. 130–32, gives a detailed account of the siege. Basil's father Alousianos was the son of the last Bulgarian king Ivan Vladislav and appeared in 1040 as commander of Theodosioupolis and supporter of a Bulgarian revolt. Bar Hebraeus, p. 246, trans. Budge, p. 219.

106 Sibṭ b. al-Jawzī, p. 144 (14 Rabīʿ II 463); Ibn al-ʿAdīm, p. 261 (who locates the camp near the Nahr al-Jawz in the region of Bīra).

107 Sibṭ b. al-Jawzī, p. 144, ll. 1–2, 18.

108 Sibṭ b. al-Jawzī, p. 144, ll. 19–20 (*min al-ʿIrāqiyyīn ʿaskar Ṭughril Beg*).

109 Bar Hebraeus, p. 246, trans. Budge, p. 219, in addition to the sum of Edessa, mentions a tribute of 100,000 dinars paid by Mayyāfāriqīn and 1,000 dinars paid by al-Suwaydāʾ/Siverek.

110 Sibṭ b. al-Jawzī, pp. 144–45.

111 Ibn al-Athīr, 6:245, trans. Richards, *Annals*, p. 169; Sibṭ b. al-Jawzī, pp. 145–46.

112 Ibn al-ʿAdīm, p. 262.

113 Sibṭ b. al-Jawzī, p. 146.
114 Sibṭ b. al-Jawzī, p. 146, ll. 5–14; Ibn al-ʿAdīm p. 264 (who mentions the date 1 Shaʿbān); for brief reports, see Ibn al-Qalānisī, p. 99 (dating the departure of the Seljuk army from Aleppo to 23 Rajab 463 = 26 April 1071); al-Iṣfahānī/al-Bundārī, p. 38; Ibn al-Athīr, p. 244, trans. Richards, *Annals*, pp. 169–70 (both give a summary of Sibṭ b. al-Jawzī's version); ʿAẓīmī, p. 15 (Arabic text), p. 19 (trans.).
115 Attaleiates, p. 105; Sibṭ b. al-Jawzī, pp. 146–47.
116 Sibṭ b. al-Jawzī, p. 147, l. 12.
117 Attaleiates, p. 107, ll. 5–9; Sibṭ b. al-Jawzī, p. 146.
118 Attaleiates, pp. 108–11, for the battlefield near Sebasteia, ibidem, p. 110, ll. 16–23.
119 Sibṭ b. al-Jawzī, p. 146, ll. 16–18, p. 147, ll. 13–16; Ibn al-ʿAdīm, p. 264.
120 Ibn al-Athīr, 6:246: "The news reached Sultan Alp Arslān while he was in the city of Khuwayy in Azarbeijan;" Ibn al-ʿAdīm p. 264: "He had reached Azerbaijan when news reached him that the emperor of the Romans had set off for Khilāṭ." For details concerning the imperial army's march route in 1071, see Hild and Restle, *Kappadokien*, pp. 103–104, and Haldon et al., "Marching across Anatolia," pp. 212–14 (with a map).
121 Attaleiates, p. 111, ll. 15–21.
122 Attaleiates, p. 111, ll. 8–9: διὰ χώρας ἀοικήτου καὶ καταπεπατημένης τοῖς ἔθνεσι.
123 Attaleiates, pp. 111–12.
124 Attaleiates, pp. 115–16 and p. 118, ll. 4–7.
125 Attaleiates, pp. 119–21, esp. p. 120, ll. 8–14 (τῶν ἐφεδρευόντων αὐτῷ τις, ἐξάδελφος ὢν τῷ τοῦ βασιλέως προγόνῳ Μιχαήλ), and p. 121, ll. 16–24 (the emperor's capture).
126 Attaleiates, pp. 112–13.
127 Sibṭ b. al-Jawzī, pp. 147, 148, l. 16.
128 Sibṭ b. al-Jawzī, p. 147, ll. 16–17: *wa-lam yara l-rujūʿ li-jamʿ al-ʿasākir fa-takūnu hazīma.*
129 Attaleiates, p. 113, ll. 1–2: προκατέλαβεν ὁ σουλτάνος ἀκηρυκτεὶ καὶ τὰ δοκηθέντα τελεσθῆναι διεκωλύθησαν.
130 Attaleiates, pp. 118–19.
131 Attaleiates, pp. 119–21.
132 For the details of the encounter between Alp Arslān and Emperor Romanos IV and the treaty concluded on this occasion, see Attaleiates, pp. 122–23; Ibn al-Qalānisī, p. 99; Nīshāpūrī/Rashīd al-Dīn, pp. 36–39; al-Rāwandī, pp. 119–20; al-Ḥusaynī, pp. 52–53; Ibn al-Athīr, 6:247–48, trans. Richards, *Annals*, pp. 171–72; Sibṭ b. Jawzī, pp. 149–51; for modern interpretations, see Yinanç, *Anadolu'nun Fethi*, pp. 76–77; Turan, *Selçuklular Târihi*, pp. 184–88; Sevim, *Anadolu'nun Fethi*, pp. 69–72; Vryonis, "Eight-Day Captivity," pp. 439–50; Leveniotis, *Collapse*, pp. 177–80; Sevim and Merçil, *Selçuklu Devletleri*, pp. 87–91; Öngül, *Selçuklular*, 1:63–66; Özgüdenli, *Selçuklular*, pp. 157–58, esp. n. 99.
133 For the treaty, see the careful analysis of Leveniotis, *Collapse*, pp. 177–80; in addition, see Sevim and Merçil, *Selçuklu Devletleri*, pp. 89–90; Öngül, *Selçuklular*, 1:157; Özgüdenli, *Selçuklular*, pp. 157–58.
134 Psellos 7.144–46, 148–52, pp. 271–72, 274–76; Attaleiates, p. 125, ll. 3–18.
135 Attaleiates, p. 123, l. 26 (ὀλίγους πάνυ καταλαβὼν τῶν φυγάδων τῆς μάχης στρατιωτῶν), p. 124, l. 1–2 (μετὰ τῶν συνελευθερωθέντων [...] τὸ δ' ἄλλο πλῆθος συνείλεκτο παρὰ τῶν προσοίκων τῶν ἐκεῖσε κωμῶν τε καὶ πόλεων), p. 126, ll. 8–9 (τῶν Φράγγων οἱ πλείους), p. 126, ll. 12–13 (πολλοὺς τῶν Καππαδοκῶν [...] κηρύγμασί τε καὶ γράμμασι μετεπέμψατο), p. 127, ll. 15–20 (Χατατούριος [...] συνέθετο τούτῳ καὶ τῆς ἐκείνου μοίρας ἐγένετο), p. 127, l. 25 (δύναμιν ἑτέραν in Cilicia). Psellos, 7.152, 161, pp. 276, 281, more elusively mentions a "large number of troops" and refers to the army of Khatatourios.
136 Psellos, 7.162, p. 282 (περσικὴν συμμαχίαν ἤλπιζε πρὸς αὐτὸν αὐτίκα ἀφίξασθαι); Attaleiates, p. 127, ll. 26–27.

137 Attaleiates, p. 127, ll. 2–13; Psellos, 7.153, p. 276 (being less accurate with respect to the emperor's itinerary, mentions Amaseia).

138 Psellos, 7.155, p. 278 (εἰς δὲ τὴν τῶν Κιλίκων χώραν ἀπαγαγὼν καὶ εἰς τὴν ἐξ ἐφόδου φυλακὴν τὰ τέμπη τῆς Κιλικίας αὐτοῦ προβαλόμενος); Attaleiates, p. 127, ll. 15–25.

139 Attaleiates, p. 129, ll. 10–11.

140 Psellos 7.154, 157, pp. 276–77, 279; Attaleiates, p. 126, ll. 3–4 (Constantine), p. 128, ll. 17–18 (Andronikos).

141 Attaleiates, p. 126, ll. 4–6 (τοὺς παρατυχόντας τῶν στρατιωτῶν [...] καὶ ἄλλους τῶν ἐπαρχιῶν), p. 126, ll. 21–25 (Crispin).

142 Attaleiates, p. 128, ll. 1–16.

143 Attaleiates, pp. 128–29, esp. p. 129, ll. 4–5.

144 Attaleiates, pp. 129–30.

145 Attaleiates, p. 122, esp. ll. 23–24: ὁπότε καὶ ἡ τοῦ Θεοῦ κρίσις μετὰ τῶν ἄλλων κἀνταῦθα δικαία καὶ ἀρρεπὴς κατεφάνη.

146 Attaleiates, p. 130, ll. 11–21.

147 Attaleiates, p. 131, ll. 14–19.

148 Psellos 7.163–64, pp. 283–84 (Ὃ δὴ καὶ γενόμενον ἠγνοεῖτο τῷ βασιλεῖ).

149 Merçil, *Büyük Selçuklu Devleti*, pp. 70–71; Özgüdenli, *Selçuklular*, pp. 159–61.

150 For details, see below, pp. 205–206.

Part II

Decay of imperial authority and regionalization of power, 1071–96

4 Sulaymān b. Qutlumush and the first Turkish lordships in Syria

Sulaymān b. Qutlumush in the light of modern scholarship

As the grandson of Arslān-Isrā'īl, who had died in 1032 as prisoner of Maḥmūd of Ghazna, and the son of Ṭughril Beg's seditious cousin Qutlumush, who had been killed in late 1063/early 1064 fighting Sultan Alp Arslān, Sulaymān was the scion of a very prominent Seljuk lineage, which for decades was in rivalry and sometimes even in open hostility with the dynasty's main branch represented by the descendants of Mīkā'īl.[1] It thus comes as no surprise that he and his brothers made their first appearance in the light of history as restless warlords along with a number of competing Turkmen bands striving for power in northern Syria. Several years later, the same persons reappeared as chiefs of a considerable military force in Bithynia in western Asia Minor, only a few days march from Constantinople. As raiders, military commanders, and valuable allies of Byzantine rebels and emperors, such as Nikephoros III Botaneiates and Alexios I, Sulaymān b. Qutlumush and his companions laid the foundations for the formation of a new political entity that soon acquired distinct Muslim-Turkish characteristics. Within a time span of five years, from the imperial government's recognition of Sulaymān as an autonomous ruler in about June 1081 until his premature death in the battle of ʿAyn Saylam in June 1086, this Seljuk chieftain succeeded in establishing his rule in Nicaea and in conquering parts of Cilicia and Byzantium's main center in the southern section of the eastern borderland, the city of Antioch.[2]

Modern scholars generally agree on the outcomes and long-lasting effects of Sulaymān's ventures, but there are widely differing views and interpretations with respect to his political concepts and practices and the nature of the principality that he brought to life. Most remarkably, there is a broad gap between Western and Turkish perceptions of Sulaymān's historical significance, which is closely related to the diverging viewpoints and research interests in Europe and the modern Republic of Turkey. Specialists of Byzantium and the crusades deal with Sulaymān b. Qutlumush only insofar as he was involved in the empire's disintegration during the 1070s and 1080s or in the formation of the Muslim-Turkish powers opposing the First Crusade in the 1090s. Modern Turkish historiography, instead, presents Sulaymān b. Qutlumush as a central figure in the creation of a Turkish nation and its collective historical memory in Anatolia.

Ferdinand Chalandon's monograph on the reign of Alexios I devotes no more than a few lines to Sulaymān's activities in Asia Minor, describing him as a chieftain entrusted by his cousin, Sultan Malikshāh, with the war against the empire and as loosely attached to the Seljuk Empire by bonds of vassalage.[3] The success of his troops in taking control of Bithynia is explained by the civil strife within the empire. The first full-length study on the Turkish conquest of Asia Minor by Joseph Laurent also does not attach any outstanding importance to Sulaymān, presenting him as just one of many Seljuk warriors who in about 1080 were pillaging Byzantine territories as far as the shores of the Bosphorus.[4] Unlike Chalandon, Laurent considered Sulaymān an undisciplined rebel, who disregarded the authority of his master, the Sultan of Persia, and struggled for independence in accordance with the customary practice of incessant intra-dynastic conflicts among the Seljuk chiefs.[5] Moreover, Laurent firmly stressed the lack of obedience, discipline, and organization as a common feature in the behavior of Turkish warriors, who were generally speaking reluctant to submit to any supreme authority, preferring instead to follow the most powerful in pursuit of easy profits and temporary advantages.[6] Consequently, in Laurent's view the establishment of Seljuk troops in Byzantine towns and fortified places certainly did not result from well-defined political goals and carefully thought-out strategies, but should rather be ascribed to the conduct of competing Byzantine generals, who opened for them the gates to these places by employing them as mercenaries. By and large, Laurent's interpretation found broad acceptance in the Western bibliography and, apart from some slight modifications regarding the untamed nature of the Turks, has been widely adopted by younger generations of scholars.

Referring to diverging opinions concerning the relationship between the Seljuk Turks in Anatolia and those in the central Muslim lands, Claude Cahen rejected the notion of an official appointment as a legitimizing strategy of later Persian historiography. As regards the position of the Turks in Asia Minor, however, he further developed Laurent's thesis by combining the fact of their permanent establishment in Bithynia with the statement of certain Byzantine authors that at about that time Sulaymān came to be called "sultan" by his partisans. Given that the use of this title conflicted with the claims of the Great Seljuk Sultan Malikshāh and thus could not have been officially bestowed upon Sulaymān by the caliph, Cahen's argument goes, it must have been the recognition of his rule by the Byzantines that caused his companions to concede him this title.[7] Another new element in Cahen's presentation is his explanation of Sulaymān's expansionist policy towards Cilicia and Antioch, which is described as an attempt to maintain bonds with the main body of Turkish forces in order to avoid being absorbed by the numerically superior Byzantine population.[8]

Speros Vryonis, Michael Angold, and Dimitri Korobeinikov adopted many of the previous views of Sulaymān without further questioning.[9] More than had been previously done, Korobeinikov included Armenian and late Seljuk chronicles in his discussion, thus supporting the emergence of a strong Turkish dominion in western Asia Minor from about 1075 onwards, but his interpretation combines near-contemporary Byzantine and later sources without sufficiently taking into account the particularities of each historiographical tradition. Taken together, although it is generally accepted that Sulaymān's presence in western Asia Minor had deep and often-irreversible effects on the political situation of Byzantium, Western scholars have never proceeded to a thorough examination of Sulaymān's role and activities. The main reason for the rapid establishment of Turkish warriors in western Asia Minor is usually sought in intra-Byzantine conflicts, in which the Turks became more or less coincidentally involved. This view also reflects the perception of Byzantine narratives, which refer to these events from the viewpoint of the Byzantine ruling elite.

As far as Turkish scholarship in the Republican period is concerned, Mükrimin Halil Yinanç's monograph on the Seljuk conquest of Anatolia (first published in 1934) provided the first systematic examination of the available source material and put in place the basic elements for a new interpretation, embedding the figure of Sulaymān b. Qutlumush into the context of Anatolian Turkish nationalism.[10] According to the author's political convictions, favoring the concept of a Turkish nation based in an Anatolian homeland (*Anadoluculuk*) in contrast to Pan-Turkism or Ottoman dynastic concepts,[11] Yinanç described Sulaymān as the "greatest and most respected father of the Anatolian Turks" (*Anadolu Türklerin en büyük ve en muhterem babası*).[12] As the last and greatest commander in the conquest of a region that after wars and battles lasting more than half a century came to be called Turkey, Yinanç argued, Sulaymān was honored by all historians with the title of the conqueror of Anatolia. In his view, this man ranks among the most prominent conquerors and *ghāzī* warriors of Islam, on the same level as the heroes of the Muslim expansion in the seventh century. Moreover, for Yinanç, Sulaymān has to be considered the most important of all Islamic conquerors in that he led the Turkish race to the Mediterranean Sea, founded a new Turkish fatherland (*yeni bir Türk vatanı*), and first brought the Turks into contact with Greeks, Latins, Slavs, and Germans. The borders of the conquered region by and large correspond with the present ones of Anatolia, i.e., the Republic of Turkey as defined in the Treaty of Lausanne of 1923. Besides, the territory bearing the name "land of the Romans" forms part of the 12 provinces of the Great Seljuk Sultanate or the Turkish Empire (*büyük Selçuklu sultanlığı yani Türk imparatorluğu*) and thus belongs to one of the princes of the sultanic dynasty on a hereditary basis.[13]

Yinanç thus integrated Sulaymān b. Qutlumush and his notion of a Turkish Anatolian ethnicity into the broader context of far-reaching expansionist movements like the Islamic conquests and the Seljuk Empire. Accordingly, the relationship between Sulaymān and Malikshāh is described as that of a faithful subordinate commander depending upon the sultan as his overlord. Reports of a decree conferring the whole of Anatolia to Sulaymān made Yinanç believe that the title of sultan indicated the position of a general governor of Anatolia (*Anadolu vali-i umumisi*), while his military exploits allowed him to acquire additional honorifics, such as *shāh* and *ghāzī*.[14] As regards Sulaymān's attitude towards Byzantium, Yinanç, like European scholars, pointed out the importance of coalitions with Byzantine rebels for the seizure of urban centers. In contrast to Western views, however, these alliances are not regarded as resulting from the Turkish warriors' desire for booty, but rather from a well-prepared and designed strategy of conquest. The choice of Nicaea (Iznik) as the new state's residence and administrative center, for example, is explained by its vicinity to Constantinople, allowing quick expansion as far as the shores of the Sea of Marmara and future attacks on the Byzantine capital itself.[15] In this way, the Seljuk warlords appear to be like generals of modern armies moving their forces in accordance with far-reaching strategic considerations and well-defined military targets.

Ibrahim Kafesoğlu, Yinanç's assistant at the University of Istanbul in the 1940s,[16] devoted a chapter of his PhD thesis on the Great Seljuk Empire under Sultan Malikshāh to the situation in Anatolia and the rise of Sulaymān.[17] In the main points of his analysis, he was fully in line with his academic mentor, regarding both the conceptual framework and the reconstruction of historical facts. Some of Laurent's views providing a somewhat negative image of the Turkish expansion in Asia Minor are submitted to harsh criticism. In particular, Kafesoğlu argued against the opinion that the Turks ravaged Asia Minor without conquering it, that they did not settle or found a state prior to 1080, and that they lacked discipline and organization.[18] As evidence to the contrary, he referred to episodes of destruction going back to previous periods or the civil wars, to agreements with Byzantine emperors and rebels, and to pre-existing institutions of the Turkish tribal society.

A decisive step in bringing new aspects and important modifications of Sulaymān's image in Turkish historiography was the work of Osman Turan.[19] Like his predecessors, Turan highlighted Sulaymān's pivotal role as founder of a new political entity, the Seljuk State of Turkey (*Türkiye Selçuklu devleti*), as he called it, but much more than previous scholars he underlined the integrative force of this leader, who managed to unify widely dispersed Turkmen groups under his banner and thus inaugurated a new period in the history of Anatolia.[20] In contrast to older views insisting on an organic unity between Seljuk rule in Asia Minor and the sultanate of Iran, Turan argued that an important aspect of Sulaymān's policy consisted in the maintenance of his independence against the aggressive attempts of Malikshāh to force the Turks of Asia Minor into obedience.[21] The fact that this state even survived the chaotic years of the interregnum following Sulaymān's death, his argument goes, proves the strong foundations and the vitality of the new power and indicates the existence of "a new national unity" (*yeni bir millî birlik*) among the Turkmen people in Asia Minor.[22] In addition, Sulaymān is credited with outstanding civilizing capacities and organizing talents. He transformed a land suffering from decay and civil strife into a flourishing Turkish homeland, thus securing the survival of the Turkish nomads, for whom settlement in Anatolia was a matter of life or death.[23] He adopted a favorable attitude towards the indigenous Christian peasantry, which in turn was ready to submit to Seljuk rule, thus acquiring freedom and landed property. In this way, he increased agricultural production, settled Oghuz nomads in uncultivated areas, and introduced a well-functioning administrative system.[24] These and other achievements made Sulaymān a legendary figure celebrated as *ghāzī*, the first Seljuk ruler of Anatolia, and forefather of the Ottomans.[25] Osman Turan brought the idealized presentation of a highly talented ruler, military leader, and visionary state founder to completion. Sulaymān represents a prototype of ethnic leadership, preparing the ground for the creation of a new homeland and protecting the people against external threats.

Gradually, this image was further embellished with a set of character traits that, though not mentioned by any primary source, can easily be derived from widely circulating images of heroic nation builders. Ali Sevim, for instance, attributed the successful transformation of Anatolia into a Turkish homeland to Sulaymān's strong determination (*büyük azmi*), political intelligence (*eşsiz siyasî zekasıyla*), endurance in incessant conflicts (*bitip tükenmeyen mücadeleleri*), and Turkish consciousness (*Sulaymānşah'ın sahip olduğu Türklük bilinci*).[26] The same author also indicated broader historical dimensions by presenting Sulaymān's conquests as something that brought the Turks to the Mediterranean shores and into contact with European nations and thus made them forerunners of the Ottoman expansion on the Balkans.[27]

In a recent edited volume on the civilization of the Anatolian Seljuks and the beylik period, Salim Koca supports very similar arguments: Sulaymān is credited with sharp political intelligence, enabling him to make astute movements in Anatolia and northern Syria and to exploit the historical opportunities provided by the internal instability of the Byzantine Empire.[28] As every great state founder, he was both a conqueror and an organizer (*hem fatih hem de teşkilâtçı bir hükümdar*). He built up a strong and disciplined army and laid the foundations for a stable and permanent rule, but he did not have enough time to create well-functioning administrative structures. In contrast to previous scholars, Koca also finds shortcomings in Sulaymān's policy in that, without firmly establishing himself in Anatolia, he pursued an expansionist policy outside Anatolia, thus provoking a major conflict with the vassals of the Great Seljuk dynasty.[29] What Turan highlighted as a sign of autonomy constitutes in Koca's eyes political recklessness and overconfidence.

In summary, modern scholarship, both Western and Turkish, on the founder of the Seljuk State in Anatolia is largely unsatisfactory. An obvious lack of interest on the part of European scholars goes hand in hand with anachronistic interpretations related to the modern discourse on national history on the part of Turkish scholarship. Basic questions, therefore, remain open for further discussion: What was the driving force behind Sulaymān's advance into western Asia Minor? Why did he succeed in concluding his alliances with the Byzantine ruling elite and how did he manage to obtain recognition from the imperial government as a territorial ruler in Bithynia? Muslim sources mainly refer to his early activities in northern Syria and, thereafter, to the conquest of Antioch and his ensuing downfall in the years 1084–86. Byzantine sources, instead, refer to his presence in western Asia Minor from the late 1077s onwards. This gives us the opportunity to investigate different historiographical traditions with respect to parallels and common behavioral patterns in Syria and Asia Minor.

The emergence of the Qutlumush clan

As regards the political role of the Qutlumush clan prior to 1070, our knowledge largely depends on the *Saljūq-nāma* tradition. Pieces of information scattered in Arabic chronicles and in the chronicle of John Skylitzes certainly provide useful additional material, but they do not elucidate the general framework in which individual events have to be placed. If we follow the oldest surviving version of the *Saljūq-nāma* attributed to Ẓahīr al-Dīn Nīshāpūrī, Arslān-Isrā'īl, having been invited to the court of Maḥmūd of Ghazna and answering his host's questions concerning his military strength, boasted of the uncountable numbers of troops he would be able to muster. Maḥmūd, full of suspicion, gave the order to imprison Isrā'īl in the castle of Kālinjār in the Indian borderland, where seven years later he died of poisoning (ca. 1032).[30] His son Abū l-Fawāris Qutlumush, unable to free his father, entered the service of his paternal uncles.[31] On Mikā'īl's death, his sons Jaghrī Beg and Ṭughril Beg took over the leadership in the Seljuk family.[32] Nevertheless, in a letter written to Caliph al-Qā'im bi-Amr Allāh after the battle of Dandānqān and the conquest of Khurāsān, it was explicitly stated that Isrā'īl was "our leader and chief" (*muqaddam wa sarwar-i mā*). Qutlumush then reappeared as a prominent commander under Ṭughril Beg, who charged him with the conquest of the provinces of Jurjān, Dāmghān, and Qūmis.[33] From the city of Tabriz in Azerbaijan, shortly before his betrothal to the caliph's daughter, Ṭughril Beg sent Qutlumush to subdue Mosul, the Diyār Rabī'a province, and Syria and appointed him ruler over the provinces of Ṭabaristān and Mazāndarān. Ṭughril's death in September 1063 and the succession of his nephew Alp Arslān, however, provoked Qutlumush to start a rebellion, laying claim to his paternal rights to supreme leadership: "The sultanate comes to us, for which reason our father, who was the best and eldest of the tribe, was killed."[34] Of crucial significance for the Seljuk dynasty's official definition of the relationship between its Iranian and Anatolian branches is the story related immediately after Qutlumush's death and defeat in the battle of Isfarā'īn in late December 1063:

> Alp Arslān wanted to kill everyone who belonged to him and his followers and he ordered them to execute his son Sulaymān-shāh, although he was young. Niẓām al-Mulk the vizier did not consider this correct and said: "Killing them would be a mistake and a sacrilegious act." Alp Arslān therefore sent them to the border of the realm so that they would settle in the frontier region of Islam and the insignia of the emirate and the royal rank would be taken from them. As a result they would be in contempt and misery. They appointed them to Diyār Bakr and Ruhā. Sulaymān-shāh is the father of the sultans of Rūm.[35]

This account has to be seen in connection with another referring to the time after Alp Arslān's murder on 24 November 1072 and the succession of his son Malikshāh to the Great Seljuk sultanate:

> In the time of Sultan Malikshāh, with the approval of vizier Niẓām al-Mulk, they sent Sulaymān to rule the land of the Romans, so that he would put an

> end to the conflicts among the emirs and a region would be added to the lands of the Padishah. If he were to be killed, a thorn would be removed from the foot of the dynasty.[36]

In summary, the *Saljūq-nāma* clearly expresses the idea that, because their forefather Isrā'īl was the eldest and most respected representative of the entire clan, the descendants of Qutlumush rightfully took precedence over the rest of their relatives, but they were deprived of their pre-eminence because of their forefather's violent death in captivity. Consequently, Qutlumush's rebellion against his cousin Ṭughril Beg is not completely condemned as a lawless act of usurpation, but partly justified on the grounds of Ṭughril's ignoring Qutlumush's claims in favor of Jaghrī Beg's son Alp Arslān. Obviously, a strong faction within the dynasty's innermost circle, despite the prevailing position of Mīkā'īl's sons, continued to support the opinion that Isrā'īl's offspring were by no means inferior to their cousins. This awareness of pre-eminence swiftly became associated with the legitimizing strategies for Qutlumush's sons' newly acquired rule in the "land of the Romans," on the basis of which the sultanate of Rūm was integrated into the concept of dynastic legitimacy with the creation of the notion of an official appointment and transmission of power on the part of the Great Seljuk sultan in Iran. To this effect, two basic elements defining the relationship between the two sides are especially emphasized. First, after Qutlumush's death, Alp Arslān on the advice of his vizier Niẓām al-Mulk, is said to have spared the lives of his sons by instead depriving them of their royal status and exiling them to remote frontier regions in Upper Mesopotamia. Second, after mounting the throne Malikshāh is said to have partly restored their status as leading commanders of the dynasty by sending them to Byzantine territories both as overlords of the competing emirs in the region and as conquerors.

Apparently, this legitimizing tendency was readily adopted and further enhanced by Sulaymān's descendants and successors in Anatolia. In particular, over time it became associated with the concept of an autonomous sultanate based on the conferral of sovereign rights by the dynasty's supreme lord, Alp Arslān. There is no trace of this extension of the original concept in the *Saljūq-nāma* tradition, which at least before the thirteenth century is to a large extent centered on the historical memory of the Iranian Seljuk branches, nor in the bulk of local and universal Muslim chronicles. But the Anatolian Seljuks' sultanic ideology seems to have been put into circulation among their Byzantine neighbors and the Christian subjects of the Muslim-Turkish lords. Anna Komnene first spoke about a "sultanate" based in Nicaea, as will be shown below, and thereafter the Syriac author Michael the Syrian referred to the proclamation of a sultan.[37] It thus becomes clear that the original ideas of the sultan's forbearance towards his seditious relatives and of Sulaymān's appointment to the post of a subordinate military leader were gradually transformed in the course of the twelfth century into a true proclamation going back to the founder of the Seljuk State in Asia Minor. As an additional element further highlighting the lawful character of this ceremony, the account introduced the dispatch of royal insignia and a confirmation by the Abbasid caliph, the supreme spiritual authority of Islam. As various Turkish scholars have already pointed out, such an act would have been completely unacceptable for the eleventh-century leaders of the Great Seljuk Empire.[38] It would also presuppose the existence of a firmly consolidated dominion as well as a fully developed dynastic awareness on the part of the Anatolian Seljuk lords.

As far as the size and composition of the Qutlumush clan is concerned, the secondary bibliography usually refers to one brother of Qutlumush, whose name was Rasūltakīn, and to four sons, called Sulaymān, Manṣūr, Alp Ilik/Ilek, and Dawlāt (Devlet/Dolat).[39] One should bear in mind, however, that only Sulaymān figures prominently in Christian and Muslim sources, while the other individuals are mentioned in very few and isolated cases. Even more confusion results from the fact that, especially as regards the first appearances of these persons, the available Arabic accounts discuss a certain Ibn Qutlumush without further specifying his identity. Dawlāt b. Quṭlumush is mentioned only once, in the chronicle of al-ʿAẓīmī, on the occasion of his death during an attack on the city of A'zāz in 516/1122–23.[40] Given that this event dates to more than 35 years after the death of Sulaymān in 1086 and the Seljuk dynasty of Asia Minor had reached its third generation, it is highly doubtful that the aforementioned person actually was one of Sulaymān's brothers. The same holds true for another individual who figured as member of the Qutlumush clan and whose name is usually reconstructed as Alp Ilek/Ilik. Just as Dawlāt, he is mentioned only once, on the occasion of his death by poisoning in the city of Edessa in 1095 or 1096. Michael the Syrian calls him *Alpīragh amīrā Tūrkāyē* (the emir of the Turks), whereas in the chronicle of Matthew of Edessa he appears as "the sultan al-Faraj, who was descended from Kutulmish," which is the only indication that he might have been a brother of Sulaymān.[41] The details concerning the circumstances of his death are confused. According to Michael the Syrian, Gabriel, the Byzantine lord of Melitene, brought the Turkish emir to Edessa and poisoned him there. Matthew of Edessa, instead, relates that the Armenian *kouropalates* Tʿoros had invited him to Edessa to deliver the city into his hands, but after a brief reign of one month he killed him with poison. In these reports Alp Ilek is depicted as operating independently from the other Turkish emirs, such as Suqmān b. Artuq of Mārdīn, Balduk of Samosata, Riḍwān b. Tutush of Aleppo, and Yaghi-Siyān of Antioch, who in the years before and/or after the arrival of the First Crusade were the leading potentates in the region.[42] On the other hand, the chroniclers do not tell us from where he came and what the basis of his power was. If he was in fact a brother of Sulaymān, we cannot say anything about his role in the years following Sulaymān's death in 1086.

Thus, the only fully trustworthy piece of information concerning the sons of Qutlumush is transmitted by the Byzantine historian Nikephoros Bryennios, who explicitly speaks of two brothers, Manṣūr and Sulaymān.[43] A weak echo of the presence of two Qutlumush brothers in western Asia Minor can be found in the chronicle of Bar Hebraeus, who mentions "a certain emir from the lineage of the Seljuks, whose name is Qatlamīsh, the son of Yabbāgū Arslān, the son of Seljuk, who had fled from Sultan Alp Arslān and sought refuge to the dominion of the Romans."[44] The passage obviously conflates the two brothers' father with events and circumstances pertaining to the period 1077/78. The man in question is said to have been an ally of Nikephoros Botaneiates and to have supported him in his uprising against Emperor Michael VII. Another episode mentioned by Bar Hebraeus is Qatlamīsh's struggle with the Seljuk commander Bursuq, who had been sent by Sultan Malikshāh to bring him back. Eventually Qatlamīsh was killed by unfair means during a duel, and the remainder of his people joined Sulaymān.[45] This report reflects some of the events that took place in the time of Malikshāh's Syrian campaign and Bursuq's expedition against Sulaymān b. Qutlumush's companions in Asia Minor in 1086. Moreover, the negotiations between Bursuq and the emperor are described in the same manner as those of Afshīn concerning the handing over of Arīsghī/Chrysoskoulos mentioned in Muslim sources. Bar Hebraeus certainly mixed up different persons and chronological layers, so there are serious doubts regarding the trustworthiness of the related details. It is noteworthy, however, that he distinguishes between two different persons of the Qutlumush clan operating in western Asia Minor, something that seems to refer to a historical core represented by the brothers Sulaymān and Manṣūr. Although in the early years of his activities as chief of Turkish warriors Sulaymān was operating along with one or several of his brothers and perhaps other relatives, he gradually emerged as the supreme commander and uncontested leader of the family branch, the one who came to establish himself in Anatolia.

The formation of the first Seljuk lordships in Syria

The situation in which the sons of Qutlumush made their appearance in the political setting of Syria and the Byzantine borderland in the early 1070s was characterized, on the one hand, by incessant conflicts among numerous regional factors, such as Fatimid governors, Arab tribes, local potentates, town militias (*aḥdāth*), and Byzantine commanders, and, on the other, by a broad spectrum of Turkish warrior groups, whose activities ranged from large-scale invasions to geographically confined raids and short-lived alliances. At about the same time as Alp Arslān's Syrian campaign in 1070/71, the Turkmen commander Atsiz b. Uwaq al-Khwārizmī undertook incursions into Palestine and central Syria, while a number of independent Turkish warlords were operating on their own account in order to gain booty and establish power bases.[46] As we have already seen with respect to the emirate of Aleppo, these developments unavoidably entailed a further weakening of both Byzantine and Fatimid influence in Syria, along with an overall increase of disorder and confusion. Due to the incessant hostilities, many regions and urban centers suffered severe devastation, supply shortages, depopulation, and famine. Nevertheless, the vacuum of power that resulted from the elimination of pre-existing elites also enabled the establishment of new political powers controlled by Turkmen chiefs.[47]

Available sources tell us very little about the composition and nature of these groups. In most cases, we know nothing more than the names of the commanders and some terms referring to discernible ethnic or tribal characteristics of the warriors under their command. Nevertheless, through these accounts we learn a great deal about the aims, behavioral patterns, and strategies of these groups during their political and military activities in Syria and Palestine. Just as in the case of the Iraqi Turkmen and the groups operating in the Diyār Bakr province and the region of Aleppo, one comes across a multi-layered process of gradual penetration of areas and political structures. The accumulation of wealth and power on the basis of booty and captives prepared the grounds for building up coalitions with other raiders or the local elites and for establishing permanent power bases in or near important urban centers and residences of emirs. These, in some cases, could also form the core of a gradually growing radius of territorial control and the creation of a rudimentary lordship. At this point, new concerns and methods aiming at the consolidation of stable rule and the acquisition of legitimacy in a contest with other competing forces came into play.

Syria was the first region within the Byzantine sphere of influence in which the Turks proceeded to establish permanent political entities and played a pioneering role for similar developments in Anatolia. As we have seen already with respect to other regions, the complexity of these processes cannot be sufficiently explained through a bipolar model juxtaposing conquerors and conquered. An outstanding quality of the Turkish warlords consisted in their astonishing ability to adapt to the particularities of each region and to creep into local social fabrics and personal networks. Both the indigenous groups and the Turkish invaders were too divided and uncoordinated to be able to impose their hegemony by force. The key to the success of the Seljuk expansionist movement was the swift adoption of local practices and concepts in conjunction with the exploitation of friction and antagonism among the local factors.

The fading influence of supra-regional powers, such as Byzantium and the Fatimid caliphate, was an additional feature favoring the intrusion of Turkish warrior groups into the enfeebled and disintegrating structures of the political landscape in Syria. This in part answers the question of whether the Turkish invaders at that time were primarily attached to nomadic or to sedentary patterns. Even if nomadic features still prevailed in their lifestyle, fighting technique, social organization, and self-identity, the available sources, which were all written from the viewpoint of outside observers, hardly refer to these elements with respect to their political achievements. What really mattered for the Turks was to make the transition from raids on rural areas to the exercise of effective control over urban centers by establishing relations with sedentary communities and by adopting their institutional framework and administrative apparatus. Hence, the dichotomy of nomadic *vs.* sedentary lifestyles, which is so often referred to in discussions about the Turkish conquests, should be supplemented by a thorough analysis of the mechanisms of transition and of the grey zones and overlaps between the two spheres.

With respect to procedures of legitimization, from the second half of the tenth century onwards, large parts of Syria were influenced by a long-standing tradition of Fatimid rule based on Ismaili Shiite doctrines and ideological concepts related to the caliphate of Cairo. This mainly applies to Palestine, central Syria with Damascus as its main center, and the littoral as far as Tripoli, but at times Fatimid suzerainty also extended to the emirate of Aleppo and various petty emirates between the Euphrates and the Orontes Valley.[48] The big confederations of Arab nomad tribes, i.e., the Kilāb in the environs of Aleppo, the Kalb in the hinterland of Damascus, and the Ṭayyi' in Palestine, according to the constantly changing balances of power in the region vacillated between acceptance of Fatimid supremacy and autonomous tendencies. Occasionally, the Byzantine imperial government took advantage of these constellations by including Arab chieftains and emirs in its own sphere of influence through coalitions with the ducate of Antioch and the bestowal of court titles.[49]

In this environment, Seljuk dynastic ideas and Iranian models of kingship that the Turkish warriors brought to Syria constituted a novelty. The rapid emergence of political entities in Syria required the implementation of hierarchical concepts defining the relations among the sultan, inferior family members, subordinate commanders, and vassals in various regions of Syria according to the models known from Iran and Iraq. In contrast to the predominant Shiite circles related to the Fatimid caliphate, most Turkish rulers adhered to the doctrines of Sunni Islam and the Seljuk claims to supremacy over the Abbasid caliphate. This was usually articulated through the replacement of the Fatimid Friday prayer by the Abbasid one, so that the new rulers appeared as subjects of the Abbasid caliph, who legitimized their authority through letters of appointment, honorifics, honorary robes, and other symbols of power. Nevertheless, there were also attempts to create bonds of allegiance with the caliphate of Cairo, and thus the religious and ideological identity of the Turks in Syria cannot be considered consistent and uniform.

After the invasions and temporary settlement of various Turkish groups beginning in the early 1060s, the activities of the Turkmen chief (*muqaddam al-Atrāk al-Ghuzz*) Atsiz b. Uwaq al-Khwārizmī in central Syria and Palestine mainly led to the emergence of a Seljuk lordship in the region. The sequence of events is debatable in some points, but it seems that already before September 1071, both Jerusalem and al-Ramla in Palestine had been conquered and attacks on Damascus and its environs had begun.[50] In addition to Atsiz's forces, there were other Turkmen bands that seem to have been loosely associated with the former but were largely operating on their own.[51] The local elites frequently established first contacts with the Turkish invaders by proposing that they enter their service and fight on their behalf in exchange for payments and booty. In a second stage, such collaborations could lead to the acquisition of domains for permanent settlement and agricultural exploitation. Hence, the nature of these alliances varied according to the investments that individual potentates were willing to make and ranged from salaries and grants of booty to landed estates. The Turkish warriors, for their part, had the opportunity to gain considerable amounts of money and economic power, which later enabled them to take hold of towns and the surrounding areas. At this point the local rulers were no longer able to exert control over them, and the allies easily turned into independent territorial lords.

Let us take a closer look at some characteristic examples of these phenomena. Among the governors who were operating in the Fatimid territories of Syria during the 1060s we come across Badr al-Jamālī, the future vizier and commander in chief (*amīr al-juyūsh*) in Egypt, who in 1063 had been appointed governor of Damascus and later appeared as commander of important coastal towns, such as Acre/ʿAkkā and Sidon/Ṣaydā.[52] His efforts to take hold of Tyre/Ṣūr prompted the local ruler to summon Turkish warriors for help and thus to fend off the Fatimid aggressor. In 462/20 October 1069-8 October 1070 the potentate and judge (*qāḍī*) of Tyre, Ibn Abī ʿAqīl, came into contact with the Turkmen chief Qaralī/ū/Qurlū (*muqaddam al-Atrāk*), who had come to Syria and Palestine along with other warlords like the nephew of al-Malik b. Khān, Atsiz b. Uwaq and his brothers.[53] The Turkmen chief managed to relieve the pressure on Tyre by laying siege to the port of Sidon with a considerable force of 6,000 horsemen. Qaralū's action seems to have been effective, for Badr al-Jamālī, despite the desperate situation in Tyre, was forced to lift the siege for some time. When he reassumed it, encircling the town by land and by sea for one year and causing a serious shortage of foodstuffs, he still was unable to achieve his goal "because of the opposition of the Turks in Syria."[54]

This example shows that within a few years Turkish warrior groups had turned into a dangerous military force that was able to seriously undermine the attempts of the Fatimid government and their representatives in Syria to exert control over the region. But this does not mean that the Turkmen leaders pursued any consistent strategy focusing on the support of local rulers to the detriment of Fatimid governors. The only recognizable pattern regarding the choice of allies was a sort of who-pays-best policy. A case in point is Ibn Khān, the powerful supporter of the Mirdāsid emirs, who after splitting off from the rulers of Aleppo entered the service of the said Ibn ʿAqīl in Tyre. During the one-year siege by Badr al-Jamālī, Ibn Khān suddenly switched sides. Hence, Ibn ʿAqīl ordered two of Ibn Khān's slave soldiers to kill him. Contemporary witnesses and chroniclers were obviously embarrassed by the commander's treachery, for the report quoted by Sibṭ b. al-Jawzī emphatically stresses Ibn ʿAqīl's generosity, for which the Turk did not reward him adequately. After his murder, Ibn Khān's head was publicly exhibited in Tyre, something that shows that the execution was actually perceived as punishment for the chief's disloyalty. Nevertheless, many of his soldiers switched to Badr al-Jamālī's camp, apparently because the prospects of success and revenues were much better there after their leader's demise.[55] Allegiances among the Turkish warriors were still highly fluctuating in their interactions with the Syrian elites. Ideological bonds with supreme authorities only gained importance when the Turks themselves started to build up permanent forms of territorial rule.

Be that as it may, the military role of the Turkish chiefs was by no means confined to intervening in conflicts between local rulers and Fatimid forces, but it also affected the internal strife of opposing factions within the local elites. After Ibn Khān's departure, the rulers of Aleppo continued to employ Turkmen warriors for their purposes. Maḥmūd b. Naṣr of Aleppo faced an attempt by his uncle ʿAṭiyya to drive him out of his residence. After Alp Arslān's retreat from the city in May 1071, 'Aṭiyya concluded an alliance with the Byzantine *doux* of Antioch Khatatourios and the Banū Kilāb, attacking the region of Ma'arrat Miṣrīn south of Aleppo with joint forces.[56] In response to this threat, Maḥmūd asked the Turkmen chieftains in Palestine for their support in exchange for salaries, and thus the aforementioned Qaralū intervened in the affairs of Aleppo.[57] His troops, which according to one source amounted to 1,000 men, supported the emir during the ensuing hostilities until the Byzantines of Antioch sometime after April 1072 retreated, most probably because of the developments following the battle of Manzikert.[58]

Disputes over expected rewards easily became a source of instability and unrest, turning useful allies into dangerous enemies. In the year 464/1071 September 29-1072 September 16 the Fatimid governor of Acre, Badr al-Jamālī, seriously threatened by local Arab tribes, called in a group of Turkmen warriors (*al-Nāwakiyya*) who reportedly were fleeing from Alp Arslān.[59] The source gives no other details about this group, but on the basis of the events mentioned in this context, they may once again be identified with the forces of Qaralū. Badr al-Jamālī conceded to them the booty they gained from the Arabs but was not willing to pay them salaries or to give them land grants (*iqṭā'*).[60] In this case, Badr's refusal caused serious friction with the Turkmen warriors, who terminated their coalition with the Fatimid governor. Subsequently they established themselves in Tiberias of Galilee, distributing estates and crop yields among themselves. Badr al-Jamālī thus began to collaborate with local Arab tribes against his former mercenaries who launched attacks on Tripoli and the Balqā' region (modern northern Jordan).[61] Changes in the political constellations were closely related to migrations and the occupation of new territories.

It was most probably at this time that Qaralū succeeded in taking possession of al-Ramla, which formerly had been seized by the troops of Atsiz b. Uwaq and was described as a destroyed site.[62] The Turkmen warriors rebuilt the town, brought the peasants back, and took measures for the cultivation of the surrounding estates.[63] In 1072, Qaralū's warriors laid siege to Damascus and Acre. The townspeople of the former were forced to pay the sum of 50,000 dinars. During the fights with Badr al-Jamālī and the Banū Kalb Arabs, who inhabited the environs of Acre, Qaralū lost his life, but his soldiers under the command of one of his relatives caused great damage to the entire region and extended their activities as far as Tyre. A detachment supposedly advanced as far as Egypt.[64]

Qaralū and his companions considered warfare, above all, a very lucrative business allowing them to accumulate wealth at the expense of various opposing parties. Apart from short-lived agreements with clearly defined objectives, there were hardly any factors creating cohesion or bonds of allegiance. As soon as one of the potentates refused to make further concessions, the Turks sought to operate on their own or turned against their former employer. It is also noteworthy that the Turks of Qaralū engaged in different activities at various levels. While gaining booty and extorting tribute during their extensive military ventures, they began cultivating and exploiting land and peasants in the region of al-Ramla.

These patterns clearly demonstrate that these people swiftly adapted to the cultural environment they came to live in and easily switched from nomadic preoccupations to sedentary forms of agricultural production. Qaralū did not live long enough to consolidate his rule, and his followers were swiftly absorbed by larger groups.

The case of the Turkish commander Atsiz illustrates the successful accomplishment of the next step, from accumulating wealth and domains to establishing a viable territorial lordship bolstered by the legitimization of a supreme authority.[65] Once he and his followers had managed to build up a power base in the newly acquired regions in Palestine, they started to develop legitimizing strategies, as is clearly expressed in a letter to Caliph al-Qā'im of Baghdad.[66] Therein Atsiz announced that he had conquered Jerusalem and had established the *khuṭba* in the name of the Abbasid caliph. He treated the inhabitants well and defeated the Egyptians without fighting, for he did not intend to attack the sanctuary of God but only wished to establish the prayer in the name of the Abbasid imam and the sultan. After negotiations with the Fatimid governor, the starving city was handed over in exchange for a guarantee of safety and the concession of domains to the governor. Atsiz further assured the caliph that he had not appropriated any of the vast riches of the town and had ordered his soldiers to protect the inhabitants. In this way, Atsiz presented himself as a subordinate commander acknowledging the supreme authority of the sultan and the Abbasid caliph and supporting the Seljuk dynasty's program of Sunni restoration. His newly established lordship in the city of God's sanctuary forms part of a greater political and religious entity, while his lenient attitude towards the inhabitants demonstrates the moral integrity of his pursuits.

As a result, the sources began calling him "lord of al-Quds and al-Ramla" or "lord of Syria/al-Shām," and he is said to have arbitrarily adopted the title of *al-malik al-mu'aẓẓam* (the honored king).[67] In this capacity he continued to pursue his expansionist plans in Syria, undertook campaigns against the Syrian hinterland and coastal towns, such as Aleppo, Rafaniyya, Jaffa, and Tyre, and after a series of annual attacks he eventually seized Damascus on 1 July 1076.[68] In doing so Atsiz faced the opposition of both people belonging to the sultan's entourage and other Turkmen chieftains operating in Syria. The situation during this first stage of Seljuk intrusion in Syria was highly conflict-ridden. The superiority of one group over the other largely depended upon a commander's ability to build up and maintain a power balance among the local warlords and to secure the support of the Seljuk dynasty and the Abbasid court. This is clearly articulated in a letter that Atsiz sent to Sultan Malikshāh in response to the sultan's intention to replace him with his brother Tāj al-Dawla Tutush as governor of Syria:

> I am the obedient servant and deputy in these provinces that I have conquered on my own without causing him troubles or asking for help. I established the prayer in his name and did not deceive him with respect to the money that I am able to pay.[69]

Irrespective of the historicity of these words, this letter gives a good description of what was to be expected from a loyal Seljuk governor regarding his attitude towards the sultan. The reasons for Tutush's appointment are nowhere explicitly mentioned, but it seems that there was fear that Atsiz, in contrast to what he had promised in his letter, would develop into an unruly potentate. He was to become simply too powerful a ruler in such a crucial province bordering the Fatimid realm.[70] At Niẓām al-Mulk's instigation, on this occasion Atsiz received a number of insignia as a token of the sultan's benevolence and the close relationship between the governor and his lord.[71] But eventually this was no obstacle to the materialization of Malikshāh's plans, and two years later Tāj al-Dawla Tutush actually seized power in Syria.[72]

A decisive turning point in Atsiz's career was his disastrous expedition to Egypt in late 1076. The event illustrates both the strengths and weaknesses of his lordship. The official recognition of his rule by the sultan and the ambitious plan to strike the Fatimid archenemy in the very center of his realm provided Atsiz with a strong unifying force. He is said to have gathered a large army of several thousand troops consisting of Turks, Kurds, and Arabs, and the first part of his campaign was quite successful. Outside Cairo, however, Atsiz's army suffered a terrible defeat at the hands of the forces of Badr al-Jamālī, and the Syrian army was further decimated during its retreat via Gaza and al-Ramla. On arriving in Damascus on 7 February 1077, Atsiz was penniless and had no more than 15 horsemen accompanying him.[73] Doubtlessly, this defeat was a terrible blow to his prestige. In addition, the people of Damascus were facing a serious famine, which further undermined his position as supreme ruler and enabled Badr al-Jamālī and the pro-Fatimid forces to initiate a revolt striving for the restoration of Cairo's supremacy in the region.[74] Atsiz' lordship managed within a short period to secure a strong basis of legitimacy and to build up an impressive military power, but it was not able to establish internal cohesion and stability.

Internal conflicts of Turkish warlords

Another crucial aspect of the developments in Syria was exhibited by the conflicts between competing Turkish warlords. These had repercussions for the situation in Asia Minor as well, because of the direct involvement of the sons of Qutlumush. Atsiz's position in Syria was challenged by a Turkmen commander called Shuklī (*amīr al-Turkumān*), who managed to seize Acre in November 1074 and made an attempt to carve out an independent lordship in Syria.[75] While Shuklī and his warriors were looting and ravaging the surroundings of Acre, a certain Ibn Saqḥā', a high-ranking official of the powerful Fatimid army commander (*amīr al-juyūsh*) Badr al-Jamālī, after losing a precious shipload of Badr's personal fortune, agreed with some local notables to hand the city over to the Turkmen chief. Shuklī executed the governor, the judge, and other local officials of Badr, appropriated his possessions, imprisoned his wife and children, and married his daughter. Shuklī, at a single blow, acquired an important coastal town along with large amounts of money and formally consolidated his position by establishing bonds of marriage with the family of the most powerful man in Fatimid Egypt at that time. Politically, he distanced himself from the Fatimid government by killing and expelling its representatives and by collaborating with the local nobility of Acre. At the same time, he began to forge alliances with the lord of Damascus, Muʿallā b. Ḥaydara b. Manzū, by giving him his sister in marriage, and with the Banū Kilāb tribe, by exchanging oaths and hostages.[76] Muʿallā b. Ḥaydara was a Fatimid officer of the Kutāma Berbers, who had come to Damascus along with his father Ḥiṣn al-Dawla Ḥaydara and ruled as governor on behalf of Badr al-Jamālī in the period between July 1069 and August 1075. Because of its repressive and unjust character, his rule is said to have been especially hated by the local population.[77] Apparently, the expansion of Atsiz b. Uwaq and other Turkish lords in Syria seems to have advanced to such an extent that the governor of Damascus deemed it more advantageous to collaborate with the new Turkish lord of Acre than to respect his allegiance to his former overlord Badr al-Jamālī. Shuklī, in turn, gained support from the most important urban center in central Syria and through his alliance with the Banū Kilāb from the most powerful tribe in the Aleppo region.

Atsiz, who himself nourished serious ambitions towards Damascus, doubtlessly considered Shuklī's exploits a dangerous threat to his own predominance in the region. As a result, Atsiz sought the recognition of his supremacy in Syria by asking Shuklī to deliver him the imprisoned members of Badr's family and half of the booty taken in Acre. Shuklī's refusal articulated in an insulting response signaled the outbreak of an open conflict between the two warlords.[78] This example illustrates the highly antagonistic spirit that emerged among Turkish chieftains as soon as they managed to create the nucleus of a lordship. As territorial lords exerting authority over major urban centers as important as Jerusalem, Acre, or al-Ramla, the Turkish warlords quickly gained control over large revenues and military forces, something that, in turn, secured them a certain degree of autonomy and increased their readiness to use violence against each other.

At that time the Qutlumush clan became involved for the first time in the power struggle of the competing Turkish factions in Syria.[79] The only available account referring to these events does not further specify the identity of Shuklī's ally, merely calling him "the son of Qutlumush, the Turk" (*Ibn Qutlumush al-Turkī*) and locating him in the Byzantine borderland (*wa-kāna fī aṭrāf al-Rūm*).[80] This laconic phrase does not allow us to determine whether Shuklī was dealing with Sulaymān himself or with one of his brothers. Nor can we say with any certainty in which part of the borderland the sons of Qutlumush were operating at the time in question. Most probably, they were not too far from central Syria, perhaps in the region of Antioch or slightly further northeast in the Euphrates region.

A passage from a letter that Shuklī reportedly wrote to Ibn Qutlumush reveals that this coalition, apart from securing military support, aimed at creating a basis of dynastic legitimacy:

> 'You belong to the Seljuk family (*al-Saljūqiyya*) and to the house of kingship (*bayt al-mulk*). If we be obedient to you and enter your service, we will be

> honored by you and filled with pride. Atsiz does not belong to the house of kingship and we are not willing to follow and to obey him.' And he set out before him the whole matter concerning Atsiz and Syria as something easy and said: 'Promises concerning money reached us from Egypt if we destroy and remove him from Syria.'[81]

Given that Atsiz b. Uwaq had been officially recognized as governor of Jerusalem and al-Ramla by Sultan Malikshāh, Shuklī had to seek ways to pass over Atsiz's claims to superiority by connecting himself with the Seljuk dynasty. As immediate descendants of one of the most prominent forefathers of the ruling dynasty, whom a large confederation of Turkish warriors known as "Iraqi Turkmen" considered their leader and figurehead, the sons of Qutlumush possessed a remarkable amount of legitimizing power. Because of their seditious past, this capacity was certainly not recognized by Malikshāh, but a great part of the warriors attached to the Seljuk dynasty and its political principles may have deemed the Qutlumush branch a serious alternative to existing power structures. Atsiz, instead, may have been acknowledged by the ruling sultan, but he still was a man of inferior standing among the leading representatives of the Seljuk military elite. Thus, Shuklī's strategy to bolster his attempts to gain a leading position in Syria by proclaiming his allegiance to other leaders endowed with royal qualities certainly had good prospects for success.

A novelty that appeared in the context of the alliance between Shuklī and the sons of Qutlumush was the unconcealed collaboration with the Seljuk dynasty's and Abbasid caliphate's archenemy, the Fatimid government of Cairo. During the 1050s Sultan Ṭughril Beg was frequently confronted with various pro-Shiite and pro-Fatimid movements in Iraq, but these usually drew their support from groups outside the Seljuk army. In this case Turkish military chiefs and even dynastic members were prone to ally themselves with the Fatimid caliphate in order to expel their opponent and Malikshāh's supreme representative from Syria. It may well be that, after his takeover in Acre, Shuklī had made serious attempts to gain the support of Badr al-Jamālī, perhaps with the aid of local notables and his newly acquired ally in Damascus. It should also be noted that the emirate of Aleppo, despite its formal submission to Seljuk rule, still remained under Fatimid influence. The hope apparently was that the strong Fatimid presence in Syria could act as a counter-weight to the pressure to be exerted by the Seljuk sultanate. This example also illustrates that, despite the explicit pro-Abbasid and pro-Sunni attitude that had been so extensively propagated by the Seljuk chiefs ever since the early 1040s, there was still considerable freedom of action with respect to their political options. The Seljuk branch of the sons of Qutlumush and their followers apparently wished to take advantage of the long-lasting tradition of Fatimid rule in Syria and to use the caliphate of Cairo as a source of legitimacy in exchange for the restoration of Fatimid suzerainty in the region. Consequently, after uniting their forces Shuklī and Ibn Qutlumush went to Tiberias, where they openly proclaimed their obedience to the Fatimid caliph.[82] Turkmen warriors had developed a strong sense of loyalty towards the Seljuk dynasty, which they considered "their house of kingship," but they were still flexible with respect to Shiite and Sunni doctrines.

The conflict ended with a violent clash on the battlefield: Atsiz went forth from Jerusalem to take action against his opponents, and thus Shuklī and Ibn Qutlumush supported by the townspeople encountered him outside Tiberias. Despite the backing of the locals, the pro-Fatimid Turkish allies suffered a disastrous defeat. Shuklī was killed; Ibn Qutlumush, a younger brother, and a cousin were taken prisoner. The sources also refer to seven concubines of Ibn Qutlumush who preferred being killed to falling into the enemy's hands. Only Shuklī's son Ṣabrā managed to escape to Acre, but the townspeople refused to let him in and surrendered to the Fatimid governor of Tyre, Jawhar al-Madanī, thus re-establishing Egyptian rule over the city. Most likely, Atsiz's victory was due to his superior military forces, for Malikshāh is said to have sent a contingent of 3,000 slave soldiers (*ghilmān*) in his support.[83] Another survivor was Shuklī's father, who managed to escape to Cairo. At the time of Atsiz's Egyptian expedition in 1077 he appears as a supporter of Badr al-Jamālī, trying to alienate Turkmen warriors from Atsiz's army.[84] The fact that he won over a considerable number of soldiers shows that the sentiments of allegiance among the various warrior groups could persist years after their leader's death.

At about the same time, in the summer/autumn of 1075, another brother of Ibn Qutlumush reportedly came from Byzantine territory to the region of Aleppo and Antioch.[85] After skirmishes with Emir Naṣr b. Maḥmūd and the town militia (*aḥdāth*), he agreed to lift the siege in return for a sum of money. Modern scholars usually identify this man as Sulaymān,[86] but again the question cannot be determined with any certainty. The commander in question moved southward to Salamiyya east of Ḥamāh, where he sent word to Atsiz, asking for his brothers. During the further course of the expedition, he became engaged in another fight with the town militia of Aleppo; besieged Antioch, thereby extorting an annual tribute of 20,000 dinars in return for halting his attacks on the city's cultivated lands; and undertook new raids in the region of Aleppo.[87]

In all likelihood, we are dealing with retaliatory attacks that started after the defeat of Tiberias and perhaps were aimed at putting pressure on Atsiz in order to force him to deliver his prisoners. Nevertheless, the game seems to have been irreversibly lost, and the assaults had no lasting results. With the failure of the Turkmen-Fatimid coalition, the previous status quo was immediately re-established. The emir of Aleppo and Atsiz both presented themselves as loyal governors of the Seljuk sultan and denounced the operations of the sons of Qutlumush as seditious acts directed against their overlord's authority. Thus, Naṣr b. Maḥmūd urged Ibn Qutlumush to depart if he was obedient to the sultan, and Atsiz replied with respect to the fate of the imprisoned brothers that he would do with them whatever the sultan asked him to do.[88] In December 1075/January 1076 an emissary of Atsiz brought the prisoners to Baghdad.[89] Thereafter we once more lose track of the sons of Qutlumush until they suddenly re-appear in a completely different setting, the Byzantine province of Bithynia in 1078, during the uprising of Nikephoros Botaneiates against Emperor Michael VII.

Turkish warlords and the breakdown of Mirdāsid rule in Aleppo

Unlike many regions in central Syria and Palestine that gradually turned into centers of newly established Turkish lordships, the emirate of Aleppo continued to be in the hands of members of the Mirdāsid dynasty, until the city was besieged between May and late August 1079 by a strong coalition of Turkish and Arab forces under the command of Tāj al-Dawla Tutush and ultimately fell to the ʿUqaylid lord of Mosul, Sharaf al-Dawla Abū l-Makārim Muslim b. Quraysh, who took possession of the city in September/October 1080.[90] The last years of Mirdāsid rule in Aleppo are characterized by an undiminished struggle for power among various local elements and foreign potentates. Within these groupings Turkish warrior groups featured prominently, but they were heavily restricted in their activities by other competing forces or by conflicts among themselves. A case in point is Aḥmad Shāh al-Turkī, "the emir of the Turks" (*amīr al-Atrāk*),[91] who closely collaborated with both Naṣr b. Maḥmūd (January 1075-May 1076) and his brother Sābiq (May 1076-June 1080). It is noteworthy that his followers are explicitly located in the "rural areas" (*ḥāḍir*) of Aleppo, which indicates that they kept their nomadic lifestyle and did not merge with the townspeople and the urban environment of the city.[92] There even seems to have been a certain distrust between the two sides, for on the approach of Tāj al-Dawla Tutush, instead of seeking refuge within the walled town, the Turks retreated to the fortress Ḥiṣn al-Jisr in order to protect their possessions and families. Ibn al-ʿAdīm's account refers to the bad memories from the time of Ibn Khān.[93] Moreover, some of Aḥmad Shāh's people seem to have camped in the Euphrates region east of Aleppo.[94]

In comparison to the Turks of Atsiz, Shuklī, and other commanders in Syria, this group maintained its social character as non-sedentary nomads and refrained from mingling with the local urban elites. Their military activities, however, were broadly in line with the behavioral patterns known from other warrior groups. In some cases one gains the impression that Aḥmad Shāh at times played a central role as supreme commander of the emirate's forces. In September/October 1075 he participated in Naṣr b. Maḥmūd's expedition against Manbij, one of the last Byzantine strongholds, and in the summer of 1077 he led a campaign against Antioch.[95] In early 1076 he appeared as commander in heavy battles with Atsiz's brother Jāwulī in the region of Ḥamāh,[96] and in July 1076 he successfully warded off a strong coalition consisting of Sābiq's seditious brother Waththāb and the Banū Kilāb tribe and gaining tremendous amounts of booty by looting the enemy's camp.[97] Hence, he obviously was involved in all the important military operations of the emirate, including raids against the Byzantine neighbors and fights with dangerous internal and external adversaries. The revenues of all these ventures must have been considerable, although the figures mentioned with respect to the victory over the Banū Kilāb—100,000 camels, 4,000 sheep, 10,000 slaves, and a large number of slave girls—was certainly an exception.[98]

Aḥmad Shāh maintained especially close relations with Emir Sābiq b. Maḥmūd, as can be deduced from Aḥmad's leading position in the conflict with Waththāb,[99] but there were also serious clashes among members of the emirate's elite. For unknown reasons, Naṣr b. Maḥmūd imprisoned Aḥmad Shāh in the citadel of Aleppo and mounted an attack on the Turkish camp, which eventually cost him his life.[100] Muḥammad b. Damlāj, a Turkish commander who allied with Aḥmad in June 1076, also imprisoned Aḥmad in order to extort a large ransom from Sābiq. Our source speaks of 10,000 dinars and 20 horses.[101] This discord seems to have been motivated by easily gained material benefits and does not reveal any deep-rooted antagonism or long-term strategy aiming at political superiority. Aḥmad Shāh was eventually killed during the siege of Aleppo by the forces of Tāj al-Dawla Tutush.[102] We do not hear anything about the fate of his Turkish fighting force, but we may assume that his troops were absorbed by one of the supra-regional powers operating in the area. All in all, Aḥmad Shāh and his ally Muḥammad b. Damlāj exemplify the persistence of independent small-size groups that did not manage to take hold of important urban centers but played a considerable role as local military forces, thus contributing to the diversification of political factions in the region. During their activities in Syria and in the first stage of their presence in Bithynia, the sons of Qutlumush largely worked at the same level.

The fact that both Atsiz b. Uwaq and Tāj al-Dawla Tutush, despite various attempts, failed to take possession of Aleppo was of decisive importance for the development of the political groupings in northern Syria during the 1080s. In the time of his conquest of Damascus, the former also led a campaign into the districts south of Aleppo. But he was obviously too weak to besiege the city, and negotiations with Naṣr b. Maḥmūd did not bring any results.[103] His brother Jāwulī took hold of Ranafiyya southwest of Ḥamāh for some time and ravaged the surrounding area, but he, too, was forced to retreat to Damascus.[104] Much more dangerous was the three-month siege of Aleppo by Tāj al-Dawla Tutush. On this occasion Malikshāh made his first attempt to establish a broad alliance encompassing numerous Turkish warlords and local forces in order to create a strong basis for centralized rule over large parts of Syria. This was the only way to put a definite end to the incessant series of local conflicts and the predominance of Fatimid rulers in the region. The coalition supporting the siege of 1079 consisted of Sābiq's brother Waththāb, his close companions and the leaders of the Banū Kilāb, a number of prominent Turkish warriors, such as Afshīn b. Bakjī, Ṣunduq al-Turkī, Muḥammad b. Damlāj, Ibn Ṭūṭū, and Ibn Birīq, and the forces of Muslim b. Quraysh of Mosul.[105] Had the military situation in Aleppo led to a successful outcome, Tāj al-Dawla would have been able to exert a formal suzerainty over the emirate on behalf of the sultan and with the support of parts of the Mirdāsid establishment. The enterprise failed and instead of Aleppo Tāj al-Dawla Tutush took possession of Damascus, expelling Atsiz b. Uwaq. Nevertheless, the emergence of Tāj al-Dawla Tutush and the new coalition of forces initiated by his campaign brought about radical changes to the political geography in the whole of Syria, including the emirate of Aleppo.[106]

A large-scale campaign under the command of Afshīn in central Syria and Antioch in late 1079 had disastrous consequences for agriculture and food supplies in central and northern Syria. A number of places and districts between Rafaniyya and Maʿarrat al-Nuʿmān were pillaged and their fortifications dismantled.[107] A piece of information indicating that caravans and merchants on their way from Rafaniyya to Tripoli were trapped and killed by the invaders shows that these raids also caused serious damage to the overland trade connecting the Syrian hinterland with the main ports of the littoral.[108] The report of Ibn al-ʿAdīm speaks about extensive looting, unrestrained killing, and large numbers of captives. "When al-Afshīn departed from Syria," the author characteristically concludes, "there was no more inhabited domain in the region between al-Maʿarra and Aleppo."[109] Equally disastrous seems to have been the ensuing attack on the territory of Antioch.[110] The same source characterizes this campaign as an event of unheard-of dimensions, which provoked a disastrous famine causing people to commit cannibalism and grain prices to increase tremendously.[111] People who were able to do so left the country for the territories of Muslim b. Quraysh, who treated the refugees well and provided them with foodstuff.[112] In the winter months of 1079–80 the political situation in Syria was largely dominated by Tāj al-Dawla Tutush and his commanders, against whom both local potentates and Turkish chieftains were powerless to resist. Likewise, Byzantine Antioch, which at that time was under the rule of the semi-independent potentate Philaretos Brachamios,[113] was not able to put up effective resistance against invasions coming from the Muslim territories. It may be assumed that during the last phase of the conflict-ridden reign of Nikephoros III Botaneiates there was hardly any communication between Constantinople and Antioch and the defense of the region fully depended upon the potential of Brachamios' military power.

Nevertheless, the campaigns of Tāj al-Dawla Tutush and Afshīn with their devastating results apparently made the potentates in northern Syria reluctant to seek an understanding with the new Seljuk ruler of Damascus. Tutush, for the time being, was unable to impose his rule over Aleppo by force. Small Turkish bands, which formerly had formed detachments of larger warrior groups, still moved around central Syria, but they were not willing to submit to Aleppo or Damascus. On the approach of Tutush's troops, a certain Arslān Tāsh, who was outside Kafarṭāb, fled into Byzantine territory.[114] Seditious Turks under the command of a certain Khaṭlaj, a former companion of Aḥmad Shāh, marauded in the region of Aleppo and took captive Abū Manṣūr, the son of the leader of the town militia of Aleppo, Ḥasan b. Hibatallāh al-Hāshimī al-Ḥutaytī.[115] On the other hand, the lack of food supplies in Aleppo made the townspeople inclined to recognize the authority of a man who was able to offer them swift relief from their starvation.[116] This was the chance for Muslim b. Quraysh of Mosul to take advantage of the situation. During the spring of 1080 he came to an understanding with both Sābiq b. Maḥmūd and the Banū Kilāb tribe regarding the surrender of Aleppo, and thus he made camp outside the city walls on 8 June 1080.[117] Through the mediation of al-Ḥutaytī's son and that of Sadīd al-Mulk Abū l-Ḥasan b. Munqidh, a high-ranking dignitary of the Mirdāsid elite, Muslim b. Quraysh won the support of the town militia and other sections of the local population. Sābiq and his brothers were compensated with domains in A'zāz, al-Athārib, and al-Raḥba whereas Muslim b. Quraysh consolidated his claims to succeed to the Mirdāsid emirate by marrying Manī'a, a sister of Sābiq.[118] In this way, in September/October 1080 the new emir assumed rule over Aleppo on the basis of a strong coalition comprising the 'Uqaylids of Mosul, the Banū Kilāb, the Mirdāsid family of Aleppo, and the leading elements among the townspeople.[119] This alliance was strong enough to impede the Turkish penetration of the emirate for another five years until the conquest of Antioch by Sulaymān b. Qutlumush in late 1084 and the ensuing conflict between Sulaymān and Muslim b. Quraysh, which prepared the ground for Malikshāh's Syrian campaign of 1086.

Notes

1 For Qutlumush and his descendants, see Cahen, "Qutlumush," pp. 14–27; Sevim, *Süleymanşah*, pp. 21–22; Sevim and Merçil, *Selçuklulu Devletleri*, pp. 26–27, 34, 44–45, 59–62; Öngül, *Selçukluleri*, 1:8, 19, 22–23, 30–31, 35–39; Özgüdenli, *Selçuklular*, pp. 132–33, 137–39.

2 For details of Sulaymān's political career, see Sevim, *Suriye*, pp. 107–26; Sevim, *Süleymanşah*, pp. 26–42; Sevim and Merçil, *Selçuklulu Devletleri*, pp. 113–16, 133–39, 442–47, 521–29; Öngül, *Selçukluleri*, 1:58, 85–92, 106, 419–24, 2:1–14.

3 Chalandon, *Comnène*, 1:71–72.

4 Laurent, *Turcs*, p. 97.

5 Laurent, *Turcs*, p. 101.

6 Laurent, *Turcs*, pp. 99–100.

7 Cahen, "Pénétration," p. 35 (despite the statement of later Persian historiography, the sons of Qutlumush were independent and hostile to their Iranian cousins), pp. 42–44: "En somme les Grecs ont fait de lui un Sultan dans l'Empire byzantin." Cahen, *Pre-Ottoman Turkey*, pp. 75–76: "it is clear that it was the Byzantines themselves who encouraged the Turks to advance further [...] and provided their leaders with the basis of solid power by throwing open to them towns." Cahen, *Formation*, pp. 8–9; see also Talbot-Rice, *Seljuks*, pp. 44–46, who in contrast to Cahen talks about an appointment as "Governor of Rum" and a self-proclamation as Sultan.

8 Cahen, "Pénétration," p. 44.

9 Vryonis, *Decline*, p. 113: "Sulayman's Turks apparently had their first major introduction into the urban centers as garrisons of Botaneiates [...] the reign of the new emperor was the decisive step in their [the Bithynian towns'] occupation." Angold, *Empire*, pp. 118–19: "For the task of restoring imperial authority in Anatolia the Byzantine government ironically called in the Turks [...]. In this instance, the arbiter of Byzantium's fate turned out to be Suleiman, the son of Kutlumush." Angold, "Époque," p. 610, declaring the alliance with Sulaymān "a colossal miscalculation on Botaneiates' part." Korobeinikov, "Raiders," pp. 706–707: "His arrival at Nicaea in the summer or autumn of 1075 transformed the situation in Asia Minor to the Turks' advantage [...] the Turkish incursions spread as far as the Bosporus at this time. Suleiman's chance came in October 1077, when Nikephoros Botaneiates [...] began his rebellion against Michael VII."

10 Yinanç, *Anadolu'nun Fethi*, pp. 85–86, 104–109, 114–34.

11 Strohmeier, *Geschichte*, pp. 91–101.

12 Yinanç, *Anadolu'nun Fethi*, p. 128.

13 Yinanç, *Anadolu'nun Fethi*, p. 129.

14 Yinanç, *Anadolu'nun Fethi*, p. 106.

15 Yinanç, *Anadolu'nun Fethi*, p. 106.

16 Strohmeier, *Geschichte*, p. 165.
17 Kafesoğlu, *Melikşah*, pp. 68–85.
18 Kafesoğlu, *Melikşah*, pp. 77–78, n. 58.
19 Strohmeier, *Geschichte*, pp. 151–63.
20 Turan, *Türkiye*, p. 77–79.
21 Turan, *Türkiye*, p. 80.
22 Turan, *Türkiye*, p. 77.
23 Turan, *Türkiye*, p. 79.
24 Turan, *Türkiye*, pp. 79–80.
25 Turan, *Türkiye*, p. 81.
26 Sevim, *Süleymanşah*, pp. viii, 40.
27 Sevim, *Süleymanşah*, pp. 41–42; these views reappear unaltered in the works mentioned above, n. 2.
28 Koca, "Süleyman-Şâh," p. 34.
29 Koca, "Süleyman-Şâh," p. 35.
30 Nīshāpūrī/Rashīd al-Dīn, pp. 7–11, trans. Luther, pp. 30–33. See also Merçil, *Büyük Selçuklu Devleti*, pp. 7–9; Sevim and Merçil, *Selçuklu Devletleri*, pp. 25–27; Öngül, *Selçukluleri*, 1:7–8; Özgüdenli, *Selçuklular*, pp. 55–56.
31 Nīshāpūrī/Rashīd al-Dīn, p. 11, trans. Luther, p. 33.
32 Nīshāpūrī/Rashīd al-Dīn, p. 18, trans. Luther, p. 39; Sevim and Merçil, *Selçuklu Devletleri*, pp. 27–29; Öngül, *Selçukluleri*, 1:8–10; Özgüdenli, *Selçuklular*, pp. 56–57.
33 Nīshāpūrī/Rashīd al-Dīn, p. 20, trans. Luther, p. 40.
34 Nīshāpūrī/Rashīd al-Dīn, p. 28, trans. Luther, p. 45: Salṭanat bi-mā mī-rasad wa-pidar-i mā kih bihtar u mihtar-i qawm būd bi-īn wāsiṭa kushte shud. For this revolt, see Sevim and Merçil, *Selçuklu Devletleri*, pp. 59–60; Öngül, *Selçukluleri*, 1:35–36; Özgüdenli, *Selçuklular*, pp. 132–33.
35 Nīshāpūrī/Rashīd al-Dīn, p. 28, trans. Luther, p. 45–46: Alp Arslān khwāst kih har kih az khwīshān u atbā'-i ū bāshad hame-rā bi-kushad wa pisarash Sulaymān-shāh-rā agar-chih khurd būd, farmūd kih halāk kunand. Niẓām ul-mulk wazīr ṣawāb nadīd, guft: khwīshān-rā kushtan khaṭā u nā-mubārak buwad, Alp Arslān īshān-rā bi-sar-ḥadd-i mamlakat firistād tā dar s̱ughūr-i islām iqāmat kunand, wa-az īshān rusūm-i imārat u malikī barāndāzand tā dar maẕallat u maskanat mī bāshand, pas Diyār Bakr wa-Ruhā mu'ayyan kardand, wa Sulaymān-shāh pidar-i salāṭīn-i Rūm ast, wa Alp Arslān dar Ẕū l-Ḥijja-i īn sāl bi-āmad.
36 Nīshāpūrī/Rashīd al-Dīn, p. 39, trans. Luther, p. 53: Dar zamān-i sulṭān-i Malikshāh bi-istiṣwāb-i Niẓām ul-Mulk wazīr Sulaymān-rā bi-ḥukūmat-i mulk-i Rūm firistādand tā mukhālafat miyān-i umarā qaṭ' kunad wa iqlīmī dar mamālik-i pādishāh afzūda bāshad, wa agar kushta shawad khārī az pā-yi dawlat bīrūn āmada bāshad.
37 Michael the Syrian 15.4, 3:172 (trans.), 4:579, col. a (Syriac text).
38 Turan, *Türkiye*, pp. 62–64; Sevim and Merçil, *Selçuklu Devletleri*, pp. 522–23 (Süleymanşah'ın kurduğu Türkiye Selçuklu Devleti'nin [...] hukukî bakımdan Büyük Selçuklu Imparatorluğuna (Sultan Melikşah'a) tâbi bir devlet olduğu görülmektedir); Öngül, *Selçukluleri*, 2:4–5.
39 Turan, *Türkiye*, pp. 45–49.
40 'Aẓīmī, p. 37 (Arabic text), p. 45 (trans.): *aghāra Dawlāt b. Quṭlumush 'alā balad 'Azāz fa-qatalahū Kulyām ṣāḥib 'Azāz*.
41 Michael the Syrian 15.6, 3:179 (trans.), 4:584 (Syriac text); Matthew of Edessa 2.106, p. 163.
42 For these personalities, see below, pp. 203, 248, 251–59.
43 Bryennios 4.2, pp. 258–59: πρὸς τοὺς τῶν Τούρκων ἐξάρχοντας ἐν Νικαίᾳ τῆς Βιθυνίας διατρίβοντας· ἤστην δὲ τούτω Μασοὺρ καὶ Σολυμάν, οἱ τοῦ Κουτλουμοῦς παῖδες.
44 Bar Hebraeus, p. 254, trans. Budge, p. 226: *hānā eṯhayyaḏ 'am amīrā nāsh men shāqā dh-Salgūqāyē dha-shmēh Qatlamīsh bar Yabbāgū Arslān bar Salgūq d-men sūlṭān Alb Arslān 'raq-(h)wā wa-ṭpas b-ūḥdānā dh-Rhōmāyē*.

45 Bar Hebraeus, p. 257, trans. Budge, p. 227. See also Sevim and Merçil, *Selçuklu Devletleri*, pp. 523–24, and Öngül, *Selçukluleri*, 2:5–6, who erroneously, in my opinion, interpret the elusive pieces of information regarding Manṣūr's death as Sultan Malikshāh's reaction to a revolt initiated by Manṣūr against his brother Sulaymān.

46 For details, see Sevim, *Suriye*, pp. 63–74; Sevim, *Selçuklu Komutanları*, pp. 33–40; El-Azhari, *Saljūqs of Syria*, pp. 34–40; Sevim and Merçil, *Selçuklu Devletleri*, pp. 422–37; Öngül, *Selçukluleri*, 1:404–14.

47 For a brief overview of general developments in Syria between the tenth century and the arrival of the Seljuks, see Brett, "Near East," pp. 123/288-24/89, 130/296-33. He mainly emphasizes the expansion of tribal chieftains and their impact on social structures and institutions of urban life; the economic growth of ports and urban centers, the political diversity, and corridor position of Syria between Iraq and Egypt as factors impeding the consolidation of Fatimid rule in Syria and favoring the emergence of qāḍī rulers in coastal cities, such as Acre, Tyre, and Tripoli, and various petty dynasties in the hinterland.

48 Halm, *Kalifen*, pp. 99–108, 151–57, 332–39, 359–62; Brett, "Near East," pp. 124/290–26/92.

49 Todt, Antiocheia, pp. 189–245; Halm, *Kalifen*, pp. 359–62.

50 Ibn al-Qalānisī, pp. 98–99; Ibn al-Athīr, 6:248, trans. Richards, *Annals*, p. 172 (the report is in both sources *sub anno* 463/9 October 1070–28 September 1071). Ibn al-Athīr describes Atsiz as "one of the emirs of Sultan Malikshāh," while Ibn al-Qalānisī calls him "chief of the Oghuz Turks." See also Sibṭ b. al-Jawzī, p. 152: "In this year [463/9 October 1070–28 September 1071] appeared Atsiz b. Uwaq, the commander of the Oghuz Turks, and conquered al-Ramla and Jerusalem (*Bayt al-Maqdis*) and put pressure on Damascus. He continued the raids against the city and devastated Syria." Ibid., p. 169, erroneously dates the conquest of Jerusalem to Shawwāl 465/June 10-July 8 1073. For further details, see Sevim, *Suriye*, pp. 64–66; Sevim and Merçil, *Selçuklu Devletleri*, pp. 425–26; Öngül, *Selçuklular*, 1:406–407.

51 Sibṭ b. al-Jawzī, pp. 157–58 (*al-Turkumān al-Nāwakiyya* under the command of "their chief who is called al-Qaralī").

52 For this person, see EI^2, 1:869–70, s. v. Badr al-Djamālī (C. H. Becker); Bianquis, *Damas*, pp. 623, 643; Halm, *Kalifen*, pp. 403, 419–20. For Badr's conflict with various potentates and factions in Damascus, see Sibṭ b. al-Jawzī in Ibn al-Qalānisī, pp. 96–97, n. 1.

53 Ibn al-Qalānisī, p. 98. For Qaralū's arrival in Syria, see also Ibn al-ʿAdīm, p. 269; Sibṭ b. al-Jawzī, p. 153. For his activities in general, see Sevim, *Suriye*, pp. 64–65 and n. 110, 112; Sevim and Merçil, *Selçuklu Devletleri*, pp. 423; Öngül, *Selçuklular*, 1:404–405. The vocalization of the name is uncertain, Sevim and other Turkish scholars opt for "Kurlu."

54 Ibn al-Qalānisī, p. 98: *li-khtilāf al-Atrāk fī l-Shām*; see also Bianquis, *Damas*, p. 644.

55 Sibṭ b. al-Jawzī, p. 143 *sub anno* 462/20 October 1069–8 October 1070; see also Bianquis, *Damas*, p. 644 (his distinction between two brothers, Hārūn b. Khān and Ibn Khān, is unnecessary).

56 Ibn al-ʿAdīm, p. 269.

57 Ibn al-ʿAdīm, p. 269; Sibṭ b. al-Jawzī, p. 153; for the military clash with the Byzantine *doux*, see Ibn al-Qalānisī, pp. 101–104 (departure of Emir Maḥmūd and his Arab troops towards Aʿzāz on 22 Rajab 464 = 14 April 1072); ʿAẓīmī, p. 15 (Arabic text), p. 20 (trans.).

58 Ibn al-ʿAdīm, p. 153: *wa-rtabaṭa Maḥmūd min al-Turkumān naḥwa alf ghulām*, "Maḥmūd allied with about 1,000 slave soldiers from the Turkmen"; for details, see Sevim, *Suriye*, pp. 52–53.

59 Sibṭ b. al-Jawzī, p. 153: *istawlā al-Nāwakiyya alladhīna harabū min Alb Arslān 'alā l-Shām*, "the Turkmen, who fled from Alp Arslān, took possession of Syria."

60 Sibṭ b. al-Jawzī, p. 153: "They demanded money from Badr, who was residing in 'Akkā. He responded: 'I have no money and I gave you power over the Arabs only on the condition that you be content with looting them, and I will not give you landed estates in Syria.'"
61 Sibṭ b. al-Jawzī, p. 153; for details, see Sevim, *Suriye*, pp. 51–52.
62 Sibṭ b. al-Jawzī, p. 153: "They came to al-Ramla, which was in ruins. Nobody was there and the town's market had no gates."
63 Sibṭ b. al-Jawzī, p. 153: "They transferred peasants there and cultivated the region. They pledged themselves to pay the sultan's share amounting to 30,000 dinars from the olive trees and decided to split the land into two parts. It is said that they sold the olives for 300,000 dinars this time and so the Turkmen gave 30,000 dinars and kept the rest."
64 Sibṭ b. al-Jawzī, pp. 157–58; for details, see Sevim, *Suriye*, pp. 53–54.
65 For Atsiz b. Uwaq in general, see Sevim, *Suriye*, pp. 63–84; Sevim, *Selçuklu Komutanları*, pp. 33–45; Sevim and Merçil, *Selçuklu Devletleri*, pp. 425–37; Öngül, *Selçuklular*, 1:406–14.
66 Sibṭ b. al-Jawzī, p. 169; for details concerning the conquest of Jerusalem, see Sevim, *Suriye*, pp. 64–66; Sevim, *Selçuklu Komutanları*, pp. 35–36; Sevim and Merçil, *Selçuklu Devletleri*, pp. 425–26; Öngül, *Selçuklular*, 1:407.
67 Ibn al-Qalānisī, p. 108: *al-Malik Atsiz b. Uwaq muqaddam al-Atrāk*, "the King Atsiz b. Uwaq, the commander of the Turks;" Sibṭ b. al-Jawzī, p. 172: *Atsiz al-Turkī ṣāḥib al-Quds wa-l-Ramla wa-kāna mutaqaddiman 'alā jamī' al-Turk wa-l-Nāwakiyya bi-l-Shām*, "Atsiz, the Turk, the lord of Jerusalem and Ramla, who was the commander of all the Turks and Turkmen nomads in Syria;" ibid., p. 178: *Atsiz al-Turkumānī ṣāḥib al-Shām*, "Atsiz, the Turkmen, the lord of Syria;" *Atsiz al-Khwārizmī ṣāḥib al-Shām*, "Atsiz, the Khwārizmian, the lord of Syria;" Ibn al-'Adīm, p. 282: *wa-kāna qad sammā nafsahū al-malik al-mu'aẓẓam*, "he called himself the honored king."
68 Ibn al-Qalānisī, pp. 108–109; Ibn al-'Adīm, pp. 281–82 (in 468/16 August 1075–4 August 1076 Atsiz arrived in the southern districts of Aleppo, negotiations with Naṣr b. Maḥmūd brought no results); ibid., p. 282: *fa-nahaba kull mā qadara 'alayhi wa-malaka Rafaniyya wa-sallamahā ilā akhīhi Jāwulī*, "he looted whatever he could and took possession of Rafaniyya and handed it over to his brother Jāwulī"; Ibn al-Athīr, 6:269, trans. Richards, *Annals*, p. 99 (the final siege started in Sha'bān 468/10 March-7 April 1076, after negotiations about a guarantee of safety the city surrendered and the first Friday prayer in the name of the Abbasid caliph was held on 26 Dhū l-Qa'da 468/1 July 1076); 'Aẓīmī, p. 17 (Arabic text), p. 21 (trans.); Sibṭ b. al-Jawzī, pp. 179–80 (conquest of Damascus in Dhū l-Qa'da 468/6 June-5 July 1076, Atsiz's letter to Caliph al-Muqtadī about this event arrived in Baghdad in Dhū l-Ḥijja/6 July-4 August 1076); ibid., p. 178 (conquest of Rafaniyya), p. 185 (attacks on Jaffa and Tyre); for the conquest of Damascus, see Sevim, *Suriye*, pp. 72–74; Sevim, *Selçuklu Komutanları*, pp. 39–40; Bianquis, *Damas*, p. 649; Sevim and Merçil, *Selçuklu Devletleri*, pp. 429–30; Öngül, *Selçuklular*, 1:410–11.
69 Sibṭ b. al-Jawzī, p. 178; see also Sevim, *Suriye*, p. 71; Mouton, *Damas*, p. 26; Sevim and Merçil, *Selçuklu Devletleri*, pp. 428–29; Öngül, *Selçuklular*, 1:409–10.
70 Sevim, *Suriye*, p. 71; Sevim and Merçil, *Selçuklu Devletleri*, p. 428; Öngül, *Selçuklular*, 1:409, arrived at a similar conclusion.
71 Sibṭ b. al-Jawzī, p. 179.
72 Ibn al-Qalānisī, p. 112 (Tāj al-Dawla Tutush arrived in Syria in 470/25 July 1077–13 July 1078; he seized Damascus and killed Atsiz in Rabī' I 471/11 September-10 October 1078); Ibn al-Athīr, 6:277, trans. Richards, *Annals*, pp. 197–98 (*sub anno* 471); Sibṭ b. al-Jawzī, pp. 178–79 (Sultan Malikshāh first decided to send his brother Tāj al-Dawla Tutush to Syria in 468/16 August 1075–4 August 1076, perhaps after Jumādā I/12 December 1075–10 January 1076); ibid., p. 195 (Tāj al-Dawla Tutush arrived

in Syria in 470/25 July 1077–13 July 1078); ibid., pp. 197–98 (operations of Tutush and other commanders in the region of Aleppo and the Diyār Bakr province in early 471/14 July 1078–3 July 1079; after various diplomatic contacts, the sultan prevented Tutush from attacking Atsiz in central Syria); ibid., p. 201 (Tutush seized Damascus and killed Atsiz before Rabīʿ II 472/1-30 October 1079, the report is erroneously placed *sub anno* 472 instead of 471); see also Sevim, *Suriye*, pp. 78–84; Sevim, *Selçuklu Komutanları*, pp. 42–45; Bianquis, *Damas*, pp. 649–50; El-Azhari, *Saljūqs of Syria*, pp. 47–49; Sevim and Merçil, *Selçuklu Devletleri*, pp. 432–33; Öngül, *Selçuklular*, 1:412–14.

73 Sibṭ b. al-Jawzī, pp. 182–84; for the Egyptian expedition, see Sevim, *Suriye*, pp. 74–78; Sevim, *Selçuklu Komutanları*, pp. 41–42; El-Azhari, *Saljūqs of Syria*, pp. 40–47; Sevim and Merçil, *Selçuklu Devletleri*, pp. 430–32; Öngül, *Selçuklular*, 1:411–13.

74 Sibṭ b. al-Jawzī, pp. 184–85; see also Sevim, *Suriye*, pp. 79–83; Sevim and Merçil, *Selçuklu Devletleri*, pp. 431–32; Öngül, *Selçuklular*, 1:412–13.

75 Sibṭ b. al-Jawzī, p. 171 (Shuklī seized ʿAkkā in Rabīʿ I 467/25 October-23 November 1074); see also Sevim, *Suriye*, pp. 68–71; Sevim, *Selçuklu Komutanları*, pp. 36–38; Bianquis, *Damas*, p. 648; Sevim and Merçil, *Selçuklu Devletleri*, pp. 426–27; Öngül, *Selçuklular*, 1:407–408.

76 Sibṭ b. al-Jawzī, p. 172.

77 Ibn al-Qalānisī, pp. 95–96; for further details, see Bianquis, *Damas*, pp. 640–43, 646–47.

78 Sibṭ b. al-Jawzī, p. 172.

79 For these events, see Sevim and Merçil, *Selçuklu Devletleri*, pp. 426–28; Öngül, *Selçuklular*, 1:407–409.

80 Sibṭ b. al-Jawzī, p. 174.

81 Sibṭ b. al-Jawzī, pp. 174–75.

82 Sibṭ b. al-Jawzī, p. 175: *sārā ilā Ṭabariyya wa-aẓharū ṭāʿat ṣāḥib Miṣr*, "they went to Ṭabariyya and showed their obedience to the lord of Egypt."

83 Sibṭ b. al-Jawzī, p. 175: "In this month 3,000 slave soldiers from the troops of Malikshāh had come to Atsiz in Syria, for he had written a letter to them;" for this battle, see Sevim and Merçil, *Selçuklu Devletleri*, p. 427; Öngül, *Selçuklular*, 1:408–409.

84 Sibṭ b. al-Jawzī, p. 182.

85 Sibṭ b. al-Jawzī, p. 175: *wa-warada ayḍan akh li-Ibn Qutlumush kāna fī l-Rūm ilā Ḥalab fa-ḥaṣarahā* [...] *fa-qaṣada Ibn Qutlumush Anṭākiya*, "There also arrived a brother of Ibn Qutlumush, who was in [the land of] the Romans, outside Aleppo and he besieged it [...] then Ibn Qutlumush headed towards Antioch."

86 Sevim, *Suriye*, pp. 69–70.

87 Sibṭ b. al-Jawzī, pp. 175–76.

88 Sibṭ b. al-Jawzī, p. 175: "[Naṣr b. Maḥmūd] I am a deputy of the sultan (*nāʾib al-sulṭān*) and if you are obedient to the sultan, go away from us [...], [Atsiz] I have sent a message to the sultan because of him and I am expecting the response. If he orders it, I will send him to him, if he orders something else, it will happen."

89 Sibṭ b. al-Jawzī, p. 178: "In [the month] Jumādā I/12 December 1075–10 January 1076 an emissary of Atsiz the Turkmen, the lord of Syria, arrived [in Baghdad]. He had with him the imprisoned son of Qutlumush and a younger brother of him. Saʿd al-Dawla al-Kawharāʾīn received them and sent them to the sultan."

90 Ibn al-ʿAdīm, pp. 288–89, 299–301; for details, see Sevim, *Suriye*, pp. 85–102; El-Azhari, *Saljūqs of Syria*, pp. 60–61; Mouton, *Damas*, p. 26; Sevim and Merçil, *Selçuklu Devletleri*, pp. 440–42; Öngül, *Selçuklular*, 1:416–18.

91 Ibn al-ʿAdīm, pp. 281, 286; for details concerning this person, see Sevim, *Suriye*, pp. 85–90.

92 Ibn al-ʿAdīm, pp. 282, 284, 289.

93 Ibn al-ʿAdīm, p. 289.

94 Ibn al-ʿAdīm, p. 282.
95 Ibn al-ʿAdīm, pp. 281, 289.
96 Ibn al-ʿAdīm, p. 282.
97 Ibn al-ʿAdīm, pp. 286–87.
98 Ibn al-ʿAdīm, p. 287.
99 Ibn al-ʿAdīm, p. 286.
100 Ibn al-ʿAdīm, p. 284.
101 Ibn al-ʿAdīm, pp. 287–88.
102 Ibn al-ʿAdīm, p. 289.
103 Ibn al-ʿAdīm, pp. 281–82.
104 Ibn al-ʿAdīm, p. 282; for details see Sevim, *Suriye*, pp. 69–70.
105 Ibn al-ʿAdīm, pp. 288–89; for details, see Sevim, *Suriye*, pp. 91–95; Sevim and Merçil, *Selçuklu Devletleri*, pp. 438–40; Öngül, *Selçuklular*, 1:415–16.
106 Sevim, *Suriye*, pp. 96–99; Mouton, *Damas*, p. 26; Sevim and Merçil, *Selçuklu Devletleri*, pp. 439–40; Öngül, *Selçuklular*, 1:416.
107 Ibn al-ʿAdīm, pp. 297–99: The places mentioned as targets of Afshīn's campaign were Rafaniyya (10 jumādā I/8 November 1079, the invaders stayed there for ten days), Ḥiṣn al-Jisr, which was under the rule of Abū l-Ḥasan b. Munqidh, Kafarṭāb, Qasṭūn (the invaders stayed there more than 20 days), the towers of Jabal al-Summāq, Sarmīn, Jabal Banī ʿUlaym, the domains of Maʿarrat al-Nuʿmān (whose towers and fortresses were conquered by force), Tall Mannas (which could not be taken by force, the invaders were content with a tribute of 5,000 dinars), Maʿartāriḥ near Kafarṭāb; see also Sevim, *Suriye*, p. 97, n. 231.
108 Ibn al-ʿAdīm, p. 298.
109 Ibn al-ʿAdīm, p. 299.
110 Ibn al-ʿAdīm, p. 299.
111 Ibn al-ʿAdīm, p. 299.
112 Ibn al-ʿAdīm, p. 299.
113 For this personality, see below, pp. 00.
114 Ibn al-ʿAdīm. p. 299.
115 Ibn al-ʿAdīm, p. 300.
116 Ibn al-ʿAdīm, p. 299: *wa-kāna dhālika l-iḥsān minhu akbar al-asbāb fī mamlakatihī Ḥalab*, "his good treatment [of the refugees who had come to his territory] was the most important reason for his taking possession of Aleppo."
117 Ibn al-ʿAdīm, pp. 299–300.
118 Ibn al-ʿAdīm, p. 302.
119 Ibn al-ʿAdīm, pp. 299–303 (Rabīʿ II 473/19 September-17 Oktober 1080); see also Sevim, *Suriye*, pp. 99–102; Sevim and Merçil, *Selçuklu Devletleri*, pp. 440–42; Öngül, *Selçuklular*, 1:416–18.

5 Revolts and Byzantine-Turkish coalitions in Asia Minor, 1071–86

Historiographical viewpoints and perceptions

This chapter deals with the developments in Byzantine Asia Minor in the decade between the aftermath of Manzikert and the rise to power of Alexios I Komnenos. Only a few months after his coronation in early April 1081 and in view of the imminent Norman attack, the new emperor concluded a treaty with Sulaymān b. Qutlumush, thus recognizing the existence of a Muslim-Turkish sphere of influence in Bithynia.[1] In this sense, the dynastic change of 1081 constitutes a decisive step in the Turkish expansion in Asia Minor. Muslim and Eastern Christian authors very rarely and elusively refer to central and western Anatolia. Therefore, our reconstructions and interpretations of this period largely depend upon the viewpoints and perceptions of Byzantine accounts. This unavoidably entails a change of perspective with respect to some leading figures operating in both Muslim and Byzantine regions. As we have seen in the previous chapter, the activities of the sons of Qutlumush in Syria are only known from Arabic sources, whereas their establishment in Asia Minor is mainly documented by Byzantine reports. Needless to say, these opposing views result in widely diverging images. The comparison of behavioral patterns and practices mentioned in both traditions allows us to bridge the gap between Muslim and Byzantine perceptions to a certain degree and to arrive at conclusions concerning comparable structures and processes in Syria and the Byzantine territories. At the same time, of course, we also have to be aware of diverging perspectives within the Byzantine historical tradition.

The battle of Manzikert and the ensuing downfall of Romanos IV form a watershed in the narrative of Michael Attaleiates. Due to the author's direct involvement as an eyewitness, the eastern campaigns of the years 1068–71 are related in the form of a detailed report of troop movements, military clashes, and personal judgments. In contrast, the account covering the reign of Michael VII and the rise of Nikephoros III Botaneiates mainly serves propagandistic purposes. This part of the narrative, almost one half of the whole text in extent,[2] first and foremost aims at creating a sharp contrast between the man in power, a model case of a totally incapable ruler surrounded by malicious favorites and immoral advisors, and the successful rebel, who came to the fore as God-sent savior, for whom the empire's suffering subjects had been waiting in desperation. In this conceptual framework the Turkish raids occupy a central position as a manifestation of divine anger because of the Doukas clan's *coup d'état*, which had culminated in Diogenes' sacrilegious blinding: "A manifestation of anger sent by God reached the East, for the Turks emerging from Persia made campaigns against the Roman themes."[3]

Nevertheless, the narrative is no longer primarily concerned with the military situation in Asia Minor and the ever-increasing pressure of the Turks, but rather focuses on internal conflicts among the leading commanders and members of the ruling elite. In this respect, the Turkish danger does not appear as the predominant matter of life and death for the survival of the Byzantine administration in the East, as modern historians may expect, but as a secondary theme subject to the overarching topic of the imperial government's political and moral decay. In many cases, Attaleiates, when referring to Turkish warriors, provides very few details concerning their origin, their activities, or their relations with other political groups. He describes them only insofar as they are of direct relevance for the affairs and struggles of the Byzantine elite, thus employing them as a mirror reflecting the incompetence of the men in power or, as the narrative proceeds, illustrating the superior skills of the future emperor Botaneiates. Statements regarding the devastation of towns and territories and the expansion of Turkish invaders are not necessarily based on objective assessments of the actual state of affairs, but are subject to the narrative's intention to juxtapose a bad emperor and a good rebel.[4]

A hiatus of approximately 50 years lies between Attaleiates and the first historians of the Komnenian era, Nikephoros Bryennios and his wife Anna Komnene. Bryennios' unfinished *Hyle historias* covering the years 1070–79 has a focus similar to that of Attaleiates with respect to the empire's internal power struggle, but, instead of Botaneiates, his heroes are the young Alexios Komnenos and the rebel Nikephoros Bryennios, the author's father and grandfather.[5] The text is structured along the same sequence of events regarding developments in Asia Minor, but it has plenty of additional details and episodes resulting from the narrative's eulogizing tendency. The particularities of Bryennios' literary concept, embedding historical facts into a romance-like narrative embroidered with numerous fictional and idealizing features, make it difficult for us to distinguish between the factual core and the retrospective perceptions emanating from the collective memory of Alexios I's reign.

A central feature of Bryennios' idealization is the projection of aristocratic values that determine the conduct and attitudes of the ruling elite. In this context, Alexios Komnenos is portrayed as the model of a young Byzantine nobleman gifted with all the talents and virtues of a ruler and thus pre-destined to be elevated to the imperial throne. With respect to the Turks, Bryennios, apart from providing a number of names and details not mentioned in other sources, in many points differs from Attaleiates' point of view by highlighting Alexios' role as a chief commander who successfully accomplished all the tasks assigned by the regime of Michael VII. Certain actions that Attaleiates presents as signs of the imperial government's decay appear in Bryennios' narrative as praiseworthy achievements; the assessment of the situation in Asia Minor before and after Botaneiates' rise to power is much more balanced in that Bryennios does not shrink from pointing out the negative consequences of the new ruler's attitude towards the Turks; the seizure of Byzantine cities in western Asia Minor by Turkish warriors, especially with respect to the revolt of Nikephoros Melissenos, is explicitly stated.[6] The first book of Anna Komnene's *Alexias*, as far as the situation in Asia Minor is concerned, largely summarizes Bryennios' narrative without adding any substantial information and fully adopts the latter's point of view.[7]

(Near-)contemporary witnesses to the aftermath of Manzikert

As for the situation in Asia Minor after the battle of Manzikert and the defeat of Romanos IV Diogenes, all historiographical traditions agree on the ethical dimension of the crime committed against the dethroned emperor as well as on the disastrous consequences of the new regime's refusal to implement the treaty concluded with Sultan Alp Arslān. The motif of divine wrath striking the empire as a result of its rulers' moral failure, as expressed by Attaleiates, appears in a great number of sources. The Muslim accounts of Ibn al-Athīr and Sibṭ b. al-Jawzī have Romanos Diogenes after his resignation addressing Michael VII, praising the sultan's benevolence and bounty, and summoning his successor to respect the concluded treaty:

> I did not shrink from any effort nor was I overwhelmed by faint-heartedness or weakness; it was rather God's judgment and power that let Islam and its people gain the victory. Nobody has power over Him and nobody is able to refuse Him. When I fell into the hands of this man [i.e., the sultan], he demonstrated a magnanimity that I did not expect and he imposed a sum of money upon me for the conclusion of the peace treaty. He was merciful and released me. I came up to this fortress [i.e., of Dokeia] in order to resign from the imperial office and became a monk. I praised God—may he be exalted—, for I had reached a rank that you deserve more than me, and I am obliged to expose to you the sultan's well-being, his excellence, and generosity. If you agree with my words, I am ready to mediate between the two of you in order to preserve the Christian faith.[8]

In the context of Alp Arslān's portrayal as champion of the Muslim faith, Romanos appears to have been overwhelmed by the superior forces of Islam and the outstanding virtues of its supreme lord. Having abdicated the throne and become a monk, he figures in the Arabic narrative as spokesman of the Muslim side, addressing his successor in a sort of moral exhortation. According to Muslim legal concepts concerning the establishment of peaceful relations with non-Muslims on the basis of treaties, special emphasis is placed on the importance of respecting the agreements with the sultan, for they offer a suitable framework for the protection of all Christians. At the same time, the great victory most naturally engenders a strong sentiment of Muslim superiority. The Muslim version thus sees the reason for the empire's downfall in the imperial government's disrespect for the peace treaty.

Romanos paid part of the tribute, the account continues, but Michael soon came into conflict with Romanos and thus the latter was imprisoned and blinded by "Sinakhārīb, the king of the Armenians." In this way the Byzantines violated their oaths and disregarded the sultan's virtues. Sinakhārīb reportedly shifted Romanos' soldiers onto his side, pillaged the region of Konya, seized Melitene, extracted taxes from the inhabitants, and promised to support the sultan. These details, albeit spurious to a large extent, seem to reflect some knowledge about the activities of Armenian potentates in Cappadocia at that time. The name as it is spelled in Arabic makes us think of Senek'erim Artsrouni, the ex-king of Vaspurakan, and his descendants.[9] The idea of Armenian opposition to Romanos certainly contradicts what more reliable sources tell us about the Armenians' loyalty to the dethroned emperor. A case in point is Chatatourios, the governor of Antioch, who actively supported Romanos during the civil war, or Philaretos Brachamios, who from the early 1070s onwards, in opposition to Constantinople, was establishing a semi-independent lordship in the southern flank of the Byzantine borderland.[10] Yet it is still noteworthy that the Muslim account ascribes the empire's disintegration to the treacherous behavior of the Byzantines and the activities of local lords in the borderland, but it does not refer to any Seljuk plans of conquest or centrally organized campaigns into the interior of Asia Minor. The Muslim historical tradition after Manzikert mainly concentrates on Alp Arslān's march to the easternmost provinces of his empire and his murder on 20 November 1072.[11]

The Seljuk court historiography represented by Ẓahīr al-Dīn Nīshāpūrī's *Saljūq-nāma* and its derivatives ascribes the foundation of a number of Turkmen principalities, which would dominate the political landscape of eastern Anatolia during the twelfth century, to a decision made by Sultan Alp Arslān immediately after the battle of Manzikert. According to this version, it was the Byzantine emperor's refusal to pay the tribute that caused the sultan to order his emirs to invade and to take possession of the Byzantine territories:

> When the king of the Romans reached his own country, the Satan of disappointment nested in his heart and the demon of temptation in his brain and so he showed deficiency and delay in the sending [of the money] to the treasury. When they revealed this state of affairs to his majesty the sultan, he ordered the emirs to invade the provinces of the Romans; each district they were to conquer and take possession of would belong to him [i.e., one of them] and his children and grandchildren; except for him, nobody would have access to or control over it [...] authority and dominion was established in the best possible way. Each year they made their summer quarters in a pleasant steppe land and spent their time in pleasure. Sometimes discord occurred among them and because of pride and arrogance contentions made their appearance.[12]

The text obviously intends to underpin the legitimacy of the Turkmen lordships in Anatolia by introducing the idea of an official bestowal by the Great Seljuk sultan of hereditary rights of sovereignty upon the leading commanders who had fought in the battle of Manzikert. Because of the emperor's disobedience, the Turkish chieftains are entitled to seize his territories and to establish their dominion over them. In addition, the account underlines two characteristic features of the ruling elites in these newly established principalities, namely their maintenance of nomadic and migratory forms of rule and their proclivity to quarrels and conflicts among themselves. In contrast to western and central Asia Minor and to Syria, where the Turkish military elite quickly assimilated to the indigenous urban and sedentary cultures, in eastern Anatolia, most likely due to the absence of large cities and urban traditions and the predominance of mountainous areas and vast steppe lands, the nomadic character of the Turkmen immigrants persisted throughout the twelfth century and formed an essential part of their rulers' self-awareness. In particular, our source mentions (a) Emir Saltuq ruling over Erzurum (Arzan al-Rūm) and its dependencies; (b) Emir Artuq ruling over Mārdīn, Āmid, Manzikert, Melitene (Malaṭya), and Kharput (Charpete); (c) Emir Dānishmand ruling over Kaisareia (Qayṣariyya), Tzamandos (Zamandū), Sebasteia (Sīwās), Gabadonia (Dawalū), Dokeia (Tūqāt), Neokaisareia (Nikīsār), and Amaseia (Āmāsiya); (d) Emir Chāwuldur ruling over Germanikeia (Marʿash) and Sarūs (Saros/Sayḥān River); and (e) Emir Mangūjak Ghāzī ruling over Erzincan, Kamākh, Koloneia (Kūghūnīya), and other districts. This catalogue roughly covers the entire eastern frontier zone stretching from Cappadocia and Commagene through Upper Mesopotamia, the Anti-Taurus Mountains, and the Armenian highlands, as far as the Lykos (Kelkit) and Halys (Kızılırmak) Valleys. The idea of a distribution of clearly defined territories evokes the image of firmly established lordships that were closely linked with Alp Arslān's great victory and based on a common allegiance to the Seljuk sultanate's supreme authority. In this way, the model of Seljuk dynastic rule, which had emerged in various Iranian provinces and was to prevail in Syria in the years of Tāj al-Dawla Tutush and Malikshāh, was transferred to former Byzantine territories of eastern Anatolia and Armenia. The region in question could thus be conceived of as a part of the Muslim world and the Seljuk Empire. The new Turkish-Muslim elites in these areas consolidated their position through the creation of a shared identity grounded on a common foundation myth. Chronologically, 1071 became a point of reference for much later developments.[13]

It is certainly true that all of these territories actually passed into the hands of the aforementioned rulers during the reign of Alexios I, but it is hardly possible to trace their origins back to the battle of Manzikert and its aftermath. The first Saltukid lord of Erzurum, called Emir ʿAlī, appears in the context of the civil strife between Sultan Barkyāruq and Sultan Muḥammad Tapar in Rabīʿ I 496/13 December 1102–11 January 1103 as an ally of the latter.[14] Without other sources it is impossible to say how long prior to this event he had been ruling there and what relationship he had with the founder of the dynasty. A Turkmen commander called Artouch is first mentioned by Bryennios, who describes him as a man raiding the eastern provinces and in about 1074 allying with Emperor Michael VII against Roussel de Bailleul.[15] Thereafter we lose track of him until he reappears in 1084 participating in a campaign of Seljuk troops under the command of one of Malikshāh's viziers against the Marwānid emirate of Diyār Bakr and again in 1086 during the expedition of Malikshāh's brother Tutush to Aleppo. In the meantime the latter appointed him governor of Jerusalem.[16] The establishment of the Artuqid lordships in the Diyār Bakr province is a later development resulting from the repercussions of the Frankish conquests during the First Crusade and internal conflicts of the Seljuk dynasty. Artuq's son Suqmān in 1101 was granted Ḥiṣn Kayfā by the emir of Mosul, while some years later, in 1108, his brother Īlghāzī took possession of Mārdīn.[17]

The first securely identifiable representative of the Mangūjak (Mengücek) dynasty is a certain "Emir Mangūg, lord of Kamākh," who according to Michael the Syrian pillaged the region of Melitene on 15 March 1118.[18] Modern scholars, though admitting that the emirate's formative period is generally obscure, have made efforts to detect earlier traces of the dynasty's presence in the northernmost part of the Upper Euphrates region by combining archaeological and textual evidence. One of the tombs on a pilgrimage site outside the citadel of Kamākh, called *Sultan Melik türbeleri*, is designated in an inscription as the burial place of Mengücek Gazi.[19] This piece of information, while reflecting a much later tradition, certainly points to the memory of a saint-like ancestor, who can be linked to various corrupted names of Turkmen leaders mentioned in the sources. The strongest evidence may be a short note concerning the arrival of a certain Ibn Manjāk, who according to Ibn al-ʿAdīm reinforced Sulaymān b. Qutlumush with 300 cavalrymen after the conquest of Antioch in December 1084.[20] It is thus believed that the founder of the Mangūjak emirate arrived in about 1080 in the region, establishing his first residence in Kamākh and from there expanding his rule over the surrounding districts.[21]

As regards the origins of the Dānishmand emirate, the most reliable pieces of information are provided by Michael the Syrian and Ibn al-Athīr. According to the former, "in the year 1396/1084–1085 a certain emir of the Turks called Tanūshmān invaded the province of Cappadocia, taking possession of Sebasteia, Kaisareia, and other places in the northern region, and thus the rule of the house of Tanūshmān began."[22] The latter, under the year 493/17 November 1099-5 November 1100, provides some additional details: "Gumushtakīn b. al-Dānishmand Ṭāylū, who was only called Ibn al-Dānishmand because his father had been a teacher of the Turkmen (*mu'alliman li-l-Turkumān*) and whose fortunes prospered to such an extent that he became a ruler as lord of Malaṭya, Sīwās, and other places."[23] Combining these statements with data provided by inscriptions, coins, and the legendary narrative of the *Dānishmand-nāma*, scholars have drawn the conclusion that the historical founder of the dynasty may have been called Gumushtakīn Aḥmad, son of Ṭāylu ʿAlī, the Dānishmand, i.e., "the teacher, wise man." Perhaps a relative of Sulaymān b. Qutlumush, he may have come to Asia Minor in about 1080, probably sent into exile by Malikshāh because of seditious tendencies, and devoted himself to the conquest of the northeastern part of the central Anatolian plateau, while Sulaymān concentrated on the regions further west.[24] This reconstruction, which pre-supposes the existence of a well-coordinated strategy of conquest, is certainly too schematic, but, on the other hand, there is no necessity to follow the skepticism of Cahen, who rejects any definite knowledge about Dānishmand prior to 1095.[25]

As regards Chāwuldur, the available evidence is extremely scarce. The only otherwise known personality bearing a similar name would be Atsiz's brother Jāwulī, who in 1075/76 appears as commander during a campaign in central Syria.[26] But this identification can hardly be correct, for the city of Marʿash soon became one of the main strongholds of Philaretos Brachamios, who in 1084/85 made it a residence of an Armenian *katholikos* and thereafter used it as a final refuge.[27] There may have been a short period of Turkish rule in the time before the arrival of the crusaders in 1097. Taken together, except for Artuq, there is no evidence supporting the arrival of the aforementioned commanders as early as the 1070s. There are some details pointing to the 1080s as time of their first appearance, but they did not come even then as conquerors of specific regions granted to them, but rather as rebels and chiefs of raiders, who in the course of time managed to gain hold of certain fortresses. From these points they gradually widened their sphere of influence over the towns and territories listed in Nīshāpūrī's catalogue.

Sulaymān B. Qutlumush's first appearance in Anatolia

It is striking that very few early Muslim sources transmitting material about the Turkish expansion in Asia Minor clearly refer to the activities of Sulaymān b. Qutlumush in the time preceding his expedition to Antioch. The mid-twelfth century author al-Aẓīmī briefly notes *sub anno* 467/27 August 1074-15 August 1075: "Sulaymān b. Quṭlumush conquered Nicaea and its territories (*Nīqīya wa-a'mālahā*)."[28] Likewise, the slightly younger chronicler of Mayyāfāriqīn, Ibn al-Azraq al-Fāriqī, in a passage referring to Qilij Arslān I explains: "The king (*al-malik*) Sulaymān b. Quṭlumush had come from Malikshāh and had conquered the land of the Romans (*bilād al-Rūm*), Malaṭya, Qaysāriyya, Aqṣarā—the underlying word is Aq Sarā, which means 'white city'—Qūniyā, Sīwās, and the whole territory of the Romans (*jamī' wilāyat al-Rūm*)."[29] Many scholars have taken these scraps of information at face value, and thus the year 1075 became a sort of widely accepted foundation date for the Seljuk principality in Asia Minor, which extended from the Propontis coastland as far as the banks of the Euphrates.[30] An anonymous *Saljūq-nāma* from the second half of the fourteenth century came to support this version with additional legendary material. Sulaymān is said to have been originally granted the rule over Syria and Diyār Bakr, but being unable to impose his authority, he decided to fight the Romans. Along with Turkmen warriors from Khurāsān he conquered Konya and Nicaea, seized the treasures of the imperial government, and received the tribute of the local population.[31] Hence, the image of Sulaymān is further developed into that of a powerful conqueror and champion of *ghazā*, who managed within a short time to gain wealth and to establish a strong lordship, earning the respect of the Byzantines. As will be shown in more detail below, our Byzantine witnesses hardly refer to any form of Turkish control over Nicaea or other cities in Bithynia and central Anatolia prior to 1080/81.[32] The only thing that seems to be certain is that the sons of Qutlumush, who escaped death and captivity after the failure of their Syrian adventure in 1075, fled with their companions to the interior of Asia Minor. They may actually have raided the old capital of Lycaonia and its environs and thence proceeded, following the Byzantine road system in a northwestern direction, to Phrygia and Bithynia. There they quickly established contacts with the Byzantine aristocracy, among them Nikephoros Botaneiates and other rebels.[33]

Ibn al-Azraq's laconic phrase may imply a sort of official appointment on the part of the sultan, but in general the early Muslim tradition, most likely because of the seditious past of the sons of Qutlumush, does not count them among the loyal commanders of the Seljuk dynasty. They were primarily perceived as being associated with the rebellious Nāwakiyya Turkmen, who intruded into Asia Minor in an attempt to escape the sultan's control. A characteristic case in point is Malikshāh's aunt and ex-wife of the rebel Arīshgī, Jawhar Khātūn, who, because of serious discord with her nephew in March 1076, tried via Azerbaijan to join groups of Turkish invaders heading to Byzantine territory, but eventually she was stopped and killed.[34]

Twelfth-century Christian texts, despite their diametrically opposed viewpoint, in some aspects share the ideas expressed in Seljuk and other Muslim chronicles. Matthew of Edessa, who presents the Byzantine defeat of Manzikert as the "beginning of the second devastation and final destruction of our country by the wicked Turkish forces,"[35] construes Diogenes' death as an event causing the sultan's anger. The sacrilegious crime against Alp Arslān's treaty partner demonstrates the Byzantines' godless nature and prompts the sultan to nullify all existing agreements, sending his soldiers on new raids against Christian territory.[36] In a very similar way Nikephoros Bryennios notes that, when the Turks learned what had happened to Diogenes, they violated the agreements and treaties that he had concluded for the benefit of the Romans and began to pillage the entire East.[37] Michael the Syrian was the first Christian historian to make a direct causal link between the battle of Manzikert and the further Turkish expansion into the interior of Asia Minor. Michael agrees with Matthew that the immediate result of the sultan's military success was the Turks' holding sway over Armenia. This view is confirmed by other sources referring to the outcome of Alp Arslān's campaigns in the years 1064-71, in which a series of major strongholds between the Caucasus Mountains and Vaspurakan had been subjected to Seljuk rule. Michael also shows similarities with Nīshāpūrī and Ibn al-Azraq in using the motif of the commanders' official appointment by the sultan, applying it to Sulaymān b. Qutlumush:

> Their sultan, Alp Arslān [...] sent his cousin Sulaymān to the lands of Cappadocia and the Pontus (*l-athrawāthā dh-Qappadhūqāyā wa-dh-Pūnṭūs*) and gave him the authority to proclaim himself sultan (*d-nettakhraz sūlṭān*). When

> he came, the Romans took to flight before him. He seized the cities of Nicaea and Nikomedeia (*l-Nīqīyā wa-l-Nīqūmūdhīyā*) and took up rule over them, and the whole region was filled with Turks. When the caliph of Baghdad (*khālīphā dh-Baghdād*) learned about this, he sent a banner and other objects, and he himself crowned Sulaymān and proclaimed him sultan, that means king, and thus his authority was confirmed. Thus the Turks had two kings (*l-Tūrkāyē hāllēn trēn malkē*), one in Khurāsān and the other one in the land of the Romans (*bēth Rōmāyē*), apart from those of Margiana (*hāllēn da-bh-Margānī*).[38]

It may be assumed that in composing this passage, which along with the rest of the chronicle reflects the historical knowledge of the second half of the twelfth century, Michael the Syrian was influenced by Seljuk dynastic concepts, the existence of the powerful sultanate of Konya in the years of Qilij Arslān II (1155-92) and the idea that the Abbasid caliph had the right to bestow titles and appoint governors by handing over the insignia of office. Just as in the Seljuk tradition, without any historical foundation the concession to Sulaymān of territories in Anatolia is connected with the memory of Sultan Alp Arslān and the victory of Manzikert. Moreover, Michael was certainly well acquainted with the ceremonial of the court of Konya, where the caliph's conferral of banners and other symbols of authority must have been already a firmly established practice. A new element, however, that contradicted Seljuk political concepts and thus could not have been derived from Muslim sources was the idea that the Seljuk sultan would concede the title of sultan to subordinate commanders. In this way, Michael obviously tried to explain why in his time there were two sultans pertaining to the same lineage. As we have already seen with respect to the alleged letter of the Turkish chief Shuklī to Ibn Qutlumush,[39] kinship with the Seljuk dynasty from early on was a strong element forging unity and cohesion among the Turkish warriors. What is more, many Turkmen groups favored the pre-eminence of the descendants of Arslān-Isrā'īl and Qutlumush among the various branches of the Seljuk clan. Later on, the lords of Konya also underlined their close relationship with the Great Seljuk sultanate. Hence, an outside observer could be led quite easily to the conclusion that in its institutional basis the sultanate of Rūm was rooted in an official bestowal of the title upon its founder.

A similar tendency can be observed in the terminological nuances used in historical texts of the early Komnenian period. Anna Komnene, for instance, alternately labels Sulaymān and other Seljuk rulers *soultan* or *amer* and speaks of the residence in Nicaea as *soultanikion* (sultan's palace).[40] Byzantine intellectuals in the 1130s/1140s were aware of the firmly established sultanate of Konya, but they did not possess any specific knowledge about the gradually emerging structures and institutions of the Turkish-Muslim principalities in Asia Minor. Just as Michael the Syrian, they projected their contemporary experiences back to the time of the Turks' first arrival.

As the geographical horizon of the extant accounts after the defeat of Romanos IV shifted to central and northwestern Asia Minor, Byzantine sources, except for some glimpses at the situation in Antioch, hardly yield any information about the eastern borderlands during the 1070s. The imperial government obviously maintained a kind of formal authority by appointing officials and conferring court titles, and the structures of the Byzantine administrative system remained largely intact,[41] but it is hard to say to what extent Constantinople was still able to exert effective control. In any event, from a military point of view after the civil strife of 1071–72 the government of Constantinople was no longer able to put up any resistance against invading warrior groups, whereas the Seljuk sultanate increased its influence over the Muslim potentates in the regions stretching between the Caucasus Mountains, Lake Van, and Aleppo. These developments certainly contributed to a growing permeability of the frontier zone and the unbroken influx of new groups of Turkmen invaders. The number of Turks arriving on the central Anatolian plateau certainly increased, but there are no traces of any permanent establishment in certain regions or towns. The available evidence exclusively concerns relatively small bands that were moving rapidly in various parts of Asia Minor. In contrast to Syria, where Turkish chiefs, such as Atsiz b. Uwaq and Tāj al-Dawla Tutush, quickly intermingled with local elites, established themselves in urban centers, and thus founded new political entities, in central and western Anatolia the Turkish warrior groups persevered in rural areas for quite a long time, dominating river valleys and roads. They pursued raiding activities and formed profitable coalitions with members of the local aristocracy, but they did not yet develop mechanisms supporting the control of territories and the creation of durable lordships.

First Turkish advances to the Sangarios Basin and Bithynia, 1073

In the civil strife between Romanos IV and the Doukas clan, the Komnenos family, by that time mainly represented by the *kouropalatissa* Anna Dalassene and her sons, sided with the latter and thus regained its influential position at court, establishing bonds of marriage with the ruling house and holding some of the most important military posts.[42] After Manuel's premature death, his younger brothers, Isaac (born ca. 1050) and Alexios (born 1057), despite their young ages, began to play a leading role in the military affairs of the East. The starting point of this development was the appointment of Isaac to the rank of *domestikos ton scholon tes anatoles* and his expedition against the Turks in 1073.[43] Both Attaleiates and Bryennios explain this new campaign as resulting from extensive Turkish raids, which, on the grounds of the itinerary of the imperial troops via Konya to Kaisareia, can be located in Cappadocia and the eastern fringes of the Anatolian plateau.[44]

While attacking Turks marauding the region of Kaisareia, Isaac's troops suffered a serious defeat, in which many soldiers were killed and captured—Isaac too was taken prisoner—and the camp and the baggage train were pillaged.[45] The accounts of Attaleiates and Bryennios differ substantially in that the former stresses the personal responsibility of the commander, who attacked the enemy without taking necessary precautions, while the latter turns the report into a eulogy on Alexios, who as companion of his elder brother is presented as the central protagonist of the events despite his very young age of about 17. He is said to have made heroic attempts to raise the morale of the soldiers and to organize the defense of the Byzantine camp.[46] During the soldiers' flight in the dark of the night he escaped over the mountains to the city of Gabadonia (Develi), where the townspeople gave him shelter.[47] Subsequently, all his efforts concentrated on ransoming his brother from Turkish captivity.

It is hard to assess the exact relationship between the historical facts and the literary elaboration of Bryennios' account, but as regards the problem of Turkish expansion, it is noteworthy that Alexios is said to have pursued the Turks who were holding his brother in custody in a northwesterly direction as far as Ankara.[48] The old capital of the province of Galatia and the Boukellarion theme, situated on the northern part of the Anatolian plateau between the Sangarios and the Halys Valleys,[49] appears here for the first time as a target of Turkish raiders. The most important invasion route ran through the southern parts of the Anatolian plateau from Cappadocia to Lycaonia, Phrygia, and the Upper Meander (Büyük Menderes) Valley.[50] Another remarkable detail is that, while encircling the city and harassing the inhabitants with their assaults, the Turks had no ambition but obtaining a ransom for their high-ranking prisoner.[51] This example clearly shows that in 1073 the Turks had not yet developed a strategy beyond the customary aims of accumulating booty and wealth.

Having arrived on the northern Anatolian plateau, the Turks apparently found no obstacles to crossing the Sangarios River to Bithynia and advancing into the coastland of the Propontis. After the release of Isaac, who was freed in exchange for money collected in the region and a number of hostages, the two Komnenian brothers reportedly followed this path as far as a village near Nikomedeia (Izmit), where they were ambushed by a band of 200 Turkish warriors.[52] Byzantine soldiers defected to the Turks in order to save their lives while in a fervent speech Alexios tried to raise the fighting spirit of his companions.[53] These details are certainly part of the idealizing tendency in Bryennios' romance-like presentation of young Alexios' heroic exploits. Nevertheless, the episode is one of the few pieces of evidence suggesting that Turkish groups in Anatolia, just as in Syria and Iran, incorporated local elements into their ranks. Moreover, it shows that from 1073 onwards northwestern Asia Minor had become permeable from the northern plateau around Ankara to the Propontis coastland. After the defeat of the imperial troops in Cappadocia, the Byzantine administration no longer possessed any defensive structures in the Sangarios Valley and Bithynia with which to put a halt to the invaders' advance.[54] This was the first step towards the ensuing intrusion of Sulaymān b. Qutlumush and his companions, who found a largely unprotected region.

In the context of the changing structures of the Byzantine military system, with its increasing dependency upon mercenary troops, an important factor of this period was a strong contingent of Norman mercenaries under the command of Rouselios/Ourselios, i.e., Roussel de Bailleul, formerly a subordinate officer of Crispin and participant in Romanos IV's expedition of 1071.[55] Until his imprisonment in 1075, he was a powerful player who, in his attempt to create an independent sphere of influence in regions of central and northern Anatolia, partly rose up against and partly collaborated with the Byzantine ruling elite while pursuing coalitions with Turkish chieftains. His conflict with the imperial government forms one of the main themes of Byzantine historical accounts concerning these years.[56]

The 1073 campaign marked the beginning of this confrontation. Roussel, who had been ordered to accompany Isaac's troops with a contingent of 400 Frankish soldiers, split with the Byzantine commander in Konya and abandoned the main body of the imperial forces, heading towards Melitene or Sebasteia.[57] The disruption of administrative links and lines of communication between the center and the periphery allowed local factors to take hold of revenues and to exert political authority. After the withdrawal of Isaac and Alexios, Roussel de Bailleul wielded power over towns and villages in Galatia and Lycaonia and levied taxes from them.[58] Apparently, the Norman soldiers' military force was strong enough for them to impose their will upon the local population and to fend off Turkish attacks. Both Attaleiates and Bryennios ascribe the government's failure to take effective measures to safeguard the threatened regions to the ruler's lack of imperial virtues and his minister Nikephoritzes' bad influence.[59] In this way, the chief representatives of the old regime were blamed for the overall disintegration, which in 1073 apparently started to spread from the borderlands to central and western Anatolia.

Byzantine rebels and Turkish warriors in central Asia Minor, 1074–75

The imperial government tried to face the precarious situation in Asia Minor by dispatching new military forces and by using diplomatic means to establish alliances with warrior groups operating in the region. The court of Constantinople was already well acquainted with Turkish defectors who had been integrated into the Byzantine military apparatus. As a result, the imperial palace entered negotiations with Turkish invaders and tried through gifts and promises to win them over for temporary coalitions. The growing power of Roussel's Norman forces caused the imperial government to seek a strong counter-weight, which at that time only the Turks could provide. In this way, the practice of undermining local elites through short-lived military alliances, one of the main factors fostering the Turkish expansion in northern Syria and other Muslim regions, was transferred to Asia Minor in 1074.[60] Once again, the Byzantine government could hardly control the Turkish chieftains and, within a short time, they came to be directly involved in serious power struggles.

The new campaign against Roussel de Bailleul was under the command of Michael VII's uncle, the *kaisar* John Doukas, whom the emperor had appointed *strategos autokrator*. Bryennios ascribes this decision to a conspiracy of the *logothetes tou dromou* Nikephoritzes, who allegedly wished to get rid of his strongest rival at court, but the exact nature of these constellations can hardly be elucidated.[61]

The first hostile encounter took place at the bridge *tou Zombou*, one of the most important crossings of the Sangarios River, on the eastern bank of which Roussel was encamped while John approached from Dorylaion. The battle ended with a disastrous defeat of John Doukas. His troops were dispersed, his son Andronikos was seriously wounded, and he himself was taken prisoner. Only Nikephoros Botaneiates, the commander of the rear guard, managed to escape with his men.[62] Further strengthened by this victory, Roussel proceeded with his troops through Bithynia to the coastland opposite Constantinople. The details our two main narratives provide are contradictory at some points, but, if we believe Attaleiates, Roussel set up camp near Chrysopolis (Üsküdar) within sight of the imperial palace with a considerable force of 3,000 Frankish soldiers, pillaging the area and setting fire to houses in the nearby town.[63] The objectives of this campaign are not entirely clear, but in all likelihood he intended to put pressure on the imperial government in order to extort important concessions.[64] The subsequent proclamation of John Doukas as emperor, which is explained as a means to gain broader backing among the local population and to gather more soldiers,[65] is in line with this explanation, although it cannot be said for certain whether John Doukas had serious personal ambitions to take the imperial crown from his nephew.[66]

How serious a threat this advance was considered in Constantinople is articulated in the descriptions referring to the panic overwhelming Michael VII and the court elite and the measures they took. An embassy sent to Roussel's camp promised gifts and the title of *kouropalates*, which was still reserved to relatives of the ruling house and very high-ranking Christian vassal lords.[67] Moreover, the emperor set Roussel's wife and children free in order to appease him.[68] Another plan of the imperial government aimed at establishing an alliance with Turkish raiders operating in the Propontis region, which seems to have become even more accessible to the Turkish invaders because of the conflict with Roussel. The sources speak of the arrival of Turks in the area of the Sophon Mountain (Sabanca Dağı), thus forming an immediate threat to Roussel, who retreated with his troops to Nikomedeia and the fortress of Metabole located at the foot of the said mountain.[69] Bryennios explicitly mentions the chieftain Artouch, who is usually identified with the well-known governor of Tāj al-Dawla Tutush and forefather of the homonymous dynasty in the Diyār Bakr region.[70] At that time he was operating in the area east of the Sangarios River, from where he was summoned by Michael VII to invade Bithynia and to fight Roussel de Bailleul.[71] During the ensuing skirmishes both Roussel and John Doukas were captured.[72] Once more, the way Artouch treated his captives clearly shows the absence of any far-reaching political ambitions. The Turks could have used two of the most influential personalities of the Byzantine court elite as a highly effective means to exert all sorts of pressure on the imperial government, but they were content with ransoming them. Attaleiates explicitly points out the advantages the Turks could have achieved. According to the words put into the mouth of the *protovestes* Basileios Maleses, by proclaiming John Doukas emperor the Turks would have earned great profit from Byzantine towns, villages, and authorities.[73]

After being released in exchange for a sum paid by his wife, Roussel retreated to the Pontus region, where he seized fortresses and built up a new network of territorial control in the region south of Samsun near the Iris River (Yeşilırmak), i.e., the area of the Armeniakon theme. Soon he became strong enough to bring important urban centers, such as Amaseia and Neokaisareia, under his control and to attack Turks approaching his realm.[74] As has been suggested, in that time Roussel was able to collect tax revenues, strengthen his military power through fortified strongholds, and may have even possessed personal domains in the region, although there is no clear evidence with respect to the latter.[75] All in all, we can speak of some rudimentary structures of a local lordship held by an independent group of Norman soldiers, who had gained the support of the local aristocracy, be it by force or by favorable agreements and the advantages resulting from the Normans' effective military protection.

At the time under discussion, Turkish groups were invading parts of Paphlagonia, the northern Anatolian plateau, and the Sangarios Valley. Although the emergence of warlords like Dānishmand, Mangujak, and Saltuk most probably dates to one or two decades later, it may be assumed that the Turkish presence within the Halys basin in northern Cappadocia and the regions east of the Armeniakon district must have been at least equally strong. Hence, the territories controlled by Roussel's soldiers were exposed to the influx of Turkish elements from all sides, something that made the presence of a strong fighting force guaranteeing a certain amount of security and stability especially valuable.[76]

The imperial government increasingly failed to control and integrate the various centrifugal forces making their appearance in the eastern provinces and to offer an effective defensive system for the provincial population.[77] At the same time, it faced serious intra-dynastic issues requiring an urgent settlement. John Doukas' proclamation as emperor certainly caused serious disturbances in the relations between the ruling emperor and his uncle. When on the senate's approval the court of Constantinople eventually paid the ransom for John Doukas, the latter had to make clear that he had no ambitions to question the rights of his nephew and gain the imperial throne for himself. Therefore, he presented himself before the emperor dressed as a monk and thereafter retreated from court politics to the monastery of Stoudiou.[78] On the basis of this symbolic gesture peace could be restored within the imperial family, but John's defeat and double captivity, first at the hands of Roussel and then of Artouch, must have caused a serious loss of prestige. Doubts concerning the military skills and suitability of the men in power may have become increasingly stronger.

Bryennios and Attaleiates offer widely differing interpretations of these events. While the former considers the Norman commander above all a rebel who had to be subjected to imperial rule,[79] the latter acknowledges his outstanding abilities in military matters and the strength of his troops, which could have been of great value for the Byzantine defensive system.[80] This assessment has to be viewed in the context of the author's harsh critique of Michael VII. Attaleiates took pains to blame Botaneiates' predecessor for the rapid Turkish expansion and the overall chaos in the eastern provinces.[81] His failure to fulfill his duty to protect his subjects from hostile attacks constituted one of the main arguments justifying his violent overthrow. The emperor considered it to be of secondary importance, Attaleiates argues, that the Turks attacked the Romans, slaughtered the Christians, pillaged villages and territories, and captured and killed countless people. As a result "the whole East" was thrown into a panic and the Turks were scattered in all Roman themes. Moreover, he accused Michael VII of preferring the Turks to control Roman affairs to having the Franks settle somewhere to fend off Turkish attacks.[82]

Viewed objectively, it is quite obvious that in 1073–74 Roussel's Normans were a similarly destabilizing factor in Asia Minor to the Turks and certainly a greater and more immediate threat to the imperial government, especially in view of the proclamation of John Doukas. Indeed, the warriors of Artouch certainly took advantage of this situation, but this was not Michael VII's preference. It was the unavoidable consequence of the Turks' involvement in this conflict. With the benefit of hindsight, Attaleiates inverted the historical facts by contrasting the image of a potential Norman ally with that of destructive Turkish raiders. According to our sources, after their successes in the Propontis coastland the Turks withdrew to Upper Phrygia, which probably means the region around Amorion south of the Sangarios River.[83] We may assume that by 1074 the Turks had significantly strengthened their presence in certain regions of Galatia and Phrygia. They were still far from establishing a territorial lordship or from taking possession of towns, but they may have possessed rallying points serving as support bases for incursions into western Asia Minor.

The last phase in the conflict between the imperial government and Roussel de Bailleul is marked by an expedition in 1075 under the command of Alexios Komnenos, who according to our sources was appointed supreme commander in the East on this occasion. This decision certainly has to be seen in connection with the balance of power among the leading persons at the imperial court and seems to have strengthened the alliance between Nikephoritzes and the Komnenian family, although the young Alexios may have actually held a much lower title during this campaign.[84] Be that as it may, the personal involvement of the future emperor gave rise to widely differing presentations of this campaign by Attaleiates and Bryennios. The former makes a brief and very critical appraisal, blasting Michael VII's policy, which, in his view, achieved nothing but drawing the Turks to the coastal area opposite Constantinople.[85] Bryennios, instead, in the context of his eulogizing narrative, portrays his hero as a skillful commander and diplomat, who successfully fulfilled his mission and eventually brought the dangerous enemy in fetters to Constantinople. Accordingly, Roussel's capture appears either as a major accomplishment or as fatal mistake accelerating the breakdown of Byzantine military power.

On his way to the East, Alexios reportedly gathered troops, among them a small unit of Alan soldiers, and went to Amaseia in order to force the inhabitants of this and adjacent towns to suspend their payments to Roussel. At that time a Turkish group under the command of a certain Toutach was operating in the area, and both Roussel and Alexios entered negotiations with him.[86] Bryennios used this episode for an elaborate presentation of Alexios' diplomatic skills and rhetorical persuasiveness. Allegedly, he convinced the Turkish chieftain by presenting the idea of two legitimate rulers collaborating against an outlaw who was causing troubles for both of them. By turning Roussel in, Toutach would profit in a threefold manner by gaining money, the emperor's favor, and the sultan's benevolence.[87] An intriguing detail is that the Seljuk sultan, i.e., Malikshāh, is portrayed as being amicably disposed towards the Byzantine emperor and as ruling over the Turkmen warriors in Asia Minor. The image thus evoked is that of two supreme authorities of equal rank exerting power over their respective spheres of influence and creating bonds of allegiance with subordinate commanders moving between the two realms. According to this idea, which expressed what was thought to have been the official stance of the imperial government in the 1070s, there was no essential difference between Frankish and Turkish chiefs with respect to their relations with the emperor and the sultan.[88]

Bryennios' description of an uprising of the people of Amaseia instigated by the *archontes* of the town provides a glimpse at the social tensions in the provincial towns of Anatolia. Once Toutach had taken Roussel prisoner, Alexios had to find the ransom money for the captive and secure his transport back to Constantinople. The local aristocracy, however, collaborated with Roussel and was not interested in restoring imperial rule over Amaseia. Upon Alexios' request for financial support, riots broke out in the town. Alexios supposedly calmed the inhabitants by delivering a speech in which he pointed out the diverging interests of the aristocrats and the lower strata of the population: The *archontes* profit both by securing their property through collaboration with Roussel and by receiving gifts from the emperor; the other citizens, instead, have to bear all reprisals, suffering massacres, imprisonment, blinding, and mutilation.[89] Alexios put an end to the riots by pretending to blind Roussel and thus disseminating the impression that the Norman chief was no longer capable to command his troops.[90]

The aforementioned details illustrate some noteworthy political attitudes that Bryennios ascribed to the milieu of Anatolian provincial towns. Political utility and military strength formed the main criteria for the establishment of alliances, which came into being irrespective of ethnic and religious divides. Allegiance to Constantinople was of significance only as long as the emperor was able to maintain his influence and to guarantee safety with the aid of his army. Hence, the local elites of Amaseia concluded agreements with the Norman soldiers, while Roussel closely collaborated with Toutach before his imprisonment. As a result, the provincial population was confronted with arbitrary encroachments of both local aristocrats and foreign warriors, Turks and Normans alike. The estrangement between the central government and the provincial population favored the formation of close links between local aristocrats and intruding invaders. Bryennios presents Alexios' negotiations with the townspeople of Amaseia as an attempt to undermine this collaboration by shifting broader portions of the inhabitants to his side. Regardless of the fictional elements in this report, it can be assumed that it actually reflects the social groupings and tensions among the groups living in Anatolian provincial towns during the 1070s.[91]

It is hard to make a more precise assessment of the Turkish activities in the northern parts of Asia Minor, but the overall impression conveyed by Bryennios' account is that numerous warrior groups followed the Halys Valley in a north-westerly direction until they reached Paphlagonia and the Pontus coastland. Alexios reportedly achieved the surrender of most places under Roussel's control and headed back along the coastland of Paphlagonia and the Boukellarion theme to the port of Herakleia (Ereğli), where he embarked on a ship for Constantinople. The region he crossed is described as being seriously threatened by the Turks. The domains of the Komnenoi family in Kastamona were abandoned and exposed to Turkish attacks; the environs of Herakleia were full of raiders.[92] The routes and mountain passages connecting the imperial city with the Pontus region apparently were under the constant threat of invaders. The Turks seem to have exerted considerable pressure on the towns and villages in the region, but as in other regions they did not yet control any fortified places.[93]

All in all, Bryennios stresses the successful outcome of this expedition, claiming that Alexios would have continued to fight the Turks were it not for urgent messages from the emperor calling him back to Constantinople.[94] Attaleiates, instead, presents a very negative view, suggesting that the imprisonment of Roussel removed the last obstacle to the Turks' advance to the Propontis coastland so that they began to attack the environs of Chalkedon and Chrysopolis.[95] In fact the Turks had already reached Bithynia, coming from the Sangarios Valley further south, and thus his remark concerning Roussel's importance seems somehow exaggerated and has to be seen in the context of his severe criticism of Michael VII. For the same reason, the author strongly condemns the agreement between the emperor and Toutach. Doing so, the historian combines the ethnographic stereotype of the barbarians' treacherous and unreliable nature with the image of Michael VII as a careless and pitiless ruler. The Turks, he argues, betray friendship for money and consider it a legal precept (παράγγελμα νόμιμον) to deceive, to kill, and to betray the Romans, disregarding their oaths. Michael VII, in turn, is depicted as totally ignoring the Turkish threat and the rumors concerning the Turks' raiding in the vicinity of the capital as though it were a foreign country.[96] As regards Roussel, the emperor was not willing to make a decision in accordance with the ideas of imperial tolerance and generosity and thus to preserve such a great commander for the empire in order to gain his gratitude and use him for the defense of the East.[97] The emperor's wrath deprived the Byzantine State of a capable military leader and effective manpower. This view is in sharp contrast with the facts transmitted in Bryennios' report presenting Roussel primarily as a dangerous rebel. While repudiating the alliance with the Turks, Attaleiates overemphasizes Roussel's military force and draws parallels between the Turks' inferior human qualities and the emperor's immorality. Having lost the characteristics of a good ruler, the argument goes, the emperor became one with the barbarians, insensible to their cruelties.[98]

In summary, the eastern provinces in the years 1073–75 experienced a significant expansion of Turkish activities from Cappadocia to Galatia, northern

Phrygia, Paphlagonia, the Sangarios Valley, Bithynia, and the Propontis coastland. In this way, the southern invasion route leading from Cilicia and the Euphrates region to Lycaonia, southern Phrygia, Pisidia, and the Meander Valley was supplemented by a northern one. Movements and assaults of Turkish warrior groups affected the entire central Anatolian plateau and parts of northwestern Asia Minor as far as the Pontic coastland around Herakleia (Ereğli). Their aims and strategies were still mainly focused on the acquisition of booty, money, and captives. But due to the political constellations, there was a stronger involvement in intra-Byzantine power struggles among the central government, the provincial aristocracy, and independent mercenary groups. As a result, the Turks intensified their control over rural areas, roads, and river valleys and established advanced rallying points enabling them to remain permanently in regions of central Anatolia. A part of the Byzantine historiographical tradition ascribes these developments to the personal failure of Emperor Michael VII and his advisors. But on the basis of the opposing views proposed by the historians it becomes quite clear that the eastern provinces faced a situation in which the imperial government, no longer able to exert effective control, had lost its integrative and unifying force while various centrifugal and local powers were still not able to prevail and establish viable territorial lordships. The Turks successfully took advantage of a power vacuum and offered their services to all parties involved. In the next stage they were increasingly drawn into the political and ideological sphere of the Byzantine imperial court.

Asia Minor during the Revolts of Nikephoros Botaneiates and Alexios I, 1077–81

The decisive phase for the permanent establishment of Turkmen warrior groups and nomads in Bithynia and other parts of western Asia Minor roughly coincides with the period between the revolt of Nikephoros Botaneiates in June 1077 and the revolt of Alexios Komnenos in April 1081.[99] As we have seen, in the years 1073–75 the Turks enjoyed more or less unhindered access to Bithynia and penetrated the Propontis coastland as far as the Asian suburbs of Constantinople. If we believe Attaleiates, who establishes a causal link between the revolt of Botaneiates and the Turkish raids,[100] until 1077 the Turkish presence in western Asia Minor was constantly increasing. The same source mentions masses of refugees who arrived day after day in Constantinople, fleeing the marauding barbarians and the threat of famine.[101] One gets the impression that numerous bands of raiders were roaming around the region, causing vast devastation, disruption of routes and transportation networks, and a high degree of insecurity for the rural population, travelers, and military units. The image of wholesale destruction in the entire East is evoked.[102] Considering Attaleiates' intention to create the impression of a sharp contrast between a corrupt regime and a just rebel, it is questionable to what extent these descriptions reflect the reality of these years. What does "the entire East" really include, at a time when the Turks still did not possess any urban centers or fortified places? With their raids they certainly put considerable pressure on military units and the rural population, but they were not yet able to exert any territorial control.

The most characteristic feature of these years is the frequent involvement of Turkish warriors in Byzantine rebellions, a factor that had become tangible for the first time during the conflicts with Roussel de Bailleul. The Turks not only achieved considerable financial gains, but they also became deeply involved in the power struggle between members of the Byzantine elite. This drew the Turkish invaders closer to the imperial circles of Constantinople and contributed to the dissemination of Byzantine political concepts among them. The final outcome was an official treaty by which, in the months after his accession to the throne, Alexios I conceded to Sulaymān b. Qutlumush and his companions a certain degree of legitimate authority and territorial rule in parts of Bithynia.[103]

The reconstruction of the developments is complicated by the fact that both Attaleiates and Bryennios have a gap in their narrative covering the time span between the end of Alexios' expedition in 1075 and the beginning of Botaneiates' revolt in 1077. This is all the more regrettable in that we do not have any information about the immediate results of the first massive arrival of Turkish groups in Bithynia. In particular, the Byzantine sources do not provide any details about the first appearance of the sons of Qutlumush in western Asia Minor. They suddenly come to the foreground with Botaneiates' advance towards Constantinople.[104]

The accounts of Attaleiates and Bryennios show increasing divergences because of the strong encomiastic elements in the former's presentation of his hero.[105] This tendency entails not only a change of style from a relatively straightforward narrative to a particularly verbose and ornate description but also a quite radical re-appraisal of the political events. Aspects of the Turkish expansion, which with respect to previous years are interpreted as symptoms of decay in the imperial government and as signs of God's wrath, are now described as challenges that the new God-chosen ruler successfully handled. Bryennios, instead, certainly explains Botaneiates' victory as an accomplishment enabled by God's providence, but he does not especially highlight the qualities of this man.[106] He appears as one of a whole series of rebels, the most outstanding of whom in Bryennios' view is, as one may expect, his namesake father or grandfather.[107]

A crucial question that needs further clarification is in what way the collaboration between Byzantine rebels and Turkmen warriors changed the political and ideological framework of their relations and to what extent the Turkish invaders transformed this mutual approach into a formative power enabling the establishment of rudimentary structures of domination and administration.[108] Nikephoros Botaneiates was a distinguished general who, after a long career beginning under the reign of Constantine IX, held the post of *strategos* of the Anatolikon theme. In about October 1077 he openly revolted against Michael VII, setting off from Phrygia for Constantinople.[109] From the outset it seems that both the emperor and Botaneiates were taking pains to gain support from the Turks who were roaming the territories between Phrygia and Bithynia. Sulaymān b. Qutlumush and his men occupied a crucial position in these contacts. If we believe Bryennios, the decision-makers in Constantinople first approached Sulaymān through an emissary,[110] thus applying the same strategy as in the war against Roussel de Bailleul in 1075. In the meantime Botaneiates and his followers proceeded via Kotyaion (Kütahya) and a stronghold on the Sangarios River towards Nicaea, where he first had skirmishes with Sulaymān's Turks. Botaneiates' advantage in this situation was the fact that one of his closest companions was the Seljuk lord Arīsghī/Chrysoskoulos, who had taken refuge at the court of Constantinople in 1070 because of discord with Sultan Alp Arslān.[111] This man entered negotiations with Sulaymān, persuading him to retreat in exchange for a sum of money, and thus the men of Botaneiates gained access to Nicaea.[112] It becomes evident that the Turks controlled the routes and rural areas in the vicinity of this city. The presence in Botaneiates' camp of a Turkish nobleman, who despite his defection several years earlier may still have been an awe-inspiring personality because of his bonds with the Seljuk dynasty of Persia, in all likelihood played an important role for the successful outcome of the talks with Sulaymān, an important scion of the same family. It may be assumed that the mediation of a Turkish dignitary with close relations to the Seljuk house and the Byzantine court elite was an important factor for acquainting the sons of Qutlumush with elements of the Byzantine mentality and political culture.

Bryennios does not mention any further agreements between the two sides, stressing, instead, the enthusiastic reception Botaneiates had among the people of Nicaea.[113] This gap can be filled with the report of Attaleiates, who refers extensively to contacts with the Turks, albeit with a strong tendency to glorify. According to the traditional ideal of the victorious emperor, which forms an intrinsic part of encomiastic speeches, the author presents his protagonist as an irresistible commander, who "terrified all Huns who were ravaging the East and filled them with astonishment and perplexity, and [so] an enormous Turkish crowd started to gather around him in a slavish attitude. They came to him as defectors professing their servitude and exposing that talking to him and seeing him is an enormous benefit."[114] The image of a ruler desperately at pains to find allies among hostile invaders even to the detriment of the empire, as presented in the case of Michael VII, is now reversed for Botaneiates by highlighting the rebel's powerful attractiveness in drawing Romans and enemies close to him.[115] People fleeing to Botaneiates' camp went without fear of the marauding Turks, and the latter did not prevent anybody from reaching his destination.[116] While Michael VII eagerly tried to win over the Turks as intimate friends, sending them countless gifts and stirring them up with all sorts of promises, God's providence arranged another outcome, and so they joined Botaneiates, swore servitude, promised to make an alliance, and sided with his faction.[117] God, who in Attaleiates' view had prepared the grounds for Botaneiates' rebellion, appears once again as a transcendental power causing the Turks to support the rebel. These statements prepare the description of the establishment of the official alliance between Botaneiates and the sons of Qutlumush:

> For this reason some of the noblemen of Persia came to Nicaea. They were brothers in flesh and nature, drew the eponym of Koutloumouses from their

> father's name and strove for the sultan's title and power opposing the chieftain of the Huns. Therefore, they fled to the land of the Romans to gain [the support of] a power rivaling him. What because of their royal descent they would never have accepted to do for any king of the Persians or the Romans, they unexpectedly showed to him: they bent their knees and declared that with much confidence they would lead the way of his march to the imperial city. After making them more obedient and well disposed with prudent words and gestures, he inflamed them so as to submit and show allegiance to him and made them fervent supporters of his majesty to such an extent that they turned into completely different persons, as the saying goes, made an agreement with the Romans accompanying him and became one union and lordship in the unification of allegiance and honest friendship.[118]

Attaleiates' account resembles the Muslim-Seljuk tradition in that it points to the rebellious past of the sons of Qutlumush and their power struggle with the Great Seljuk sultan. This version is in sharp contrast to the idea of an official appointment of Sulaymān b. Qutlumush as conqueror and ruler of territories in Asia Minor, as described by Michael the Syrian and later Seljuk chronicles. By presenting the sons of Qutlumush as refugees arriving in Byzantine territory in search of a strong power to back their claims, Attaleiates emphasizes the outstanding political profile of Botaneiates, who thus is portrayed as the most appropriate person to offer the sons of Qutlumush the support and protection they need. An intriguing new feature is the prostration of the Turkish warlords before the Byzantine rebel, a symbolic gesture that not only underlines Botaneiates' imperial aspirations but also underscores the rebel's position ideologically. With the prostration performed by Persian descendants of royal blood, Attaleiates alludes to a concept of spiritual affinity, on the basis of which members of outstanding ruling houses share common rights of sovereignty and supreme rule. Rebellious Turks and Romans agree to fight side by side under the aegis of Botaneiates' leadership, thus recognizing his overarching integrative force and legitimatizing potential. The Turks, so stubbornly insisting on their struggle against all previous emperors, are now ready to be absorbed into the Byzantine political and cultural sphere, thus being transformed into useful supporters of the empire. We are dealing with a central feature of political thought in Byzantium, going back to the period of the empire's confrontation with the barbarian migrations in Late Antiquity. For instance, the ideas that historians and court orators expressed on the occasion of the Gothic-Roman treaty of 382 in many respects resemble Attaleiates' vision of a Byzantine-Turkish coalition.[119]

In contrast to Syriac and later Muslim texts stressing that Sulaymān b. Qutlumush was fully integrated into the Muslim sphere because of his official appointment, the Byzantine version offers a genuine Roman interpretation, according to which Sulaymān acquired authority through his alliance with the Byzantine rebel and future emperor. In this respect it is noteworthy that, in his brief report of the alliance between Botaneiates and the Turks, John Zonaras presents a very different version of the circumstances of Sulaymān's arrival.[120]

He is the only Byzantine author to support the idea of an official appointment in accordance with Michael the Syrian, albeit with some remarkable peculiarities. While Qutlumush and the sultan were striving for power, he argues, the caliph left his palace in fear of a civil war and went to the two rivals, persuading them to refrain from fighting. It was agreed that the sultan would keep his empire undiminished but would help his relative, in every possible way, conquer Roman territories and hold sway over them. Sulaymān's invasion thus appears as result of an intra-dynastic compromise initiated by the caliph. In the early twelfth century, when Zonaras was writing, the idea of a Roman-Turkish coalition had already been superseded by the events of Alexios I's reign. Seljuk rule in Anatolia had become a political reality and thus disseminated its own concepts of legitimacy based on the supreme authorities of Islam. As regards the actual state of affairs in about 1078, there apparently was intense antagonism between Emperor Michael VII and Nikephoros Botaneiates in gaining the support of Turkish warrior groups. Especially for the latter, securing open routes for his march towards the imperial city and for people coming to his camp was vital for success. The rural areas between Phrygia and Bithynia could no longer be controlled without taking the Turkish factor seriously into account.[121]

According to Attaleiates, in March 1078 the united Turkish and Byzantine forces under Botaneiates' command proceeded to Chalcedon and Chrysopolis, where they pitched camp. The atmosphere is depicted as one of "great joy" due to the fact that for a long time no Romans had come to this place, which had become a shelter for Turks and a place stained with the blood of many Christians. But once the insignia of Roman dominion made their appearance all the inhabitants of Constantinople took courage and held hopes of victory. The coastal towns on the Asian shores of the Propontis joyfully opened their gates to Botaneiates' soldiers.[122] These were in all likelihood Byzantine soldiers, for Attaleiates explicitly refers to "infantrymen," not to soldiers on horseback as would apply to Turkish forces. The latter seem to have controlled the routes between the coast and Nicaea, thus enabling the people of Constantinople to reach Botaneiates' camp without obstacles.[123]

While Michael VII was compelled to resign and become a monk, Nikephoros Botaneiates entered the imperial city and was crowned emperor in late March 1078.[124] As was to be expected, the successful rebel first had to expand his circle of supporters by generously distributing lavish gifts, titles, and privileges.[125] Among those waiting for their awards were "the barbarian company" (ἡ ἐθνικὴ μερίς) or the "Qutlumush Turks" (Κουτουλμούσιοι Τοῦρκοι). "For keeping their servile devotion and loyalty towards the emperor," as Attaleiates puts it, they received many goods. In particular, he distinguishes between the sons of Qutlumush, who day by day were showered with lavish gifts from the imperial treasury, and the Turkish commanders, who entered the city in servile habit and came out with their hands and bags full of gold and precious textiles.[126] The Turkish military elite was thus given the opportunity to visit Constantinople in person, to form an impression of Byzantine court life, and to amass considerable amounts of precious objects and artisan products. This certainly further strengthened the cultural and ideological influence of the Byzantine elite on its Turkish allies. The fact that the Turks, as Attaleiates asserts, with drumbeats and acclamations publicly projected their allegiance to and recognition of Botaneiates' authority shows that they had become a part of the new ruler's propaganda strategy, disseminating the image of a generous and powerful emperor, who had transformed the empire's dangerous enemies into obedient subjects.[127]

As the strategy followed by various Turkmen warrior groups in the Muslim territories of Syria and Mesopotamia has demonstrated, establishing bonds of allegiance with the local elites was the first step towards erecting an independent territorial rule within the framework of pre-existing political entities. Likewise, in the Byzantine eastern provinces of the 1070s, warrior groups bound together by a strong spirit of cohesion could quickly turn into autonomously operating political factors, trying to increase their revenues and spheres of influence. Roussel de Bailleul and his Norman soldiers were on the verge of achieving the establishment of a local lordship, but they were frustrated by a Byzantine-Turkish coalition in conjunction with a lack of support from the provincial population. Very soon, the sons of Qutlumush would not find any serious rival to stop them.

The successive emergence of other seditious movements, in which the Turkmen warriors of the Qutlumush clan were actively involved, decisively fostered further Turkish penetration of the inner circles of Byzantine imperial power. Already in November 1077, Nikephoros Bryennios, the *doux* of Dyrrachion, had started his rebellion in the western provinces, having secured the support of many aristocrats and the greatest part of the western military units of the empire.[128] In the weeks following Botaneiates' accession to the throne Bryennios marched towards Constantinople, forcing the new regime to react as quickly as possible. Alexios Komnenos had switched sides early enough, persuading Michael VII to resign. As a reward, he was appointed *megas domestikos* and entrusted with the campaign against Bryennios.[129] While the palace was negotiating with Bryennios about a peace agreement, Alexios once more made use of the alliance with the Qutlumush Turks. "He sent a message to the Turkish chiefs who resided in Nicaea of Bithynia. These were Masur and Solyman [Manṣūr and Sulaymān], the sons of Koutloumous, and they immediately sent allies not fewer than 2.000 and swiftly prepared others."[130]

This is the first statement of a Byzantine author indicating that the sons of Qutlumush and their Turkmen warriors not only raided or controlled rural areas but were actually in possession of an important fortified town. Given that Attaleiates, referring to events that took place only a few weeks earlier in the context of Botaneiates' rise to power, describes the new emperor's Turkish allies as camping outside the Asian suburbs of Constantinople, the question arises whether Bryennios' statement should be taken at face value or reflects a later stage in the process of Turkish establishment in Bithynia. The available source material does not allow for a definitive conclusion. In the first case one may assume that, after Botaneiates' entrance into Constantinople, the Turkish allies, who previously secured the routes between the coastland and Nicaea, came with the emperor's consent to fill the vacuum created by the transfer of local forces to the capital, thus forming a sort of rearguard protecting the hinterland of Bithynia against other seditious elements or Turkish raiders. On the other hand, it seems highly doubtful that in the moment of his greatest triumph Botaneiates would have handed over such a significant stronghold situated a short distance from Constantinople to military forces whose loyalty could hardly inspire confidence. More likely Nicaea came under Turkish control on some later occasion, when the political situation became more insecure because of the persisting internal unrest, and many regions in western Asia Minor slipped further from the control of the central government.

A detachment of Turkish warriors participated in the battle of Kalobrye near Selymbria in the Thracian hinterland of Constantinople. Alexios Komnenos and his forces were about to be defeated by the numerically superior enemies, so the Turkish soldiers, arriving on the battlefield in the last moment with their combat technique of shooting arrows from horseback and luring enemies into ambushes, turned the battle into a victory of the imperial troops and managed to capture Nikephoros Bryennios.[131] This success, a matter of vital importance for the political survival of Botaneiates, certainly much increased Botaneiates' esteem for his allies and further strengthened their position within the Byzantine administrative and military apparatus. Unfortunately, the sources do not indicate in what way the Turkish warriors were rewarded for their support.

While other minor uprisings occurred in the western part of the empire in the following years, it was not before the autumn of 1080, a few months prior to Alexios Komnenos' usurpation, that Asia Minor once more formed the setting of a large-scale rebellion, this time under the command of Nikephoros Melissenos, a high-ranking officer holding posts in Asia Minor and the West, who since Alexios' rise to power was closely associated with the Komnenian clan through the title of *kaisar* and the bond of marriage with the emperor's sister Eudokia.[132] According to Bryennios' account, the main source for these events, Melissenos started his revolt from his exile in Kos, from where he came into contact and established an alliance with several Turkish chieftains, whose identity is not revealed.[133] The area of his first seditious activities is located in the provinces of Asia, Phrygia, and Galatia, which roughly correspond to the administrative units of the Anatolikon and Boukellarion themes.[134] It seems that Dorylaion was an especially important stronghold for Melissenos.[135] With the aid of his Turkish allies, the report goes, he put on the red shoes that visualized his bid for the imperial throne and began subduing the towns of the region, the inhabitants of which were ready to accept his authority. In this way he gathered a considerable number of troops consisting of both local elements and Turkish auxiliary forces and eventually seized the city of Nicaea.

As we do not have accurate information about the identity of his allies, it is hard to arrive at conclusions as to their relationship with the Qutlumush Turks. A brief reference to the "sultan" (σουλτάνος) who was to be fought in the region of Dorylaion,[136] the only time Bryennios uses the word with respect to a Turkish ruler in Asia Minor, certainly points to the Seljuk clan of Sulaymān, but the occurrence of the title in this context is doubtlessly anachronistic. Likewise, it is unclear whether and to what extent the Qutlumush Turks were able to extend their sphere of influence beyond Bithynia to the interior of Asia Minor in the years after 1078. As a result, it cannot be decided whether Melissenos' allies were subjects or vassals of Sulaymān or independent groups of Turkmen warriors. The assertion that Melissenos and his troops seized Nicaea clearly contradicts Bryennios' previous statement concerning the city's role as residence of the sons of Qutlumush. Had it been in their hands, they would never have handed it to the Byzantine rebel to serve as a basis for his further advance to Constantinople. Moreover, given that in 1078 the Qutlumush Turks were loyal allies of Botaneiates, supporting him against Michael VII and Nikephoros Bryennios, the question arises as to why in 1080/81 they would have abandoned him, siding with one of his most dangerous opponents. One assumes that the amicable relations between the two sides, based on considerable payments and gifts from the imperial treasury, had begun to crumble and the former alliance had lost its validity, but the sources do not provide any clue for the reasons for such a change. The overall picture emerging from this report is highly fragmentary and inconclusive, and thus it is hardly possible to draw conclusions regarding the political role of the Qutlumush Turks or other Turkmen warrior groups in western Asia Minor and their relations with the Byzantine elite during the years 1078–81.[137]

It is remarkable, however, that in this context Bryennios explicitly mentions the surrender of Anatolian towns to Turkish forces for the first time. After putting the towns under his control, Melissenos was forced against his will to hand them over to the Turks. "Thus it happened within a short time that the Turks took hold of all towns in Asia, Phrygia, and Galatia."[138] At about the same time it may be assumed that the Turks took possession of Kyzikos.[139] It is also noteworthy that Bryennios repeatedly stresses the military superiority of the Turkish forces. Alexios is said to have refused to command an expedition against Melissenos because his troops were much inferior to the power of the Turks.[140] Therefore, the *protovestiarios* John was entrusted with the campaign, but more experienced senior officers like George Palaiologos and Basil Kourtikes advised him not to besiege Nicaea under these circumstances. As was to be expected, the Byzantines were forced to retreat, and it was only at great risk that George Palaiologos managed to rescue John and his troops from total annihilation. A plan aiming at an advance towards Dorylaion was also rejected.

These details make us believe that the military situation in western Asia Minor around 1080 became increasingly precarious and gradually shifted against the Byzantine side. Apparently, the Turks were still unable to conquer fortified towns by themselves. In order to occupy the urban centers, they depended upon the collaboration of Byzantine representatives, who found acceptance among the local population. On the other hand, the Byzantine commanders and rebels were obviously no longer able to restrain the expansive tendencies of the Turks and to restrict their activities to rural areas.[141] Bryennios gives no explanation for Melissenos' handing the towns to the Turks, nor does he specify which towns came under Turkish control. In any case it may be assumed that the incessant upheavals and bids for power seriously jeopardized the central government's presence in the provinces of Asia Minor. Apparently, Melissenos relied much more on Turkish support than had Botaneiates three years earlier for putting his plan into practice. Thus, he was forced to make many more concessions, allowing the establishment of Turkish garrisons in fortified places and towns. The fact that shortly before Alexios Komnenos' usurpation Melissenos reached an agreement with the former and thus renounced his claims to the throne in exchange for the title of *kaisar* and some other prerogatives while the imperial troops had no opportunity to re-establish their control over the territories of western Asia Minor certainly meant that the Turks took advantage of a vacuum of power to further consolidate their sway over the region.

Peter Frankopan recently proposed an interpretation suggesting that twelfth-century Komnenian historiography consciously created a rather obscure and negative image of Nikephoros Melissenos because of his former role as a dangerous rival of the Komnenian clan, thereby accusing him of being responsible for the loss of the Anatolian towns, losses that may actually have occurred after Alexios' rise to power.[142] This theory, while persuasive regarding the unfavorable depiction of Melissenos, is problematic as far as providing a satisfactory explanation for the sudden increase in the Turks' military strength. The fact that Alexios I had to concentrate the empire's forces in the West in order to confront the Norman invasion may have strengthened the Turkish expansionist tendencies, but the seizure of towns also pre-supposes an important change in the Turks' strategy and military technique. The cooperation with Byzantine rebels, therefore, better explains the Turkish infiltration of the urban centers of western Asia Minor, which at least in the initial stage seems to have happened without causing greater disturbances and destruction. Another argument rebutting Frankopan's theory can be drawn from the fact that Alexios I's treaty of 1081 with Sulaymān b. Qutlumush pre-supposes the latter's firm hold over Nicaea, which is much more likely to have been achieved in the course of Melissenos' advance, at the latest, than in the weeks after Alexios' ascent to the throne.

Be that as it may, the expansion of Turkish influence from rural areas and villages to urban centers certainly was a decisive turning point. The Turks now gained access to the tools and infrastructure of the Byzantine provincial administration and thus for the first time were able to levy taxes from the local population on a regular basis in order to secure their sources of income and to establish mechanisms of state-like control. This must also have been an important step towards transforming their nomadic or semi-nomadic lifestyle into a sedentary one. By settling in the urban environment of the Byzantine cultural sphere, the sons of Qutlumush were ultimately in a position to exert rudimentary forms of political authority, such as taxation, the distribution of landed estates, and the dispensation of justice. Accordingly, their retinue of Turkmen warriors tied together by bonds of kinship, nomadic customs, and a sense of allegiance to the Seljuk house was gradually transformed into a new ruling elite based on elements of Turkish, Muslim-Persian, and Byzantine origin.

It is very difficult to estimate the territorial extension of this nascent principality in western Asia Minor. From Bryennios' report one gets the impression that the whole area between Dorylaion and Nicaea north and south of the Sangarios Valley was already under firm Turkish control, but, as stated before, it is uncertain whether this region came under the sway of only one commander. Anna Komnene's statement claiming that the Turks had spread over all regions between the Black Sea, the Aegean coastland, and Cilicia around the time of Bryennios' revolt is greatly exaggerated.[143] An expansion over the whole of Asia Minor is unrealistic even in the years of the strongest Turkish presence in the western littoral prior to the First Crusade. It seems that statements like this primarily serve to underline the importance of Alexios' restoration of Byzantine rule achieved in the wake of the crusaders' march through Asia Minor, rather than to give a reliable assessment of the actual situation in 1078. Since it is impossible to assess the total number of Turkmen warriors and nomadic groups penetrating Asia Minor in the 1070s, no safe conclusion can be drawn as to the degree of Turkish presence in single regions. It can be taken for granted, however, that their presence was of a sporadic nature, concentrating on certain assembly points and suitable transit routes near rivers and pasture areas and, from 1080/81 onwards, on fortified places in provincial towns, from which a certain amount of control could be exerted over the surrounding areas. This is also suggested by the way in which the sources usually describe the size of dominions and principalities that came into existence on Byzantine soil, be they Turkish or not. The usual definition consists of a list of important towns as central strongholds around which a ruler's area of control is structured.[144] At least with respect to the decades following the establishment of the Turks it is likely that the new men in power exerted their authority by retaining the pre-existing Byzantine administrative system with its functioning staff. The introduction of structures and institutions originating from the Muslim-Persian tradition has to be dated several decades after the initial expansion.

Anna Komnene's perception of the Turks in Asia Minor before the first crusade

From a Byzantine viewpoint, the most important narrative describing the Turkish expansion in Asia Minor in the years after Alexios I's accession to the throne is Anna Komnene's *Alexiad*.[145] As has already been pointed out, the numerous details and interpretations this text provides must be viewed in the context of the author's thought-world reflecting the perceptions and ideological attitudes of Komnenian Constantinople and the imperial court in the 1130/40s.[146] As regards the macro-structure of Anna's reports about the Turks in Asia Minor, apart from the passages adopted from the chronicle of her husband Nikephoros Bryennios, the relevant material falls into three large thematic units: (1) Books III, VI, VII, IX, and the first part of book XI relate events in western Asia Minor and relations with the Great Seljuk sultanate from 1081 up to the arrival of the First Crusade in 1096. (2) Books X and XI describe the developments from the crossing of the crusader contingents to Asia Minor up to Bohemond's departure for Italy in late 1104; book XII, while mostly dealing with Bohemond's campaign in the region of Dyrrachion, adds two chapters on the situation in Cilicia and the Pontus region in 1105. (3) Books XIII and XV give detailed accounts about the Turkish attacks and the Byzantine campaigns in western Asia Minor in the years 1109–16.

It is noteworthy that, except for the reports concerning the First Crusade, which can be compared with a great number of Latin and some Oriental sources, the bulk of information on central and western Asia Minor before 1096 and the military activities of the years 1109–16 is known to us exclusively through the *Alexiad.* Given the lack of additional evidence, a source-critical approach to Anna's text has to focus primarily on an accurate analysis of the way she selects, arranges, presents, and interprets the historical facts to which she refers. Wherever it is possible, her descriptions should be checked against the background of data known from other regions in order to detect parallels and similarities in the behavioral patterns of Turkish warrior groups. Unavoidably, the overall image remains highly fragmentary, and it is not always possible to draw a clear distinction between twelfth-century Byzantine perceptions and the underlying reality of late eleventh-century Asia Minor.

Let us start with some characteristic features of Anna Komnene's discourse on the Turks and the political situation in Asia Minor. A central idea repeatedly evoked in her accounts is the notion of an overwhelming threat encompassing the entire East. Regarding the military situation during the revolt of Nikephoros Bryennios, the author asserts that

> "[...] the troops of the East are scattered here and there, whereas the Turks have spread and hold sway over almost everything that is between the Black Sea, the Hellespont, the Aegean, and the Syrian Sea, the Saros [Seyhan] and the other rivers, especially those that cross Pamphylia and Cilicia and flow into the Egyptian Sea."[147]

Passing over the Armenian provinces and the borderlands of Syria and Upper Mesopotamia, she focuses on the shorelines of Asia Minor, presenting all the provinces in the interior as having come under Turkish rule. Accordingly, the author depicts Sulaymān b. Qutlumush in Nicaea as "ruling over the whole East" and, in the context of a brief review of the territorial extension of the ancient Roman Empire, she notes that in her days, i.e., the mid-1080s, the boundaries of the Roman scepter were the Bosphorus in the east and the city of Adrianople in the west.[148] In the same passage, Anna also expounds Alexios' political program to recover the Roman territories as far as the Adriatic Sea in the west and the banks of the Euphrates and Tigris in the east. The strategy the emperor implemented to this end aimed at gaining a foothold on the Bithynian coast, whence he would gradually recover one city after the other and thus expand Roman dominion. Had not the incessant struggles and frequent troubles and dangers distracted him from his intention, he would have restored the empire to its former magnitude.[149] Hence, Anna's insistence on the Turks' invincible power becomes comprehensible. At the time of writing, the author had certainly realized that her father had not achieved his goals. His son and successor John II continued this policy, undertaking a number of campaigns to the East and further stabilizing the Byzantine defense system in western Asia Minor, but central and eastern Anatolia had become the heartlands of firmly established Muslim-Turkish principalities and the Euphrates River was no more than an ideologically charged reminiscence from the time prior to the Komnenians' rise to power.[150] Accordingly, Anna's intentions are both encomiastic and apologetic. On the one hand, she has to explain why the plan of restoring Byzantine control over the eastern provinces has eventually failed. The reason, in her opinion, lies in the great number of hostile threats Alexios had to cope with. On the other, she highlights the remarkable results that had been achieved under these difficult circumstances. With Alexios' rise to power, the message goes, the enemies had been driven out from the coastland opposite Constantinople; the emperor's step-by-step strategy brought important results; the Komnenian dynasty was able to meet the requirements of successful imperial rule as prescribed by the principles of Byzantine political theory.[151]

Another characteristic feature of Anna Komnene's account is the fact that the various Turkish protagonists no longer appear as mere raiders, warriors, and troublemakers, as was the case in sources referring to the previous period, but as well-established potentates residing in fortified towns and exerting political authority over the surrounding regions or even larger territorial units. This image is anachronistic to a certain extent and reflects the realities of the first half of the twelfth century. But it is also true that during the 1080s and 1090s there was a clearly discernible tendency among Turkish warrior groups in Asia Minor to establish themselves permanently in fortified places and develop rudimentary forms of administration, including the settlement of Turks in the environs of Byzantine provincial towns, the formation of regular military units, the integration of migrating Turkmen nomads and other newcomers from the East, the adoption of pre-existing administrative structures, the exertion of authority over the indigenous population, and the control of public revenues and tax levies. The evidence for this process is extremely tenuous, and thus it is all the more important to offer an accurate interpretation of the available details based on a comparison with data from other regions.

The lordship of Sulaymān b. Qutlumush in Nicaea

The landscape of the nascent Turkish lordships in western Asia Minor, as presented by Anna Komnene, had two main centers, one in Bithynia and a second one on the Gulf of Smyrna. Sulaymān b. Qutlumush (*Solymas*) was located in Nicaea, which was called the *soultanikion* (the sultan's court),[152] but this by no means indicates that Anna had a clear idea about the titles used among the first Turkish potentates in Anatolia. She speaks of a sultan only rarely and refers to Sulaymān in most cases as *amer* (= *amīr*) or without any further specification.[153] The activities of his warriors are presented as raids in the whole of Bithynia reaching the Propontis, the coastal suburbs of Constantinople on the Bosphorus, and the plains around Damalis (Üsküdar). They are said to have gained much booty and entered many fortresses and churches without meeting any obstacles,[154] but nothing points to a permanent establishment. The first defense measures taken by the emperor soon after his takeover in Constantinople were nighttime attacks of small detachments going on boats and descending on small groups of raiders who were lingering near the shores. Buildings and fortified places near the coast were suitable for laying ambushes. In this way the Turks were forced to retreat further inland, while the Byzantines were able to undertake more effective assaults supported by horsemen and expel the invaders from the environs of Nikomedeia and other regions of Bithynia.[155]

These skirmishes, datable to April/May 1081, prepared the ground for the conclusion of a peace treaty including the formal recognition of a borderline along the Drakon River in exchange for the Turks' promise to stop their assaults against the coastal region.[156] As regards the reasons for this treaty, Anna states that the emperor's military successes against the Turks forced Sulaymān to ask for peace, but she also refers to Robert Guiscard's war preparations, which made Alexios joyfully accept the peace proposal.[157] At first sight this explanation seems not very conclusive, but this is due to the fact that the author sought to present the agreement as a successful achievement of the imperial policy without completely concealing the dire straits in which the emperor was at that time. With a strong element of exaggeration, she first asserts that the Turks were expelled from not only the Bosphorus and the coastland but also from the whole of Bithynia and the environs of Nikomedeia, whereas finally she openly admits that the territory that had been rescued from hostile attacks did not reach beyond Damalis and the littoral.[158] Furthermore, she clearly points out the dangerous weakness of the state and its young ruler, who possessed neither troops nor money to face Robert's aggression. In light of these details, Anna, despite all embellishing brushstrokes, makes it sufficiently clear that Alexios I, with his empire still balancing on a knife's edge, simply had no choice but to seek peace with Sulaymān's Turks at all costs. The concluding phrase, "presenting them with gifts, he compelled them to accept the peace treaty,"[159] illustrates Anna's device to present matters of diplomatic etiquette and Alexios' flattery under the guise of terms suggesting Byzantine superiority.

It was the first formal peace treaty between a Byzantine emperor and a Seljuk chieftain, regulating territorial rights and thus *de facto* recognizing the existence of an independent political entity within the confines of the Byzantine State. Sulaymān was no longer an ally providing auxiliary forces, as happened under Nikephoros III Botaneiates, but a ruler exerting political authority within a certain radius of action centered in Nicaea and the areas along the northern and southern shores of the Gulf of Nikomedeia. Despite Anna's elusive statements, it seems that the city of Nikomedeia itself remained under Seljuk control, while on the peninsula of Thynia (Kocaeli Yarımadası) the Turks were not to extend their influence beyond the stipulated boundary at a considerably safe distance from the Asian suburbs of Constantinople, such as Chalkedon and Damalis. When the Norman troops of Robert Guiscard took Aulona (Vlora) and Corfu and put

Dyrrachion (Durrazzo) under siege in May/June 1081,[160] in his search for allies Emperor Alexios also sought the support of Sulaymān, who sent him auxiliary forces to fight on the side of the Byzantines against the western invaders.[161]

We do not hear anything else about Sulaymān's activities in Bithynia until his departure for Antioch, which on the basis of Muslim sources can be dated very accurately to November 1084.[162] It is also difficult to say which other regions of Asia Minor were under Sulaymān's control during the time span between 1081 and 1084. Ibn al-Athīr calls him lord of Konya and Aqṣarā (Aksaray).[163] The latter is to be identified with the Byzantine stronghold of Koloneia, a rallying point of troops east of Lake Tatta (Tuz Gölü) situated on a juncture of roads leading to Syria and Sebasteia in northeastern Anatolia. In this way, the town was connected with the two metropolitan seats of southwestern Cappadocia, Tyana and Mokissos (Viranşehir). Archaeological evidence attests to the significance of these places as ecclesiastical centers and fortified dwellings in the middle-Byzantine period, perhaps up to the tenth and eleventh centuries.[164] Koloneia may have benefited from the proximity of these urban centers. According to Michael the Syrian, Sulaymān was sent to Cappadocia and conquered Konya, Nicaea, and Nikomedeia.[165] Al-ʿAẓīmī mentions only Nicaea and its environs.[166] Al-Ḥusaynī is the only source to associate the appointment of Rukn al-Dīn Sulaymān b. Quṭlumush b. Isrāʾīl b. Saljūq with Malikshāh's Syrian campaign, stating that the sultan "thereafter [went to] Constantinople, besieged it, imposed upon them 1,000,000 gold dinars, and seized al-Qūniya, Āqsarā, Qayṣariyya, and the whole land."[167] This version, apart from being chronologically unsound, obviously contains some elements of exaggeration, linking the Seljuk sultanate with the traditional Muslim views of the Byzantine capital as one of the main targets of Holy War. An anonymous fourteenth-century Seljuk chronicle provides additional material interwoven with a highly idealized presentation of Sulaymān's conquests in Asia Minor:

> Sulaymānshāh, being vigilant against the big crowd of soldiers of the alliance of the Syrian emirs, was not able to stay and set off to raid [the land of] Rūm. Good luck came to the foreground and a good turn of fortune made its appearance. The Turkmens of Khurāsān turned their faces towards him. First he came to Antioch but he could not conquer it. He passed by and invaded [the land of] Rūm. First he took Konya from Marṭā and Kūstā and the fortress of Kavāla from Romanos Makri. In short, within a few days he took the well-fortified castles, which are in that region, and brought them to Islam. He took the treasures of the kings of Rūm with a strike of his sword. Horror filled the hearts of the infidels. From Kūniya [Kughūnīya?] as far as the city of Nicaea he conquered everything with bravery. No army was able to resist him. They brought tribute from the cities of the infidels to Konya, and the noblemen of Rūm turned their faces towards the ground of his royal residence.[168]

This report stands at the end of a process transforming the historical memory of Sulaymān b. Qutlumush from a seditious warlord to a Muslim model conqueror and founder of a principality on Byzantine soil. Apart from repeating facts already known from older sources, such as the conflict with the opponents in Syria and the seizure of Konya and Nicaea, the account creates the image of a hero of *ghazā* or Holy War, who with the support of powerful Turkmen forces and by means of his personal bravery (*mardigānī*) swiftly took possession of the towns and treasures of the Byzantines, was paid taxes, and received the submission of the indigenous elite. Aspects of an all-embracing royal authority, such as invincible military power, total control of territories and revenues, and the obedience of all subjects, are evoked. The names of the Byzantine commanders may stem from widely circulating oral traditions about legendary battles between Turkish-Muslim warriors and their Christian adversaries, as known from the *Dānishmand-nāma* and similar tales. The fortress of Kavāla situated on the Tekeli Dağ in the environs of Konya makes sense as an example of important and well-known strongholds in Lycaonia.[169] If *Kūniya* actually is a misspelling of *Kughūniya*, i.e., Koloneia, and not just a variant reading of *Qūniya*, it can be identified with the homonymous Byzantine stronghold near Lake Tatta, which is mentioned in older Muslim sources as Aqṣarā.

Anna Komnene at first sight seems to confirm the image outlined by the Seljuk chronicle. On the occasion of Sulaymān's departure to Antioch, the author speaks of the appointment of *satrapai* in the coastland, Cappadocia, and the whole of Asia,[170] whereas a certain dignitary known as Apelchasem—a name that is usually interpreted as a phonetically garbled transliteration of the Arabic *kunya* Abū l-Qāsim/Ebulkasım—was established as "custodian of Nicaea and the supreme leader of all leaders" or as *archisatrapes* of Nicaea.[171] This terminology suggests that there was a strictly controlled realm extending from the western coastland to Cappadocia and a group of loyal local commanders and governors subordinate to the chief emir and the Seljuk ruler residing in Nicaea. From other urban centers in Syria and Mesopotamia we know of the appointment of judges, castellans, and officials responsible for the financial administration, and we may surmise that similar measures were taken in former Byzantine towns of Asia Minor, thus laying the foundations of a rudimentary administrative system. Apelchasem seems to have been a high-ranking person of Sulaymān's entourage, who fulfilled the tasks of a deputy during the ruler's absence. Anna's description is too elusive, however, to allow a comparison with one of the leading officials of the Seljuk court of Konya known from later periods. Due to his position in the innermost circle of the Seljuk ruling elite, other commanders seem to have respected him as a sort of supreme chief. The fact that after Sulaymān's unexpected death he managed to maintain his leading role in Nicaea and, at the same time, to establish his brother Poulchazes as governor in Cappadocia shows that he possessed a family background closely connected with the Seljuk clan.[172] Yet it is too early to assume the existence of a fully developed hierarchy of dignitaries.

In view of Sulaymān's expansionist attempts towards Cilicia and northern Syria it makes sense to accept that a number of strongholds in Lycaonia and Cappadocia situated near the main routes crossing the central Anatolian plateau and the Taurus Mountains actually were under his direct control. But what about the numerous regions that, though not explicitly mentioned, would be included in Sulaymān's domains if we took Anna Komnene's and the Seljuk chronicle's wording at face value? As will be shown below, the regions between the Sangarios Valley and the Pontus, i.e., Paphlagonia, Galatia, Phrygia, and the entire Aegean coastland between Mysia and Lycia, do appear in the context of Turkish invasions, Byzantine counter-attacks, and the activities of Turkish potentates trying to establish local lordships. But there is no evidence connecting these areas with a newly emerging central authority based in Nicaea. Potentates like Tzachas of Smyrna and others are presented as acting independently and trying to carve out their own lordships, drawing on different political concepts and sources of legitimacy. Tzachas, for instance, is explicitly described as ally and father-in-law of Sulaymān's son Qilij Arslān,[173] and thus the relationship between the two leaders certainly stood on an equal footing.

It becomes clear that both Anna's and the Seljuk chronicle's description of a centrally controlled realm covering large parts of central and western Asia Minor is nothing but a retrospective reconstruction drawing on realities that hardly took shape before the second quarter of the twelfth century. In both cases, the projected image serves propagandistic purposes from different perspectives. For Anna, it was of prime importance to underline the success of Alexios I's attempts to restore imperial rule in Asia Minor, so the previous situation had to be portrayed in the most negative way. From the viewpoint of the fourteenth-century chronicler, Sulaymān's time represented a remote and legendary past that served to underpin claims referring to the Seljuk legacy in the highly fragmented situation of fourteenth-century Anatolia. A process of dismemberment was at the heart of the developments in late eleventh-century Asia Minor as well. The centrally organized provincial administration of the Byzantine imperial system was replaced by a conglomeration of widely scattered and isolated strongholds controlled either by remnants of the Byzantine military elite or by Turkish warlords. Gradually, certain fortresses developed into political centers exerting their influence over an ever-increasing radius of action and thus became the cores of new lordships, which formed new territorial units and partly overlapped with pre-existing administrative areas. In this sense, Nicaea and Nikomedeia under Sulaymān's rule can be interpreted as centers of a small-scale principality, which was limited in the west by the Propontis shoreline along the Gulf of Nikomedeia and was gradually losing its influence in the territories situated eastward and southward.

As far as we can see from the reports of crusader witnesses, who crossed these areas about a decade after Sulaymān's departure to the East,[174] the villages and rural areas in the environs of the major strongholds did not undergo any deep-rooted structural changes in the time following the termination of the raids. In all likelihood, they continued to pay the same taxes and fulfill the same obligations as before, with the only difference that erstwhile Byzantine landowners and imperial officials were replaced by Turkish commanders. More remote and mountainous regions became transit areas of pastoralist nomad groups, which were wandering about in search for winter and summer pastures. It can be safely assumed that Sulaymān's dominion over Konya and Aksaray had similar characteristics. Hence, the first core of the Seljuk principality of Konya consisted of a number of widely scattered strongholds straddling regions between the Propontis coast and the central Anatolian plateau and controlling agricultural areas, river valleys, and road networks in western and central Asia Minor. With respect to the period between 1080/81 and the First Crusade, we certainly cannot speak yet about unified and centrally governed territories, for the consolidation and defense of which the sons of Qutlumush at first do not seem to have possessed the necessary means in view of the overall chaotic situation and the activities of various Turkish and Byzantine rival forces. The establishment of Turkish warriors in fortified places may have brought about a certain stabilization in the areas controlled by them and contributed to a revival of agricultural production and economic activities, perhaps even an increasing exchange between the local sedentary population and the nomads, but we do not yet find state-like administrative structures.

The conquest of Antioch and Sulaymān's downfall

As mentioned before, in most Muslim chronicles Sulaymān b. Qutlumush makes his first appearance as ruler in former Byzantine regions of Asia Minor on the occasion of his conquest of Antioch in late 1084.[175] While almost all available information for the activities of the Qutlumush Turks in Bithynia and central Anatolia from the late 1070s onwards has to be gathered from Byzantine and, to some extent, crusader sources reflecting the state of affairs in about 1096–97, the Muslim tradition suddenly speaks about a well-established territorial lord controlling central Anatolian urban centers like Konya and Aqsarā, eager to extend his rule towards Cilicia and northern Syria.[176] Likewise, the Antioch expedition gives Muslim authors the opportunity to present Sulaymān as a warlord and politician fully attuned to Muslim ideals of public authority and Seljuk dynastic legitimacy. There are no traces of any seditious tendencies or tensions with Sultan Malikshāh, nor do these narratives refer to any Byzantine influence or previous agreements with the imperial government of Constantinople. Sulaymān is described as exerting rule over his territories just as any other Muslim emir in the central lands of Islam would have done. Furthermore, he appears to have pursued a clearly defined strategy vis-à-vis the local population and the city of Antioch, where he was to exert his authority as a loyal subject of the Seljuk sultan.[177] Since Christian sources referring to these events focus on other aspects,[178] there is no possibility to gauge the Muslim accounts against independent material, but they doubtlessly reflect later reconstructions.

Sulaymān's eastward expansion apparently resulted from a deliberate plan, as the gradual penetration of Cilicia in the years between 1082 and 1084 illustrates.[179] Evidently, Sulaymān drew on the previous experience of the sons of Qutlumush in interfering with Syrian affairs and, to some extent, resumed the pursuits given up after the disastrous defeat of Emir Shuklī and his allies in 1075. At the time under discussion Antioch stood no longer under the immediate control of the Byzantine central government but had been held for several years by the Byzantine-Armenian potentate Philaretos Brachamios.[180] Hence, the city may have lost some of its significance as a pivotal stronghold of the Byzantine administration and military system in the East but it was still a densely populated urban center, which also had outstanding significance as a patriarchal see and place of worship. The fact that the Kassianos Church of Antioch was transformed into a mosque, as Michael the Syrian and Ibn al-ʿAdīm note,[181] especially underlines the high prestige the Turkish conquerors gained by seizing this place. The weakness of the imperial government, which was still involved in the Norman war, in conjunction with the absence of any other Muslim lord openly claiming rule over Antioch, may also have provided a strong incentive.[182] Philaretos had nominally recognized the suzerainty of Nikephoros III Botaneiates, but his relations with the Komnenian regime were rather loose.[183] The ducate of Antioch as an integrative unit of the Byzantine Empire had practically ceased to exist. But even under these favorable conditions it is questionable whether Sulaymān would have had the necessary military power to force a city of this size to surrender. In all likelihood, he just grasped a good opportunity, taking advantage of especially favorable conditions that arose from serious tensions among members of Philaretos' entourage. The reports of both Anna Komnene and the Muslim tradition imply that the group opposing Philaretos first approached Sulaymān in order to gain him as an ally. The Muslim account transmitted in slightly differing versions by the chronicles of Ibn al-Athīr and Sibṭ b. al-Jawzī speaks about a conflict between Philaretos (*al-Firdūs al-Rūmī*) and his son, who had been imprisoned on his father's order and thus came to an agreement with the local governor (*al-shiḥna*) to allow Sulaymān to take possession of the city.[184] Anna Komnene, most likely under the influence of rumors referring to Philaretos' conversion to Islam, gives a religious interpretation of this conflict, claiming that the Armenian ruler's son, despairing of his father's sacrilegious plan, fled to Sulaymān in Nicaea, summoning him to fight his father and to seize Antioch.[185] The argument justifying the course of action of Philaretos' son lacks logic; however, Anna is in accord with the Muslim version regarding the serious intra-familiar discord between father and son that led to the alliance with Sulaymān and constituted the main reason for the successful outcome of the expedition. In this way Sulaymān secured the support of a substantial segment of the local elite, although many inhabitants may not have been willing to submit to Turkish rule. This can be concluded from the brief but determined resistance put up by the people who had fled into the citadel of Antioch.[186]

After taking possession of the city, Sulaymān b. Qutlumush faced several crucial issues, the successful handling of which formed a pre-condition for cementing his position in the newly gained locale. The first one was related to the problem of treating of the local populace in a just and moderate manner. During the fighting, many people seem to have been killed, and the surrender of the citadel gave Sulaymān the opportunity to gain large amounts of booty. But as soon as the hostilities were over, the townspeople were granted amnesty, were allowed to repair damaged buildings, and received guarantees for their property rights, thus preventing Turkish warriors from mingling with the local population and from settling in houses within the city.[187] Hence, the Muslim tradition took pains to assert that the personal status of the townspeople was by no means negatively affected by the Seljuk takeover. No doubt this was also the best way to avoid the emergence of any new seditious movements seeking to establish contacts with the remaining Christian potentates in the region or to restore Philaretos' rule.

Another thorny question was the problem of legitimacy. According to Christian accounts, Sulaymān and his subordinate commanders became Antioch's new rulers. But in the Muslim tradition reflecting Seljuk dynastic principles Sulaymān's conquest had to be presented as a victory of Sultan Malikshāh. Consequently, Sulaymān is described as a loyal subject of the Great Seljuk sultan. In a letter announcing the conquest, Sulaymān is said to have presented himself as an obedient follower, thus attributing his success to the sultan. Likewise, court poets composed encomiastic works celebrating the sultan as conqueror of Antioch.[188] It is hard to say to what extent this presentation is shaped by idealized models and what Sulaymān actually intended at that stage of his expansionist policy. The fact is that in view of the Seljuk predominance in Syria, based mainly on the powerful principality of Malikshāh's brother Tāj al-Dawla Tutush in Damascus, Sulaymān could not afford to enter into an open conflict with his Seljuk relatives. Moreover, after having spent a period of several years in Byzantine Anatolia in order to create a new base of power there, it was the first time that Sulaymān dynamically returned to the Muslim sphere of influence. Hence, he had to pursue an effective strategy of legitimization in order to be accepted by the Muslim lords surrounding his newly acquired stronghold. At the same time, this was a good opportunity to finally get rid of the stigma of being a recalcitrant rebel and thus be upgraded to the position of an equal member of the Seljuk dynasty.

At first this strategy seems to have worked, but due to an overestimation of both his own abilities and the sultan's support of his cause Sulaymān failed in handling his relations with the neighboring rulers. Obligations Philaretos had undertaken towards the emirate of Aleppo led to a major clash between Sulaymān and Sharaf al-Dawla Muslim b. Quraysh.[189] On the latter's demand to receive the tribute that Philaretos formerly paid, Sulaymān brought forward an argument based on his different status and religious identity. As a faithful subject of the sultan and a good Muslim, he argued, he was not obliged to pay any money, whereas Philaretos was an infidel who had to pay the poll tax.[190] Again there is a possibility that later chroniclers retrospectively construed this statement. Yet it is very convincing in underlining the Seljuk conqueror's need to integrate himself into the framework of Muslim legal principles in order to stabilize his authority and to reject the claims of rival potentates.

Sulaymān obviously crossed the acceptable boundaries when he began to undermine the existing balance of power in the region by seeking to expel Muslim b. Quraysh from Aleppo and take possession of the city himself. A part of the local population seems to have been willing to collaborate.[191] There were also some dubious elements among the Turkmen warlords of inferior standing, who on various occasions interfered in local conflicts, siding with whoever happened to be advantageous regarding their goals. A case in point is the Turkmen emir

Jubuk (*amīr al-Turkumān*), who in 1083 participated in an uprising of the Numayrid Arabs of Ḥarrān against the overlord Muslim b. Quraysh and later re-appeared in the conflict between the latter and Sulaymān b. Qutlumush. On the day of the decisive battle fought on 20 June 1085 near Qurzāḥil at the ʿAfrīn River, Jubuk suddenly threw in his lot with Sulaymān and thus contributed to Muslim b. Quraysh's defeat and death.[192] After the battle, however, neither the Banū ʿUqayl Arabs in the emirate nor the chief of the town militia al-Ḥutaytī showed any readiness to collaborate with Sulaymān.[193] Hence, the latter besieged Aleppo in vain for several months, and al-Ḥutaytī summoned the sultan's powerful brother Tāj al-Dawla Tutush, who eventually defeated his relative in the battle of ʿAyn Saylam outside Aleppo on 4 June 1086. Sulaymān was killed by Tutush's soldiers or, according to other reports, committed suicide.[194]

He had obviously underestimated the internal cohesion of the forces supporting the ʿUqaylid elite of Aleppo, which preferred to maintain the existing structures and thus to control the city on its own instead of introducing a Turkish ruler into the city, who would have been eager to transfer his residence from the Byzantine regions in Anatolia to Antioch and Aleppo. The open clash with Tutush also shows that the preceding proclamations of allegiance did not suffice to exclude rivalries among the members of the Seljuk clan. Dynastic peace was restored with the takeover of Sultan Malikshāh, who in the months following Sulaymān's death managed to establish a system of centralizing control over the three major centers of northern Syria and Upper Mesopotamia, Antioch, Aleppo, and Edessa. In this sense, the battle of ʿAyn Saylam was of decisive significance for the subsequent demarcation of spheres of influence among the competing forces within the Turkish military elite and the Seljuk dynasty. In the decades to come, subordinate commanders of the sultan and descendants of Tāj al-Dawla Tutush were to dominate the political setting of Syria with its two main centers in Aleppo and Damascus. The regions north and west of the Euphrates as far as the western fringes of the Anatolian plateau continued to be penetrated by Turkish warlords who, despite various centralizing attempts on the part of the Seljuk sultanate, largely maintained their independence.

Notes

1 The significance of this treaty is especially emphasized by Turkish scholars. See, for instance, Kesik, *1071 Malazgirt*, pp. 157–58; Sevim and Merçil, *Selçuklu Devletleri*, pp. 524–25; Öngül, *Selçuklular*, 2:6.
2 Attaleiates, pp. 133–229.
3 Attaleiates, p. 135.
4 For the description of political agency and the tension between history and encomium in Attaleiates' work in general, see Krallis, *Michael Attaleiates*, pp. 126–34, 142–70, who contends that the deplorable state of affairs in the late 1070s prevented the author from fully applying the conventional rules of the encomiastic genre even in the case of Botaneiates.
5 For the author and his work, see Carile, "Niceforo Briennio," pp. 429–54; idem, "Ὕλη Ἱστορίας," pp. 56–87, 235–82; Hunger, *Literatur*, 1:394–400, mainly pp. 396–99; Karpozilos, *Ιστορικοί*, 3:357–70.

6 Bryennios, *Histoire* 4.1 and 31, pp. 259, 301. For details, see the argumentation below.
7 For the author and her work, see Hunger, *Literatur*, 1:400–409; Karpozilos, Ιστορικοί, 3:397–425.
8 Sibṭ b. al-Jawzī, p. 154; Ibn al-Athīr, 6:248, trans. Richards, *Annals*, p. 172 (summarizing Sibṭ's version).
9 For this personality, see ODB, 1:161 s. v. Arcruni.
10 For Chatatourios, see Bryennios 1.21.24, pp. 126–27, 132–37: Ἀνὴρ γάρ τις ἐξ Ἀρμενίας τὸ γένος ἀνέλκων, τὴν γνώμην βαθύς, τὴν χεῖρα γενναῖος — ὁ Χατατούριος ἦν —, ἀρχήν τινα παρὰ τοῦ Διογένους τῶν μεγίστων λαβών. For Philaretos Brachamios, see Yarnley, "Philaretos," pp. 331–53; ODB, 1:319 s. v. Brachamios; and above all the detailed analysis of Dédéyan, *Arméniens*, pp. 5–357, containing all available data and sources for Philaretos' life; for Armenian loyalty to Romanos IV, see ibidem, pp. 40–41.
11 ʿAẓīmī, p. 16 (Arabic text), p. 20 (trans.); Ibn al-Qalānisī, p. 106; Nīshāpūrī/Rashīd al-Dīn, pp. 40–42, trans. Luther, pp. 53–55; al-Bundārī/ʿImād al-Dīn, pp. 45–47; Ibn al-Athīr, 6:251, trans. Richards, *Annals*, pp. 176–77; Sibṭ b. al-Jawzī, p. 160; for details and the historical context, see Turan, *Selçuklular Târihi*, pp. 188–91; Merçil, *Büyük Selçuklu Devleti*, pp. 70–71; Merçil and Sevim, *Selçuklu Devletleri*, pp. 93–95; Öngül, *Selçuklular*, 1:68–70; Özgüdenli, *Selçuklular*, pp. 159–61.
12 Nīshāpūrī/Rashīd al-Dīn, pp. 38–39, trans. Luther, pp. 52–53.
13 For the traditional view of modern Turkish historiography, which speaks of systematic conquests and the formation of a Turkish nation in the time after 1071, see Kesik, *1071 Malazgirt*, pp. 131–32.
14 Ibn al-Athīr, 6:431, trans. Richards, *Chronicle*, 1:71; for the historical background, see Özaydın, *Sultan Muhammed*, pp. 32–33.
15 Bryennios 2.17-18, pp. 178–81: τὸν Ἀρτοὺχ τοῖς τῆς ἑῴας τηνικαῦτα μέρεσιν ἐπιχωριάζοντα.
16 Ibn al-Athīr, 6:290–91, 299, trans. Richards, *Annals*, pp. 213–14, 223–24.
17 Cahen, "Diyar Bakr," pp. 227–32; Turan, *Doğu Anadolu*, pp. 157–64; Sevim and Yücel, *Türkiye*, pp. 213–14; Hillenbrand, "Najm al-Dīn İl-Ghāzī," pp. 254–67; eadem, "Artuqid Power," pp. 131–36; see also the detailed discussion below, pp. 249, 256–58, 326, 332–37, 341–43.
18 Michael the Syrian 15.12, 3:204 (trans.), 4:598, col. B, lines 24–26 (Syriac text): *amīrā Mangūg mārāh d-Qamāḥ.*
19 Sakaoğlu, *Mengücekoğulları*, pp. 51–54.
20 Ibn al-ʿAdīm, p. 314.
21 Turan, *Doğu Anadolu*, pp. 73–78; Sakaoğlu, *Mengücekoğulları*, pp. 36–50.
22 Michael the Syrian 15.4, 3:173 (trans.), 4:580, col. B, lines 18–21 (Syriac text): *(ʾ)nāsh amīrā menhōn d-Tūrkāyē da-shmēh Tanūshmān … w-men hādhē sharyath rēshnūthā dh-bhēth Tanūshmān.*
23 Ibn al-Athīr, 6:394, trans. Richards, *Chronicle*, 1:32.
24 Yinanç, *Anadolu'nun Fethi*, pp. 89–103; İslâm Ansiklopedisi, 3:468–79 s. v. Dânişmendliler (M. H. Yinanç), especially at pp. 468–69 (with a highly critical stance towards the existing source material); Turan, *Türkiye*, pp. 112–22; Merçil, *Türk Devletleri*, p. 228.
25 Cahen, *Pre-Ottoman Turkey*, pp. 82–83; idem, *Formation*, p. 11.
26 See above, pp. 189–190, 195, n. 68.
27 Matthew of Edessa 2.82-83, p. 150.
28 ʿAẓīmī, p. 16 (Arabic text), p. 21 (trans.).
29 Ibn al-Azraq, p. 272.
30 Cahen, "Première pénétration," p. 42; idem, *Formation*, p. 8; and Vryonis, *Decline*, pp. 112–13, are more careful on this point, talking about a retreat of the sons of Qutlumush to Anatolia in 1075 and their involvement in Byzantine seditious movements from 1078 onwards; less so Turan, *Türkiye*, pp. 53–56; Turan, *Selçuklular Târihi*, p. 202; Sevim, *Anadolu'nun Fethi*, p. 81; Sevim, *Süleymanşah*, p. 26 (O, 1075 yılında Bizans başkenti Istanbul'un hemen yanıbaşında … İznik'i fethetti ve burasını,

temellerini atmakta olduğu Türkiye Selçuklu Devleti'nin başkenti yapmak suretiyle, devletini kurdu); Sevim and Merçil, *Selçuklu Devletleri*, pp. 113–14, 522; Öngül, *Selçuklular*, 1:85–87, 2:3–5; Korobeinikov, "Raiders," pp. 706–707. Yinanç, *Anadolu'nun Fethi*, pp. 104–105, speaks about the conquest of Konya according to the anonymous Saljūq-nāma but gives no date; Kesik, *1071 Malazgirt*, p. 144–45, referring to the same source dates the event to 1078.

31 *Tārīkh-i Āl-i Saljūq*, p. 36 (Persian text), pp. 23–24 (trans.); Turan, *Türkiye*, pp. 54–55, quotes the same source in conjunction with 'Aẓīmī, thus criticizing the Western scholars' ignorance of Muslim sources and supporting the reliability of this information. See also Yinanç, *Anadolu'nun Fethi*, p. 104; Kesik, *1071 Malazgirt*, p. 144; for an extensive analysis of this passage, see this chapter, p. 228–29.

32 See this chapter, pp. 215–24.

33 Turan, *Türkiye*, pp. 50–53.

34 Sibṭ b. al-Jawzī, p. 173 (dated Sha'bān 467/10 March-7 April 1076): *al-Nāwakiyya al-mutaraddidīn ilā bilād al-Rūm*, "the *Nāwakiyya* who were frequently invading the land of the Romans." See also the obituary of Sulaymān b. Qutlumush, ibidem, p. 243: "It is said that he belonged to *al-Turkumān al-Nāwakiyya*, who came to Syria, and it is said that he is the forefather of the kings of the Romans (*jadd mulūk al-Rūm*) and he conquered numerous territories of the Romans."

35 Matthew of Edessa 2.55, p. 129.

36 Matthew of Edessa 2.57, p. 135.

37 Bryennios 2.3, p. 145.

38 Michael the Syrian 15.4, 3:172 (trans.), 4:579, col. b-580, col. a (Syriac text).

39 See above, pp. 186–87.

40 For details, see the analysis in Beihammer, "Ethnogenese," pp. 610–12; for further details, see the analysis in this chapter, pp. 220–24.

41 These aspects have been discussed by Cheynet, "Résistance aux Turcs," pp. 131–47.

42 Bryennios 2.1, pp. 142–43 (Alexios' elder brother Isaac married a cousin of Michael VII's wife, the Alan princess Maria); for details, see Chalandon, *Comnène*, 1:28–30; Angold, *Empire*, p. 116.

43 Bryennios 2.3, pp. 146–47; Chalandon, *Comnène*, 1:28–29; Angold, *Empire*, p. 116; Leveniotis, *Στασιαστικό κίνημα*, pp. 105–106; Kesik, *1071 Malazgirt*, p. 133.

44 Attaleiates, pp. 135–36; Bryennios 2.3, pp. 146–47.

45 Attaleiates, p. 136 (τῇ Καισαρέων μητροπόλει); Bryennios 2.5-6, pp. 148–53 (κατὰ τὰ Καππαδοκῶν ὅρια).

46 Attaleiates, p. 136 (ἀποτυχὼν δὲ τῆς ἐπιβουλῆς); Bryennios 2.5-6, pp. 150–53 (ὦ νεανία, ὁ σωτήρ, ὁ κυβερνήτης, ὁ τῆς περισωθείσης τῆσδε Ῥωμαϊκῆς στρατιᾶς ῥύστης).

47 Bryennios 2.6, pp. 152–53; see also Leveniotis, *Στασιαστικό κίνημα*, pp. 110–11; Kesik, *1071 Malazgirt*, pp. 133–34; for a church of Saints Cosmas and Damian at Develi, pointing to Byzantine building activities and thus the wealth of the local community in the tenth century or later, see Decker, "Frontier Settlement and Economy," p. 242.

48 Bryennios 2.7-8, pp. 154–57.

49 ODB, 1:816 s. v. Ankyra; for the historical and archaeological data related to Byzantine Ankara, see Foss, "Late Antique and Byzantine Ankara," pp. 29–85, esp. 82–85 for the time of the Turkish raids. The fortifications of the castle date to the period between the seventh and the ninth centuries, but there seem to be no traces of the Seljuk conquest.

50 See above, pp. 146, 151.

51 Bryennios 2.8, pp. 156–57 (διὰ τὸ μὴ πάνυ τι πόρρω τοὺς Τούρκους ἔτι στρατοπεδεύειν ... ὡς βούλοιντο τιμῆς αὐτὸν ἀποδιδόναι οἱ βάρβαροι).

52 Bryennios 2.9, pp. 156–59 (ξυνέβη Τούρκους περί που διακοσίους κατιέναι ἐπὶ προνομῇ).

53 Bryennios 2.10-13, pp. 158–67.

54 Kesik, *1071 Malazgirt*, pp. 134–35.

55 Attaleiates, p. 111: ἐπαπέστειλε [i.e., Romanos IV] δὲ καὶ Γερμανοὺς τοὺς λεγομένους Φράγγους μετά τινος ἡγουμένου τούτων, ἀνδρὸς εὐσθενοῦς κατὰ χεῖρα, Ῥουσέλιος τούτῳ τὸ ὄνομα. Bryennios 2.4, p. 147: ὁ Φράγγος Οὐρσέλιος, τῆς ἑταιρείας ὢν τοῦ Κρισπίνου; for this personality, see ODB, 3:1814–15 s. v. "Roussel de Bailleul;" Leveniotis, *Στασιαστικό κίνημα*, pp. 74–102 (for his early career).

56 Krallis, *Michael Attaleiates*, pp. 157–69, places special emphasis on Attaleiates' sympathetic attitude towards the Norman commander. Despite his ample use of literary conventions referring to Roussel's barbarian characteristics, the historian saw in this person "a solution to the state's troubles" and "a viable alternative to the failed policies of the Doukas regime" (ibidem, p. 163). Again, Krallis insinuates an implicit criticism of Botaneiates (ibidem, p. 168).

57 Attaleiates, pp. 135–36 (Melitene); Bryennios 2.4, pp. 148–49 (Sebasteia); Leveniotis, *Στασιαστικό κίνημα*, pp. 108–109.

58 Bryennios 2.14, pp. 166–67: Ὁ δὲ Οὐρσέλιος ἀδείας λαβόμενος περιῄει τὰς μεταξὺ Γαλατίας καὶ Λυκαονίας κώμας και πόλεις, καὶ τὰς μὲν ἐπόρθει, τὰς δὲ πειθοῖ ἑαυτῷ παρίστα, ἐκ δὲ τῶν χρήματα εἰσπράττετο.

59 Bryennios 2.2, pp. 144–45.

60 For an analysis of the diplomatic relations and alliances among the imperial court, the Seljuk sultanate, and the Turkish chieftains in Anatolia, see Leveniotis, Στασιαστικό *κίνημα*, pp. 145–49. In contrast to prevailing scholarly opinions, because of the autonomous character of most warrior groups operating in the interior of Anatolia I think that it is rather unlikely that there was a direct interrelationship among the contacts with Sultan Malikshāh and the various coalitions formed with chieftains in Asia Minor.

61 Attaleiates, p. 136; Bryennios 2.14, pp. 166–67; for details, see Leveniotis, *Στασιαστικό κίνημα*, pp. 115–21; Kesik, *1071 Malazgirt*, p. 135.

62 Attaleiates, pp. 136–37; Bryennios 2.14-15, pp. 168–73. For details, see Leveniotis, Στασιαστικό *κίνημα*, pp. 123–29; Krallis, *Michael Attaleiates*, p. 160.

63 Attaleiates, pp. 138, 139; Bryennios 2.16, p. 173, omits these details and passes on to Roussel's encampment on the foot of the Sophon Mountain.

64 For details, see Leveniotis, Στασιαστικό *κίνημα*, pp. 133–39.

65 Attaleiates, pp. 139–40: Βουλεύεται τοίνυν τοὺς στρατιώτας τῶν Ῥωμαίων ὑποποιήσασθαι καὶ εἰς πλῆθος μέγα τὸν οἰκεῖον ἀγεῖραι στρατόν ... βασιλέα Ῥωμαίων τοῦτον ἀνίστησιν; Bryennios 2.17, p. 177: ἡ δὲ ἦν βασιλέα τὸν καῖσαρα ἀνειπεῖν Ῥωμαίων καὶ οὕτω περιέρχεσθαι τὰς πόλεις καὶ ὑποχειρίους ποιεῖν ἑαυτῷ.

66 For details, see Leveniotis, Στασιαστικό *κίνημα*, pp. 140–42; Kesik, *1071 Malazgirt*, pp. 135–36.

67 Attaleiates, p. 138.

68 Attaleiates, p. 139.

69 Attaleiates, p. 140; Bryennios 2.18, pp. 178–79. Foss, "Byzantine Malagina," pp. 166–72, identifies a castle on a steep hill above the village of Paşalar northwest of Pamukova with Metabole and dates the main phases of its walls to the seventh century and the time of Manuel Komnenos respectively. Likewise, he identifies the adjacent plain of the Sangarios between Mekece and Geyve with the place of Malagina. For the fortifications of Metabole/Malagina, see also Foss and Winfield, *Byzantine Fortifications*, p. 140.

70 See Leveniotis, Στασιαστικό *κίνημα*, p. 150, and above, pp. 202–203.

71 Attaleiates, p. 139: μεταπέμπεται δὲ καὶ τοὺς Τούρκους λαθραίως ἤδη τῇ Ῥωμαίων προσβαλόντας ἐπικρατείᾳ καὶ πολλαῖς ὑποσχέσεσι πείθει τῷ Ῥουσελίῳ ἀνταγωνίσασθαι; Bryennios 2.17, pp. 178–79: πρὸς τοὺς Τούρκους διεπρεσβεύσατο καὶ τὸν Ἀρτοὺχ τοῖς τῆς ἑῴας τηνικαῦτα μέρεσιν ἐπιχωριάζοντα, 2.18, pp. 178–179: Ὁ δὲ Ἀρτοὺχ περαιωθεὶς τὸν Σαγγάριον καὶ ἐπὶ τὴν Μεταβολὴν φθάσας.

72 Attaleiates, pp. 140–41; Bryennios 2.18, pp. 180–81; for details, see Leveniotis, Στασιαστικό *κίνημα*, pp. 149–53.

73 Attaleiates, p. 142; Kesik, *1071 Malazgirt*, pp. 136–39. For Maleses' close relationship with Attaleiates, see Krallis, *Michael Attaleiates*, pp. 164–65.
74 Attaleiates, p. 146; Bryennios 2.19, pp. 182–83.
75 Leveniotis, Στασιαστικό *κίνημα*, pp. 156–67; Kesik, *1071 Malazgirt*, p. 140.
76 This opinion is clearly reflected in Attaleiates' narrative: Krallis, *Michael Attaleiates*, pp. 162–63, 164.
77 See also Kesik, *1071 Malazgirt*, p. 139.
78 Attaleiates, pp. 142–43; Bryennios 2.18, pp. 180–81; for details, see Leveniotis, Στασιαστικό *κίνημα*, pp. 153–56; Kesik, *1071 Malazgirt*, p. 139.
79 Bryennios 2.5, pp. 148–49.
80 Attaleiates, pp. 146, 151–52.
81 For instance, Attaleiates, pp. 143–45.
82 Attaleiates, p. 146; see also Krallis, *Michael Attaleiates*, pp. 165–67.
83 Bryennios 2.18, pp. 180–181: ἀπῄει ὡς ἐπὶ τὴν ἄνω Φρυγίαν.
84 Leveniotis, Στασιαστικό *κίνημα*, pp. 169–71; Kesik, *1071 Malazgirt*, p. 140.
85 Bryennios 2.20-27, pp. 184–201; Attaleiates, pp. 146–47, 151–52.
86 Bryennios 2.21, pp. 186–87: τοῦ Τουτὰχ ἐκ Περσίδος κατελθόντος ἐπὶ τὰ Ῥωμαίων ληΐζεσθαι ξὺν πλήθει Τούρκων πολλῶν.
87 Bryennios 2.21, pp. 186–89: "Friends, my dear, are the emperor of the Romans and the sultan, but Ourselios is hostile to both of them, for he pillages the land of the Romans and attacks the Turks as well. As he now saw your emir approaching and feared that he might be eliminated by both of them, he put on the mask of friendship and went to him in order to gain time. When it passes by, he will be again an enemy of the Turks, as he has been before. But if he listens to me, he should give him to me when he comes again for a lot of money. From this he will gain three very important things: a lot of money, intimacy with the emperor of the Romans, from which he will obtain great favors, and thirdly the sultan of the Turks' joy about the fact that he got rid of his enemy."
88 Kesik, *1071 Malazgirt*, pp. 140–41.
89 Bryennios 2.23, pp. 190–93.
90 Bryennios 2.24, pp. 192–193; see also Kesik, *1071 Malazgirt*, pp. 141–42.
91 For further details and bibliography, see Leveniotis, Στασιαστικό *κίνημα*, pp. 173–84.
92 Bryennios 2.24-26, pp. 195–201; see also Leveniotis, Στασιαστικό *κίνημα*, pp. 184–86.
93 For further details, see Leveniotis, Στασιαστικό *κίνημα*, pp. 186–90; Kesik, *1071 Malazgirt*, pp. 142–43.
94 Bryennios 2.27, pp. 198–99: καὶ ἐβούλετο καρτερεῖν ἐν τοῖς τῆς Ἡρακλείας ὁρίοις, εἴ που ἐντυχεῖν δυνηθείη Τούρκοις εἰς προνομὴν κατελθοῦσιν· ἐβούλετο γὰρ αὐξῆσαι τὰ τρόπαια καὶ οὕτως εἰς τὴν μεγαλόπολιν πένταθλος εἰσελθεῖν στεφανίτης.
95 Attaleiates, p. 147: φῆμαι καταλαμβάνουσαι τοὺς Τούρκους λέγουσαι περὶ Χαλκηδόνα καὶ Χρυσόπολιν κατατρέχειν, ἄρτι πρῶτον τῇ τοιαύτῃ πλησιοχώρῳ ἐπιφοιτήσαντας γῇ.
96 Attaleiates, p. 147.
97 Attaleiates, p. 152.
98 My interpretation differs from that of Krallis, *Michael Attaleiates*, pp. 157–69, in that I assume that both the Normans and the Turks were primarily perceived as destabilizing factors by the Byzantine ruling elite, whereas Attaleiates deliberately construed an overwhelmingly positive image of Roussel as antipode of Michael VII's regime.
99 Chalandon, *Comnène*, 1:33–50; Cahen, "Première pénétration," pp. 42–43; Vryonis, *Decline*, pp. 113–14; Cahen, *Formation*, pp. 8–9; Cheynet, *Pouvoir*, pp. 83–90, 350–57, 359–60; Angold, *Empire*, pp. 123–28; Cheynet, "Résistance aux Turcs," pp. 132–34; Kesik, *1071 Malazgirt*, pp. 144–53; for a revisionist view, see Frankopan, *The First Crusade*, pp. 42–56, who argues that Byzantine rule over Asia Minor at the beginning of Alexios I's reign was "relatively stable" and the Byzantine administrative structures widely intact. Although it is certainly true that the Turkish penetration of Asia

Minor brought about much less social and institutional disruption than is usually assumed, I disagree with most of Frankopan's conclusions regarding the maintenance of Byzantine central control and the extent and character of Byzantine-Turkish collaboration.

100 Attaleiates, pp. 155–56: Ἤσχαλλον πάντες καὶ ἐδυσχέραινον καὶ διηνεκῶς ἐποτνιῶντο πρὸς τὸν Θεὸν [...] προσδεξάμενος γὰρ τὴν αἴτησιν αὐτῶν ὁ ἐν ἐλέει ἀμέτρητος Κύριος, ἀνίστησιν ἄνδρα κρείττονα τῆς εὐχῆς τῶν φοβουμένων αὐτὸν [...]. Ἦν δὲ οὗτος ὁ τὸ κράτος δηλονότι ἐκ τοῦ ἐπουρανίου βασιλέως μνηστευθεὶς καὶ ἄξιος αὐτῷ λογισθείς, Νικηφόρος κουροπαλάτης ὁ Βοτανειάτης [...].

101 Attaleiates, p. 155.

102 Attaleiates, p. 156: καὶ πᾶσαν τὴν ἑῴαν τοῖς πολεμίοις ἀνάστατον [...]. Καὶ τῆς Τούρκων ἔτι ζεούσης ἐπιφορᾶς καὶ πολέμων πανταχόθεν ἀναρριπιζομένων σφοδρῶς, p. 173: τῶν ὁδοσκοπούντων καὶ τῆς ὑπαίθρου κρατούντων Τούρκων τὸ πλῆθος [...] ὅτιπερ οἱ Τοῦρκοι τῆς Ἀνατολῆς πάσης κυριεύσαντες ἤδη, p. 192: [the region of Chalcedon and Chrysopolis] Τούρκων γὰρ ἐπὶ τῶν ἡμερῶν τοῦ Μιχαὴλ ἐγίνετο καταγώγιον καὶ πολλῶν αἱμάτων χριστιανικῶν μολυντήριον, καὶ το πᾶν ἔρημος καὶ ἀοίκητος καὶ ἄβατος ἦν. Frequently statements of this kind are taken at face value; see, for instance, Kesik, *1071 Malazgirt*, p. 139.

103 For details, see below in this chapter, pp. 227–28.

104 Attaleiates, p. 191.

105 Attaleiates, pp. 156–95.

106 Bryennios 3.16-23, pp. 238–51, esp. 3.17, p. 243: Οἱ γὰρ ξὺν αὐτῷ πρὸς ἀποστασίαν χωρήσαντες οὐ πλείους ἦσαν τριακοσίων ἀνδρῶν, οἵτινες [...] ὑπὸ τῆς θείας προνοίας ἀσινεῖς διεσώθησαν.

107 Bryennios 4.15-17, pp. 280–83.

108 See, for instance, Kesik, *1071 Malazgirt*, p. 146: "Mikhail Doukas'ın son sultanat yılı plan 1078 yılı geldiğinde, Türkler Anadolu'yu kontrol altına almışlardı. Kendi çıkarları doğrultusunda Bizans tahtında meydana gelen olaylara müdahale ederek Anadolu'da edindikleri mevkii korumaya çalışıyorlardı."

109 Cheynet, *Pouvoir*, pp. 84–85.

110 Bryennios 3.16, pp. 240–41: πρὸς τὸν τῶν Τούρκων διεπρεσβεύοντο ἄρχοντα - ἦν δὲ τηνικαῦτα τούτων κατάρχων Σολυμάν, ὁ τοῦ Κουτλουμοῦς υἱός.

111 Bryennios 3.15, pp. 238–39; Kesik, *1071 Malazgirt*, pp. 146–47.

112 Bryennios 3.16, pp. 240–41.

113 Bryennios 3.17, pp. 242–43.

114 Attaleiates, p. 157: καὶ πρῶτον μὲν καταπλήττει τοὺς Οὔννους ἅπαντας ὅσοι τὴν ἑῴαν κατέτρεχον καὶ θάμβους καὶ ἀπορίας πληροῖ καὶ ἤρξατο συρρεῖν ἐπ' αὐτὸν πλεῖστον ὅσον τουρκικὸν πλῆθος ἐν δουλικῷ τῷ φρονήματι.

115 Attaleiates, p. 158.

116 Attaleiates, p. 173.

117 Attaleiates, p. 174.

118 Attaleiates, p. 191; see also Kesik, *1071 Malazgirt*, pp. 147–48.

119 Heather, Peter, *The Goths*, The Peoples of Europe (Oxford, 1998); pp. 135–37; Leppin, Theodosius, pp. 49–52.

120 Zonaras 18.18.4-6, p. 718.

121 For the various groups supporting Botaneiates, see Cheynet, *Pouvoir*, pp. 351–52, who suggests that they mainly represented the interests of the local aristocracy in western Asia Minor, which hoped for a restoration of Byzantine rule in their regions under the command of an experienced military leader.

122 Attaleiates, pp. 191–92: [...] πολλὴν θυμηδίαν τοῖς πολίταις ἐνῆκαν [...] χρόνος γὰρ παρελήλυθεν ἱκανὸς ἀφότου Ῥωμαίους οὐκ ἔσχεν ὁ τόπος ἐκεῖνος ἐπιφανέντας τὸ σύνολον [...].

123 Attaleiates, p. 193: πεζοὺς στρατιώτας. Cheynet, *Pouvoir*, p. 352, explains Constantinople's support for Botaneiates by the presence of many refugees and influential

ecclesiastical hierarchs from Asia Minor, such as Isaias of Konya and Aemilianos of Antioch; Kesik, *1071 Malazgirt*, p. 149.

124 Angold, *Empire*, p. 124.

125 Attaleiates, pp. 193–99; Bryennios 3.18-19, pp. 242–47; Zonaras 18.18.10-17, pp. 719–20.

126 Attaleiates, pp. 198–99.

127 Krallis, *Michael Attaleiates*, pp. 153–54 (who sees an implicit criticism in this passage of the fact that Botaneiates so heavily relied upon Turkish forces and was limited to Constantinople in his political authority); Kesik, *1071 Malazgirt*, p. 150.

128 Cheynet, *Pouvoir*, pp. 83, 351–52.

129 Chalandon, *Comnène*, 1:35–36; Angold, *Empire*, pp. 124–25.

130 Bryennios 4.2, p. 259: [...] διεπέμπετο πρὸς τοὺς τῶν Τούρκων ἐξάρχοντας ἐν Νικαίᾳ τῆς Βιθυνίας διατρίβοντας· ἤστην δὲ τούτω Μασοὺρ καὶ Σολυμάν, οἱ τοῦ Κουτλουμοῦς παῖδες, καὶ αὐτίκα ἐκεῖνοι συμμάχους ἐξέπεμπον οὐκ ἐλάττονας δισχιλίων καὶ κατὰ πόδας ἑτέρους ηὐτρέπιζον.

131 Attaleiates, pp. 206–208; Bryennios 4.5-13, pp. 266–79; for this battle, see also Chalandon, *Comnène*, 1:35–36; Cheynet, *Pouvoir*, p. 353; Kesik, *1071 Malazgirt*, pp. 150–53, especially emphasizes the decisive role the Qutlumush Turks played in Botaneiates' gaining the throne and defeating his adversary Bryennios: "Tahtını büyük ölçüde Selçukluların desteğiyle elde eden Botaneiates, şimdi yine onların yardımıyla tahtını koruyabilmiş oldu."

132 Chalandon, *Comnène*, 1:40, 43, 47; Cheynet, *Pouvoir*, pp. 88–89, 355–56; Angold, *Empire*, p. 128; Frankopan, "Fall of Nicaea," pp. 153–62; Kesik, *1071 Malazgirt*, pp. 155–57.

133 Bryennios 4.31, pp. 300–301: τὰς Τούρκων δυνάμεις καὶ τοὺς Τούρκων ἄρχοντας ἑλκύσας πρὸς ἑαυτόν. See also Kesik, *1071 Malazgirt*, pp. 155–56.

134 Bryennios 4.31, pp. 300–301: περὶ τὴν Ἀσίαν τε καὶ Φρυγίαν καὶ τὴν Γαλατίαν.

135 Bryennios 4.33, pp. 302–303: εἴτε εἰς τὸ Δορύλαιον ἀπελθόντας.

136 Bryennios 4.33, pp. 302–303.

137 For a different view, see Kesik, *1071 Malazgirt*, p. 156, who supports the opinion that Melissenos proceeded with Sulaymān's help to Nicaea and was backed by both him and other Turks in Anatolia.

138 Bryennios 4.31, pp. 300–301: Ὁ δὲ καὶ ἄκων τοῖς Τούρκοις ἐνεχείριζεν, ὡς συμβῆναι διὰ βραχέος καιροῦ κἀκ τούτου τοῦ τρόπου πασῶν τῶν περὶ τὴν Ἀσίαν τε καὶ Φρυγίαν καὶ τὴν Γαλατίαν πόλεων κατακυριεῦσαι τοὺς Τούρκους.

139 Anna Komnene 2.3.1, p. 60: τῆς πόλεως τοίνυν Κυζίκου κατασχεθείσης παρὰ τῶν Τούρκων. See also Kesik, *1071 Malazgirt*, p. 156.

140 Bryennios 4.31, pp. 300–301; Kesik, *1071 Malazgirt*, p. 156.

141 For a different view, see Kesik, *1071 Malazgirt*, p. 157: The Seljuk Turks were now able to expand in all regions of Anatolia and to seize places they had not conquered yet. As a result of the foundation of the Seljuk State of Turkey and Sulaymān's successful conquests in 1080, Turkish groups started in great numbers to come from Azerbaijan to Anatolia.

142 Frankopan, "Fall of Nicaea," pp. 153–84, esp. 176–84.

143 Anna Komnene, *Alexias* 1.4.4, p. 19.

144 See above, pp. 201–204.

145 For a discussion of the current state of research, see Karpozilos, *Ιστορικοί*, 3:397–425. Despite the rich bibliography on the *Alexias*, there is no special study devoted to the image of the Turks. The cursory remarks of Buckler, *Anna Comnena*, pp. 418–31, are largely outdated.

146 For reflections of later realities in the *Alexiad*, see Magdalino, "Pen of the Aunt," pp. 15–43; for the date of composition, see Karpozilos, *Ιστορικοί*, 3:406–407 (shortly after 1136/37 until 1148).

147 Anna Komnene 1.4.4, p. 19, ll. 37–42.

148 Anna Komnene 3.11.1, p. 114, l. 40, and 6.11.3, p. 193, ll. 7–16.
149 Anna Komnene 6.11.2-3, p. 193, ll. 3–5 and ll. 16–24.
150 On John II's policy against the Turks and his eastern policy in general, see Angold, *Empire*, pp. 184–90; Parnell, "John II," pp. 149–60; Papageorgiou, "Image," pp. 149–61.
151 On Byzantine twelfth-century imperial ideology with respect to the wars in Asia Minor, see, Beihammer, "Orthodoxy," pp. 15–36.
152 Anna Komnene 3.11.1, p. 114, ll. 40–42: τοῦ Σολυμᾶ τῆς ἑῴας ἁπάσης ἐξουσιάζοντος καὶ περὶ τὴν Νίκαιαν αὐλιζομένου (οὗ καὶ τὸ σουλτανίκιον ἦν, ὅπερ ἂν ἡμεῖς βασίλειον ὀνομάσαιμεν).
153 Anna Komnene 3.11.4, p. 116, l. 84 (τὸν σουλτάνον), 4.2.1, p. 122, ll. 75–76 (τῷ σουλτάνῳ), 6.9.1, p. 186, l. 54 (μετὰ τοῦ Σολυμᾶ), p. 186, l. 60 (ὁ ἀμὴρ Σολυμᾶς), 6.9.2, p. 187, l. 76 (τῷ ἀμὴρ Σολυμᾶ), p. 187, l. 79 (ὁ Σολυμᾶς), 6.9.3, p. 187, l. 89 (τὸν ἀμὴρ Σολυμὰν), p. 187, l. 92 (τοῦ ἀμὴρ Σολυμᾶ), p. 187, l. 93 (οἱ τοῦ Σολυμᾶ), 6.10.1, p. 188, l. 42 (τοῦ ἀμὴρ Σολυμᾶ).
154 Anna Komnene 3.11.1, pp. 114–15, ll. 42–48: ληιζομένου ἅπαντα τά τε περὶ τὴν Βιθυνίαν διακείμενα και Θυνίαν, καὶ μέχρις αὐτῆς Βοσπόρου τῆς νῦν καλουμένης Δαμάλεως ἱππηλασίας καὶ ἐπιδρομὰς ποιουμένους καὶ λείαν πολλὴν ἀφαιρουμένους [...] ἀφόβως πάντῃ ἐνδιατρίβοντας ἐν τοῖς περὶ τὰς ἀκτὰς διακειμένοις πολιχνίοις καὶ ἱεροῖς τεμένεσι μή τινος ἐκεῖθεν αὐτοὺς ἀπελαύνοντος.
155 Anna Komnene 3.11.2-4, pp. 115–16.
156 The localization of this river remains uncertain. Chalandon, Comnène, 1:72, n. 2, puts it on the Bozburun Peninsula, the westernmost cape of the southern shore of the gulf of Nikomedeia. Yinanç, *Anadolu'nun Fethi*, p. 114, and, after him, Turan, *Türkiye*, p. 62, n. 50, think of modern Orhantepe, which is located below Maltepe on the seaside of the Asian part of the greater Istanbul area between Çetin Emeç Bulvarı and Üsküdar Caddesi. Turan's localization would fit to Anna's account about the fighting along the coastland opposite Constantinople. For the peace treaty, see also Chalandon, *Comnène*, 1:72; Cahen, *Pre-Ottoman Turkey*, pp. 76–77; Vryonis, *Decline*, p. 114; Sevim, *Anadolu'nun Fethi*, pp. 85, 87; Sevim, *Süleymanşah*, p. 30; Sevim and Merçil, *Selçuklu Devletleri*, p. 115, 524–25; Dölger and Wirth, *Regesten*, no. 1070a; Beihammer, "Defection," pp. 609–10; Öngül, *Selçuklular*, 1:87, 2:6; Frankopan, *The First Crusade*, pp. 46–50, argues that Sulaymān on the basis of the 1081 treaty "became Alexios' agent, securing strategically important locations in Asia Minor." I do not share this opinion.
157 Anna Komnene 3.11.4-5, p. 116, ll. 80–95.
158 Anna Komnene 3.11.4-5, p. 116, ll. 93–94: ἔνθέν τοι καὶ τοὺς Τούρκους διὰ παντοίας μεθόδου τῆς τε Δαμάλεως καὶ τῶν περὶ αὐτὴν παραλίων τόπων ἐκδιώξας.
159 Anna Komnene 3.11.4-5, p. 116, ll. 94–95: ἅμα καὶ δώροις δεξιωσάμενος, ἐξεβιάσατο εἰς εἰρηνικὰς ἀπονεῦσαι σπονδάς.
160 Chalandon, *Comnène*, 1:73–74.
161 Anna Komnene 4.2.1, p. 122, ll. 74–75: δέον ἔκρινεν ἐκ τῆς ἑῴας Τούρκους μετακαλέσασθαι, καὶ τηνικαῦτα περὶ τούτου δηλοῖ τῷ σουλτάνῳ.
162 Ibn al-Athīr, 6:293, trans. Richards, *Annals*, p. 218: Antioch fell in Shaʿbān 477 (3–31 December 1084).
163 Ibn al-Athīr, 6:293, trad. Richards, *Annals*, p. 216: *Sulaymān b. Qutlumush, ṣāḥib Qūniya wa-Aqṣarā wa-a'māliha min bilād al-Rūm.*
164 For Koloneia (Aksaray), see Hild and Restle, *Kappadokien*, pp. 207–208; Decker, "Frontier Settlement and Economy," pp. 242–45, mentions tenth-century church components and a seal of an eleventh/twelfth-century bishop for Tyana and summarizes the main results of the Mokissos survey. This site appears as a hill town of impressive size with rich material remains.
165 Michael the Syrian 15.4, 3:172 (trans.), 4:579, col. a (Syriac text).
166 ʿAẓīmī, p. 16 (Arabic text), p. 21 (trans.).
167 Al-Ḥusaynī, p. 76, trans. Lügal, p. 49.

168 Tārīkh-i Āl-i Saljūq, p. 36 (Persian text), pp. 23–24 (trans.): *Sulaymānshāh az anbūhī-yi lashkar-i ittifāq-i amīrān-i Shām iḥtiyāṭ natawānast qarār kardan qaṣd-i ghazā-yi Rūm kard; sa'ādat bi-istiqbāl āmad wa-dawlat rūy numūd; Turkumānān-i Khurāsān rūyhā-yi ū nihādand; awwal bar sar-i Anṭāqiya āmad, natawānast fatḥ kardan, guzasht, bi-Rūm dar āmad, awwal Qūniya-rā sitad az Mārṭā wa Kūstā wa qal'a-i Kawālah-rā az Rūmānūs Mākrī sitad; fī l-jumla bi-andak rūzgār qal'ahā-yi muḥkam-rā ki dar ān nāḥiyat girifta bi-Islām āward. Ganjhā-yi pādishāhān-i Rūm-rā bi-zakhm-i shamshir sitad; haybat bar dal-i kāfirān uftād, az Kūniya tā bi-dar shahr-i Īznīk bi-mardigānī sitad, hīj lashkar birābir-i ū na-tawānast īstādan, kharāj az-shahrhā-yi kuffār bi-Qūniya āwardand wa-sar-kashān-i Rūm pīsh-i sarāparda-i ū rūy bar khāk nihādand.*

169 For the place, see Belke and Restle, *Galatien und Lykaonien*, pp. 182–183 (s. v. Kabal[l]a).

170 Anna Komnene 6.10.1, p. 188, ll. 46–48: διαφόροις σατράπαις τά τε κατὰ τὴν παραλίαν καὶ τὴν Καππαδοκίαν καὶ τὴν ἅπασαν Ἀσίαν ... ἀνέθετο.

171 Anna Komnene 6.9.2, p. 187, ll. 80–81: κατέλιπε φύλακα τῆς Νικαίας ὑπερέχοντα πάντων τῶν ἡγεμόνων ἡγεμόνα τοῦτον κατονομάσας, 6.10.1, p. 188, ll. 49–50: ὁ δὲ Ἀπελχασὴμ ἀρχισατράπης τῷ τότε τῆς Νικαίας ὢν ταύτην κατασχών.

172 Anna Komnene 6.10.1, pp. 189–89, ll. 50–51; Sevim and Merçil, *Selçuklu Devletleri*, pp. 528–29.

173 Anna Komnene 9.3.2, p. 264, ll. 8–9.

174 For these sources, see above, pp. 36–44.

175 For this event and its consequences in general, see Yinanç, *Anadolu'nun Fethi*, pp. 122–25; Vryonis, *Decline*, p. 114; Cahen, *Pre-Ottoman Turkey*, pp. 77–78; Turan, *Türkiye*, pp. 69–76; Sevim, *Suriye*, pp. 107–24; Sevim, *Anadolu'nun Fethi*, pp. 88–94; Sevim, *Süleymanşah*, pp. 31–40; Sevim and Merçil, *Selçuklu Devletleri*, pp. 442–47; El-Azhari, *Saljūqs of Syria*, pp. 62–64; Öngül, *Selçuklular*, 2:8–14; Özgüdenli, *Selçuklular*, p. 177; Frankopan, *The First Crusade*, pp. 50–52, argues that Sulaymān's conquest of Antioch was an attempt to restore Byzantine control over the city and, consequently, Sulaymān's defeat was "major setback for Byzantium." This opinion can hardly be supported by the available sources.

176 See, for instance, Sibṭ b. al-Jawzī, p. 243: "He was a cousin of the sultan and it is said that he belonged to the Nāwakiyya Turkmens who had come to Syria. It is also said that he is the forefather of the kings of the Rūm and that he conquered numerous lands of the Romans and the last place he conquered was Antioch;" see also Ibn al-Athīr, 6:293, trans. Richards, *Annals*, p. 217; Ibn al-'Adīm, p. 313.

177 Ibn al-Qalānisī, pp. 117, 118–19; 'Aẓīmī, pp. 19–20 (Arabic text), 24–25 (trans.); Ibn al-'Adīm, pp. 313–23; Ibn al-Athīr, 6:293–94, trans. Richards, *Annals*, pp. 217–18; Sibṭ b. al-Jawzī, pp. 229–30, 234–35, 237, 238–39.

178 Matthew of Edessa 2.78, 81, 84, pp. 147–149, 151–52; Anna Komnene 6.9.2-3, pp. 186–87, ll. 65–69; Michael the Syrian 15.4, 3:173, 179 (trans.), 4:580, 584 (Syriac text).

179 For details, see below, pp. 291–292.

180 For this personality, see below, pp. 285–286.

181 Michael the Syrian 15.4, 3:174 (trans.), 4:580 (Syriac text); Ibn al-'Adīm, p. 314: "The Muslims performed the prayer on Friday, Sha'bān 15/17 December 1084, in al-Qasyān. On that day there were 110 muezzins calling to prayer and a great gathering of people from Syria."

182 For the situation in Syria in the time of the conquest of Antioch, see Sevim, *Suriye*, pp. 112–16.

183 Anna Komnene 6.9.2, p. 186, ll. 70–71: ἀλλ' ἀποστασίαν μελετήσας τὴν τῆς Ἀντιοχείας ἐξουσίαν ἑαυτῷ περιεποιήσατο.

184 Ibn al-Athīr, 6:293, trans. Richards, *Annals*, p. 217; Sibṭ b. al-Jawzī, p. 229; Ibn al-'Adīm, p. 313, is more elusive in this point: "He [Sulaymān] pretended that al-Filāradūs had summoned him to come."

185 Anna Komnene 6.9.2, pp. 186–87, ll. 65–81; for these events, see also Sevim, *Suriye*, pp. 108–109; Sevim and Merçil, *Selçuklu Devletleri*, pp. 442–43; Öngül, *Selçuklular*, 1:419.

186 Ibn al-Athīr, 6:293, trans. Richards, *Annals*, p. 218; Sibṭ b. al-Jawzī, p. 229; Ibn al-ʿAdīm, pp. 314–15: The city fell on 1 Kānūn I/1 Dezember 1084 and Sulaymān besieged the citadel until 12 Ramaḍān/12 January 1085; Sevim, *Suriye*, pp. 109–10; Sevim and Merçil, *Selçuklu Devletleri*, pp. 443–44; Öngül, *Selçuklular*, 1:419–20.

187 Ibn al-Athīr, 6:293, trans. Richards, *Annals*, p. 218; Sibṭ b. al-Jawzī, p. 229; Ibn al-ʿAdīm, p. 314; Sevim, *Suriye*, pp. 111–12; Sevim and Merçil, *Selçuklu Devletleri*, pp. 443–44; Öngül, *Selçuklular*, 1:419–20.

188 Ibn al-Athīr, 6:293, trans. Richards, *Annals*, p. 218.

189 Ibn al-ʿAdīm, p. 316.

190 Ibn al-Athīr, 6:294, trans. Richards, *Annals*, p. 218; Sibṭ b. al-Jawzī, p. 229; for a slightly different version, see Ibn al-ʿAdīm, p. 316.

191 Ibn al-Athīr, 6:294, trans. Richards, *Annals*, p. 219; Sibṭ b. al-Jawzī, pp. 229–30; further details can be found in the detailed account of Ibn al-ʿAdīm, pp. 316–17: Sulaymān allied with the Banū Kilāb, who pillaged the territories of Aleppo, attacks on Sarmīn and Buzāʿā.

192 Ibn al-Athīr, 6:277, 294, trans. Richards, *Annals*, pp. 210, 219; for Jubuk, see Heidemann, *Renaissance*, pp. 130–31, 132.

193 For the battle, see Ibn al-Athīr, 6:294, trans. Richards, *Annals*, p. 219; Sibṭ b. al-Jawzī, p. 234 (in both sources dated 24 Ṣafar 478/20 June 1085); Ibn al-ʿAdīm, p. 317 (who gives the exact place and date of the battle); for a description of this battle from a Christian viewpoint, see Matthew of Edessa 2.81, p. 149; for subsequent events after the battle, see Ibn al-Athīr, 6:295, trans. Richards, *Annals*, pp. 219–20; Sibṭ b. al-Jawzī, p. 235; for further details concerning this battle, see Sevim, *Suriye*, pp. 114–19; Mouton, *Damas*, p. 28; Sevim and Merçil, *Selçuklu Devletleri*, pp. 444–45; Heidemann, *Renaissance*, pp. 132–33; Öngül, *Selçuklular*, 1:420–22.

194 Ibn al-Qalānisī, pp. 118–19; ʿAẓīmī, p. 20 (Arabic text), p. 25 (trans.); Ibn al-Athīr, 6:299–300, trans, Richards, *Annals*, pp. 223–24; Sibṭ b. al-Jawzī, p. 238; Ibn al-ʿAdīm, pp. 318–20 (with various details concerning Sulaymān's activities following Muslim's defeat, such as the conquest of Maʿarrat al-Nuʿmān, Kafarṭāb, and Laṭmīn, the exaction of tribute from Shayzar, negotiations with the notables of Aleppo, the re-fortification of Qinnasrīn, and the marriage with Manīʿa, a daughter of the former Mirdāsid emir Maḥmūd and widow of Muslim); Matthew of Edessa 2.84, pp. 151–52; Anna Komnene 6.9.3, p. 187; for all known details concerning Sulaymān's defeat against Tutush, see Sevim, *Suriye*, pp. 119–24; Mouton, *Damas*, pp. 28–29; Sevim and Merçil, *Selçuklu Devletleri*, pp. 445–47; Öngül, *Selçuklular*, 1:422–24.

6 Seljuk rule between centralization and disintegration, 1086–98

General lines of development

The demise of Sharaf al-Dawla Muslim b. Quraysh and Sulaymān b. Qutlumush in the battles of Qurzāḥil at the ʿAfrīn River on 20 June 1085 and of ʿAyn Saylam near Aleppo on 4 June 1086, respectively, put an end to the expansionist objectives in northern Syria of both the Qutlumush clan and the ʿUqaylid dynasty of Upper Mesopotamia. The political power in the entire region was to be redistributed.[1] As the local chiefs preferred to submit directly to Sultan Malikshāh rather than to his brother Tāj al-Dawla Tutush, the latter did not benefit from the victory over his recalcitrant relative and was unable to wield power over the emirate of Aleppo. All in all, the 1086/87 campaign of Malikshāh brought about a decisive, albeit temporary, strengthening of the Seljuk sultanate's predominance in Syria and contributed to a stabilization of existing alliances and bonds of allegiance.[2] In turn, this prevented the remnants of the Byzantine military elite as well as local Armenian potentates, who had come to power as governors on behalf of Philaretos Brachamios, from restoring control over the region, thus sealing the collapse of the local Christian lordships until the arrival of the Frankish crusaders in 1097/1098.

This chapter intends to present an outline of the most important developments of Seljuk political structures in Syria and Upper Mesopotamia in the time between Malikshāh's predominance and the eve of the First Crusade. This 11-year period witnessed a rapid sequence of upheavals and changes in the political setting of the wider region, during which the antagonism between local centrifugal and supra-regional centralizing forces entered its most decisive stage. The developments in the said regions were of direct relevance for the situation in Anatolia, for they largely conditioned the objectives and activities of the Great Seljuk sultanate and various local emirates in the territories of the former Byzantine borderlands as well as their relations with the Turkish potentates operating in the Armenian highlands and the interior of Asia Minor.

The Turkish penetration of central and western Anatolia advanced rapidly during the years 1086–98. Apart from some Byzantine enclaves in the Pontus region and a number of Byzantine-Armenian lordships in Cilicia and the Euphrates Valley, the entire area between the Caucasus Mountains and Cappadocia in this period came to be increasingly dominated by various Turkmen rulers. With the disintegration of the Byzantine central power, which ever since 1073 had been progressing in strides, and the acquisition of fortified places in western Asia Minor from 1080/81 onwards, the Turks met no further obstacles in penetrating the Anatolian plateau as well as the river valleys and road networks leading to the Aegean coastland. Evidently, the defeat of Roussel de Bailleul, the incessant contentions among the warring factions of the Byzantine aristocracy, and the war against the Normans (1081–85) deprived the eastern provinces of the last remnants of their military forces.[3] The raids and hostilities during the 1070s and 1080s doubtlessly caused casualties, displacements of captives, and movements of refugees heading for safer regions, but it is virtually impossible to make a reliable assessment of the actual impact of these phenomena. The fact that there were no large-scale concentrations of armed forces moving through Asia Minor in the time between the end of the Byzantine aristocratic uprisings and the arrival of the crusading armies must have brought a certain relief.[4] This is to say that military activities were carried out by rather small units and remained regionally confined. Hence, the overwhelming majority of the rural population and townspeople could live largely undisturbed. As has been shown already with respect to the city of Amaseia,[5] the provincial population's sense of allegiance to the central government of Constantinople was dwindling in a time of civil strife, and the inhabitants were increasingly prone to submit to the authority of military groups offering safety and stability at a local level. Their gradual absorption by the nascent Turkish powers was only a logical consequence of this development, especially in those cases where the takeover by the Turks was peacefully achieved, and the integrity, property rights, and religious freedoms of the local population were guaranteed by agreements.[6] It was in this period that the first phenomena of close collaboration and interaction between indigenous Byzantine elements and Turkish immigrants occurred, as can be grasped from the descriptions of certain urban centers in crusader chronicles.[7] The Turkish conquerors, too, underwent a profound change in these years. From warriors and marauding raiders, they gradually turned into potentates and state builders, who started to focus on the consolidation of their rule and the security of the agricultural and financial resources of the territories they came to control.

The period of Sultan Malikshāh's supremacy in Syria coincided with the culmination of his efforts to hold sway over the Turkish potentates in Asia Minor through military interventions and diplomatic contacts with the Byzantine imperial court.[8] The outbreak of civil strife following the death of Sultan Malikshāh in November 1092 suddenly brought this process to an end and caused a precarious destabilization of the political units in Syria and Upper Mesopotamia. This was mainly due to the fact that, besides various factions supporting different sons of Malikshāh, Tāj al-Dawla Tutush was one of the chief protagonists in these conflicts until his death in early 1095.[9] We have very little and elusive information about the impact of the Seljuk civil war on the Turkish rulers in Asia Minor. Yet it is quite evident that the survival of the principality founded by Sulaymān b. Qutlumush in Bithynia has to be seen in conjunction with this confrontation and with the broader developments in Syria and the Muslim heartlands. They prepared the ground for the succession of Sulaymān's son Qilij Arslān I in 1093 and for the first appearance of a clearly discernible dynastic identity related to this branch of the Seljuk family.

The Syrian campaign of Sultan Malikshāh, 1086–87

The intervention in northern Syria of the two leading chiefs of the Seljuk dynasty at that time, Tāj al-Dawla Tutush and Sultan Malikshāh,[10] has to be viewed in connection with the attempts of local rulers in Aleppo to maintain their independence against the claims of Sulaymān b. Qutlumush by seeking the protection of a superior, though geographically more remote, authority. The decision makers in Aleppo were Abū ʿAlī l-Ḥasan b. Hibatallāh al-Hāshimī al-Ḥutaytī, the chief of the local urban militia (*mutaqaddim al-aḥdāth wa-raʾīsuhum*), and Sālim b. Mālik, a relative of Muslim b. Quraysh and commander of the citadel. While organizing their resistance against Sulaymān, who was harassing the environs of Aleppo, the defenders rejected the proposal to hand the city over to another member of the ʿUqaylid clan, Quraysh's brother Ibrāhīm, and offered it to Sultan Malikshāh. When it became clear that the arrival of the sultan's army would be delayed, the potentates of Aleppo established contact with Tāj al-Dawla Tutush, who set off for a campaign in northern Syria in April/May 1086.[11] After the battle of ʿAyn Saylam, however, al-Ḥutaytī refused to fulfill his commitments towards Tutush under the pretext that letters from Malikshāh were announcing the mobilization of the sultan's troops.[12] With the support of a local merchant, on 11 July 1086 Tutush managed to seize parts of the ramparts and towers, al-Ḥutaytī surrendered, and parts of the town militia sided with Tutush, whereas Sālim continued to put up resistance in the citadel. Nevertheless, a month later, when Tutush had heard that Malikshāh's army had reached the banks of the Euphrates, he abandoned his plans and returned to Damascus.[13]

The detailed report in Ibn al-ʿAdīm's chronicle makes perfectly clear that the remnants of the ʿUqaylid elite in Aleppo preferred to be under the suzerainty of the Seljuk sultanate centered in Iran rather than the ruler of Damascus. Tutush already held sway over large parts of Syria and maintained close relations with many of the local elites. He therefore was in a position to interfere with the internal affairs of the emirate. The ʿUqaylid rulers feared that Tutush's power would enable him to expel them whenever it was in his interest. Hence, al-Ḥutaytī and Sālim tried to reduce Tutush's role to that of a temporary counterweight, which was to be removed as soon as the threat of Sulaymān was eliminated.[14] Sultan Malikshāh, instead, may have been eager to place the old marches of the Byzantine Empire under his immediate control, but the main focus of his activities certainly lay elsewhere, in the vast Muslim heartlands between Iraq and Khurāsān. The sultan demanded obedience and loyalty from the local elites, but they hoped that he would not bring radical changes to the regional power structures.[15] Eventually, Malikshāh acted differently than the potentates in Aleppo had expected: He replaced the old regime with his own governor. This decision was facilitated by the internal opposition of part of the citizenry to al-Ḥutaytī. It is also evident that Tutush was not interested in defying his brother's overlordship and provoking a conflict about pre-eminence in northern Syria. Thus, the sultan gained full freedom of action with respect to the re-organization of the political structures in the entire region between the Diyār Bakr province and the Mediterranean coast.[16]

The itinerary of Malikshāh's army basically followed the same route as Alp Arslān's 1070/71 campaign. Setting out from Iṣfahān in September/October 1086, the army made its way via Mosul to Ḥarrān, Edessa, and Qalʿat Jaʿbar (Dawsar), all of which passed under the sultan's control. After crossing the Euphrates, Malikshāh took Manbij and proceeded towards Aleppo, which on 6 December 1086 was handed over to him by Sālim b. Mālik. With the submission of the lord of Shayzar, Naṣr b. al-ʿAlī b. Munqidh, the sultan extended his sway further south to the Orontes Valley, including towns like Kafarṭāb and Afāmiya. To the west, the sultan took control of Laodikeia, one of the most important ports at the Syrian coast, which less than 15 years later would become an apple of discord between Byzantium and the crusaders. Malikshāh moved on to Antioch, which was handed over to him by Sulaymān's vizier al-Ḥasan b. Ṭāhir, eventually reaching the Mediterranean coast at the harbor of al-Suwaydiyya. The sultan prolonged his stay in Aleppo until the day of fast breaking (*ʿīd al-fiṭr*) on 9 January 1087, whence he started the way back to the East. In March 1087 he arrived in Baghdad, where in a series of publicly performed ceremonial acts he re-affirmed his relationship with the Abbasid caliphate and celebrated the marriage of his daughter to the caliph in the following month.[17]

The arrangements made during his stay in northern Syria reflect the sultan's ambition to apply a system of centralizing rule based on the appointment of new governors drawn from the circle of his most loyal *ghulām* commanders, on the one hand, and on the strengthening of bonds of allegiance with the old local elites in places of minor significance, on the other. At the same time, Malikshāh respected the preponderant position of Tāj al-Dawla Tutush in Damascus, the southern part of Syria, and Palestine, perhaps as a reward for his peaceful withdrawal from Aleppo before the arrival of the sultan's forces. Indicative of the overall situation is the fact that the newly acquired cities in the north—Antioch, Edessa, and Aleppo, the first two of which until recently had formed the backbone of the Byzantine military administration in the frontier zone—were given to newcomers, who did not possess any previous links with the Syrian nobility or the Turkmen chiefs operating in the region.[18] More specifically, the city of Edessa, the Armenian governor of which surrendered after a siege of several months in March 1087, passed under the administration of Būzān, who was one of the chief commanders in the sultan's vanguard.[19] Aleppo was given to Qasīm al-Dawla Aqsunqur, who took residence in the city along with a garrison of 4,000 horsemen. In addition, the sultan installed a certain Nūḥ al-Turkī as commander of the citadel and a nobleman from al-Raḥba called Tāj al-ru'asā' Abū Manṣūr b. Khallāl as head of the city's financial administration. Aqsunqur is said to have been a military slave (*mamlūk*) and a companion (*laṣīq*) of Malikshāh and was married to the sultan's nurse. Aqsunqur most probably nourished especially strong feelings of deference to the sultan, and thus the latter continued to exert direct influence over this highly important place.[20] The former commander of the citadel, Sālim b. Mālik, was compensated with Qalʿat Jaʿbar (Dawsar) and al-Raqqa, two fortresses situated further east in the Euphrates region.[21] Al-Ḥutaytī, instead, despite the loyal attitude he had demonstrated to the sultan, was removed from Aleppo at the demand of discontented townspeople and reportedly died in the Diyār Bakr province in severe poverty.[22] These measures certainly enhanced the position of the new Seljuk administration by fulfilling the expectations of a powerful group of citizens and, simultaneously, by appeasing the ʿUqaylid clan and its followers. No doubt, relieving tensions between political factions by means of pre-existing personal ties was a primary objective of Malikshāh's strategy in Aleppo. The sultan applied the same policy to Antioch, where he appointed another newcomer, Yaghī Siyān b. Alp, governor while he installed Sulaymān's former vizier, al-Ḥasan b. Ṭāhir, as head of the financial administration.[23] Here, too, the sultan's primary goal was to secure close cooperation between the new commander and a leading figure of the old administration established by Sulaymān b. Qutlumush.

Along with Būzān, a certain Bursuq also made his appearance at that time as commander of the sultan's vanguard in Syria.[24] He did not receive any governorship in the newly acquired territories, but we find him again as chief of Seljuk forces operating against Turkish potentates in Asia Minor and Bithynia. Anna Komnene mentions two distinct expeditions led by Prosouch (= Bursuq) and Pouzanos (= Būzān). The chronological details in her account are quite confused and unreliable. While presenting the new raids in Bithynia as the immediate result of Apelchasem's takeover in Nicaea, Anna states that Prosouch was sent along with 50,000 men by "the recently installed sultan Pargiarouch [i.e., Barkyāruq]."[25] Apparently, the historian had only a rough idea about the state of affairs in the Seljuk sultanate during the time in question. She knows of the pre-eminent position of the sultan's brother Tutush in Syria as well as of his role in the ensuing civil war, but ignores the identity of the Χοροσὰν σουλτάν.[26] She confuses Malikshāh with his sons Barkyāruq and Muḥammad and identifies Pargiarouch as the "son of the murdered sultan Tapares," which was the Turkish name of Muḥammad.[27] Muslim sources attest that in Muḥarram 480/8 April-7 May 1087 Bursuq was in Baghdad and took part in the wedding procession of Malikshāh's daughter. This indicates that the operations in Asia Minor were carried out simultaneously with those in Syria. After the end of the Syrian campaign, the Seljuk commander returned immediately to the East. This is indirectly supported by Ibn al-ʿAdīm and Seljuk dynastic chronicles, which speak of parallel operations in Syria and Byzantine regions, though in a very elusive way.[28] As for Būzān's expedition, Matthew of Edessa dates it to 1092,[29] which explains to a certain degree why Anna Komnene combines the events of Asia Minor with details concerning the Seljuk civil war in the years 1093–95.[30] In both expeditions, Sultan Malikshah attempted to use the Seljuk strongholds in Syria and Upper Mesopotamia to force the Turks of Anatolia, and especially the followers of his recalcitrant relatives, into submission. The diplomatic relations the sultan maintained with the imperial government show that he did not intend to conquer new territories in Byzantine regions.[31] But in the context of his centralizing ambitions he strove to become recognized as supreme leader of all Turkish warriors, just as his father Alp Arslān had attempted to do with Afshīn's campaign in 1070.[32]

In sum, Malikshāh's policy relied upon both loyal *ghulām* officers and members of the old local elite, who were compensated either with grants of other territories (Sālim b. Mālik) or with appointment to profitable positions in the local administration (al-Ḥasan b. Ṭāhir). This, in turn, led to a tightening of relations between the Seljuk sultan and his new subjects, who because of the generous treatment they experienced were well disposed towards the new men in power. In this respect, it may be safely assumed that there was no fundamental difference between Christian-ruled Edessa and the Muslim-ruled cities of Antioch and Aleppo. For the people of Edessa, too, before surrendering to Būzān's forces, had expelled their governor Parsama and thus had shaken off their dependence upon the rulers established by Philaretos Brachamios while prospecting for better conditions under Seljuk rule.[33]

Malikshāh's policy in the Diyār Bakr province

Similar developments took place at that time further east in the province of Diyār Bakr. Some years prior to the Syrian campaign, the Marwānid emirate had already begun to disintegrate under the attacks of the former vizier of the Abbasid caliph, Fakhr al-Dawla b. Jahīr, and his clan. With the support of Sultan Malikshāh, who in 1083 assigned the rule over Diyār Bakr to Fakhr al-Dawla and reinforced him with troops, the latter engaged in a series of campaigns in the region, eventually achieving the conquest of Āmid, Mayyāfāriqīn, and Jazīrat b. ʿUmar in 1085.[34] It is noteworthy that during these expeditions Fakhr al-Dawla enjoyed the support of a broad coalition of forces. Saʿd al-Dawla Kawharāʾīn was military prefect (*shiḥna*) of Baghdad and a loyal companion of Malikshāh and frequently served as intermediary between the caliphal court and the sultanate. He reinforced Fakhr al-Dawla during the siege of Mayyāfāriqīn.[35] Leading officers of the Seljuk army like Artuq b. Aksab and Qasīm al-Dawla Aqsunqur cooperated with the Jahīr clan in attacks on Āmid and Mosul.[36] The sources on these attacks also refer to local Arab potentates from Iraq, such as the emir of Ḥilla, Bahāʾ al-Dawla Manṣūr b. Mazyad, and his son Sayf al-Dawla Ṣadaqa.[37]

Apparently, Sultan Malikshāh made every endeavor to unite Turkish commanders and local potentates in a common front against the Marwānid principality in order to increase his influence in the Diyār Bakr region before starting his own advance towards Syria. Again, close cooperation with an influential local clan formed the basis for the consolidation of Seljuk influence in Upper Mesopotamia. The Banū Jahīr was a prominent family of Mosul and, in the early stages of his career before 1062, Ibn Jahīr served the ʿUqaylids, the Mirdāsids of Aleppo, and the Marwānids of Diyār Bakr.[38] Although by the time of Malikshāh's

Syrian campaign Fakhr al-Dawla was replaced by a prominent jurist called Abū ʿAlī al-Balkhī, in early 1090 the Jahīr family returned to Mayyāfāriqīn with the appointment of Fakhr al-Dawla's son ʿAmīd al-Dawla, who like his father had served as vizier at the Abbasid court and was married to a daughter of the Seljuk vizier Niẓām al-Mulk.[39] Likewise, shortly before the Syrian campaign began, Malikshāh allotted territories of the Diyār Muḍar province including the towns of al-Raḥba, Ḥarrān, Sarūj, al-Raqqa, and al-Khābūr to Muḥammad, a son of the ʿUqaylid chief Sharaf al-Dawla, and married him to his sister Zulaykhā Khātūn.[40] In this way, the prominent Arab dynasty of Mosul, which during the wars against the Marwānids had opposed the sultan's policy in various ways and had suffered a serious blow with the loss of Aleppo, was reconciled and inserted into the circle of the Seljuk dynasty's kinsmen by marriage.

Local conflicts and balance of power

During the last years of his reign between 1087 and 1092, Malikshāh had managed to forge a hitherto unknown unity among the various political players in the marches of northern Syria and Upper Mesopotamia.[41] For the Seljuk military elite, this was a period of stabilization and consolidation based on firmly established governors in Antioch, Aleppo, and Edessa and on loyal local elements residing in the Euphrates region and the Diyār Bakr province. Tendencies of fragmentation were curbed, and concepts of Seljuk dynastic legitimacy supporting Sultan Malikshāh's suzerainty over all potentates in Syria began to gain broader acceptance. In this way, a new balance of power emerged, in which the sultan's governors and military leaders in the northern marches as well as Tāj al-Dawla Tutush in central Syria were able to negotiate their mutual relations and, if need be, join forces in a common front against recalcitrant local rulers or the remaining pockets of Fatimid presence on the Syrian littoral.

We have only very scarce information about the situation in the adjacent regions of Cilicia, the Pyramos/Jayḥān Valley, and the lands north of the Anti-Taurus range. But it is quite obvious that the remnants of the Byzantine administration and local Christian potentates of Armenian and Syriac pedigree were mostly confronted with Turkish warrior groups coming from the interior of the Anatolian plateau, not with attacks from the south. Even the Seljuk expeditions of Bursuq and Būzān to western Asia Minor were primarily targeting Turkish adversaries who were to be subjugated to the sultan's rule. They did not intend to seize Byzantine territories.[42] Hence, there doubtlessly was no policy of conquest that would have been initiated by the Seljuk commanders in northern Syria. This is of course not to say that the military conflicts in the region came to an end, but their focus shifted to the annexation of semi-independent lordships in central Syria and the coastland.[43]

In 481/27 March 1088-15 March 1089 Qasīm al-Dawla Aqsunqur undertook an attack on Shayzar and ravaged the town.[44] In October 1089 the same commander seized Barzūya, the last Christian stronghold in the region of Antioch, which was held by an Armenian garrison and must have been one of the places previously controlled by Philaretos.[45] In 483/6 March 1090-22 February 1091, after complaints about acts of robbery, Sultan Malikshāh ordered Aqsunqur, Yaghī Siyān, and Būzān to join forces with Tutush in an expedition against Khalaf b. Mulā'ib of Ḥimṣ. During this campaign they also conquered 'Arqa north of Tripoli and, in the following year 484/23 February 1091-11 February 1092, Afāmiya. The commanders eventually fell out with each other while besieging Tripoli, which at that time was in the hands of Jalāl al-Mulk b. 'Ammār. According to Ibn al-Athīr, the latter, by bribing Aqsunqur with gifts, managed to enter negotiations with him and showed him diplomas of appointment issued by the sultan. As a result, Aqsunqur refused to fight and maintained that he would not support Tutush in disobedience to the sultan.[46]

The episode is another example illustrating how Malikshāh's ascendancy within the Seljuk dynasty was used as a means to oppose the claims of his brother Tutush. The account suggests that the real motive behind Aqsunqur's attitude was money rather than concerns of legitimacy, yet it is still remarkable that matters related to the sultan's supreme authority played so crucial a role in the political discourse in the time of Malikshāh's reign. Nevertheless, Ḥimṣ and certain strongholds at the Syrian coast fell into Tutush's hands, something that implies that he, too, profited to a large extent from the stabilization in northern Syria. Nevertheless, many of the coastal towns of Syria and Palestine remained under Fatimid rule, and the period in question witnessed a number of conflicts between Tutush and the Fatimid caliphate about control over the Syrian coast. Fatimid troops invaded Syria, and important ports like Beirut, Tyre/Ṣūr, and Sidon/Ṣaydā repeatedly changed hands. If we believe Ibn al-Athīr, during a visit of the Syrian governors in Baghdad, Malikshāh ordered Aqsunqur and Būzān to support Tutush in taking hold of the Syrian shores and thereafter to attack Egypt.[47] Doubtlessly, the power relations had changed ever since the 1070s and the Fatimid army was much weaker than it had been when fighting with the Byzantine governors of Antioch in the late tenth or early eleventh century. The Seljuk rulers, however, were still facing a dangerous threat from the Shiite caliphate of Cairo, as is evidenced by the sudden upswing of Fatimid expansionism in the time of chaos following Tutush's defeat in early 1095 during the Seljuk dynastic strife.

The Seljuk succession crisis and Tāj al-Dawla Tutush's grip on power, 1093–95

A decisive turning point in the further development of the political constellations in Seljuk Syria was Sultan Malikshāh's death on 19 November 1092 and Tāj al-Dawla Tutush's attempt to lay claim to the sultanate.[48] The ensuing conflicts caused the death of most chief commanders in Syria and, eventually, that of Tutush himself. Hence, by early 1095 the greatest part of the Seljuk military elite was eliminated and, while Sultan Barkyāruq was hardly able to intervene in the internal matters of the western fringes of his empire, the vacuum of power was filled by Tutush's sons Riḍwān and Duqāq and their followers, who established themselves in Aleppo and Damascus, respectively.[49] Tutush's failure in 1095 brought about a total breakdown of the system that had come into being after Malikshāh's Syrian campaign in 1086 and caused a sudden and violent fragmentation of the political situation in Syria.

When Turkān Khātūn's four-year-old son Maḥmūd was proclaimed sultan, the first clashes with the Niẓāmiyya Mamlūks (the slave soldiers of the defunct vizier Niẓām al-Mulk, who supported the sultan's eldest son Barkyāruq) occurred in early 1093 in the region between Iṣfahān and Rayy. Aqsunqur at first proclaimed the Friday sermon for Maḥmūd but then, along with Yaghī Siyān and Būzān, he agreed to side with Tutush and to help him seize the lands of his brother.[50] In the spring of 1093 Tutush successfully extended his sway beyond the Euphrates, took al-Raḥba and Nisibis, defeated and killed Ibrāhīm b. Sharaf al-Dawla, and thus wielded power over Mosul with the aid of Ibrāhīm's widow and Malikshāh's aunt Ṣafiyya and her son ʿAlī. Eventually he also seized the former Marwānid territories in the Diyār Bakr province. While Tutush was advancing farther towards Azerbaijan, however, Barkyāruq put up open resistance to his uncle's claim. This, in turn, prompted Aqsunqur and Būzān to switch sides and join the defunct sultan's son.[51] According to Ibn al-ʿAdīm, the two emirs were in rivalry with Yaghī Siyān because of Tutush's great affection for the latter. The fact that none of the newly conquered territories was granted to the two commanders may have been another possible motive.[52] Whatever the real reason for this breakup may have been, it is evident that, apart from internal discords among the Seljuk governors, the old bonds of loyalty with the head of the dynasty still played an important role. Aqsunqur's argument justifying his defiance of Tutush during the siege of Tripoli shows that the idea of Malikshāh's precedence over his brother was widely accepted among the Seljuk military elite. This was a substantial shortcoming in Tutush's claims to the throne vis-à-vis the deceased sultan's offspring. As a result, Tutush was forced to retreat to his base in Damascus. He further cemented his alliance with Yaghī Siyān by marrying his son Riḍwān to a daughter of his ally during a meeting near Ḥamāh in Rabīʿ I 487/21 March-19 April 1094.[53]

Aqsunqur and Būzān were well received at the court of Barkyāruq. In collaboration with other emirs, they murdered Ismāʿīl b. Yāqūtī b. Dā'ūd, a cousin of Malikshāh, who for some time was vacillating between the two factions.[54] On 3 February 1094, Barkyāruq was proclaimed sultan in Baghdad with the support of Caliph Muqtaḍī bi-Amr Allāh, just one day before the latter's sudden death.[55] In the meantime, the civil strife in Syria continued with undiminished violence: Aqsunqur and Būzān came back to Syria with reinforcements made available by the sultan and gathered a strong coalition consisting of troops from Mosul, Edessa, Antioch, al-Raḥba, the Kilāb Arabs, the urban militia of Aleppo, as well as Daylamī and Khurāsānī soldiers.[56] In late May 1094, Tutush defeated and thereafter executed Aqsunqur in a battle near Aleppo, seized the city, killed Būzān, and took possession of Ḥarrān and Edessa. Emir Karbūqā, who had been sent by Barkyāruq in order to support the sultan's followers in Syria, was imprisoned in Ḥimṣ. Yaghī Siyān was granted Maʿarrat al-Nuʿmān and Laodikeia in reward for his loyalty. Tutush advanced via Diyār Bakr and Khilāṭ to Azerbaijan and Hamadhān. In October/November 1094, Tutush defeated Barkyāruq in Azerbaijan and forced him to flee to Iṣfahān along with the rest of his companions.[57] In the city, both Maḥmūd and his mother Turkān Khātūn suddenly died of smallpox, something that decisively strengthened the position of the surviving elder brother and caused an increasing number of emirs to throw in their lot with him. This turn of events anulled Tutush's preceding agreements with Turkān about a marriage.[58] Tutush was eventually defeated and killed in a decisive battle against the superior forces of Barkyāruq in the vicinity of Rayy in February 1095.[59]

All in all, the aforementioned events resulted in the elimination of the Seljuk commanders installed in 1086/87 and in a sudden breakdown of Tutush's lordship in Syria and Palestine. The stability that had been achieved until 1093 under the aegis of the sultanate's centralizing mechanisms fell apart and gave way to a fierce power struggle among the remnants of the old elite and a new group of Turkish chieftains belonging to the retinue of the Great Seljuk sultanate. It is noteworthy that neither the leading representative of the Qutlumush lineage, Qilij Arslān I, nor any other Turkmen chief in Anatolia actively participated in the struggles of the Seljuk civil war or otherwise benefited from the decay of Seljuk rule in Syria. Seemingly, the internecine strife among Malikshāh's relatives completely distracted the emirs in Syria from the goings-on in Anatolia, whereas the Turks there were pre-occupied with carving out new lordships. A case in point is Qilij Arlsān's attempt to take hold of Melitene, a target that would have been too risky had the old Seljuk elite still been in place. The civil war, thus, significantly contributed to a clear-cut separation between the Seljuk emirates of Syria and Upper Mesopotamia and their peers on former Byzantine soil.

Power struggles in Aleppo, Damascus, and the Jazīra, 1095–98

As a result of his victory, Sultan Barkyāruq secured his ascendancy in the heartlands of the Seljuk empire for some years but was not able to rebuild the patchwork of personal ties on which the centralizing policy of his father had been based. The power vacuum in Syria that occurred after the elimination of most of Malikshāh's commanders came to be filled by Tutush's sons, dignitaries from Tutush's entourage, and a group of newcomers. Due to the lack of a commonly accepted representative of the Seljuk dynasty in Syria, the *atabegs*, i.e., Turkish military chiefs of servile origin serving as tutors and regents of Seljuk princes, managed to assume a leading role in the political affairs of post-1095 Syria.[60] Whereas before 1092 Tutush and the Seljuk governors of Antioch, Aleppo, and Edessa mostly collaborated for common goals, after Tutush's death in 1095 the rulers of Aleppo and Damascus and their allies engaged in a fierce struggle for territorial expansion and supremacy. In the course of these conflicts existing coalitions were repeatedly overthrown, and it is hardly possible to detect any consistent strategies or overarching objectives apart from the accumulation of territories and the increase of political influence. Besides the mutual rivalry of Antioch, Aleppo, and Damascus, emirs from the retinues of Tutush and Barkyāruq took possession of key points in the Euphrates region and Diyār Bakr and seized Mosul, as it was the main center in the northern Jazīra. In addition, the Egyptian conquest of Jerusalem in August 1096 brought about a temporary increase of Fatimid influence in Syria and thus further compounded the destabilization overall.[61]

As regards the situation immediately after Tutush's death, the accounts of the Arab chronicles especially emphasize the high degree of insecurity menacing all surviving members of the old ruling elite. Riḍwān learned about his father's death while encamped near ʿĀna at the banks of the Euphrates. In fear of his persecutors, he immediately made his way back to Aleppo, where, with the aid of his father's vizier, he took hold of the city and the citadel. Two younger brothers of Riḍwān, Abū Ṭālib and Bahrām, were also detained in the city and later executed. Janāḥ al-Dawla al-Ḥusayn b. Aytakīn, Riḍwān's *atabeg* and husband of his mother, who had survived the battle of Rayy and had managed to escape to Aleppo, persuaded the garrison in the citadel to recognize Riḍwān as their ruler and assumed the administration of the city.[62]

When Tutush conquered the province of Diyār Bakr, he entrusted his second son Duqāq and his *atabeg* Ẓahīr al-Dīn Ṭughtikīn with the governorship of this region. Both of them participated in the battle of Rayy, from which the former managed to flee to Aleppo while the latter was taken captive. The relationship between the two brothers quickly deteriorated, and thus, upon receiving messages from Sāwtikīn al-Khādim, Tutush's *nāʾib* in Damascus, Duqāq secretly left Aleppo and took possession of his father's main residence.[63] This conflict-ridden atmosphere was tempered to a certain degree by the fact that in the months following Tutush's death, Sultan Barkyāruq, in exchange for a formal recognition of his suzerainty, re-established peaceful relations with the adherents of his former rival in Syria. This not only averted the danger of a new clash with the sultanate but also allowed the release of the prisoners taken in the battle of Rayy. Hence, Ṭughtikīn joined his pupil in Damascus, killed Sāwtikīn, married Duqāq's mother Ṣafwat al-Mulk, and assumed the administration of the political affairs in the city.[64]

Under the umbrella of Barkyāruq's formal suzerainty, the two most important urban centers of Syria had come under the rule of those Seljuk princes who represented the continuity of Tutush's lineage while ceding much of their political authority to their educators and stepfathers. This was a highly fragile constellation of power constantly vulnerable to rivalries both within the cities and at a supra-regional level. Thus, not surprisingly, the period from the summer of 1095 until the arrival of the crusader troops outside Antioch in the late summer of 1097 is marked by an incessant series of clashes among the competing members of Tutush's family and their subordinate commanders. No faction was strong enough to prevail over the other, and thus the disintegration of the political authority in Syria further progressed.

Yaghī Siyān of Antioch was the only Seljuk governor of the old generation to not only survive Tutush's downfall but also maintain his position. He was joined at that time by another Turkish commander of Tutush's retinue, a certain Yūsuf

b. Abaq/Ābiq. Shortly before the battle of Rayy, this man had been sent as military prefect (*shiḥna*) to Baghdad with his warriors. They had caused serious troubles in the environs of the city before they retreated towards Aleppo on the news of their lord Tutush's death.[65] For some time in 488/1095, he collaborated with Yaghī Siyān so as to oppose Janāḥ al-Dawla and gain power in Aleppo. Yūsuf and Janāḥ al-Dawla clashed in a battle at Marj Dābiq north of Aleppo, in which Yūsuf was routed and forced to flee to Antioch.[66] Thereafter, in search of reconciliation, he sent word to Riḍwān and requested permission to take up residence in Aleppo and enter his service.[67] Ibn al-ʿAdīm also mentions Manbij and Buzāʿā as being in the possession of Yūsuf and his followers, but it is not clear if he had taken hold of these places earlier or acquired them as a reward for throwing his lot in with Riḍwān. Be that as it may, Yūsuf did not have time to execute his plans in Aleppo, for in January 1096 he fell victim to an attempt against his life, which was carried out by the chief of the urban militia (*ra'īs al-aḥdāth*) on the instigation of Riḍwān and his *atabeg*. Obviously, his presence in the city was considered too dangerous to be tolerated by the local magnates.[68]

Yaghī Siyān of Antioch, though a loyal companion of Tutush, was constantly at odds with the *atabeg* of Aleppo and his Seljuk prince. Only in the beginning of Janāḥ al-Dawla's rule did he ally with him for a joint expedition to the Diyār Bakr province.[69] The campaign was eventually directed against Edessa, where the Greek *kouropalates* Theodore/Tʿoros had been established as governor on behalf of Būzān. Matthew of Edessa speaks of a 65-day siege and heavy assaults culminating in a temporary penetration of the town. But at the end Tʿoros, who is praised by both Muslim and Christian witnesses for his vigor, managed to keep the city. According to the Muslim sources, during the siege a quarrel broke out between Janāḥ al-Dawla and Yaghī Siyān, who tried to remove the former from his tutelage over Riḍwān. After an assault, Janāḥ al-Dawla fled to Aleppo and the siege was lifted.[70] Ever after, the relations between Antioch and Aleppo were mostly hostile, with Riḍwān and his *atabeg* making every effort to extend their sway in northern Syria. At that time, Yaghī Siyān seems to have held Maʿarrat al-Nuʿmān south of Aleppo, so that the local rulers allied with Waththāb b. Maḥmūd, the chief of the Kilāb Arabs from the Mirdāsid clan, in order to expel their opponent.[71]

In 489/31 December 1095-18 December 1096 Aleppo mounted new attacks on domains of followers of Yaghī Siyān in Tall Bāshir and Shayḥ al-Dayr, as well as on the territory of Antioch.[72] Given that Aʿzāz had been handed over to Riḍwān already in 1095,[73] it is evident that within a year the rulers of Aleppo managed to wield power over a swathe of land stretching from the Euphrates to the strongholds near the Quwayq River north of Aleppo and Maʿarrat al-Nuʿmān in the south. From Ramaḍān 489/23 August-21 September 1096 onwards Riḍwān and his allies concentrated their efforts on their relatives in Damascus, while Yaghī Siyān sided with the latter, and thus an axis of collaboration between Antioch and Damascus came into being.[74]

***

The territories east of the Euphrates came under the possession of various newcomers, some of whom had belonged to Tutush's entourage and others of whom had penetrated the region of Upper Mesopotamia as military chiefs subject to Sultan Barkyāruq. One of them was Sukmān/Suqmān b. Artuq, whose father Artuq b. Aksab had been in 1084 a commander in Malikshāh's army. Sukmān/Suqmān fought with Fakhr al-Dawla in Diyār Bakr and thereafter entered the service of Tutush and was appointed governor of Jerusalem.[75] His participation in the battle of 'Ayn Saylam is another incident attesting to this warlord's direct involvement in northern Syrian affairs.[76] It comes as no surprise thus that Suqmān was able to take advantage of the power vacuum emerging in 1095 and seize the city of Sarūj shortly before being expelled by Fatimid forces along with his brother Īlghāzī b. Artuq and other kinsmen from their base in Jerusalem.[77] On Tutush's order, Īlghāzī had accompanied Riḍwān on his march to Iraq before the battle of Rayy,[78] which shows that the Artuq clan abided by its loyalty to Tutush and his offspring until the final defeat. When in 1095 during its march to Edessa, Riḍwān's army made an attempt to seize Sarūj, the two sides, through the mediation of local dignitaries, reached an agreement and Riḍwān confirmed Suqmān's rule over Sarūj.[79] According to Matthew, Suqmān even participated in the siege of Edessa.[80] Later on, Riḍwān invited Suqmān to support him. The latter sided with the potentates of Aleppo in the battle of Marj Dābiq against Yūsuf b. Abaq and was allotted the city of Ma'arrat al-Nu'mān as a reward.[81]

It was also during the siege of Edessa that Balduk, the son of Amīr Ghāzī, made his first appearance as emir of Samosata/Sumaysāṭ (Samsat) at the banks of the Euphrates northwest of Edessa.[82] Ibn al-'Adīm seems to refer to the same person when talking about an ally of Riḍwān that appeared in the conflicts with Duqāq of Damascus in 1097, but he calls him Sulaymān b. Īlghāzī.[83] Hence, there is confusion regarding the name and the parentage of the emir of Samosata. Matthew of Edessa associates him with Dānishmand (= Amīr Ghāzī) and Ibn al-'Adīm with the Artuqid potentate Īlghāzī. The inconsistencies are too great to be harmonized in a satisfactory way. It must therefore remain open to question whether Balduk/Sulaymān had links of kinship with the Artuq clan or other Turkmen rulers operating in the region.[84] Matthew mentions him again under the year 547/1098–99 as fending off a joint attack of Armenian and crusading forces against Samosata.[85] This implies that he had managed temporarily to consolidate his rule over a section of the Euphrates Valley, which at that time was primarily dominated by Byzantine-Armenian lords. Apparently, he was still able to resist hostile assaults when the crusaders took hold of Edessa.

In Dhū l-Qa'da 489/21 October-19 November 1096 another high-ranking officer belonging to Sultan Malikshāh's retinue and survivor of the civil war, Qiwām al-Dawla Abū Sa'īd Karbūqā, seized the city of Mosul at the banks of the Tigris River in the eastern edge of Upper Mesopotamia. Originally supporting the faction of Turkān Khātūn and her son Maḥmūd, he later sided with Barkyāruq against Tutush and defended Aleppo against the latter until he was defeated and imprisoned in Ḥimṣ.[86] After Tutush's death, Riḍwān released him and his brother Altūntāsh on the order of Sultan Barkyāruq.[87] With a large number of "unemployed soldiers" (*kathīr min al-'asākir al-baṭṭālīn*), apparently troops that were looking for new activities after the end of the civil war, they crossed the Euphrates and took Ḥarrān. Thereafter, they involved themselves in the power struggle of the 'Uqaylid princes then ruling in Niṣibīn and Mosul, where they had been appointed in the time of Tutush's advance. Eventually, Karbūqā turned against both of them, first taking hold of Niṣibīn and, after a siege of nine months, of Mosul.[88] After killing his brother Altūntāsh, he secured broad acceptance among the local elites, reduced the Turkmen emir dwelling farther to the north, Jokermish of Jazīrat b. 'Umar, to vassal status, and seized al-Raḥba on the Euphrates River.[89] Thus within a short time, Karbūqā managed to expel the last 'Uqaylid rulers in tandem with the proponents of Seljuk claims to suzerainty represented by Tutush and his sons and to carve out an independent lordship in the Diyār Rabī'a region southeast of the newly emerging Turkish emirates in the former Marwānid territories of Diyār Bakr.[90] It is noteworthy that as a result of the gradual intrusion of seditious warlords the personal bonds between the political centers of Syria and the northern Jazīra were disrupted. The conquest of Edessa and the surrounding territories east of the Euphrates by the crusading armies in 1097–98 further aggravated these divides and the overall fragmentation of the region. What in the years of the Seljuk expansion up to Malikshāh's death in 1092 had been a transition zone for Turkmen warrior groups, in which the first Seljuk sultans made concerted efforts to build up a cluster of personal ties and mechanisms of centralizing rule, at the close of the eleventh century turned out to be a deeply fragmented conflict area of competing local forces emerging from a Syrian or Iraqi background.

* * *

In Ramaḍān 489/23 August-21 September 1096, the conflict between Aleppo and Damascus escalated when Riḍwān and Janāḥ al-Dawla made an assault upon Damascus. Unable to achieve anything against Duqāq and his allies, Riḍwān's troops made a southward advance towards Nāblus and Jerusalem but were forced to retreat the whole way back through the Syrian desert to Aleppo while being chased and severely harassed by the troops of Duqāq, Ṭughtikīn, and Yaghī Siyān.[91] For some time the center of hostilities shifted back to the north, and the troops of Damascus and Antioch ravaged and imposed tribute on Kafarṭāb (17 February 1097) and Ma'arrat al-Nu'mān.[92] Suqmān b. Artuq and his companions were compelled to give up this city and retreated to the territory of Aleppo, while Riḍwān mustered a new fighting force consisting of Turks, Arabs, and the urban militia of Aleppo. Peace talks at the Quwayq River outside Qinnasrīn brought no tangible results, and a new battle took place on 22 March 1097, which ended with the defeat of the Antioch-Damascus coalition.[93] In the wake of this battle the pre-existing coalitions suddenly collapsed and new groupings appeared. Facing conspiracies of Riḍwān, Janāḥ al-Dawla fled to Ḥimṣ along with his wife, Riḍwān's mother, whereas Yaghī Siyān entered the service of the lord of Aleppo, to whom he gave his daughter Khātūn Jijek in marriage.[94]

At this point Riḍwān's objectives with respect to his brother in Damascus coincided with attempts of the government of Cairo to extend its influence in Syria and Palestine. These efforts had been initiated by a large-scale campaign under the command of the *amīr al-juyūsh* al-Afḍal b. Badr al-Jamālī against Jerusalem in Shaʿbān 489/August 1096, shortly before Riḍwān's attack on Damascus. After a heavy siege, Artuq's sons, Suqmān and Īlghāzī, surrendered to the Fatimid commander, who treated them respectfully and granted them safe conduct. As a result, Suqmān went back to his ally Riḍwān in Aleppo, while Īlghāzī took refuge with Duqāq in Damascus and thereafter set off for Iraq where he entered the service of Barkyāruq's half-brother and rival Muḥammad.[95]

The Fatimid caliphate and its Shiite dogma, once again, had become powerful factors in Syrian affairs. Hence, it comes as no surprise that within a short time thoughts came up that the Fatimid caliphate in Palestine and the emirate of Aleppo could successfully collaborate against their common opponent in Damascus. Neither loyalty to the Seljuk sultanate nor Sunni teaching seems to have been the primary concern of the Seljuk leaders in northern Syria. An exchange of emissaries between Aleppo and al-Afḍal b. Badr al-Jamālī prompted Riḍwān to introduce the Friday prayer in the name of the Fatimid caliph. Thus, on 17 Ramaḍān 490/28 August 1097, the emir was mentioned in the prayer along with Caliph al-Mustaʿlī for the first time. Presumably, the ruler of Aleppo hoped for substantial support in his conflict with his brother Duqāq as a reward for this action. Moreover, Riḍwān clearly felt safe from any intervention on the part of Sultan Barkyāruq, whose claims to formal suzerainty in Syria were seriously undermined by Aleppo's change of allegiance. The alliance with Fatimid Cairo, however, did not last long. According to one version, a mere four weeks after the alteration of the Friday prayer, Riḍwān's allies Suqmān b. Artuq and Yaghī Siyān came to Aleppo complaining loudly about Riḍwān's defiance towards the Abbasid caliphate and the Seljuk sultanate, so that the Abbasid prayer was quickly restored. Other sources speak about four months or even assert that it was only in June 1099 that Riḍwān returned to Abbasid obedience.[96] Be that as it may, the alliance between Aleppo and the Fatimids remained a short, though meaningful, interlude indicating that, just as in the troublesome times of Tutush's first arrival in Syria in the 1070s, members of the Seljuk elite still considered Shiism a potential alternative. The estrangement between the Syrian emirs and the Great Seljuk sultanate in the years 1093–95 seems to have made local potentates more inclined to switch allegiance to the rival caliphate of Cairo in order to create a counter-weight to the encroachments of the Seljuk emirs based in Iraq and the Jazīra.

By that time, Riḍwān sought to mobilize Suqmān and his newly acquired ally Yaghī Siyān for a campaign against his former tutor Janāḥ al-Dawla in Ḥimṣ. But worrying news about the Franks' advance towards Antioch brought about a total reversal of fortunes. From Shayzar, where these messages had reached them, Suqmān headed to his territories in Diyār Bakr and Yaghī Siyān hastened back to Antioch, feverishly seeking for allies against this unexpected threat. With the crusader army's march through Anatolia in the months between May and October 1097, the provinces of northern Syria faced the invasion of powerful Christian forces able to undertake large-scale attacks and conquests for the first time since the campaign of Emperor Romanos IV in 1068. It is not clear to what extent the contemporary witnesses of these events in the Muslim territories of Syria were actually aware of the size, character, and purpose of this expedition.[97] But there is no doubt that from the outset it was conceived of as a major menace that urgently required attention. This explains why local potentates, who for years were relentlessly fighting each other, suddenly joined forces to oppose this new enemy. For this purpose, Yaghī Siyān sent letters and emissaries, among them his sons Shams al-Dīn and Muḥammad, to Duqāq and Ṭughtikīn in Damascus, Janāḥ al-Dawla in Ḥimṣ, the chief of the Kilāb Arabs Waththāb b. Muḥammad, Karbūqā of Mosul, the Turkmen chiefs, and other Muslim emirs.[98] The sudden emergence of an external threat had strong unifying effects on the Turkish chieftains in Syria and Upper Mesopotamia.

In sum, in the time span between 1086 and 1098 the Turkish potentates in Syria and parts of Upper Mesopotamia went through three different stages: a first one of centralizing rule exerted by the Great Seljuk sultanate (1086–92); a second one of fierce intra-dynastic struggle between the factions of Tāj al-Dawla Tutush and Barkyāruq (1093–95); and a third one of highly destructive regional conflicts extending over the whole area in question.[99] The personal loyalties of Turkish *ghulām* commanders and their coalitions with the local elites were largely controlled by the supreme head of the Seljuk dynasty. After Malikshāh's death the greatest part of the Turkish chieftains remained faithful to the sultan's descendants, and thus Tutush faced many difficulties in finding allies among them and imposing his authority. By the time of Tutush's violent death in early 1095, most of Malikshāh's chief commanders had lost their lives, which unleashed new centrifugal dynamics. These dynamics manifested themselves in incessant conflicts among Tutush's sons Riḍwān and Duqāq, surviving members of the old regime, and newcomers from Sultan Barkyāruq's retinue.

Damascus, Ḥimṣ, Antioch, Aleppo, Edessa, and Mosul turned into mutually rivaling, semi-independent, small-size lordships. Smaller towns and strongholds, such as Shayzar, Ma'arrat al-Nu'mān, Manbij, Sarūj, Ḥarrān, and Jazīrat b. 'Umar, became targets of various competing forces and domains of tiny vassal lords. Simultaneously, the Fatimid government of Egypt once again came to the foreground as a powerful political factor by expelling the Seljuk commanders from Palestine and extending its authority over parts of the Syrian littoral. In this way, the Turkish potentates in Syria lost much of their internal cohesion. They became fully integrated with the local urban elites and developed close ties with other military forces, such as town militias and Arab nomadic tribes. Despite the sudden decay of the Seljuk dynastic project in Syria, the Turkish chiefs gained the recognition of the indigenous population in most major cities as emirs and thus became an integral part of the political structures in Syria. Unlike their predecessors in the 1060s and 1070s who mostly operated as supporters of various local factions, after 1095 the Turkish chiefs had become commonly accepted by the local populations as rulers who further consolidated their position by promoting the interests of the local aristocracy and religious elite. Conversely, overarching structures of imperial rule, which aimed at cultivating widely ramified clusters of vassal lords, as was the case with Byzantium and the Fatimid caliphate until the 1070s or the Seljuk sultanate until 1092, ceased to exist by the end of the eleventh century. Most areas of the old Byzantine-Muslim borderland were transformed into a disparate and highly fragmented patchwork of tiny local lordships consisting of one or two main towns and a number of smaller strongpoints. The same model of political authority came to apply to many territories in central and eastern Anatolia, which had slipped away from Byzantine control. Thus, many aspects of the process of state building and political change in Muslim and former Byzantine regions show similar patterns.

Notes

1 For the battles and their consequences, see Ibn al-Athīr, 6:294–95, 299, trans. Richards, *Annals*, pp. 218–20, 223–24; Ibn al-ʿAdīm, pp. 317–18, 320; see also Sevim and Merçil, *Selçuklu Devletleri*, p. 444–47; Öngül, *Selçuklular*, 1:420–24; Özgüdenli, *Selçuklular*, pp. 177–78.

2 Sevim, *Suriye*, pp. 112–32; Sevim, *Süleymanşah*, pp. 35–39; Sevim and Merçil, *Selçuklu Devletleri*, p. 134–39; Öngül, *Selçuklular*, 1:109–12.

3 See, for instance, the summarizing remarks of Leveniotis, *Στασιαστικό κίνημα*, pp. 39–41, 213–22.

4 See the details gathered by Leveniotis, *Στασιαστικό κίνημα*, pp. 129–33 (general decay of the Byzantine military forces in Asia Minor), pp. 134, 151 (Roussel commanded 2,700–3,000 soldiers), pp. 149–50 (Artuk led 5,000–6,000 men), pp. 167–68, 169–70 (campaigns in Asia Minor organized by the imperial government lacked manpower).

5 See above, pp. 212–213, and Leveniotis, *Στασιαστικό κίνημα*, pp. 176–84.

6 See, for instance, Turan, *Türkiye*, pp. 78–80, who, like many other Turkish scholars before and after him, exaggerates the positive effects of this policy by describing the state of Sulaymān b. Qutlumush as establishing a fully developed institutional framework for the peaceful co-existence of nomadic Oghuz Turks and free Christian peasants.

7 For details, see above, pp. 36–44.

8 Turan, *Türkiye*, pp. 84–87.

9 Turan, *Selçuklular Târihi*, pp. 227–30; Sevim and Merçil, *Selçuklu Devletleri*, pp. 176–85; Öngül, *Selçuklular*, 1:145–55; see also Irwin, "Impact," p. 137/303, who greatly emphasizes the death of Malikshāh as a turning point in the history of the Middle East.

10 For a detailed analysis of all events related to Malikshāh's Syrian campaign, see Turan, *Selçuklular Târihi*, pp. 206–207; Kafesoğlu, *Melikşah*, pp. 86–94; Sevim, *Suriye*, pp. 119–32; Bosworth, "Political History," pp. 97–98; El-Azhari, *Saljūqs of Syria*, pp. 63–70; Sevim and Merçil, *Selçuklu Devletleri*, pp. 136–39; Ripper, *Marwāniden*, pp. 229–40; Öngül, *Selçuklular*, 1:109–12.

11 Ibn al-ʿAdīm, pp. 318–20.

12 Ibn al-ʿAdīm, p. 321.

13 Ibn al-ʿAdīm, pp. 322–23; for further details, see Kafesoğlu, *Melikşah*, pp. 90–91; Sevim, *Suriye*, pp. 124–26; Sevim and Merçil, *Selçuklu Devletleri*, pp. 134–36; Öngül, *Selçuklular*, 1:109–10.

14 Ibn al-Athīr, 6:300, trans. Richards, *Annals*, p. 225, explicitly states that Ibn al-Ḥutaytī invited Malikshāh because of his fear of Tutush.

15 Kafesoşlu, *Melikşah*, p. 91, and Sevim, *Suriye*, p. 127, refer to a later version transmitted by Aqsarāʾī, according to which Sultan Malikshāh had decided to concede Antioch and Aleppo to Sulaymān b. Qutlumush. When he was informed about the latter's death, he wrote an angry letter to Tutush and set off for the Syrian campaign. This is a narrative's construction of claims underpinning the idea of an official appointment of Sulaymān b. Qutlumush by the Seljuk sultan.
16 El-Azhari, *Saljūqs*, pp. 68–69, points to Tutush's weak military position vis-à-vis the sultan's army and to the former's wish to secure his position in Damascus; for the Seljuk administrative system established in the regions in question, especially with respect to the urban centers, see Heidemann, *Renaissance*, pp. 145–46, 149–56.
17 For the sultan's itinerary, see Ibn al-Athīr, 6: 300–301, trans. Richards, *Annals*, pp. 225–26; for the advance to Antioch and the Syrian coast, see Ibn al-ʿAdīm, p. 324; for the sultan's celebrations in Baghdad in Dhū l-Ḥijja 479/9 March-7 April 1087 and Muḥarram 480/8 April-7 May 1087, see Ibn al-Athīr, 6:305–06 and 309–09, trans. Richards, *Annals*, pp. 227–29 and pp. 232–33; other sources: Ibn al-Qalānisī, p. 119; ʿAẓīmī, pp. 20–21 (Arabic text), p. 26 (trans.); Matthew of Edessa 2.85-86, pp. 152–53; Bar Hebraeus, pp. 259–60, trans. Budge, p. 231; see also Kafesoğlu, *Melikşah*, pp. 91–94; Sevim, *Suriye*, pp. 127–31, El-Azhari, *Saljūqs*, pp. 65–68; Mouton, *Damas*, pp. 28–29; Sevim and Merçil, *Selçuklu Devletleri*, pp. 136–44; Öngül, *Selçuklular*, 1:110–16.
18 Heidemann, *Renaissance*, pp. 149–51, stresses the emirs' twofold function as governors and iqṭāʿ holders, though it seems that in terms of administrative practices it is hardly possible to draw a clear distinction between the two roles.
19 For the surrender of Edessa, see Matthew 2.88, p. 154; for Būzān, see Ibn al-Athīr, p. 333, trans. Richards, *Annals*, p. 251; Ibn al-ʿAdīm, pp. 328, 323.
20 Ibn al-Athīr, 6:309, trans. Richards, *Annals*, p. 233; Ibn al-ʿAdīm, pp. 325–26, 327; ʿAẓīmī, p. 21 (Arabic text), p. 26 (trans.); for Aqsunqur, see also Sevim, *Selçuklu Komutanları*, pp. 72–81.
21 Ibn al-ʿAdīm, p. 324.
22 Ibn al-Athīr, p. 301, trans. Richards, *Annals*, p. 226.
23 Ibn al-ʿAdīm, p. 324.
24 Ibn al-ʿAdīm, p. 323.
25 Anna Komnene 6.10.3, p. 189, ll. 73–75.
26 Anna Komnene 6.12.5-8, pp. 195–97.
27 Anna Komnene 6.12.7, p. 196, l. 33: ὁ τοῦ ἀναιρεθέντος Ταπάρη σουλτὰν υἱός, ὁ Παργιαρούχ.
28 Ibn al-ʿAdīm, p. 323; al-Bundārī/ʿImād al-Dīn, p. 55; al-Ḥusaynī, p. 72, trans. Lügal, p. 49.
29 Matthew of Edessa 2.96, pp. 157–58, *sub anno* 541/1092-93.
30 For similar conclusions concerning the chronology, see Turan, *Türkiye*, p. 85.
31 For these contacts, see below, pp. 268–69.
32 For this campaign, see above, pp. 150–51, 153.
33 For the appointment of Seljuk governors in northern Syria, see also Kafesoğlu, *Melikşah*, pp. 91–93; Sevim, *Suriye*, 127–31; El-Azhari, *Saljūqs*, pp. 65–68; Sevim and Merçil, *Selçuklu Devletleri*, pp. 136–39; Öngül, *Selçuklular*, 1:110–12.
34 Ibn al-Athīr, 6:287–88, 290–91, 296–97, trans. Richards, *Annals*, pp. 209–10, 213–15, 220–22; Ibn al-Azraq, pp. 206–14; for details and other sources, see Yinanç, *Anadolu'nun Fethi*, pp. 136–50; Kafesoğlu, *Melikşah*, pp. 46–54; Ripper, *Marwāniden*, pp. 220–29.
35 Ibn al-Athīr, 6:263, 270, 297, trans. Richards, *Annals*, pp. 183, 191, 221; Ibn al-Azraq, pp. 211–12.
36 Ibn al-Athīr, 6:290–92 trans. Richards, *Annals*, pp. 213–16; Ibn al-Azraq, p. 210.
37 Ibn al-Athīr, 6:291, trans. Richards, *Annals*, p. 214; for this dynasty, see EI^2 6:965–66 s. v. Mazyad, Banū (C. E. Bosworth).
38 Ripper, *Marwāniden*, p. 212–20.

39 Ibn al-Athīr, p. 307, trans. Richards, *Annals*, p. 230; Ibn al-Azraq, pp. 206–207; for details, see Ripper, *Marwāniden*, pp. 235–38.
40 Ibn al-Athīr, 6:307, trans. Richards, *Annals*, p. 229; see also Kafesoğlu, *Malikşah*, p. 87; Ripper, *Marwāniden*, p. 231 and n. 174.
41 Sevim, *Suriye*, p. 132, claims that, as result of Malikshāh's intervention, northern Syria was directly connected to the Great Seljuk Empire and thus the political and military activities of Tutush could be kept under control.
42 It was only in the late twelfth- and early thirteenth-century Seljuk dynastic chronicles of 'Imād al-Dīn/al-Bundārī, p. 55, and al-Ḥusaynī, p. 72, trans. Lügal, p. 49, that the campaigns to western Asia Minor were described as attacks on Constantinople, but this has to be seen in the context of later tendencies glorifying the Seljuk historical memory.
43 For the situation in general, see Kafesoğlu, *Melikşah*, pp. 98–101; Sevim, *Suriye*, pp. 133–36; El-Azhari, *Saljūqs*, pp. 69–72.
44 Ibn al-Qalānisī, pp. 119–20; 'Aẓīmī, p. 21 (Arabic text), p. 26 (trans.); Ibn al-Athīr, p. 313, trans. Richards, *Annals*, p. 238; Ibn al-'Adīm, p. 327; see also Kafesoğlu, *Melikşah*, p. 98; Sevim, *Suriye*, p. 133.
45 Ibn al-'Adīm, p. 327.
46 Ibn al-Athīr, pp. 333–34, trans. Richards, *Annals*, pp. 251–52; Ibn al-'Adīm, p. 328; Ibn al-Qalānisī, pp. 121–22, and al-'Aẓīmī, pp. 21–22 (Arabic text), p. 27 (trans.), are more accurate concerning the chronological sequence. According to their reports, Ibn Mulā'ib, after the conquest of Ḥimṣ, escaped to Egypt, from where he returned to Afāmiya. When this town was seized by Qasīm al-Dawla, he took Ibn Mulā'ib captive again and sent him to the East (Ibn al-'Adīm mentions Iṣfahān); see also Kafesoğlu, *Melikşah*, pp. 99–100; Mouton, *Damas*, p. 30; Sevim, *Suriye*, pp. 135–36.
47 Ibn al-Qalānisī, pp. 120–21; al-'Aẓīmī, pp. 21–22 (Arabic text), pp. 26–27 (trans.); Ibn al-Athīr, 6:333, trans. Richards, *Annals*, p. 251; for further details, see Kafesoğlu, *Melikşah*, pp. 98–100; Sevim, *Suriye*, pp. 133–36; El-Azhari, *Saljūqs of Syria*, pp. 69–72.
48 For Malikshāh's death, see, for instance, 'Aẓīmī, p. 28 (Arabic text), p. 22 (trans.); Ibn al-Qalānisī, p. 121 (erroneously 6 Shawwāl 485); Ibn al-Athīr, 6:338–39, trans. Richards, *Annals*, pp. 258–59 (middle of Shawwāl 485/19 November); see also Brett, "Near East," p. 134/300; Irwin, "Impact," p. 137/303; Sevim and Merçil, *Selçuklu Devletleri*, pp. 168–72; Öngül, *Selçuklular*, pp. 1:137–40; Merçil, *Büyük Selçuklu Devleti*, pp. 91–92; Özgüdenli, *Selçuklular*, pp. 189–92.
49 Turan, *Selçuklular Târihi*, pp. 229–30; Sevim, *Suriye*, pp. 137–63; Sevim and Merçil, *Selçuklu Devleti*, pp. 176–85, 447–60; Merçil, *Büyük Selçuklu Devleti*, pp. 95–96; Özgüdenli, *Selçuklular*, pp. 197–201.
50 Ibn al-Athīr, 6:344, trans. Richards, *Annals*, p. 265; Ibn al-'Adīm, pp. 328–29; for the Seljuk succession crisis in the years 1092–95 and its impact on the situation in Syria in general, see Köymen, *Selçuklu Devri*, pp. 72–77; Turan, *Selçuklular Târihi*, pp. 227–29; Sevim, *Suriye*, pp. 137–58; Bosworth, "Political History," pp. 103–107; El-Azhari, *Saljūqs*, pp. 73–78; Sevim and Merçil, *Selçuklu Devletleri*, pp. 176–85; Öngül, *Selçuklular*, 1:141–55, 424–33; Merçil, *Büyük Selçuklu Devletleri*, pp. 93–96; Heidemann, *Renaissance*, pp. 165–69 (with special emphasis on the situation in the Diyār Muḍar region); Hanne, *Caliph*, pp. 126–29; Başan, *Great Seljuqs*, pp. 98–100; Özgüdenli, *Selçuklular*, pp. 193–201; Peacock, *Great Seljuk Empire*, p. 76.
51 Ibn al-Qalānisī, pp. 122–24; Ibn al-Athīr, 6:344–46, trans. Richards, *Annals*, pp. 265–67; Ibn al-'Adīm, pp. 329–30.
52 Ibn al-'Adīm, p. 330; see also Mouton, *Damas*, pp. 30–31.
53 Ibn al-'Adīm, p. 331; for details, see Sevim, *Suriye*, pp. 137–45.
54 Ibn al-Athīr, 6:347, trans. Richards, *Annals*, pp. 267–68; Ibn al-'Adīm, p. 330.
55 Ibn al-Athīr, 6:350–51, trans. Richards, *Annals*, pp. 271–72.

56 Ibn al-Qalānisī, p. 124; Ibn al-ʿAdīm, pp. 330–32 (they arrived in Aleppo in Shawwāl 486/25 October-22 November 1093).
57 Ibn al-Qalānisī, pp. 126–27; Ibn al-Athīr, 6:352–54, trans. Richards, *Annals*, pp. 273–75; Ibn al-ʿAdīm, pp. 332–35; for details, see Sevim, *Suriye*, pp. 145–50; Sevim and Merçil, *Selçuklu Devletleri*, pp. 450–51; Öngül, *Selçuklular*, 1:149–50, 428–29.
58 Ibn al-Qalānisī, p. 127; Ibn al-ʿAdīm, pp. 329–30, 335.
59 Ibn al-Qalānisī, pp. 128–30; Ibn al-Athīr, 6:360–61, trans. Richards, *Annals*, pp. 278–79; Ibn al-ʿAdīm, pp. 335–36 (Tutush entered Rayy in Muḥarram 488/11 January-9 February 1095 and the battle took place on 16 Ṣafar/26 February); for details, see Sevim, *Suriye*, pp. 150–58; Mouton, *Damas*, p. 31; Sevim and Merçil, *Selçuklu Devletleri*, pp. 452–55; Öngül, *Selçuklular*, 1:151–55, 429–33.
60 EI^2 1:731–32, s. v. atabak (C. Cahen); Peacock, *Great Seljuk Empire*, pp. 93–94.
61 For a general overview, see Sevim, *Suriye*, pp. 161–78; Mouton, *Damas*, pp. 32–33; El-Azharī, *Saljūqs*, pp. 79–90.
62 Ibn al-Qalānisī, p. 130 and p. 189, for the killing of Riḍwān's younger brothers; Ibn al-Athīr, 6:361, trans. Richards, *Annals*, pp. 279–80; Ibn al-ʿAdīm, p. 336; see also Sevim, *Suriye*, pp. 161–63; Mouton, *Damas*, p. 62; El-Azhari, *Saljūqs*, pp. 79–80; Sevim and Merçil, *Selçuklu Devletleri*, pp. 458–60; Öngül, *Selçuklular*, 1:434–35.
63 Ibn al-Qalānisī, p. 130; Ibn al-ʿAdīm, pp. 336–37; Ibn al-Athīr, 6:362, trans. Richards, *Annals*, p. 281.
64 Ibn al-Qalānisī, pp. 130–31; Ibn al-ʿAdīm, pp. 337–38; Ibn al-Athīr, 6:362–63, trans. Richards, *Annals*, p. 281; see also Sevim, *Suriye*, pp. 166–67; Mouton, *Damas*, p. 32; El-Azhari, *Saljūqs*, pp. 80–82; Sevim and Merçil, *Selçuklu Devletleri*, pp. 460–61; Öngül, *Selçuklular*, 1:436–37.
65 Ibn al-Athīr, 6:359–60, trans. Richards, *Annals*, p. 278.
66 Ibn al-ʿAdīm, pp. 339–40.
67 Ibn al-ʿAdīm, p. 340.
68 Ibn al-ʿAdīm, p. 340; Ibn al-Athīr, 6:366–67, trans. Richards, *Annals*, pp. 285–86; see also Sevim, *Suriye*, pp. 166–67 and 169–70; Sevim and Merçil, *Selçuklu Devletleri*, p. 461; Öngül, *Selçuklular*, 1:434–36.
69 Ibn al-Athīr, 6:361, trans. Richards, *Annals*, p. 280.
70 Ibn al-Athīr, 6:326, trans. Richards, *Annals*, p. 280; Ibn al-ʿAdīm, pp. 338–39; Matthew of Edessa 2.105, pp. 162–63; for further details of this event, see Heidemann, *Renaissance*, pp. 169–71.
71 Ibn al-ʿAdīm, p. 339; see also Sevim, *Suriye*, pp. 164–65.
72 Ibn al-ʿAdīm, pp. 340–41.
73 Ibn al-ʿAdīm, p. 338.
74 Ibn al-ʿAdīm, p. 341; see also Sevim, *Suriye*, pp. 166–68 and 169–71; El-Azhari, *Saljūqs*, pp. 82–85; Sevim and Merçil, *Selçuklu Devletleri*, pp. 462–63; Öngül, *Selçuklular*, 1:437–38.
75 Turan, *Doğu Anadolu*, pp. 153–54; Hillenbrand, "Najm al-Dīn İl-Ghāzī," pp. 254–55; for further details on Artuq b. Aksab, see above, p. 249.
76 Ibn al-Athīr, 6:299–300, trans. Richards, *Annals*, pp. 223–24; Turan, *Doğu Anadolu*, p. 153.
77 Cahen, "Diyar Bakr," p. 228; Turan, *Doğu Anadolu*, p. 157; Hillenbrand, "Najm al-Dīn İl-Ghāzī," p. 255.
78 Ibn al-Athīr, 6:361, trans. Richards, *Annals*, p. 279.
79 Ibn al-Athīr, 6:361–62, trans. Richards, *Annals*, p. 280.
80 Matthew of Edessa 2.105, p. 162; Turan, *Doğu Anadolu*, p. 158.
81 Ibn al-ʿAdīm, pp. 339–40; Turan, *Doğu Anadolu*, p. 158.
82 Matthew of Edessa 2.105, p. 162; Cahen, "Diyar Bakr," p. 228; Turan, *Doğu Anadolu*, p. 157; for this personality, see Heidemann, *Renaissance*, pp. 169–70.
83 Ibn al-ʿAdīm, pp. 341–42.

84 Cahen, "Diyar Bakr," p. 228, n. 3; Turan, *Doğu Anadolu*, p. 158, n. 21.
85 Matthew of Edessa 2.117, pp. 168–67.
86 Özaydın, "Kürboğa," pp. 405–407; for Mosul, see EI^2 6:899–901 s. v. al-Mawṣil (E. Honigmann and C. E. Bosworth).
87 Ibn al-Athīr, pp. 6:338–39, 347, 352–53, 368, trans. Richards, *Annals*, pp. 259, 267, 273–74, 286; Özaydın, "Kürboğa," pp. 407–408.
88 Özaydın, "Kürboğa," pp. 408–10.
89 Ibn al-Athīr, 6:368–69, trans. Richards, *Annals*, pp. 286–87; Özaydın, "Kürboğa," p. 410.
90 Cahen, "Diyar Bakr," p. 227; Özaydın, "Kürboğa," pp. 409–10; Heidemann, *Renaissance*, pp. 173–75.
91 Ibn al-Athīr, 6:375, trans. Richards, *Annals*, p. 293; Ibn al-ʿAdīm, pp. 340–41.
92 Ibn al-ʿAdīm, p. 341.
93 Ibn al-Athīr, 6:375, trans. Richards, *Annals*, pp. 293–94; Ibn al-ʿAdīm, p. 342; al-Maqrīzī, *Ittiʿāẓ*, 3:19 (dating the reception of Riḍwān's emissaries in Cairo to 16 Ṣafar 490/1097 February 2); see also Sevim, *Suriye*, pp. 169–73; El-Azhari, *Saljūqs*, pp. 84–86; Sevim and Merçil, *Selçuklu Devletleri*, pp. 462–63; Öngül, *Selçuklular*, 1:438–39.
94 Ibn al-Qalānisī, p. 133; Ibn al-Athīr, 6:375, trans. Richards, *Annals*, p. 294; Ibn al-ʿAdīm, pp. 342–43; see also Sevim, *Suriye*, pp. 173–74; Sevim and Merçil, *Selçuklu Devletleri*, p. 463; Öngül, *Selçuklular*, 1:439.
95 Ibn al-Qalānisī, p. 135; Ibn al-Athīr, 6:383, trans. Richards, *Chronicle*, 1:21; Hillenbrand, Najm al-Dīn İl-Ghāzī," pp. 255–56; Sevim and Merçil, *Selçuklu Devletleri*, pp. 463–64; Öngül, *Selçuklular*, 1:439–40.
96 Ibn al-Athīr, 6:375, trans. Richards, *Annals*, p. 294; Ibn al-ʿAdīm, pp. 343–44; see also Sevim, *Suriye*, pp. 174–76; El-Azhari, *Saljūqs*, pp. 87–90; Sevim and Merçil, *Selçuklu Devletleri*, pp. 463–65; Öngül, *Selçuklular*, 1:439–40.
97 For Muslim perceptions of the First Crusade in general, see Hillenbrand, *Crusades*, pp. 38–54, esp. pp. 44–47, where she discusses the possibility that the Fatimids knew about the crusaders' march to Palestine before the latter arrived there. In this context she assumes that there were collaborations between the Fatimids and the crusaders against Seljuk predominance in Syria. The Fatimids may have underestimated the crusaders' objectives while cherishing hopes for an alliance with the Byzantine Empire. It should be noted, however, that any allusions in the sources to Byzantine warnings concerning the arrival of the Franks or other details indicating Fatimid measures taken in view of the imminent Frankish invasion are highly questionable. Near-contemporary crusader chronicles are very vague with respect to the goals of the crusade. People in the East, therefore, could hardly have had a clear idea about the crusaders' advance to Palestine prior to 1099. See, for instance, Fulcher of Chartres' version of Pope Urban II's crusader sermon held on the Council of Clermont in November 1095: 1.3.2-8, pp. 132–38. For the question of motives in general, see Asbridge, *First Crusade*, pp. 40–49, 65–78; for the main factors facilitating the Frankish expansion in the western parts of Seljuk-held territories, see Heidemann, *Renaissance*, pp. 175–79.
98 Ibn al-Qalānisī, p. 134; Ibn al-ʿAdīm, pp. 344–45; see also Heidemann, *Renaissance*, pp. 178–79.
99 El-Azhari, *Saljūqs*, p. 87.

7 Turkish and Byzantine-Armenian lordships in Asia Minor

The Turks of Nicaea under Apelchasem, 1086–93

In the time span between Sulaymān's death in June 1086 and the beginning of the intra-dynastic civil strife in the Seljuk empire in early 1093, the situation in western Asia Minor was marked by the gradual crystallization of Turkish local lordships centered in provincial capitals and coastal towns along the shores of the Propontis and the Aegean Sea. All of these powers were certainly at odds with the imperial government, yet it would be misleading to assume that they formed a unified block of conquerors imposing their rule upon the local population. As has been shown in the previous chapters, the Turkish penetration of these regions was based on a cluster of personal links and forms of collaboration with Byzantine aristocrats, whereas the relations among the various Turkish warrior groups were frequently characterized by rivalries and competition. Hence, an adequate analysis of the newly emerging constellations of power in Asia Minor prior to the First Crusade has to take into account the particularities of each political entity and its specific environment.

The province of Bithynia in the years after 1086 was dominated by Apelchasem, while his brother Poulchazes seems to have controlled parts of Cappadocia.[1] Although it is not certain, in view of the details known about the strongholds under Sulaymān b. Qutlumush's control it is likely that Poulchazes resided in Koloneia/Aqṣarā.[2] In these years the relations with the government of Constantinople went through two clearly distinct stages. At first the Turkish potentate no longer considered himself bound by the treaty of 1081 and resumed the raids into the Propontis coastland, thus initiating a new phase of military conflicts. These were superseded by a period of peaceful negotiations culminating in a visit of the Turkish ruler to Constantinople, during which the emperor bestowed court titles upon Apelchasem and concluded a new peace treaty with him. It is noteworthy that the emir's political ambitions are described as going far beyond looting and accumulating wealth, thus gaining a new dimension in comparison to those of Sulaymān b. Qutlumush. Given that at that time Nikomedeia was occupied by the Turks of Nicaea,[3] it seems plausible to accept Anna's assertion that Apelchasem made every effort to increase his hold over the coastland of the nearby gulf and other regions of the Propontis area and to further extend his sway over the offshore islands by constructing a fleet. Anna even talks about the emir's wish to "adorn himself with the scepters of the Roman Empire."[4] Despite the evident exaggeration of this statement, it is noteworthy that Anna here introduces a new feature in the portrayal of Turkish potentates operating in Asia Minor. She implies that the Turks, who up to then excelled as raiders, powerful allies, and local potentates, began to show an increasing interest in the Byzantine imperial sphere and its ideology. Apelchasem is the first Turkish warlord to be granted the title of *sebastos*, an honor hitherto exclusively reserved for high-ranking members of the imperial dynasty.[5] This event thus marks the beginning of a gradual accommodation of the practices of Turkish warrior groups to Byzantine political concepts. In contrast to northern Syria and the provinces of eastern Anatolia, where the remnants of the Byzantine elite were gradually absorbed by the newly emerging Muslim-Turkish milieu, in western Asia Minor the Byzantine cultural and political substrate persisted and continued to exert a strong influence on the Turkish newcomers.

As regards the military threat in the time after the end of the Norman war in the summer of 1085 and prior to the Pecheneg invasion on the Balkans that required new operations in late 1086,[6] Alexios I was able to react more dynamically by launching two campaigns under the command of Tatikios. The second was further supported by the naval forces of Manuel Boutoumites. The Byzantine forces did not succeed in recovering territories in Bithynia or defeating the Turkish troops, but they removed the Turks from the coastland and destroyed a number of recently constructed ships.[7] The arrival of Bursuq's army in Bithynia, however, changed the balance of power in the region to the detriment of both the Byzantines and Apelchasem. Tatikios is said to have stopped his attacks on Nicaea as soon as he was informed about Bursuq's advance.[8] Apelchasem accepted the emperor's peace proposals in fear of Bursuq's imminent arrival and a possible siege of Nicaea.[9] It is especially noteworthy that according to Anna's narrative it was Malikshāh's attempt to bring the Turks in Asia Minor under his immediate control that caused the local Turkish warlords and the Byzantines to seek a rapprochement and to join forces against the external threat. Anna's presentation of the Turks' reasoning, "it is better to be called servants of him [i.e., the emperor] than to extend our hands to Porsouch,"[10] is reminiscent of similar statements made by Byzantine historians with respect to Arīsghī in 1070 and to Sulaymān b. Qutlumush in 1078 and can therefore be regarded as a recurring literary motif. However, Anna's words contain a kernel of truth, reflecting the progressive estrangement between the central authority of the Seljuk dynasty and the Turkish potentates in the remote frontier zones of Asia Minor. Anna presents the Byzantine course of action as part of a well-conceived plan aiming at the gradual restoration of imperial authority in the provinces of Asia Minor. According to his daughter's idealized image, Alexios acts with prudence and diplomatic skillfulness and in the stratagems he used against Apelchasem is comparable to Alcibiades and his handling of the Spartans, as described by Thucydides.[11] When two enemies like Apelchasem and Bursuq were fighting against each other, the emperor had to support the weaker one, not in order to make him stronger but to fend off the other and thus to find a way to recover lost territories.[12] The Byzantines thus appear as morally and mentally superior, although the imperial government, no doubt, was in an extremely precarious position while seeking to regain a foothold in regions close to the Asian suburbs of Constantinople. For this reason, we should be cautious in accepting the explanations Anna gives in order to elucidate the underlying motives of certain actions. Actually, the diplomatic steps Alexios took had nothing to do with superiority but were born out of the necessity of handling the danger of two hostile forces operating in the vicinity of Constantinople without being able to confront them militarily. The meager results of Tatikios' and Boutoumites' expedition had demonstrated that, apart from some minor successes, it was hardly possible to achieve substantial gains in Bithynia. The Turks were already too firmly established to be driven out from their territories. An alliance based on the well-known practice of incorporating former opponents into the Byzantine court hierarchy was the only possibility to neutralize the enemy's military power and to avert a possible cooperation between Apelchasem and Bursuq.

According to Anna's account, Alexios sent a letter to Apelchasem summoning him to stop fighting and to accept a peace treaty in order to enjoy the emperor's presents and honors.[13] Apelchasem complied with these requests and departed for Constantinople, where he was granted an honorable reception. During his sojourn, he received regular payments and was offered a lavish amusement program, comprising sightseeing in the boulevards of the imperial city, horse races in the Hippodrome, hunting, and visits to public baths. Eventually, the emperor showered him with another load of gifts and granted him the title of *sebastos*.[14] Given that during Apelchasem's stay the *droungarios* of the fleet, Eustathios, and his men erected a fortress in the vicinity of Nikomedeia, it can be assumed that this visit lasted at least several weeks.[15] Bursuq's army approached Nicaea when the emir entered negotiations with the emperor and besieged the city for three months.[16] Upon Apelchasem's entreaties, Alexios sent forces in support of his ally. They took possession of the so-called castle of George on the northern shore of the Lake of Nicaea.[17] Fearing that the emperor would confront them in person, Bursuq's soldiers broke off the siege. For their part, the Byzantine units were alarmed by the arrival of new Turkish forces and did not dare proceed towards Nicaea. Because of this, for the time being Alexios' ambitions to regain the capital of Bithynia came to naught.[18]

As a whole, there were no changes from the *status quo* of 1081. The Byzantine government was not able to extend its sway over the Bithynian littoral. Nor did Bursuq's campaign bring any tangible results with respect to a strengthening of Seljuk influence in Asia Minor. What actually changed was the relationship between the imperial government and Apelchasem. The emir managed to consolidate his position as uncontested ruler in Nicaea and the adjacent regions of Bithynia and, at the same time, created close links with Constantinople as holder of a high-ranking court title. This entailed an important gain in prestige vis-à-vis the Byzantines and his subjects, an increase of his political authority, as stipulated in the treaties of 1081 and 1086, and more income in the form of gifts and payments from the imperial treasury. Moreover, the emir was drawn into the cultural sphere of the Byzantine ruling elite. The amusements Apelchasem enjoyed during his stay in Constantinople brought him into contact with expressions of Byzantine court life. The chieftain was exposed to the empire's monuments and historical memory and so made first-hand acquaintance with elements of imperial ideology. Titles, symbols of power, precious artifacts, and elements of self-representation on coins and seals could be used to enhance the Turkish ruler's claims to legitimacy and facilitated his fluency with Christian-Byzantine culture. The oldest surviving copper coins dating to the period of Sultan Mas'ūd I (1116–55) clearly illustrate this process: the obverse shows the half-length portrait of a Byzantine emperor wearing the imperial crown and bearing a labarum and a globe in his hands, while the reverse has an Arabic inscription consisting of the title *al-sulṭān al-mu'aẓẓam* and the ruler's name.[19] The sovereign is associated with timeless symbols of Byzantine imperial power, thus representing the merging of Muslim terms of lordship with Byzantine concepts of statehood. The first step in this direction was the bestowal of the title of *sebastos*, which was closely associated with the dynastic ideals of the Komnenian house and the principles of imperial rule.

Turkish lordships in western Asia Minor

The earliest traces of Turkish presence in the region of Paphlagonia are related to a man called Charatikes, i.e., Karatekin, who is mentioned by Anna Komnene as ruler of Sinope (Sinop), one of the most important Black Sea ports, which had been fortified by a large citadel in the eighth or ninth century.[20] It is not known when and under what circumstances this place surrendered to Turkish warriors, but given that the environs of the nearby town of Kastamona (Kastamonu) were subject to Turkish raids already in the mid-1070s,[21] it may be assumed that the conquest of Sinope occurred at a rather early stage, perhaps at the same time as the penetration of Bithynia by the Turks of Sulaymān b. Qutlumush or the raids of Dānishmand Ghāzī in the lands east of the Halys River. Certain indications provided by the Turkish epic tradition as well as the fact that important towns and fortresses of Paphlagonia like Kastamona and Gangra at the time of the arrival of the Lombard crusading forces in 1101 were under Dānishmand's control[22] suggest close relations between the latter and Charatikes, but without further evidence it is impossible to arrive at firm conclusions. Moreover, the invasions of Turkish warriors into Bithynia certainly disrupted communication between Constantinople and the Paphlagonian coast and thus may have allowed the intrusion of other groups coming from the lands east of the Halys. As regards Charatikes' activities in Sinope, Anna only tells us that for some time he benefited from the tax revenues he collected and that he destroyed a local church dedicated to the Virgin Mary (Theotokos). His downfall occurred soon after Sulaymān's defeat in Syria and was due to Malikshāh's efforts to strengthen his influence over Asia Minor. The Seljuk emissary Siaous, obviously a Greek transliteration of the well-known Iranian name Siyāwush, forced Charatikes to hand over Sinope to imperial troops by means of a sultanic decree ordering the Turkish commanders to surrender in the event that a treaty with the emperor was achieved. Born of a Georgian mother and a Turkish father, the emissary is described as an intelligent man (νουνεχῆ ἄνδρα) who in the time of the sultan's Syrian campaign had been sent to Constantinople in order to enter negotiations with the emperor about an alliance and a marriage between the two families. Reportedly, Alexios exploited Siaous' twofold ethnic identity in order to win him over and persuade him to become baptized and to work on his behalf.[23] Other Turkish emirs are said to have surrendered as well on this occasion, but the geographic position of their strongholds is not indicated and thus it is unclear whether Siaous' activities extended to regions beyond Paphlagonia.

Turkish scholars tried to establish a link between Anna's Charatikes and a character who figures in the *Dānishmand-nāma* as Ḳara Tegin.[24] In the epic tale's eleventh session (*on birinci meclis*) Artukhī, one of Dānishmand Ghāzī's chief companions, is in search for his beloved Efromiya, who has been imprisoned in the fortress of Manḳuriya (Çankırı). On his way, Artukhī comes across Ḳara Tegin, who expresses the wish to join him after telling him the story of his family: his father, a merchant originating from Baghdad, fell in love with the daughter of the Christian priest Ṭamāsūn. Being forced to become Christian in order to marry her, he converted but remained a faithful Muslim in his heart. After a long time, his wife, who had given birth to two sons, also converted to Islam secretly. The priest gave his village to his son-in-law and thereafter was killed by the Muslim hero Sayyid Baṭṭāl Ghāzī. The Romans in the region, regarding them as Christians, never embarrassed them and thus the family continued to live there as crypto-Muslims. In dream visions the Prophet Muḥammad summoned Ḳara Tegin to return to Islam and to support Artukhī in his attempt to free Efromiya from prison. The two warriors arrive in Manḳuriya, where a Greek girl called Meryem helps them to free Efromiya and other Muslim captives imprisoned in the town's citadel. Eventually, the Muslim champions kill the local lord Ḥamīrān and take hold of the town. In this way, Ḳara Tegin becomes the new *beg* of Manḳuriya and establishes his authority as an exemplary Muslim ruler along with his wife Meryem.[25]

As has been pointed out by Irène Mélikoff, except for the name and a certain geographic proximity, there are hardly any factual similarities between Charatikes and the epic Ḳara Tegin.[26] Nevertheless, the narratives of Anna Komnene and the *Dānishmand-nāma* present one theme in common, albeit from diametrically opposed perspectives. Both Anna and the Turkish epic tale focus on religious zeal as a key motive for the protagonists' actions. In Anna's version, Charatikes, upon destroying the Theotokos church in Sinope, was punished by a demon, who took possession of him while he wriggled on the ground foaming at the mouth. For his part, Emperor Alexios made every effort to win Siaous for the Christian faith. As reward for his valuable service, Siaous was made a member of the Byzantine court aristocracy and was appointed *doux* of Anchialos.[27] Hence, the emperor and Charatikes form two antipodes representing the true and the wrong faith respectively. Siaous, in turn, represents a person of mixed origin rooted in both societies, who by switching sides and adopting the Christian faith achieved considerable social advancement and gained a prestigious position within the hierarchy of the Byzantine elite.

The account of the *Dānishmand-nāma* is based on a very similar idea: Ḳara Tegin and Meryem, despite their Christian background, were attracted to the champions of Islam, converted, and excelled as members of the Muslim community. In this way, they contributed to the creation of a new political entity based on the principles of Muslim rule. After the conquest, some of the townspeople converted to Islam, whereas the rest undertook to pay *kharāj* and to settle in a suburb outside the town. On the site of Ḥamīrān's palace a mosque was erected. The new rulers appointed a *ḥāfiẓ* to teach the Quran as well as an *imām*, a *khaṭīb* (preacher), and a *ḳāḍī* (judge) from among the Muslim jurists. Ḳara Tegin and his wife distributed the goods of the town among the faithful and began to study the principles of Muslim law.[28] Without referring to specific historical facts, the epic tale epitomizes the establishment of what can be considered the most essential components of a Muslim institutional framework.

Both texts deal with the topics of conversion and counter-conversion and stress the advantages individual converts would gain by adopting the other faith. Such issues certainly became common experiences for many people in the wake of the crusades and the gradual consolidation of the Turkish-Muslim principalities in twelfth-century Asia Minor. In the context of Christian-Muslim antagonism, the historical figure of Karatekin could be portrayed in two different ways: In the collective memory of the Anatolian Turks, he became a symbol for the emergence of Muslim institutions in Paphlagonia, as is evidenced by his *türbe* in the castle of Çankırı. On the basis of stylistic elements, this building can be dated to the second half of the twelfth century and thus is quite close to the period of the Turkish conquest.[29] The new Turkish-Muslim elite of the house of Dānishmand established a site of remembrance symbolizing the beginning of a new era and a break with the Christian past. Anna, instead, placed emphasis on the demonic threat emanating from Islam, which her father confronted so successfully.

* * *

Another "chief satrap" called Elchanes appears in Anna Komnene's account as lord of Kyzikos and Apollonias on the Rhyndakos River (Mustafakemalpaşa/Orhaneli Çayı)[30] in the coastland west of Nicaea between the peninsula of Kyzikos (Kapıdağı Yarımadası) and Lake Lopadion (Ulubat Gölü).[31] Turan interprets the name as a Greek transliteration of the Turkish title *Īlkhān* and describes the man as a *beylerbey* subordinate to the ruler of Nicaea and perhaps identifiable with a governor of Nicaea called Muḥammad.[32] Both assumptions seem questionable, for the title of *Īlkhān* does not appear before the thirteenth century, and the term *archisatrapes* is used by Anna not in a technical sense indicating a hierarchy of emirs but as designation for powerful local rulers.[33] The name of the well-known Turkmen commander Hārūn b. Khān shows that the Turkish royal title could also be used as personal name, which in the case of *Elchanes* may have been combined with the Arabic article '*al*'.[34] Like the Turks of Nicaea, he was active in ravaging the littoral as far as the stronghold of Poimanenon (Eski Manyas).[35]

As Anna refers to a first seizure of Kyzikos shortly before the Komnenian *coup d'état*,[36] it seems that Turkish warriors took possession of the region in early 1081. Her account does not yield further details, and it remains unclear whether these conquerors are to be identified with Elchanes' troops. Chronologically, Anna places the Byzantine campaigns in the region and its re-conquest immediately after the takeover of Qilij Arslān in Nicaea in 1093, but it is doubtful whether all events mentioned in the relevant passage actually took place in one sequence. Elchanes is described as commanding a strong fighting force, which during the siege of Kyzikos by Byzantine troops was reinforced by a considerable number of allies coming perhaps from Bithynia or other nearby areas.[37] His retinue consisted of kinsmen and a number of high-ranking Turkish chiefs, among them a certain Skaliarios, who because of his future role as commander in the Byzantine army is mentioned by name.[38] These details point to a lordship commanding considerable military power and maintaining close relations with other Turkish rulers in western Asia Minor, by means of which it could put up effective resistance against Byzantine attacks in the southwestern part of the Propontis coastland.

According to Anna Komnene, Apollonias was besieged twice by Byzantine troops, with a first expedition under the command of Alexander Euphorbenos and a second one under Constantine Opos, both of whom were faithful generals of Alexios I and fought in operations against the Normans, the Turks, and later on the crusaders.[39] Euphorbenos led his troops on boats via the Makestos River (modern Simav/Çapraz/Susurluk Çayı) from the Propontis coast into Lake Lopadion, from where they put Apollonias under siege. Upon taking the outer walls of the town, Euphorbenos was forced to retreat because of the arrival of strong relief forces and suffered a heavy defeat while trying to escape through the mouth of the aforementioned river. The second campaign seems to have been carried out by stronger and better-equipped forces, which advanced overland, took Kyzikos and Poimanenon, and again put Apollonias under siege. This time Elchanes surrendered, apparently after entering negotiations with Opos, in which he secured generous payments and gifts for himself and his relatives.[40] Anna's report does not clarify the circumstances of Elchanes' defeat. It is tempting to think that, apart from Opos' powerful forces and the emperor's enticing offers, there were also other reasons prompting Elchanes to seek an understanding with the Byzantines. A possible explanation is that Euphorbenos' expedition occurred before Nicaea was under Apelchasem's firm control,[41] whereas Opos' campaign took place in the time after Būzān's attack on Nicaea. The Turks of Bithynia were deprived of any effective leadership in the period between Apelchasem's murder and the takeover of Qilij Arslān I. The Turkish chiefs in Apollonias could no longer expect reinforcements and may have seen entrance into the service of the imperial government as more profitable. Another motive may have been given by the example of Apelchasem, who, as holder of one of the most important Byzantine court titles, demonstrated how many political and financial benefits collaboration with Constantinople could bring.

Just as in the case of Siaous, Anna once again celebrates Alexios as a successful Christian emperor disseminating the true faith among barbarians and infidels. She evokes the idea of a mission aiming at the conversion of Muslims, not only among the Turkish nomads of Asia Minor but also in the central lands of Islam like Egypt, Libya, and Persia.[42] Presumably, Elchanes and his relatives were baptized not immediately after their surrender but at some time after being subsumed into the ranks of the Byzantine military elite. Conversion to the Christian faith was the last step in a gradual process of assimilation transforming Turkish-Muslim chieftains into Byzantine commanders and court officials. As regards the military activities of Elchanes and Skaliarios, they are mentioned as commanders of auxiliary forces in the region of Anchialos. During an attack of Kumans and Vlachs over the Danube, they were sent together with Byzantine commanders to Therma.[43] Anchialos, thus, seems to have become a region to which dignitaries of Turkish origin were commonly sent.

* * *

The Gulf of Smyrna in the 1080s became the core region of the principality of Tzachas (Çaka), certainly the most prominent figure among the Turkish potentates in western Asia Minor during the reign of Emperor Alexios I.[44] Anna Komnene's *Alexias* transmits almost all historical facts known about this person while the chronicle of John Zonaras adds some minor details. Yet in his case too scholars have tried to establish a link with the epic tradition of the *Dānishmand-nāma*, which mentions a character called Çavuldur Çaka.[45] Unlike Ḳara Tegin, however, who is one of the protagonists in a whole section, Çavuldur Çaka is mentioned only very briefly. He first appears at the beginning of the epos as a warrior sent to the coastland of Karaman and on a second occasion as one of the champions of the Holy War, who managed to reach Istanbul, to seize the city, and to defeat the emperor.[46] Certain references to naval activities and to an attack on Constantinople may lead us to think that these are reminiscences of Tzachas, but the evidence is too meagre to sustain this identification conclusively. Since the epic tradition adds no new information, we have to concentrate on the available narratives, which should be interpreted against the background of the known facts concerning western Asia Minor in the period under discussion.

While conducting raids in Asia Minor as a young man (μειράκιον), Tzachas was taken prisoner and handed over to Nikephoros III Botaneiates, who as a reward for loyal services bestowed the title of *protonobelissimos* upon him.[47] His close relationship with the Byzantine military aristocracy strongly indicates that he must have belonged to the circle of leading Turkish warlords. This is also confirmed by the fact that later on his daughter was married to the Seljuk chief of Nicaea, Qilij Arslān I.[48] Apart from that, we have no information about his origin. With Alexios I's rise to power, Tzachas lost his privileged position at court, fled to the western littoral of Asia Minor, where the imperial government in the time of the Norman war was hardly able to exert efficient control, and took possession of Smyrna. Having spent some years at the court of Constantinople,

Tzachas had certainly been influenced by the cultural values, ideology, and political concepts of the Byzantine milieu in which he had lived. The principality he came to carve out in the region of Smyrna, therefore, seems to have had a mixed Byzantine-Turkish character. His military forces consisted for the most part of Turkish warriors.[49] On the other hand, Tzachas managed to construct a fleet with the aid of local people from Smyrna,[50] and his political ambitions, apart from extending his rule over the ports and islands in the vicinity of Smyrna, were emulating Byzantine dynastic concepts of the ruling elite in Constantinople. In the negotiations with the general Constantine Dalassenos, a maternal kinsman of Alexios I, he demanded the restoration of the rights, revenues, and privileges he had formerly enjoyed at court and proposed a marriage between his own and the emperor's children.[51] Likewise, in Smyrna he is said to have used the title of *basileus* and the imperial insignia,[52] thus being one of the earliest known instances of an independent ruler employing Byzantine symbols of sovereignty at a local level, as became widespread in the second half of the twelfth century. It is hard to say what his actual ambitions were, but Anna's statement that he intended "if possible, to climb even the peak of the imperial office"[53] should be viewed in the broader political and ideological context of his activities.[54] The military advantages offered by a well-equipped fleet certainly encouraged Tzachas to undertake attacks against poorly defended coastal towns and islands, and his alliance with the Pechenegs may have caused Anna to think that his plans were directed against Constantinople.[55] On the other hand, her account makes clear that his operations were mostly limited to the Gulf of Smyrna.[56] Hence, Tzachas' lordship was, above all, a local power, and if certain actions appear as direct assaults against the Byzantine capital, they were not more than brief and isolated incidents. What actually matters is the strong dynastic character of Tzachas' political program aiming at the establishment of close relations with the ruling family.

Again, it is impossible to give an accurate chronological account of the events, but apparently in the years after 1081, while Alexios was fighting the Normans and the Pechenegs, Tzachas with the support of a local shipbuilder constructed a strong naval force and extended his sway over the coastal towns of Klazomenai (Urla) and Phokaia (Foça). Thereafter, Tzachas took possession of Mitylene in Lesbos, forcing the Byzantine governor Alopos to retreat. But Methymna on the northern coast of the island refused to surrender and received reinforcements. In the meantime, Tzachas also seized the castle of Chios. A first naval expedition under the command of Niketas Kastamonites failed and Tzachas captured many ships. But a new fleet under Constantine Dalassenos put the fortress under siege and after heavily damaging the ramparts forced the local garrison to enter peace negotiations. While the capitulation was postponed Tzachas managed to arrive with relief forces, and the fighting was resumed. The Byzantines kept the port and town of Bolissos in the island's northeastern edge under their control. As the peace talks brought no results, Tzachas retreated to Smyrna in view of the arrival of another naval force under the command of the renowned general and *doux* of Dyrrachion, John Doukas.[57] None of the islands, thus, came under the full control of Tzachas while Byzantine pressure continued to be very strong.

Nevertheless, it seems that as long as the hostilities with the Pechenegs were going on, the imperial government was unable to attack Tzachas' residence in Smyrna directly. His power reached its zenith with the escalation of the Pecheneg war and the spread of hostilities to Thrace as far as the suburbs outside the walls of Constantinople in 1090/91.[58] At that time, Tzachas further strengthened his naval forces and conducted raids from Lesbos towards the Dardanelles straits.[59] His emissaries summoned the Pecheneg leaders to occupy the Thracian Peninsula (Gelibolu Yarımadası) and strove to persuade Turkish mercenaries from the East to side with Tzachas against the emperor. Most likely, these messages were addressing soldiers of Apelchasem, who on the basis of the existing peace treaty supported the imperial troops by fending off the Pecheneg attacks.[60] One of the coastal towns, which at that stage seems to have been totally destroyed by Tzachas' raids, was Adramyttion (Edremit) situated in the gulf opposite Lesbos.[61] With the Byzantine counter-attack in the first months of 1091 and the decisive defeat of the Pechenegs at the foot of Mount Levounion on 29 April 1091,[62] Alexios put a definite halt to their destructive activities in the Balkans and thus, in the summer and autumn of 1091, was able to prepare a major campaign against Tzachas' stronghold in Smyrna itself.[63]

Farther south, the town of Ephesus, or properly speaking the fortified settlement around the church of John the Theologian (near Selçuk), was in the hands of two warlords called Tangripermes and Marakes, whose names are usually interpreted as transliterations of Turkish variants like Tanrıpermiş/Tanrıvermiş and Marak/Barak respectively.[64] Anna Komnene also alludes to some other warlords in the region but without further specifying or locating them. The picture she draws is one of ongoing naval raids directed against Chios, Rhodes, and other islands, which caused extensive devastation in the coastland.[65] Here too a certain degree of exaggeration is evident, for her account clearly intends to exalt the emperor's feats when she reports his restoration of imperial rule in these regions in 1098.[66] Yet the turmoil caused by the Turkish raids in the southwestern edge of Asia Minor is clearly reflected in contemporary imperial documents that are preserved in the archive of the monastery of St. John the Theologian in Patmos. They refer to the bestowal of landed estates in Cos and other islands to the monk Christodoulos and his companions, who in view of the Turkish threat were forced to abandon their monastic community on Mount Latros (Beşparmak near Bafa) in Caria.[67] A chrysobull issued by Alexios I in March 1085 confirms a previous donation by Nikephoros III in 1080 and explicitly refers to "the newly founded monastery." Hence, the Turkish raids can be dated to the early 1080s and have to be viewed in connection with the overall upheaval in western Asia Minor in the time of the Byzantine power struggles. Most likely, the attacks on the Latros monasteries were conducted by the Turks of Ephesus, who extended their raiding activities towards the southern coastland. In sum, the imperial government in the early 1090s succeeded in restoring its control over the Gulf of Nikomedeia and the rest of the Propontis coastland, but it proved much more difficult to check the newly established maritime powers of the Turks in Smyrna and Ephesus. For almost two decades, the Byzantine army was unable to afford any effective protection to the coastland of Lydia and Caria. This explains why the Turkish emirs were so successful in mounting their attacks on nearby islands, monasteries, and coastal towns and why sections of the local population feeling forsaken by the central government actively supported them. The fact, however, that the emperor's donations to Christodoulos concerned islands in the immediate vicinity of the coastland shows that the Turkish threat did not provoke a total collapse of Byzantine administrative structures in this area. Despite all the unrest, there must have been periods of tranquility, probably based on agreements with the local emirs, which allowed the monks to re-organize their monastic centers and develop their economic activities.[68]

Qilij Arslān I's rise to power

In the months following Malikshāh's death on 20 November 1092, Sulaymān b. Qutlumush's eldest son Qilij Arslān managed to return from the sultan's court to Asia Minor and take hold of the lordship his father had left in Nicaea.[69] Doing so, he not only secured his own and his followers' political survival during the early stage of the power struggle in the Seljuk sultanate but also ensured the preservation of the Qutlumush dynasty in Anatolia. Sulaymān's deputy Apelchasem, who had wielded power in Nicaea from the time of his lord's departure for the East in late 1084 until his assassination in 1092, had taken important steps towards the further consolidation of the Bithynian principality by warding off the attacks of Malikshāh's commanders through his coalition with the imperial government of Constantinople. He had prevented the Seljuk sultan and his representatives in Syria from extending their influence over the Turkish chiefs in the central and western parts of Anatolia. Moreover, through the peace treaty with Emperor Alexios I and the title of *sebastos* that had been granted to him, Apelchasem had gained access to the imperial household and had introduced elements of the Byzantine court hierarchy into the political practices of the Turkish ruling elite in Bithynia. Presumably, his unexpected assassination would have caused the disintegration of his lordship, had not Malikshāh's death forestalled such a development. The destabilization of Seljuk rule in Syria, which resulted from Tāj al-Dawla Tutush's grip on the sultanate, channeled the Seljuk elite's political ambitions away from Anatolia to the Muslim heartlands. Thus, Qilij Arslān was given the opportunity to build upon the foundations his predecessors had left.

The evidence concerning the circumstances of Qilij Arslān's takeover in Nicaea is, as in many other cases, highly elusive. Anna Komnene, our earliest and most detailed source, distorts the facts due to her inner-Byzantine viewpoint and the chronological distance of almost 50 years. Near-contemporary Latin, Muslim, or Eastern Christian texts are more or less silent about Qilij Arslān's rise to power. Additional evidence can only be gleaned from fourteenth-century Seljuk chronicles, which are characterized, however, by strong idealizing tendencies. A common feature of these accounts is the idea of a well-established royal lineage governed by clearly defined succession procedures transferring rights of leadership from the father to the son and legitimized through official recognition by the sultan. Although in some details there is a certain resemblance with the facts transmitted by older sources, these reports mostly present conceptions of statehood originating from the Muslim heartlands in an attempt to project the image of a fully developed political authority back into the period of the formation of Seljuk power in Anatolia.

> In short, Sulaymānshāh had two boys, Qilij Arslān and Qulān Arslān. Malikshāh gave the rule over these people to Qilij Arslān and sent him a robe of honor. He [Qilij Arslān] grew stronger day by day and once the signs of nobility and maturity became obvious in his person, as time went by, pleasing effects came into being from his actions.[70]
>
> The Sultan [Malikshāh] was angry with his brother because of this action [i.e., Tutush's killing of Sulaymān], and the rule passed over to Dāwūd, and Dāwūd became the head of this lordship [...] Dāwūd in Konya ascended the throne of the emperor in the year 480 [1087/88] and ruled for 20 years and died in the year 500 [1106/07] [...] his brother Qilij Arslān b. Sulaymān became *pādishāh* after him; he held the sultanate for 40 years.[71]

Both Aqsarā'ī and Qazwīnī, writing in the 1320s, mention a brother of Qilij Arslān, who is alternately called Qulān Arslān or Dāwūd. The former considers him as merely a close companion to his brother; the latter includes him in the list of Seljuk rulers in Konya. The existence of a brother is corroborated by Anna Komnene, and Matthew of Edessa notes that a son was born to Sulaymān in Antioch immediately after his victory over Sharaf al-Dawla of Aleppo.[72] It is impossible that this was Qilij Arslān, as the chronicler wants to make us believe, for in 1093 the latter is described as a ruler of full age. Presumably, Qilij Arslān had a younger brother, who at the time of his takeover in Nicaea may still have been an eight-year-old boy. Qazwīnī's version refers to the approximate time span of 20 years between the death of Sulaymān and that of Qilij Arslān and calculates this period as the reign of the alleged sultan Dāwūd. Ignoring Apelchasem and the actual reign of Qilij Arslān, he confuses the latter with his son Mas'ūd, who in fact died approximately 40 years after his father in 1155. Qazwīnī apparently intends to present the dynastic succession as unbroken by referring to Qilij Arslān's brother in the absence of more specific information on the post-1086 situation in Anatolia.

Other anachronistic elements of these accounts are the idea of an official investiture performed by the sultan (Aqsarā'ī) and the existence of an imperial throne (*takht-i qayṣar*) in Konya (Qazwīnī). The image of this city as residence of Qilij Arslān and his successors is certainly much older as it is found already in twelfth-century sources. Michael the Syrian puts it as follows: "When Sulaymān, the first of the Turks who ruled in Iconium, was killed, Qilij Arslān, who was the first to come to Melitene, ruled after him."[73] Accordingly, the same author labels him elsewhere as "sultan of Iconium."[74] Ibn al-Athīr employed a similar designation although he, as opposed to Michael the Syrian, does not use the title of sultan: "the lands of Qilij Arslān b. Sulaymān, which are Konya and other [territories]," "Qilij Arslān b. Sulaymān b. Qutlumush, the lord of Konya."[75]

It was mainly in the years of Masʿūd I (1116–55) that the old metropolis of Lycaonia gradually developed into the residence and capital of the Seljuk sultanate of Asia Minor, the oldest surviving archaeological evidence of which is the 1155 inscription on the *minbar* situated in the *miḥrāb* area of the Alaeddin Mosque on the citadel hill of Konya, the oldest known piece of Rūm Seljuk art.[76] The close association between Qilij Arslān I and Konya in various narrative sources reflects an awareness of the significance that the city had for the Seljuk elite, but it should be noted that no source makes mention of any activities of Qilij Arslān having to do specifically with this place. Similarly, various sources refer to Qilij Arslān's father, Sulaymān, as the conqueror of Konya, but whether he actually exerted any authority there is unknown. With the further crystallization of the Qutlumush lineage's dynastic consciousness, Masʿūd I and his successors apparently attempted to assert the importance of the place of their main residence in the historical recollections of their dynasty and to project this significance back to the early days of Sulaymān and Qilij Arslān I.

As regards the situation after the surrender of Nicaea in June 1097,[77] the information given by the Frankish historians is hardly conclusive. The *Gesta Francorum* and the authors depending on them describe Konya as a rich town, the inhabitants of which kindly received the armed pilgrims and supplied them with plenty of water and foodstuff. For its part, the town of Herakleia (Tont Kalesi near Ereğli),[78] which is situated further east near the Cilician Gates, appears as being in the hands of a strong Turkish garrison.[79] This would suggest that at that time only the strongholds close to the Taurus Mountains and Cilicia were under firm Turkish control, while the western fringes of the Anatolian plateau, at least after the first defeats of the Turks by the crusaders, turned into a sort of no-man's land. On the other hand, according to Fulcher of Chartres the whole region between Antioch of Pisidia and Herakleia had undergone extensive devastations from Turkish attacks, and thus the crusaders frequently had difficulty finding provisions.[80] Only Albert of Aachen asserts that the Christian inhabitants of Philomelion, Konya, and Herakleia were subject to the Turks of *Solimannus* (Qilij Arslān).[81] All in all, the region of Konya was heavily affected by Turkish raids, and it formed a corridor for warrior groups moving between Cilicia and the provinces of Lycaonia and Phrygia, but it was not yet permanently held by the Seljuk Turks as a strongpoint or administrative center. Albert of Aachen is the only witness who speaks about a sort of Seljuk dominion in the region. If we believe the same author, the situation changed in the years before 1101. In his report about the Lombard crusade he refers to the contingent of Count William II of Nevers, who is said to have taken the route from Ankara to Konya. There he found "a Turkish garrison and forces in the fortress." Despite fierce attacks, William's men were not able to take the city.[82] Hence, in the years after 1097 Konya actually became a well-defended fortress controlled by Turkish warriors. Presumably, this is related to the establishment of the Norman lordship of Antioch and the partial restoration of Byzantine rule in regions of western Asia Minor, two events that forced the Turks of Nicaea and other warrior groups to move the center of their political activities to the Anatolian plateau. Since Albert also refers to combined forces of Qilij Arslān and *Donimannus* (Dānishmand), who were embarrassing the Franks during their advance towards Konya,[83] it can be assumed that after the setback of 1097 the Turks in the regions between Galatia, Lycaonia, Cappadocia, and the Armenian highlands had succeeded in significantly stabilizing their military strength. In this framework, Konya became a well-protected stronghold, but there is still no evidence pointing to the existence of a residence there. After 1101, Qilij Arslān's ambitions were directed much more towards Melitene and the Upper Euphrates region than the Anatolian plateau.[84] What made Konya the actual center of the Seljuk principality was mainly determined by the post-1107 developments under Qilij Arslān's sons and successors.

Another text emphasizes the leading position of Qilij Arslān among the Turkish warlords in Asia Minor:

> When he decided to set off from Konya, he made his son Qilij Arslān heir to the throne. Qilij Arslān became the great pādishāh and all the emirs of Rūm submitted to his authority, in the beginning of his sultanate he reached Ablastayn and conquered Malatya […].[85]

The anonymous *Tārīkh-i Āl-i Saljūq* dating from the second half of the fourteenth century speaks of a kind of supreme authority of the "great pādishāh" and underlines the numerous conquests he has made. Qilij Arslān is portrayed as a powerful Muslim ruler of an outstanding lineage exerting control over a great number of emirs operating in the land of Rūm (Byzantine Asia Minor). Hence, Konya as the place of the pādishāh's throne appears as the political center of the land of Rūm. To sum up, the Muslim source material is largely dominated by anachronistic views reflecting the dynastic memory of the Seljuk sultanate of Anatolia at the heyday of its power. Western sources exclusively focus on Qilij Arslān's role in his conflicts with the Frankish crusaders, thus allowing us to draw some conclusions about the situation in the Anatolian plateau in the years 1097–1101. As useful as the crusader sources are, they have limitations; we may find even more accurate insight into the circumstances of Qilij Arslān's takeover in Nicaea and his subsequent activities in the writings of Anna Komnene.

When Apelchasem set off on his trip to the court of Sultan Malikshāh, her account goes, it was his brother Poulchazes who took control of Nicaea. During this short period of several months between 1092 and 1093, Emperor Alexios I made another attempt to recover the city by means of diplomacy. Assuming that the Turkish leaders were weakened by their chief's absence, he sent an emissary to Nicaea, who promised rich gifts if Poulchazes would hand over the city. Poulchazes pretended to be willing to do so but protracted the negotiations, sending one message after the other and biding his time, for he expected Apelchasem's return.[86] It becomes clear thus that the Turkish commanders in Nicaea still preferred to hold out whereas the emperor was not strong enough to exert any military pressure.

While these attempts came to nothing, Sulaymān's two sons, who are said to have been imprisoned by Malikshāh, managed to escape after the sultan's unexpected death and headed straight back to Nicaea. Anna describes their take-over in their father's former stronghold as a joyful event, giving rise to a sequence of spontaneous decisions.

> When the people in Nicaea (οἱ ἐντὸς Νικαίας) saw them, they received them joyfully like in a tumultuous gathering (δημοκρατοῦντες οἷον περιχαρῶς ἐδέξαντο), and Poulchazes readily handed Nicaea over to them just like a share of the paternal inheritance. The firstborn of the two, who is called Klitziasthlan, was proclaimed sultan. This man invited the women and children of those who at that time were present in Nicaea and settled them there, thus turning this city into a residence of sultans, as one might say (σουλτάνων [...] κατοικητήριον). While arranging the affairs of Nicaea in this way, he removed Poulchazes from power and entrusted the government over the satraps who were in Nicaea to the *archisatrapes* Mouchoumet. Thus he left the town and set off for Melitene.[87]

No doubt, this complicated succession procedure could hardly have been carried out in such a spontaneous manner but required careful preparation through a series of preliminary contacts and negotiations. Apparently, the phrase οἱ ἐντὸς Νικαίας means the Turkish ruling elite and their soldiers, not the Christian population of the city, and thus is synonymous with τῶν [...] ἐν Νικαίᾳ παρόντων and τῶν ἐν Νικαίᾳ ὄντων σατραπῶν. The Turkish commanders deemed it advantageous to implement a dynastic rule based on the succession of the descendants of Sulaymān b. Qutlumush. Although six to seven years had passed since the latter's death, it seems that the idea of having a ruler originating from an illustrious branch of the Seljuk family still constituted a unifying force among the Turkish warriors.

This attitude is also reflected in some of the older Arabic accounts of the death of Sulaymān in the battle of ʿAyn Saylam. Ibn al-ʿAdīm, for instance, refers to Tāj al-Dawla Tutush, who is said to have easily identified Sulaymān's bloodstained body among the dead on the battlefield since (as he stated) "his foot resembles my foot, for the feet of the sons of Saljūq resemble each other."[88] According to the same report, Tutush also performed a public act of repentance, expressing his grief about his relative's death by shedding tears and uttering formulas of penitence in the Turkish language. Eventually, Sulaymān's body was buried in a solemn funeral ceremony. Tutush wrapped the corpse in a precious shroud, said a prayer, and let it be transported to Aleppo, where he was interred side-by-side with his former opponent Muslim b. Quraysh.[89] It can be assumed that the members of the Seljuk dynasty in the years of Sultan Malikshāh had actually developed a strong sense of belonging to a select group of people determined to rule.

This fits perfectly with the way Anna Komnene describes Qilij Arslān's rise to power in Nicaea. Turkish warlords in Asia Minor and the Muslim lands were tempted to use the prestige of members of the Seljuk family to achieve their political objectives. The Turks of Nicaea succumbed to this temptation and recognized Qilij Arslān as their ruler. In spite of this, it may be surmised that Qilij Arslān had to make concessions in order to be accepted by Poulchazes and his companions. Anna's wording is highly elusive, but, if we accept the details mentioned in this report, in all likelihood the settlement of wives and children within the city indicates that houses and landed estates were granted to Turkish warriors. Given that Nicaea was never seized by force, it seems that until 1093 the Turkish presence within the city was limited to the installation of a garrison for defense purposes and the levy of taxes from the local population. With Qilij Arslān's takeover, Nicaea was transformed into a residential city of the Turkish elite, which may have entailed the adaptation of buildings to the needs of the new owners, perhaps also the transformation of churches into mosques.[90] The citadel district of Konya, which may have already possessed a Byzantine fortress at the time of the Seljuk takeover, seems to have played a central role in this process. It has been assumed that either the church of St. Amphilochios, later on known as Eflatun Mesjid, or more likely an older church building that existed on the site of the Alaeddin mosque was used as first Friday mosque of Konya.[91]

It remains doubtful, however, whether one should accept Anna's phraseology regarding the proclamation of the sultan. The word δημοκρατοῦντες, which seems to refer to the gathering of a big crowd of people, suggests a public ceremony in which the Turkish soldiers officially welcomed Qilij Arslān and escorted him into the town. He seems to have been proclaimed their leader with the consent of these people, but the title of sultan presupposes an official bestowal by the caliph and thus could not be obtained through such a ceremony.[92] Be that as it may, Qilij Arslān, as a result of this proclamation, became the head of a loyal group of Turkish warlords who were transforming Nicaea and its environs into a power base for their political and military activities in Bithynia and other regions of Asia Minor. Qilij Arslān's prestige certainly increased the attractiveness of Nicaea for other chieftains operating in the region at that time. The *archisatrapes* Mouchoumet, (Muḥammad), who according to Anna was appointed governor of Nicaea, i.e., commander of the garrison and/or head of the local administration of tax revenues, most likely belonged to the circle of Qilij Arslān's close intimates or was a high-ranking dignitary from the time of Qilij's predecessors.[93] It remains unclear whether this appointment took place in the course of the establishment of the new ruler or later on but before Qilij Arslān's departure for Melitene in 1096.[94]

Unfortunately, Anna refers nowhere to the indigenous population and its involvement in these procedures. Apparently, for the time being a *modus vivendi* had been achieved, and there were no attempts aiming at a restoration of the imperial administration. Nor is it possible to find any evidence for the fate of the Byzantine land-holding aristocracy. More specifically, it cannot be said if and to what degree the better-off people abandoned their holdings, were expelled, or subsumed into the newly established principality. The information provided by the crusader chronicles,[95] at least, points to some extent of unbroken continuity in agricultural production, urban economic activities, and the social fabric of the subject population.

Qilij Arslān I's network of alliances

The establishment of relations with Turkish potentates in other parts of Asia Minor was a pre-condition for the further consolidation of Qilij Arslān's principality in Bithynia and adjacent regions. After the short-lived lordship of Elchanes in the Propontis coastland quickly succumbed to the attacks of Emperor Alexios I,[96] Tzachas of Smyrna became the leading power in the western coastland of Asia Minor in the years before 1091. Nothing is known about how Tzachas and Qilij Arslān first came into contact, but it seems that the two lords started to collaborate almost immediately after the proclamation of the latter in Nicaea. Their alliance was strengthened by Qilij Arslān's marriage to a daughter of Tzachas.[97] Both sides profited from this arrangement. Qilij Arslān could henceforth rely upon the support of Tzachas' military forces stationed in the western littoral of Asia Minor, whereas the latter bolstered his position through his personal ties with a branch of the prestigious Seljuk family and other Turkish chieftains in central Anatolia. Besides the integration of Turkish warriors into the social fabric of urban centers, the development of networks in order to increase influence and military strength was clearly a highly effective instrument of consolidation.

On the other hand, the potentates could not afford to risk dangerous conflicts by lending reckless support to one of their allies. Hence, it would not have been in Qilij Arslān's interest to be drawn into a major clash with the Byzantine government, because of his alliance with Tzachas.[98] With his attack in 1093 against the straits of the Hellespont near Abydos,[99] the emir of Smyrna seriously undermined Constantinople's strategy of keeping the Propontis coast under its firm control until Byzantine military forces were strong enough to move further inland. Under these circumstances, Qilij Arslān decided to continue his predecessors' policy of peaceful relations with the Byzantine emperor and to turn against his father-in-law. He may also have hoped to extend his sway over his ally's territories by using Tzachas' daughter as a means to establish the legitimacy of his claim over them. Anna Komnene presents these events primarily as the result of her father's shrewd scheming aimed at dividing the Turkish rulers. Her report is embroidered by various literary clichés underlining the Turks' moral inferiority.[100] Moreover, Anna quotes a letter the emperor is said to have sent to the Seljuk emir in order to highlight strategic and ideological aspects of their alliance.

> You know, most glorious sultan Qilij Arslān, that the sultanate (τὸ σουλτανικὸν ἀξίωμα) belongs to you as an inheritance from your father. Even if your father-in-law Tzachas by all appearances takes up arms against the empire of the Romans by calling himself *basileus*, this is but an evident pretext. As he is a very experienced man, it cannot remain hidden from him and he knows very well that the empire of the Romans does not belong to him and that it is impossible to take hold of such a dominion. The whole enterprise, no doubt, is directed against you. Therefore, you should not tolerate him nor should you draw back, but you should be vigilant so that you will not be removed from your dominion. With God's support, I will banish him from territories

> subject to the empire of the Romans. Since I am troubling myself on your account, I ask you to take care for your own dominion and principality. You should hasten to subjugate him either with a peace proposal or, should he refuse, with the sword.[101]

Although Anna Komnene is generally considered trustworthy as regards quotations of official letters and charters, it is unlikely that Qilij Arslān in 1093 would have been addressed as μεγαλοδοξότατε σουλτάν. What is authentic in Anna's quotation, however, is the emperor's assertion of the son's hereditary right to the father's throne, by which the imperial government articulated its recognition of Qilij Arslān's political authority and dynastic legitimacy. Certainly, one may wonder why Constantinople should have openly accepted an independent potentate's sovereignty in a region that less than 15 years earlier was still part of the empire. Yet the argument tallies fully with the treaty of 1081 and the subsequent agreements with Apelchasem and Poulchazes, according to which the Turks' presence in Nicaea was tolerated as long as they would abstain from raids in the coastland. The novelty of this letter lies in the fact that Constantinople for the first time explicitly acknowledges the dynastic rights of the descendants of Sulaymān b. Qutlumush. Given that Qilij Arslān had just gained power in Nicaea, the ideological backing offered by the imperial government must have been especially welcome. It gave him the opportunity to present himself to all potential opponents as the legitimate heir to the Seljuk ruling dynasty who enjoyed the esteem and favor of the Byzantine emperor. In exchange, Alexios received Qilij Arslān's support in denouncing Tzachas as an illegitimate usurper who was to be removed from power. In order to do so, Tzachas had to be defamed as an enemy of the empire and traitor against his son-in-law, whom the emperor's letter presents as the main target of Tzachas' aggression. Rhetorical persuasion had to prevent the two Turkish potentates from joining forces against the empire.

It is doubtful whether Qilij Arslān was actually convinced by this argument. Apart from the political benefits resulting from an alliance with the emperor, the ruler of Nicaea may have been wary of Tzachas' expansionist plans in the region of Abydos and the Dardanelles straits, a strategic point of outstanding importance. Qilij Arslān most probably knew that such a move would have brought the emir of Smyrna dangerously close to his sphere of influence in nearby Bithynia.[102] This might have been the real reason lying behind the Seljuk emir's decision to side with the imperial government and to do away with his father-in-law. As a result, Tzachas suddenly found himself trapped by the Byzantine army, Qilij Arslān's forces, and the garrison of Abydos. His only way out was to seek an understanding with his former ally by resuming negotiations in a personal meeting.

The rest of the story is described by Anna as a treacherous act against the Seljuk emir's father-in-law.[103] As for the murderous outcome of this conflict, she explicitly accuses the Turks' barbarian mentality, but one may wonder to what extent it was the emperor who was pulling the strings behind the scenes. The report consists of a series of commonplaces of betrayal: Qilij Arslān receives Tzachas friendly and joyfully; as is customary, the table is set and the two potentates share a joint meal, during which Qilij Arslān sees to it that his father-in-law becomes drunk and then kills him with his own hands. Thereafter an embassy is sent to Constantinople to negotiate a peace treaty. The way in which Anna so closely combines the two events certainly suggests a causal link, but further details cannot be known. Anna tells us that Alexios accepted the Turkish ruler's request, but it is evident that the two sides were equally interested in affirming their peaceful relations with a new treaty.[104] Again the author points to the "usual procedure" without dwelling on the details of the negotiations or the clauses of the treaty.[105]

Anna's concluding phrase "the coastal regions remained intact"[106] indicates that, due to the defeat of Elchanes in Apollonias and the failure of Tzachas' attack on the Dardanelles straits, Byzantine dominance in the Propontis coastland was decisively strengthened. In addition, it can be assumed that in 1090 the city of Nikomedeia was restored to Byzantine rule. This was due to an expedition of 500 Frankish horsemen, who had been sent to Constantinople by Robert of Flanders in the time of the Pecheneg attacks in Thrace. The emperor ordered them to guard the region of Nikomedeia against attacks of Apelchasem.[107] Hence, in all likelihood, the Drakon borderline of 1081 was no longer valid and the imperial government had managed to extend its sway over the Peninsula of Thynia (Kocaeli) and the Gulf of Nikomedeia. Yet, the elimination of Tzachas hardly brought about major changes in the political situation of western Asia Minor. The fact that Anna Komnene in her report on the siege of Antioch by the crusaders continues to speak about Tzachas of Smyrna is certainly an error,[108] but it shows that, after the emir's assassination in 1093, the city and its environs remained in the hands of his warriors, perhaps under the command of one of his sons or close relatives. Nevertheless, Tzachas' violent death curbed the Turkish chief's ambitions for expansion in the coastland. In this respect, the peace treaty of 1093 brought about a certain stabilization until the emergence of the next major upheaval caused by the arrival of the crusading hosts in 1096. Accordingly, in the years 1093–95 Alexios I could devote himself to campaigns against Serbian chiefs in the Balkans without facing any serious challenges in Asia Minor.[109]

The only episode of this period that Anna considered worth recording is the construction of fortifications in the region of Nikomedeia.[110] Her account refers to the Black Sea coastland west and east of the mouth of the Sangarios River, which Turkish invaders were seemingly crossing without meeting obstacles, whence they proceeded as far as the Gulf of Nikomedeia.[111] Anna mainly explains this by the fact that nobody prevented them from passing through the land of the Maryandenoi, i.e., the coastland around Herakleia (Ereğli).[112] Since the center of Qilij Arslān's lordship was located southwest of Nikomedeia, Anna's geographical description does not match the realm of the Turks of Nicaea, who seemingly abided by their treaty with the emperor. Apparently, these were different warrior groups, who were perhaps based in Herakleia or somewhere further east in the Pontus region and threatened the Bithynian coastland with their attacks. The association of Gangra, Kastamona, and other Paphlagonian towns with the relevant epic tradition may suggest that these were warriors subject to the principality of Dānishmand,[113] but there is no positive evidence attesting to raids from the

Dānishmandid territories across the Sangarios River. The fortifications designed to protect an ancient manmade channel connecting Lake Baane (Sabanca Gölü) with the Sangarios River.[114] Alexios decided to make this channel deeper and to erect a strong fortress called *Sidera* near the junction between the channel and the river in order to prevent invading bands from advancing westward.[115] The most remarkable aspect of this defensive measure is the fact that the Byzantine government had managed to restore its control over a substantial strip of land stretching from the Gulf of Nikomedeia as far as the western banks of the Sangarios River. This is another indication that Byzantine troops continued to hold sway over Thynia and with small steps were advancing further inland.

Alexios' defensive measures in Bithynia chronologically coincide with Qilij Arslān's eastward advance towards Melitene (Malatya). The available sources do not explain the reasons for the Turkish chief's sudden involvement in the affairs of the Euphrates region, but most likely, as in his flight to Asia Minor in 1093, this decision had to do with the developments in northern Syria and Upper Mesopotamia after Tutush's death in early 1095. With the collapse of the administrative structures built up by Sultan Malikshāh, the whole region once again turned into an area of fierce strife among numerous competing forces, both Christian and Muslim. Controlling Melitene offered Qilij Arslān the possibility to extend his power towards the Pyramos/Jayḥān Valley, the towns and fortresses situated along the course of the Euphrates farther south, and the Diyār Bakr province.

The fragmentation that resulted from the new conflicts starting in 1095 was also an opportunity for making easy conquests and enormous profit. Qilij Arslān may also have hoped to be able to compete with the Seljuk chiefs in Syria, Tutush's sons Riḍwān and Duqāq, in creating a new network of vassals and allies among the Turkmen warlords in the region. At the height of his power, Tutush would have been much too strong for Qilij Arslān. Syria and Mesopotamia, no doubt, were much more attractive than western or central Asia Minor, where the ambitions of the Byzantine imperial government in combination with an overwhelmingly Greek-speaking population posed a constant threat to Qilij Arslān's principality. There, moreover, the economies of the urban centers and the revenues from agriculture and trade were of much smaller size than those in the regions beyond the Euphrates and the Anti-Taurus Mountains, which were closely connected with the trade routes of the Muslim central lands.[116] These may have been some of the incentives prompting Qilij Arslān to turn his attention back towards the East. It is unlikely that at that stage the Seljuk chief already anticipated the military operations he would later carry out in Upper Mesopotamia, but a stronghold on the banks of the Euphrates doubtlessly constituted a pre-condition for extending his sway over the old Byzantine-Muslim borderland and for maintaining contacts with other Turkish groups in the Muslim lands.

The siege of Melitene can be dated quite accurately on the basis of Michael the Syrian. According to his account, Saʿīd bar Ṣabūnī, a prolific theologian writing in Syriac and Greek, was ordained metropolitan of Melitene on Ascension Day (22 May 1096) in Qanrat near Āmid and thereafter entered the city of Melitene while it was attacked by the Turks and "the sultan of Konya" laid siege to it.[117]

With the advance of the crusader army towards Nicaea in early May 1097, Qilij Arslān was forced to return to western Anatolia.[118] One can safely assume that the siege lasted a little less than a year. Between May and July 1097, we find him fighting against the Frankish host outside the walls of Nicaea and in the bloody battle of Dorylaion before he withdrew with the rest of his army into the interior of Anatolia.[119] As will be shown in the following chapter in more detail, these defeats were heavy blows to the power and prestige Qilij Arslān had gained ever since his takeover in 1093. Bithynia and other parts of western Asia Minor slipped away from his control, and it is unclear whether by 1097 he was able to exert any authority in the provinces of Lycaonia and Cappadocia. This goes a long way towards explaining why Qilij Arslān after his failure at Dorylaion suddenly disappeared from the scene, being completely absent both during the siege of Antioch by the crusaders and the attacks of Dānishmand against Melitene.

Philaretos Brachamios and the Byzantine-Armenian aristocracy

The Armenian provinces in the East and the Anti-Taurus region, which since the 1060s and 1070s were transit zones for Turkmen warrior groups or passed under the rule of local emirs, had a fate unlike that of the southwestern section of the borderland stretching from Cilicia to the Diyār Muḍar province. It was during the civil strife between Romanos IV Diogenes and the Doukas clan that the Armenian officer Chatatourios, who had been appointed *doux* of Antioch in 1069 and was a fervent supporter of the dethroned emperor, managed to exert some degree of independent rule over much of Cilicia and the ducate of Antioch.[120] With Diogenes' defeat in the spring of 1072, Chatatourios too lost his position, and for some years Antioch came under the direct rule of Constantinople. Yet the Byzantine-Armenian aristocracy, which at that time began to establish itself in the region, largely escaped imperial control. From 1072 onwards Philaretos Brachamios began to carve out his lordship from his strongholds in Marʿash, Lykandos, Samosata, and Melitene.[121] Subsequently, this potentate managed to unite a large part of the local Armenian and Syrian aristocracy, the most important urban centers of the region, and the ecclesiastical leadership under the umbrella of his authority. Thus, he maintained a semi-independent status vis-à-vis the imperial government while impeding the penetration of these areas by Turkmen groups. Philaretos gradually extended his sway over the cities of Cilicia and the two key points in this Byzantine frontier region, Antioch and Edessa.[122] Although, in the absence of detailed reports, it is difficult to reconstruct the various steps in the formation of this political entity, Philaretos' powerful position in this vast area until the Seljuk conquest of Antioch in late 1084 shows that he mainly benefited from the vacuum of power resulting from Byzantine civil strife and the overall instability in the neighboring Muslim regions.

The lead seals surviving from his rule show that, on the condition of his formal recognition of Nikephoros III's and Alexios I's suzerainty, he was granted the office of δομέστικος [τῶν σχολῶν] τῆς Ἀνατολῆς in conjunction with important court titles, such as *kouropalates*, *sebastos*, and *protosebastos*.[123] In this way he was subsumed into the circle of the highest court dignitaries. He liaised with the ruling dynasty and held a position that under normal conditions would have invested him with substantial military power.[124] In the years 1078–84, these titles were still important signifiers of legitimacy warranting his claims to political authority over the aforesaid regions and projecting a semblance of imperial rule embodied by his person. Yet there is no scrap of evidence indicating that he was acting on behalf of the emperor or was supported by Byzantine troops.[125] Philaretos exerted his authority just as independently as did the Turkish potentates Apelchasem and Qilij Arslān in Bithynia or Tzachas in Smyrna. For many years, there was no other major potentate, Christian or Muslim, who would have been in a position to lay claim to Philaretos' territories. At the same time, the latter successfully expanded his cluster of allies and subordinate princelings within the Armenian aristocracy and church while exploiting Byzantine political concepts in order to enhance his authority.

It was only with the centralizing efforts of the much more powerful forces of Sultan Malikshāh and the firm establishment of Seljuk rule in northern Syria that Philaretos' principality came to ruin. After the loss of Antioch to Sulaymān b. Qutlumush in late 1084, he failed to gain the sultan's recognition as his vassal and consequently retreated to Marʿash. Thus, most of his territories were quickly seized either by Seljuk commanders acting on behalf of Malikshāh or by Turkish potentates invading from Cappadocia or central Anatolia.[126] Nevertheless, one can hardly speak of a full-scale conquest of these regions. What actually happened was a gradual disintegration of Philaretos' principality that was largely conditioned by the accessibility of individual regions: The cities of the Cilician plain were seized by the warriors of Sulaymān b. Qutlumush and other Turkish chiefs from Anatolia. Antioch and Edessa became residences of Seljuk commanders within months after Malikshāh's campaign. The situation was much more complicated in the adjacent mountain regions, in which various pockets of retreat consisting of some impregnable strongholds came into being. For the most part, those occupying these fortresses were members of the local Byzantine-Armenian aristocracy. They had originally belonged to Philaretos' retinue and, after his fall, continued to maintain bonds of kinship and a certain ideological cohesion based on shared religion and Byzantine imperial ideology. Their political attitudes and survival strategies were determined by the threats emanating from the powerful Seljuk presence in northern Syria and Upper Mesopotamia and, from 1097/98 onwards, by the establishment of crusader principalities in Antioch and Edessa, which became a third power in the region.

In order to give a full account of the structure of a particular hegemonic group, it is of the utmost importance to determine the means and mechanisms by which it maintained its independence, developed forms of cooperation with the Turkish-Muslim elite and the Frankish potentates, or integrated itself into the Seljuk-Muslim system of rule. Generally speaking, one comes across a broad range of interactions irrespective of ethnic and religious boundaries: We see

Christian garrisons fighting side-by-side with Muslim forces, Armenian or Greek dignitaries being appointed governors on behalf of Turkish overlords, and Armenian patriarchs negotiating their flocks' rights with the Seljuk sultan. Warfare certainly continued or was resumed from time to time, but the primary objective of the Turkish rulers in the consolidation period after 1086 was the implementation of a workable *modus vivendi* and effective administrative tools securing incomes and stability. These efforts have to be seen in connection with the general framework of Sultan Malikshāh's centralizing policy and his attempts to create a stable balance of power among the Seljuk potentates in Syria and Upper Mesopotamia. In the course of this process the sultanate and the Abbasid caliphate became central points of reference for religious matters and basic principles of political ideology. Most intriguingly, the Christian subjects living in Seljuk territories were obviously involved in this procedure and, if the need arose, could appeal to the sultan's supreme authority.

The picture we get from the sources remains unavoidably fragmentary because we depend almost exclusively on Christian sources referring to the regions in question, whereas Muslim authors are mostly silent about the relations of Seljuk chiefs with their non-Muslim subjects. Most of the information we have concerns Cilicia and the Pyramos/Jayḥān region, Melitene, and Edessa. The most detailed accounts are transmitted in the chronicle of Matthew of Edessa. In contrast to his often extremely negative and emotionally charged descriptions of the Turkish raids in the previous decades, he frequently expresses very positive and laudatory assessments of the Muslim rulers operating in the region in this later period. Accordingly, Sultan Malikshāh during his Syrian campaign is not depicted as a merciless conqueror like his father Alp Arslan, but as a man full of "benevolence, gentleness, and compassion for the Christians," who "showed fatherly affection for all the inhabitants of the lands."[127] Likewise, Aqsunqur of Aleppo is characterized as "benevolent and pacific, kind to everyone, and a benefactor of peoples,"[128] and Malikshāh's maternal uncle Ismāʿīl b. Yāqūtī is depicted as "a benevolent and very merciful man," who after being appointed governor of Armenia made the land "prosper once again" and protected all monasteries.[129] An exception was Yaghī Siyān of Antioch, who appears as "a vicious, vile, invidious and savage-minded man."[130] This person does not figure very prominently in Matthew's chronicle. His role as defender of Antioch during the siege by the crusaders is not especially emphasized,[131] and there are only a few other occasions in which he comes to the foreground. Most likely, his role as loyal companion of Tutush in the civil strife with Barkyāruq explains his bad reputation. In particular, the chronicle mentions an assault on an otherwise unknown Armenian castle called Zarinak/Zōrinak, where he is said to have "slaughtered an innumerable amount of Christians."[132] It is also remarkable that the transition from Christian to Muslim rule in some cases is presented as a positive event causing "great rejoicing." This applies to the city of Edessa, where "the wicked Philaretos" is said to have appointed as governor a Greek eunuch bearing the title of *parakoimomenos*, who in turn was assassinated by a certain Parsama. This man had to face the three-month siege of the city by Būzān, which caused famine and despair among the inhabitants. Accordingly, Parsama's surrender on the basis of a guarantee of safety for the townspeople is described as a joyful event.[133] It is certainly an exaggeration to interpret these statements along with Turkish scholars as an indication that Armenian Christians actually preferred Turkish-Muslim rule to that of the crusaders.[134] Yet they point to workable forms of co-existence, in which local monasteries and clerics had managed to secure conditions of safety and economic prosperity in exchange for the ecclesiastical leaders' willingness to show political loyalty and to mediate between Christian subjects and Muslim overlords.

Christian rulers frequently acknowledged the sovereignty of Turkish potentates as a result of negotiations and agreements, although these efforts did not always have the expected outcome. After the loss of Antioch in 1084, Philaretos tried to secure at least the remaining parts of his territories by presenting himself with loads of precious gifts before Sultan Malikshāh and paying him homage. According to Matthew, the sultan treated him with contempt so that Philaretos, in an act of despair, even adopted the Muslim faith.[135] The actual circumstances of his conversion cannot be accurately reconstructed. Michael the Syrian suggests that Philaretos abjured the Christian faith as part of his submission in order to obtain diplomas from the sultan and the caliph granting him his lands.[136] Both authors agree that the apostate eventually had no benefit from his conversion and lost his territories despite all attempts to curry favor. "Having lost both his faith (*haymānūthā*) and his principality (*rēshānūthā*)," Michael adds, he died in Marʿash.[137]

More successful seems to have been the mission of another Greek governor belonging to Philaretos' circle, Gabriel of Melitene (*Gabhrā'īl*).[138] He was the last of a series of known commanders in this city, namely Theodore, the son of Hetum (*Todorūs bar Hetūm*), who is called a "Greek," i.e., an Armenian of Chalcedonian denomination, the Armenian Hāreb, and a certain Balāṭīnūs.[139] According to their seals, both Theodore and Gabriel held the office of *doux* or *amīr* and bore the title of *kouropalates* and *protokouropalates/protonobelissimos* respectively and thus enjoyed the same rank as Philaretos before his promotion to the rank of *sebastos* by Alexios I.[140] Gabriel is said to have sent his wife to the caliphal court of Baghdad in order to obtain a letter granting him the city of Melitene (*kthābhā dh-mezdqīn lēh rēshānūthā dh-Mīlīṭīnī*).[141] The reason given for this action is that "the Turks have defeated the Greeks," a laconic phrase that perfectly epitomizes the results of the breakdown of Byzantine administration in the region. Philaretos' principality had vanished; the Upper Euphrates region had turned into a transit area for Turkmen warrior groups moving back and forth between central Anatolia and northern Syria. Consequently, the only legitimizing authority respected by the Muslim potentates in the region was the court of Baghdad. Hence, sending his wife as petitioner on his behalf to the caliph was the only chance Gabriel had to secure his position under the threat of incessant sieges and the internal discords he had with the Syrian population and ecclesiastical representatives. The city was eventually conquered by Dānishmand Ghāzī on 18 September 1101.[142]

A different course of affairs can be observed in the city of Edessa, where Būzān appointed a Turkish officer (*sālār*) called *Khulukh* in 1087.[143] After Būzān's death in 1094, Tutush is said to have employed Theodore/T'oros, the son of Hetum, apparently the same person who had previously served as lieutenant of Philaretos in Melitene.[144] With the downfall of Tutush's rule in early 1095, Theodore, for a brief period until the arrival of Baldwin's forces, established an independent rule by means of appropriating legitimating elements of the imperial court.[145] Gabriel and Theodore, apart from their common bonds of allegiance with Philaretos, were also relatives by marriage, for Gabriel was father-in-law or brother-in-law of the latter.[146] It is evident that the Byzantine-Armenian nobility residing in places of Philaretos' former realm preserved a strong sense of cohesion relying on a common religious identity—they were Orthodox in contrast to the overwhelming majority of the local populace adhering to the Armenian dogma—and on close inter-familial relations. The persistence of elements related to the Byzantine administrative system and court hierarchy points to a common political ideology rooted in Constantinopolitan imperial concepts. As regards the Muslim environment these people came to live in, just as Gabriel managed to obtain a diploma of appointment issued by the caliph, Theodore was invested by Tāj al-Dawla Tutush, i.e., a man who in the eyes of his followers was the legitimate sultan of the Seljuk Empire. Through a switch of allegiance from Constantinople to the Muslim sovereigns in Syria and Iraq, remnants of the Byzantine aristocracy in the Upper Euphrates region became a part of the newly established institutional framework of the Seljuk sultanate. They inserted themselves into this framework along with their social network, their religious tenets, and their ideological self-awareness.

Similar processes were at work in the ecclesiastical sector: The Armenian patriarch of Ani, Barsegh Pahlavuni (1081–1105) set off in 1090 for a mission to Sultan Malikshāh accompanied by a considerable number of dignitaries and carrying a large amount of gifts.[147] If we believe Matthew's account, his endeavor was crowned by full success. Facing serious harassments and heavy levies imposed upon churches, monasteries, and bishoprics, the *catholicos* requested and obtained written guarantees exempting Armenian clergymen and monks from all dues. Barsegh's paying homage to the sultan was rewarded by honorable treatment, decrees confirming the privileges of the church, and a group of eminent persons assigned to the patriarch. Thus he achieved not only an essential improvement of the status of the Armenian church under Seljuk rule but also an elevation of his own position, which allowed him to present himself as a spiritual leader endowed with the favor and respect of the sultan. After his return from the Seljuk court, Barsegh undertook a trip through all the provinces under his jurisdiction, which led him from the Jayḥān district to Edessa, Kaisareia in Cappadocia, and Antioch.

The ecclesiastical representatives proved to be an important instrument for the implementation and stabilization of Seljuk rule in the former marches of the Byzantine Empire. The laudatory expressions used by Matthew for Malikshāh and other Turkish rulers should not be regarded as lip service to new political authorities or as indicative of the Christians' enthusiasm for liberal Muslim rule,[148] but as statements reflecting the successful incorporation of the old Byzantine-Armenian secular and ecclesiastical elite into the nascent structures of the Seljuk administration. Matthew's rejoicing certainly results from the well-being of the Armenian Christians in total but has also much to do with the fact that the ecclesiastical hierarchy secured its power, wealth, and status. Moreover, it reflects awareness that the decay of the Byzantine government eventually resulted in the emergence of a new order, in which the church enjoyed the protection of the sultanate and, for their part, the leading clerics supported the implementation of Muslim rule over the Christian population.

Armenian aristocrats and Turkish invaders in Cilicia

Despite Philaretos' temporary ascendency, the Armenian aristocratic clans penetrating Cilicia from the early 1070s onwards developed separately from the potentates in the Euphrates region. They contrived their own strategies for carving out their lordships and faced the challenges posed by the neighboring Turkish-Muslim powers. Emperor Michael VII appointed Aplgharip Artzruni, a scion of a noble lineage originating from Vaspurakan, *strategos* of Tarsus, and added the adjacent castles of Lambrun, Papeṙawn, and perhaps Mamistra to his jurisdiction.[149] In about 1073, Gagik, the Bagratid ex-king of Ani, who had settled with his retinue in Cappadocia, came to visit Aplgharip in Tarsus, but their negotiations—most likely regarding a matrimonial alliance—ended in intense discord. Eventually, Gagik was assassinated by a group of local Greek magnates.[150] Taking advantage of the presence of Armenian warlords in Cilicia, Aplgharip created a network of vassals serving as commanders of strongholds on his behalf. One of his most important followers was Ōshin, an Armenian lord from Ganjak, who was allotted the castle of Lambrun and, thereafter, married a daughter of Aplgharip. On the basis of his position, he was able to succeed his father-in-law after the latter's death in 1078.[151]

A very similar process can be observed with respect to the Rupenid lordship in the region of the Upper Saros (Seyhan) Valley.[152] The elusive evidence of the available sources points to the province of Khanzit east of Melitene as the family's place of origin and suggests links with Gagik II in Cappadocia. Certain reports point to a massive dispersion of Armenian vassals after the ex-king's assassination in 1073 and allow us to conclude that the Rupenids, too, started their expansionist efforts after this event.[153] The sources are confused in matters of chronology and disagree as to whether Rupen or his son and successor Kostandin/Constantine has to be considered the actual founder of the principality. The starting point of Rupen's political activities in the region seems to have been the town and district of Kōsitar/Kopitaṙ (Bostan Kalesi), which can be identified with the village and river valley of Gök Dere situated about 10 miles northwest of the subsequent center of Rupenid power in Sis (Kozan). From there, Rupen and his son from about 1076/77 onwards extended their sphere of influence over other castles and villages in the region, such as Kōṙomozol (Gürümze), Barjrberd (Meydan Kalesi), and Vahka (Feke). In the vicinity of the latter one finds Rupen's and Constantine's burial place and a first dynastic site of remembrance, the monastery of Kastaghawn (Karakilise).[154] Rupen's and Constantine's death dates are a matter of controversy, but certain indications seem to support the years 1093 and 1100, respectively.[155]

There are reports about the transfer of relics from the Armenian families' lands of origin and about the foundation of monasteries and churches, which in some cases were dynastic burial places and became centers of commemoration. These features bear witness to the gradual introduction into Cilicia of Armenian ideological concepts, religious traditions, and political practices, which came to merge with the local Greek cultural substrate and Byzantine institutions. Aplgharip, for instance, was both a representative of the imperial government bearing the title of *magistros* and an Armenian feudal lord building up a largely independent principality in collaboration with other Armenian aristocrats.[156]

We have very insufficient information about the Turkish penetration of the Cilician plain in the time prior to the First Crusade.[157] The chronicle of Sibṭ b. al-Jawzī transmits two short notes mentioning conquests of Sulaymān b. Qutlumush in Cilicia. The first note under the year 475/1 June 1082–20 May 1083 refers to the seizure of "the fortress of Ṭarsūs from the Romans" and adds that on Sulaymān's request Ibn ʿAmmār of Tripoli sent a judge (*qāḍī*) and a prayer leader (*khaṭīb*) to the recently acquired city. This piece of information points to the earliest importation of rudimentary Muslim institutions. The fact that the said dignitaries were brought from Syria suggests that there were not yet any Muslim jurists able to fulfill such tasks in Sulaymān's territories in Asia Minor. The second note mentions more towns and gives 30 Rajab 477/2 December 1084 as the date of their conquest: "Sulaymān b. Qutlumush conquered Nīqīyā [*sic*], which is a town on the coast and resembles Anṭākiya, as well as places in its vicinity, such as Ṭarsūs, Adhana, Maṣṣīṣa (Mamistra), and ʿAynzarba (Anazarbos)."[158] Except for the first toponym, which seems to be a garbled variant of an unidentifiable coastal town, all aforesaid places are key points in the Saros, Kydnos, and Pyramos Valleys as well as the eastern Cilician plain.[159] The chronicle of al-ʿAẓīmī corroborates these details but does not associate them with Sulaymān's men and dates the conquest a year earlier to 476/21 May 1083-9 May 1084.[160] Michael the Syrian links this event with Malikshāh's Syrian campaign.[161] Furthermore, Matthew of Edessa under the year 534/1085–86 mentions "a certain emir named Pōltachi," who seized the Jayḥān district from Philaretos.[162] Most likely, this person is identical to Anna Komnene's Poulchazes, the brother of Apelchasem and ruler in Cappadocia.[163]

All in all, a part of the Muslim tradition connected, albeit vaguely, the Turkish penetration of Cilicia with Sulaymān's campaigns and/or his expedition against Antioch. Al-ʿAẓīmī and Michael the Syrian, instead, speak of Turks without further specification and give different chronological details. We may think of several incursions, which may have begun in 1082 and were carried out by Sulaymān's men and other warrior groups. Matthew's reference to the Jayḥān region suggests that the collapse of Philaretos' principality significantly facilitated the intrusion of Turks into Cilicia. Since Pōltachi/Poulchazes of Cappadocia can be associated with the Qutlumush clan, it seems that this commander eventually consolidated the results of previous operations. It is impossible to further clarify other crucial issues, such as the identity of the Turks in Cilicia and the outcome of their activities. Under the year 477/10 May 1084-28 April 1085, Sibṭ b. al-Jawzī mentions an alleged conquest of Melitene by a maternal uncle of Sulaymān b. Qutlumush.[164] This piece of information is completely unfounded, but there seems to be a kernel of truth in it. The chronicler may have mistakenly mixed up raids carried out by followers or kinsmen of Sulaymān with the campaign launched by Qilij Arslān I a decade later.[165]

As has been pointed out above, the Turkish raids basically resulted in the elimination of Philaretos' principality. The situation is more complicated with respect to other Armenian lords, such as Ōshin and the Rupenids and the remaining Greek potentates in the region. They were certainly affected by hostile attacks and suffered territorial losses, but the sources do not mention any specific details about their relations with the Turkish emirs. We may gain better insights into this situation via crusader chronicles' accounts of the Cilician expedition of Bohemond's nephew Tancred and Baldwin of Boulogne in mid-September 1097.[166] According to a statement of Ralph of Caen, "at this time the Turks ruled, the Greeks obeyed, and the Armenians protected their liberty in the difficult conditions provided by their mountains."[167] Turkish garrisons held sway over the fortified towns as well as the indigenous, mainly Greek-speaking population in the Cilician plain. Upon the arrival of Tancred's and Baldwin's forces, neither the Turks in Tarsus nor those in Mamistra were able to put up strong resistance or to coordinate their defensive efforts under the command of a supreme leader. The local garrisons thus forsook their cities after the first skirmishes or even before being attacked.[168] Adana is described as being in the hands of an Armenian lord called Ursinus, who was "an inhabitant of the mountains" in the years of Turkish domination. He is usually identified with Aplgharip's former vassal Ōshin of Lambrun. In the wake of an uprising initiated by the people of Adana against the Turkish lords, Ursinus/Ōshin supported the local population in expelling the Turks from the city. In this way, Adana appears as a Christian lord's stronghold surrounded by an overwhelming host of Turkish enemies.[169] The fact that relatively small contingents of crusader forces met hardly any effective resistance, however, indicates that the fighting force of the Turks in Cilicia was not very strong at that time.

Generally speaking, the cities of the Cilician plain and the valleys of the nearby Taurus Mountains present a very different image from the urban centers in the Euphrates region. This is partly due to the perspective of the crusader chronicles, which primarily stress the conflicts between the local Christians and the Turkish invaders. Accordingly, the said Ursinus/Ōshin is depicted as a champion of resistance against the Turkish rulers in Adana. Another aspect of this differing image is exhibited by the geographic particularities of Cilicia, the mountainous areas of which could hardly be controlled from the fortresses in the plain and formed impregnable strongholds for local warlords. In these places, they found protection from hostile assaults and were able to mount attacks against the plain.

A third aspect, which has to be taken into account, is the different character of the Turks who established themselves in Cilicia. As has been pointed out above, they were most likely related to the warrior groups of Sulaymān b. Qutlumush and to the Turks operating in Cappadocia. This is to say that they did not maintain any links with the Seljuk commanders in the Syrian urban centers and were hardly influenced by the centralizing attempts of Sultan Malikshāh. The Turkish chiefs in Cilicia remained largely isolated from the developments and institutional changes that occurred east of the Amanus Mountains. As a result, they hardly managed to strengthen their position in the cities of Cilicia and could be easily expelled from there at the first appearance of Frankish troops.

Armenian lordships in the Jayḥān and Euphrates Valleys

The political units in the swathe of land stretching from the Upper Pyramos/Jayḥān Valley to the Euphrates River and the Anti-Taurus Mountains exhibited especially strong tendencies toward fragmentation in the years following Philaretos Brachamios' downfall. The key points in the Byzantine borderlands, such as Antioch, Edessa, and Melitene, after a brief interlude of semi-independent local rule, fell into the hands of supra-regional Muslim powers or became centers of newly founded crusader principalities. On the contrary, the region in question was outside of the main invasion routes and was dominated by more remote strongholds in well-protected, mountainous areas. Some of them became centers of short-lived, small lordships claimed by Byzantine-Armenian aristocrats, Turkish emirs, and, from 1097 onwards, Frankish crusaders.

A case in point is the city of Marʿash. In about 1084/85 it was one of the major strongholds of Philaretos Brachamios, in which he organized the election and consecration of the Armenian catholicus Paul.[170] After Sulaymān's conquest of Antioch and substantial territorial losses, Philaretos made the city his last residence. Seljuk dynastic historiography preserves the memory of a certain Chāwuldur, who reportedly took hold of Marʿash and Sarūs, i.e., the Saros/Sayḥān Valley, in the years after the battle of Manzikert,[171] but this piece of information hardly tallies with the evidence for Philaretos' predominance. There seems to have been a short period of Turkish rule under the said Chāwuldur in the time between Philaretos' death and the arrival of the crusading forces before Marʿash in 1097. The Turks, who had oppressed the city for many years "by means of undue force and unfair tributes," are said to have taken flight. The Frankish chiefs, in turn, formally handed the city over to the Byzantine emperor.[172]

The region of Gargar (Gerger) and the monastery of Barṣawmā in the Anti-Taurus range northeast of Sumaysāṭ (Samsat) constituted a base of power for local chiefs of Syrian and Armenian origin. Michael the Syrian specifically mentions the Syrian Sanbīl family, which was represented by the brothers Qūsṭanṭīn, Tābhtūgh (David), and Krīstofūr and resided in the mountains around Barṣawmā. Moreover, there was a group of Armenian potentates called Constantine of Gargar, Michael of Gaqtay, and Ōhannēs of Būlā that became powerful in the region and merged with the Sanbīl family.[173] The isolated position of these places enabled them to maintain their independence and to fend off occasional raids carried out by transient warriors.

Perhaps the most powerful lordship in the Euphrates region in the years before and after the First Crusade was that of Kogh-Basil. Close ties with the local Armenian nobility, alliances with Frankish and Muslim potentates, and effective defensive measures against hostile attacks seem to have been the main components of his success.[174] Starting his career as a follower of Philaretos, he wielded power over the towns of Raʿbān (Araban) and Kayshūn (Keyşun) situated northwest and north of the Euphrates respectively, in the vicinity of Sumaysāṭ (Samsat). From there, he extended his sway as far as Ḥiṣn Manṣūr.[175] The fortifications of Kayshūn were repaired, and thus the city became Kogh-Basil's principal residence.[176] Apart from territorial expansion, he strengthened his position among the local Armenian clans by adopting a scion of the Kamsarakan family, who was called Dgha-Basil, and by marrying the child's nurse.[177] In addition, he created links with the Armenian military aristocracy, the surviving members of the Bagratid and Pahlavid royal families, and the incumbents of the Armenian patriarchal see.[178] It has correctly been pointed out that Kogh-Basil's association with the most noble Armenian lineages may be part of an encomiastic idealization constructed by Matthew of Edessa because of the chronicler's close personal relation with this ruler.[179] In any case, these features of constructed kinship perfectly fit into the consolidation strategies of a powerful upstart and have numerous parallels in other newly established lordships.

One of Kogh-Basil's vassals called Kurtig contributed substantially to the ideological and economic consolidation of his overlord and the Armenian Church. Michael the Syrian relates that Kurtig took hold of Bēth Ḥesnē (Besni) and Qalʿa Rūmaytā/Qalʿat al-Rūm, two fortresses situated in the vicinity of Kogh-Basil's residence.[180] He is strongly criticized for supporting Kogh-Basil's wife in dispossessing Syrian monks of the monastery of Karmir-Vankʿ near Kayshūn. This place was granted to the catholicus Gregory and Armenian monks and later on served as Kogh-Basil's burial place. Thus this sacred place of worship became closely associated with the ruling house's dynastic identity. Kurtig also expelled other Syrian monastic communities and exacted money from them. In retaliation for his misdeeds, a Frankish (Greek?) woman called *Qalāmarī* is said to have poisoned him.[181]

Despite some setbacks and internal frictions, the formation of a firmly established territorial lordship was well underway. Gérard Dédéyan especially stresses Kogh-Basil's adherence to the Armenian Church, something that provided him with a stronger footing among the local Armenian population and a sort of national legitimacy.[182] This view perhaps overemphasizes religious identity as a vehicle of ethnic cohesion but correctly underlines the distinct character of Kogh-Basil's principality. On the basis of evidence provided by lead seals, Werner Seibt argues that Kogh-Basil bore the important court title of *sebastos* and may have been a relative of Philaretos.[183] The identification of the seals in question, however, is rather hypothetical, and thus it is hardly possible to verify this assumption. At the time of his death in 1112, Kogh-Basil's authority was strong enough that his adopted son found acceptance among the local noblemen with the aid of Patriarch Barsegh and succeeded to his stepfather's position.[184]

All in all, the situation in Mar'ash, Gargar, and the Euphrates Valley very much resembled that of Cilicia with respect to its high degree of fragmentation among numerous local clans and Byzantine-Armenian chieftains. Kogh-Basil, the most successful of them, pursued strategies similar to those of Aplgharip and the Rupenids, which included the adoption of Byzantine court titles, the creation of local networks of vassals, and the establishment of ecclesiastical and dynastic sites. The Armenian lords in Cilicia and the Euphrates Valley thus gradually transformed their domains and castles into centers of dynastic identity and key points of distinct territorial lordships. Clearly, this process was frequently hampered by conflicts with both local forces and foreign invaders. Unlike Cilicia, which had to endure several waves of Turkish invasion and conquest coming from central Anatolia and Cappadocia, the mountainous areas in the river valleys farther east were more isolated from outside attacks. Malikshāh's governors in Syria and the Diyār Bakr province paid no attention to the regions bordering their territories to the north and beginning in 1093 were distracted by Seljuk civil strife. The situation suddenly changed in 1097–98 with the emergence of a new conflict zone of Frankish crusaders, Byzantines, and Turkish-Muslim emirs.

Notes

1 For his activities, see Chalandon, *Comnène*, 1:100–101; Kafesoğlu, *Melikşah*, pp. 102–107; Cahen, *Pre-Ottoman Turkey*, pp. 77–81; Vryonis, *Decline*, p. 115; Turan, *Türkiye*, pp. 83–87; Merçil and Sevim, *Selçuklu Devletleri*, pp. 528–29.

2 Turan, *Türkiye*, p. 84, speaks of "Kapadokya (Kayseri) vâliliğine tâyin etmişti," but this is not supported by any source. For Sulaymān's territories, see above, pp. 227–31.

3 Anna Komnene 6.10.9, p. 191, ll. 48–50.

4 Anna Komnene 6.10.5, p. 190, ll. 91–94: ἐπιθυμητικῶς γὰρ εἶχε τὰ σκῆπτρα τῆς Ῥωμαίων ἀναδήσασθαι ἀρχῆς.

5 For details, see Beihammer, "Feindbilder," p. 79; Beihammer "Defection," pp. 612–13, and the discussion below, p. 268.

6 Chalandon, *Comnène*, 1:93–94, 101–10; for the Pechenegs, see also Malamut, "Image," pp. 135–38.

7 Anna Komnene 6.10.2-7, pp. 189–91.

8 Anna Komnene 6.10.3, p. 189.

9 Anna Komnene 6.10.8, p. 191.

10 Anna Komnene 6.11.1, p. 193, ll. 89–90.

11 Anna Komnene 6.10.11, p. 192.

12 Anna Komnene 6.11.2, p. 193, ll. 95–94.

13 Anna Komnene 6.10.8, p. 191, ll. 34–38; see also Dölger and Wirth, *Regesten*, no. 1163 (erroneously dated to 1092 on the basis of Malikshāh's date of death).

14 Anna Komnene 6.10.8-9, 10, p. 191, ll. 38–48, p. 192, ll. 59–69; for the title, which, though in use from the mid-eleventh century onwards, gained special significance from the reform of Alexios I and was mainly reserved for members of the ruling family, see ODB 3:1862–63, s. v. sebastos.

15 Anna Komnene 6.10.9, pp. 191–92, ll. 48–59.

16 Anna Komnene 6.10.8, p. 191, ll. 38–41, 6.11.1, p. 192, ll. 84–86.
17 For the location of the castle τὸ τοῦ κυροῦ Γεωργίου ὀνομαζόμενον πολίχνιον, see Reinsch, *Anna Komnene*, p. 223, n. 169.
18 Anna Komnene 6.11.1-4, pp. 193–94; for these events in general, see Chalandon, *Comnène*, 1:100–101; Kafesoğlu, *Melikşah*, pp. 103–105; Turan, *Türkiye*, pp. 83–85; Cahen, *Pre-Ottoman Turkey*, pp. 79–80, who unanimously date them to the year 1086.
19 Erkiletlioğlu and Güler, *Türkiye Selçuklu Sultanları*, pp. 45–46; Aykut, *Türkiye Selçuklu Sikkeleri*, pp. 187–89; for the broader context, see Shukurov, "Self-identity," pp. 259–76.
20 Anna Komnene 6.9.5-6, p. 188; for a geographical definition of Paphlagonia as the region between the Parthenios River (Bartın Suyu) and the Halys (Kızılırmak), see Belke, *Paphlagonien*, pp. 41–43; for the personality of Charatikes/Karatekin in general, see Yinanç, *Anadolu'nun Fethi*, pp. 126–27; Kafesoğlu, *Melikşah*, p. 85; Turan, *Türkiye*, p. 86, n. 11; Cahen, *Pre-Ottoman Turkey*, p. 80; Vryonis, *Decline*, p. 115; Çakmakoğlu Kuru, "Çankırı Fatihi," pp. 63–84; for the citadel of Sinope and its development in Seljuk times, see Redford, "Medieval Anatolian Arsenals," pp. 543–49.
21 Belke, *Paphlagonien*, p. 228 (s. v. Kastamōn).
22 Belke, *Paphlagonien*, p. 196 (s. v. Gangra), p. 228 (s. v. Kastamōn).
23 Anna Komnene 6.9.4-5, pp. 187–88, ll. 9–31.
24 Yinanç, *Anadolu'nun Fethi*, pp. 126–27; Turan, *Türkiye*, p. 86 with n. 11.
25 Dānishmand-nāma, pp. 176–83, trad. Mélikoff, pp. 360–69.
26 Mélikoff, *Geste*, p. 85 and n. 2, p. 128.
27 Anna Komnene 6.9.4-5, pp. 187–88, ll. 15–19, 31–34, 40–41.
28 Dānishmand-nāma, p. 183, trans. Mélikoff, p. 368.
29 Çakmakoğlu, "Çankırı Fatihi," pp. 71–74.
30 The site of Apollonias can be identified with a promontory near modern Gölyazı adası on the northeastern shore of Lake Ulubat: Aybek and Öz, "Archeological Survey," pp. 1–25; for a description of the surviving walls, see Foss and Winfield, *Byzantine Fortifications*, pp. 139.
31 For this personality, see Chalandon, *Comnène*, 1:136; Yinanç, *Anadolu'nun Fethi*, p. 133; Cahen, *Pre-Ottoman Turkey*, p. 81; Turan, *Türkiye*, p. 97; Vryonis, *Decline*, p. 116.
32 Turan, *Türkiye*, p. 97; the rank of *beylerbey* as translation of the Greek ἀρχισατράπης is also accepted by Cahen, *Pre-Ottoman Turkey*, p. 81.
33 The inconsistency of the Byzantine terminology is well illustrated by Anna Komnene 7.7.4, p. 222, ll. 63–66, quoted in the introduction below, p. 00. This passage demonstrates that the word "*satrapes*" is used as synonym of the Arabic term *ameras*, the prevailing designation for chiefs of Turkish warrior groups. Hence, the word *archisatrapes* obviously refers to chief emirs of outstanding importance but hardly designates a specifically defined hierarchical rank.
34 See above, pp. 110, 117–118.
35 Anna Komnene 6.13.1-4, pp. 197–99. Poimanenon was occupied by Elchanes' soldiers: 6.13.3, p. 198, l. 94–95.
36 Anna Komnene 2.3.1, p. 60, ll. 46–47 (τῆς πόλεως τοίνυν Κυζίκου κατασχεθείσης παρὰ τῶν Τούρκων, πυθόμενος τὴν τῆς πόλεως ἅλωσιν ὁ αὐτοκράτωρ [i.e., Nikephoros III Botaneiates]), 2.3.2-3, p. 60–61, ll. 63–65, 73–74. The passage (2.3.1-4, pp. 60–61) describes a meeting in the imperial palace, to which the emperor summoned the Komnenian brothers Alexios and Isaac on the arrival of letters announcing the conquest of Kyzikos.
37 Anna Komnene 6.13.1, pp. 197, ll. 58–59 (ὁ δὲ Ἐλχάνης ἀρχισατράπης μετὰ τῶν ὑπ' αὐτόν), 6.13.2, p. 197, ll. 70–71 (καὶ δὴ στρατιὰν βαρβαρικὴν ἀξιόμαχον ἐπικαταλαμβάνουσαν εἰς ἀρωγὴν τοῦ Ἐλχάνη).
38 Anna Komnene 6.13.4, p. 197, ll. 5–9 (αὐτὸς δὲ μετὰ τῶν καθ' αἷμα προσηκόντων [...] ὅ τε Σκαλιάριος [...] ἀρχισατράπαι δὲ καὶ οὗτοι τῶν ἐπιφανῶν).
39 Anna Komnene 6.13.1, p. 197, ll. 63–64, 6.13.3, p. 198, ll. 90–91.

40 Anna Komnene 6.13.4, pp. 198–99, ll. 6–10 (καὶ μυρίων ἐπαπολαύει δωρεῶν [...] τὰς εἰς τὸν Ἐλχάνην φιλοφροσύνας καὶ δαψιλεῖς δωρεάς).

41 Vryonis, *Decline*, p. 116, points to the erection of the fortress of Kibotos in the Gulf of Nikomedeia, identifying it with the castle Σιδηρά, but Anna Komnene 10.5.1-3, pp. 295–96, refers to a place more eastward near the modern Sabanca Gölü and dates the event to the time before the arrival of the First Crusade, that is 1095–96. The two facts are not reconcilable with the expeditions against Elchanes.

42 Anna Komnene 6.13.4, p. 199, ll. 11–17.

43 Anna Komnene 10.2.6, p. 286.

44 For this personality in general, see Chalandon, *Comnène*, 1: 126–29, 146–48; Kurat, *Çaka Bey*; Mélikoff, *Geste*, pp. 73, 81, 85–88, 122; Cahen, *Pre-Ottoman Turkey*, p. 81; Turan, *Türkiye*, pp. 87–95; Vryonis, *Decline*, p. 115; Savvides, "Εμίρης," pp. 9–24, 51–66. The older scholarly literature strongly emphasizes his political significance during the time under discussion: according to Chalandon he was an extremely dangerous enemy, who made an attempt to blockade Constantinople with his fleet, to destroy the maritime trade in the region, and to organize a large-scale attack on Constantinople in collaboration with Apelchasem of Nicaea and the Pechenegs in Thrace in order to gain the Byzantine throne. A similar view is supported by Savvides, "Εμίρης," p. 11, n. 2: "Ὁ Τζαχᾶς – παρὰ τὶς λεηλασίες, ὠμότητες καὶ βαρβαρότητες τὶς ὁποῖες κατὰ διαστήματα διέπραξε – ὑπῆρξε ἀναμφισβήτητα σημαντικὴ καὶ πολὺ δραστήρια προσωπικότητα μὲ ὑπέρμετρη φιλοδοξία, καὶ ἡ καριέρα του δείχνει ὅτι σχεδὸν πάντοτε ἐνεργοῦσε βάσει προκαθορισμένου σχεδίου." Frankopan, *The First Crusade*, pp. 58–60, also argues that Tzachas' activities brought about a "rapid downturn in Asia Minor." The Turkish scholarly and popular opinion sees in Çaka the founder of the first Turkish principality in Izmir and its environs, a capable organizer and intelligent commander, who has a special place in Turkish maritime history as constructor of the first Turkish fleet, and a farsighted politician planning the conquest of Thrace and Istanbul: Kurat, *Çaka Bey*, p. 59. In 2008 the municipality of Çeşme celebrated the opening of a memorial site in his honor (*Çaka Bey anıtı*). The person also figures as character of Turkish historical romances: Yavuz Bahadıroğlu, *Çaka Bey* (Istanbul, 2001); Mehmet Dikici, *Çaka Bey* (Ankara, 2007).

45 Kurat, *Çaka Bey*, pp. 15–16; Mélikoff, *Geste*, p. 122; Savvides, "Εμίρης," pp. 9–10.

46 Dānishmend-nāma, p. 17, trans. Mélikoff, p. 201 (*iki biñ dahı Ḳara Toñaya ve Çavuldura verdiler kim bu yaña deñiz kenārından Ḳaramān Ṭağlarından yaña varalar*), p. 223, trans. Mélikoff, p. 404 (*birinüñ adı dahı Çavuldur Çakadur … Ḳayṣariyadan tā Istanbul sinūrınadek ne ḳadar şehir varise harāb ḳıldı … Istanbulı aldılar. Andan Ḳayṣarı ṭutub boğazından aṣaḳodılar*).

47 Anna Komnene 7.8.7, p. 225, ll. 70–76.

48 Anna Komnene 9.3.9, p. 264, l. 9 and 9.3.4, p. 265, l. 32.

49 Anna Komnene 7.8.3, p. 223, ll. 5–7 (the garrison in the fortress of Chios were Turks who used the Greek language while asking for peace); ibid. 7.8.4, p. 223, ll. 18–19 (8,000 Turkish soldiers were sent by Tzachas from Smyrna to Chios).

50 Anna Komnene 7.8.1, p. 222, ll. 70–74.

51 Anna Komnene 7.8.7, p. 225, ll. 76–85.

52 Anna Komnene 9.1.2, p. 258, ll. 21–22.

53 Anna Komnene 9.1.2, pp. 259, ll. 24–25: καὶ εἰς αὐτὴν δὲ εἰ δυνατὸν τὴν τῆς βασιλείας ἀνενεχθῆναι περιωπήν.

54 Turan, *Türkiye*, p. 90; Savvides, "Εμίρης," pp. 52–54.

55 Anna Komnene 9.1.2, pp. 258–59, ll. 23–24: μέχρις αὐτοῦ φθάσαι Βυζαντίου.

56 John Zonaras 18.25.14, p. 737, ll. 4–5 (καὶ τὴν Σάμον τήν τε Ῥόδον ὑφ' ἑαυτὸν ἐποιήσατο καὶ πλείους ἄλλας τῶν νήσων) is not supported by Anna Komnene.

57 Anna Komnene 7.8.1-8, pp. 222–26. For these events, see also Kurat, *Çaka Bey*, pp. 24–38; Turan, *Türkiye*, pp. 87–91; Savvides, "Εμίρης," pp. 14–24. Tzachas' conquests are approximately dated to the period 1087–89 while the campaign of Constantine Dalassenos took place in 1090.

58 Anna Komnene 8.1-3, pp. 236–42; for details, see Kurat, *Çaka Bey*, pp. 39–43; Turan, *Türkiye*, pp. 92–93; Demirkent, *Kılıç Arslan*, p. 16. Contemporary reactions of members of the Byzantine elite to this threat are reflected in a speech delivered by John the Oxite in the spring of 1091: Frankopan, *The First Crusade*, p. 59.

59 Anna's wording is too unclear to allow a more accurate geographic location of his activities: 8.3.2, p. 241, ll. 67–74: τὰ παρὰ θάλατταν ἅπαντα κατατρέχοντος [...] ὡς ἤδη πλείονα στόλον ἐκ τῶν παραλίων κτησάμενος ὁ Τζαχᾶς καὶ τὰς ἐπιλοίπους, ὧν προφθάσας κατέσχε νήσων, πορθήσας.

60 Anna Komnene 8.3.2, p. 241, ll. 73–78.

61 Anna Komnene 14.1.4, p. 423, ll. 45–48.

62 Chalandon, *Comnène*, pp. 132–34; Angold, *Empire*, p. 133.

63 Anna Komnene 9.1.3, p. 259.

64 Anna Komnene 11.5.1, p. 335, ll. 24–27, 11.5.5, p. 337, l. 86 (Marakes); for the names, see Kurat, *Çaka Bey*, p. 56; Mélikoff, *Geste*, p. 86; Turan, *Türkiye*, p. 95; Demirkent, *Kılıç Arslan*, p. 32. For the development of the fortified hill of Theologos, the emergence of which was connected with the silting of the ancient harbor of Ephesus, see Foss, *Ephesus*, pp. 117–37, esp. 118–22. In the time preceding the first Turkish conquests, Ephesus/Theologos was a flourishing country town "of some commercial importance" and a pilgrimage center because of its holy sites and the nearby monastery of the stylite Saint Lazarus on Mount Galesion.

65 Anna Komnene 11.5.1, pp. 335–36, ll. 20–30.

66 Anna Komnene 11.5.1, p. 335, ll. 20–23.

67 Ἔγγραφα Πάτμου, no. 4, pp. 31–39, no. 5, pp. 40–54; for Christodoulos, see ODB, 1:1140–41 s. v. Christodoulos of Patmos, and 2:1188–89 s. v. Latros.

68 For a different view, see Frankopan, *The First Crusade*, pp. 59–66, who argues for a "rapid and spectacular" collapse of Byzantine Asia Minor in the early 1090s. He is certainly right in adducing further evidence from the archive of Patmos, which attests to the dangers threatening Christodoulos' monastic communities. Yet Schreiner, "Brief des Alexios I. Komnenos," pp. 111–40 and Gastgeber, "Schreiben Alexios I. Komnenos," pp. 141–85, have convincingly demonstrated that the surviving version of Alexios I's alleged letter to Robert of Flanders exhibits no trace whatsoever of Byzantine rhetorical conventions or chancery practices and therefore has to be regarded as a western fabrication. Consequently, this text cannot be used as evidence reflecting the state of affairs in Asia Minor in the early 1090s but rather as a western piece of propaganda based on widely circulating rumors about the deadly menace to Eastern Christianity.

69 Chalandon, *Comnène*, 1:135–36; Cahen, *Pre-Ottoman Turkey*, pp. 80–81; Turan, *Türkiye*, pp. 95–97; Demirkent, *Kılıç Arslan*, pp. 15–16.

70 Aqsarā'ī, p. 21, trans. Öztürk, pp. 15–16: *al-qiṣṣa, Sulaymānshāh-rā dū pisar būd, Qilij Arslān wa Qulān Arslān, Malikshāh imārat-i ān qawm bi-Qilij Arslān dād wa tashrīf firistād wa ū har rūz taraqqī mī kard wa čūn āṣ ār-i rushd wa najābat dar wujūd-i ū ẓāhir būd har rūz az af'āl-i ū kārhā-yi pasandīda dar wujūd mī āmad.*

71 Qazwīnī, pp. 334–36: *sulṭān bedīn ḥarakat az barādar bi-ranjīd wa bi-nām-i Dāwūd b. Sulaymān ḥukm nāfiẓ shud wa Dāwūd mutaṣaddī-yi ān shughl gasht ... Dāwūd dar Qūniya bar takht-i qayṣar nishist dar sana-i ṣamānīn u arba'ami'a wa muddat-i bīst sāl ḥukm kard wa dar sana-i khamsmi'a dar-gasht ... barādarash Qilij Arslān b. Sulaymān ba'd az ū pādishāh shud, muddat-i čihil sāl dar sulṭanat bi-mānd.*

72 Anna Komnene 6.12.8, p. 197, l. 46 (τοῦ μεγάλου Σολυμᾶ δύο υἱεῖς); Matthew of Edessa 2.81, p. 149.

73 Michael the Syrian 15.8, 3:187 (trans.), 4:588, col. b (Syriac text): *kadh ethqṭel Sūlaymān haw d-qadhmāyā men Tūrkāyē amlekh-(h)wā bh-Īqūniyūn amlekh bāthrēh Mīgharslān* [sic! To be read as *Qilīgharslān*] *w-haw qadhmāyā ethā l-Mīlīṭīnī.*

74 Michael the Syrian 15.8, 3:185 (trans.), 4:586, col. a (Syriac Text): *sūlṭān dh-Īqūniyūn d-hū Mīgharslān* [sic!].

75 Ibn al-Athīr, 6:378, trans. Richards, *Chronicle*, 1:14: *wa-waṣalū ilā bilād Qilij Arslān b. Sulaymān b. Qutlumush, wa-hiya Qūniya wa-ghayruhā*, ibid. 6:420–21, trans. Richards, *Chronicle*, 1:59: *Qilij Arslān b. Sulaymān b. Qutlumush ṣāḥib Qūniya*.
76 Redford, "Alaeddin Mosque," pp. 54–74, esp. pp. 55–56.
77 Asbrigde, *First Crusade*, pp. 124–31.
78 Hild and Restle, *Kappadokien*, pp. 188–89 (s. v. Hērakleia).
79 Gesta Francorum 4.10, p. 23: [...]*appropinquavimus Yconio. Habitatores vero terrae illius suadebant et ammonebant nos ... pervenerunt at Erachiam, in qua erat Turcorum nimia congregatio, exspectans et insidians*; Robert the Monk 3.18-19, pp. 766–67, trans. Sweetenham, p. 115: [...]*et intraverunt Lycaoniam, provinciam omnibus bonis uberrimam, et venerunt Iconium* [...]. *Est autem Iconium civitas opulentissima temporalibus bonis* [...] *bonis terrenis repleti sunt. Quumque digredi a civitate placuit, suadentibus incolis, aquam in vasis* [...] *venerunt ad civitatem quae Heraclea memoratur, in qua Turcorum maxima multitudo aggregabatur.* Peter Tudebode, p. 57: [...]*appropinquavimus Hiconium, habitatores enim illius terre suadentes atque ammonentes* [...] *pervenerunt ad Herchliam, in qua erat nimia Turcorum congregatio expectans atque insidians.*
80 Fulcher 1.13.1, pp. 199–201: *Tunc venimus Antiochiam, quam parvam praenominant, in provincia Pisidiae, deinde Iconium, in quibus regionibus saepissime pane cibariisque satis indiguimus. Nam Romaniam* [...] *invenimus nimis a Turcis vastatam et depopulatam.*
81 Albert of Aachen 3.3, p. 140: [...]*ad urbes Finiminis, Reclei et Stancona descendit, in quibus Christiani cives habitabant Turcis viris Solimanni subiugati.*
82 Albert of Aachen 8.27, p. 620: [...]*viam arripuerunt, que ducit ad civitatem Stancona*; 8.29, p. 620: *Stanconam descenderunt, ubi Turcorum custodiam et vires in presidio reperientes.*
83 Albert of Aachen 8.28, p. 621.
84 See below, pp. 338–47.
85 Tārīkh-i Āl-i Saljūq, p. 37: *dar waqtī-ki az Qūniya mī-khwāst 'azm kardan pisarash Qilij Arslān walī 'ahd karda būd. Qilij Arslān pādishāh-i buzurg shud, cumla-i umerā-yi Rūm bi-ṭā'at-i ū dar-āmadand, dar awwal-i sulṭanat Ablūstān rāstad wa-Malāṭya-rā fatḥ kard* [...].
86 Anna Komnene 6.12.8, p. 197, ll. 39–44; see also Turan, *Türkiye*, pp. 96–97.
87 Anna Komnene 6.12.8, p. 197, ll. 48–57.
88 Ibn al-'Adīm, p. 321.
89 Ibn al-'Adīm, p. 321.
90 A similar conclusion is expressed by Turan, *Türkiye*, p. 96: "İznik'de bulunan muhariblerin kadın ve çocuklarını getirerek şehirde yerleştirdi ve şehri kendisine payitaht yaptı."
91 For the archaeological details concerning the citadel district and churches in Konya, see Tekinalp, "Palace Churches," pp. 154–60.
92 Turkish scholars take Anna's wording at face value and interpret the relationship of the ruler of Nicaea with other Turkish emirs in accordance with a theory of Turkish feudalism. In this context they describe the political program of Qilij Arslān as an attempt to restore the political unity of the Turkish lords in Anatolia: Turan, *Türkiye*, pp. 96–97: "Büyük kardeş Kılıç Arslan *sultan* unvanını aldı ... Kılıç Arslan, Sultan sıfatıyle, Süleyman'a tâbi bulunan diğer feodal Anadolu beylerinin de hükümdarı oldu ise de fiiliyatta bunlar babasının ölümünden sonra müstakil bir durum kazanmışlar idi." Demirkent, *Kılıç Arslan*, p. 15: "Kılıç Arslan, bir taraftan babası Süleymanşah'ın ölümünden beri dağılmış bulunan devletin birliğini kurmaya çalışırken."
93 Turan, *Türkiye*, p. 97, and Demirkent, *Kılıç Arslan*, p. 16, identify him with Elchanes, but this opinion is not supported by Anna's account.
94 For the dating of this event, see below in this chapter, pp. 284–85.
95 See above, pp. 41–44.
96 Anna Komnene 6.13.1-4, pp. 197–99.
97 Anna Komnene 9.3.2, p. 264, l. 9, and 9.3.4, p. 265, l. 32, see also 11.2.5, p. 326, ll. 49–50: τῇ γυναικὶ τοῦ σουλτάνου, ἥτις θυγάτριον ἦν, ὡς ἐλέγετο, τοῦ Τζαχᾶ; see also Kurat, *Çaka Bey*, p. 43; Turan, *Türkiye*, p. 97; Demirkent, *Kılıç Arslan*, pp. 15–16, 17.

98 For further details, see Kurat, *Çaka Bey*, pp. 49–55 (who, pointing to the changes caused by the First Crusade, dates the event prior to 1097); Cahen, *Pre-Ottoman Turkey*, p. 81; Turan, *Türkiye*, pp. 97–98; Demirkent, *Kılıç Arslan*, pp. 17–18; Savvides, "Εμίρης," pp. 63–66 (who dates the incident to 1106, ignoring, however, that the political setting in the region changed completely in the wake of the First Crusade and that Qilij Arslān in 1106 was operating in Upper Mesopotamia and Mosul).

99 Anna Komnene 9.3.1-4, pp. 263–65.

100 Anna Komnene 9.3.1, pp. 263–64, ll. 93–94: ὁ δέ γε Τζαχᾶς ἀνὴρ ὢν φιλοπόλεμος δραστηριότητι γνώμης οὐκ ἤθελεν ἠρεμεῖν. Ibid. 9.3.4, p. 265, l. 28: τοιοῦτον γὰρ τὸ βάρβαρον ἅπαν ἕτοιμον πρὸς σφαγὰς καὶ πολέμους.

101 Anna Komnene 9.3.2, p. 264; see also Dölger and Wirth, *Regesten*, no. 1169 (dating the letter to the spring of 1093, but Qilij Arslān is erroneously located in Konya).

102 For a similar view, see Demirkent, *Kılıç Arslan*, p. 18: "Esasen Çaka'nın gittikçe güçlenmesini kendi hâkimiyeti açısından endişe verici bir gelişme olarak."

103 Anna Komnene 9.3.4, p. 265, ll. 35–44.

104 The treaty is ignored by Dölger and Wirth, *Regesten*.

105 Anna Komnene 9.3.4, p. 265, ll. 42–43: καὶ τῶν εἰρηνικῶν σπονδῶν ὡς ἔθος τελεσθεισῶν; see also Demirkent, Kılıç Arslan, p. 18.

106 Anna Komnene 9.3.4, p. 265, ll. 43–44: ἐν καταστάσει τὰ παρὰ θάλασσαν ἦσαν ὅρια.

107 Anna Komnene 7.7.4, pp. 221–22, ll. 57–67. In the first months of 1091 this contingent along with other units under the command of Nikephoros Melissenos was sent to Ainos (Enez) to defend this region against the Pechenegs: ibidem 8.3.5, p. 242, l. 97–98. The remains of the castle of Nikomedeia display elements of brickwork datable to the Comnenian period and hypothetically to the time after the recapture by Alexios I: Foss, "Defenses of Asia Minor," pp. 200–201.

108 Anna Komnene 11.5.1, p. 335, ll. 23–24: ὁ μὲν γὰρ Τζαχᾶς τὴν Σμύρνην ὥσπερ ἴδιόν τι λάχος κατεῖχεν.

109 Chalandon, *Comnène*, 1:149–54.

110 Anna Komnene 11.5.1-3, pp. 295–96.

111 Anna Komnene 11.5.1, p. 295, ll. 55–56: τοὺς Τούρκους τὰ ἐντὸς Βιθυνίας κατατρέχοντας εὗρε καὶ ληιζομένους ἅπαντα.

112 Anna Komnene 11.5.2, p. 295–96, l. 66–68: διά τε Μαρυανδηνῶν καὶ τῶν πέραν Σαγγάρεως ῥᾳδίως κατεληίζοντο καὶ μᾶλλον τὴν Νικομήδους ἐπέθλιβον τὸν ποταμὸν διαπεραιούμενοι.

113 See above, pp. 268–70.

114 Anna Komnene 11.5.2, p. 296, ll. 71–80.

115 Anna Komnene 11.5.3, p. 296, ll. 80–98. The phrase τὸν θερινὸν τροπικὸν τοῦ ἡλίου διαπορευομένου clearly indicates that the works were carried out during the summer of 1096, a few months prior to the arrival of the People's Crusade of Peter the Hermit.

116 For the economic situation in Syria and Upper Mesopotamia in Seljuk times, see Heidemann, *Renaissance*, pp. 297–435.

117 Michael the Syrian 15.7, 3:185 (trans.), 4:585, col. c-586, col. a (Syriac text): *w-'all lāh la-mdhīttā khadh mettaqrbhā-(h)wāth men Tūrkāyē w-beh b-yawmā dh-'all lāh ettehdhāh tar'ēh wa-shrā 'alēh sūlṭān dh-Īqūnīyūm* ("and he entered the city when it was attacked by the Turks and on the day he entered it the door was closed and the Sultan of Iconium laid siege to it").

118 Michael the Syrian 15.8, 3:187 (trans.), 4:588, col. b (Syriac text).

119 Asbridge, *First Crusade*, pp. 124–39.

120 Dédéyan, *Les Arméniens*, 1:39–46. This and the following subchapters reproduce parts of my article "Christian Views of Islam in Early Seljuq Anatolia: Perceptions and Reactions," in A. C. S. Peacock, Bruno de Nicola, and Sara Nur Yıldız, eds., *Islam and Christianity in Medieval Anatolia* (Ashgate: Aldershot, 2015), pp. 51-76.

121 Dédéyan, *Les Arméniens*, 1:32 (nous le voyons présent dans les thèmes de Mârach et de Lykandos [...] et dans les thèmes de Samosate et de Mélitène, qui seront bientôt partie intégrante de sa principauté); for the process of consolidation after 1072, see ibidem, pp. 47–55.

122 Attaleiates, pp. 99–100 (Philaretos appears in 1069 as a high-ranking officer in the army of Romanos IV, in which he commands a military unit defending the region of Melitene), pp. 215–16 (he does not recognize the authority of Michael VII, rules independently, and occupies imperial cities [τῷ προβεβασιλευκότι ἀκαταδούλωτος ἦν καὶ κατ' ἐξουσίαν τὰ ἑαυτοῦ προμηθούμενος καὶ πόλεις βασιλικὰς εἰς ἑαυτὸν οἰκειούμενος], but submits to Nikephoros III [δοῦλος αὐτεπάγγελτος γέγονε]); Matthew of Edessa 2.60, pp. 137–38 (attack against T'ornik the lord of Sasun; extremely negative image of Philaretos as a "most wicked chief" exercising "a tyrannical rule"; he is supported by "the Frankish count Rmbaghat [Raimbaud?] with eight hundred men"); Michael the Syrian 15.4, 3:173–74 (trans.), 4:580, col. b, l. 24–581, col. a, l. 20 (Syriac text) (brief account of his rise to power with a list of territories being under Philaretos' control: most of his fortified places are in Cilicia, Tarsus, Mopsuesteia, Mar'ash, Kayshūm, Ra'bān, Edessa, Anazarba, Antioch, the province of Jayḥān, Melitene). For Philaretos in general, see Laurent, *Turcs*, pp. 81–90; Yarnley, "Philaretos," 331–53; Cheynet, *Pouvoir*, p. 82; Dédéyan, *Les Arméniens*, 1:287–357; Ersan, *Ermeniler*, pp. 37–42; Pryor and Jeffreys, "Euphrates' Frontier," pp. 35–38.

123 Pryor and Jeffreys, "Euphrates' Frontier," p. 83 (with a list of all known seals).

124 Pryor and Jeffreys, "Euphrates' Frontier," pp. 41–44.

125 This contradicts the conclusion of Pryor and Jeffreys, "Euphrates' Frontier," p. 38: "But after 1078 he returned to Byzantine political orthodoxy." The signification of legitimacy and subsidies linked with court titles are hardly evidence that Philaretos's acknowledgement of imperial suzerainty was more than nominal or that he was actually supported by the troops of the imperial government, which was not able to back its claims of sovereignty with military force.

126 Matthew of Edessa 2.85, pp. 152–53; Michael the Syrian 15.4, 3:173 (trans.), 4:580–81 (Syriac text); see also Ersan, *Ermeniler*, pp. 42; Beihammer, "Defection," pp. 616–17.

127 Matthew of Edessa 2.86, p. 153. The author articulates a similar opinion on the occasion of the sultan's death: ibid. 2.97, p. 158.

128 Matthew of Edessa 2.86, p. 154.

129 Matthew of Edessa 2.98, p. 158. See also ibid. 2.103, p. 160: "[...] a benefactor of all the Armenians; moreover, he was an embellisher of monasteries and a supporter of monks, besides which he protected the [Christian] faithful against harassment from the Persians [...] the Armenians lived in happiness [and security]."

130 Matthew of Edessa 2.86, p. 154.

131 Matthew of Edessa 2.113, p. 167.

132 Matthew of Edessa 2.104, p. 161.

133 Matthew of Edessa 2.85, p. 152: "the illustrious Roman official, who was the *paracoemomenus*, a benevolent and pious eunuch," 2.88, p. 154.

134 Turan, *Türkiye*, pp. 110–11; for a more moderate interpretation, see Ersan, *Ermeniler*, pp. 34–35.

135 Matthew of Edessa 2.85, pp. 152–53 (the connection between the murder of the *parakoimomenos* in Edessa and the sultan's contempt for Philaretos is undoubtedly a narrative construction by the historian).

136 Michael the Syrian 15.4, 3:173 (trans.), 4:580–81 (Syriac text).

137 For further details, see Beihammer, "Defection," pp. 616–17. Anna Komnene 6.9.2, pp. 186–87, ll. 65–84 (καθ' ἑκάστην δὲ τῶν Τούρκων ληιζομένων τὰ πέριξ [...] ἐσκέψατο προσελθεῖν τοῖς Τούρκοις καὶ περιτμηθῆναι) provides a different version, according to which Philaretos considered converting to Islam even before the fall of Antioch and thus his son summoned Sulaymān to come and conquer the city. Anna's story is

hardly convincing, but it tallies with the other versions insofar as the conversion is viewed as resulting from enemy military pressure.

138 For more details concerning this person, see Mutafian, *Arménie*, 1:56–57; Ersan, *Ermeniler*, pp. 73–76; Pryor and Jeffreys, "Euphrates Frontier," pp. 70, 82 (with a list of his seals).

139 Michael the Syrian 15.4, 3:173–74 (trans.), 4:581, col. a (Syriac text). For T'oros, see Pryor and Jeffreys, "Euphrates Frontier," p. 69, 84 (with a list of his seals).

140 Pryor and Jeffreys, "Euphrates Frontier," pp. 82, 84.

141 Michael the Syrian 15.6, 3:179 (trans.), 4:584, col. b (Syriac text).

142 Michael the Syrian 15.8, 3:188 (trans.), 4:590, col. b (Syriac text).

143 Matthew of Edessa 2.88, p. 154.

144 Matthew of Edessa 2.104, p. 161; Michael the Syrian 15.7, 3:183 (trans.), 4:587, col. a (Syriac text); Pryor and Jeffreys, "Euphrates Frontier," p. 69, incorrectly refer to Theodore's appointment in Edessa immediately after Malikshāh's takeover in 1087.

145 Pryor and Jeffreys, "Euphrates Frontier," p. 69, with further bibliographical references in n. 157.

146 Matthew of Edessa 2.108, p. 163–64; see also Mutafian, *Arménie*, 1:56, who because of Theodore's advanced age assumes that he must have been Gabriel's brother-in-law.

147 Matthew of Edessa 2.92, pp. 156–57; see also Ersan, *Ermeniler*, pp. 34–35. For Barsegh's personal relation with Matthew of Edessa, see MacEvitt, "The Chronicle of Matthew of Edessa," pp. 165–66.

148 For these views, see the literature cited above, n. 134.

149 Hild and Hellenkemper, *Kilikien und Isaurien*, pp. 328–30 (s. v. Lambrun), 373–74 (s. v. Papeṙawn); Dédéyan, *Les Arméniens*, 1:307–11; Pryor and Jeffreys, "Euphrates Frontier," pp. 67–68, 82 (with a list of his surviving seals).

150 Matthew of Edessa 2.74, pp. 144–45, who dates the king's death to 528/1079-80; for an earlier date, see Samuel of Ani, p. 449, and the argumentation of Dédéyan, *Les Arméniens*, 1:375–76.

151 Dédéyan, *Les Arméniens*, 1:311–19; Pryor and Jeffreys, "Euphrates Frontier," p. 67.

152 Hild and Hellenkemper, *Kilikien und Isaurien*, pp. 398–99.

153 Dédéyan, *Les Arméniens*, 1:368–74, 376–82; Pryor and Jeffreys, "Euphrates Frontier," p. 68.

154 Matthew of Edessa 2.113-14, pp. 166–67; *Lignages d'Outremer*, ed. Nielen, p. 131; see also Michael the Syrian 15.8, 3:187 (trans.), 4:589, col. b (Syriac text): "There were also Armenians (*Armenāyē*) who seized places in the region of Cilicia, those who were called *Benē Rupen*." For details, see Hild and Hellenkemper, *Kilikien und Isaurien*, pp. 207–208 (s. v. Baka), pp. 210–11 (s. v. Barjrberd), p. 295 (s. v. Kastaławn), pp. 312–13 (s. v. Koṙomozol), Dédéyan, *Les Arméniens*, 1:378–86; Mutafian, *Arménie*, pp. 63–64.

155 Dédéyan, *Les Arméniens*, 1:388–91.

156 Dédéyan, *Les Arméniens*, 1:308–12, 381–84; Pryor and Jeffreys, "Euphrates Frontier," p. 82.

157 Turan, *Türkiye*, pp. 69–71; Dédéyan, *Les Arméniens*, 1:338–40; Ersan, *Ermeniler*, p. 40.

158 Sibṭ b. al-Jawzī, pp. 217, 229.

159 Hild and Hellenkemper, *Kilikien und Isaurien*, pp. 154–58 (s. v. Adana), pp. 178–85 (s. v. Anazarbos), pp. 351–59 (s. v. Mopsuestia), 428–39 (s. v. Tarsos).

160 ʿAẓīmī, p. 19 (Arabic text), p. 24 (trans.): "The Turks conquered the frontier strongholds and the mountain passes (*al-thughūr wa-l-durūb*) and Adhana, ʿAynzarba, and al-Maṣṣīṣa."

161 Michael the Syrian 15.6, 3:179 (trans.), 4:584, col. b (Syriac text): *nsabh(u) Tūrkāyē l-Tarsūs w-Mṣīṣtā w-Anāzarbā w-šarkā dh-mdhī(n)ttā dh-Qīlīqiyā*, ("The Turks seized Tarsus, Mamistra, Anazarbos, and other cities of Cilicia").

162 Matthew of Edessa 2.81, pp. 149–50.

163 Anna Komnene 6.10.1, pp. 188–89.

164 Sibṭ b. al-Jawzī, p. 233.
165 Cahen, *Pre-Ottoman Turkey*, p. 77; Turan, *Türkiye*, pp. 69–70; Ersan, *Ermeniler*, p. 110, implies the idea of a systematic expansion of Sulaymān b. Qutlumush's state in a southeastern direction.
166 Asbridge, *First Crusade*, pp. 140–47; Tyerman, *God's War*, pp. 131–32.
167 Ralph of Caen, *Gesta Tancredi* 34, p. 630, trans. Bachrach and Bachrach, p. 58: *Ea namque tempestate Turcis dominari contigerat, Graecis famulari, Armenis montium arduitate tueri libertatem.*
168 Ralph of Caen, *Gesta Tancredi* 34–36, 41, pp. 630–32, 636, trans. Bachrach and Bachrach, pp. 57–60, 66.
169 Ralph of Caen, pp. 634–36, trans. Bachrach and Bachrach, pp. 63–65.
170 Matthew of Edessa 2.82-83, p. 150.
171 Rashīd al-Dīn/Nīshāpūrī, p. 39, ed. Luther, p. 53.
172 Albert of Aachen 3.27, pp. 182–83: *Turci qui adventum tantorum ac tot principum intellexerant ab urbis presidio aufugerunt quam iniqua vi et iniustis tributis ante multos hos annos subpresserunt.*
173 Michael the Syrian 15.11, 3:198 (trans.), 4:595, col. b (Syriac text); see also Mutafian, *Arménie*, 1:62.
174 Mutafian, *Arménie*, 1:56; Ersan, *Ermeniler*, pp. 67–70; Pryor and Jeffreys, "Euphrates Frontier," pp. 69, 84; for a detailed analysis of the development of Kogh-Basil's principality on the basis of all available sources, see Dédéyan, *Les Arméniens*, 2:1057–1137. For lead seals ascribed to this ruler, see Seibt, "Vasil Goł," pp. 153–58.
175 Dédéyan, *Les Arméniens*, 2:1076–79; Seibt, Vasil Goł, p. 153; for Ḥiṣn Manṣūr, see Matthew of Edessa 3.38, p. 220.
176 Michael the Syrian 15.8, 3:187 (trans.), 4:589, col. b (Syriac text): *Kūgbāsīl d-aḥīth l-Kayshūm da-l-Ra'bān.*
177 Michael the Syrian 15.9, 3:199 (trans.), 4:595, col. b-596, col. b (Syriac text); Matthew of Edessa 3.57, p. 212; Seibt, "Vasil Goł," p. 153.
178 Matthew of Edessa 3.38, p. 200, 3.57, p. 211, 3.25, pp. 195–96.
179 MacEvitt, "Chronicle of Matthew of Edessa," pp. 165–66.
180 Mutafian, *Arménie*, 1:63.
181 Michael the Syrian 15.11, 3:199 (trans.), 4:595, col. b-596, col. b (Syriac text); for further details, see Dédéyan, *Les Arméniens*, 2:1090–95; Seibt, "Vasil Goł," p. 154.
182 Dédéyan, *Les Arméniens*, 2:1057–60.
183 Seibt, "Vasil Goł," pp. 156–57.
184 Matthew of Edessa 3.57, p. 212.

Part III

The crusades and the crystallization of Muslim Anatolia, 1096–ca. 1130

8 Seljuk reactions to the First Crusade

General remarks

What consequences did the First Crusade have for the nascent Turkish principalities in Asia Minor? In what respect did the unexpected arrival of hosts of armed pilgrims from the West influence or change the developments that had been initiated by the expansion of Turkish warrior groups in Anatolia? Historians of Byzantium and the crusades usually do not pay much attention to these questions.[1] They are much more concerned with the relations between Alexios I and the crusader chiefs as well as the emperor's conflict with the Normans of Antioch.[2] They also concentrate on the hardships and perils the crusaders faced while crossing Anatolia and besieging Antioch. In this context, the Turks are normally described as dangerous enemies who at times were able to threaten the very existence of the crusading army. Yet there are no systematic attempts to approach the topic from the opposite viewpoint and examine the challenges the newly established Turkish lordships were facing in the time of the crusade's advance.[3] Turkish scholars partly fill this gap.[4] Their view, however, is biased by a very negative image of the crusaders, which depicts them as unruly and rapacious hosts, driven by religious fanaticism, unrestrained violence, and avarice. The crusaders' arrival, therefore, is perceived as a great disaster for the Turks, who were forced to retreat from the Propontis and Aegean shores towards central Anatolia and to give up Cilicia. Only two decades after its foundation, the young Seljuk emirate was tottering on the edge of demise and being forced to fight a desperate, but heroic, struggle for survival.

In what follows, I will try to draw a more balanced picture of the first encounter among Byzantines, Franks, and Turks in Asia Minor. A comparative analysis of Byzantine, Latin, and Muslim accounts presenting crucial moments in this process should lead us to a better understanding of the particular problems each side confronted in its conflicts and interactions with the others. The relatively well-studied Frankish experience has to be supplemented by an adequate interpretation of Turkish reactions and strategies vis-à-vis the crusaders. Likewise, it is important to obtain a more accurate insight into the particularities of the Byzantine policy, which for all its coordination with the Frankish aims also pursued its own agenda and could rely on a much higher degree of acquaintance with the Turks of Asia Minor. The establishment of Frankish rule over Antioch and Edessa further raises the question of how these new entities influenced the Byzantine military structures in the southern coastland of Asia Minor and the development of Muslim-Turkish emirates in central Anatolia, Syria, and Upper Mesopotamia. A secondary aspect is the imperial government's diplomacy towards the Frankish and Muslim powers in this broad area.

The story of the crusaders' march across Anatolia has been told countless times, and there is no need to repeat it here. It suffices to recall some basic facts: In September/October 1096 expeditionary forces of Peter the Hermit's host were trapped in the fortress of Xerigordos near Nicaea, while the main body of his army was almost completely destroyed near Kibotos/Civitot in the Gulf of Nikomedeia. On 18 June 1097, after a siege of more than seven weeks, the Turkish defenders of Nicaea surrendered and submitted to the Byzantine emperor. While continuing its march through Phrygia, the crusader army was attacked by strong Turkish forces under Qilij Arslān I near Dorylaion on 1 July 1097. Warding off this last major offense, the army advanced in a southeasterly direction via Nakoleia (Seyit Gazi) and Kedrea (Bayat) across the Sultan Mountains to Antioch of Pisidia (Yalvaç) and Konya[5] and thence across the Anatolian plateau to Herakleia near the Cilician Gates. There, the main body of the army took the longer route via Cappadocia and the Anti-Taurus Mountains and proceeded via the Jayḥān Valley and Marʿash to Antioch. As a preparatory measure for the campaign against Antioch, an expeditionary force under Baldwin of Boulogne and Bohemond's nephew Tancred invaded Cilicia in September and October 1097 and subjugated the Cilician cities of Tarsus, Adana, and Mamistra. No doubt, the most critical turning point in the whole expedition was the eight-month siege of Antioch between 20 October 1097 and 3 June 1098, followed by the counter-attack of Karbūqā's relief forces and the crusaders' risky, but successful, sortie on 29 June 1098. A few months earlier in February/March, Baldwin had concluded an alliance with Thoros of Edessa and had taken possession of the city, thus laying the foundation for the Frankish principality of Edessa.[6]

The elimination of Peter the Hermit's People's Crusade and the main army's crossing of Asia Minor were but brief episodes, yet they had long-lasting effects on the political situation in Anatolia. The surrender of Nicaea to Alexios' officers inaugurated the restoration of Byzantine rule in the western littoral and river valleys as far as the port of Attaleia at the Lycian coast. With the conquest of Antioch and Edessa, the Franks not only forced a number of Armenian, Greek, and Turkish lords into submission but also engendered radical shifts in the balance of power between the political groupings of the entire region. After 1098, the princedom of Antioch and the county of Edessa quickly came to form a Christian-Frankish block of feudal lordships, which maintained close links with the kingdom of Jerusalem, the imperial government of Constantinople, and local Byzantine-Armenian potentates. This unavoidably affected the position of the Muslim emirs in Asia Minor, northern Syria, and Upper Mesopotamia.

The surrender of Nicaea

The surrender of Nicaea to Emperor Alexios I on 18 June 1097 is a well-documented example of successful Byzantine-Turkish negotiations that resulted in the restoration of Byzantine rule and the absorption of parts of the Seljuk military leadership by the imperial elite.[7] During the siege Alexios I had his headquarters at some distance from Nicaea near a place at the northern shore of the Gulf of Nikomedeia called Pelekanos (near Hereke), where he organized markets supplying the army and monitored the military operations.[8] His officers Manuel Boutoumites and Tatikios, who commanded a Byzantine contingent outside the city walls, served as go-betweens for the emperor, the Franks, and, most intriguingly, the Turkish defenders. This twofold strategy embracing military and diplomatic means attests to the close relationship the Turks of Nicaea and the imperial court had developed ever since their first formal treaty in 1081.

The fact that both Anna Komnene and the crusader chronicles report extensively on these events allows us to compare both perspectives directly. As is to be expected, the Byzantine historian primarily focuses on the activities of the imperial government whereas the Frankish accounts extoll the feats of the crusading army during their attacks on the impregnable city walls and in the battle against the relief forces of Qilij Arslān. The older Latin chronicles are not explicit about this point, but Anna and William of Tyre agree that, despite the oaths of allegiance the Frankish leaders had sworn to the emperor, there was still a great deal of distrust between the two sides.[9] The Franks considered the conquest of Nicaea as one of their obligations towards the emperor and a task they had to complete before continuing their march to the Holy Land. For the Byzantines, instead, the recovery of Nicaea had been a prime objective ever since the early 1080s.[10] Furthermore, the Franks saw in the siege of Nicaea an opportunity to take rich booty as a reward for the hardships they had had to endure during the siege.[11] In contrast, the imperial government wanted to make sure that the crusaders would respect the agreements concerning the emperor's sovereignty and would not perpetrate any acts of violence. The Byzantines, therefore, could argue that their attempts to come to an understanding with the Turkish defenders served the purpose of averting the danger of potential Frankish acts of aggression.[12]

Due to their religious zeal and lack of experience, the Franks regarded the Turks above all as mortal enemies of Christendom who had to be eliminated for the benefit of the Christian faithful and the divinely ordained pilgrimage to Jerusalem. The notion of a deadly threat to Christian territories and ecclesiastical institutions in Asia Minor was also one of the incentives that stood at the beginning of the crusade, as Fulcher's version of Pope Urban II's speech in Clermont clearly demonstrates.[13] The Byzantines shared the crusaders' defensive ambition to liberate Christian subjects from the Turkish yoke. Aside from that, however, they made strong efforts to subsume the Turks into the ranks of the imperial army and the higher echelons of the court hierarchy. Rather than eradicating them by force, they preferred to benefit from their military potential as staunch allies, willing to support Constantinople in its efforts to regain its territories in Asia Minor.

Anna construes her version of the siege of Nicaea in accordance with these principles of the imperial strategy. The diplomatic skills of the emperor's representative and chief negotiator, Manuel Boutoumites, and imperial chrysobulls promising impunity, generous sums of money, and titles as a reward for the surrender of the town were important means of projecting the emperor's reconciliatory attitude.[14] Another factor working in favor of the Byzantine plans was the Turks' fear of the mistreatment they would suffer should the Franks seize the city. The Turkish chiefs in Nicaea were enticed by the emperor's offer but kept their loyalty to Qilij Arslān until the latter failed to break the siege and the emperor, with the aid of vessels, managed to cut the supply lines over Askanian Lake.[15] Anna's report then focuses on Boutoumites' and Tatikios' tricky task of organizing a smooth takeover in Nicaea while facing the danger of potential assaults by the Franks from outside and the Turks from within the city.[16] Anna's description extolls the astuteness of the Byzantine officers in handling this situation. Boutoumites is said to have outwitted his Frankish allies by ordering Tatikios to launch a feigned attack against the city walls while he lifted the imperial banners and acclaimed the emperor on the ramparts. In the most precarious moment, Boutoumites prevented the Franks from entering the city while urging the Turkish emirs to depart as quickly as possible to the imperial camp. Due to their proficiency in colloquial Turkish, the officers Rodomeros and Monastras successfully handled an angry outburst among the Turks, who had gathered at the shore of Askanian Lake. Monastras was of mixed origin, and Rodomeros had spent a long time among the Turks as a captive.[17] The restoration of Byzantine rule over the city thus appears to be the result of a negotiated consensus between Byzantines and Turks, the latter of whom were attracted by the prospects of benefiting from the emperor's wealth and bounty. Seemingly, the example of Nicaea was designed to form a counterpart to what happened in Antioch and to highlight the legitimacy and manifold advantages of imperial rule. Moreover, the incident with the two bilingual officers illustrates that a group of people who possessed linguistic skills and cross-cultural competence played a crucial role in resolving conflicts and developing forms of interaction between the two sides.

The crusader chronicles reflect some knowledge of the emperor's generous attitude towards the Turks of Nicaea, in particular towards *Solimannus*' (= Qilij Arslān I's) wife and her two under-age sons, who were honorably received and released by the emperor.[18] The author of the *Gesta Francorum* harshly criticizes the emperor's decision to grant them safe conduct, for these people would create more obstacles and cause further damage to the Franks.[19] Albert of Aachen, instead, expresses a rather positive view: Tatikios, whom the chronicler apparently mixed up with Manuel Boutoumites, is said to have intervened with the Frankish chiefs to ensure that the Turks would leave the city unharmed and surrender to the emperor. The capitulation brought about great rejoicing among the crusading troops, who shortly afterwards continued their march to the East.[20] William of Tyre is the only Frankish author to refer to the negotiations of *Tatinus Grecus* (= Tatikios, in fact Boutoumites) with the Turkish chiefs. The words William puts into the Byzantine officer's mouth are similar to those reported by Anna

Komnene: the Turks would greatly benefit from the protection and clemency of the emperor who was to recover a city that had been unlawfully wrested away from the empire. Reportedly, Tatikios also contrasted the powerful and ever-present emperor with the Frankish barbarians, who undertook this siege only in passing while bearing other objectives in mind.[21] In the eyes of the crusading chiefs, it was the priority of other goals that justified their consent to the surrender of Nicaea to the emperor.[22] Although the crusaders did not claim the city for themselves, rank-and-file soldiers were greatly concerned about the compensation they expected for their hardships during the seven-week siege. The emperor rebuffed their request to keep the booty and captives they had previously taken and lavished gifts upon the Frankish chiefs instead. This attitude caused overall indignation. For the first time there was loud complaining that the emperor had violated the treaty.[23] All in all, Byzantine and Frankish attitudes towards the Turks differed fundamentally long before the relations between the two allies were strained because of their discord regarding Antioch. The Turks had the advantage of never being confronted with a united Christian front. They could develop their channels of communication with the imperial government without being compromised by the crusaders. This most likely was one of the reasons giving rise to accusations of Byzantine sympathies towards the Muslim foe or even Byzantine-Turkish coalitions against the Franks.

Central Anatolia after the battle of Dorylaion, 1 July 1097

Anna Komnene and the Frankish chronicles give only cursory accounts of the crusading army's march across the Anatolian plateau, mainly describing the hardships the pilgrims had to endure while advancing through dry steppe land in blistering heat. Accordingly, remarks concerning the situation of the Turkish potentates are scarce and frequently unreliable. This is to say that in contrast to Cilicia, Antioch, and the Euphrates region, which are treated more extensively because of their significance for the crusaders, we have only a very fragmentary picture of the situation in central Asia Minor in the time after the battle of Dorylaion.

According to Albert of Aachen, *Solimannus* (Qilij Arslān) after his retreat from Nicaea gathered new forces from Antioch, Tarsus, Aleppo, and other cities in Romania occupied by the Turks.[24] Anna asserts that the Seljuk ruler was supported by Τανισμὰν ὁ σουλτάν (Dānishmand) and Ἀσάν (a certain Ḥasan) who is said to have commanded 80,000 men.[25] This gives the impression that Qilij Arslān managed to gather all Turkish potentates in Anatolia and northern Syria in order to expel the crusaders, but it is certainly an exaggeration. As has been shown above, the situation in northern Syria in the years after Tutush's death was extremely conflict ridden and Muslim sources hardly refer to any alliances prior to the siege of Antioch.[26] It is very unlikely, therefore, that Qilij Arslān gained the support of Aleppo and Antioch. Tarsus and other cities in the Cilician plain in 1097 actually were in Turkish hands, but one may wonder if they were strong enough to send troops to fight in western Anatolia. Dānishmand is also mentioned in the chronicle of al-ʿAẓīmī as an ally of Qilij Arslān in the struggle against the crusading army and reappears in this capacity in the war against the Lombard crusaders in 1101.[27] Anna identifies the aforementioned Asan elsewhere as ruler of Cappadocia,[28] but it is questionable whether he actually fought on Qilij Arslān's side in the battle of Dorylaion or merely opposed the crusaders while they were marching through his territories. Presumably, the conquest of Nicaea alerted the Turks in the regions east of the Halys River and in Cappadocia and prompted them to support the Seljuk chief.[29] There was a great danger that the crusaders' advance would affect their own territories as well, and thus they had to join forces against the common threat.

As regards the geographical details concerning the military clashes in the provinces of Phrygia and Pisidia, Anna mentions the places of *Hebraike* and *Augustopolis*, which can presumably be located in the region northeast of Akroinos (Afyonkarahisar) and in the Akar Çayı Valley east of the same town.[30] The account is confused, and it may well be that some of the events referred to have to be located further to the east. It becomes clear, however, that Turkish warrior groups, despite their setback near Dorylaion, still exerted some control over the region between Akroinos and Antioch of Pisidia. This is also supported by crusader accounts referring to the implementation of a scorched-earth policy in the region: the Turks ravaged churches and houses, carried off animals and victuals, and burned down whatever could be of use for the Franks.[31] These scraps of evidence also show that prior to the events of 1097 the economic and social structures of the region in question were largely intact. Accordingly, the crusaders while marching eastward faced serious supply problems and a shortage of water.

The Turks continued to put up resistance but were not able to confront the crusaders in a pitched battle. The defeat of Dorylaion was not only a military setback causing a considerable loss of manpower but also an economic disaster for Qilij Arslān and his followers. This is due to the fact that the crusaders managed to seize the Turkish camp with its huge quantities of booty, including grain, wine, livestock, gold, silver, and tents.[32] The Seljuk leader suffered a heavy blow that undermined his prestige as ruler and military commander. The descriptions of Anna Komnene and William of Tyre evoke chaotic scenes of disintegration with Turkish warriors forsaking towns and cultivated areas along with their families and livestock and seeking refuge in remote mountainous areas.[33] The regions affected by the passage of the crusading army in Phrygia, Pisidia, Lycaonia, and Cappadocia were devastated twice, first by the scorched earth tactics of the fleeing Turks and then by the crusading army seeking to cover its supply needs. It is not possible to estimate the extent of depredation and destruction caused by the two groups, but given that since the time of Romanos IV's eastern campaigns no hosts of comparable size had made their appearance in Anatolia it may be assumed that the damages of 1097 were much more extensive than those caused by the Turkish raids in the 1070s and 1080s. Despite all signs of continuity in social and economic structures, the events of 1097 seem to have had a profound impact on the urban and rural population in parts of western and central Asia Minor. This mainly has to be ascribed to the large numbers of people making their way through Anatolia at that time.

Another aspect of the massive influx of Frankish Christians and their encounter with Muslim Turks was the problem of apostasy and conversion. Such phenomena are reported from time to time with respect to Greek Orthodox and Armenian Christians ever since the first Seljuk invasions. As has been already stated, it is highly improbable that Turkish warriors would have exerted any systematic pressure in matters of faith. They were mainly interested in raids and booty and had not yet adopted a clear concept of *jihad* to justify their attacks on the Christian population of Asia Minor. Narratives referring to such incidents do not appear prior to the 1130s and thus have to be seen in conjunction with the changes engendered by the crusades and the gradual crystallization of Muslim institutions in the nascent Turkish principalities. Individual cases of apostasy among elite members, however, actually did occur and resulted from the attempts of certain persons to secure their position under foreign rule or to join a rival group because of other benefits. With the beginning of the crusades, new incidents of apostasy occurred, which had mainly to do with the adversities and perils of war. A case in point is Rainald, the commander of a contingent of the People's Crusade that in September 1096 advanced towards Nicaea.

> Their leader Rainald concluded a secret treaty with the Turks, preferring to hold onto the temporary life rather than suffer such a martyr's death for Christ. So, drawing up his forces, he pretended to launch an attack on the enemies; but soon, as he came out, he changed direction towards them with many others [...] he shrank from suffering martyrdom and renounced profession of the Christian faith despite being in good shape, on horseback and armed. It was only fitting that he deserved to lose God's grace and fall to the lot of he who chose to reside in the North.[34]

This incident transmitted in the *Historia Iherosolimitana* of Robert the Monk contains all the characteristic features of a high-ranking nobleman's defection to the enemy's camp:[35] preceding agreements securing the successful outcome of so risky an action; the enemies' willingness to include the apostate into their own ranks; his conversion to the enemies' religion; the defector's denouncement by his compatriots and co-religionists. The temptation to seek security by switching sides in view of unbearable hardships or unavoidable death in battle obviously was a reality with which the crusaders were constantly confronted. Moreover, the Turkish warlords were open to all sorts of collaboration with non-Muslims in order to strengthen their own ranks. This positive attitude is in full accordance with the practices implemented during their contacts with Byzantine and Armenian commanders in the eastern borderlands or with Muslim lords in Syria and Upper Mesopotamia.[36] The crusaders were no exception from the rule despite the strong religious sentiment that came to dominate their relations with the Muslims. Rainald's apostasy apparently was no isolated incident of an individual fallen into despair but reflects widespread behavioral patterns in the confrontation between Turks and Franks.

In his report about the siege of Nicaea, Albert of Aachen presents an example for the opposite case of a Turk converting to the Christian faith. Qilij Arslān supposedly dispatched two messengers to the crusaders' camp "with the false outward appearance of Christians in the manner of the pilgrims" in order to gather intelligence about the state of affairs in the Frankish army and to inform the people of Nicaea about the sultan's imminent attack. On their way, one of them was killed while the other was captured and brought to the Frankish chiefs. During the interrogation, the envoy not only begged for his life but also "urged with many and most humble pleas that with the confession of the Christian faith he might receive baptism and take communion with the Christians according to Christian law."[37] Albert explains this behavior as a result of the envoy's fear of death but also stresses the high esteem the man gained when the crusaders succeeded in fending off Qilij Arslān's attack as a result of his warnings. The Franks took pity on him and admitted him to the circle of the supreme leaders' intimates.[38] Just as in Rainald's case, we are dealing with a person acting under the threat of death. Albert gives no further details about the man's identity, but it can be assumed that a spy being ordered to mingle unnoticed with the Christians must have possessed linguistic skills and a certain familiarity with the other side. Again we come across the motif of successful personal advancement resulting from conversion.[39] The apostate on proving his devotion to the Christians' cause was requited with an influential position securing him access to the Frankish princes.

The transgression of moral and religious boundaries by Christians and Turks is exemplified by a German nun from the convent of St. Mary *ad Horrea* near Trier. She had survived the elimination of Peter the Hermit's People's Crusade in Bithynia and was released from captivity during the negotiations about the surrender of Nicaea. During the ensuing interrogation she admitted that she had had intercourse with a Turkish warrior and his companions. But with the aid of a German knight, who knew her personally, she obtained forgiveness from Duke Godfrey and the papal legate. The Turk, however, "who had been inflamed by passion for the nun's inestimable beauty," urged her to come back to him, even promising to become a Christian. Eventually the nun rushed back "for no other reason than the intolerability of her lust."[40] This intriguing episode involving a woman of lower social standing accompanying the baggage train of the crusading knights gives us one of the few insights into the day-to-day experiences of common people who came in contact with the Turks of Asia Minor. Albert obviously relates this story as an admonition in view of the dangers people had to face during their arduous march through the lands of the infidels. The fact that captives, while being detained by the enemies, could be in various ways attracted to the environment they came to live in constitutes the empirical background of this story. This also applies to men and women devoted to God, Albert argues, for even they might face moral temptations emanating from contacts with the Turks. Behavioral patterns of people exposed to cross-cultural contact situations under extreme conditions are denounced as reproachable incidents of moral defilement. Rainald, the Turkish messenger, and the German nun stand for a noteworthy side effect of the crusaders' passage through Asia Minor: the Turks for the first time came into contact with larger groups of Frankish Christians and developed various forms of interaction with them. While earlier relations with Frankish rebels and mercenaries in the empire's service did not go beyond ephemeral coalitions, the events of 1097 laid the groundwork for a limited degree of mutual permeation. Henceforth, small numbers of Franks were incorporated into Turkish warrior groups and vice versa.

Byzantine operations in western Asia Minor, 1098

At a military level, the crusaders' passage through Anatolia triggered the Byzantine campaigns in the spring of 1098, aimed at recovering the coastland and river valleys of western Asia Minor while the crusading army besieged Antioch.[41] The state of affairs in the region in the years following Tzachas' assassination in about 1093 obviously did not evince any major changes. The Byzantine government increased its hold over the Propontis littoral. As long as Nicaea and the greater part of Bithynia were in Qilij Arslān's hands, however, the emperor was unable to extend his control beyond the Dardanelles straits. The Turks of Tzachas continued to hold sway over Smyrna and the nearby islands of the eastern Aegean. The fact that Anna Komnene despite her detailed report about Tzachas' death speaks of this potentate as though he were still alive has led to various speculations in the scholarly literature.[42] It may be a mere error, but one may think of a parallel with the crusader chroniclers' convention of calling the ruler of Nicaea *Solimannus*. Turkish lordships and the warriors gathering around them were frequently identified with and named after their chief, and it may well be that the same practice applied to Smyrna. It is of secondary importance whether the actual man in power was a son, brother, or some other member of Tzachas' entourage.

Apparently, the conquest of Nicaea and the ensuing collapse of Turkish rule in Phrygia and Pisidia had a sort of domino effect on the remaining potentates in western Asia Minor. The Byzantine campaign under the command of Alexios' brother-in-law John Doukas within a short time resulted in the recovery of a considerable number of strongholds and territories stretching from the Gulf of Smyrna to the valleys of the Hermos and Meander Rivers. Several attempts of local Turkish emirs to put up resistance against the Byzantine troops quickly ended in failure. Just as the Turks of Nicaea did, a large section of the warrior groups who had established themselves in the western coastland and river valleys retreated towards the Anatolian plateau. A noteworthy detail highlighted by Anna is the fact that John Doukas was accompanied by Tzachas' daughter, who had been taken captive in Nicaea. The Byzantine commander employed her as a means of exerting psychological pressure on the Turks in order to undermine their fighting spirit.[43] Nicaea had been marked out as an especially powerful center of Turkish dominion in western Asia Minor and, at least since Qilij Arslān's takeover in 1093, as a place bearing the hallmark of Seljuk ascendancy.

The symbolic value of detaining a renowned member of the ruling family, therefore, could be harnessed to cause distress and despair among the emirs in the coastland and to break their resistance.

As regards the course of events according to Anna Komnene, the military operations started with a simultaneous attack of Byzantine naval and military forces on Smyrna. Facing the superiority of the hostile army in conjunction with the fact that after the fall of Nicaea there was no possibility of obtaining reinforcements from elsewhere, the Turkish garrison quickly surrendered to John Doukas.[44] More difficult was the subjugation of Ephesos, which was achieved only after heavy fighting. Anna speaks of many dead and about 2,000 captives, whom the emperor ordered to be dispersed over the islands.[45]

The remaining Turks fled through the Meander Valley towards Polybotos (near Bolvadin), a Phrygian town east of Akroinos (Afyonkarahisar) in the plain of Lake Tessarakonta Martyron (Eber/Akşehir Gölü).[46] Setting forth from Ephesos, John Doukas pursued the fleeing Turks towards the Anatolian plateau and occupied a number of places in the reach of his troops. He moved in a northeasterly direction, taking Sardis (near Salihli) and Philadelpheia (near Alaşehir), and then across the Meander River to Laodikeia (near Denizli), whence he continued his advance eastward to Choma (Akkale near Gümüşsu) and Lampe, two fortresses and partly overlapping military districts situated between the Upper Meander Valley and Lake Acıgöl. Arriving in Polybotos, John Doukas won another victory against the Turks, who had taken refuge in that place, and killed and captured a great number of them.[47]

The Byzantine strategy during this campaign aimed at keeping the recovered strongholds under tight control by appointing governors from among the leading officers in Alexios I's army. Thus, John Doukas appointed the fleet commander Kaspax as *doux* of Smyrna. After the latter's assassination during a riot, the position was conferred on a certain Hyaleas, who had distinguished himself as a brave officer.[48] Ephesos, the region of Sardis and Philadelpheia, and the especially sensitive area of Choma and Lampe were entrusted to Petzeas, Michael Kekaumenos, and Eustathios Kamytzes respectively, a new group of outstanding commanders who were to play an important role in the wars against the Turks over the next decades.[49] The only exception was Laodikeia, the inhabitants of which immediately submitted to the Byzantine commander and thus were allowed to remain in their hometown without being placed under the control of a governor.[50] The phrase αὐτοῖς μὲν ὡς αὐτομόλοις χρησάμενος καὶ τεθαρρηκώς (he treated them as defectors and put his faith in them) allows us to assume that there were not only local Greeks who submitted to Byzantine rule but also Turks, who preferred to stay in their newly acquired homes. If this is true, we are dealing with a group of people who had taken root in this region and were no longer willing to return to a semi-nomadic lifestyle. An inscription datable to 1094 and surviving walls provide archaeological evidence for fortification work in Didyma (near Didim) at the Carian coast south of Miletos.[51] We may assume that similar improvements of defense structures were undertaken in many other strongholds of the newly conquered areas.

Alexios I's troops advanced from their camp at Pelekanos as far as the Phrygian stronghold of Philomelion (Akşehir) situated on the northern slopes of the Sultan Mountains.[52] This juncture on one of the variants of the route leading from Dorylaion to Konya was the easternmost outpost Byzantine troops reached in central Anatolia ever since the rebellion of Nikephoros Botaneiates in 1077. It was to be exceeded only very rarely before the expeditions of Emperor Manuel I in the 1140s.[53] Apart from a brief note referring to heavy fighting with the Turks and the pillaging of towns, we have no piece of information about the itinerary of the imperial troops in 1098. It can be assumed, however, that they approximately followed the same route as the crusading army, which in the summer of 1097 advanced via Antioch of Pisidia along the southern slopes of the Sultan Mountains. This goes a long way towards explaining why Alexios I reached this point without meeting any serious resistance. The region must have been still largely abandoned and devastated. Moreover, the troops of John Doukas from their position in Polybotos covered the rear of the imperial forces.

In June 1098, just a few days before the successful sortie against Karbūqā's forces on 28 June, Alexios I and a group of Frankish lords, who in view of the growing danger had deserted from Antioch, had their well-known meeting in the camp of Philomelion. Stephan of Blois, William of Grandmesnil, and others persuaded the emperor that the situation of the Frankish army had reached so desperate a point that any further advance would be of no avail.[54] Crusader historians have long dwelled on the question as to the actual motives behind the emperor's decision and the breach of his promises to the Frankish chiefs. The issue gained major importance because of its being used as a pretext for Bohemond's claims to rule over Antioch.[55] In the scholarly discussion, this aspect fully overshadows the fact that Alexios' decision not to advance beyond Philomelion was a crucial juncture in the wars against the Turks. Crusader sources and their modern interpreters would have us believe that Alexios was mainly concerned with the desperate situation in Antioch. Anna's report, however, makes plain that the emperor was seriously pondering the overall situation of Asia Minor irrespective of the fate of the crusading army. After an aggressive phase in the years 1097–98, which aimed at restoring imperial rule over large parts of northwestern Asia Minor, Alexios I made a deliberate shift to more defensive attitudes since he realized that at least for the time being it would be extremely difficult to maintain further territorial gains while new waves of Turkish warrior groups were penetrating Anatolia. The experience of the past decades taught the decision makers in Constantinople that with the Turks in Antioch, the Upper Euphrates Valley, and in the lands east of the Halys River, it was virtually impossible to control central Anatolia.

These views are reflected in the argument Anna put forward in her attempt to account for her father's behavior. She stresses the emperor's will to lend support to the crusaders in Antioch but also points to the major challenges posed by the Turks, who were threatening both his troops and the civil population in the region.[56] "The sultan of Khurāsān," her report goes, had gathered innumerable forces and had put it under the command of his son Ismāʿīl, ordering him to attack the emperor before he arrived in Antioch.[57] Alexios, in turn, took measures for the protection of the local populace: he summoned them to gather their movable goods and to follow his troops to safer regions. While the main body of the army along with the civilians and captives was heading back to Constantinople, reconnaissance patrols were dispatched into various directions to fend off marauding enemies.[58] This version corresponds to reproaches uttered by pro-Norman spokesmen blaming Alexios for treason. The emperor is described as placing the safety of his empire and subjects above his undertakings towards his allies in Antioch, who, apart from being threatened by complete elimination, were unreliable and had no military discipline.[59]

As for the identity of the "sultan of Khurāsān," the geographical term is used here with the same meaning as *regnum Corruzana* and similar expressions in contemporary crusader sources and thus refers to the eastern Muslim lands beyond the Euphrates.[60] Ekkehard of Aura considers *terra Chorizana* the homeland of the Turks and distinguishes between the Turkish-Muslim regions of eastern Anatolia and the rest of Asia Minor, which, irrespective of the westward expansion of the Turks, is still called *Romania*.[61] The Great Seljuk sultanate in the time of the struggle between Barkyāruq and Muḥammad Tapar was unable to take any concerted action against the Byzantines or the crusaders threatening Antioch. Accordingly, Anna most likely refers to a Turkish potentate in eastern Anatolia, but it is not possible to illuminate the background of this event. Probably, Qilij Arslān in the time following his defeat at Dorylaion managed to re-organize his forces and allied with Dānishmand Ghāzī for a new campaign against the imperial troops. The *archisatrapes* Ismāʿīl, who appears as the sultan's son and leader of the Turkish forces, is usually identified with a son of Dānishmand Ghāzī, but there is no other source confirming this assumption.[62] Being informed about the emperor's retreat, Ismāʿīl took a different route and encamped at the Akampsis (Çoruh) River in order to besiege Paipert (Bayburt), which recently had been taken by Theodore Gabras.[63] Geographically, this event leads us far away from central Anatolian affairs to the Pontus region. We may assume that Anna combined originally unrelated events in order to offer a sound explanation for the emperor's course of action. The dangers emanating from the Turkish warriors based in the regions beyond the Halys River and a potential alliance with the Turks on the Anatolian plateau were the main factors lying behind this reasoning.

Paphlagonia and the central Anatolian plateau during the Lombard crusade of 1101

In the context of the aforementioned developments, the arrival in 1101 of new crusading hosts coming from Lombardy, southern France, and Germany was a decisive turning point with manifold repercussions for the balance of power in Asia Minor.[64] After some serious setbacks in the wake of the First Crusade, the seizure of Antioch, and the ensuing re-conquests of western Asia Minor by Byzantine troops, the newly arriving armies encountered a strong alliance consisting of various powerful Turkish chiefs, such as Qilij Arslān, Dānishmand

Ghāzī, Riḍwān of Aleppo, and a certain *Karageth*. The latter may be identified with Qarāja, a former slave soldier (*mamlūk*) of Sultan Malikshāh, who had been appointed lord of Ḥarrān.[65] Another commander mentioned in this context is *Balas de Sororgia*,[66] who doubtlessly can be identified with Balak b. Bahrām of Sarūj, a nephew of Suqmān b. Artuq. If we believe Matthew of Edessa, Qilij Arslān took the initiative in creating this alliance by sending letters to Dānishmand and other emirs.[67] Although this detail cannot be verified, it seems quite plausible, for Qilij Arslān had been more seriously affected by the events of 1097/98 than any other Turkish chief in Anatolia. It must have been of high priority for him to avert the danger of another disastrous setback, which certainly would have meant the end of his political existence.

The geographic terms "mountains of Paphlagonia" and "all the kingdom of Antioch" used by Albert of Aachen in order to designate the origin of the warriors fighting under the leadership of the said emirs should not be taken literally. Rather, they are vague localizations circumscribing broader areas, comprising the province of Paphlagonia and the Pontus region east of the Halys River, on the one hand, and northern Syria and Upper Mesopotamia, on the other. Remarkably, this new coalition included not only warrior groups immediately affected by the crusaders' invasion but also many Turks living in regions adjacent to the nascent crusader strongholds of Antioch and Edessa. Obviously, the massive arrival of fresh troops made them apprehensive of a potential increase of Frankish pressure.

The situation in Paphlagonia and the Pontus region is especially well documented by the reports about the Lombard contingent, which stood under the command of Bishop Anselm of Milan, the brothers Albert and Guido of Biandrate, Count Guibert of Parma, and other Italian chiefs.[68] This is due to the unorthodox decision of the Lombard chiefs, instead of taking the shortest route to Syria, to head in a northeasterly direction to the *regnum Corruzana*, i.e., the "kingdom of Khurāsān." In this case, the term apparently means the territories of Dānishmand Ghāzī. Their goal was to liberate Bohemond, who was imprisoned in the citadel of Neokaisareia.[69] The Norman lord had been captured in July 1100 outside Melitene and was to stay in prison until the summer of 1103.[70] According to Albert's account, the crusaders soon after Easter (21 April 1101) crossed the Bosphorus straits and marched to Nikomedeia, where the forces of Conrad, constable of the German emperor, as well as the troops of Count Stephen of Blois and other French knights joined them. At Pentecost (9 June 1101) the chiefs made their fatal decision.[71] The crusaders were accompanied by a detachment of Byzantine Turcopole forces under the command of a certain Tzitas and by Raymond of Toulouse, who served as an intermediary between the Byzantine emperor and the crusading chiefs. Both Albert and Anna Komnene assert that the emperor and other people advised them to desist from this route, but the Lombard commanders put all their trust in the military superiority of their troops.[72]

The detailed descriptions of the crusaders' advance and their disastrous defeat near Merzifon in early August 1101 give us valuable insights into the state of affairs of the Turkish forces in this area. Ankara was defended by a tiny garrison of 200 soldiers who were easily overwhelmed and killed. The fortifications of Gangra, however, because of their location on a steep hill, were considered impregnable. Thus, the Franks confined themselves to ravaging the crops and cornfields in the region.[73] Continuing their way towards Kastamona, the Franks were offered gifts and provisions from many fortified places in the environs, which thus averted hostile attacks.[74] Despite the scarcity of evidence we gain the impression that the hinterland of Paphlagonia was under firm control of Turkish emirs who collected taxes from the surrounding villages and agricultural areas. The military predominance of the Turks does not necessarily imply that all towns were actually manned by Turkish garrisons. Anna Komnene describes a town situated east of the Halys River on the road to Amaseia as being governed by the indigenous Greek population.[75] The local priests, wearing their sacred robes and carrying Gospels book and crosses, reportedly came to meet the crusaders. This unmistakable demonstration of obedience and unity in faith, however, did not prevent the crusaders from cruelly slaughtering the townspeople. The historicity of this account cannot be verified, but it is highly probable that the crusaders passed many towns and villages that were subject to the Turks but maintained a purely Christian character.

Ambushes, incessant skirmishes, a rough and arid landscape, and lack of supplies led the crusaders increasingly into dire straits.[76] In a mountainous area,[77] which can be located in the region of the Ilgaz Mountains, the Lombard crusaders, while constantly suffering from famine and Turkish assaults, hastened eastward across the Halys River, where they eventually fell upon the main host of the Turkish forces. The exhaustion of the men and horses caused by the hardships of the march and the massive Turkish attacks supported by skillful archers were the main reasons for the crusaders' defeat.[78] According to Albert of Aachen, Raymond of Toulouse's flight spread panic among the soldiers and caused them to abandon the camp along with the womenfolk and non-combatants and to seek refuge in the coastal towns, which stood still under Byzantine administration.[79] Albert mentions two ports affording protection and sea connections with Constantinople, namely Pulveral (Bafra) and Sinope (Sinop).[80] Although a great number of crusaders seem to have been killed on the way, some are said to have survived the whole way back to Constantinople.[81]

An important aspect in the accounts of the crusaders' defeat was the idea of an alleged Byzantine-Turkish conspiracy against the Franks. The case of Nicaea had demonstrated that the Byzantines pursued different goals and possessed more effective tools of communication with the Turks.[82] Moreover, in 1101 the imperial government had already gone through various stages of open conflict with the Normans of Antioch.[83] As a result, at least a section of the Frankish elite harbored anti-Byzantine sentiments and was generally ill disposed towards the emperor's involvement in crusading activities against the Muslims. It was most probably the result of Norman propaganda that Raymond of Toulouse was accused of acting treacherously against the defeated crusaders because of his hasty flight from the battlefield near Merzifon. Albert of Aachen also refers to rumors arguing that it was on the emperor's instigation that Raymond led the crusaders through devastated regions in order to weaken them. Yet the author himself rejects this possibility and points to the emperor's warnings to avoid this route.[84] Furthermore, he mentions Alexios' indignation about Raymond's flight.[85]

Ekkehard of Aura was a German eyewitness of the 1101 crusade who participated in the contingent of Duke Welf of Bavaria and included a brief report about this expedition in his *Chronicon Universale.* Unlike Albert, he fully adopted the negative views of Emperor Alexios as a traitor who favored the Turks more than the Christians and stirred the former up through his messengers. "This perfidious Alexios had usurped the imperial crown from his lord Michael and now he wished to make the Franks fight with the Turks as much as dogs rip each other to pieces. For this reason all people cursed and condemned him and all people called him not emperor but traitor."[86] Equally harsh is the judgment of Matthew of Edessa, who accused both the Byzantine emperor and Raymond of having driven the Franks to disaster and of having instigated the Turks against them.[87] This is not to say, however, that the Armenian author was a spokesman of the anti-Byzantine party, for in the same passage he blames the Franks for their wickedness and abandoning God's precepts. In his view, it was a combination of Greek treachery and Frankish vileness that caused God's anger and led the Turks to victory. Apart from unfounded accusations resulting from prejudice and propaganda, there was a kernel of truth in the statements of non-Byzantine chroniclers. The indigenous Greek population of Paphlagonia, which continued to live under Turkish rule, had developed peaceful forms of co-existence with their new overlords. The imperial government and certain army commanders evinced a high degree of familiarity with the local conditions and living habits of the Turks and maintained channels of communication through diplomatic contacts and skillful in-betweens. In the event of Byzantine-Frankish frictions, these aspects could easily be interpreted as signs of conspiracy.

Details regarding the situation in the southern parts of the central Anatolian plateau can be gleaned from the accounts of the expedition of Count William II of Nevers. He followed the route of the Lombard contingent as far as Ankara, but then turned southward towards Konya.[88] In 1101 this town already had a strong garrison fending off the crusaders' attack, so that the latter moved on to Herakleia, which is described as "ruined and empty of inhabitants."[89] Frequent ambushes and attacks by the troops of Qilij Arslān and Dānishmand Ghāzī in combination with thirst, famine, and physical exhaustion caused by the march through the waterless Anatolian plateau in mid-summer had similar results as in the case of the Lombard army in Paphlagonia. In addition, the Turks had destroyed all cisterns and wells in Herakleia, and thus the exhausted crusaders were an easy prey for the Turks, who killed a great many soldiers and non-combatants in the valley outside the town.[90] Just like the fugitive Lombards in Paphlagonia, Count William and the knights who survived the slaughter strove to reach territories under Byzantine control. They moved from the environs of the Cilician Gates southward to the Taurus Mountains. From there they may have hoped to reach one of the safe harbors at the coast.

The town of Germanicopla (Ermenek) situated in the mountains north of Anamourion (Anamur) is mentioned as being controlled by a garrison of imperial Turcopoles.[91] This provides evidence for the fact that, from their strongholds at the southern shores, the Byzantines had managed to build up outposts in the Taurus Mountains. In this way they monitored the routes leading from the Anatolian plateau to the coastland and were able to fend off invading raiders or nomad groups. Most probably, the soldiers of Germanicopla and their likes were also active as unruly brigands in regions far from any centralizing authority. This is illustrated by the fate of Count William, who was robbed by these soldiers despite their promises to escort him to Antioch.

Philomelion, which three years earlier had been evacuated by the army of Alexios I, in 1101 was in Turkish hands. The same applies to a place called Salimia southeast of Konya, which is identified with the modern town of İsmil.[92] These pieces of information can be gleaned from Albert's report about the third crusader contingent commanded by William IX of Aquitaine and Duke Welf of Bavaria. The crusaders attacked these towns and ravaged their environs but were not able to take possession of them.[93] Heavily exhausted by the Turkish strategy of scorched earth, this contingent, too, suffered a disastrous defeat near Herakleia by the allied forces of Qilij Arslān, Dānishmand, and others.[94]

The overall picture emerging from these accounts is that Qilij Arslān and other Turkish emirs considerably consolidated and reorganized their rule in the years after their setbacks in 1097/98. Vast areas of the Anatolian plateau including the western fringes in Phrygia between the Sultan Mountains and Lake Akşehir as well as the mountainous areas of Paphlagonia were firmly under Turkish control. Konya, which in 1098 had still been an easy prey for the crusaders, had turned into an impregnable fortress. Philomelion, which controlled one of the main access routes to the Anatolian plateau, was equally well defended, thus impeding the imperial government's attempts to extend its sway eastward. The weak defenses of Ankara may suggest that the Turks initially did not anticipate Frankish attacks in the northern parts of Galatia but concentrated their forces in areas affected by the onslaught of the First Crusade, as the strong garrison in Philemelion shows. Nevertheless, the presence of Turkish units in towns like Kastamona, Gangra, and Amaseia demonstrates that the Byzantines maintained their strongholds along the Pontic shoreline but had completely lost control of the hinterland. The entire region could easily be penetrated by warrior groups coming from the territories of Dānishmand Ghāzī east of the Halys River. The devastated state of Herakleia in the southeastern edge of the Anatolian plateau seems to point to a swathe of no man's land in the region north of the Armenian territories of Cilicia.

Another remarkable feature of the situation in 1101 was the improved network of communication between the emirs in the Anatolian highlands and those based in northern Syria and Mesopotamia. One of the first lessons Turkish warlords had to learn in their confrontation with the crusading armies was that they could cope with them solely with the support of broad alliances and large contingents. This was a new element of Turkish warfare in Anatolia, which came into being in reaction to the crusader hosts. In other words, the crusades prompted the Turks of Anatolia to strengthen their fighting force, to form larger units, and to improve their military capacities beyond incursions and raids to large-scale operations in pitched battles. The Byzantine re-conquests in the wake of the First Crusade had certainly brought about a dwindling of the Turkish sphere of influence in Asia Minor. In return, Lycaonia, Cappadocia, parts of Paphlagonia, Galatia, Phrygia, and the lands east of the Halys River had become hardly accessible for both Byzantine and Frankish troops. This was an important factor contributing to the imperial government's strategic re-orientation towards the southern littoral of Asia Minor, which had become the only route of communication with Cilicia and northern Syria.

Byzantine consolidation at the southern littoral of Asia Minor, 1098–1108

The conquest of Antioch and the defeat of Emir Karbūqā of Mosul in June 1098 not only laid the foundations for the princedom of Antioch but also had a strong impact on the political situation in the southern coastland of Asia Minor and the region between the Gulf of Iskenderun and Tripoli.[95] Bohemond of Taranto's efforts to keep Antioch under his sway and the ensuing struggle with the Byzantine emperor, though primarily a conflict between Byzantium and the crusaders, affected the Turkish emirs as well. The operations in the coastal regions brought about a strong increase in Frankish and Byzantine military pressure. The Muslim local lords in the ports at the Syrian coast were often trapped in isolated enclaves exposed to the attacks of both Frankish and Byzantine troops. Aleppo and other strongholds south of Edessa and the Diyār Bakr province came to form a new Christian-Muslim frontier. The Turkish warrior groups in Anatolia lost access to Cilicia and the Jayḥān Valley and were largely confined to regions north of the Taurus Mountains.[96] Byzantium may have failed to impose its will on the Normans, but it took advantage of the enfeeblement of various Muslim powers, which were increasingly involved in the conflicts with the Franks.

After his retreat from central Anatolia in June 1098, the emperor pursued the twofold goal of undermining the Norman base in Antioch and wielding power over the coastland between Lycia and Cilicia.[97] Under these circumstances, the Byzantine navy turned out to be an instrument of outstanding significance for the empire's military strategy. It took defensive actions against western fleets arriving from Pisa and Genoa and bolstered expansionist attempts in the coastal areas, which could be reached much more easily from the seaside than from the Anatolian hinterland. At that time, the island of Cyprus emerged as the easternmost outpost of the Byzantine military administration and as a hub of naval operations in the eastern Mediterranean.[98] After suppressing a local insurrection led by a certain Rapsomates in 1092/93, the imperial government realized the necessity of establishing a strong local administration on the island and appointed a judge and tax collector as well as a military chief commanding a contingent of ships and horsemen.[99] The fleet unit stationed on Cyprus enabled the imperial government to exert some control over the surrounding coastal areas. This first became evident during the siege of Antioch, in which the island served as a post for supply and retreat. When the Normans eventually took possession of Antioch and the Byzantines consolidated their hold on Attaleia, Cyprus proved especially useful for imperial strategy as an advanced bridgehead situated at short distance from the contested strongholds on the Syrian coast.[100]

The fortification of Cyprus was accompanied by a substantial expansion of Byzantine naval forces in 1099.[101] In that year the imperial government faced the advance of the Pisan fleet of Archbishop Daimbert, which made its way through the Aegean and along the coast of Asia Minor towards the East.[102] Constantinople reacted to this threat by levying vessels from the provinces and by constructing a new type of battleship equipped with fire spitting mechanisms.[103] The supreme command over the new fleet was entrusted to officers who were familiar with both naval warfare and the fighting skills of Frankish soldiers. The emperor chose Tatikios, who had distinguished himself during the crusaders' march through Asia Minor, and a certain Landoulphos, apparently a man of Italian origin, who is described as expert in naval battles. The latter was appointed chief commander, bearing the title of *megas doux*. In their fighting skills the new units seem to have lagged behind the experienced sailors of the Italian cities but were strong enough to defend Byzantine-held positions and support attacks and sieges in the coastal region.

In the skirmishes with Daimbert's fleet, the Byzantine navy failed to destroy the well-equipped Italian ships but drove them back from the empire's islands and ports. In a battle fought at some point between Rhodes and the port of Patara (Gelemiş west of Kastelorizo), the Byzantine fleet faced problems of discipline and coordination, thus failing to inflict serious damage upon the enemies. Conversely, when the Pisans made an attempt to attack Cyprus, Eumathios Philokales put them immediately to flight. Hence, they continued their way to Laodikeia to support Bohemond in the siege of this port.[104] In the following year (1100) the Byzantines fought back Genoese ships coming in support of Bohemond off the coast of the Peloponnese and near the Syrian shore.[105] Landoulphos' fleet had been dispatched to intercept them before they passed the easternmost cape of the Laconian Gulf and enter the Aegean Sea. A storm caused substantial damage to Landoulphos' ships, and thus the Genoese continued their journey towards the Syrian coast without meeting further obstacles.[106] The Byzantine fleet again proved too weak to prevent western ships from reaching their Norman allies. Over the first year of their activities, the new naval contingents had suffered some setbacks and were partly destroyed. Yet the naval base on Cyprus had passed its initial trial, and the imperial government managed to increase its hold over the region.

Taking possession of and fortifying the castles of Kourikon/Korykos (Kız Kalesi) and Seleukeia (Silifke) were decisive steps in this direction.[107] These strongholds at the straits of Cilicia just opposite the northern shores of Cyprus significantly buttressed the defensive system in the region and made the passage of Italian ships heading to or returning from the Syrian coast or possible attacks of the Normans of Antioch much more difficult. Alexios entrusted the eunuch

Eustathios with this mission, a man who fulfilled both civil and military functions as *epi tou kanikleiou* and *megas droungarios* of the fleet.[108] Given that the same person had been charged with the erection of a fortress near Nikomedeia in the time of Apelchasem's rule,[109] it can be assumed that he was an expert in fortifications.[110] The stationing of a garrison and naval contingent in the port of Seleukeia frustrated Bohemond's plans to wield power over the Cilician coastland and thus strengthen his coalition with the Italian naval forces.

The events related to the catastrophe of the Lombard, French, and German crusader hosts near Merzifon and Herakleia in 1101[111] illustrate another vital function fulfilled by Byzantine ports and naval bases at the shores of Asia Minor. As has been shown above, many survivors escaped the disaster via the ports of Paphlagonia and Cilicia. These strongholds were supporting a network of seaborne traffic transporting troops, weapons, and supplies between Constantinople and the remnants of the Byzantine territories in Asia Minor. If need be, they also served as places of refuge for military units and non-combatants afflicted by hostile attacks in the hinterland.

Besides consolidating its defensive structures, the imperial government shortly after the conquest of Antioch organized a series of military operations targeting cities on the Syrian littoral. Due to its frontier position, Cyprus offered great strategic advantages for these activities. After Bohemond's retreat in 1099, the emperor ordered Raymond of Toulouse to hand Laodikeia over to the Byzantine officer Andronikos Tzintziloukes. Simultaneously, the fortresses of Bāniyās and Maraqiyya situated further south were placed under the command of subordinate officers of Eumathios Philokales, thus establishing direct links between the units in Syria and the headquarters in Cyprus.[112] When Raymond in 1102 began to blockade Tripoli by erecting a fortress on the so-called Pilgrim's Mountain opposite the town, he was effectively supported by the *doux* of Cyprus, who at the emperor's bidding sent building material and workers to the site in question.[113] The imperial strategy apparently aimed at strengthening the alliance with Bohemond's archrival Raymond of Toulouse by lending military support through a naval network embracing Cyprus and a number of fortified places between Laodikeia and Tripoli. In this way Byzantine strongholds and naval contingents increasingly tightened the loop they had made around Antioch and the Gulf of Iskenderun.

In the years between 1101 and 1104, the rivalry between Byzantium and the Normans of Antioch further escalated in a series of heavy conflicts for control over Cilicia and the Syrian littoral. Generally speaking, the Byzantine naval forces proved too weak to gain permanent footholds in the coastal areas east of Seleukeia, and various diplomatic overtures to the Norman chiefs were of no avail. Temporary setbacks of Antioch in its conflicts with neighboring Muslim forces, however, encouraged the Byzantines to resume their attacks and to regain lost ground.[114]

In the spring of 1101, shortly after the arrival of Tancred, who in the time of Bohemond's captivity ruled Antioch on behalf of his uncle, the Normans in a quick campaign seized the main towns of Cilicia, such as Mamistra, Adana, and Tarsus.[115] The conquest of Laodikeia proved more difficult and required a one-and-a-half-year blockade. The Byzantine naval forces from Cyprus failed to provide sufficient support for the defense of the city. As we lack reliable chronological details, the seizure of the town can only approximately be dated to the second half of 1102 or early 1103.[116] Pressured by Norman attacks and the famine raging in the town, Tzintziloukes sent urgent messages to Cyprus. Being unable to protract his resistance without effective relief, he eventually surrendered to Tancred.[117]

The Frankish defeat of Ḥarrān on 7 May 1104, in which Suqmān b. Artuq and Jokermish decimated Bohemond's troops and took Tancred and Baldwin of Edessa captive, tipped the scales in favor of the imperial government and its goals in the East. This setback gave the Byzantines breathing time, which they used to restructure their forces in the region.[118] Alexios I launched a last campaign against Cilicia and the Syrian coast with Antioch as its final objective. Large forces under Manuel Boutoumites were sent via Attaleia by sea to Cilicia. A second contingent under Kantakouzenos proceeded further ahead to the Syrian coast, attacking Laodikeia and other places.[119] From a military point of view, the operations were by and large successful despite some minor setbacks. Arriving in Cilicia, Boutoumites found the Armenians allied with Tancred. Thus, he passed the towns of the Cilician plain and seized Marʿash in the Jayḥān Valley, where he left Monastras with strong forces.[120] The latter continued the expedition by taking Tarsus, Adana, and Mamistra.[121] Kantakouzenos put siege to Laodikeia and managed to take the harbor and the town, but the citadel was supplied by Bohemond from the outside and held out. At the same time, Byzantine troops took other fortresses south of Laodikeia, such as Argyrokastron/Qalʿat al-ʿUlayqa, Jabala, and Marqab, advancing southward as far as Tripoli, which was still under siege by Raymond's forces.[122]

All in all, the military predominance established by Byzantine forces over Cilicia and parts of the Syrian coastlands in this campaign was highly fragile and short lived. The imperial army took temporary possession of some major towns and fortresses, but there were no adequate military structures to consolidate these territorial acquisitions. The inability of the naval forces in Cyprus to lend effective support to the garrison of Laodikeia during the Norman siege is indicative of the difficulties the imperial government was facing in sustaining larger combat-capable contingents in the area. In contrast to previous periods, the Byzantine administration could no longer resort to any hinterland or supply areas supporting the outposts with provisions and manpower. The situation was further exacerbated by ongoing Norman aggression and the unwillingness of the Armenian lords to submit to Byzantine rule. It thus comes as no surprise that the expansion towards Cilicia and the Syrian littoral collapsed as soon as the local Christian powers recovered from the Muslim strikes they had endured.[123] What is more, in late 1104 Bohemond returned to the West in order to start his propaganda campaign for a large-scale expedition against Byzantium.[124]

The main junction between Cyprus, Seleukeia, and the ports of the Aegean Sea was the city of Attaleia, a well-fortified port and naval base at the coast of

Pamphylia.[125] As a result of the reconquests achieved in 1098, by about 1104 the city was firmly controlled by Byzantine troops. Rich archaeological evidence bears witness to Komnenian building activities in the adjacent towns of the Lycian coastland. Sections in the walls of Makre-Telmessos (Fethiye), Kyaneai (Asar Tepe), and Limyra (on a foothill of Toçak Dağı), as well as traces of rebuilding in churches on the island of Lebissos (Gemile Ada, Kayaköy), Xanthos (Kınık), and especially Myra (Kale/Demre) with its monastery of St. Nicholas point to an improvement of defenses, perhaps even to a "whole chain of coastal forts."[126] There is no piece of information attesting to any form of Turkish rule in Lycia before 1098, but it may be safely assumed that the region was heavily exposed to raiding activities.[127] Written and archaeological evidence concurs in that the restabilization of Byzantine control brought about an overall recovery of the entire region of the Lycian coast, although it is hardly possible to assess to what extent the mountainous areas in the hinterland were included in this safety zone. The situation in the Pamphylian coastland east of Attaleia seems to have remained more unstable. This at least becomes clear from the state of affairs in the port of Side. Despite its significance as an entrepot of local agricultural products and as a hub on the maritime routes between the Levant and the West in earlier centuries, the city never recovered from its decline in the eleventh century and seems to have been in complete disrepair in the early twelfth century.[128] It may be assumed that Side was replaced by the port of Kalon Oros (Alanya) situated further east.[129] Certain indications point to a full restoration of the city walls in the Komnenian period, perhaps already under Alexios I, and these fortifications seem to have remained intact until the Seljuk conquest in 1221.[130] There is hardly any conclusive evidence for the situation in the hinterland. Ceramic finds from the excavations on the Alexander Hill of Sagalassos (Ağlasun) north of Attaleia show no signs of an increase of pastoralism, which would point to a permanent presence of nomadic groups.[131]

A snapshot view of the situation in the broader area is provided by an incident mentioned by Anna Komnene. She refers to the unruly behavior of Bardas and the imperial cupbearer (*archioinochoos*) Michael, two young officers in Alexios' retinue, who were to accompany Manuel Boutoumites on his expedition to the East. The chief commander was ordered to send them from Attaleia to Cyprus, where they were put under the custody of the *doux* Euphorbenos Konstantinos.[132] Since they continued their insurgent activities (such as their instigation of suspicious individuals on the island), Kantakouzenos had to take them back onboard during a stopover in Keryneia (Girne).[133] Anna says nothing about the backgrounds of these schemes, but in her account we catch a glimpse of the seaborne traffic in the coastal areas of southern Asia Minor and of the handling of recalcitrant elements by the Byzantine authorities. Attaleia and the port of Keryneia situated on the northern shore of Cyprus were closely connected through warships moving between the Pamphylian coast and the Cilician straits. Keryneia seems to have been an intermediate station for naval contingents heading towards Syria. The surviving lead seal of a certain Leon, *kommerkiarios* of Cyprus and Attaleia, shows that there also were close administrative links between the two places.[134]

The imperial administration evinced a high degree of cautiousness in checking and, if need be, removing insurgent people from these sensitive strongholds. Due to its exposed frontier position, Cyprus seems to have been regarded a suitable place of exile for unruly elements. On the other hand, the island's proximity to the crusader states and Muslim territories made it especially vulnerable to insurrections of marginalized local elements and susceptible to undesired enemy contacts undermining the allegiance of the population. Rapsomates' uprising in 1092 had shown that dangerous situations could be produced by local seditious movements, and thus Byzantine officials had to be especially alert to these phenomena. This seems to have been the reason for the quick removal of the two officers when they continued stirring up trouble.[135]

The territorial gains achieved in 1104 did not persist for long, because Bohemond's preparations for a large-scale campaign in the West forced the emperor to recall his most capable officers, such as Kantakouzenos and Monastras, from their posts in Laodikeia and Cilicia and to replace them with second-string personnel.[136] This decision proved especially disastrous in the case of Cilicia, where Alexios in 1105/06 appointed an Armenian nobleman called Aspietes to the rank of a commander-in-chief of the entire East (*stratopedarches pases anatoles*). Apparently, the man was no newcomer, for he had already distinguished himself for his bravery in the wars against Robert Guiscard two decades earlier. On the basis of sigillographic evidence, this individual can be identified with the *kouropalates* and *protonobelissimos* Aspietes Pakourianos, whose titles suggest that he was invested with a position similar to his semi-independent Armenian compatriots in the Jayḥān region and the Upper Euphrates Valley.[137] When Tancred mounted an attack on Mamistra, it turned out that the Byzantine defense was completely insufficient. Anna puts the blame on Aspietes' personal incapability.[138] More likely, the reason lies in the fact that the Norman campaign in the West unavoidably weakened the Byzantine military presence in the East. Laodikeia could be held a little longer. It was under the command of Petzeas, one of the leading officers of Alexios' 1098 expedition, who had served as governor of Ephesos for some time. In 1108, however, the city likewise surrendered to Tancred of Antioch.[139] As a result, the Byzantine Empire lost its strongholds in Cilicia and northern Syria for several decades until John II in his eastern campaign of 1137–38 recovered the cities of the Cilician plain and imposed his overlordship on Antioch.[140]

Despite these setbacks, Constantinople preserved its predominance over the southern shores of Asia Minor as far as Seleukeia and its naval base on Cyprus. The natural barrier of the Taurus Mountains, which seem to have become a kind of no-man's land, separated these ports from the principality of Qilij Arslān. After the expulsion of the crusaders in 1101, Qilij Arslān further strengthened his position in the central Anatolian plateau and stabilized his sphere of influence vis-à-vis the Byzantine territories and the Armenian and Frankish lordships in the southeast.[141] As we have seen, the Byzantines maintained some advanced outposts in the mountains, which protected the access routes to the littoral. Most likely, there were Turkish raiders and nomad groups moving around in search of booty and pastureland during the summer months. After the definite loss of

Cilicia, however, the Seljuk elite desisted from any attempts at expanding towards the southern coastland.

Diplomatic activities vis-a-vis Muslims and crusaders

The Byzantine military operations against the Normans and their allies were accompanied by brisk diplomatic activities embracing both Frankish and Muslim potentates in the region. By doing so, the imperial government advanced its claims to political supremacy over Antioch and forged its relations with Raymond of Toulouse and other potential proponents of its cause.[142] Muslim powers, which at times inflicted crushing defeats on the Franks, provided ample opportunity for the emperor to intervene in favor of high-ranking prisoners and thus enhance his image as protector of all Christians in the East. These overtures may not have brought the expected results with respect to Antioch, but they bolstered Alexios' efforts to engage in Muslim-Frankish conflicts as a regulating factor and mediating authority.

The first Byzantine emissaries to meet the crusader lords after the fall of Antioch were dispatched in response to the embassy of Hugh of Vermandois and arrived in the Frankish camp before ʿArqa on 10/11 April 1099. They conveyed complaints about Bohemond's perjury and renewed the emperor's promises of lavish gifts should the Franks await his arrival in order to jointly proceed under the emperor's command to Jerusalem.[143] The crusading chiefs would not comply with these proposals, but the imperial government seems still to have cherished hopes of maintaining supreme control over the crusading army through a peaceful settlement of its discord with Bohemond. To this effect, it evoked its sovereign rights over the contested territories and the Norman chiefs' oaths of allegiance. John Pryor and Michael Jeffreys have recently argued that the imperial court's initial objective was the recreation of the *Domestikaton of the East*, as had been held until the late 1080s by Philaretos Brachamios. Through a complicated line of argument juxtaposing Anna's reports on the 1097 negotiations, the treaty of Devol, numerous details provided by Latin chronicles, and Byzantine lead seals, the authors try to show that the Byzantine strategy aimed at a restoration of direct imperial rule over the ducate of Antioch while Bohemond was to take hold of Philaretos' lands farther east as far as Edessa.[144] According to this theory, Bohemond was to be transformed into a Byzantine court dignitary and powerful ally exerting territorial rule on the basis of Byzantine concepts of legitimacy.

As usually happens when evidence is scarce and elusive, it is hard to say whether all the conjectures in Pryor's and Jeffrey's argumentation correspond to the historical facts. It is beyond doubt, however, that Alexios treated Bohemond in more or less the same way as he did his Turkish allies and opponents in western Asia Minor. This is to say that the emperor's prime objective was to subsume the Norman lord into his network of eastern alliances. Despite all conflicts Alexios never ceased to pursue a policy of appeasement vis-à-vis his rival. During Bohemond's siege of Laodikeia in 1099, the chief-commanders of the fleet and the *doux* of Cyprus Eumathios Philokales ordered Manuel Boutoumites to enter peace negotiations with Bohemond, but the emissary was detained for 15 days and thereafter chased away under the pre-text that his real purpose was to burn the ships in the harbor.[145] Following the Norman conquest of Laodikeia in 1102/03, Alexios reportedly sent a letter to Bohemond in which he reminded him of his oath and ordered him to stay away from Antioch and other fortresses, which legally belonged to the empire. Bohemond once again is described as ruthless and irreconcilable, accusing the emperor of having betrayed them during the siege of Antioch.[146] In terms of practical results, all efforts to negotiate a compromise with the Normans were of no avail.

As has been pointed out, Alexios closely collaborated with Raymond of Toulouse as Bohemond's chief opponent and the main representative of pro-Byzantine attitudes among the crusader lords.[147] The emperor, however, failed to set the relations with the nascent county of Tripoli on a firm basis. Raymond's reception at the court of Constantinople in early 1100 was an event of high political and symbolic significance, which underlined the fact that one of the most powerful Frankish princes had become a staunch ally of the emperor.[148] For some years, Raymond proved very useful in promoting the imperial government's goals in the conflicts with the Turks of Asia Minor and the Normans of Antioch. But after Raymond's death in February 1105 things changed quickly. Alexios instructed the *doux* of Cyprus to appoint a man called Niketas Chalintzes as emissary to William II Jourdain in order to renew the oath of allegiance taken by his predecessor.[149] Most likely, Anna's silence about the results of this mission suggests that the new chiefs in the region of Tripoli were no longer interested in maintaining their vassal relationship with the emperor.[150] Hence, by 1105 Alexios I lost one of the pillars on which his influence over the Syrian coastland and the crusader states was based. As a result, the Cypriot naval base and the Byzantine officers on the island gained further importance in regional military operations and official contacts with the Franks. The Cypriot base certainly facilitated the temporary occupation of strongholds in Cilicia and the Syrian coastland in the years 1104–1108, although it was not strong enough to secure these gains.[151]

Ransoming high-ranking Frankish prisoners was an effective means of projecting ascendency in conjunction with traditional imperial virtues, such as philanthropy and love of peace. After the defeat of King Baldwin I by the Fatimid army outside al-Ramla on 19 May 1102,[152] Alexios sent a certain Bardales to Cairo to ransom the counts who had been captured in the battle. The emperor's show of solicitousness resulted in an equally sympathetic response on the part of the Fatimid court, which set the prisoners free without accepting the ransom money.[153] We may suppose that there were more things at stake in these negotiations than the fate of some prominent Frankish knights. The Aleppo chronicle of al-ʿAẓīmī refers to Byzantine-Fatimid contacts even prior to the arrival of the crusaders,[154] a scrap of evidence that, however spurious it might be, seems to point to an understanding regarding the maintenance of amicable contacts even in times of open conflict with the Franks. Simultaneously, the emperor sought to increase his influence on the governing elite of Jerusalem by hosting the released counts in Constantinople and lavishing rich gifts on them before they returned to Palestine. A very similar scenario recurred in about 1105 with the embassy of Niketas Panoukomites to Cairo.[155] This shows that the emperor's demeanor was based on a consistent long-term strategy. Different purposes were exhibited by the embassy of Gregory Taronites, who was charged with a mission to Dānishmand Ghāzī to ransom Bohemond.[156] In this case, the emperor primarily aimed at taking hold of his archenemy and thus to extract concessions with respect to Antioch and other objectives in the East. In short, high-ranking Frankish prisoners, who with the growing Muslim resistance increased in number, proved an effective means to promote the idea of the empire's abiding power and resourcefulness in Byzantine-Muslim diplomatic contacts and widened the circle of potential supporters of Byzantium among the Frankish nobility in the East.

Granting lavish receptions to fugitives was another important tool bolstering the emperor's efforts to forge a network of personal ties with the Franks. A case in point is the arrival of the chiefs of the 1101 crusade following their crushing defeat in the battle of Merzifon in August 1101. Raymond of Toulouse, Constable Conrad, Stephen of Burgundy, and others, deprived of all their belongings in the wake of their hasty flight, were granted splendid gifts and permitted to recuperate for months in Constantinople. As the bishop of Milan passed away during his sojourn in the imperial city, he was buried with all due funerary celebrations.[157] The same treatment was conceded to Count William II of Nevers, who on arriving at the straits of the Bosphorus in June 1101 was granted lavish receptions in the imperial palace for two weeks on a daily basis. At the same time, all his soldiers received financial support to cover their needs.[158] According to Matthew of Edessa, William of Aquitaine showed an especially arrogant attitude towards the emperor by addressing him as "eparch" instead of emperor. Despite his haughtiness, Alexios did not desist from summoning him to court or from purveying a magnificent reception with lavish gifts and sumptuous spectacles in his honor.[159] All these examples garnered from Latin and Armenian sources concur in underlining the imperial government's assiduous endeavor to attract and gain the confidence of the crusading lords. This was all the more important at a time when the enmity with the Normans of Antioch was already underway and Bohemond's propaganda increasingly denigrated the emperor. There was a great danger that the Frankish leaders, who followed the footpaths of their predecessors and set forth to liberate Bohemond from Dānishmandid captivity, would be inveigled to make a stand against Byzantium and to flock to the Norman camp. In view of this contingency, the emperor had to project his role as the crusaders' generous supporter and savior from dire plights at all costs.

Soon after the disastrous outcome of the 1101 crusade with all the ensuing accusations of breach of pledges, deceit, and treason spelled out obliquely or forthrightly by various circles against the Byzantine emperor, a decisive step towards an improvement of relations with the kingdom of Jerusalem was achieved by an embassy sent by King Baldwin I soon after Easter (6 April) 1102 to Constantinople. The emissaries requested the emperor's assistance for the Christians and the church of Jerusalem, an end to Byzantine contacts with the Turks and Saracens, and free trade between the kingdom and the Byzantine provinces.

Being well disposed towards these propositions, the emperor agreed to a treaty of friendship with King Baldwin and on oath asseverated his innocence as to the Lombards' defeat. Eventually, with a mission to Pope Paschal II led by the bishop of Barcelona, Alexios solicited absolution from the Holy See.[160] In this way, he belied all accusations disseminated by the pro-Norman propaganda and strengthened his influence in Jerusalem.

Taken together, the diplomatic efforts during the years of 1099–1105 failed to resolve the conflicts with the Normans or reduce their influence in northern Syria before Bohemond's departure for the West to prepare his invasion. Nevertheless, ransoming prisoners, granting sanctuary to fugitives, and lavishing gifts upon Frankish noblemen highlighted the emperor's role as mediating authority between Christians and Muslims and contributed to a stabilization of personal ties between Constantinople and the royal court of Jerusalem. The contacts with Dānishmand Ghāzī and the Fatimid caliphate of Egypt show that the imperial government for all its setbacks and territorial losses still enjoyed a powerful and prestigious position among its Muslim neighbors. Moreover, the negotiations regarding Bohemond's release provided the emperor with one of the first occasions to establish official contacts with a Turkish emirate in northeastern Anatolia and thus to extend his diplomatic network to regions that for many decades had totally escaped the influence of the imperial court. Relations with Egypt and certain emirs in the former Armenian provinces could be used as a counterweight against the gradually crystallizing predominance of Antioch and the newly emerging Muslim powers in Upper Mesopotamia.

The Artuqids in Diyār Bakr

It was certainly of major significance that the consolidation and expansion of Qilij Arslān I's Anatolian principality after his victories over the crusaders coincided with a new phase in the internecine struggle between Malikshāh's sons, Barkyāruq and his half-brother Muḥammad Tapar.[161] Unlike the preceding conflicts, in which the Seljuk elite of Syria was deeply involved, the civil strife of the years 1099–1104 was centered on Iraq, Baghdad, Azerbaijan, and western Iran and thus did not directly affect the regions of northern Syria and Upper Mesopotamia. A definite influence, which the Great Seljuk sultanate in the time after Tutush's death had still been able to exert, frayed irremediably after 1099. Hence, the local Muslim lordships formed their power relations without interference from supra-regional forces. A great number of conflicts and military clashes in the wider area resulted from the gradual strengthening of the crusader principalities of Antioch and Edessa and the Armenian lordships farther north. These wars proved to be a strong unifying factor among the Muslim emirs in that they favored the forging of alliances against the Christians and the crystallization of a strong *jihad* ideology. For the first time, Turkish emirs came to the foreground as champions of Islam and thus gained access to a new source of legitimacy and military prestige.

The Artuqids, who had been staunch supporters of Tutush, played a leading role in this process when they managed to carve out new lordships in the Diyār Bakr province. In the wake of their overlord's defeat in 1095 many Turkish emirs lost their territories in Palestine, the Syrian coastland, and the region around Edessa and were forced to move eastward. In this time members of the Artuqid clan seized the fortresses of Sarūj and Samosata.[162] Suqmān b. Artuq first became involved in the affairs of Diyār Bakr sometime after 1098, when he backed the Turkmen commander of Āmid against an attack of the emir of Mosul, Qiwām al-Dawla Karbūqā. Suqmān was defeated while his nephew Yāqūtī was taken captive and imprisoned in the citadel of Mārdīn. Yāqūtī thereafter inserted himself into the local elite by creating close ties with the lord of Mārdīn, a former singer at the court of Barkyāruq, who had been given the town as a land grant (*iqṭāʿ*). By engaging in military activities against local Kurds, he gained control over Mārdīn, but later on lost his life in a battle against Jokermish, a slave soldier from Sultan Malikshāh's entourage who after the end of the civil war had become involved in the affairs of Upper Mesopotamia as emir of Jazīrat b. ʿUmar.[163] On his mother's request, Suqmān mounted an attack on Jokermish to take revenge for Yāqūtī's death. Eventually, Suqmān took possession of Mārdīn, thus preventing Yāqūtī's brother ʿAlī from surrendering to Jokermish.[164]

A turning point in these rivalries between Turkish warlords from Syria and local potentates associated with Barkyāruq's entourage was the death of Karbūqā in Dhū l-Qaʿda 495/17 August-15 September 1102.[165] During the succession struggle among Karbūqā's followers, a certain Mūsā al-Turkumānī called on Suqmān b. Artuq to support him against Jokermish. As a reward, Mūsā was to give him the town of Ḥiṣn Kayfā (Hasankeyf) and a sum of 10,000 dinars. Jokermish, however, proved stronger and seized Mosul while Suqmān took possession of Ḥiṣn Kayfā, a castle of great strategic importance on the banks of the Tigris River about halfway between Jazīrat b. ʿUmar and Āmid.[166] In sum, the Artuqid expansion from the Euphrates region to the key points of Mārdīn and Ḥiṣn Kayfā resulted in an expulsion of emirs belonging to Sultan Barkyāruq's retinue by members of Tutush's entourage. With his takeover in Mosul, Jokermish became the most powerful ruler in northern Jazīra. Unlike his predecessor, however, he adopted an accommodating attitude towards the Artuqids and entered coalitions with them. This prepared the ground for a first anti-Frankish alliance of Turkish emirs based in Upper Mesopotamia.

Their victory in the battle of Ḥarrān in May 1104 was the most remarkable success of this policy. Count Baldwin of Edessa and Joscelin I of Tall Bāshir, who had attacked Ḥarrān with the support of Antiochene troops, were defeated and taken captive by the allied forces of Suqmān and Jokermish. Despite some discord about the sharing of the booty, both rulers drew great profit from their military triumph. Jokermish failed to seize Edessa but was recognized as lord of Ḥarrān, and Suqmān seized a number of smaller fortresses in the region. The captivity of the two princes, which was to last until 1108, temporarily weakened the county of Edessa and prevented the Franks from any southward expansion.

The easternmost outpost of the crusader states no longer posed a serious threat to the Turkish lords in Upper Mesopotamia.[167]

What is more, with the victory of Ḥarrān, Suqmān gained a great deal of fame and prestige among the Muslim lords in Syria. Shortly after the battle, the lord of Tripoli and Ṭughtikīn of Damascus summoned him to assume the protection of their respective realms.[168] Victory on the battlefield and the capture of some of the most prominent crusader lords founded his reputation as a powerful commander in the war against the Christians. On his way to Damascus, Suqmān suddenly died in the village of al-Qaryatayn in October 1104.[169] In this context the Muslim historiographical tradition began to attribute elements of *jihad* ideology to him. While concluding their alliance, Jokermish and Suqmān are said to have announced their readiness to sacrifice themselves for God and his reward.[170] Another source states even more explicitly that they made their agreement in order to conduct the *jihad* against the enemies of God, the Franks.[171] In a similar vein, Suqmān on falling ill during his march to Damascus insisted on continuing his journey, stating that God should not see him neglecting the struggle against the infidels for fear of death.[172] These statements certainly reflect a later, fully developed concept of *jihad* in the wars of the Syrian emirs against the crusaders. Yet it is still remarkable that they first appear in the aftermath of the battle of Ḥarrān as a means of describing the Artuqid lord as a Muslim champion of Holy War successfully fending off Frankish aggression. In this way, Suqmān's lordship enhanced its legitimacy and strengthened its ties with local Syrian lords and Tutush's descendants ruling in Damascus and Aleppo.

With the gradual expansion of the county of Edessa, other members of the Artuqid clan were compelled to retreat from the banks of the Euphrates into the interior of Upper Mesopotamia. A case in point is Suqmān's nephew, Balak b. Bahrām, who had been entrusted with the administration of Sarūj but lost it to the Franks. Dodging the territories of his relatives and of Jokermish, in Muḥarram 497/October 1103 he marched southward and took possession of the towns of ʿĀna and al-Ḥadītha, which were in the hands of a local Arab tribe and the Mazyadids of Ḥilla.[173] In the following year 498/23 September 1104-12 September 1105, we find him in the service of his second uncle Īlghāzī b. Artuq, at that time the military prefect of Iraq (*shiḥna l-ʿIrāq*), who entrusted him with the protection of the Khurāsān road against marauding Turkmen groups.[174]

Upper Mesopotamia in the time of Muḥammad Tapar's sultanate

The prolonged period of destabilization in the Great Seljuk sultanate was further protracted by the turmoil resulting from the premature death of Sultan Barkyāruq on 21 December 1104 while traveling from Iṣfahān to Baghdad. Shortly before passing away, he had designated his four-year old son Malikshāh (II) as successor and had appointed Emir Ayāz as his *atabeg*. A few weeks later, on 19/20 January 1105, Malikshāh was proclaimed sultan in Baghdad. He was initially backed by a number of powerful emirs. But this coalition proved too weak to withstand the claims of Barkyāruq's half-brother Muḥammad Tapar. In February 1105 the two parties reconciled, and in exchange for the recognition of Muḥammad's sultanate Ayāz was honorably received. The agreement did not prevent the sultan from doing away with him at the first convenient occasion on 1 April 1105 and from blinding Barkyāruq's infant son shortly afterwards.[175] A few months after his rise to the throne, Sultan Muḥammad successfully suppressed the insurrection of a relative called Mengü Bars in Nihāwand and thus for the first time after long years of incessant civil strife confirmed his position as undisputed ruler.[176]

This power shift within the Great Seljuk ruling elite had a deep impact on the Jazīra region. The principality of Jokermish faced increasingly aggressive attempts of Muḥammad Tapar to put Mosul under his immediate control and the sultan's proponents in the wider area were decisively strengthened. A case in point is Sukmān al-Quṭbī, a former follower of Malikshāh's cousin Quṭb al-Dawla Ismāʿīl b. Yāqūtī and his son Mawdūd. After the latter's death on 27 December 1102, Sukmān along with the rest of the deceased prince's soldiers entered the service of Muḥammad, who ceded him the cities of Arjīsh and Khilāṭ at the northern shores of Lake Van as a land grant (*iqṭāʿ*).[177] A battle between Barkyāruq and Muḥammad outside the gates of Khoy in early 1103 forced the latter to retreat to Sukmān's holdings in Khilāṭ, where the sultan also established contacts with Emir ʿAlī b. Saltuk of Erzurum.[178] Having thus created the nucleus of a new dynasty in the region, the so-called Shāhs of Armenia (*Shāh-i Arman*), Sukmān remained a loyal follower of Muḥammad Tapar and accompanied him in early 1105 from Mosul to Baghdad.[179] Unlike the independent emirs in the region of Mosul and Diyār Bakr, the potentates in the Armenian highlands maintained close ties with the Great Seljuk sultanate.

The status of the Turkish emirs in Upper Mesopotamia was contingent upon the last peace treaty concluded between Barkyāruq and Muḥammad Tapar in January 1104. This and previous agreements provided for a shared rule over Seljuk territories. Barkyāruq would control the provinces south of the Caspian Sea and in southwestern Iran (Ṭabaristān, Khūzistān, Fārs) as well as the Iraqi Highlands (al-Jabal) and Muḥammad the provinces of Azerbaijan, Armenia, and the greatest part of Iraq. Their younger brother Sanjar ruled in Khurāsān and the eastern Iranian provinces. According to a new clause included in the latest version of the treaty, Barkyāruq took Iṣfahān while Muḥammad was allotted Syria and the provinces of Diyār Bakr and Jazīra, which previously had been under the suzerainty of Barkyāruq. Moreover, Muḥammad was recognized as overlord of Mosul and the lands of Sayf al-Dawla Ṣadaqa, the Mazyadid lord of Ḥilla. Both brothers were to be mentioned in the Friday prayer and on coins as sole suzerains in their respective territories. The correspondence between the two sides was to be carried out by the two sultans' viziers. The soldiers were free to choose the ruler they preferred.[180] Hence, both factions abided by their claims to supreme overlordship of all provinces forming part of their father Malikshāh's empire. Until about 1115, the developments in northern Syria and Upper Mesopotamia were marked by attempts on the part of the Great Seljuk elite to enforce these claims in various ways. Most local emirs strove to preserve their autonomy, first by vacillating between the opposing parties and, after Barkyāruq's death, by forging regional alliances against the sultanate's centralizing ambitions.

While Iṣfahān was handed over to Barkyāruq without resistance, the situation proved more complicated in Baghdad. According to the stipulations of the treaty, Barkyāruq was entitled to be proclaimed sultan there. This caused a conflict between Īlghāzī b. Artuq, the *shiḥna* of Baghdad, who arranged Barkyāruq's proclamation, and Sayf al-Dawla Ṣadaqa, who in a letter to the caliph accused Īlghāzī of a breach of allegiance to Sultan Muḥammad.[181] A military clash could be avoided at that time, but the seeds for future rivalries were sown. After Barkyāruq's death, Ṣadaqa actively supported Muḥammad's takeover in Baghdad along with his two sons Badrān and Dubays and his powerful troops.[182] Thereafter he appeared as an important member of Sultan Muḥammad's retinue and participated in the assassination of Emir Ayāz.[183]

Under these circumstances, Mosul and the northern Jazīra turned into a highly contested conflict area, where Turkish emirs, local elites, and the proponents of the Great Seljuk sultanate clashed repeatedly in a fierce power struggle. In the months following the treaty with Barkyāruq, Muḥammad tried to impose his rule over Mosul by launching an attack in October/November 1104 from his residence in Tabriz.[184] It is noteworthy that during this conflict both sides put forward claims emanating from separate agreements with Barkyāruq. Muḥammad is said to have presented Barkyāruq's letters and oaths, according to which Mosul and the Jazīra provinces were subject to Muḥammad's authority and were to be handed over to him. Jokermish, therefore, was called to submit and to proclaim the Friday prayer in Muḥammad's name so that the sultan would confirm him in his position as governor. Jokermish, however, invoked a letter of Barkyāruq that ordered him not to give Mosul to anyone else.[185] Apparently, Barkyāruq, despite the agreements with his brother, was keen to maintain his links with Jokermish and to control this vital place in the Jazīra. The siege wore on until 27 January 1105, when Jokermish and the people in Mosul were informed about Barkyāruq's death. Under these circumstances, they agreed to submit to Muḥammad and entered negotiations through the mediation of the sultan's vizier Saʿd al-Mulk Abū l-Maḥāsin.

The conflict was resolved by a public act of submission, in exchange for which Muḥammad reconciled with Jokermish and treated him favorably. The ritual aspects of this encounter were further highlighted by the active participation of the townspeople of Mosul. When Saʿd al-Mulk led Jokermish to the sultan's camp outside the town, the inhabitants began to cry, to wail, and to put dust on their heads, thus articulating their grief about their ruler's departure. Upon the populace's demonstration of loyalty towards the emir, Sultan Muḥammad received him cordially. After embracing him he immediately ordered him to return to his subjects, for "their hearts are with you and they are awaiting your return." Jokermish's deference and the townspeople's message prompted Muḥammad to show generosity. Jokermish prostrated himself before the sultan and offered him a solemn entrance into the town, but the sultan refused, instead sending a number of his notables into the city. The ceremony ended with a banquet outside the walls with rich gifts offered to Muḥammad and his vizier.[186] In this way, mutual confidence was restored and the sultan officially recognized Jokermish as his subordinate governor. The rivalry between the two sides was settled on the basis of a precarious equilibrium, in which the sultan was conceded symbols of formal suzeraintzy while he respected the existing bonds of allegiance between Jokermish and the local people.

Jokermish's political success largely depended upon his ability to extend his cluster of allies and to check the activities of rivals based in adjacent territories. Through the acquisition of Nisibis/Niṣībīn and Ḥarrān in 1104 he had extended his sphere of influence as far as the borders of the County of Edessa and the Artuqid territories in Diyār Bakr.[187] Kurdish rulers in the Iraqi highlands, such as the lord of Irbil, Abū l-Hayjā' b. Mūsak, were well disposed towards Jokermish.[188] The town of Sinjār was in the hands of a son-in-law called Albī b. Arslān Tāsh and, after a short period of unrest, fell to the latter's uncle Tamīrak.[189] In Mosul itself Jokermish seems to have been generally accepted by the local notables (*a'yān al-balad*). One of his slave soldiers (*mamlūk*) called Ghuzzoghlī was appointed commander of the citadel and was in charge of the defense of the city.[190] Indicative of the situation is the fact that after Jokermish's defeat by Jāwulī Saqāw in a battle near Irbil, the former's adopted son Zankī was immediately recognized as successor.[191] Apparently, Jokermish had already taken important steps towards securing the succession of his descendants in the territories under his sway. The possession of Mosul not only gave him access to the revenues of one of the wealthiest urban centers in the Jazīra but also formed the basis of a principality with firm administrative and military structures.

A dangerous threat to Jokermish's rule resulted from a coalition between Īlghāzī b. Artuq, a prominent member of the Artuqid clan, and forces from northern Syria. After losing his post of *shiḥna* in Baghdad due to his loyalty to Barkyāruq, Īlghāzī in early 1106 allied with Riḍwān of Aleppo and other emirs to attack Jokermish's territories and put Nisibis under siege.[192] The coalition quickly fell apart and Riḍwān came to an agreement with Jokermish. On the latter's instigation, Riḍwān made an attempt to arrest his ally, but Īlghāzī escaped to the citadel of Nisibis. Fiercely attacked by the Turkmen soldiers of Īlghāzī, Riḍwān was forced to retreat and returned to Aleppo.[193] Hence, Īlghāzī managed to take temporary hold of the city and to involve himself in the affairs of Upper Mesopotamia, which prepared the ground for his subsequent interventions in the Diyār Bakr province.

The conflict with Īlghāzī and the emir of Aleppo shows how sensitive a position Jokermish's lordship occupied in the network of forces in Syria, Upper Mesopotamia, and Iraq. This seems to have been the main incentive prompting Sultan Muḥammad to disregard the agreements of early 1105 and remove Jokermish from power. In September 1106, the sultan ordered Jāwulī b. Saqāw, a former *atabeg*, governor, and temporary rebel in the Iranian provinces of Khūzistān and Fārs, to launch a campaign against the Franks. Ibn al-Qalānisī explains this decision with letters sent by the *atabeg* Ẓahīr al-Dīn and Fakhr al-Mulk b. 'Ammār of Tripoli, who complained about the Frankish depredations and conquests in Syria as well as the threats to Tripoli in particular. The sultan is said to have asked Sayf al-Dawla Ṣadaqa and Jokermish to support his jihad with money and troops.[194] At this point the accounts of Ibn al-Athīr and Ibn al-Qalānisī differ from each other. According to the former, Jāwulī was given Mosul, Diyār Bakr, and the Jazīra as land grants (*iqṭāʿ*), because Jokermish neglected his services and payments to the sultan. Ibn al-Qalānisī, instead, asserts that Jāwulī had been granted al-Raḥba and territories near the Euphrates as *iqṭāʿ* but was expelled from there by Sayf al-Dawla Ṣadaqa and thus moved against Mosul.[195] These irreconcilable details notwithstanding, both sources link Jāwulī's campaign with the situation in Syria and the war against the Franks. This allows us to assume that Muḥammad Tapar, after having secured his dominant position in Baghdad, Iraq, and western Iran, sought to strengthen the sultanate's leading role in Upper Mesopotamia and Syria by fostering the *jihad* movement against the crusader principalities.[196] Mosul was a stronghold of vital significance for intensifying Seljuk military pressure on the territories subject to the County of Edessa and for increasing the sultanate's influence over the Turkish, Arab, and Kurdish emirs in the Diyār Bakr province and the Armenian highlands.

According to Ibn al-Athīr's account, Jāwulī departed from Baghdad in the beginning of Rabīʿ I 500/31 October 1106, advancing via al-Bawāzīj and Irbil towards Mosul. In a village outside Irbil, Jokermish made an attempt to stop him in a pitched battle but was defeated and captured.[197] As has been mentioned above, the notables of Mosul abided by their loyalty to his son Zankī, and Ghuzzoghlī made efforts to secure the support of the remaining troops by distributing Jokermish's money among them. Unable to face this threat on his own, Ghuzzoghlī was in desperate need of allies and sent letters to various powerful men, such as Sayf al-Dawla Ṣadaqa, Aqsunqur al-Bursuqī, the new *shiḥna* of Baghdad, and Qilij Arslān in Anatolia.[198] In this way, Jokermish's principality and the question of hegemony over Upper Mesopotamia became the objects of a last major clash between the Anatolian Seljuks and the Great Seljuk sultanate.

Qilij Arslān I and Dānishmand Ghāzī, 1101–1104

The developments in Anatolia following the victories of 1101 against the crusading armies were characterized by a sudden outbreak of serious contentions between the Seljuks and the Dānishmandid Turks.[199] This was the first time that the two newly established local powers in former Byzantine territories were driven into a large-scale conflict. In part, this was due to their strengthening after 1101. Another reason lay in the fact that the two sides had a common ambition to expand their influence towards the Euphrates region. Michael the Syrian poignantly speaks of the "Turks of Cappadocia and Bithynia" (*Tūrqāyē dha-bh-Qappadhūqāyā w-Bhīthūnīyā*), who were fighting with the Greeks or against each other because "the sultan of the Arabs" (*shūlṭānā dh-Arabhāyē*) had completely lost control of these regions.[200] The statement is inaccurate with respect to the political and institutional context, for the author conflates the idea of a central power ruling the Arab lands with the Great Seljuk sultanate. Yet it clearly illustrates the high degree of isolation into which the Turkish rulers in the regions west of the Euphrates had fallen because of the establishment of the crusader states and the ongoing civil strife among the claimants to Sultan Malikshāh's heritage. The Seljuk elites gathering around Barkyāruq and Muḥammad Tapar were hardly able to reach their kinsmen in Anatolia. After being expelled from Cilicia, the Jayḥān Valley, and the region of Antioch, the Turkish potentates in Anatolia were largely cut off from what was going on in Syria and Upper Mesopotamia. Most naturally, the absence of a strong supra-regional Muslim authority further exacerbated the antagonism between the contending local forces in Anatolia, which strove for the acquisition of strongholds at the banks of the Euphrates. Fortified places, which formerly had loomed large among the military structures of the Byzantine borderlands and had not yet fallen into the hands of the crusaders, were of great importance for the Turks in their attempts to entrench themselves vis-à-vis the principalities of Edessa and Antioch and to gain access to the emirates in the Diyār Bakr and Jazīra provinces. This makes the fact that Dānishmand's success in seizing Melitene engendered "incurable hatred and hostility" (*men hārkā senāthā wa-bh'eldebhābhaw[hy] metasyanīthē*) understandable, as Michael the Syrian asserts.[201]

The discord between Qilij Arslān and Dānishmand seems to have been further exacerbated because of the release of Bohemond of Antioch in May 1103. Given that there are very few Muslim or Eastern Christian sources referring to this issue, we mostly depend upon the Frankish perspective reflected in the narratives of the crusader historian Albert of Aachen and the English monk Orderic Vitalis. Their reports, though very detailed, are richly embroidered with romance-like features and primarily intend to highlight the Frankish lords' virtues and the benefits the infidels were to gain from keeping peace with them.[202] Basic elements in Albert's version can be corroborated by other sources and thus seem to reflect some first-hand knowledge about Bohemond's ransoming and the Seljuk-Dānishmandid dispute resulting therefrom. Orderic's version, instead, is a piece of politico-religious propaganda, which extolls the Christian faith's persuasiveness in drawing high-ranking Muslims to conversion and presents Bohemond as a highly revered Christian ruler embodying all moral and martial virtues of the western aristocratic value system. The second protagonist of Orderic's account, besides Bohemond, is *Melaz, filia Dalimanni principis*, who in her admiration for the Frankish knights and their religion persuaded Bohemond to fight on her father's side against his enemy *Solimannus* (Qilij Arslān) and thereafter supported him and his companions by forcing her raging father to release them and to conclude a treaty of friendship with them. Expectedly, Melaz converted to Christianity and left her father along with the Frankish lords.[203] Apparently, the author transformed Bohemond's defeat and captivity into a triumph of Christianity. The story of Melaz served as an edifying example outweighing reports about Christian captives' and exhausted soldiers' proneness to convert to Islam.

Albert of Aachen evinces the same idealizing tendency and adds elements of literary elaboration, such as letters and direct speeches but in general stays closer to the political facts. In particular, he refers to the attempts of Emperor Alexios I who, through his emissaries and letters, sought to persuade Dānishmand to deliver Bohemond against a sum of 260,000 *bezants* so that he would get hold of his dangerous enemy.[204] Alexios' diplomatic efforts are confirmed by a reliable contemporary source, namely a letter of Archbishop Theophylaktos of Ochrid to Gregory Taronites, *doux* of Trebizond, in which the latter is praised for his successful negotiations with Dānishmand concerning the release of Bohemond.[205] In view of the final outcome, Theophylaktos clearly exaggerates the achievements of his addressee. But there is no doubt that Gregory Taronites actually maintained close relations with Dānishmand, thus consolidating his own position in the region of Trebizond vis-à-vis other Turkish emirs and the central government of Constantinople.[206]

The reason behind the conflict between the two Turkish potentates, according to Albert, was Dānishmand's refusal to give Qilij Arslān a share of the ransom money the emperor was to pay. The eulogizing tendency in this narrative becomes stronger in the description of Bohemond's intervention. He is said to have convinced Dānishmand of the advantages of coming to an agreement with him rather than the emperor. He would give only half of the sum but would take an oath of loyalty and friendship along with all his Christian compatriots and fellow princes in Antioch, Edessa, and Jerusalem and thus support him in fighting his Seljuk opponent and conquering Byzantine territories. Against the sum of 100,000 *bezants* collected from Bohemond's relatives and friends, a treaty of friendship came into being.[207] The main points of this report are corroborated by Matthew of Edessa, who mainly concentrates on the role of the Armenian lord Kogh-Basil as intermediary.[208]

The overall image resulting from these accounts is that Bohemond's release was framed by a newly established coalition between Dānishmand and the Franks of Antioch and Edessa, which aimed at stabilizing the situation in the contested regions of the Euphrates Valley and Upper Mesopotamia. It is rather improbable that it was the ransom money itself that triggered the conflict between the two Turkish potentates. The actual problem, which is at least alluded to in the western accounts mentioning some military clashes with Qilij Arslān, seems to have been the Seljuk chief's aggressive stance in view of Dānishmand's conquest of Melitene and the growing threat of large-scale attacks in the region. The fact that Dānishmand maintained friendly relations with the Byzantine *doux* of Trebizond shows that in general he deemed it advantageous to be at peace with his Christian neighbors as long as he faced the menace of his rival in central Anatolia. Emperor Alexios I's proposal and Qilij Arslān's alliance with Constantinople may have been additional factors in these negotiations, but it is misleading to assume that there was a well-functioning Seljuk-Byzantine axis of collaboration.[209] It is certainly noteworthy that in the years between 1101 and 1107 there were hardly any military activities in the western and northern fringes of the Anatolian plateau. Qilij Arslān actually supported the emperor with auxiliary troops in the 1107 war against Bohemond. But this is not to say that the two powers collaborated in any systematic or concerted way against the Franks of Antioch or the

Dānishmandid emirate. The two competing rulers merely continued to pursue the customary tactics of forging coalitions with local powers irrespective of their ethnic and religious identity.

In the months following Bohemond's release, Qilij Arslān mounted an attack on Antioch. While advancing towards the city in August 1103, the Seljuk chief joined in a battle with the forces of Dānishmand near Marʿash and put them to flight.[210] Thereupon Qilij Arslān intruded deep into northern Syria, where he exchanged emissaries with Aleppo and asked for supplies and provisions and thus caused great rejoicing among the townspeople, as Ibn al-Qalānisī asserts.[211] Despite the clash with Dānishmand, the report seems to suggest that the prime objective of this expedition was not his Turkish rival but a strike against the Frankish princedom and a tightening of relations with the Muslim heartlands. Perhaps this expedition has to be seen in connection with Count Baldwin of Edessa's attack on Emir Ulugh-Salar of Mārdīn.[212] The assault apparently constituted a dangerous extension of Frankish raiding activities into the Diyār Bakr region. Due to the escalating aggressiveness of all factions involved, the time was ripe for a new power shift in Upper Mesopotamia. Under these circumstances, the Seljuk ruler achieved major success in both enfeebling his inner-Anatolian opponent and making his own presence felt in the Muslim territories bordering the crusader states. This seems to have been an important step in preparing the policy he was going to pursue in the following years until his death in 1107.

In 1104 Dānishmand Ghāzī died in his northern residence town of Sebasteia, leaving behind 12 sons. Matters of succession obviously had not been arranged beforehand, and thus the emirate underwent a time of unrest until the late emir's son Gümüshtekīn Ghāzī (1105?–1134/5) managed to prevail and put many of his brothers to death.[213] The demise of Duqāq of Damascus in June, who soon was replaced by his *atabeg* Ṭughtikīn,[214] that of Suqmān b. Artuq, lord of Ḥiṣn Kayfā, in October, and that of Sultan Barkyāruq in December 1104 further weakened pre-existing power structures and favored the ambitions of determined newcomers. This was the right moment for Qilij Arslān to renew his claims to Melitene and prepare his intrusion into the lands east of the Euphrates River.

The Jayḥān and upper Euphrates Valleys after the First Crusade

The Byzantine-Armenian enclaves in the Jayḥān and Euphrates Valleys, which survived the onslaught of the First Crusade, faced a highly precarious situation. On the one hand, they had to cope with the threats emanating from the expansionist tendencies of neighboring Turkish warlords and the Franks of Antioch and Edessa. On the other, they were unavoidably drawn into the struggles between the nascent crusader principalities and the local Muslim emirates. The only way to survive under these circumstances was to come to terms with the dominant powers in the region and to establish links of allegiance with them. Apart from the brief period of direct Byzantine rule in Cilicia between 1104 and 1107, the imperial government was no longer able to lend active support to these potentates, but court titles and personal ties with the Komnenian elite continued to serve as a source of legitimacy for them.

The city of Marʿash after 1097 came under the rule of "the Roman general, the Prince of Princes (= ἄρχων τῶν ἀρχόντων), whose name was Tʿatʿul." This man exerted his authority on behalf of Emperor Alexios I.[215] Lead seals corroborate the details provided by Matthew of Edessa. They attribute to Tʿatʿul the aforesaid honorific, which seems to have been reserved for high-ranking Armenian dignitaries, along with the title of *protonobelissimos*.[216] As in the case of Tʿoros of Edessa and Gabriel of Melitene, we are dealing with a Byzantine-Armenian nobleman who formally recognized the emperor's suzerainty.

The Jayḥān Valley was largely out of the reach of Turkish emirs operating in central Anatolia, Syria, or Upper Mesopotamia. When Dānishmand Ghāzī and Qilij Arslān from 1101 onwards extended their sway to Melitene, the nearby princedom of Antioch and other local powers prevented them from invading the adjacent provinces. Marʿash, therefore, rarely faced Turkish attacks but was drawn into the Byzantine-Norman conflict. Tʿatʿul sided with the emperor and warded off Bohemond's attempt to seize the city in 1100.[217] Eventually, however, he was forced to surrender to Joscelin of Courtenay and found refuge in Constantinople.[218] Despite all efforts to wield power over Cilicia and the Syrian coast, the Byzantines failed to exert actual control over the Jayḥān Valley. As has been shown above, the expedition of 1104 resulted in the appointment of a Byzantine governor in Marʿash. Yet the Byzantine troops were too weak to build up enduring defensive structures, and thus the Franks became the dominant power in the region.[219]

The situation was different in the remote and isolated region around Gargar. Both the Franks of Edessa and the Artuqid emirs were mainly interested in economically more profitable areas east of the Euphrates and the Diyār Bakr province. Turkish pressure increased only after 1107 with the establishment of the Seljuk prince Ṭughril Arslān in Melitene and the conquest of Būlā (Palu) and Kharpete/Ḥiṣn Ziyād by Balak b. Bahrām.[220]

A remarkable exception was the lordship of Kogh-Basil, who played a very active role in the local power struggle between Turkish and Frankish potentates. In 1103 he loomed large in the negotiations about Bohemond's release from Dānishmandid captivity. Kogh-Basil contributed a sum of 10,000 *dahekans*, delivered the ransom money, and hosted Bohemond in his residence. This initiative paid off and allowed Kogh-Basil to forge close ties with the Norman ruler, who in a ceremony of oath taking declared himself his liberator's adopted son.[221] In the same vein, in 1108 Kogh-Basil granted a lavish reception to Baldwin of Edessa and Joscelin of Courtenay after their release from Muslim captivity and joined a broad coalition of forces against Tancred of Antioch with a contingent of troops from Raʿbān.[222] This gave rise to open hostility between Kogh-Basil and Tancred. In 1112 the latter temporarily occupied Kayshūn and only withdrew when the two sides agreed on a new peace treaty.[223] In 1107 and 1108 Kogh-Basil warded off Turkish attacks, which most likely were mounted by the Seljuks of Melitene and mainly afflicted the region between Marʿash and Ḥiṣn Manṣūr. In a siege of Edessa in 1110 by Emir Mawdūd of Mosul, Kogh-Basil along with his vassal Ablgharib of Bira joined the Frankish relief forces and in 1111 participated in an expedition against Shayzar.[224] Matthew of Edessa describes Kogh-Basil and his followers as courageous soldiers accomplishing admirable feats of war and celebrating their victories in triumphal entrances into Kayshūn.[225] Military success significantly increased Kogh-Basil's prestige as warlord and strengthened the cohesion among the Armenian nobility. What is more, Muslim victories over the Franks of Antioch and Edessa allowed Kogh-Basil to extend his influence. By contributing to the ransoming of Frankish chiefs he distinguished himself as a valuable ally and go-between enjoying the esteem of both Turks and Franks and strengthened his bonds with members of the Frankish elite. After Bohemond's departure to the West, Kogh-Basil mainly relied upon his coalition with the county of Edessa in order to check Antioch's expansionist ambitions and to fight the Muslims. This strategy proved largely successful, allowing him to preserve his independence in a highly sensitive section of the Christian-Muslim conflict zone in the Euphrates region.

The struggle for Upper Mesopotamia

After Dānishmand Ghāzī's death, Melitene for some time remained under the control of one of his sons called Aghūsiyān (= Yaghī Siyān).[226] Michael the Syrian's detailed report reveals that Qilij Arslān besieged and severely attacked the city between 28 June and 2 September 1105. Aghūsiyān apparently received no reinforcements from Sebasteia or elsewhere and thus surrendered in exchange for a guarantee of safety.[227] Earlier this year Qilij Arslān had invaded the Diyār Bakr province in order to take hold of Mayyāfāriqīn (Silvan). Formerly the city had been under the suzerainty of Duqāq of Damascus, but after his death the vizier Ḍiyā' al-Dīn Muḥammad had offered it to Qilij Arslān. Upon arriving there in February 1105, the Seljuk emir appointed one of his father's slave soldiers (*mamlūk*) called Khumartāsh al-Sulaymānī as governor and, in compensation, granted Muḥammad Ablastayn as *iqṭā'*.[228] Most likely, the local nobility was unable to maintain its independence in the region and thus sought the protection of another powerful ruler supplanting Damascus' overlordship.

At that time, Qilij Arslān seemingly enjoyed the highest respect amongst the rulers in the eastern parts of Upper Mesopotamia, as can be seen from the list of people who are mentioned by Ibn Azraq al-Fāriqī as having paid homage to the Seljuk lord: Emir Ibrāhīm of Āmid (Diyarbakır); al-Saba' al-Aḥmar (= Qizil Arslān) of Is'ird (Sıırt); perhaps Sukmān al-Quṭbī of Khilāṭ; Emir Shārūkh, who formerly had been lord of Arzan and then received the lordship of Ḥānī (Hani); and Ḥusām al-Dīn Tumushtakīn of Bidlīs (Bitlis) and Arzan.[229] All major strongholds in the region stretching from Mayyāfāriqīn to the western shores of Lake Van are included in this catalogue. Within a few months, Qilij Arslān turned into a predominant ruler in Upper Mesopotamia along with the Artuqids and Jokermish of Mosul.

The sudden impact of this formidable gain in power is also reflected in Ibn al-Athīr's account of Emir Ayāz's assassination on 1 April 1105.[230] On that day, the report goes, Sultan Muḥammad convened a council of supreme commanders in his palace in Baghdad in order to discuss the attacks of Qilij Arslān b. Sulaymān b. Qutlumush, which were to be fended off by Ayāz and Sayf al-Dawla Ṣadaqa.[231] It becomes clear that the chiefs in Baghdad regarded the Seljuk ruler even prior to his conquest of Melitene as a serious threat to their own ambitions.

The details mentioned with respect to early 1105 are in line with Qilij Arslān's subsequent activities, for already in the spring or summer of the next year we find him again mounting an attack on the Franks of Edessa.[232] Jokermish's people in nearby Ḥarrān reportedly expressed their willingness to surrender. He actually took possession of the town but fell seriously ill and was forced to return to Melitene. Ḥarrān, however, remained in the hands of his troops. The account does not expand on the reasons for the notables' course of action, but it vaguely refers to their zeal for the *jihad* against the Franks. This is to say that, because of his previous feats of war against the crusaders and his taking hold of Melitene and the Euphrates region, Qilij Arslān was considered the right person to assume a leading role in the wars against the Christian enemies. The attitude of the people of Ḥarrān reflects a growing esteem for the Anatolian potentate, who had grown into a ruler of supra-regional importance for the Muslims in Upper Mesopotamia. Ghuzzoghlī's plan to invite Qilij Arslān to Mosul seems to have been motivated by the same expectations.

This leads us to the circumstances following the battle of Irbil in November 1106, when Ghuzzoghlī on behalf of Jokermish's under-age son made every effort to ward off Jāwulī Saqāw. Since the latter acted as the sultan's subordinate commander, Sayf al-Dawla Ṣadaqa refrained from intervening in this conflict and abided by his allegiance to the sultan. Aqsunqur al-Bursuqī, the *shiḥna* of Baghdad, was unable to find supporters among the other parties.[233] Qilij Arslān thus was the only potentate to become actively involved in the struggle for Mosul.[234] At that moment he apparently felt strong enough to oppose Sultan Muḥammad Tapar and his supporters. In the meantime Jāwulī Saqāw put Mosul under siege and exerted psychological pressure on the defenders by parading Jokermish before the city walls until he died.[235] Jāwulī tried to win over high-ranking notables and former companions of Jokermish, but his efforts were of no avail because of the townspeople's resistance.[236] In early 1107 Qilij Arslān eventually sallied forth and encamped outside Nisibis in order to enlist more troops. The notables and military chiefs of Mosul entered negotiations and exchanged oaths with him, and thus he entered the city on 22 March 1107.[237]

Who supported this campaign apart from Jokermish's adherents? Ibn al-Athīr stresses the fact that in the year of the Mosul expedition Qilij Arslān backed Emperor Alexios I in his war against Bohemond. Although Bohemond's invasion actually took place several months after Qilij Arslān's death in October 1107, it is clear that the preparations had already begun in early 1106.[238] This makes it perfectly plausible that Alexios I during 1106 communicated with Qilij Arslān about sending auxiliary troops in view of the imminent Norman invasion. On account of previous agreements and his enmity with Bohemond, Qilij Arslān complied with the emperor's request. The bulk of the troops participating in his eastern campaign came not from Anatolia, but from the Euphrates region and the Diyār Bakr province. Ibrāhīm b. Yināl of Āmid and Muḥammad b. Jabaq of Kharput/Ḥiṣn Ziyād commanded two strongholds of outstanding significance in the region.[239] Another loyal companion was the lord of al-Raḥba, Muḥammad b. al-Sabbāq, from the Banū Shabbān clan, who had originally been installed by Duqāq of Damascus but became independent after the latter's death and recognized Qilij Arslān as his overlord.[240] After taking hold of Melitene, the Seljuk lord within a short period extended his sphere of influence over the lands south of the Anti-Taurus Mountains and, through the acquisition of Ḥarrān, over territories situated in the vicinity of the Frankish-ruled city of Edessa.[241]

Nevertheless, Mosul was not taken by force but through a consensus between the Seljuk chief, his allies, and the representatives of Jokermish's regime. The available accounts do not yield many details about the negotiations leading to this result but concentrate on the public events, through which Qilij Arslān's installation as legitimate ruler was stage managed. On arriving at the outskirts of Mosul, Qilij Arslān was escorted into the city by Jokermish's son, which shows that the Seljuk chief took up the government of the city with the support and approval of the local elite. In a second step, he removed Sultan Muḥammad's name from the Friday prayer and introduced his own along with that of the caliph. This was tantamount to an act of defiance against the sultan and his claims to Jokermish's inheritance. With a number of additional measures, Qilij Arslān consolidated his position in Mosul and presented himself to the townspeople as a righteous ruler struggling to overcome the grievances of the past. He appointed a new castellan instead of Ghuzzoghlī, a new judge (*qāḍī*), and a new city chief (*ra'īs*); he abolished unjust taxes and dispensed justice in public assemblies.[242]

The Muslim tradition stresses the Seljuk leader's qualities as an autonomous ruler, who distinguishes himself from the governors and *iqṭā'* holders subject to Sultan Muḥammad. In contrast to his predecessor Jokermish, Qilij Arslān drew his legitimacy directly from the caliph, as is expressed in the formula employed in the Friday prayer. This doubtlessly was an important step towards the creation of an independent principality, which was solely based on the authority of the Anatolian Seljuk branch and forthrightly discarded the Great Seljuk sultan's claim to supremacy. The conquest of Mosul was only a brief episode but had long-lasting effects on the Anatolian Seljuks' ideology. For the first time, they assumed the role of a supra-regional power, which extended its influence from central Asia Minor deep into the Muslim heartlands of the northern Jazīra. There are striking similarities with the procedure followed 14 years earlier (1093) in Nicaea. In this case, too, Anna Komnene, our only extant source, speaks of measures bolstering the newly arrived Seljuk scion, such as the bestowal of prerogatives upon the Turkish military chiefs, the reorganization of the local administration, and public acts highlighting the new ruler's claims to legitimacy. Qilij Arslān heavily relied upon the legacy of his father Sulaymān in his attempt to introduce a concept of dynastic succession. It may be assumed, however, that his monarchical ambitions grew much stronger after his victories against the Franks in 1101 and again after the conquest of Melitene in 1105. Qilij Arslān's entry into Mosul in March 1107 formed the pinnacle of this gradual rise to uncontested sovereignty.

Both the seizure of Nisibis and the takeover in Mosul were acts of defiance towards the political groups in the region. Threatened by this dangerous encroachment on his realm, Īlghāzī b. Artuq sided with Jāwulī. So did a large section of Jokermish's troops.[243] Upon his initial failure to take possession of Mosul, Jāwulī retreated to Sinjār. There he received a letter from Riḍwān of Aleppo that called upon him to fight the Franks in Syria, for nobody else was able to repel them. Seemingly, Jāwulī deemed himself too weak to engage in a pitched battle with Qilij Arslān and thus moved westward in compliance with the instructions Sultan Muḥammad had given to him. After securing the support of Riḍwān of Aleppo, to whom he pledged loyalty and support in his struggle against the Franks, he turned against the lord of al-Raḥba, one of Qilij Arslān's vassals in the Euphrates region.[244] The treacherous behavior of a group of soldiers from the local garrison enabled him to seize and sack al-Raḥba on 19 May 1107, and so the local ruler Muḥammad b. al-Sabbāq was forced to submit to Jāwulī's rule. In view of his growing strength, Qilij Arslān's coalition of forces began to disintegrate.

The two armies met halfway between al-Raḥba and Mosul at a site near the Khābūr River. On 13 July 1107 Jāwulī attacked the enfeebled troops of Qilij Arslān and routed them. Realizing that the battle was lost, Qilij Arslān plunged into the river on horseback, was swept along by the flow and drowned. Qilij Arslān's newly established realm in Upper Mesopotamia, which within such a short period came to extend over a broad strip of land from Melitene to Ḥarrān, al-Raḥba, and Mosul, collapsed, and Mosul fell into the hands of Jāwulī Saqāw.[245] He restored the Friday prayer in the name of Sultan Muḥammad and sent Qilij Arslān's son Malikshāh (= Shāhinshāh), who had been left behind by his father along with an emir and a detachment of his army, as prisoner to the sultan's court. Ḥabashī, a son of Jokermish and lord of Jazīrat b. ʿUmar, and Ghuzzoghlī were forced to pay a tribute of 6,000 dinars in exchange for a peace treaty.[246]

A remarkable detail concerning the political concept lying behind the Seljuk chief's expansionist objectives is revealed in Ibn al-Athīr's concluding statement: "When Qilij Arslān saw his soldiers being defeated, he knew that, if he were captured, they would do with him what someone who has broken a peace treaty is supposed to suffer, especially because he had opposed the sultan in his lands and with respect to the title of sultan (*ism al-salṭana*)." This is the only explicit reference to the fact that Qilij Arslān's invasion of Upper Mesopotamia was connected with an attempt to lay claim to the title of sultan. The omission of the sultan's name in the Friday prayer of Mosul had made plain that the new ruler openly rejected the suzerainty of Muḥammad Tapar and the Great Seljuk dynasty in the region. The perennial civil strife among the kinsmen and sons of Sultan Malikshāh and various insurrections initiated by other family members must have seriously undermined the claims of Malikshāh's descendants to possess exclusive pre-eminence within the dynasty. Nothing indicates that Qilij Arslān was actually proclaimed sultan by his followers, but Ibn al-Athīr's allusion implies that the Seljuk lord intended to establish a rival sultanate based in Anatolia and Upper Mesopotamia with favorable prospects for further expansion.

Notes

1 For recent surveys with further bibliographical references, see, for instance, Asbridge, *First Crusade*; Tyerman, *God's War*, pp. 92–164; Asbridge, *Kreuzzüge*, pp. 60–103; for the Byzantine viewpoint, see Lilie, *Crusader States*, pp. 1–60; Harris, *Crusades*, pp. 53–71; for Muslim perspectives, see Hillenbrand, *Crusades*, pp. 31–88; for aspects of mutual perception, see Völkl, *Muslime*; for a recent revisionist view, see Frankopan, *The First Crusade*, esp. pp. 6–11, who argues that the "true origins of the First Crusade" have to be found in Constantinople and the policy of Alexios I rather than the initiative of Pope Urban II.

2 Shepard, "Greek meets Greek," pp. 185–278; Lilie, *Crusader States*, pp. 1–28; Thomas, "Anna Comnena's account," pp. 269–312; Shepard, "Cross-purposes," pp. 107–29; Harris, *Crusades*, pp. 53–71; and most recently Pryor and Jeffreys, "Euphrates Frontier," pp. 31–86, with a very thorough discussion of primary sources and rich bibliographical notes.

3 Asbridge, *First Crusade*, pp. 89–240; Tyerman, *God's War*, pp. 124–48.

4 Turan, *Türkiye*, pp. 98–104; Demirkent, *Kılıç Arslan*, pp. 24–33; Durmaz, "Haçlılar," pp. 38–45; Sevim and Merçil, *Selçuklu Devletleri*, 191–97, 466–86; Öngül, *Selçuklular*, 1:163–72, 2:23–34.

5 For further details, see Belke and Mersich, *Phrygien und Pisidien*, pp. 106–107.

6 For the details, see, for instance, Runciman, "The First Crusade: Constantinople to Antioch," pp. 280–324; Mayer, *Kreuzzüge*, pp. 43–55; Demirkent, *Kılıç Arslan*, pp. 21–34; Asbridge, *First Crusade*, pp. 100–240; Tyerman, *God's War*, pp. 98–148; Asbridge, *Kreuzzüge*, pp. 62–97; for details concerning Karbūqā's defeat, see Heidemann, *Renaissance*, pp. 184–86; for the Frankish takeover in Edessa and the first coins issued by the new rulers, see ibidem, pp. 180–83.

7 For the siege of Nicaea, see, for instance, Runicman, "The First Crusade: Constantinople to Antioch," pp. 288–91; Lilie, *Crusader States*, pp. 28–29; Demirkent, *Kılıç Arslan*, pp. 24–28; Sevim and Merçil, *Selçuklu Devletleri*, pp. 192–93; Öngül, *Selçuklular*, 1:25–26; Asbridge, *First Crusade*, pp. 118–31; Frankopan, *The First Crusade*, pp. 138–44; for repairs in the walls and towers of Nicaea datable to the Comnenian period or even to the time after Alexios I's takeover, see Foss, "Defenses of Asia Minor," pp. 197–98; Foss and Winfield, *Byzantine Fortifications*, pp. 81, 96, 102, 106, 114.

8 Anna Komnene 10.9.11, p. 314, ll. 11–13, 11.1.1, p. 322, ll. 14–15. For the location, see Reinsch, *Anna Komnene*, p. 351, n. 179.

9 Anna Komnene 10.11.10, p. 321: ἐδεδίει δὲ τὸ αὐτῶν ἀναρίθμητον πλῆθος. William of Tyre 3.13, p. 211: *Sed et principes eundem imperatorem circa pactorum tenorem maliciose versatum constanter asserebant.*

10 Albert of Aachen 2.37, pp. 124–25: *claves urbis polliciti reddere in manus imperatoris Constantinopolis.* William of Tyre 3.12, p. 210: *hic peregrinorum exercitus* [...]*ad alia properabat negocia* [...]*sed incidenter et quasi pretereundo in eam descendissent obsidionem.*

11 William of Tyre, 3.13, p. 211: *ut de spoliis captivorum civium et de substantia multiplici infra urbem reperta rerum suarum dispendia* [...] *resarcire possent.*

12 Anna Komnene 11.1.2, pp. 322–23, ll. 19–29, 11.2.2, p. 325, ll. 4–15, 11.2.5, p. 326, ll. 44–52.

13 Fulcher, pp. 133–34: *Turci, gens Persica, qui apud Romaniae fines terras Christianorum magis magisque occupando, lite bellica iam septuplicata victos superaverunt, multos occidendo vel captivando, ecclesias subvertendo, regnum Dei vastando.*

14 Anna Komnene 11.1.2, p. 322, l. 24–25: τὰς τοῦ βασιλέως φιλοφροσύνας [...] ἀπαγγείλας καὶ τὰς ἐγγράφους ὑποσχέσεις ὑποδείξας, 11.2.5, p. 326, ll. 46–51: [...] ὑποδείκνυσι

τὸν χρυσόβουλλον λόγον, ὅνπερ ὁ βασιλεὺς αὐτῷ προενεχείρισεν [...] δι' οὗ ὑπισχνεῖτο ὁ βασιλεὺς οὐ μόνον ἀπάθειαν, ἀλλὰ καὶ δαψιλῆ δόσιν χρημάτων τὲ καὶ ἀξιωμάτων τῇ τε ἀδελφῇ καὶ τῇ γυναικὶ τοῦ σουλτάνου [...] καὶ πᾶσιν ἁπλῶς τοῖς ἐν Νικαίᾳ βαρβάροις.

15 Anna Komnene 11.1.2-3, pp. 322–23, ll. 21–33 (Manuel Boutoumites' negotiations with the Turks of Nicaea); see also William of Tyre 3.8, pp. 204–205.

16 Albert of Aachen 1.2-7, pp. 106–109; Anna Komnene 11.1.3-5, pp. 323–24, ll. 31–59: [...] τοῖς ἐντὸς Νικαίας Τούρκοις τὸ ἐνδόσιμον δίδωσι „πράσσετε τοῦ λοιποῦ", λέγων, „πᾶν ὅπερ βέλτιον κρίνετε". ᾔδει γὰρ πρὸ καιροῦ τῷ βασιλεῖ μᾶλλον προαιρουμένους παραδοῦναι τὴν πόλιν ἢ παρὰ τῶν Κελτῶν ἁλῶναι, ibidem 11.2.5, p. 326, ll. 36–52.

17 Anna Komnene 11.2.5-10, pp. 326–28.

18 Albert of Aachen 2.37, p. 126; William of Tyre 3.13, p. 212.

19 Gesta Francorum 2.8, p. 17: *imperator, plenus vana et iniquia cogitatione, iussit illos impunitos abire sine ullo timore* [...] *Quos studiose servabat, ut illos ad Francorum nocumenta et obstacula paratos haberet.* The same opinion is expressed by Robert the Monk 3.5, p. 758, trans. Sweetenham, p. 106.

20 Albert of Aachen 2.37, pp. 126–28: *exercitus Dei viventis hanc diem in magno gaudio et exultatione ibidem in castris exegit.*

21 William of Tyre 3.12, pp. 209–10.

22 William of Tyre 3.12, p. 211: *Nos enim, urbe tue celsitudini resignata, iter quod semel assumpsimus auctore domino prosequi non differemus.*

23 William of Tyre 3.13, pp. 211–13.

24 Albert of Aachen 2.39, p. 130: *Solimannus* [...]*auxilium et vires contraxit ab Antiochia, Tharsis, Halapia et ceteris civitatibus Romanie a Turcis sparsim possessis.*

25 Anna Komnene 11.3.5, p. 331, ll. 97–98.

26 See above, S. 257–60.

27 ʿAẓīmī, p. 24 (Arabic text), p. 30 (trans.): *wa-wāqaʿahum al-Dānishmand wa-Ibn Sulaymān, wa-aḥraqū bayna aydīhim al-maʿāqil wa-saddū l-manāhil*, "Dānishmand and Ibn Sulaymān attacked them and burned down the strongholds before them and clogged the wells."

28 Anna Komnene 14.1.5, p. 426, ll. 65–66: ἀρχισατράπης δε τις Ἀσὰν τὴν κλῆσιν, ὁ τὴν Καππαδοκίαν κατέχων.

29 See also Mélikoff, *Geste*, p. 92.

30 Belke and Mersich, *Phrygien und Pisidien*, pp. 196–97 (s. v. Augustopolis), p. 268 (s. v. Hebraïkē); Mélikoff, *Geste*, p. 93, locates the events further east in the vicinity of Kaisareia.

31 Gesta Francorum 4, pp. 22–23: *Tunc veniebamus nos persequentes iniquissimos Turcos, cotidie fugientes ante nos. At illi venientes ad cuncta castra sive urbes* [...]*spoliabant ecclesias et domos et alia omnia* [...]*et ardebant ac devastabant omnia convenientia sive utilia, fugientes et paventes valde ante faciem nostram.* For a similar account, see Robert the Monk 3.18, p. 766, trans. Sweetenham, pp. 114–15.

32 Albert of Aachen 2.43, pp. 136–37.

33 Anna Komnene 11.3.6, p. 331, ll. 14–17: κἀντεῦθεν πίπτει τὸ βάρβαρον, οἱ δέ γε σωθέντες ἄλλος ἀλλαχῇ διεσπάρησαν τάς τε γυναῖκας καὶ τοὺς παῖδας καταλίποντες, ὡς τοῦ λοιποῦ μὴδ' ἀντωπῆσαι τοῖς Λατίνοις ἰσχύοντες. William of Tyre 3.19, p. 221: *Transcursa igitur Pissidia Licaoniam ingressi, Yconium* [...] *pervenerunt, quam vacuam reperientes alimentorum maximam penuriam passi sunt. Turci enim* [...] *in nulla urbium suarum resistendi habebant fiduciam, sed expoliatis urbibus et vastata regione universa cum uxoribus et liberis, gregibus et armentis et omnimoda substantia ad montes confugiebant inperivos.*

34 Robert the Monk 1.9, p. 734, trans. Sweetenham, p. 86.

35 For typological observations on forms of defection during the period in question, see Beihammer, "Defection," pp. 597–651.

36 See the incidents mentioned above, pp. 104–11, 117–24.

37 Albert of Aachen 2.25-26, pp. 102–105: *Flebili voce, humili vultu et lacrimarum continua inundatione, de vita et salute sua multum precatur, omnibus trepidans membris* [...] *Instabat etiam*

multa et humillima prece, quatenus Christianitatis professione baptismum susciperet, et Christiano iure Christianis communicaret, sed hoc pocius petebat timore suspecte mortis, quam aliquot catholice fidei amore.

38 Albert of Aachen 2.27, pp. 108–109: *privatus inter familiares summorum procerum diligebatur.*

39 See above, pp. 268–70.

40 Albert of Aachen 2.37, pp. 126–29: *quedam sanctimonialis femina de cenobio Sancte Marie ad Horrea Treverensis ecclesie* [...]*et abhominabili cuiusdam Turci et ceterorum commixtione habuisse conquesta est* [...]*quod ad eundem Turcum reversa sit in exilio quo erat, non alia de causa, nisi propter libidinis sue intolerantiam.*

41 Chalandon, *Comnène*, 1:195–98; Kurat, *Çaka Bey*, pp. 56–58; Turan, *Türkiye*, p. 95; Cahen, *Pre-Ottoman Turkey*, pp. 84–85; Vryonis, *Decline*, p. 117; Savvides, "Εμίρης," pp. 60–62; Demirkent, *Kılıç Arslan*, pp. 32–33; Frankopan, *The First Crusade*, pp. 145–46.

42 Anna Komnene 11.5.1, p. 335, ll. 23–24 (ὁ μὲν γὰρ Τζαχᾶς τὴν Σμύρνην ὥσπερ ἴδιόν τι λάχος κατεῖχεν), 11.5.1, p. 336, l. 31, 11.5.3, p. 336, l. 65; Chalandon, *Comnène*, 1:147, 196, n. 2 (il aurait frappé d'un coup d'épée [...] une tentative d'assassinat); Kurat, *Çaka Bey*, pp. 54–55 (given that Çaka must have died before 1097, the details referring to Çaka's rule over Smyrna and the islands must be erroneous, perhaps the relevant reports refer to his brother Yalvaç); Turan, *Türkiye*, p. 95, n. 37 (Bazı âlimler [...] aslında onun oğlu olduğunu söylerken); Demirkent, *Kılıç Arslan*, p. 32 (Çaka'nın oğlu); Cahen, *Pre-Ottoman Turkey*, p. 85 (the piratical strongholds of Chaka's successors).

43 Anna Komnene 11.5.2, p. 356, ll. 39–45.

44 Anna Komnene 11.5.3, p. 336, ll. 48–66.

45 Anna Komnene 11.5.5, p. 337, ll. 83–96.

46 Anna Komnene 11.5.5, p. 337, ll. 1–3; Belke and Mersich, *Phrygien und Pisidien*, pp. 177–78 (s. v. Akroinos), 363–64 (s. v. Polybotos).

47 Anna Komnene 11.5.6, p. 338, ll. 8–20; Belke and Mersich, *Phrygien und Pisidien*, pp. 222–23 (s. v. Choma), 321–22 (s. v. Lampe), 323–26 (s. v. Laodikeia).

48 Anna Komnene 11.5.3-4, pp. 336–37, ll. 66–83.

49 Anna Komnene 11.5.5, p. 337, l. 4–5, 11.5.6, p. 338, ll. 11–12, 15–16; see also Frankopan, *The First Crusade*, pp. 146.

50 Anna Komnene 11.5.6, p. 338, ll. 12–15.

51 Foss, "Defenses of Asia Minor," pp. 157–58.

52 Anna Komnene 11.6.1, p. 338, ll. 21–25: πολλοὺς ἐν τῷ μεταξὺ κτείνας βαρβάρους, πολλὰς δὲ καὶ πόλεις δῃωσάμενος ὑπ' αὐτῶν κατεχομένας; Belke and Mersich, *Phrygien und Pisidien*, pp. 359–60.

53 Angold, *Empire*, pp. 192–93.

54 Anna Komnene 11.6.1-3, pp. 338–39, ll. 21–58; Gesta Francorum 27, pp. 63–65; Albert of Aachen 4.40-41, pp. 310–15; William of Tyre 6.10-12, pp. 319–23. For more details and primary sources, see the literature cited below, n. 55.

55 Chalandon, *Comnène*, 1:198, 203; Lilie, *Crusader States*, pp. 38–39; Tyerman, *God's War*, pp. 147–48; Asbridge, *First Crusade*, pp. 227–29; Frankopan, *The First Crusade*, pp. 168–69; Pryor and Jeffreys, "Euphrates Frontier," pp. 48–51.

56 Anna Komnene 11.6.1, p. 338, ll. 22–23: ὁ βασιλεὺς ἑτοιμασθεὶς εἰς ἀρωγὴν τῶν περὶ τὴν Ἀντιόχειαν φθάσαι Κελτῶν.

57 Anna Komnene 11.6.2, p. 338, ll. 31–38: ὁ τοῦ Χοροσὰν σουλτάν [...] τὸν ἴδιον υἱὸν Ἰσμαὴλ τὴν κλῆσιν ἀπείρους δυνάμεις ἀπό τε τοῦ Χοροσὰν ἀπό τε τῶν πορρωτέρω μερῶν συναγαγών.

58 Anna Komnene 11.6.4-5, pp. 339–40, ll. 63–77: οἱ ἔποικοι τῶν μερῶν Φιλομηλίου [...] εἵλοντο μὲν οὖν εὐθὺς ἅπαντες συνέψεσθαι τῷ βασιλεῖ.

59 Anna Komnene 11.6.3, p. 339, ll. 48–58.

60 See, for instance, Albert of Aachen 8.7, p. 594, and Ekkehard of Aura, MGH SS 6:221: *contra terram Chorizanam, quae Turcorum est patria.*

61 Ekkehard of Aura, MGH SS 6:220: *Igitur totus ille tantusque populus per Romania miter dirigere disponebat*, p. 221: *contra Nicomediam vertitur, indeque Romaniam declinans.*
62 Chalandon, *Comnène*, 1:241; Turan, *Türkiye*, p. 136, n. 82.
63 Anna Komnene 11.6.6, p. 340, ll. 77–86.
64 The most circumstantial source is Albert of Aachen 8.1-48, pp. 586–637. Shorter, but still important, accounts can be found in Ekkehard of Aura, MGH SS 6:220–23; Anna Komnene 11.8.1-5, pp. 346–47; Matthew of Edessa 3.4-6, pp. 184–86; for the 1101 crusade in general, see Gate, "Crusade of 1101," pp. 343–67; Turan, *Türkiye*, pp. 104–106; Tyerman, *God's War*, pp. 170–75; Sevim and Merçil, *Selçuklu Devletleri*, pp. 534–35; Öngül, *Selçuklular Tarihi*, 2:33–35.
65 Albert of Aachen 8.13, p. 602: *ecce Turci Donimannus, Solimannus, Carageth, Brodohan de Halapia et a montanis Flaganie et omni regno Antiochie*; Ibn al-Athīr, 6:438, trans. Richards, *Chronicle*, 1:79.
66 Albert of Aachen 8.23, p. 616.
67 Matthew of Edessa 3.6, p. 186.
68 Albert of Aachen 8.1, p. 586.
69 Albert of Aachen 8.7, p. 595: *ac Boemundum de captivitate Turcorum aut extorquere et liberare, aut in virtute sua civitatem Baldac, que est caput regni Corruzana, obsidere et destruere.*
70 For Bohemond's captivity and ransoming with the mediation of Kogh-Basil, see below in this chapter, pp. 342–43; Ralph of Caen 147, p. 709, trans. Bachrach and Bachrach, p. 164; Matthew of Edessa 3.14, pp. 191–92.
71 Albert of Aachen 8.3-6, pp. 588–94.
72 Albert of Aachen 8.5, p. 592, and 8.7, p. 594; Anna Komnene 11.8.2, p. 346. Despite his hostile attitude towards Alexios I in the early stage of the crusade, Raymond of Toulouse sided with the emperor because of his opposition to Bohemond. In June 1100 he went in person to Constantinople, where he was entrusted with the said mission: Lilie, *Crusader States*, p. 67; for the conflict between Raymond and Bohemond, see Shepard, "Greek meets Greek," pp. 205–208, 215–16, 232–33, 263–68.
73 Albert of Aachen 8.8, p. 596.
74 Albert of Aachen 8.9, pp. 596–98.
75 Anna Komnene 11.8.2, p. 346, ll. 69–75.
76 Albert of Aachen 8.9-11, pp. 596–601.
77 Albert of Aachen 8.12, p. 602: *difficultate locorum, montium et valium.*
78 Albert of Aachen 8.13-17, pp. 602–11, esp. 8.16, p. 606–607: *pondus belli sufferre non valens, et precipue equorum defectione qui fame attenuate nil poterant* [...] *cum manu diu fame macerata et viribus exhausta* [...] *multi eorum sunt prostrati ac sagittis imminuti, bellumque Turcorum nimis invaluit*; 8.21, p. 614: *supra centum sexaginta milia illic in gladio et sagitta ferocium Turcorum ceciderunt, facile ab hostibus superati ac detruncate, pre fame diuturna, qua nimium afflicti et viribus exhausti, nulla virtute resistere potuerunt.*
79 Albert of Aachen 8.17-18, p. 610: *idem comes Reimundus, nescio qua formidine correptus et vite diffisus, cum omnibus suis et cunctis Turcopolis imperatoris, equos frenis et sellis stravit, fugamque iniit.*
80 Albert of Aachen 8.17-18, p. 610: *ad castellum imperatoris Pulveral nomine venisse perhibetur* [...]*usque ad Synoplum presidium imperatoris.*
81 Albert of Aachen 8.18-21, pp. 610–15, and 8.22, pp. 614–15.
82 See above in this chapter, pp. 309–11.
83 See below in this chapter, pp. 323–28.
84 Albert of Aachen 8.46, pp. 634–37.
85 Albert of Aachen 8.24, pp. 616–17.
86 Ekkehard of Aura, MGH SS 6:220–21.
87 Matthew of Edessa 3.4, p. 185 and 3.5, p. 186; Albert of Aachen 8.41-42, pp. 630–33. It is noteworthy that on returning to Antioch in March 1102, Raymond was imprisoned by Tancred with the accusation of treachery, but shortly afterwards he was set free on the entreaties of other princes or the Latin patriarch. For Raymond's

agreement with the Normans of Antioch and his subsequent activities until his death on 28 February 1105, see Lilie, *Crusader States*, pp. 68–72.

88 Albert of Aachen 8.25-27, pp. 618–21.

89 Albert of Aachen 8.29, pp. 620–23: *Stanconam descenderunt, ubi Turcorum custodiam et vires in presidio reperientes* [...] *ad civitatem Reclei applicuerunt* [...] *Sed tantum ab hac civitatem dirutam et habitatoribus vacuam prosexerunt.*

90 Albert of Aachen 8.30, pp. 622–23.

91 Albert of Aachen 8.30-31, pp. 622–25.

92 Belke and Restle, *Galatien und Lykaonien*, pp. 220–21.

93 Albert of Aachen 8.37-38, pp. 628–29.

94 Matthew of Edessa 3.6, p. 186, speaks of 400 horsemen accompanying the count of Poitou on his flight; Albert of Aachen 8.39, pp. 630–31, mentions Countess Ida, the widow of Margrave Leopold II of Austria, who was either killed in the tumult or taken captive by the Turks. In the latter case, this would be the first known instance of a Frankish noblewoman ending up in Turkish captivity.

95 Besides Asbridge, *Antioch*, pp. 24–46, see Pryor and Jeffreys, "Euphrates Frontier," pp. 31–86, who present a new interpretation of the relationship between Alexios I and Bohemond on the basis of a thorough analysis of primary sources and secondary literature.

96 For details, see Fink, "Foundation of the Latin States," pp. 370–73.

97 Fink, "Foundation of the Latin States," pp. 373–74; Lilie, *Crusader States*, pp. 61–62; Harris, *Crusades*, pp. 69–70.

98 For the broader context, see Lilie, *Crusader States*, p. 62; Lounghis, *Byzantium in the Eastern Mediterranean*, pp. 31–38; Asdracha, "Κύπρος υπό τους Κομνηνούς," pp. 309–28, esp. p. 326: Τὸ ὅτι ἡ Κύπρος, στὸ ἰδιάζον κλῖμα τῶν Σταυροφοριῶν, ἔτυχε τῆς ἰδιαίτερης φροντίδας τοῦ αὐτοκράτορος γιὰ τὴν ἐνίσχυσή της ὡς ναυτικῆς πολεμικῆς βάσεως καὶ ὡς κέντρου γιὰ τὴν διεκπαιρέωση τῶν ἀποφάσεων ποὺ ἀφοροῦσαν στὶς σχέσεις μεταξὺ Βυζαντίων καὶ Σταυροφόρων φαίνεται [...].

99 Anna Komnene 9.2.4, p. 263: The two officials were Kalliparios and Eumathios Philokales. For the revolt of Rapsomates, see Cheynet, *Contestation*, pp. 97–98 (no. 126), 410–11; Savvides, "Consolidation," pp. 3; Asdrachas, "Κύπρος υπό τους Κομνηνούς," pp. 307–312; Lounghis, *Byzantium in the Eastern Mediterranean*, pp. 32–33. This local uprising is usually viewed in connection with the simultaneous revolt of a certain Karykes in Crete: Cheynet, *Pouvoir*, p. 98 (no. 127). In both cases, the leaders were people of inferior standing without any relations to prominent aristocratic families: Cheynet, *Pouvoir*, pp. 409–10. Certain details in Anna's report may indicate that Rapsomates was commander of a local force of *Athanatoi* soldiers, but it remains unclear what his position and competences on the island were. Cheynet assumes that Rapsomates held a post in the fiscal administration. Some scholars try to establish links between the rebels in Crete and Cyprus and the Turkish warlord Tzachas of Smyrna, but this assumption is hardly supported by the sources. Anna does not disclose the rebels' motives and aims or the deeper reasons leading to the uprising. Excessive tax burdens, the decay of the defensive system and naval power, as well as the general maladministration may lay behind these attempts. For the appointment of the new governors and the patronage of Eumathios Philokales on Cyprus, see Savvides, "Consolidation," pp. 3–4; Asdrachas, "Κύπρος υπό τους Κομνηνούς," pp. 312–13.

100 Savvides, "Consolidation," pp. 5–6; Asdrachas, "Κύπρος υπό τους Κομνηνούς," pp. 317–22.

101 Asdrachas, "Κύπρος υπό τους Κομνηνούς," pp. 323–24.

102 Chalandon, *Comnène*, 1:215–16; Fink, "Foundation of the Latin States," p. 374; Lilie, *Crusader States*, p. 62; Asdracha, "Κύπρος υπό τους Κομνηνούς," pp. 323–24.

103 Anna Komnene 11.10.1-2, p. 350.

104 Anna Komnene 11.10.3-6, pp. 351–52; for Daimberts arrival in Jaffa at about Easter (1 April) 1100, see Ralph of Caen 140, p. 704, trans. Bachrach and Bachrach, p. 156; for the details concerning the alliance between Daimbert and Bohemond as well as their trip to Jerusalem at Christmas 1099, see Fink, "Foundation of the Latin States," pp. 374–75.
105 Chalandon, *Comnène*, 1:235.
106 Anna Komnene 11.11.1-2, pp. 353–54.
107 Anna Komnene 11.10.9-10, p. 353; Fink, "Foundation of the Latin States," p. 373; Asdrachas, "Κύπρος υπό τους Κομνηνούς," pp. 325–26.
108 For this person, see Asdrachas, "Κύπρος υπό τους Κομνηνούς," pp. 325–26, n. 82.
109 Anna Komnene 6.10.9, p. 191.
110 For the walls of Korykos, which mainly date to the Byzantine period and may still display some traces of the re-fortification in the late eleventh and early twelfth centuries, see Foss, "Defenses of Asia Minor," pp. 158–59; Foss and Winfields, *Byzantine Fortifications*, pp. 21–22.
111 See above, pp. 00.
112 Anna Komnene 11.7.4, pp. 343–44; Fink, "Foundation of the Latin States," p. 374; Savvides, "Consolidation," pp. 5–6; Asdrachas, "Κύπρος υπό τους Κομνηνούς," pp. 315–16.
113 Anna Komnene 11.4.6, p. 345: ὁ δὲ βασιλεὺς τῷ δουκὶ Κύπρου τὴν τοῦ τοιούτου πολιχνίου κτίσιν ἀνέθετο; Fink, "Foundation of the Latin States," p. 396; Lilie, *Crusader States*, p. 70; Savvides, "Consolidation," p. 6; Asdrachas, "Κύπρος υπό τους Κομνηνούς," p. 326.
114 Fink, "Foundation of the Latin States," pp. 387–91; Savvides, "Consolidation," pp. 6–7.
115 Ralph of Caen 143, p. 706, trans. Bachrach and Bachrach, pp. 158–59; Fink, "Foundation of the Latin States," p. 387.
116 Chalandon, *Comnène*, 1:232–33 ("dans la deuxième moitié de l'année 1102"); Fink, "Foundation of the Latin State," pp. 387–88 ("in the spring of 1103, after a siege of a year and a half"); Lilie, *Crusader States*, pp. 70–71 ("in the first months of 1103"); Harris, *Crusades*, p. 70; for the siege and its duration, see Ralph of Caen 144, 146, pp. 706–707, 708–709, trans. Bachrach and Bachrach, pp. 159–60, 162–63.
117 Anna Komnene 11.7.7, p. 345: [...] βοήθειαν ἐκεῖθεν ᾔτεῖτο. βραδυνόντων δὲ τῶν ἐν τῇ Κύπρῳ [...].
118 Ibn al-Athīr, 6:438–40, trans. Richards, *Chronicle* 1:79–80; Ralph of Caen 148–49, p. 710–11, trans. Bachrach and Bachrach, pp. 164–66; Matthew of Edessa 3.19, pp. 193–94; Fink, "Foundation of the Latin States," pp. 389–90.
119 Anna Komnene 11.9.2-4, pp. 349–50 and 11.11.3-7, pp. 354–55; Fink, "Foundation of the Latin States," p. 390; Lilie, *Crusader States*, p. 72; Harris, *Crusaders*, p. 71.
120 Anna Komnene 11.9.4, p. 350; Fink, "Foundation of the Latin States," p. 390.
121 Anna Komnene 11.11.7, p. 355; Chalandon, *Comnène*, 1:232; Fink, "Foundation of the Latin States," p. 390; Lilie, *Crusader States*, p. 72.
122 Anna Komnene 11.11.3-7, pp. 354–55; Chalandon, *Comnène*, pp. 235–36; Fink, "Foundation of the Latin States," p. 390; Lilie, *Crusader States*, p. 72.
123 Fink, "Foundation of the Latin States," p. 392.
124 Chalandon, *Comnène*, pp. 236–39; Fink, "Foundation of the Latin States," pp. 390–91; Lilie, *Crusader States*, pp. 73–75.
125 ODB, 1:228–29 s. v. Attaleia; Hellenkemper and Hild, *Lykien und Pamphylien*, 1:297–341 s. v. Attaleia.
126 Foss, "Lycian coast," pp. 1–51, esp. 5 (Telmessos), 8 (Lebissos), 12 (Xanthos), 21 (Kyneai), 35 (Myra), 51 (quotation); Foss, "Lycia in History," pp. 25–32, esp. 26; for detailed lists of historical data and archaeological remains, see Hellenkemper and Hild, *Lykien und Pamphylien*, 1:342–59 s. v. Myra, 2:671–75 s. v. Kyaneai, 2:681–83 s. v. Lebissos, 2:686–90 s. v. Limyra, 2:704–709 s. v. Makre, 2:911–15 s. v. Xanthos.

127 Hellenkemper and Hild, Lykien und Pamphylien, 1:348–49 s. v. Myra, point to the evidence provided by Nicephorus' report about the relics of St. Nicholas, which merchants from Bari in 1087 transferred to their hometown: *habitatoribus civitatis Myreae, qui pro metu Turcorum hinc aufugerant in montem absentem quasi a duodecim stadia.*

128 Foss, "Cities of Pamphylia," pp. 24–47, esp. 46–47; Hellenkemper and Hild, *Lykien und Pamphylien*, 1:373–94 s. v. Side; a letter of Theophylaktos of Ochrid dated to about 1100 points to the presence of a metropolitan (ibidem, p. 378), but it is doubtful whether this piece of information indicates an unbroken continuity of local ecclesiastical institutions.

129 Hellenkemper and Hild, *Lykien und Pamphylien*, 2:587–94 s. v. Kalon Oros.

130 Redford, "Medieval Anatolian Arsenals," pp. 549–50.

131 Vionis, Poblome, De Cupere, Waelkens, "Byzantine Pottery Assemblage," pp. 459–60.

132 For this person, see Asdracha, "Κύπρος υπό τους Κομνηνούς," pp. 313–14, 330–33. He served already during the 1090s as *doux* of Cyprus alternately with Eumathios Philokales and then again from ca. 1102–1108. In addition to that, he appears as prominent military commander on several other frontiers.

133 Anna Komnene 11.9.3-4, pp. 349–50; Savvides, "Consolidation," p. 6.

134 Savvides, "Consolidation," p. 6 and n. 45; Foss, "Cities of Pamphylia," p. 9; Metcalf, *Lead Seals*, pp. 259–60, no. 217–18.

135 For this episode, see also Asdracha, "Κύπρος υπό τους Κομνηνούς," p. 331.

136 Anna Komnene 12.2.1, p. 362.

137 For this person, who is sometimes fallaciously identified with Oshin of Lampron, see ODB, 1:211–21 s. v. Aspietes, and Seibt, "Vasil Goł," p. 155 with n. 21, who refers to a lead seal preserved in Munich (Sammlung Zarnitz) and published by V. P. Stepanenko.

138 Anna Komnene 12.2.1-7, pp. 362–64; for the conquest of Mamistra, see Fink, "Foundation of the Latin States," p. 392.

139 Anna Komnene 12.2.1, p. 362, ll. 90–91: ἐς μὲν γὰρ τὴν Λαοδίκειαν τὸν Πετζέαν μεθ' ἑτέρων ἐκπέμπει δυνάμεων; for the new conquest of Laodikeia, see Fink, "Foundation of the Latin States," p. 392; Lilie, *Crusader States*, pp. 83–84.

140 Lilie, *Crusader States*, pp. 117–25; Angold, *Byzantine Empire*, p. 187.

141 Fink, "Foundation of the Latin States," pp. 371–72.

142 Lilie, *Crusader States*, pp. 66–72.

143 Raymond of Aguilers 18, p. 286; William of Tyre 7.20, pp. 368–69: *Advenerant preterea Constantinopolitani imperatoris legato, multum conquerentes de domino Boamundo* [...]. For the details of these negotiations, see Chalandon, *Comnène*, 1:214–15; Runciman, "First Crusade: Antioch to Ascalon," p. 329; Lilie, *Crusader States*, pp. 42–45; Harris, *Crusaders*, pp. 69–70; Frankopan, *The First Crusade*, pp. 169, 172; for the details concerning the siege of 'Arqa between 14 February and 13 May 1099, mostly under the command of Raymond of Toulouse, see Runciman, "First Crusade: Antioch to Ascalon," pp. 328–30.

144 Pryor and Jeffreys, "Euphrates Frontier," pp. 31–86, esp. 33–40, 44–64, 76–79.

145 Anna Komnene 11.10.7, p. 352; Lilie, *Crusader States*, p. 63; Savvides, "Consolidation," pp. 5–6; Asdracha, "Κύπρος υπό τους Κομνηνούς," pp. 324–25; for the siege of Laodikeia by Bohemond, see Fink, "The Foundation of the Latin States," p. 374.

146 Anna Komnene 11.9.2, p. 349; see also Lilie, *Crusader States*, p. 71.

147 Raymond of Aguilers pp. 126–27; William of Tyre 7.20, p. 369.

148 Lilie, *Crusader States*, p. 67.

149 Anna Komnene 11.8.5, pp. 347–48; for details, see Lilie, *Crusader States*, pp. 82–83; Savvides, "Consolidation," p. 7.

150 Lilie, *Crusader States*, pp. 82–83, points to the rather conflict-ridden relations between the imperial government and William over the following years and to the

emperor's alliance with Raymond's son Bertrand, who set off in late 1108 in order to lay claim to his father's heritage. After William's murder he managed to take hold of all territories formerly controlled by his father; see also Asdracha, "Κύπρος υπό τους Κομνηνούς," p. 331.

151 See above, pp. 323–28.

152 Matthew of Edessa 3.7, p. 187; for this battle, see Asbridge, *Kreuzzüge*, pp. 145–52.

153 Anna Komnene 11.7.3, p. 343; see also Lilie, *Crusader States*, p. 71.

154 'Aẓīmī, p. 26 (Arabic text), p. 30 (trans.) *sub anno* 489/31 December 1095–18 December 1096; see also Hillenbrand, *Crusades*, p. 44.

155 Anna Komnene 12.1.3, p. 360.

156 Matthew of Edessa 3.14, p. 192; Albert of Aachen 9.33, pp. 680–81: *Alexis imperator Constantinopolis, cui semper Boemundus susceptus erat, ne eum a regno expelleret, pecuniam ducentorum et sexaginta milium bysantiorum creberrimis legationibus epistolarum obtulit Donimanno magnifico principi Turcorum*; Dölger and Wirth, *Regesten*, pp. 1214g; Lilie, *Crusader States*, p. 71.

157 Albert of Aachen 8.24, pp. 616–17.

158 Albert of Aachen 8.25, pp. 618–19.

159 Matthew of Edessa 3.5, p. 185.

160 Albert of Aachen 8.45-47, pp. 634–37; see also Lilie, *Crusader States*, pp. 71; Dölger and Wirth, *Regesten*, no. 1218 (1102 before August).

161 For details, see Turan, *Selçuklular Târihi*, pp. 231–32; Bosworth, "Political History," pp. 108–11; Sevim, *Büyük Selçuklu Devleti*, pp. 99, 104; Sevim and Merçil, *Selçuklu Devletleri*, pp. 198–201; Öngül, *Selçuklular*, 1:172–75; Özgüdenli, *Selçuklular*, pp. 212–16; for the role of Baghdad and the caliphate in this period, see Hanne, *Caliph*, pp. 136–38.

162 Cahen, "Diyar Bakr," p. 228; Väth, *Fürstentümer*, pp. 44–45; Heidemann, *Renaissance*, p. 183; Öngül, *Selçuklular*, 2:326–27.

163 For Jokermish, see Hillenbrand, "Career of Zengi," p. 114.

164 Ibn al-Athīr, 6:449–50, trans. Richards, *Chronicle*, 1:90–91; Cahen, "Diyar Bakr," pp. 228–29; Turan, *Doğu Anadolu*, pp. 162–63; Väth, *Fürstentümer*, pp. 48–51; Özaydın, "Kürboğa," pp. 419–20; Öngül, *Selçuklular*, 2:327; for Mārdīn, see EI^2, 6:539–42 s. v. Mārdīn (V. Minorsky and E. C. Bosworth).

165 Özaydın, "Kürboğa," pp. 420; Heidemann, Renaissance, pp. 189–90, who argues for a stabilization of the region in the last years of Karbūqā's rule.

166 Ibn al-Athīr, 6:419–20, trans. Richards, *Chronicle*, 1:58–59; Cahen, "Diyar Bakr," p. 229; Turan, *Doğu Anadolu*, pp. 161–62; Väth, *Fürstentümer*, pp. 47–48; Öngül, *Selçuklular*, 2:327–28; for Mūsā, see Özaydın, "Kürboğa," pp. 420–21; for Ḥiṣn Kayfā, see EI^2, 3:506–509 s. v. Ḥiṣn Kayfā (S. Ory).

167 Albert of Aachen 9.38-40, pp. 688–95; Matthew of Edessa 3.18, pp. 192–93; Ibn al-Qalānisī, p. 143; Ibn al-Athīr, 6:438–40, trans. Richards, *Chronicle*, 1:79–80; for the battle of Ḥarrān, in general, see Turan, *Doğu Anadolu*, p. 162; Väth, *Fürstentümer*, pp. 52–54; Öngül, *Selçuklular*, 2:328–29; Heidemann, *Renaissance*, pp. 192–97 (who gives a very detailed analysis of all available sources); Tyerman, *God's War*, p. 186; Asbridge, *Kreuzzüge*, pp. 156–58.

168 Ibn al-Qalānisī, p. 146; Ibn al-Athīr, 6:448, trans. Richards, *Chronicle*, 1:90.

169 Ibn al-Qalānisī, pp. 146–47; Ibn al-Athīr, 6:448–49, trans. Richards, *Chronicle*, 1:90; see also Elisséeff, *Nūr ad-Dīn*, pp. 296–97.

170 Ibn al-Athīr, 6:439, trans. Richards, *Chronicle*, 1:79: *wa-yu'limuhū annahū qad badhala nafsahū li-llāh ta'ālā wa-thawābihī*, "and announced to him that he had offered himself to God's service in return for His reward to come."

171 Ibn al-Qalānisī, p. 143: *wa-ta'āqadā 'alā l-mujāhada fī a'dā' Allāh al-Ifranj.*

172 Ibn al-Athīr, 6, trans. Richards, *Chronicle*, 1:90: *bal asīru, wa-in 'ūfītu tammamtu mā 'azamtu 'alayhi wa-lā yarānī llāh tathāqaltu 'an qitāl al-kuffār khawfan min al-mawt, wa-in*

adrakanī ajalī kuntu shahīdan sā'iran fī jihād, "No, I shall go on. If I recover I shall fulfill what I have decided to do. God shall not see me unwilling to shoulder the burden of battling the Franks for fear of death. If my fate overtakes me, I shall be a martyr marching [on the path of] jihad." The version of Ibn al-Qalānisī, pp. 146–47, is less idealized, stating that the *atabeg* Ẓahīr al-Dīn on receiving the complaints of the notables of Damascus regretted his decision to call Suqmān for help and thus greatly rejoiced at the message of his sudden death. According to the word put into the notables' mouth a comparison was drawn with the disastrous results of Atsiz b. Uwaq's takeover in Damascus.

173 Ibn al-Athīr, 6:435, trans. Richards, *Chronicle*, 1:76; see also Väth, *Fürstentümer*, p. 52; for the subsequent career of Balak as lord of Kharput/Ḥiṣn Ziyād from 1113 onwards, see Turan, *Doğu Anadolu*, pp. 164–65.

174 Ibn al-Athīr, 6:452, trans. Richards, *Chronicle*, 1:93–94.

175 Turan, *Selçuklular Târihi*, p. 232; Merçil, *Büyük Selçuklu Devleti*, pp. 104–105; Sevim and Merçil, *Selçuklu Devletleri*, pp. 217–20; Hanne, *Caliph*, pp. 138–39; Öngül, *Selçuklular*, 1:192–94; Özgüdenli, *Selçuklular*, pp. 217–20.

176 Bosworth, "Political History," p. 114; Sevim and Merçil, *Selçuklu Devletleri*, pp. 222–23; Öngül, *Selçuklular*, 1:198; Özgüdenli, *Selçuklular*, pp. 220–21.

177 Ibn al-Athīr, 6:431 and 445–46, trans. Richards, *Chronicle*, 1:71 and 87.

178 Ibn al-Athīr, 6:431, trans. Richards, *Chronicle*, 1:71: *wa-hiya min a'māl Khilāṭ min jumlat iqṭā' al-amīr Sukmān al-Quṭbī* [...] *wa-ttaṣala bihī l-amīr 'Alī ṣāḥib Arzan al-Rūm*.

179 Ibn al-Athīr, 6:446, trans. Richards, *Chronicle*, 1:87; see also Turan, *Doğu Anadolu*, pp. 102–105; Öngül, *Selçuklular*, 2:303–304; EI^2, 1:329–30 s. v. Akhlāṭ (F. Taeschner), 9:193, s. v. Shāh-i Arman (C. Hillenbrand).

180 Ibn al-Athīr, 6:436, trans. Richards, *Chronicle*, 1:77; see also Turan, *Selçukluar Târihi*, pp. 231–32; Merçil, *Büyük Selçuklu Devleti*, pp. 103–104; Hanne, *Caliph*, pp. 138–39; Sevim and Merçil, *Selçuklu Devletleri*, pp. 214–17; Heidemann, Renaissance, p. 199; Öngül, *Selçuklular*, 1:191–92; Özgüdenli, *Selçuklular*, p. 216.

181 Ibn al-Athīr, 6:437, trans. Richards, *Chronicle*, 1:78; Hillenbrand, "Najm al-Dīn İl-Ghāzī," p. 257.

182 Ibn al-Athīr, 6:446, trans. Richards, *Chronicle*, 1:87; Väth, *Fürstentümer*, pp. 59–60.

183 Ibn al-Athīr, 6:447–48, trans. Richards, *Chronicle*, 1:88–90; Öngül, *Selçuklular*, 2:338–39; for the assassination af Ayāz, see Sevim and Merçil, *Selçuklu Devletleri*, pp. 221–22; Öngül, *Selçuklular*, 1:197–98.

184 Ibn al-Athīr, 6:444–45, trans. Richards, *Chronicle*, 1:85–87; Elisséeff, *Nūr ad-Dīn*, 2:297; Heidemann, *Renaissance*, pp. 199–200.

185 Ibn al-Athīr, 6:444–45, trans. Richards, *Chronicle*, 1:86: *wa-'araḍa 'alayhi l-kutub min Barkyāruq ilayhi bi-dhālika wa-l-aymān 'alā taslīmihā ilayhi* [...] *inna kutub al-sulṭān waradat ilayya ba'd al-ṣulḥ ta'murunī an lā usallima l-balad ilā ghayrihā*.

186 Ibn al-Athīr, 6:445, trans. Richards, *Chronicle*, 1:86–87: *irja' ilā ra'iyyatika fa-inna qulūbahum ilayyka wa-hum mutaṭalli'ūna ilā 'awdika*.

187 Ibn al-Athīr, 6:457 (Nisibis), 463 (Ḥarrān), trans. Richards, *Chronicle*, 1:100, 106; Elisséeff, *Nūr ad-Dīn*, 2:296.

188 Ibn al-Athīr, 6:468, trans. Richards, *Chronicle*, 1:112.

189 Ibn al-Athīr, 6:458–59, trans. Richards, *Chronicle*, 1:100–101; Väth, *Fürstentümer*, p. 61.

190 Ibn al-Athīr, 6:469, trans. Richards, *Chronicle*, 1:112–13.

191 Ibn al-Athīr, 6:469, trans. Richards, *Chronicle*, 1:112; Elisséeff, *Nūr ad-Dīn*, 2:298–99; Väth, *Fürstentümer*, p. 62; Zankī was the son of Aqsunqur, Malikshāh's governor in Aleppo, born in about 1084–85 and came after his father's death under the tutelage of Jokermish: Hillenbrand, "Career of Zengi," pp. 112–14.

192 Ibn al-Athīr, 6:457–58, trans. Richards, *Chronicle*, 1:100–101. The siege is dated Ramaḍān 499/7 May-5 June 1106; Cahen, "Diyar Bakr," p. 230; Heidemann, *Renaissance*, p. 201.

193 Ibn al-Athīr, 6:458, trans. Richards, *Chronicle*, 1:100–101; Väth, *Fürstentümer*, pp. 61–62; Öngül, *Selçuklular*, 2:338–39.
194 Ibn al-Athīr, 6:468, trans. Richards, *Chronicle*, 1:468; Ibn al-Qalānisī, p. 156; for Jāwulī Saqāw and his activities under Sultan Muḥammad's reign, see Bosworth, "Political History," pp. 116–17.
195 Turan, *Selçuklular Târihi*, 232–33; Elisséeff, *Nūr ad-Dīn*, 2:298; Turan, *Türkiye*, p. 108; Sevim, *Suriye*, p. 205; Väth, *Fürstentümer*, p. 62; Demirkent, *Kılıç Arslan*, p. 55; Sevim and Merçil, *Selçuklu Devletleri*, pp. 223–24; Öngül, *Selçuklular*, 1:199; Peacock, *Great Seljuk Sultanate*, p. 81.
196 Bosworth, "Political History," pp. 113–14.
197 Ibn al-Athīr, 6:468–69, trans. Richards, *Chronicle*, 111–12; see also Heidemann, *Renaissance*, p. 203.
198 Ibn al-Athīr, 6:469, trans. Richards, *Chronicle*, 1:112–13; Elisséeff, *Nūr ad-Dīn*, 2:298–99; Turan, *Türkiye*, p. 108; Sevim, *Suriye*, p. 205; Demirkent, *Kılıç Arslan*, p. 55; Sevim and Merçil, *Selçuklu Devletleri*, p. 224; Heidemann, *Renaissance*, p. 204; Öngül, *Selçuklular*, 1:199–200; for Aqsunqur al-Bursuqī, see Hillenbrand, "Najm al-Dīn İl-Ghāzī," p. 258.
199 Turan, *Türkiye*, pp. 105–108; Demirkent, *Kılıç Arslan*, pp. 49–53; Öngül, *Selçuklular*, 2:34–37.
200 Michael the Syrian 15.9, 3:192 (trans.), 4:591 (Syriac text).
201 Michael the Syrian 15.9, 3:192 (trans.), 4:591 (Syriac text); Turan, *Türkiye*, p. 142; Demirkent, *Kılıç Arslan*, p. 49; Öngül, *Selçuklular*, 2:34–35.
202 Albert of Aachen 9.33-37, pp. 680–89; Orderic Vitalis 10.23, 4:139–41, 142–56.
203 Orderic Vitalis 10.23, 144–45, 149–51; Turan, *Türkiye*, p. 143–44, n. 99, typologically compares Melaz with the character of *Afrūmiya* in the Dānishmand-nāma.
204 Albert of Aachen 9.33, p. 681.
205 Theophylaktos of Ochrid, Lettre no. 81, pp. 426–33.
206 Anna Komnene 12.7.1-4, pp. 376–78.
207 Albert of Aachen 9.35-36, pp. 683–87: *amicicia et foedere percusso, adinvicem reconciliatione amici facti sunt.*
208 Matthew of Edessa 3.14, pp. 191–92.
209 Turan, *Türkiye*, pp. 143–44.
210 Ibn al-Qalānisī, p. 143 (dated Dhū l-Qaʿda 496/6 August-4 September 1103); Aqsarāʾī, p. 28, also speaks of a conquest of Ablastayn, but due to the notorious inaccuracy of this source with respect to the early period this piece of information is questionable.
211 Ibn al-Qalānisī, p. 143.
212 Matthew of Edessa 3.15, p. 192 (dated 552 Armenian era = 1103–04); Cahen, "Diyar Bakr," p. 230.
213 Matthew of Edessa 3.21, p. 194; Turan, *Türkiye*, pp. 146–47.
214 Ibn al-Athīr, 6:440–41, trans. Richards, *Chronicle*, 1:80–81; Ibn al-Azraq al-Fāriqī, p. 271.
215 Matthew of Edessa 2.133, p. 176.
216 For Tʿatʿul, see Cheynet, "Thathoul," pp. 233–42; Beech, "Lordship of Marash," pp. 38–39; Pryor and Jeffreys, "Euphrates Frontier," pp. 70, 83–84.
217 Matthew of Edessa 2.133, p. 176.
218 Matthew of Edessa 3.24, p. 195.
219 Anna Komnene 11.9.4, p. 350.
220 See below, pp. 358–60.
221 Matthew of Edessa 3.14, pp. 191–92. See Dédéyan, *Les Arméniens*, 2:1112–15 (who considers Bohemond's adoption as an attempt to make him heir of the principality).
222 Matthew of Edessa 3.39, p. 201.
223 Matthew of Edessa 3.56, p. 211; for more details, see Dédéyan, *Les Arméniens*, 2:1126–31; Mutafian, *Arménie*, 1:61–62.

224 Matthew of Edessa 3.45-46, pp. 203–205 and 3.51, p. 207; Albert of Aachen 11.40–41, pp. 814–17 (*Corvasilius de civitate Crasson*); Dédéyan, *Les Arméniens*, 2:1119–22; for Ṭughril Arslān's and his mother's rule in Melitene from 1107 onwards, see below, pp. 358–59.
225 Matthew of Edessa 3.37-38, pp. 200–201.
226 Cahen, "Diyar Bakr," p. 230.
227 Michael the Syrian 15.9, 3:192 (trans.), 4:591, col. b (Syriac text); Turan, *Türkiye*, p. 107; Demirkent, *Kılıç Arslan*, pp. 52–53; Öngül, *Selçuklular*, 2:36–37.
228 Ibn al-Azraq al-Fāriqī, pp. 272–73; Cahen, "Diyar Bakr," p. 231; Öngül, *Selçuklular*, 2:36.
229 Ibn al-Azraq al-Fāriqī, pp. 268–69, 272–73 (the list mentions Sukmān b. Artuq, but as he had already died at the time of Qilij Arslān's takeover he may have been mixed up with the lord of Khilāṭ); Cahen, "Diyar Bakr," p. 231; Turan, *Türkiye*, pp. 107–108.
230 For this event, see Peacock, *Great Seljuk Sultanate*, p. 81.
231 Ibn al-Athīr, 6:447–48, trans. Richards, *Chronicle*, 1:89.
232 Ibn al-Athīr, 6:463–64, trans. Richards, *Chronicle*, 1:106; Turan, *Türkiye*, p. 108; Demirkent, *Kılıç Arslan*, p. 54; Sevim and Merçil, *Selçuklu Devletleri*, p. 535; Heidemann, *Renaissance*, pp. 202–203.
233 Ibn al-Athīr, 6:470, trans. Richards, *Chronicle*, 1:114; Öngül, *Selçuklular*, 1:200, 2:37.
234 Turan, *Türkiye*, p. 108; Demirkent, *Kılıç Arslan*, p. 55; Sevim and Merçil, *Selçuklu Devletleri*, p. 535; Öngül, *Selçuklular*, 1:200–201, 2:38.
235 Ibn al-Athīr, 6:469, trans. Richards, *Chronicle*, 1:113.
236 Ibn al-Athīr, 6:469–70, trans. Richards, *Chronicle*, 1:113.
237 Öngül, *Selçuklular*, 1:200–201, 2:38.
238 Chalandon, *Comnène*, 1:242–43; Cahen, "Diyar Bakr," p. 231.
239 Ibn al-Athīr, 6:471, trans. Richards, *Chronicle*, 1:115; Bezer, "Harput," p. 87.
240 Ibn al-Athīr, 6:472, trans. Richards, *Chronicle*, 1:116.
241 Turan, *Türkiye*, p. 107; Demirkent, *Kılıç Arslan*, p. 54; Sevim and Merçil, *Selçuklu Devletleri*, p. 535; Öngül, *Selçuklular*, 1:201, 2:37–38.
242 Turan, *Türkiye*, pp. 108–109; Demirkent, *Kılıç Arslan*, pp. 55–56; Sevim and Merçil, *Selçuklu Devletleri*, pp. 535–36; Heidemann, *Renaissance*, p. 204; Öngül, *Selçuklular*, 2:38–39.
243 Ibn al-Athīr, 6:471, trans. Richards, *Chronicle*, 1:114.
244 Ibn al-Athīr, 6:471, trans. Richards, *Chronicle*, 1:114.
245 Ibn al-Athīr, 6:473, trans. Richards, *Chronicle*, 1:116–17; Turan, *Türkiye*, pp. 109–10; Demirkent, *Kılıç Arslan*, pp. 56–58; Sevim and Merçil, *Selçuklu Devletleri*, pp. 535–37; Heidemann, *Renaissance*, pp. 204–205; Öngül, *Selçuklular*, 1:201–202, 2:38–41.
246 Ibn al-Qalānisī, p. 158; Ibn al-Athīr, 6:473, trans. Richards, *Chronicle*, 1:117; Turan, *Türkiye*, pp. 109–11; Demirkent, *Kılıç Arslan*, pp. 58–59.

9 New contact and conflict zones

Succession and disintegration among the Anatolian Seljuks, 1107–10

Qilij Arslān's death on the battlefield brought the centralizing authority that had begun to take shape in the nascent Seljuk principality suddenly to grief. Despite the strengthening of the Anatolian Seljuks' dynastic identity in the years after 1101, the lordship's internal cohesion was still primarily contingent upon personal ties of allegiance among the Seljuk emirs, the warrior elite, and the non-Turkish indigenous populace recognizing their authority. There were as yet no mechanisms regulating succession procedures within the Seljuk family or institutions vouchsafing the central administration's stability irrespective of the supreme chief's integrative power. As a result, the ruler's death unavoidably led to the principality's disintegration into various competing factions. Their chiefs drew their strength and revenues from urban centers remaining under their control and gathered around different representatives of Seljuk dynastic claims. Broadly speaking, this was a constant feature in the internal development of the Anatolian Seljuk sultanate throughout the twelfth century.[1]

In the years after 1107 the surviving members of the Seljuk house and various groups of the Turkish military elite rallied around the deceased ruler's four sons Shāhinshāh, ʿArab, Masʿūd, and Ṭughril Arslān, something that clearly indicates that the dynastic principle established by Sulaymān b. Qutlumush and his successors had found common acceptance as a predominant source of legitimacy.[2] The eldest son, Shāhinshāh, who had accompanied his father to Mosul, seems to have remained under arrest at the court of Sultan Muḥammad Tapar for some years. In the meantime, the dowager princess (Khātūn) and her son Ṭughril Arslān established their authority in the recently acquired city of Melitene. According to Michael the Syrian, who gives plenty of information about the situation of his hometown in these years, Ṭughril's mother first did away with her son's *atabeg* Pizmish (Bozmısh) by collaborating with another local chief called Īl-Arslān. The latter became her husband but thereafter was imprisoned on account of unjust exactions from the local population and was handed over to Sultan Muḥammad Tapar.[3] Apparently, the potentates in Melitene sought to demonstrate a certain degree of obedience to the Seljuk sultan while at the same time building up a network of alliances at a local level. In 1113 Khātūn married the Artuqid emir Balak b. Bahrām, nephew of Suqmān of Ḥiṣn Kayfā and Īlghāzī of Mārdīn, who was creating his own lordship in the Khanzit district east of Melitene. He had managed to take hold of the fortress of Bula (Palu) near the confluence of the Arsanias and the Euphrates Rivers and expanded his influence towards Kharpete/Ḥiṣn Ziyād, which was to become the center of his ephemeral principality.[4] Seemingly, Balak rapidly gained a powerful position among the potentates in the Euphrates region and thus was deemed the most suitable protector of the Seljuk branch residing in nearby Melitene.[5]

Being backed up by Balak, Khātūn and her son were able to pursue their own goals in the region: the acquisition of new territories and the forging of coalitions with Christian and Muslim powers in their vicinity. In about 1114, apparently in view of the increasing pressure built up against him, the ruler of Kharpete/Ḥiṣn Ziyād (*asbasālār d-Ḥisnā dh-Ziyād*) sold his city to the "sultan of Melitene" (*sulṭān d-Mīlīṭīnī*) in exchange for a sum of money and other places. Apart from a brief interlude, during which the city was temporarily occupied by troops subject to the Great Seljuk sultan, Kharpete/Ḥiṣn Ziyād henceforth was part of the united lordships of Balak and Ṭughril Arslān, which extended over territories of the old Byzantine borderland's central section in the Euphrates and Arsanias Valleys.[6] Already prior to the marriage with Balak, in 1111 the Turks of Melitene had begun to invade areas of the Jayḥān region and thus lay claims to the lands of the lordship of Marʿash, which stood under the suzerainty of Antioch.[7] The geography of the area certainly encouraged expansionist tendencies similar to those observed several decades earlier in the time of Philaretos Brachamios. Yet in the 1110s the political situation of the Turkish emirates in the Euphrates region was also determined by a twofold pressure, which partly emanated from the Franks of Antioch and Edessa in the south and partly from the rivaling Dānishmandid and Mangujak emirates in Sebasteia and Erzincan in the north. Therefore, after Balak b. Bahrām's death in 1124, Melitene was no longer able to maintain its independence and rapidly reverted to Dānishmandid rule. For several decades, the city remained out of the Anatolian Seljuks' reach.[8]

Parts of Cappadocia northwest of the Euphrates River stood under the control of a chieftain called Asan. As has been mentioned already, he made his first appearance in 1097 in a battle fought against Bohemond's army near Herakleia.[9] Apparently, he managed to survive the onslaught of the crusading hosts and the power struggles between various Turkish emirs. Yet the scanty pieces of information provided by Anna Komnene hardly allow us to arrive at safe conclusions regarding Asan's exact relationship with the Seljuks of Konya and the Dānishmandid emirate.[10] At any rate, it is noteworthy that prior to Shāhinshāh's return to Konya Asan appears as the leader of a major campaign against Byzantine territories in western Asia Minor.[11] It may be assumed that he maintained close ties with the Seljuk scions in Konya and thus became directly involved in the military operations in central Anatolia. It remains open to question, however, whether he actually held power in Konya. Nor is there sufficient evidence to prove that he was a son of Qilij Arslān's brother Kulan Arslān, as Osman Turan suggests.[12]

As regards the situation in Konya itself, the available information is extremely scarce. The two brothers ʿArab and Masʿūd seem to have imposed their rule for some time, but it is unclear whether this happened on account of a formal proclamation by the Turkish elite in Konya. Ibn al-Qalānisī is the only source to assert that Shāhinshāh returned from captivity in early 503/31 July 1109-19 July 1110 (in about August 1109).[13] If we believe the same source, the young prince fled from Muḥammad Tapar's camp, which points to ongoing frictions with the Great Seljuk sultan and took power by killing *ibn ʿammihī* (his cousin). Turan identifies the latter with Asan, but there is no evidence supporting this assumption.[14] Bar Hebraeus, instead, claims that Shāhinshāh was "sent" by the sultan, and a later Arab historian even talks about a Muslim jurist (*faqīh*), whom people in Konya reportedly entrusted with negotiating the prince's release.[15] In this case, Muḥammad Tapar's decision could be interpreted as an attempt to intervene in the internal succession procedures of the Anatolian Seljuks and thus to increase his influence in the principality.

This version is partly corroborated by the fact that Sultan Muḥammad in this period generally sought to increase his influence on the local emirates of northern Iraq and Syria and took a much more aggressive stance towards the crusader states.[16] The leading proponent of this policy was the sultan's staunch emir Mawdūd b. Altūntakīn, who in September 1108, after a siege of several months, managed to take power in Mosul and expel the insurgent governor Jāwulī b. Saqāw.[17] Nevertheless, the greatest part of the forces supporting Sultan Muḥammad and Mawdūd were based in western Iran, Azerbaijan, the Lake Van region, and northern Iraq. The lords in Diyār Bakr and Syria, instead, tenaciously strove to maintain their independence. Hence, the rulers in central Anatolia could hardly have felt much pressure in submitting to the Great Seljuk sultan. Īl-Arslān's extradition to the sultan may indicate some temporary influence in Melitene, but this was rather an isolated incident without lasting implications. As for the events in Konya after Shāhinshāh's arrival, Michael the Syrian refers to Masʿūd's imprisonment. The chronicler implies that this was the reason for the future conflict between the two brothers, in the course of which Masʿūd allied with Emir Ghāzī b. Dānishmand and was later on ambushed and blinded his brother.[18] ʿArab's death is also noted on this occasion, but he apparently died much later in the 1120s.[19]

Putting the available evidence together, one gains the impression that we are mainly dealing with internal rivalries between Qilij Arslān's sons, who in the years after 1107 were largely isolated from what was going on in the Euphrates region and the Armenian highlands. The gradual consolidation of the local potentates in this area, such as the Dānishmandids, the Mangujak emirate, the Artuqids, and the Seljuk branch in Melitene, favored the emergence of a separate Turkish-Muslim sphere, which interacted with a complicated patchwork of Frankish and Armenian lords in the region. At that time, the influence of the Anatolian Seljuks was largely confined to the central Anatolian plateau west of Cappadocia.

The great Seljuk sultanate's last involvement in Syria and eastern Anatolia

The meager results of Sultan Muḥammad's attempts in the years 1111–15 to create a broad coalition against the crusader states clearly illustrate the deep-rooted changes the Muslim-Christian frontier zone in northern Syria and Upper Mesopotamia had undergone since the 1090s. After 1110, except for some Fatimid strongholds, all ports along the Syrian and Palestinian coast stood under Frankish control. Serious setbacks, such as the Frankish conquest of al-Athārib a few miles west of Aleppo, fomented fears that the crusaders soon would attack more Muslim territories in Syria.[20] A delegation of representatives from Aleppo, who stirred up riots in the mosques of Baghdad so as to urge the sultan to support the war against the crusaders, is indicative of the panic that spread among large sections of the local population.[21]

In this context, Muslim sources mention the arrival of a Byzantine embassy at the court of Sultan Muḥammad Tapar in Jumādā II 504/15 December 1110–12 January 1111, the first diplomatic contact with the Seljuk sultanate after the death of Malikshāh in 1092.[22] The purpose of this mission was apparently related to Emperor Alexios I's attempts to create a coalition of forces against Tancred of Antioch.

> In Jumādā II of this year an emissary from the king of the Romans (*mutamallik al-Rūm*) arrived with presents, precious objects, and letters (*murāsalāt*). His message urged [the court of Baghdad] to wage war on the Franks, to attack them, to gather forces so as to expel them from these provinces, to be no longer negligent in dealing with them, and to be eager to kill them before the mischief they have caused becomes too great and their evil too terrible. He [i.e., the emperor] claimed that he had prevented them from reaching the lands of the Muslims and had waged war on them. But since they seek to gain them [i.e., the Muslim lands] so that their troops and reinforcements continue to come to the Islamic lands, he needs to flatter them and to allow them to cross and to help them in their goals and purposes, as exigency requires. And he verbosely instigated and stirred [the Muslims] up to gather forces in order to fight them [i.e., the Franks] and to fend them off from these regions with an alliance against them.[23]

In spite of the rhetorical exaggeration in Ibn al-Qalānisī's account, there is no reason to doubt the reliability of this piece of information, the gist of which is corroborated by another independent Arabic source. The idea of instigating the Seljuk sultanate to a large-scale campaign against the Franks is in tune with the emperor's deep disappointment about the failure of his plans regarding the princedom of Antioch, as is described in great detail by Anna Komnene.[24] Within a period of two years following the treaty of Devol (September 1108), Tancred had managed to strengthen his principality significantly. Apart from a number of military achievements, this is mainly due to the agreement that King

Baldwin I and the leading Frankish potentates reached in the summer of 1109.[25] The settlement of the disputes among Tancred, Baldwin of Edessa, Raymond's son Bertrand, and others regarding their claims to the newly founded county of Tripoli and other territories as well as the ongoing Frankish expansion frustrated the implementation of what Byzantium and the Norman lords of Antioch had agreed upon in 1108. Tancred forthrightly rejected all propositions an imperial embassy submitted to him.[26] After Tancred's taking possession of Laodikeia and the main cities of the Cilician plain in 1108–1109, the Franks forced Tripoli into submission in July of 1109, seized Sidon and Beirut in 1110, and put Tyre under siege in 1111–12. Simultaneously, they achieved other territorial gains in the region east of the Orontes Valley.[27] Hence, Alexios I had two options for pursuing his goals further. He could instigate a powerful external foe against the Franks, as he attempted to do with his embassy to the sultan's court, or he could divide the Frankish coalition, as he would try to do in late 1111 and early 1112 by entrusting Manuel Boutoumites with a mission to Bertrand of Tripoli and King Baldwin I.[28] It is certainly an overestimation of Byzantine influence to assume that it was the emperor's embassy to Baghdad that induced Sultan Muḥammad to proclaim the jihad against the Franks.[29] Yet the imperial court seems to have been aware of the fact that the Frankish expansion affected both Byzantine and Muslim territories in the East and thus may have hoped to find fertile ground for its requests, as a statement of Ibn al-Athīr suggests.[30]

There certainly were strong sentiments in favor of a united Muslim front against the Franks. Yet the attitudes of the potentates in the region were by no means uniform. The disintegration caused by the Seljuk dynastic wars and the ensuing consolidation of various Turkish local lordships in the Armenian highlands and the Euphrates region had caused a rupture of ties with the Great Seljuk sultanate. This situation is clearly reflected in the composition of the allied forces participating in the conquest of Mosul and, later on, in the invasion of the Frankish territories. Apart from Mawdūd and the sultan's son Masʿūd, who held the supreme command of these expeditions, the coalition included powerful emirs of Sultan Muḥammad's entourage: the sons of Bursuq, Īlbakī, Zankī, and Bursuq of Hamadhān; Aqsunqur al-Bursuqī, the military prefect of Iraq; warlords of Azerbaijan like Aḥmadīl of Marāgha; Kurdish emirs like Abū l-Hayjā' of Irbil; Sukmān al-Quṭbī of Akhlāṭ, who in May 1109 had taken hold of Mayyāfāriqīn; and Tamīrak of Sinjār.[31]

Contrarily, the Turkish lords in regions adjacent to the Frankish territories only reluctantly collaborated with the Seljuk coalition and, at times, even preferred to side with the Franks against the united Muslim forces. Apparently, the fear of being reduced to a vassal status was greater than the Frankish menace. Īlghāzī of Mārdīn only halfheartedly dispatched his son Ayāz. Riḍwān of Aleppo forthrightly refused to collaborate with the Seljuk commanders.[32] Ṭughtakīn of Damascus, who met the allied leaders near Maʿarrat al-Nuʿmān, was suspicious of their intentions and thus started peace talks with the Franks.[33] Despite their political differences, however, Ṭughtakīn and Mawdūd seem to have established friendly relations with each other. After a series of raids carried out by King

Baldwin of Jerusalem in the spring of 1113, they eventually collaborated and undertook a counter-attack on the Jordan Valley and places in Palestine.[34] This alliance came to a sudden end with Mawdūd's murder at the hands of a Bāṭinī assassin during the Friday prayer in the mosque of Damascus on 12 September 1113.[35] His successor as governor of Mosul, Aqsunqur al-Bursuqī, was ordered to continue the war against the Franks. He relied upon largely the same coalition of forces, but after a brief siege of Edessa in April and May 1115, the Seljuk troops withdrew to Sumaysāṭ.[36]

In the same year, Aqsunqur al-Bursuqī engaged in a fierce conflict with the Artuqids of Mārdīn and Ḥiṣn Kayfā and with Ṭughtakīn of Damascus. Under the menace of military interventions by the sultan's army, these rulers concluded new treaties with the princedom of Antioch and Emir Khīr Khān of Ḥimṣ.[37] As a result, the Seljuk alliance, which had come into being in order to build up a united Muslim front against the crusader states, eventually faced a coalition of Muslim and Christian potentates in Syria and the Diyār Bakr province. This coalition enlisted large numbers of Turkmen troops for the common goal of preventing Sultan Muḥammad and the emir of Mosul from extending their influence over Syria. After some initial successes in taking Muslim- and Christian-held places like Ḥamāh, Kafarṭāb, and Buzā'ā, a last major invasion of Seljuk forces under the command of Emir Bursuq b. Bursuq of Hamadhān ended with a crushing defeat inflicted by Roger, regent of Antioch (1112–19), in the battle of Sarmīn in September 1115.[38] This event sealed the end of the *jihad* movement led by the Great Seljuk sultanate and the emirate of Mosul.

By that time, the Turkish emirates in Syria and Upper Mesopotamia had significantly cemented their position as autonomous entities and thus were able to distance themselves from the Great Seljuk sultanate as an authority claiming supreme rule over the Turkish military elite. The idea of building up a unified Muslim front against the Franks had gained momentum in view of the growing territorial expansion and military power of the Christian principalities. Yet the potentates in the Christian-Muslim frontier zone were not willing to support this policy in exchange for their submission to Seljuk claims. This overall tendency seems to have been an important factor in the formation of a dynastic ideology in the Turkish emirates of eastern Anatolia and the Armenian highlands. A secondary result was a new westward shift in the political orientation of the Anatolian Seljuks, who in the years after 1107 abandoned their expansionist attempts towards the Euphrates region and turned their military power once more against the Byzantine territories.

New defensive structures in western Asia Minor, 1109–13

While Qilij Arslān's struggle with the Great Seljuk sultanate was brought to a conclusion in Upper Mesopotamia, it was in the western parts of Asia Minor that the imperial government of Constantinople during the 1110s managed to put a halt to the Turks' westward expansion. As a result, the frontier zone separating the two sides assumed a clearer shape and certain contact and conflict areas came into being, which by and large persisted until the thirteenth century. The region in question straddled parts of the ancient provinces of Phrygia, Pisidia, and Lycaonia and can be roughly located between the fortress of Akroinon (Afyonkarahisar), the Sultan Mountains, Lake Tessarakonta Martyron (Eber/Akşehir Gölü), and Lake Pousgouse (Beyşehir Gölü).[39] The backbone of this stabilization was a new defensive system created by Emperor Alexios I and his subordinate commanders in the years 1110–16 in reaction to a series of large-scale invasions launched by the Anatolian Seljuks. In the course of these campaigns, which affected the whole area between the Propontis coastland, the western fringes of Phrygia, and the Upper Meander Valley, the Byzantine army pursued a successful strategy of warding off hostile assaults while simultaneously affording protection to the local population. Attempts to recover parts of the Anatolian plateau and the newly established Seljuk capital of Konya failed, but western Asia Minor reached its highest degree of safety and security since the 1070s.

The imperial troops succeeded in expelling the Turks from the littoral and the Meander Valley and pushed as far as Polybotos and Philomelion near the northern and southern shores of Lake Tessarakonta Martyron respectively. Yet, until the later years of Alexios I's reign, they were unable to block the invasion routes leading from Phrygia to the river valleys of western Asia Minor and the southern coastland. The overall situation remained extremely unstable, and warrior groups of varying size could easily spread in various directions. Byzantine commanders made efforts to rebuild or fortify strongpoints and to secure sensitive areas from hostile attacks, but the results were swiftly overturned by new invasions. A case in point is the expedition of Eumathios Philokales datable to about 1109.[40] Fierce conflicts on the Balkan Peninsula and especially the dangerous Norman invasion forced Alexios to transfer his troops to the West, thus neglecting the territories recovered between 1098 and 1105 in western and southern Asia Minor and at the Syrian littoral. As has been shown above, in the years after 1101 the Anatolian Seljuks were preoccupied with the conflict with the Dānishmandid emirate and Qilij Arslān I's eastward expansion. Treaties with the imperial government affirmed the *status quo* in the Byzantine-Turkish border zone and intensified certain forms of collaboration, such as the dispatch of Turkish auxiliary troops against the Normans.[41] This brought about a stagnation of military activities and a certain stabilization of political and administrative structures on both sides of the frontier in western Asia Minor. But due to other priorities, the imperial government could hardly proceed to other improvements of the existing defensive structures.

Hence, the 1109 expedition primarily aimed at rebuilding towns and fortresses along the Aegean coastland from Smyrna to Attaleia and at repopulating the region by offering incentives to the indigenous population, who had fled to safer areas, to return to their hometowns. It is not known when and under what circumstances Attaleia, one of the major ports on the southern coast of Asia Minor, was attacked and devastated by Turkish invaders.[42] As has been shown above, the place was of paramount importance not only for protecting the Pamphylian coast and its hinterland but also for maintaining lines of communication with the Byzantine strongholds further east and the naval base in Cyprus.[43] Eumathios also managed to repair Adramyttion (Edremit) and to repopulate the town, but he was unable to extend his work to other regions of the Aegean littoral because of the emergence of new Turkish invaders arriving from the East. Anna mentions warriors in the region of Lampe in the Upper Meander Valley and a large invading force of 24,000 men led by Asan, the lord of Cappadocia.[44] The former may have been a group of Turkish nomads who invaded the Meander Valley during the summer season in order to pillage towns and fertile agricultural areas along the river and its lateral valleys. Asan's forces seem to have consisted of a large gathering of troops from various Seljuk territories. Anna's report makes us believe that this expedition took place in retaliation for atrocities perpetrated by the Byzantine troops, but if this were the case one would primarily expect spontaneous counter-attacks of Turkish warriors living close to the borderland. In this case, it seems more likely that we are dealing with a well-prepared, concerted action, which materialized in collaboration with the Seljuks of Konya.

Unlike the nomads who stayed in Lampe only to be crushed by a detachment of Philokales' army,[45] Asan's troops deeply penetrated the western coastland and reached Philadelpheia, where the soldiers of Philokales had entrenched themselves, and thence split up into various directions: one group moved southwestward across the Boz Mountains towards Kelbianon (Kiraz) at the Kaystros River (Küçük Menderes); another advanced westward to Nymphaion (near Kemalpaşa) and Smyrna; and a third group headed in a northerly direction towards Chliara (Kırkağaç) and Pergamos (Bergama). The underlying strategy was to swarm out in a fan-shaped manner in order to bypass the Byzantine defenders and to take as much booty as possible. Anna's account conveys the impression that the Byzantines did not have much difficulty checking the invaders and forcing them back to the Anatolian plateau. Yet it cannot be ruled out that she glosses over problems and shortcomings that would have shed a negative light on her father's handling of the situation.[46]

During the years following this campaign, the defensive measures of the imperial government mainly concentrated on the western coastland from the Hellespont and the shores of Mysia (Biga Yarımadası) as far as the Meander Valley. Philadelpheia continued to be a strongpoint of crucial significance, controlling the access routes from the central Anatolian plateau towards the Gulf of Smyrna. Since the Byzantine re-conquest in 1098, the city was held by a strong garrison under the command of Constantine Gabras and Monastras, who both belonged to the circle of Alexios I's most intimate officers. Pergamos and Chliara were the main points blocking the routes leading across the Kaikos River (Bakir Çayı) into the northwestern edge of Asia Minor. Adramyttion situated further north at the mouth of the gulf opposite the island of Lesbos provided additional protection to the coastland of Mysia and the Propontis.[47]

In 1110 or 1111, upon the arrival of messages about the imminent attacks of the Seljuk ruler Shāhinshāh on Philadelpheia and the coastal area, the imperial government sought to further improve the defensive structures in western Asia

Minor.[48] This time, the main objective was to strengthen the military forces in the threatened region by transferring troops from Thrace across the Hellespont and the Skamandros River to the Thrakesion theme, i.e., the central section of the Aegean coast around the Gulf of Smyrna and the Hermos Valley (Gediz Nehri).[49] They were ordered to monitor the enemies' movements closely with the aid of scouts.[50] In addition, the Byzantines relied on strategic advantages offered by the geographic position of the fortress of Philadelpheia, which they used as an advanced outpost for the troops defending the Thrakesion region. Perhaps after the end of the winter season 1111/12, Constantine Gabras sallied forth with his troops from Philadelpheia and defeated the Turkish invaders near Kelbianon east of Sardis.[51] The Turks reportedly penetrated the Byzantine provinces by two different routes. A northern one "through the regions of Sinaos" may be identified with the route leading from Kotyaion (Kütahya) via Azanoi (near Çavdarhisar) to Syanos (Simav) in northwestern Phyrgia, from where another route continued southwestward towards Sardis.[52] A southern one διὰ τῆς ἰδίως καλουμένης Ἀσίας, a term usually synonymous with Thrakesion, in all likelihood can be identified with one of the connections between the Meander Valley and the Anatolian plateau leading from Philomelion or Antioch of Pisidia (near Yalvaç) to Apameia (Dinar) near the region in which the source of the Meander River is located.[53] In sum, the imperial defensive strategy proved effective. Upon the invaders' defeat, Shāhinshāh entered negotiations about a peace treaty with Emperor Alexios I, and the hostilities were temporarily terminated.[54]

The situation farther east was characterized by an overall state of insecurity and instability, which was even more exacerbated by the seditious behavior of recalcitrant local lords. Anna mentions a certain Michael of Amastris (Amasra at the Black Sea coast), who took possession of Akroinon (Afyonkarahisar) and pillaged the environs of the town. He was defeated by Byzantine troops under George, the son of Dekanos, and was brought in chains to Constantinople. The emperor at first sentenced him to death but then pardoned him and sought to win him over by lavishing gifts upon him.[55] The episode shows that the imperial government, though concentrating its defensive efforts mainly on the western shores and river valleys, still kept an eye on fortified places in the interior of Phrygia by dispatching troops and governors. At the same time, Constantinople sought to regain the loyalty of local elements that defied the authority of the central government. Emperor Alexios I apparently wished to avoid violent reactions on the part of Michael's kinsmen and followers should the rebel be executed. Granting him amnesty was a sign of good will, which signaled Alexios' intent to tighten relations with the remnants of the Greek nobility in Asia Minor. Alexios also feared that these people would end up collaborating with the Turks against the imperial government. Akroinon was a hub in the road network of central Anatolia, where routes led northwestward to Kotyaion and Bithynia and southeastward to the Meander Valley.[56] Exerting firm control over this area was of vital importance for fending off attacks directed against the Byzantine provinces in western Asia Minor.

As early as 1113, hostilities broke out again with a new Turkish invasion advancing most likely via Akroinon and Kotyaion towards Bithynia and the

Hellespont region.[57] Once again the Turkish forces split up into several detachments: one group attacked Nicaea and adjacent regions; a commander called Monolykos pillaged the territories around Askanian Lake (Iznik Gölü) and then advanced along the Propontis coastland to Prousa (Bursa), Apollonias at the Rhyndakos, Lopadion, and Kyzikos, which was seized after being abandoned by the local governor; farther south there was the contingent of two chieftains called Kontogmes and Emir Mouchoumet who, along with their booty and captives, headed towards Poimanenon (Eski Manyas), a fortress south of Lake Kuş near Kyzikos. At the same time, Monolykos continued his march, passing through the entire Hellespont region via Pareos, Abydos (Çanakkale), and Adramyttion until he reached Chliara on the Kaikos River (Bakır Çayı).[58] Over the whole distance, Monolykos met no resistance nor did he lose any of the booty he had taken.[59] The Byzantine garrisons in the aforementioned strongholds in the Hellespont region and the province of Lydia apparently adopted a passive wait-and-see attitude. They stayed behind the walls and watched the enemy's movements, perhaps in expectation of the emperor's orders or a counter-attack by the imperial troops. As is attested by the case of Eustathios Kamytzes, the governor of Nicaea, the local commanders exchanged letters with the imperial camp, through which they informed the emperor about the whereabouts of the Turkish forces and received instructions on how to behave. Kamytzes was explicitly ordered to follow the enemy with 500 horsemen and to inform the emperor in writing about their movements but to refrain from attacks.[60]

The Turks chose a place called Aorata as a rallying point.[61] It can perhaps be located somewhere in the vicinity of Poimanenon, as Anna's report may suggest,[62] but the geographical details are by no means clear. From there they started their way back towards the Turkish territories on the Anatolian plateau, but the itinerary of the invaders and their Byzantine pursuers can hardly be reconstructed. The main problem is the geographical position of a place called Akrokos and a nearby plain covered by reeds and called πεδιὰς τῆς Τεπείας.[63] Anna describes it as being located "between Philadelpheia and Akrokos,"[64] which excludes the possibility of identifying Akrokos with Akroinon, as has been proposed, because of the great distance between the two towns. Locating the place close to Philadelpheia, however, would mean that the Turkish forces, rather than heading back via Kotyaion towards Phrygia, chose a route farther south situated in regions well protected by Byzantine military contingents and far away from any supplies and reinforcements. The Turkish troops carried with them a large baggage train with booty and captives, which was in constant danger of being caught in an ambush. This alternative, therefore, seems highly improbable. The question cannot be resolved on the basis of the available data, but it is certainly much more plausible to locate the Turkish retreat somewhere on the routes leading from the Makestos or the Rhyndakos Valley eastward to Akroinon rather than in the region south of the Hermos River. It seems reasonable to adopt another theory identifying Akrokos with a fortress near Eğrigöz some 40 miles northwest of Kotyaion.[65]

Alexios I's strategy was to follow the Turks at a certain distance to a suitable place to wipe them out in a pitched battle. Being informed by Eustathios

Kamytzes about the attacks on Nicaea, he sallied forth from Damalis, crossed the Gulf of Nikomedeia at a narrow passage between Aigialoi and Kibotos and thence continued to Nicaea and Malagina at the western bank of the Sangarios River. From there he crossed a mountainous region called Basilika and descended to Alethina and Akrokon.[66] Anna's location of Basilika near the hills of the Mysian Olympus (Uludağ) is too far west from the banks of the Sangarios River, where Alexios' troops are said to have passed by. More likely, the imperial army crossed the Domaniç Mountain, which would be just north of Eğrigöz, the possible location of Akrokon. In this way, Alexios reached the said stronghold prior to the arrival of the Turks in the nearby plain of Tepeia, where he attacked and routed them.[67] This victory by no means points to an overall superiority of the Byzantine forces. Smaller contingents could be easily trapped, as is illustrated by the imprudent assault of Eustathios Kamytzes, in which the latter was taken captive by the host of Mouchoumet and Kontogmes at Aorata near Poimanenon.[68]

Another challenge for the Byzantine defensive strategy was the high mobility of nomad warriors, which enabled groups of invaders to make good their losses and to receive fresh reinforcements. Mouchoumet and his companions seem to have been on the march from the Hellespont region towards Kotyaion when they were informed about their fellow invaders' defeat against the emperor in the battle of Tepeia. In order to reinforce his troops he allied "with the Turkmens living in Asia."[69] The term *Tourkomanoi*—its first and only occurrence in the *Alexias*—obviously refers to nomad groups in contrast to the forces of the Seljuks of Konya. Accordingly, "Asia" seems to refer to the upper parts of the Hermos and Meander Valleys and the fringes of the Anatolian plateau in central Phrygia, which were frequented by transhumant pastoralists, as is testified by the 1109 attack,[70] and offered easy access to the region where Mouchoumet was operating. Despite this support, the Turkish chief was not strong enough to join battle with the emperor and thus concentrated his efforts on skirmishes with the rearguard of Alexios' army. The losses on the Byzantine side seem to have been by no means negligible.[71]

As a whole, one gains the impression that the imperial army in the 1113 campaign succeeded in ousting the Turkish troops from Bithynia and the Hellespont region and in maintaining its pre-dominance over the routes leading towards Dorylaion, Kotyaion, and farther southeastward to Akroinon and Polybotos. On the other hand, the farther east Byzantine troops advanced, the denser the presence of Turkish raiders and nomads became and the more difficult it was to wield power over important strongholds. Unavoidably, a broad swathe of land stretching from the Sangarios Valley to Phrygia, Pisidia, and the Taurus Mountains became a fiercely contested no-man's land, in which fortified places constantly changed hands and neither side was able to impose its rule. As a result, the improvements of the Byzantine defensive structures mainly concentrated on regions close to the Propontis and Aegean coastland and some more remote outposts in the western river valleys. The latter were easily defensible and could be rapidly reinforced by relief forces from the capital or the Balkan provinces. The local garrisons in fortresses like Nicaea, Prousa, Lopadion, Kyzikos, Poimanenon, Adramyttion, and Chliara confined themselves to a wait-and-watch strategy: they prevented hostile forces from entering these places, or, as happened in Kyzikos, they even withdrew in view of the enemy's numerical superiority.[72] Eustathios Kamytzes' defeat illustrates that isolated units were obviously not strong enough to check massive assaults and had to collaborate with larger mobile forces in order to take effective action. A clear disadvantage of the Byzantine defensive system was that Turkish invaders met almost no obstacles during the initial stage of their expeditions and thus deeply penetrated Byzantine territories before being warded off. Larger contingents easily bypassed outposts like Kotyaion, Malagina, and Philadelpheia. Only if the numerical ratio between defenders and invaders was balanced, these strongholds proved adequate to stop the enemies' onslaught, as is evidenced by the success of Constantine Gabras. At any rate, they served as suitable rallying points, where larger units of mobile forces could gather and prepare to advance farther. Alexios' march to Malagina and previous activities in the Phrygian frontier zone illustrate these procedures. Therefore, the maintenance and protection of advanced outposts in exposed regions was of primary importance despite all perils and hardships the local garrisons were facing.

Alexios I's last advance to the Anatolian plateau

A milestone in the formation of the Byzantine-Turkish borderland in central Asia Minor was the eventful year 1116, in which a new Seljuk invasion coincided with Emperor Alexios I's last attempt to recover Konya. Anna Komnene does not explain how and under what circumstances Konya became the capital of the Seljuk principality, but confines herself to the laconic statement that "there had been installed the *soultanikion* for Klitziasthlan."[73] In this way she linked Qilij Arslān I with the old provincial center of Lycaonia, which became the Seljuks' chief residence on the central Anatolian plateau.[74]

A general problem of Anna's narrative is its inaccuracy with respect to personal names, toponyms, and geographical details. Within the same section she calls the Seljuk ruler alternately Σολυμᾶς σουλτάν and [ὁ βάρβαρος] Κλιτζιασθλάν, although she obviously refers to one and the same person and to a period in which both Sulaymān b. Qutlumush (m. 1086) and Qilij Arslān I (m. 1107) had already passed away.[75] In other passages, the Seljuk ruler is merely called ὁ σουλτάνος.[76] Only towards the end of her report when speaking about Shāhinshāh's conflict with his brother Masʿūd does she suddenly switch to a phonetically recognizable transliteration of the sultan's name, i.e., Σαΐσάν [σουλτάνος].[77] As regards geographical terms, Anna mentions the arrival of troops from Khurāsān (Χοροσάν),[78] which has to be seen in connection with her reports concerning the Great Seljuk Empire in the time of Malikshāh and the civil strife of Tutush, Barkyāruq, and Muḥammad Tapar. Just as in contemporary crusader chronicles,[79] "Khurāsān" did not designate the eastern Iranian province known by this name but referred more broadly to the Turks' mythical homeland and center of power in the East.

In general, there is a strong tendency to conflate different chronological layers, stretching from the death of Sulaymān b. Qutlumush in 1086 to the death of Shāhinshāh in 1116, and to mix up the Seljuk sultanate in Iran and the central Islamic lands with the sultans in Asia Minor. Accordingly, the description of Konya as Qilij Arslān's residence should not be taken at face value. Nevertheless, the fact that Alexios in 1116 chose Konya as the target of his expedition because of its being the sultanate's capital is an unmistakable *terminus ante quem* for the city's gaining this position.[80] Qilij Arslān may have taken the first steps towards this direction in the time after 1101, but in view of his far-reaching ambitions in Upper Mesopotamia, it is more likely that the rise of Konya is causally linked with the restriction of Seljuk rule to the Anatolian plateau from 1107 onwards.[81]

Anna's report provides some interesting details regarding the boundaries of the Seljuk realm vis-à-vis the Byzantine territories in the West. Yet it is important to note that there was hardly any clearly demarcated frontier zone. Rather we have to imagine a loose chain of strongholds exerting military control and political authority over a certain perimeter. As for the emperor's advance towards Konya in the autumn of 1116, the imperial army in a first stage proceeded from Nicaea to the plain of Dorylaion,[82] from where it took the route leading via Santabaris (Bardakçı at the Barda Çayı) to Polybotos and Philomelion.[83] The shortest way to Konya runs along the southern shores of Lake Tessarakonta Martyron (Eber/Akşehir Gölü) and the Sultan Mountains.

As in 1098, in 1116, too, Turkish garrisons controlled Polybotos and other strongholds east of Akroinon and north of the slopes of the Emir Mountains like Kedrea (a fortress on the Asar Tepesi north of Bayat)[84] and Amorion (Hisar east of Emirdağ). The same applies to Philomelion southeast of Polybotos near the southeastern edge of Lake Eber/Akşehir. In Santabaris, Alexios is said to have dispatched detachments under the command of Eustathios Kamytzes and Michael Stypeiotes against Polybotos and Kedrea, the latter of which was in the hands of an emir called Poucheas, and against Amorion respectively.[85] The area of Akroinon, 28 miles west of Polybotos, was firmly under Byzantine control after Michael of Amastris' submission. This is attested to by the fact that it served as a camping place for the imperial army and as a meeting point for the emperor and the Seljuk ruler Shāhinshāh.[86] Remarkably, all fortresses held by Turkish garrisons could be seized without difficulty. Poucheas allegedly was warned by two Scythian (= Pecheneg?) defectors of the arrival of the Byzantine army and abandoned Kedrea without putting up any resistance. In Polybotos, Kamytzes killed a large number of Turks and encamped in the area, where he awaited the arrival of the emperor.[87] An intriguing case is the fortress of Tyragion (Ilgın), situated a few miles east of Philomelion. Anna describes the town as being inhabited by Romaioi, who were friendly towards Sultan Shāhinshāh and defended him against his internal opponents.[88] This episode took place after the renewal of the peace treaty with the emperor and the imperial army's retreat. Thus, even in areas quite close to Konya, there still were some Greek enclaves recognizing the emperor's suzerainty. Presumably, they had entered agreements with the nearby Seljuk garrisons and secured a certain degree of autonomy in exchange for payments of tribute. The attempts of the imperial army to evacuate people living in the frontier zone apparently did not entirely alter the character of the indigenous social fabric.

The Seljuk defensive structures seemingly were not prepared for attacks of this size. The Turkish strongholds rather served as rallying points of raiders invading Byzantine territory or as observation posts monitoring the native population, nomad groups moving between their winter and summer pastures, and Byzantine military garrisons stationed in Attaleia and in some isolated outposts situated in the western Taurus Mountains, the Upper Meander Valley, and Phrygia. As was noted above, the greatest part of the Byzantine troops was concentrated much farther west and thus the Turks were not expecting any immediate threats to the strongpoints they controlled. Nevertheless, for the Seljuks of Konya it was of crucial military significance to hold positions in the area bounded by Lake Eber/Akşehir, Lake Pousgouse (Beyşehir Gölü), and the Sultan Mountains. It was close to all main routes leading to Bithynia, the western coastland, the Meander Valley, and Lycia, regions that largely correspond to the objectives of Turkish raids at that time.

The Turkish campaign the imperial government was facing in the spring and summer of 1116 mainly affected the heartland of the Byzantine defensive structures in Bithynia and the Hellespont region.[89] More specifically, Anna Komnene speaks about Turkish raiders moving in the plain below the mountain ranges of Lentiana and Kotoiraikia.[90] The location of these places is unknown, but given that the main bases of the Byzantine defense in Mysia were Lopadion and Poimanenon, we may assume that the author refers to the mountainous regions south or west of these strongholds. Another detachment of Turkish warriors reached the fortress of St. George at the northern shores of Lake Askanios near Nicaea. When the Turks on receiving the message of the emperor's advance towards Nicaea retreated southeasterly, they were attacked by a Byzantine contingent under the command of Strabobasileios and Michael Stypeiotes stationed on the heights of Germia,[91] which can be located near the Dindymon Mountain (Arayit Dağı) in the southeastern part of the Sivrihisar range southeast of Dorylaion.[92] A small vanguard of Turkish warriors under the command of Monolykos entered into the region between Dorylaion and Nicaea in order to watch the moves of the imperial army and to prepare the invasion of the main force.[93]

Emperor Alexios I organized the defense against the Turkish invaders by moving back and forth between and establishing camps and defensive positions in Lopadion, certain fortresses at the Gulf of Nikomedia, such as Kibotos, Aer, and Helenoupolis, the strongholds of Nicaea and St. George at the shores of the Askanian Lake, and the Sangarios Valley. In this way, he afforded protection to the entire southern section of the Propontis littoral and large parts of Bithynia.[94] According to the exigencies of the military situation, he also extended his radius of action to other adjacent territories. In view of ongoing Turkish attacks, for instance, Alexios for some time moved his camp farther west to Poimamenon. Although he came too late to ward off the invaders, a detachment of lightly armed soldiers stopped them near a place called Kellia. Lopadion seems to have served as his headquarters over the hot summer period, for the shortage of water is mentioned as one of the reasons for a prolonged stay of three months.[95] The heights of Mount Olympus (Uludağ) and the region near Malagina were suitable for the establishment of advanced outposts controlling the access routes to the Gulf of Nikomedeia, while the imperial army reinforced by fresh mercenary troops headed back along the coast and thence eastward in order to counter new Turkish attacks.[96] Past the fortress of St. George, Alexios advanced as far as Sagoudaous (Söğüt) near the banks of the Sangarios River northwest of Dorylaion.[97] In the meantime the hostile activities in the regions of Lopadion and Nicaea went on with undiminished intensity. The mobile units of Alexios' army thus continued to cover the region between the two strongholds. They followed the route from Kios (Gemlik) situated at the mouth of the Propontis gulf north of Bursa to the town of Miskoura (perhaps Müşküle) at the southern shores of Lake Askanios. Scouts stayed back in the environs of Lopadion and observed the raiders' movements.[98] Yet the emperor shrank from mounting a full-scale attack on the sultan, perhaps in apprehension of a swift retreat of the Turks into the interior of Anatolia, where they would be out of his reach.[99]

Nikomedeia and its environs became the most important rallying point of the imperial army. It was a suitable place, which provided the necessary supplies for so large a number of men and animals for a longer period and gave the troops a respite to train fresh recruits. Alexios prepared his troops for the last phase of his operations, which targeted the very center of the Turkish dominion in Konya. It is unclear whether this expedition was part of the imperial government's original strategic considerations. According to Anna Komnene, the Turks had provoked the emperor by turning back westward and resuming their raids so that Alexios decided to inflict an even more crushing defeat on them.[100]

After departing, most likely, in late September or early October 1116, the imperial army had some initial successes and quickly advanced to the fortresses around Lake Eber/Akşehir. Yet the expedition as a whole did not bring the expected results. The aforementioned attacks of Byzantine detachments against the fortresses of Polybotos, Amorion, and Kedrea enabled the emperor, along with the main force of his army, to proceed to Kedrea in order to take the shortest possible route via Polybotos to Konya.[101] At that point, the Byzantine troops faced serious obstacles impeding their advance. A strong Turkish contingent was said to have entrenched itself in nearby strongholds that were known as "the towns of Bourtzes."[102] News arrived that the Turks had ravaged the farmland and plains along the route to Konya so that the Byzantine troops would be cut off from supplies. Other messages referred to an imminent attack by fresh Turkish hosts arriving from the East.[103] Apparently, the more the Byzantines approached the interior of the Anatolian plateau, the stronger the Turkish resistance grew and the more pressing supply problems became. Pondering these difficulties, Alexios and his generals decided to withdraw to Philomelion. The imperial headquarters had to make this sudden shift in the expedition's objectives plausible to the soldiers, who must have been concerned about the reasons behind the emperor's hesitation and the rumors about newly arriving barbarians and devastated areas further afield. Anna talks about prayers and a decision based on divine judgment, but it is quite obvious that both the rank-and-file soldiers in 1116 and Anna's audience had to be convinced that the abandoning of the campaign's initial target by no means meant that the campaign had failed.[104]

The ensuing operations aimed at gathering and evacuating inhabitants who chose to move to safer places. The Byzantine army thus organized an orderly retreat along with the non-combatants via the route along Lake Eber/Akşehir from Philomelion to Akroinon.[105] Militarily, the situation further deteriorated. On their way back from Bithynia, Monolykos' troops crossed the Sangarios River over the Zompou Bridge.[106] They intended to join forces with new warrior groups arriving from the East in order to cut off the Byzantine retreat.[107] Shāhinshāh was approaching from the region of Konya.[108] The Turkish warriors reportedly employed an irritating strategy of harassment aiming at the physical and moral exhaustion of the Byzantine soldiers. Fierce attacks by small cavalry units at daytime, a great number of fires giving the impression of large gatherings of troops, wolf-like howling, and insults hurled by bilingual warriors of mixed Greek-Turkish origin undermined the fighting morale of the imperial troops.[109] Anna stresses the importance of both strategies and psychological factors in the imperial army's success in escaping these dangers. Alexios' newly developed battle order enabled the Byzantine soldiers to fend off the assaults of Turkish archers fighting on horseback. Individual commanders demonstrated outstanding valor. Bardas Bourtzes, a descendant of the renowned tenth-century Bourtzes clan, evacuated people living in the region between Kedrea and Amorion, prevented Turkish troops from reaching Monolykos' base by routing them in the nearby plain, and warded off numerous attacks while advancing with the booty, the captives, and the non-combatants towards the emperor's troops.[110] George Lebounes excelled as a messenger crossing the enemy lines between Bourtzes' forces and the emperor.[111] Nikephoros, a young nephew of Empress Eudokia, is praised for a brave attack on a group of enemies.[112] Anna, due to the encomiastic tendencies of her work, certainly exaggerated the Byzantine feats of valor, but it is reasonable to assume that the soldiers' staunchness and perseverance during their retreat through hostile territory were decisively strengthened by their commanders' ability to maintain order.[113] On the other hand, the strong emphasis Anna places on these aspects also suggests that the Turks actually deployed a formidable fighting force in 1116 and that the emperor had no other choice than to withdraw in the quickest possible way.

Sultan Shāhinshāh's rise and fall

At that time neither side was able to defeat the other. The ongoing dynastic rivalries among the sons of Qilij Arslān further aggravated the situation in the principality of Konya. As a result, the conflicts of 1116 were terminated with a new peace treaty, which affirmed and re-defined the relations between the two sides. The emperor therefore considered it expedient to lend his full support to the man with whom he had come to terms. This attitude seems to be reflected in the account of Michael the Syrian, who claims that Shāhinshāh fled to Constantinople because of the frictions with his brother Masʿūd.[114] The lord of Konya thus appears as a refugee who was granted shelter by the imperial court from his internal enemies. This version somewhat overemphasizes the emperor's role as Shāhinshāh's protector and passes over the preceding military clashes in silence. Yet Michael and Anna Komnene concur that the peace treaty of 1116 was an important step in the formation of diplomatic and ideological relations between Constantinople and Konya.

If we believe Anna, Shāhinshāh and his emirs sought an understanding with Alexios because of a new setback that the joined forces of Monolykos and Shāhinshāh had suffered. The latter was almost taken captive by a group of Scythian soldiers, and the sultan's cupbearer fell into the emperor's hands.[115] By describing the peace treaty as a result of the Seljuk defeat by imperial troops, Anna was able to turn the meager results of the 1116 expedition into a major military and diplomatic success. Most likely in order to embroider the idealized image she wanted to convey, Anna focuses fully on the public and ceremonial aspects of the meeting the emperor and the sultan had in the plain between Akroinon and Augoustopolis.[116] She tells us nothing about the negotiation procedure and the clauses of the treaty. What matters is the new relationship, which the two rulers established as a result of their public encounter and the ritual acts performed on this occasion. The sultan and his dignitaries came into the emperor's presence, asked for peace, and demonstrated their readiness to acknowledge the emperor's superiority. Alexios is portrayed as sitting on horseback amidst his relatives and officers surrounded by a large number of soldiers. The Turkish lords, still some distance away, descended from their horses and prostrated themselves. Shāhinshāh would have acted likewise, but Alexios prevented him from doing so. After several attempts, Shāhinshāh dismounted swiftly and kissed Alexios' foot. Thereupon, the emperor extended his hand to him and instructed him to mount one of his officers' horses. As the sultan rode side-by-side with the emperor, Alexios threw his cape around the sultan's shoulders.[117]

It is very unlikely that this complicated sequence of publicly performed symbolic acts and gestures happened spontaneously, as Anna wants us to believe. We are dealing, rather, with a punctiliously prepared ceremonial encounter between two rulers, who after a period of internecine fighting came to terms and restored peace. The message conveyed to the attendants was that the Seljuk lord, as a reward for his voluntary submission, gained the emperor's respect and favor. The sultan's sitting on horseback side-by-side with the emperor and the cape belonging to the emperor's official attire were symbols for the newly founded intimacy between the two persons. This symbolism has to be seen in connection with the title of *sebastos* bestowed upon Apelchasem during his visit in Constantinople more than 20 years earlier. The ruling elite of Constantinople from early on was keen to integrate the Seljuk rulers in Asia Minor into the hierarchical structures of the imperial court. Through his title, Apelchasem had established ideological bonds linking him with the Komnenian dynasty. We may assume that Qilij Arslān I, who in the years after 1093 and again after 1101 maintained peaceful relations with Constantinople, enjoyed a similar status at the imperial court, although we do not know of any title. Shāhinshāh was the heir to this tradition. Once peaceful relations had been restored, he could be presented as one of the emperor's close confidants.

A speech put into Alexios' mouth articulates the imperial elites' claim to wield power over the whole of the eastern provinces, as had been the case in the time prior to Emperor Romanos IV.

> If you want to submit to the empire of the Romans and stop the attacks against the Christians, you will enjoy favors and honor and will henceforth have a pleasant life in the lands that belong to you and in which you previously lived before Romanos Diogenes took over the reins of the empire and suffered that defeat, when he unfortunately clashed in battle with the sultan and was captured by him. Hence, you should prefer peace instead of war and stay away from the regions under Roman rule and content yourself with your own territories. And if you comply with my words giving you good advice you certainly will not regret it, but you will obtain a great many gifts. Otherwise you should know that I shall be the destroyer of your nation.[118]

This statement is remarkable because of the ideological features ascribed to Alexios I, who appears as the empire's savior striving to restore its old splendor and power. It certainly does not reflect any realistic assessment of the political situation in 1116. In comparison to the 1081 agreement, in which Alexios for the first time officially recognized the Turks' authority in the territories beyond the Propontis littoral, in 1116 the imperial government exerted authority over western Asia Minor, the Pontus coastland, and a strip of land along the southern shores as far as Cilicia. In this respect, Alexios' policy of re-conquest over the past 35 years was crowned by considerable success. The elite of Constantinople could be optimistic that more territorial gains would be made in the near future. Referring to the ultimate objectives of the imperial policy in the East, Anna may have articulated thoughts actually uttered in the course of these negotiations. But it is hardly thinkable that such ideas would have been acceptable to the Seljuk leaders. As the terms of the treaty are not explicitly mentioned, we may only surmise that they silently presupposed the *status quo* reached in 1116 without bringing up the question of territorial gains or losses. Hence, the treaty partners committed themselves to a sort of standstill agreement. Shāhinshāh desisted from further invasions in the river valleys and coastland of western Asia Minor and, in exchange, tightened his personal links with the Byzantine ruling house. Under these circumstances, the border zone that was crystallizing in the region of the Sultan Mountains and the surrounding lakes as far as the Sangarios Valley and the Sivrihisar Mountains turned into a dividing line between Byzantine and Seljuk spheres of influence. From an ideological point of view, however, nothing prevented the Byzantines from considering the whole of Asia Minor as part of the empire that had only temporarily and illegally been occupied by hostile barbarians. Anna concludes her account about the Turks of Asia Minor by describing the rivalry between Shāhinshāh and his brother Masʿūd and the events leading to the former's assassination.[119] This section is all the more important as there are no other reports describing Shāhinshāh's downfall in Muslim or Eastern Christian sources. The Seljuk ruler's newly established alliance with the emperor may have stimulated Anna's interest in the fate of this person. After troublesome years of constant conflicts, the imperial court seems to have pinned its hopes on him as a faithful ally who would preserve peace and maintain the status quo between the two sides. With his overthrow, the achievements of Alexios I's last campaign against and treaty with the Turks were put in danger.

Towards a new order in Anatolia

The developments in the Byzantine-Turkish frontier zone in the years after 1116 are known to us only through the narratives of the next generation of Byzantine historians, namely John Kinnamos and Niketas Choniates. The chronological distance and the fact that these authors treat the reign of Alexios' son and successor John II (1118–43) rather cursorily unavoidably leads to obscurities. The two historians start their accounts about Asia Minor with the new emperor's campaigns of 1119/20. In the first expedition, John II marched from Philadelpheia, penetrated the Upper Meander Valley and seized the town of Laodikeia. In the second expedition in the following year, he advanced farther east and conquered the well-protected fortress of Sozopolis (Uluborlu) built on a steep rock close to the Kapı Mountain. Thence the imperial troops headed southwards towards Attaleia and seized a number of fortified places in the region between Lake Eğirdir and the mountainous areas of the Taurus range further afield.[120] It is not known how long the Turks had been in possession of these fortresses. Choniates explicitly mentions a breach of the treaty concluded with John's father,[121] something that would indicate a new outbreak of hostilities at some point after 1116 and may be seen in connection with Masʿūd's violent takeover. The Byzantine reports suggest that rather strong garrisons defended the conquered places. In the case of Laodikeia, Kinnamos speaks of more than 800 warriors under the command of a certain Picharas/Alpicharas.[122] We are by no means dealing with unruly groups of marauding nomads but with well-equipped military units led by renowned commanders belonging to the Seljuk elite of Konya. Hence, the imperial government was trying to halt expansionist attempts afflicting the Meander Valley and the mountainous regions spanning the Gulf of Attaleia. In this area, Sozopolis served as an import key point, since it supervised the routes leading northeastward to Philomelion and towards the coast of Pamphylia in the south. Its acquisition contributed significantly to a strengthening of local defensive structures and helped to impede invasions into the southwestern edge of Asia Minor. The newly achieved balance of power put an end to large-scale hostilities in this region for several decades.

The center of Byzantine-Turkish conflicts henceforth shifted farther north to Paphlagonia, where the cities of Kastamona (Kastamonu) and Gangra (Çankırı) were ideally located strongholds supporting invasions of warrior groups subject to the Dānishmandid emirate into the Sangarios Valley, Bithynia, and the Pontic coastland. John II's expeditions of 1132/33 aimed at subjugating these places to Byzantine rule. Yet the emperor took possession of them only temporarily, entering a short-lived alliance with Masʿūd of Konya against a Turkish chief who put up resistance against the Byzantine assault.[123] None of these feats had lasting effects. Apart from the littoral and a number of ports, Paphlagonia and the regions farther east largely remained under Seljuk and Dānishmandid influence.

As regards the situation in the Euphrates region and eastern Anatolia, above all, the principalities of Ṭughril Arslān of Melitene and Balak b. Bahrām of Ḥiṣn Ziyād/Kharpete in conjunction with the growing power of the Artuqid branches in Diyār Bakr dominated the political situation up to Balak's death in 1124. Broadly speaking, we are dealing with a complicated patchwork of local powers of Frankish, Armenian, Greek, and Turkish pedigree that were trying to strengthen their position, but none of them was strong enough to prevail over the others. This resulted in swiftly changing constellations of power alternating between fierce struggles and fragile coalitions, in which military superiority was of much greater relevance than religious or ethnic divisions.[124]

A case in point is the conflict in the years 1118–19 between Melitene and the emirate of Mangujak in Kamākh and Erzincan. During this war, Melitene allied with Edessa and the emirate with Trebizond—their respective Christian neighbors. Ibn Mangujak's aggression against Melitene prompted the Seljuk chiefs of the city to seek an understanding with Count Joscelin I.[125] The counter-attack of Ṭughril Arslān and Balak b. Bahrām on Kamākh in the following year forced Ibn Mangujak to take refuge with Constantine Gabras, the Byzantine lord of Trebizond.[126] The opposing Christian-Turkish alliances in the Euphrates and the Pontus regions prompted the predominant Muslim power in adjacent Cappadocia, Emir Ghāzī b. Dānishmand, to engage in this conflict. He was ready to collaborate with the lords of Melitene and Kharpete despite the fact that his family maintained bonds of marriage with Ibn Mangujak, his son-in-law. This would quickly lead to a conflict of interests, which in turn formed a source of discord among the allies. In a joint venture, the Greeks of Trebizond were wiped out, and Gabras and Ibn Mangujak were taken prisoner. Emir Ghāzī released the Greek potentate for ransom money but reconciled with Ibn Mangujak on account of their kinship ties.[127] Unavoidably, Ṭughril Arslān and Balak felt that they had been bamboozled. Apart from losing a considerable amount of money, they were deprived of the prospect of exploiting their victory over Ibn Mangujak through imposing a humiliating peace treaty or the like. Emir Ghāzī, for his part, must have had a keen interest in maintaining the existing balance of power in the region by restoring amicable relations with his relative. The constant objective of the Dānishmandid emirate of gaining a foothold in the Euphrates Valley and ultimately recovering Melitene may have determined his stance as well.

With the failure in 1115 of the *jihad* movement initiated by the Great Seljuk sultanate, the relations with Antioch, Edessa, and some minor Christian lordships farther north were largely contingent upon the ambitions of local Turkish emirs, who continued to engage in limited military actions against their Christian neighbors. In June 1119, Emir Ghāzī b. Dānishmand along with 7,000 Turks invaded the region of Antioch, crushed the troops of Roger of Salerno, pillaged the country, and killed a great number of monks living in the monasteries of the Amanus Mountain. In a counter-attack, King Baldwin II of Jerusalem defeated and expelled the Turks.[128] In the same year, Ṭughril Arslān extended his rule to Ablastayn and the Jayḥān region. Balak resumed this regional war in early 1121, ravaging and subjugating the lands of his Armenian tributary Michael of Gargar, who had undertaken raids in the emirate's territories.[129]

It was in about the same period that Balak's uncle Īlghāzī of Mārdīn gained the initiative in a number of ambitious large-scale strikes against the crusader principalities. By taking possession of Aleppo in 1117/18, which after Riḍwān's death had fallen into a state of decay, the Artuqid ruler, besides his domains in the Diyār Bakr region, gained a foothold of major importance in northern Syria. He thus established himself in the immediate vicinity of Antioch and became a dangerous threat to the southern fringes of the County of Edessa.[130] The following year, an alliance with Ṭughtakīn of Damascus came into being. Īlghāzī began to raise troops in the Diyār Bakr province and sent an embassy to Sultan Maḥmūd in Baghdad, through which he announced his intention to resume the war against the Franks.[131] The ensuing attack of the lords of Antioch and Edessa on the emirate of Aleppo culminated in a major clash, the battle of Balāṭ/Ager Sanguinis fought on 28 June 1119, in which Roger of Salerno was killed and a great number of Frankish knights were taken captive.[132] Temporarily, Īlghāzī fostered his fame as a champion in the wars against the crusaders, but he did not benefit from his success in terms of new territorial gains or military advantages.[133] Nevertheless, over the following years he executed a range of far-reaching plans, which culminated in a campaign against the Georgians in the Caucasus region in 1121/22.[134] Carole Hillenbrand acknowledges Īlghāzī's political abilities, which in conjunction with some favorable coincidences allowed him to carve out a powerful lordship in the Diyār Bakr region, but she also underlines his shortcomings as a military leader. In her opinion, these are exhibited by his failure to continue his campaign in 1119 and to seize Antioch and by his crushing defeat by the Georgians near Tiflis. Partly, these inadequacies can be ascribed to the unruly nature of his Turkmen warriors, who were more interested in booty and salaries than strategic military planning.[135] Although Hillenbrand's judgment certainly has some validity, she ignores the highly fragmented and constantly changing power structures in the region. Unavoidably, political ambitions were mostly based on fragile coalitions and focused on short-term objectives. Under these circumstances, Īlghāzī succeeded in maintaining his hold over Aleppo and in gaining the city of Mayyāfāriqīn, which was assigned to him by Sultan Maḥmūd.[136] This prepared the ground for the succession arrangements that were implemented after Īlghāzī's death in November 1122, with his son Ḥusām al-Dīn Timurtāsh taking possession of Mārdīn and the other son Sulaymān acquiring the lordship of Mayyāfāriqīn.[137]

Against the backdrop of Īlghāzī's formidable rise to the status of a powerful potentate operating east and west of the Euphrates, his nephew Balak b. Bahrām's intensified hostilities against Antioch and Edessa become understandable. With his ongoing assaults, he eventually provoked a counter-attack by King Baldwin II of Jerusalem (1118–31), which in May 1123 ended with the king's defeat and captivity. For a brief period, Balak, following in his uncle's footsteps, performed great feats as a champion of *jihad* and even gained hold of Aleppo. But Balak's career found an abrupt end by a deadly arrow that hit him in May 1124 outside the citadel of Manbij.[138]

Generally speaking, the Muslim-Christian frontier in northern Syria and Upper Mesopotamia in the years 1117–24 was largely dominated by branches of the Artuqid clan based in strongholds near the Euphrates River and in the Diyār Bakr province. The Seljuks of Melitene, the Dānishmandid emirate, and other minor powers thus disencumbered themselves from Frankish pressure and cemented their position under the shadow of a supra-regional Artuqid umbrella stretching from Aleppo to the banks of the Tigris River with some extensions towards central Iraq. Again, this arrangement of powers did not last for long and was soon to be substituted by a much more powerful entity created by ʿImād al-Dīn Zankī. Nevertheless, in about 1120 it had become clear that, after decades of violent penetration, disintegration, and fragmentation, the old Byzantine marches were to develop new forms of centralizing stability, which arose from amidst the Muslim-Turkish lordships in this area. The bulk of what 40 years earlier had been Byzantium's eastern frontier was transformed into a patchwork of tiny local lordships based on several fortified places and the revenues of the surrounding regions. Yet it may be assumed that Byzantine *strategoi* and Turkish emirs faced comparable challenges and resorted to similar tools of administration. Melitene, Charpete, Khilāṭ, Sebasteia, Kamākh, and other places, which had played a crucial role in the Byzantine military structures, continued to be important centers in the highly fragmented political landscape of the early twelfth century. Just as the Byzantine-Turkish frontier zone in the western fringes of the Anatolian plateau, the Euphrates region too had become a distinct political sphere, which combined the characteristic features of its Armenian, Frankish, and Turkish-Muslim lordships with a substrate of Byzantine cultural, ideological, and administrative traditions. At the same time, the potentates in the region were in close contact with and were influenced by developments in northern Syria, Palestine, Iraq, and the Armenian highlands. Hence, what radically changed in comparison to previous periods of Byzantine rule was the fact that the local elites and populations oriented themselves towards new centers of political gravity. Before its crushing defeat in the battle of Myriokephalon in 1176, the imperial government of Constantinople dreamed of restoring its political and ideological predominance over Antioch, the crusader states, and the Muslim powers in Anatolia and Syria. Yet from the 1120s onwards, it became increasingly clear that the local powers, both Christian and Muslim, were too firmly established to succumb to the ambitions of Constantinople or any of the centers in the Muslim East. The lordships in the former Byzantine borderlands had created their own identities and dynastic ideologies and had developed political mechanisms allowing them to maintain a fragile balance of power among themselves. These results were irreversible. The time of conquests was over.

Notes

1 For the viewpoint of modern Turkish historiography, see Turan, *Türkiye*, p. 148, who considers the period after 1107 as a new critical stage in the life and death struggle of the Anatolian Turks: "Seriously, the Anatolian Turks were to live in their new homelands or to die."
2 Matthew of Edessa 3.36, p. 199; for the names, see Michael the Syrian 15.10, 3:194 (trans.), 4:593, col. b (Syriac text).
3 Michael the Syrian 15.10, 3:194 (trans.), 4:592, col. b-593, col. b (Syriac text); see also Turan, *Türkiye*, pp. 149–50; Cahen, *Pre-Ottoman Turkey*, p. 87; Cahen, *Formation*, pp. 15–16.
4 Michael the Syrian 15.11, 3:199–200 (trans.), 4:596, col. a-597, col. b (Syriac text); Cahen, "Diyar Bakr," pp. 238–39; Turan, *Türkiye*, p. 152; Cahen, *Pre-Ottoman Turkey*, p. 87; Cahen, *Formation*, p. 15; Bezer, "Harput," pp. 88–89.
5 Michael the Syrian 15.12, 3:203–204 (trans.), 4:598, col. b (Syriac text).
6 Michael the Syrian 15.12, 3:204 (trans.), 4:598, col. b (Syriac text); Cahen, "Diyar Bakr," p. 239; Bezer, "Harput," p. 89.
7 Michael the Syrian 15.11, p. 3:200 (trans.), 4:596, col. a (Syriac text); for Marʿash, see Beech, "Lordship of Marash," pp. 35–52.
8 Turan, *Türkiye*, pp. 166–170; Cahen, *Pre-Ottoman Turkey*, pp. 93–94; Cahen, *Formation*, pp. 18–19.
9 See above, pp. 311–12.
10 Turan, *Türkiye*, pp. 67–68, 150, considers Asan a subject of Sulaymān b. Qutlumush, identifying him with Apelchasem's brother Poulchazes. The latter name is interpreted as a garbled Greek variant of the Arabic title Ebû l-gâzi (father of the ghāzī), which he may have been granted for his outstanding feats. Turan sees in Asan a saint-like hero in a local tradition of worship linked with warrior tombs venerated in Seljuk times on the Hasan Mountain. None of these purely hypothetical assumptions can be corroborated by the available source material.
11 See below in this chapter, p. 365.
12 Turan, *Türkiye*, pp. 153–54.
13 Ibn al-Qalānisī, p. 158.
14 Turan, *Türkiye*, p. 153.
15 Bar Hebraeus, p. 275, trans. Budge, p. 243 (*sulṭān shaddar l-Mālekshāh bar Qeleg Arslān l-Mīlīṭīnī*); the Arabic source according to C. Cahen, *Osmanlılardan önce Anadolu*, trans. Erol Üyepazarcı (Istanbul, 2000), p. 19, n. 8, is Ibn al-Furāt, MS Vienna, vol. 1, 27b.
16 Cahen, *Pre-Ottoman Turkey*, p. 88; Cahen, *Formation*, pp. 15–16, supports this opinion and follows Turan in considering Asan a cousin of Qilij Arslān.
17 Ibn al-Athīr, 6:489–90, trans. Richards, *Chronicle*, 1:136–37; Cahen, "Diyar Bakr," p. 235; for a detailed analysis of this and related events, see Heidemann, *Renaissance*, pp. 206–10.
18 Michael the Syrian 15.10, 3:194–95 (trans.), 4:593, col. b (Syriac text).
19 Michael the Syrian 16.2, 3:223–24 (trans.), 4:608–609 (Syriac text).
20 Ibn al-Athīr, 6:503–506, trans. Richards, *Chronicle*, 1:152–54 (*sub anno* 504/20 July 1110–9 July 1111); for previous conquests, see also the report of Ibn al-Qalānisī, pp. 159–64.
21 Ibn al-Qalānisī, p. 173; Ibn al-Athīr, 6:505–506, trans. Richards, *Chronicle*, 1:154.
22 Ibn al-Qalānisī, pp. 173–74; Ibn al-Athīr, 6:506, trans. Richards, *Chronicle*, 1:155; see also Peacock, *Great Seljuk Empire*, pp. 83–84.
23 Ibn al-Qalānisī, pp. 163–64.
24 Anna Komnene 14.2.1-2, pp. 427–28, ll. 18–42.
25 Lilie, *Crusader States*, pp. 82–83 (with a different assessment of the situation); Asbridge, Antioch, pp. 59–69; idem, *Kreuzzüge*, pp. 166–72.

26 Anna Komnene 14.2.3-4, pp. 428–29, ll. 42–62; Lilie, *Crusader States*, p. 84; Dölger and Wirth, *Regesten*, no. 1250a.
27 Lilie, *Crusader States*, pp. 83–84; Asbridge, *Kreuzzüge*, pp. 163, 168, 170–71.
28 Anna Komnene 14.2.5-14, pp. 429–34; Lilie, *Crusader States*, pp. 85–87; Dölger and Wirth, *Regesten*, no. 1250b, 1250c, 1250d (erroneously dated to 1110/1110 despite the correct dates given by Lilie).
29 Chalandon, *Comnène*, 1:252; Lilie, *Crusader States*, p. 85.
30 Ibn al-Athīr, 6:506, trans. Richards, *Chronicle*,1:155: "The people of Aleppo were saying to the sultan: 'Don't you fear God—may he be exalted—that the king of the Romans shows more zeal than you for Islam so that he sent an embassy to you regarding the jihad against them.'"
31 Ibn al-Qalānisī, pp. 169, 174; Ibn al-Athīr, 6:489, 507, 512, trans. Richards, *Chronicle*, 1:136, 156, 162; for Sukmān al-Quṭbī's takeover in Mayyāfāriqīn, see also Ibn al-Qalānisī, p. 164; for the sultan's announcing his campaign, see ibid., pp. 165, 173. For the targets of the various attacks, see Ibn al-Athīr, 6:507–509, trans. Richards, *Chronicle*, 1:156–57 (in the summer and autumn of 1111 siege of Edessa and Tall Bāshir, advance towards Ḥarrān, Aleppo, Maʿarrat al-Nuʿmān, Frankish attack on Shayzar); ibid., 6:511, trans. Richards, *Chronicle*, 1:160 (in July 1112 attack on Edessa and Sarūj); ibid. 6:512–13, trans. Richards, *Chronicle*, 1:162–63 (in the spring and summer of 1113 battle near al-Uqḥuwāna in the Jordan Valley, advance of the Muslim troops to Tiberias, Baysān, and places between Jerusalem and Acre); ibid. 6:516–17, trans. Richards, *Chronicle*, 1:166 (in the spring of 1115 Aqsunqur al-Bursuqī forced Jazīrat b. ʿUmar and Mārdīn into submission and made attacks on the region between Edessa, Sarūj, and Sumaysāṭ). For these campaigns in general, see Chalandon, *Comnène*, 1:251–52; Turan, *Selçuklular Târihi*, pp. 233–34; Cahen, *Pre-Ottoman Turkey*, p. 88; Cahen, *Formation*, p. 16; Väth, *Geschichte*, pp. 67–73; Lilie, *Crusader States*, p. 85; Tyerman, *God's War*, pp. 186–87, 190–91; Asbridge, *Kreuzzüge*, pp. 168–69, 173–78; Peacock, *Great Seljuk Empire*, pp. 84–85; for further details based on a very detailed analysis of the primary sources, see Sevim, *Suriye*, 210–20, 232–35, and Heidemann, *Renaissance*, p. 212–29.
32 Ibn al-Athīr, 6:507–508, trans. Richards, *Chronicle*, 1:156–57; Väth, *Geschichte*, p. 68.
33 Ibn al-Qalānisī, pp. 170, 171, 175; Ibn al-Athīr, 6:508, trans. Richards, *Chronicle*, 1:156; Sevim, *Suriye*, pp. 218–19; El-Azhari, *Saljūqs of Syria*, pp. 192–93.
34 Ibn al-Qalānisī, pp. 178, 184–87; Ibn al-Athīr, 6:508, 512–13, trans. Richards, *Chronicle*, 1:157, 162; Sevim, *Suriye*, pp. 219–20; El-Azhari, *Saljūqs of Syria*, pp. 201–204.
35 Ibn al-Qalānisī, pp. 187–88; Ibn al-Athīr, 6:512–13, trans. Richards, *Chronicle*, 1:162–63 (*sub anno* 507/18 June 1113–6 June 1114); El-Azhari, *Saljūqs of Syria*, p. 204.
36 Ibn al-Athīr, 6:516–17, trans. Richards, *Chronicle*, 1:166 (*sub anno* 508/7 June 1114–26 May 1115).
37 Ibn al-Athīr, 6:517–18, trans. Richards, *Chronicle*, 1:167–68; Sevim, *Suriye*, pp. 232–33; Väth, *Geschichte*, pp. 70–72.
38 Ibn al-Athīr, 6:521–23, trans. Richards, *Chronicle*, 1:172–73 (*sub anno* 509/27 May 1115–15 May 1116); for this battle, see Sevim, *Suriye*, p. 234; Väth, *Geschichte*, p. 73; Asbridge, *Kreuzzüge*, pp. 176–78.
39 For this region, see Belke and Mersich, *Phrygien und Pisidien*, pp. 177–78 (s. v. Akroinos) and p. 402 (s. v. Tessarakonta Martyrōn Limnē); Belke and Restle, *Galatien und Lykaonien*, p. 218 (s. v. Pusgusē Limnē).
40 Anna Komnene 14.1.1-3, pp. 424–25; see also Chalandon, *Comnène*, 1:254–55; Turan, *Türkiye*, p. 150.
41 For this detail, see above, pp. 344–45.
42 Hellenkemper and Hild, *Lykien und Pamphylien*, p. 305 (s. v. Attaleia).
43 For details, see above, pp. 326–28.
44 Chalandon, *Comnène*, 1:255–56; Turan, *Türkiye*, pp. 150–51.
45 Anna Komnene 14.1.4, pp. 425–26.

46 Anna Komnene 14.1.5-7, pp. 426–27. For the Kaystros Valley, see Foss, "Late Byzantine Fortifications in Lydia," pp. 312–14.

47 For the significance of these places and the surviving fortifications of Pergamos dating from the time of Manuel I (1143-80), see Foss, "Defenses of Asia Minor," pp. 166–71. For Pergamos, see also Foss, "'Twenty Cities' of Byzantine Asia," pp. 479–81.

48 For the 1110 campaign, see Chalandon, *Comnène*, pp. 264–65; Turan, *Türkiye*, p. 154; Belke and Mersich, *Phrygien und Pisidien*, p. 109.

49 ODB 2:2080 s. v. Thrakesion.

50 Anna Komnene 14.3.1, pp. 434–35.

51 Anna Komnene 14.3.7, p. 437, ll. 8–12. The chronological sequence results from the structure of Anna's narrative which combines the developments in Asia Minor with datable events in the empire's relations with Pisa and the crusader states: ibid. 14.3.2-4, pp. 435–36, ll. 46–77, esp. 14.3.2, p. 435, ll. 54–55, where the winter camps of Byzantine units are mentioned; see also Chalandon, *Comnène*, 1:257–59 and 264, n. 4; as Anna's conflation of different narrative strands is frequently arbitrary, we always have to reckon with certain inaccuracies. Turan, *Türkiye*, p. 154, dates the campaign to 1110; Belke and Mersich, *Phrygien und Pisidien*, p. 109, prefer 1112.

52 Belke and Mersich, *Phrygien und Pisidien*, p. 152. Foss, "Defenses of Asia Minor," pp. 189–92, assumes that the Turkish invaders passed the fortress of Pegadia (Bigadiç), which overlooks the plain of the Makestos River and is situated some 20 miles from Achyraous. The remains of both fortresses are datable to the period of John II.

53 Belker-Mersich, *Phrygien und Pisidien*, pp. 149–50; for the meaning of "Asia" in Byzantine texts, see Foss, "'Twenty Cities' of Byzantine Asia," pp. 470–71, who refers to this usage of the term in the tenth-century treaty *De thematibus* by Constantine Porphyrogennetos.

54 Anna Komnene 14.3.7-8, pp. 437–38, ll. 12–33.

55 Anna Komnene 14.3.5, p. 436; see also Belke and Mersich, *Phrygien und Pisidien*, p. 177.

56 Belke and Mersich, *Phrygien und Pisidien*, pp. 177–78.

57 Chalandon, *Comnène*, 1:265–66; Turan, *Türkiye*, pp. 154–55; Belke and Mersich, *Phrygien und Pisidien*, p. 109.

58 Anna Komnene 14.5.3, pp. 443–44.

59 Anna Komnene 14.5.3, p. 444, ll. 23–24: μετὰ πάσης αἰχμαλωσίας ἀναιμάκτως καὶ ἄνευ μάχης τινός.

60 Anna Komnene 14.5.4, p. 444, ll. 25–28.

61 Anna Komnene 14.5.4, p. 444, ll. 28–29.

62 Anna Komnene 14.5.5, p. 445, ll. 39–42.

63 Anna Komnene 14.5.7, p. 446, ll. 76–81.

64 Anna Komnene 14.6.3, p. 448, ll. 34–35.

65 Belke and Mersich, *Phrygien und Pisidien*, p. 179.

66 Anna Komnene 14.5.7, p. 446, ll. 71–76.

67 Anna Komnene 14.5.7-8, pp. 446–47.

68 Anna Komnene 14.5.4-6, pp. 444–46. Kamytzes escaped in the course of the ensuing skirmishes: Anna Komnene 14.6.3, p. 448.

69 Anna Komnene 14.6.1, p. 447, l. 8: μετὰ τῶν κατὰ τὴν Ἀσίαν οἰκούντων Τουρκομάνων.

70 See above, pp. 364–65.

71 Anna Komnene 14.6.1-2, pp. 446–47: Two commanders called Ampelas and Tzipoureles, the latter apparently a mercenary of Italian origin, came to death in these fights.

72 There is no archaeological evidence datable to the period of Alexios I, but Lopadion has a round-tower and remains of a circuit wall, which can be dated to the time of John II: Foss, "Defenses of Asia Minor," pp. 159–61; Foss and Winfield, *Byzantine Fortifications*, pp. 145–46. The walls of Achyraous, another Mysian castle south of Poimanenon (Pamukçu near Balıkesir), and perhaps the remains of a castle near

Sultan Çayırı three miles from Susurluk date to the same period: Foss, "Defenses of Asia Minor," pp. 161–66, 191–93; Foss and Winfield, *Byzantine Fortifications*, p. 146. There are no remains of fortifications in Chliara and Adramyttion: Foss, "Defenses of Asia Minor," p. 161.

73 Anna Komnene 15.1.1, p. 460, ll. 9–10.

74 Belke, *Galatien und Lykaonien*, pp. 43–44.

75 Anna Komnene 15.1.1-2, p. 460, ll. 4, 7, 9–10, 19, 25, see also 15.4.3, p. 471, l. 48, 15.5.3, p. 475, l. 73, 15.6.1, p. 476, l. 9.

76 Anna Komnene 15.1.6, p. 465, l. 62, p. 466, l. 73, 15.6.3, p. 477, l. 48, 15.6.5, p. 477, l. 71, 15.6.6, p. 478, l. 93.

77 Anna Komnene 15.6.6-10, p. 478, ll. 3, 8, p. 479, ll. 37, 39, 41, p. 480, ll. 47, 51, 61, 68, 69, 77.

78 Anna Komnene 15.1.1, p. 461, l. 5, 15.6.10, p. 480, l. 65.

79 See above, pp. 40, 317–18.

80 Anna Komnene 15.1.1, p. 461, ll. 9–10 and 15.3.5, p. 469, ll. 66–67.

81 For a different view, see Turan, *Türkiye*, pp. 153–54, who considers the sultanate of Konya in about 1110 as a firmly established institution.

82 Anna Komnene 15.3.6, p. 469, mentions as stations on this march Gaita, the bridge of Pithekas, from where the army in three days proceeded via Armenokastron and Leukai (Osmaneli) in the Sangarios Valley to Dorylaion: Belke and Mersich, *Phrygien und Pisidien*, p. 110.

83 Anna Komnene 15.4.1, p. 470, ll. 16–20.

84 Belke and Mersich, *Phrygien und Pisidien*, pp. 297–99.

85 Anna Komnene 15.4.1, p. 470, ll. 17–21.

86 Anna Komnene 15.6.4-5, pp. 477–78, esp. p. 478, ll. 73–74: τὴν πεδιάδα τὴν μεταξὺ Αὐγουστοπόλεως καὶ Ἀκρονίου.

87 Anna Komnene 15.4.1, p. 470, ll. 21–34; for the Byzantine advance, see also Chalandon, *Comnène*, 1:269–70; Turan, *Türkiye*, p. 157; Belke and Mersich, *Phrygien und Pisidien*, pp. 109–10.

88 Anna Komnene 15.6.8-10, pp. 479–80.

89 Chalandon, *Comnène*, 1:269; Turan, *Türkiye*, pp. 156–57; Belke and Mersich, *Phrygien und Pisidien*, p. 110.

90 Anna Komnene 15.1.4, p. 462, ll. 48–50.

91 Anna Komnene 15.2.3, pp. 464–65.

92 Belke, *Galatien und Lykaonien*, p. 166–68.

93 Anna Komnene 15.2.5, p. 465, ll. 53–57.

94 Anna Komnene 15.1.3, p. 462.

95 Anna Komnene 15.1.5, pp. 462–63.

96 Anna Komnene 15.1.5, p. 463, ll. 74–77.

97 Anna Komnene 15.2.3-4, pp. 464–65.

98 Anna Komnene 15.2.5, l. 465.

99 Anna Komnene 15.2.6, pp. 465–66.

100 Anna Komnene 15.2.6-3.5, pp. 466–68.

101 Anna Komnene 15.4.2, pp. 470–71, ll. 34–35, and 15.4.3, p. 471, ll. 45–47.

102 Anna Komnene 15.4.2, p. 471, ll. 36–37.

103 Anna Komnene 15.4.3, p. 471, ll. 48–52.

104 Anna Komnene 15.4.3, p. 471, ll. 52–63: Two sheets of paper, on which the two options were written, were put on an altar. After a prayer vigil a priest picked up the sheet being in favor of the retreat.

105 Anna Komnene 15.4.2, p. 471, ll. 43–44, and 15.4.9, p. 473, ll. 30–33.

106 Belke, *Galatien und Lykaonien*, p. 246: the place is perhaps to be situated on a route north of Amorion.

107 Anna Komnene 15.4.4, p. 471, ll. 63–66.

108 Anna Komnene 15.5.3, p. 475, ll. 73–75.

109 Anna Komnene 15.5.1-2, pp. 474–75, ll. 40–57, 65–72.

110 Anna Komnene 15.4.2, p. 471, ll. 39–44 and 15.4.5-7, pp. 471–72, ll. 63–95.

111 Anna Komnene 15.4.7, p. 472, ll. 1–5.

112 Anna Komnene 15.4.8, p. 473, ll. 12–21.

113 Anna Komnene 15.5.1, pp. 474–75, ll. 57–68 and 15.5.3, p. 475, ll. 78–86 (Nikephoros Bryennios, commander of the right wing, although enraged about the enemy and feeling the inner impulse to help the soldiers of the rearguard, did not move from his position and kept his troops in good order).

114 Michael the Syrian 15.10, 3:194 (trans.), 4:592 (Syriac text).

115 Anna Komnene 15.5.4-6.1, pp. 475–76, and 15.6.3, p. 477, ll. 52–55: ἀπογνοὺς μετὰ τοῦ Μονολύκου καὶ τῶν λοιπῶν σατραπῶν ἐβουλεύετο καὶ τὰ περὶ εἰρήνης ἐπιφωσκούσης ἡμέρας ᾐτεῖτο τὸν αὐτοκράτορα.

116 Belke and Mersich, *Phrygien und Pisidien*, pp. 196–97 (the position of Augoustopolis is unknown, but most probably to be located east or southeast of Akroinon).

117 Anna Komnene 15.6.4-5, pp. 477–78; for this scene, see also Beihammer, "Feindbilder," pp. 79–81; idem, "Defection," p. 613.

118 Anna Komnene 15.6.5, p. 478, ll. 83–93.

119 Anna Komnene 15.6.8-10, pp. 479–80: The Seljuk ruler on his way back to Konya is said to have been ambushed by Mas'ūd's soldiers. At first Shāhinshāh escaped, but Poucheas, pretending friendship, persuaded him to take refuge to the fortress of Tyragion (Ilgın). Eventually betraying his lord and siding with Mas'ūd, Poucheas prompted the townspeople to open the gates so that the Turks seized and blinded Shāhinshāh. Back in Konya, he was strangled by a certain Elegmos. For these events, see Turan, *Türkiye*, pp. 158–60.

120 Kinnamos 1.2, pp. 5–7; Nikephoros Choniates, p. 12–13, ll. 94–38; Michael the Syrian 15.12, 3:205 (trans.), 4:600, col. b (Syriac text); for this campaign, see Turan, *Türkiye*, pp. 160–61; Vryonis, *Decline*, p. 119; Cahen, *Pre-Ottoman Turkey*, pp. 92–93; Cahen, *Formation*, p. 17; for geographical details, see Belke and Mersich, *Phrygien und Pisidien*, pp. 387–88; for the fortifications of Sozopolis, see Foss, "Defenses of Asia Minor," pp. 153–57; Foss and Winfield, *Byzantine Fortifications*, pp. 139–40.

121 Nikephoros Choniates, p. 12, ll. 94–95.

122 Kinnamos 1.2, p. 6, ll. 1–3.

123 Kinnamos 1.5-6, pp. 13–15; Nikephoros Choniates, pp. 18–21; Turan, *Türkiye*, pp. 171–73; Cahen, *Pre-Ottoman Turkey*, p. 95; Cahen, *Formation*, pp. 19–20.

124 Turan, *Türkiye*, p. 161.

125 Michael the Syrian 15.12, 3:204 (trans.), 4:598, col. b (Syriac text); Cahen, "Diyar Bakr," p. 239; Turan, *Türkiye*, p. 162.

126 Michael the Syrian 15.12, 3:205 (trans.), 4:600, col. b (Syriac text); Cahen, "Diyar Bakr," p. 239.

127 Michael the Syrian 15.12, 3:205 (trans.), 4:600, col. b (Syriac text); Ibn al-Qalānisī, p. 202; Ibn al-Athīr, 6:571, trans. Richards, *Chronicle*, 1:227 (in both texts *sub anno* 514/2 April 1120–21 March 1121); Cahen, "Diyar Bakr," p. 239; Turan, *Türkiye*, p. 163.

128 Michael the Syrian 15.12, 3:204–205 (trans.), 4:599, col. b (Syriac text).

129 Michael the Syrian 15.12, 3:205–206 (trans.), 4:599–600, col. b (Syriac text); Turan, *Türkiye*, p. 163; Bezer, "Harput," p. 91.

130 Ibn al-Athīr, 6:535, trans. Richards, *Chronicle*, 1:187 (*sub anno* 511/5 May 1117–23 April 1118); Hillenbrand, "Najm al-Dīn İl-Ghāzī," pp. 267–69 (who considers Īlghāzī's involvement in the affairs of Aleppo as "an unfortunate lack of judgement" due to the city's lamentable financial situation and its exposed position near to the Franks' sphere of operation); for the conquest of Aleppo, see also Heidemann, *Renaissance*, pp. 231–36.

131 Ibn al-Qalānisī, pp. 199–200 (treaty with Ṭughtakīn of Damascus); Ibn al-Athīr, 6:542–43, 544, trans. Richards, *Chronicle*, 1:195–97; Mouton, *Damas*, pp. 36–37.

132 Ibn al-Qalānisī, pp. 200–201; Ibn al-Athīr, 6:550–51, trans. Richards, *Chronicle*, 1:203–205; Turan, *Türkiye*, p. 162; Hillenbrand, "Najm al-Dīn İl-Ghāzī," pp. 276–78; Asbridge, *Kreuzzüge*, pp. 182–85.

133 Hillenbrand, "Najm al-Dīn İl-Ghāzī," pp. 274–75, 278–79, 286–87: Īlghāzī is accorded an important role in the re-awakening and dissemination of jihad concepts in Syria, especially in the time after his takeover in Aleppo until the battle of Balāṭ. Hillenbrand points to the ephemeral nature of these attempts, thus excluding the possibility of a deliberate adoption of jihad propaganda. As is attested in the case of Īlghāzī's brother Suqmān, however, jihad concepts had a strong legitimating force, which contributed to a further consolidation of the emir's rule. Moreover, one should bear in mind that the Great Seljuk sultanate had already begun to make use of jihad concepts in order to justify its military interventions in Syria. Īlghāzī was by no means an isolated case.

134 Ibn al-Qalānisī, pp. 204–205; Ibn al-Athīr, 6:555, 557–59, trans. Richards, *Chronicle*, 1:209, 212–14; for the Georgian campaign, see Turan, *Türkiye*, pp. 164–66; Hillenbrand, "Najm al-Dīn İl-Ghāzī," pp. 278–80; eadem, "Artuqid Power," pp. 129–30.

135 Hillenbrand, "Najm al-Dīn İl-Ghāzī," pp. 271–75 (relations with Turkmen warriors), 276–80 (military strategy), 280–82 (political ability).

136 Cahen, "Diyar Bakr," pp. 236–37; Hillenbrand, "Najm al-Dīn İl-Ghāzī," pp. 266–67, 269–71, 285–86; eadem, "Artuqid Power," p. 132: There are different versions regarding the date and circumstances of the acquisition of Mayyāfāriqīn. Sultan Maḥmūd's bestowal may have been the formal recognition of a pre-existing situation.

137 Ibn al-Athīr, 6:559, 574–75, 583, trans. Richards, *Chronicle*, 1:214–15, 231–32, 240; Cahen, "Diyar Bakr," pp. 240–41; Hillenbrand, "Artuqid Power," pp. 131–32.

138 The most detailed source for Balak's activities is Michael the Syrian 15.13, 3:210–12 (trans.), 4:600–603, col. b (Syriac text): new attack on Antioch in 1123; the daughter of Roger of Antioch, who was to be married to Joscelin, was ambushed and taken captive; during a campaign against Balak, King Baldwin II and other Frankish dignitaries were taken captive and imprisoned in Kharpete/Ḥiṣn Ziyād; as a result of a local revolt initiated by Armenian soldiers, Baldwin and his fellow prisoners temporarily took possession of Kharpete; fighting outside the citadel of Manbij, Balak was deadly wounded. Arabic chronicles partly corroborate Michael's accounts and give additional details: Ibn al-Qalānisī, p. 208; Ibn al-Athīr, 6:575–76, trans. Richards, *Chronicle*, 1:232 (*sub anno* 515/2 April 1120–21 March 1121): attack on Edessa, Joscelin of Edessa and other Frankish dignitaries were taken captive; Ibn al-Athīr, 6:587, trans. Richards, *Chronicle*, 1:245 (*sub anno* 517/1 March 1123–18 February 1118): Balak seized Ḥarrān in Rabīʿ I/29 April-28 May 1123 and took possession of Aleppo on 1 Jumādā/27 June 11123; Ibn al-Qalānisī, pp. 209–210; Ibn al-Athīr, 6:589, trans. Richards, *Chronicle*, 1:246–47: Balak defeated King Baldwin II near Gargar and took him captive (Ṣafar 517/31 March-28 April 1123); the Frankish prisoners temporarily took possession of Kharpete; Ibn al-Athīr, 6:592–93, trans. Richards, *Chronicle*, 1:251: death of Balak, Ḥusām al-Dīn Timurtāsh took possession of Aleppo. For these events, see Cahen, "Diyar Bakr," pp. 239–40; Turan, *Türkiye*, pp. 166–67; Bezer, "Harput," pp. 89–92; for a detailed analysis, see Heidemann, *Renaissance*, p. 236–40.

Conclusions

This book focused on the political and structural changes that occurred during the earliest phase of the Turkish expansion in Byzantine Asia Minor from the late 1030s through the 1120s. This thematic choice unavoidably entailed a focus on rather traditional historiographical topics and may ignore some crucial aspects of social and economic living conditions. Yet it seems to be justified by the fact that a comprehensive book-length account of these events has never been written in any of the major western languages. I also hope to have been able to provide a number of new insights and to offer some important revisions of the modern Turkish master narrative. Moreover, it seems that certain scholarly opinions on social and economic developments in Asia Minor depend upon oversimplified interpretations of political and military events and thus may be modified in the light of a new narrative of the Turkish expansion.

The process in question was determined by a variety of factors, such as the Byzantine empire's military and administrative structures in the East, the situation in the Muslim territories of Upper Mesopotamia and northern Syria, as well as the power relations among local and supra-regional forces. Apart from the imperial government, Turkmen raiders, and Seljuk conquerors, it involved Greek, Armenian, or Syrian aristocrats, Frankish mercenaries, crusaders, Arab and Kurdish emirs, and Fatimid governors. The groupings and alliances that resulted from this intricate patchwork of political players were highly ephemeral and constantly shifting. Yet there was a key factor underlying all these phenomena: the waning influence of Constantinople and Cairo, which after the first half of the eleventh century lost their control over many of the regions in question, and the failure of the nascent Seljuk sultanate to supplant them permanently.

The explanatory models modern scholars have proposed in order to illuminate the reasons for the Turkish expansion in Asia Minor stress important aspects, but we should refrain from inappropriate generalizations or mono-causal explanations. First and foremost, it is a blatant oversimplification to consider these developments as a clash between Byzantine Christians and Turkish Muslims. Such clear-cut divides between ethnically and religiously well-defined entities are mostly due to modern nationalistic perspectives that seek to construe unbroken continuities between eleventh-century populations and their alleged descendants in modern Greece and Turkey. This study has attempted to show that from the outset there was as much collaboration as separation and conflict between Byzantine defenders and Turkish invaders. Apart from the fact that there was always a broad variety of disparate forces involved in raids and attacks, it is especially noteworthy that as soon as Turkish warrior groups gained ground in certain regions they immediately began to infiltrate pre-existing structures and create links with indigenous groups and local elites. The latter, in turn, took advantage of the newcomers by using their fighting skills for their own political objectives.

Whenever the primary sources refer to a Christian-Muslim conflict, they give expression to overarching ideological concepts related to the crusades or the revival of Muslim *jihad*, first in the context of the Seljuk imperial project and later on as a reaction of Turkish emirs to the Frankish expansion in Palestine and Syria. These ideas were used to justify specific political ambitions and underscored the legitimacy of warlords who sought to consolidate themselves in their newly created lordships, but they hardly occur beyond this context as an overall driving force of conquest in Asia Minor. In a similar vein, the notion of a Christian-barbarian conflict is frequently evoked in Byzantine and Eastern Christian accounts of raids and battles as part of a long-standing rhetorical convention harking back to late antique models, but it is rarely employed in other contexts and thus cannot be considered a common perspective in the period in question.

A large segment of the Turkish invaders, who came to Asia Minor and the borderlands either with independent warrior groups or under the leadership of the Seljuk sultanate, were nomadic pastoralists. Doubtlessly, the Turkish expansion brought an increase of nomadic elements, and the emirates in eastern Anatolia and the Armenian highlands seem to have had a distinct nomadic character. But does that mean that the Turkish expansion resulted from a clash between sedentary and nomadic groups? Natural phenomena like climatic changes, periods of drought, and the desertification of steppe lands may have triggered large-scale displacements of tribal confederations. The living conditions of the central Anatolian plateau and other areas seem to have offered an ideal habitat for the settlement of nomadic groups. The fighting techniques and high mobility of nomadic warriors may go a long way towards explaining their military superiority vis-à-vis Byzantine troops and others, especially at the time of their first appearance. There is no doubt, thus, that transhumance and nomadism played a certain role in the migrations of Turkish groups. Yet the primary sources hardly refer to these phenomena in contexts lying beyond these initial stages. Nomadic behavioral patterns cannot explain the successful intrusion into pre-existing social networks and political elites or the creation of permanent lordships, especially when they grew into larger and more powerful entities. The available primary accounts make plain that as soon as the Turkish raiders turned into lords of fortified places, urban centers, and domains, they gave up much of their nomadic habits and adapted to the sedentary practices and forms of rule that were in use in the regions in which they had established themselves. They were able to insert themselves smoothly into existing social networks and power relations, to exploit administrative tools and local resources, and thus to gain the acceptance of local elites and their subjects. This process explains how the nucleus of lordships centered in one or two towns and fortresses could evolve into a well-established principality encompassing larger territorial units.

Descriptions evoking images of total destruction, economic decay, relentless bloodshed, and a massive flight of indigenous people towards safer places are mostly to be found in Eastern Christian and sometimes in Byzantine primary sources. No doubt, such moments formed part of the harsh reality of warfare in eleventh-century Asia Minor, but the same sources also imply that these events were limited to specific areas and time periods. They can by no means be generalized as an adequate presentation of living conditions in Anatolia in the first century of the Turkish expansion. Cities that were affected by raids re-appear several years later as flourishing hubs. Turkish emirs who made chroniclers tremble because of their brutish cruelty were praised later on for their righteousness and benevolence towards their Christian subjects. Warfare in Anatolia was by no means limited to Turkish raids on towns and peasants or to clashes between Turks and Byzantines or Franks. What actually happened in times of unrest was an overall escalation of violence involving all holders of political and military authority, who for a variety of reasons turned either against each other or against the non-combatant population. Interpretations that tend to explain the transformation of Anatolia as a result of wars and conquest in conjunction with Muslim-Christian or sedentary-nomad antagonism largely ignore these facts.

Another widely accepted view is the assumption that Asia Minor fell to the Turks because of Romanos IV's defeat by Sultan Alp Arslān in the battle of Manzikert fought in August 1071. As has been shown in Chapter 4, this battle took place more or less fortuitously because Alp Arslān's retreat from his Syrian campaign coincided with the emperor's attempt to safeguard the east-west routes along the Arsanias Valley by occupying fortresses north of Lake Van. Neither side aimed at a full-front confrontation at that time, nor did the Seljuk sultan intend to conquer Byzantine territories. What he actually wanted to achieve was a high degree of control over Muslim and Christian local lords in the Caucasus region and over the Muslim emirates along the southeastern flank of the empire's borderland from the Diyār Bakr province to Aleppo. In this respect, he continued the policy first initiated by his uncle Ṭughril Beg, who aimed at imposing his suzerainty over the said region by establishing bonds of allegiance with the local emirs. This had fatal consequences for Byzantium in that the defensive structures in the eastern borderlands were gradually deprived of their screen of allies controlling the adjacent Muslim territories. Doubtlessly, this strategy also facilitated the penetration of Byzantine territories by Turkish raiders, yet there still was no semblance of an organized policy of conquest.

What made Manzikert a turning point was, once again, its presentation in near-contemporary and later accounts by both Byzantine and Muslim authors. These sources, however, attach significance to the battle for other reasons. In Arabic and Persian narratives, the battle provided an opportunity to present the sultan as a champion of Muslim *jihad*, who through his moral virtues and steadfastness in faith achieved a major victory against the supreme representative of the Roman-Christian empire. We may assume that there are inter-textual references between these accounts and the victory messages sent after the battle to the Abbasid court of Baghdad. Alp Arslān may not have conceived the idea of conquering Byzantium, but he certainly had a keen interest in spreading his image as a Muslim model-ruler, and his victory over the emperor was an extremely apt occasion to do that. Just like the battle of Dandānqān fought in 1040 in Eastern Iran, Manzikert too was later used as an event providing legitimacy to those who actually or allegedly took part in it. This came to be connected with the idea that the sultan had allotted territories in eastern and central Anatolia to Turkish emirs, but it can be easily demonstrated that this narrative contravenes facts known from elsewhere. The Byzantine eyewitness Michael Attaleiates described the battle and the emperor's captivity in Alp Arslān's camp as a symbol of the Byzantine elite's moral decay, which is juxtaposed with the sultan's paradigmatic conduct. There are Muslim and Christian reports ascribing the increase of Turkish attacks on Byzantine territories after 1071 to the fact that the dethroned emperor's opponents in the civil strife disregarded the treaty that Romanos IV had concluded with Alp Arslān. There is no reliable evidence, however, supporting the claim that the battle of Manzikert was a starting point for extensive conquests.

There are numerous salient events that, in one way or another, accelerated the advance of Turkish warrior groups into Upper Mesopotamia, Syria, and Anatolia, increased these warriors' material resources, or constituted serious setbacks in the course of their expansionist movements. Yet none of them led to a total extinction of political groupings or caused irreversible results to the existing power relations. Unlike the Muslim conquests in the seventh century, the Turkish expansion of the eleventh century was the result of an intricate long-term development that spanned almost a century. One of the main arguments put forward in this book is that Asia Minor was neither conquered nor transformed into a settlement area of nomadic pastoralists. Rather, through an interplay of internal and external factors, there was a gradual decay of centralizing imperial structures, which gave way to the emergence of small-size regional powers of Byzantine, Frankish, and Turkish origin. These owed their existence partly to the institutions and political ambitions of the Byzantine aristocracy and partly to the influx of foreign raiders. At a certain point, the Muslim-Turkish element became predominant in central Anatolia, the Armenian highlands, and parts of Upper Mesopotamia. But this outcome was by no means a foregone conclusion. Nor did it result from a conscious expansionist policy pursued by the Seljuk sultanate or Turkmen warlords. Rather, it was a gradual process that evolved in various stages.

At first, Turkish groups gained access to the river valleys of the Armenian highlands and penetrated the fringes of the Anti-Taurus Mountains and northern Syria. In this way, they advanced towards central Anatolia and became increasingly engaged in the power struggles of the local elites and mercenary groups. Ultimately, they began to infiltrate political structures and took hold of urban centers. This process engendered the creation of local bases that became centers of rudimentary lordships. The latter had no stable borders or firm administrative structures, but in the course of time they developed into durable state-like entities combining both local and newly imported institutions. Hence, we are not dealing with the replacement of one entity by another but with a merging of different cultural, religious, and ethnic elements.

Chronologically, the gradual crystallization of the Turkish presence in Anatolia can be divided into three clearly recognizable stages: A first period (ca. 1040–71) extends from the first emergence of Turkmen warriors and Seljuk troops in the Armenian highlands, Upper Mesopotamia, and Syria to Romanos IV's failure to re-stabilize the defensive structures in the East in the course of his eastern campaigns. A second period (1071–98) witnessed the gradual collapse of centralizing mechanisms of imperial government in Asia Minor and their substitution by regional powers comprising Byzantine rebels, unruly mercenaries, and Turkish invaders. In a third phase (1098–ca. 1130) the political situation of Anatolia, Syria, and Upper Mesopotamia was largely determined by the impact of the First Crusade, the creation of the crusader states, the Byzantine re-conquests, and the Seljuk dynastic wars.

In addition to these broad tendencies, there were various secondary developments that in one way or another decisively contributed to the results outlined above. The activities of Turkmen warrior groups in the years 1038–44 and the first large-scale attacks of the nascent Seljuk sultanate (1048, 1054) seriously undermined the network of Muslim vassal principalities that came into being in the wake of the Byzantine conquest of Antioch in 969 and straddled a vast swathe of land from the Armenian highlands to northern Syria. The eastern borderlands thus lost their screen of protection. The universal claims of the early Seljuk sultanate weakened the influence of the Fatimid caliphate and forced the Byzantine government to shift its diplomatic efforts in the Muslim world from Cairo to Seljuk-controlled Baghdad. In this way, the axis of collaboration between Constantinople and Cairo, which for decades had secured a fragile balance of power, suddenly vanished. Apart from this geopolitical shift, Byzantium in 1057 endured especially disastrous civil strife with fatal consequences for the defensive structures in the East. Turkish warriors, Armenian rebels, and Frankish mercenary groups began to ravage vast areas of the Armenian highlands without meeting any obstacles, and the eastern borderland became increasingly permeable. In the years 1068–71, Romanos IV ultimately failed to safeguard the defensive structures in the Arsanias and Araxes Valleys, thus enabling Turkish warriors to cross the Euphrates and to penetrate central Anatolia. The 1071–72 war between the Doukas clan and the followers of Romanos IV demonstrated that large sections of the military units in the East were still in place and ready to side with the emperor, but as a result of these conflicts the last remnants of cohesion among the eastern aristocratic families were destroyed and a large vacuum of power arose.

Another decisive factor is the impact of developments in Syria on the Byzantine provinces of Asia Minor during the 1070s and early 1080s. The collapse of Byzantine and Fatimid control over these regions gave rise to a process of particularization and regionalization of political authority. Local elements and semi-independent warlords increasingly intermingled with intruding Turkish warriors, who inserted themselves into the existing power structures. In Syria, these warrior groups quite quickly managed to build up rudimentary structures consisting of mostly short-lived, small-size lordships centered in fortified strongholds. Gradually, they acquired considerable revenues, administrative skills, and territorial rights. This process was further facilitated by the fact that the Turks operating in Syria quickly turned into leading military powers and thus took hold of large landed estates and urban centers. By invading Byzantine territories, Turkish warriors transferred some of these practices to Asia Minor, which underwent especially precarious moments of instability in the years of the Komnenos-Doukas coup and the Norman War (1081–85).

As descendants of one of the most prestigious chiefs of the Seljuk clan, the sons of Qutlumush resorted to a rich arsenal of legitimating elements and, at the same time, adopted aspects of Byzantine imperial ideology by allying with members of the ruling elite. Sulaymān b. Qutlumush was the first Turkish chieftain to found his political claims on a combination of both Byzantine and Seljuk traditions. In 1086, a united front of local potentates and Seljuk commanders under Sultan Malikshāh prevailed, and Sulaymān paid for his ambitions with his life. But even in the time of Malikshāh's undisputed predominance in Syria between 1086 and 1092, the Seljuk sultanate, despite serious military and diplomatic efforts, was not able to impose any sort of effective control over the Turks operating in Asia Minor. The chaos of the Seljuk civil strife in the years 1093–95 and ensuing rivalries among Seljuk emirs in Syria and other Muslim lands interrupted lines of communication and put an end to the influx of Turkish groups into Asia Minor. Turkish potentates in the western coastland and the central Anatolian plateau and Byzantine-Armenian aristocrats in Cilicia, the Ceyhan Valley, and the Upper Euphrates region were given the opportunity to consolidate their position against the pressure exerted from Constantinople and the Muslim central lands. A hallmark of these entities irrespective of their ethnic and religious identity is the use of disparate strategies of legitimization, including the acquisition of Byzantine court titles, the formal recognition of Seljuk authorities, local coalitions, and bonds of marriage.

The First Crusade and the establishment of the crusader principalities constituted another decisive turning point in the political transformation of Asia Minor. Large crusader hosts crossing Anatolia, numerous battles and skirmishes with the Turks settling in the regions between Bithynia and Cappadocia, and a disastrous scorched-earth strategy implemented by retreating defenders doubtlessly caused a considerable amount of devastation. The Turks who refused to submit to the emperor were forced to withdraw to the central Anatolian plateau and Cappadocia while Byzantium gradually recovered western Asia Minor and the southern coastland. At the same time, the Franks firmly established themselves in Antioch, Edessa, and the surrounding territories. The crusader principalities thus formed a new Christian frontier vis-à-vis the emirates in Syria and eastern Anatolia. Apart from incessant conflicts, this situation also led to an increase of interaction and exchange among Franks, Byzantines, Armenians, Turks, and other groups. The Byzantines frequently sought to integrate Turkish groups and individuals into their army and the imperial court hierarchy. The Franks were mostly motivated by religious aggression, but they also shared a common code of martial and aristocratic values with the Turkish chieftains. Hence, the two sides respected each other in matters of warfare and were eager to insert defectors and apostates from the other side into their ranks. In the course of its conflict with the Normans of Antioch, Byzantium suffered some serious blows regarding its position in Cilicia and the northern coastland of Syria. Nevertheless, the empire succeeded in establishing a new defensive system based on strongholds on the southern shores of Asia Minor and in Cyprus. The imperial government also developed effective diplomacy and thereby projected its salient role as a regulating factor and mediator in Christian-Muslim contacts.

A remarkable side effect of the creation of the crusader states was the penetration of Upper Mesopotamia and the Diyār Bakr province by Turkish emirs from Syria. The rise of the Artuqids, who later distinguished themselves as proponents of Muslim jihad against the crusaders, illustrates this process. In the interior of Asia Minor, the Turkish victories of 1101 prepared the ground for the consolidation of the Seljuk Turks on the central Anatolian plateau and the Dānishmandid emirate in northeastern Cappadocia. The period was characterized by expansionist tendencies and fierce power struggles among the Turkish emirs in Anatolia, northern Syria, and northern Iraq, with Melitene, the Diyār Bakr province, and Mosul being the main centers of these conflicts. The situation culminated in the temporary occupation of Mosul by Qilij Arslān I and in a deadly clash with the Great Seljuk sultanate in early 1107. All in all, Turkish wars after the crusades had a very different character from those of the previous decades. The raids and skirmishes with Byzantine and crusader armies gave way to internecine infighting among opposing factions emerging from Seljuk power struggles.

Qilij Arslān I's demise brought about a temporary disintegration of the Seljuk principality in Anatolia and thus different branches established themselves in Konya and Melitene. Despite the conflicts among Qilij Arslān's sons, however, the Seljuk emirs maintained firm control over vast areas of the central Anatolian plateau and the Euphrates region and mounted a new series of attacks on their Byzantine neighbors in the years 1109, 1111, 1113, and 1115–16. As a result of these invasions, a vast stripe of land along the western fringes of the Anatolian plateau turned into a kind of no-man's land, which was characterized by a mixed population consisting of sedentary and nomadic groups and by widely dispersed outposts held alternately by Turks and Byzantines. The imperial government built up a new defensive line, which was situated at a rather far distance from the easternmost outposts and was based on a chain of fortresses monitoring the main access routes to the western coastland.

In contrast to the relatively uniform Byzantine-Turkish frontier in the West, in the East a complicated patchwork of ethnically and religiously disparate powers had come into being. There were the crusader principalities of Antioch and Edessa; the Byzantine-Armenian lordships in Cilicia, the Ceyhan Valley, and the Euphrates region; and numerous Turkish emirates in Melitene, the Euphrates Valley, the Diyār Bakr province, Cappadocia, and the Armenian highlands. We have pointed out a set of common strategies and behaviors aiming at the political and ideological consolidation of these lordships. Apart from that, it is difficult to mark out common evolutional patterns, but the Muslim-Frankish wars in Syria, the developments in the Seljuk-controlled regions of Iraq and Azerbaijan, and an incessant series of local alliances and conflicts were certainly decisive factors for the formation of power relationships in the region in question.

In sum, by ca. 1130 the area of what up to the late 1070s had been Byzantium's eastern provinces was split into four distinct spheres: the Byzantine-held territories in western Asia Minor, parts of the Pontus region, and the southern coastland; the Seljuk principality of Konya straddling large sections of the central Anatolian plateau; a number of Muslim-Turkish emirates in Cappadocia and the Armenian highlands; and a complicated cluster of powers of different ethnic and religious identity stretching from Cilicia to Upper Mesopotamia. In the course of the twelfth century, the Komnenian emperors failed to recover the Anatolian plateau or other Turkish-held territories in Asia Minor. They were also unable to perpetuate their predominance over Antioch and the kingdom of Jerusalem. The Seljuk sultan Qilij Arslān II (1155–92), for his part, was much more successful in his expansionist attempts against the Dānishmandid emirate and other rulers in the Euphrates region and thus eventually built up a set of centralizing mechanisms in Seljuk Konya. These events did not radically alter the situation in western Asia Minor, which up to the Mongol conquest in the second half of the thirteenth century remained a region of intensive social and cultural exchange and cross-fertilization between Turks and Byzantines.

I hope I have been able to make clear that the transformation of eleventh- and twelfth-century Asia Minor should be viewed neither as Byzantine decline nor as Turkish triumph. In fact, the interaction between the two spheres was the driving force of change. Efforts at state building could have durable results only through strategies of mutual accommodation and successful incorporation of pre-existing structures. From a methodological point of view, it seems especially important to contextualize a large number of very disparate narratives into a cross-cultural discourse of texts pertaining to the Latin, Eastern Christian, and Muslim traditions. In this way we are able to discover common perceptual patterns of these transformative processes and to better understand the simultaneity, fusion, and overlap of ideological attitudes and political phenomena, which exhibit a broad spectrum of appearances oscillating between Roman-Christian and Turkish-Muslim characteristics. This approach enables us to spot long-term continuities reflecting the gradual re-interpretation of adopted cultural features within the context of new political and religious reference systems. What began in late eleventh-century Anatolia goes a long way towards explaining why 300 years later the nascent Ottoman emirate was so successful in integrating Byzantine, Muslim, and many other cultural features into a new imperial entity.

Bibliography

Primary sources

Aqsarā'ī, ed. Osman Turan, *Müsâmeret ül-Ahbâr, Mogollar zamanında Türkiye Selçukluları Tarihi, Aksaraylı Meḥmed oğlu Kerîmüddin Mahmud*, Türk Tarih Kurumu Yayınlarından III. Seri – No. 1 (Ankara, 1944); trans. Öztürk Mürsel, *Kerîmuddin Mahmud-i Aksarayî, Müsâmeretü'l-ahbâr*, Türk Tarih Kurumu Yayınları II. Dizi – Sayı 38 (Ankara, 2000).

Albert of Aachen, ed. and trans. Susan B. Edington, *Historia Ierosolimitana: History of the Journey to Jerusalem* (Oxford, 2007).

Anna Komnene, ed. Diether Roderich Reinsch and Athanasios Kambylis, *Annae Comnenae Alexias*, Corpus Fontium Historiae Byzantinae 40/1-2 (Berlin and New York, 2001).

Aristakes of Lastivert, trans. Marius Canard and Haïg Berbérian, *Récit des malheurs de la nation arménienne*, Bibliothèque de Byzantion 5 (Brussels, 1973).

'Aẓīmī, ed. and trans. Ali Sevim, *Azimî Tarihi (Selçuklular Dönemiyle İlgili Bölümler: H. 430–538)*, Türk Tarih Kurumu Yayınları XIX. Dizi – Sa. 8 (Ankara, 1988).

Bar Hebraeus, ed. Paul Bedjan, *Chronicon Syriacum e codd. mss. emendatum ac punctis vocalibus adnotationibusque locupletatum* (Paris, 1890); trans. Ernest A. Wallis Budge, *The Chronography of Gregory Abû'l-Faraj 1225–1286, the Son of Aaron, the Hebrew Physician Commonly Known as Bar Hebraeus, Being the First Part of his Political History of the World*, 1: *English Translation*, 2: *Syriac Texts* (London, 1932, reprint Amsterdam, 1976).

(al-)Bundārī/'Imād al-Dīn al-Kātib al-Iṣfahānī, ed. Theodoor Martijn Houtsma, *Recueil de textes relatifs à l'histoire des Seldjoucides*, 2: *Histoire des Seldjoucides de l'Irâq par al-Bondârî d'après Imâd ad-dîn al-Kâtib al-Isfahânî, texte arabe* (Leiden, 1889).

Dānishmand-nāma, ed. and trans. Irène Mélikoff, *La geste de Melik Dānişmend, étude critique du Dānişmendnāme*, 1: *introduction et traduction*, 2: *édition critique* (Paris, 1960); ed. Necati Demir, *Dânişmend-nâme* (Ankara, 2004).

Έγγραφα Πάτμου, 1: *Αυτοκρατορικά, διπλωματική έκδοσις, γενική εισαγωγή – ευρετήρια – πίνακες*, ed. Era L. Branousi (Athens, 1980).

Ekkehard of Aura, ed. Georg Waitz, *Ekkehardi Uraugensis Chronica*, Monumenta Germaniae Historica: Scriptores 6: Chronica et annales aevi Salici (Hannover, 1844), pp. 1–267.

Fulcher of Chartres, ed. Heinrich Hagenmayer, *Fulcheri Carnotensis Historia Hierosolymitana (1095–1127)* (Heidelberg, 1913).

Georgian Chronicles (K'art'lis C'xovreba), trans. Robert W. Thomson, *Rewriting Caucasian History: The Medieval Armenian Adaptation of the Georgian Chronicles, The Original Georgian Texts and the Armenian Adaptation* (Oxford, 1996).

Gesta Francorum, ed. and trans. Rosalind Hill, *The Deeds of the Franks and the other Pilgrims to Jerusalem*, Oxford Medieval Texts (Oxford, 1962).

(al-)Ḥusaynī, ed. Muhammad Iqbal, *Akhbār 'ud-Dawlat 'is-Saljūqiyya by Ṣadr'uddīn Abu'l Ḥasan 'Ali ibn Nāṣir Ibn 'Ali al-Ḥusaini* (Lahore: The University of the Panjab, 1933); trans. Necati Lügal, *Ṣadruddîn Ebu'l-Ḥasan 'Ali ibn Nâṣır ibn 'Ali el-Ḥüseynî, Ahbâr üd-Devlet is-Selçukiyye*, Türk Tarih Kurumu Yayınlarından II. Seri – No. 8 (Ankara, 1943); trans. C. E. Bosworth, *The History of the Seljuq State: A Translation with Commentary of the Akhbār al-dawla al-saljūqiyya*, Routledge Studies in the History of Iran and Turkey (London, 2010).

Ibn al-'Adīm, ed. Suhayl Zakkar, *Bughyat al-ṭalab fī tārīkh Ḥalab, ṣannafahū Ibn al-'Adīm al-ṣāḥib Kamāl al-Dīn 'Umar b. Aḥmad b. Abī Jarāda*, 11 vols. (Damascus, 1988); trans. Ali Sevim, *Biyografilerle Selçuklular Tarihi İbnü'l-Adîm Bugyetü't-taleb fî Tarihi Haleb (Seçmeler)*, Türk Tarih Kurumu Yayınları XIX. Dizi – Sa. 5a (Ankara, 1982).

Ibn al-'Adīm, ed. Suhayl Zakkar, *Zubdat al-ḥalab min tārīkh Ḥalab li-l-ṣāḥib Kamāl al-Dīn 'Umar b. Aḥmad b. Abī Jarāda al-mutawaffā fī sanat 660 h.*, 2 vols. (Damascus and Cairo, 1997).

Ibn al-Athīr, *al-Kāmil fī l-tārīkh li-'Izz al-Dīn Abī l-Ḥasan 'Alī b. Abī al-Karam al-Shaybānī al-ma'rūf bi-Ibn al-Athīr*, 9 vols., 4th ed. (Beirut, 1994); trans. D. S. Richards, *The Annals of the Saljuq Turks: Selections from al-Kāmil fī l-Ta'rīkh of 'Izz al-Dīn Ibn al-Athīr* (London, 2002); trans. D. S. Richards, *The Chronicle of Ibn al-Athir for the Crusading Period from al-Kamil fi'l-Ta'rikh*, 1: *The Years 491–541/1097–1146: The Coming of the Franks and the Muslim Response*, Crusade Texts in Translation 13 (Aldershot, 2005).

Ibn al-Azraq al-Fāriqī, ed. B. A. L. Awad, *Tārīkh al-Fāriqī* (Cairo, 1959); ed. and trans. Carole Hillenbrand, *A Muslim Principality in Crusader Times* (Istanbul, 1990).

Ibn Bībī, ed. Martijn Theodoor Houtsma, *Recueil de textes relatifs à l'histoire des Seldjoucides*, 4: *Histoire des Seldjoucides d'Asie Mineure d'après l'abrégé du Seldjouknāmeh d'Ibn-Bībī, texte persan* (Leiden, 1902); ed. Adnan Sadık Erzi, *İbn-i Bībī, El-Evāmirü'l-'Alā'iyye fī'l-Umūri'l-'Alā'iyye* (Ankara, 1956) (facsimile edition of MS Aya Sofya 2985); ed. Necati Lugal and Adnan Sadık Erzi, *İbn-i Bībī (el-Ḥüseyn b. Muḥammed b. 'Alī el-Ca'ferī er-Rugedī), El-Evāmirü'l-'Alā'iyye fī'l-Umūri'l-'Alā'iyye, I. Cild (II. Kılıç Arslan'ın Vefâtından I. 'Alā'ü'd-dīn Keyḳubād'ın Cülūsuna kadar)*, Ankara Üniversitesi İlâhiyat Fakültesi Yayınlarından – No. 19 (Ankara, 1957); trans. Herbert W. Duda, *Die Seltschukengeschichte des Ibn Bībī* (Kopenhagen, 1959).

Ibn al-Qalānisī, ed. Henry Frederick Amedroz, *History of Damascus 363–555 a. h. by Ibn al-Qalānisī from the Bodleian Ms. Hunt. 125, being a Continuation of the History of Hilāl al-Sābi* (Leiden, 1908).

John Kinnamos, ed. August Meineke, *Ioannis Cinnami Epitome rerum ab Ioanne et Alexio Comnenis gestarum*, Corpus Scriptorum Historiae Byzantinae (Bonn, 1836); trans. Charles M. Brand, *Deeds of John and Manuel Comnenus by John Kinnamos* (New York, 1976).

John Skylitzes, ed. Johannes Thurn, *Ioannis Scylitzae Synopsis Historiarum*, Corpus Fontium Historiae Byzantinae 5 (Berlin and New York, 1973); trans. Bernard Flusin and Jean-Claude Cheynet, *Jean Skylitzès: Empereurs de Constantinople*, Realités byzantines 8 (Paris, 2003).

John Skylitzes Cont., ed. Eudoxos Th. Tsolakis, *Ἡ συνέχεια τῆς χρονογραφίας τοῦ Ἰωάννου Σκυλίτση (Ioannes Skylitzes Continuatus)* (Thessalonica, 1968).

John Zonaras, ed. Theodor Büttner-Wobst, *Ioannis Zonarae Epitomae historiarum libri XIII-XVIII*, Corpus Scriptorum Historiae Byzantinae (Bonn, 1897).

Lignages d'Outremer, ed. Marie-Adélaide Nielen, Documents relatifs à l'histoire des Croisades 18 (Paris, 2003).

(al-)Maqrīzī, Taqī al-Dīn Aḥmad b. 'Alī, ed. J. al-Shayyāl and M. H. M. Aḥmad, *Itti'āẓ al-ḥunafā' bi-akhbār al-a'immat al-fāṭimīyīn al-khulafā' li-Taqī al-Dīn Aḥmad b. 'Alī al-Maqrīzī*, 3. vols. (Cairo 1996).

(al-)Maqrīzī, Taqī al-Dīn Aḥmad b. ʿAlī, *Kitāb al-mawāʿiẓ wa-l-iʿtibār bi-dhikr al-khiṭaṭ wa-l-āthār al-maʿrūf bi-l-khiṭaṭ al-maqrīzīya taʾlīf Taqī al-Dīn Abī l-ʿAbbās Aḥmad b. ʿAlī al-Maqrīzī al-mutawaffā 845 h.*, 2 vols. (Cairo s. a.).

Matthew of Edessa, trans. Ara Edmond Dostourian, *Armenia and the Crusades, Tenth to Twelfth Centuries, The Chronicle of Matthew of Edessa* (Lanham, New York, London, 1993).

Michael Attaleiates, ed. and trans. Inmaculada Pérez Martín, *Miguel Ataliates, Historia*, Nueva Roma 15 (Madrid, 2002).

Michael the Syrian, ed. and trans. Jean-Baptiste Chabot, *Chronique de Michel le Syrien*, 4 vols. (Paris, 1899–1910).

Michael Psellos, ed. Diether Roderich Reinsch, *Michaelis Pselli Chronographia*, 1: *Einleitung und Text*, 2: *Textkritischer Kommentar und Indices*, Millenium Studies 51 (Berlin and Boston, 2014).

Neşrî, ed. Necdet Öztürk, *Mevlânâ Mehmed Neşrî, Cihânnümâ (Osmanlı Tarihi 1288–1485)* (Istanbul, 2008).

Nikephoros Bryennios, ed. and trans. Paul Gautier, *Nicephori Bryennii Historiarum libri quattuor*, Corpus Fontium Historiae Byzantinae 9 (Brussels, 1975).

Niketas Choniates, ed. Johannes van Dieten, *Nicetae Choniatae Historia*, Corpus Fontium Historiae Byzantinae 11/1-2 (Berlin and New York, 1975); trans. Harry J. Magoulias, *O City of Byzantium, Annals of Niketas Choniatēs* (Detroit, 1984).

Niẓām al-Mulk, ed. Charles Schefer, *Siasset Namèh, Traité de Gouvernement composé pour le sultan Melik-châh par le vizir Nizam oul-Moulk* (Paris, 1891); trans. Hubert Darke, *The Book of Government or Rules for Kings, The Siyar al-Muluk or Siyasat-nama of Nizam al-mulk*, 3rd ed. (Richmond, Surrey, 2001).

Orderic Vitalis, ed. August le Prevost, *Orderici Vitalis, Angligenae, coenobii Uticensis monachi, Historiae ecclesiasticae libri tredecim*, 4 vols. (Paris, 1838–1852).

Peter Tudebode, ed. John Hugh Hill and Laurita L. Hill, *Historia de Hierosolymitano itinere* (Paris, 1977).

Qazwīnī, Ḥamdullāh Muṣṭawfī, ed. and trans. Jules Gantin, *Târîkhè Gozîdè par Hamd Ollâh Mostooufi Qazvînî, les dynasties persanes pendant la période musulmane depuis les Saffârîdes jusques et y compris les Mogols de la Perse en 1330 de notre ère*, vol. 1 (Paris, 1903).

Ralph of Caen, *Gesta Tancredi in expeditione Hierosolymitana auctore Radulfo Cadomensi*, Recueil des historiens des croisades, historiens occidentaux 3 (Paris, 1866), pp. 587–716; trans. Bernard S. Bachrach and David S. Bachrach, *The Gesta Tancredi of Ralph of Caen: A History of the Normans on the First Crusade*, Crusade Texts in Translation 12 (Farnham, 2007).

(al-)Rāwandī, ed. Muḥammad Iqbál, *The Ráḥat-uṣ-ṣudúr wa áyat-us-surúr, Being a History of the Saljúqs by Muḥammad ibn ʿAlí ibn Sulaymán ar-Ráwandí* (London, 1921).

Raymond of Aguilers, *Historia Francorum qui ceperunt Iherusalem*, Recueil des historiens des croisades, historiens occidentaux 3 (Paris, 1866), pp. 235–309.

Robert the Monk, *Historia Iherosolomitana*, Recueil des historiens des croisades, historiens occidentaux 3 (Paris, 1866), pp. 717–882; trans. Carol Sweetenham, *Robert the Monk's History of the First Crusade, Historia Iherosolimitana*, Crusade Texts in Translation 11 (Aldershot, 2005).

Samuel of Ani, *Extrait de la chronographie de Samuel d'Ani*, Recueil des historiens des croisades, documents arméniens 1 (Paris, 1869), pp. 445–468.

Sibṭ b. al-Jawzī, ed. Ali Sevim, *Mir'âtü'z-zeman fî Tarihi'l-âyan, Sıbt İbnü'l-Cevzî Şemsüddin Ebû'l-Muzaffer Yusuf b. Kızoğlu*, Dil ve Tarih-Coğrafya Fakültesi Yayınları 178 (Ankara, 1968).

Tārīkh-i Āl-i Saljūq, ed. Feridun Nâfiz Uzluk, *Anadolu Selçukluları Devleti Tarihi III: Histoire des Seldjoukides d'Asie Mineure par un anonyme*, Anadolu Selçukluları Gününde Mevlevi Bitikleri 5 (Ankara, 1952).

Theodore Prodromos, ed. Wolfram Hörandner, *Historische Gedichte*, Wiener Byzantinistische Studien 11 (Vienna, 1974).

Theophylaktos of Ochrid, ed. Paul Gautier, *Théophylacte d'Achrida, Lettres, introduction, texte, traduction et notes*, Corpus Fontium Historiae Byzantinae 16.2 (Thessalonica, 1986).

William of Tyre, ed. R. B. C. Huygens, *Chronique*, Corpus Christianorum, Continuatio Mediaevalis 63, 2 vols. (Turnhout, 1986).

Yazıcızâde Ali, ed. Abdullah Bakır, *Tevârîh-i Âl-i Selçuk [Oğuznâme-Selçuklu Tarihi]* (Istanbul, 2009).

Ẓahīr al-Dīn Nīshāpurī/Rashīd al-Dīn, ed. Ahmed Ateş, *Raşīd al-Dīn Fażlallāh, Cāmi' al-Tavārīẖ (Metin), II. Cild, 5. Cüz, Selçuklular Tarihi*, Türk Tarih Kurumu Yayınlarından III. Seri – No. 6 (Ankara, 1960); trans. Kenneth Allin Luther, *The History of the Seljuq Turks from the Jāmi' al-Tawārīkh, An Ilkhanid Adaption of the Saljūq-nāma of Ẓahīr al-Dīn Nīshāpūrī*, (Richmond, Surrey, 2001).

Modern scholarship

Agacanov, Sergey Grigoreviç, *Selçuklular*, trans. Ekber N. Necef and Ahment R. Annaberdiyev (Istanbul, 2006).

Agadshanow, S. G., *Der Staat der Seldschukiden und Mittelasien*, Turkmenenforschung 17 (Berlin, 1994).

Ahrweiler, Hélène, and Laiou, Angeliki E., eds., *Studies on the Internal Diaspora of the Byzantine Empire* (Washington, D.C., 1998).

Anderson, William, "Settlement Change in Byzantine Galatia: An Assessment of Finds from the General Survey of Central Anatolia," *Anatolian Archaeological Studies* 17 (2008), 233–240.

Angold, Michael, "The Byzantine State on the Eve of the Battle of Manzikert," *Byzantinische Forschungen* 16 (1991) (= Papers given at the Nineteenth Spring Symposium of Byzantine Studies, Birmingham, March 1985), 9–34.

Angold, Michael, *The Byzantine Empire, 1025–1204: A Political History*, 2nd ed. (London, 1997).

Angold, Michael, "Belle Époque or Crisis? (1025–1118)," in *Cambridge History of the Byzantine Empire*, ed. Shepard, pp. 583–626.

Armstrong, Pamela, "Nomadic Seljuks in "Byzantine" Lycia," in *Η Βυζαντινή Μικρά Ασία (6ος-12ος αι.)*, ed. Lampakis, pp. 321–338.

Arutjunova-Fidanjan, Viada A., "Some Aspects of the Military-Administrative Districts and of the Byzantine Administration in Armenia during the 11th Century," *Revue des Études Arméniennes* 20 (1986–87), 309–320.

Asbridge, Thomas, *The Creation of the Principality of Antioch 1098–1130* (Woodbridge, 2000).

Asbridge, Thomas, *The First Crusade: A New History* (London, 2004).

Asbridge, Thomas, *Die Kreuzzüge*, trans. Susanne Held (Stuttgart, 2010).

Asdracha, Aikaterini, "Η Κύπρος υπό τους Κομνηνούς (Α΄), in *Ιστορία της Κύπρου*, ed. Papadopoullos, pp. 293–347.

Aslanapa, Oktay, and Altun, Ara, "Anadolu Dışı Kökenler," in *Anadolu Selçukluları ve Beylikler Dönemi* 2, ed. Peker and Bilici, pp. 75–79.

Aybek, Serdar, and Öz, Ali Kazım, "Preliminary Report of the Archeological Survey at Apollonia Ad Rhyndacum," *Anatolia* 27 (2004), 1–25.

Aykut, Şevki N., *Türkiye Selçuklu Sikkeleri*, 1: *I. Mesud'dan I. Keykubad'a Kadar (510–616/1116–1220)* (Istanbul, 2000).

Babinger, Franz, *Die Geschichtsschreiber der Osmanen und ihre Werke* (Leipzig, 1927).

Bakırer, Ömür, "Kitâbeler, Vakfiyeler ve Yazarlar," in *Anadolu Selçukluları ve Beylikler Dönemi* 2, ed. Peker and Bilici, pp. 9–13.

Balard, Michel, Kedar, Benjamin Z., and Riley-Smith, Jonathan S. C., eds., *Dei gesta per Francos: Études sur les croisades dédiées à Jean Richard / Crusade Studies in Honour of Jean Richard* (Aldershot, 2001).

Başan, Aziz, *The Great Seljuqs: A History*, Routledge Studies in the History of Iran and Turkey (London and New York, 2010).

Baykara, Tuncer, *I. Gıyaseddin Keyhusrev (1164–1211) Gazi-Şehit*, Türk Tarih Kurumu Yayınları XXIX. Dizi - Sa. 20 (Ankara, 1997).

Beech, George T., "The Crusader Lordship of Marash in Armenian Cilicia, 1104–1149," *Viator* 27 (1996), 35–52.

Beihammer, Alexander D., "Die Ethnogenese der seldschukischen Türken im Urteil christlicher Geschichtsschreiber des 11. und 12. Jahrhunderts," *Byzantinische Zeitschrift* 102 (2009), 589–614.

Beihammer, Alexander D., "Feindbilder und Konfliktwahrnehmung in den Quellen zum Auftreten der Seldschuken in Kleinasien (ca. 1050–1118)," *Byzantion* 79 (2009), 48–98.

Beihammer, Alexander D., "Defection across the Border of Islam and Christianity: Apostasy and Cross-Cultural Interaction in Byzantine-Seljuk Relations," *Speculum* 86 (2011), 597–651.

Beihammer, Alexander D., "Orthodoxy and Religious Antagonism in Byzantine Perceptions of the Seljuk Turks (Eleventh and Twelfth Centuries)," *Al-Masāq: Islam and the Medieval Mediterranean* 23 (2011), 15–36.

Beihammer, Alexander D., "Muslim Rulers Visiting the Imperial City: Building Alliances and Personal Networks between Constantinople and the Eastern Borderlands (Fourth/Tenth-Fifth/Eleventh Century)," *Al-Masāq: Islam and the Medieval Mediterranean* 24 (2012), 157–177.

Belke, Klaus, *Paphlagonien und Honōrias*, Österreichische Akademie der Wissenschaften, Denkschriften der philosophisch-historischen Klasse 249 = Tabula Imperii Byzantini 9 (Vienna, 1996).

Belke, Klaus, and Mersich, Norbert, *Phrygien und Pisidien*, Österreichische Akademie der Wissenschaften, Denkschriften der philosophisch-historischen Klasse 211 = Tabula Imperii Byzantini 7 (Vienna, 1990).

Belke, Klaus, and Restle, Marcell, *Galatien und Lykaonien*, Österreichische Akademie der Wissenschaften, Denkschriften der philosophisch-historischen Klasse 172 = Tabula Imperii Byzantini 4 (Vienna, 1984).

Bezer, Gülay Öğün, "Harput'ta bir Türkmen Beyliği Çubukoğulları," *Belleten* 61 (1997), 67–92.

Bianquis, Thierry, *Damas et la Syrie sous la domination Fatimide (359–468/969–1076): Essai d'interprétation de chroniques arabes médiévales*, 2 vols. (Damascus, 1986–1989).

Blessing, Patricia, *Rebuilding Anatolia after the Mongol Conquest: Islamic Architecture in the Lands of Rūm, 1240–1330*, Birmingham Byzantine and Ottoman Studies 17 (Farnham, 2014).

Bosworth, Clifford Edmund, *The Ghaznavids: Their Empire in Afghanistan and Eastern Iran 994–1040* (Edinburgh, 1963).

Bosworth, Clifford Edmund, "The Political and Dynastic History of the Iranian World (A.D. 1000–1217)," in *The Cambridge History of Iran*, 5: *The Saljuq and Mongol Periods*, ed. Boyle, pp. 1–202.

Boyle, John Andrew, *The Cambridge History of Iran*, 5: *The Saljuq and Mongol Periods* (Cambridge, 1968).

Brett, Michael, "The Near East on the Eve of the Crusades," in *La Primera Cruzada*, ed. Ramos, pp. 119–136, reprint in *The Eastern Mediterranean Frontier of Latin Christendom*, ed. Stuckey, pp. 285–302.
Brubaker, Leslie, and Haldon, John, *Byzantium in the Iconoclast Era, c. 680–850: A History* (Cambridge, Eng., 2011).
Buckler, Georgina, *Anna Comnena: A Study* (Oxford, 1929, reprint 2000).
Cahen, Claude, "La campagne de Mantzikert d'après les sources musulmanes," *Byzantion* 9 (1934), 628–642, reprint in idem, *Turcobyzantina*, no. II.
Cahen, Claude, "Le Diyar Bakr au Temps des Premiers Urtukides," *Journal Asiatique* (1935), 219–276.
Cahen, Claude, "La première pénétration turque en Asie-Mineure," *Byzantion* 18 (1946–48), 5–67, reprint in idem, *Turcobyzantina*, no. I.
Cahen, Claude, "Le Malik-nameh et l'histoire des origines seljukides," *Oriens* 2 (1949), 31–65.
Cahen, Claude, "Une campagne du Seldjukide Alp-Arslan en Géorgie," *Bédi Kartlisa (Revue de Kartvélologie)* 41–42 (1962), 17–20, reprint in idem, *Turcobyzantina*, no. VII.
Cahen, Claude, "Qutlumush et ses fils avant l'Asie Mineure," *Der Islam* 39 (1964), 14–27, reprint in idem, *Turcobyzantina*, no. V.
Cahen, Claude, *Pre-Ottoman Turkey: A General Survey of the Material and Spiritual Culture and History c. 1071–1330*, trans. J. Jones-Williams (New York, 1968).
Cahen, Claude, *Turcobyzantina et Oriens Christianus* (London, 1974).
Cahen, Claude, *Les peuples musulmans dans l'histoire médiévale* (Damas, 1977).
Cahen, Claude, *The Formation of Turkey: The Seljukid Sultanate of Rūm, Eleventh to Fourteenth Century*, trans. Peter Malcom Holt (Harlow, Eng., 2001).
Cahen, Claude, "The Historiography of the Seljuqid period," in idem, *Peuples musulmans*, pp. 37–63.
Çakmakoğlu Kuru, Alev, "Çankırı Fatihi Emir Karatekin'in Türbesi," *Bilig* 43 (2007), 63–84.
Canard, Marius, *Histoire de la dynastie des H'amdanides de Jazira et de Syrie* (Algiers, 1951).
Canard, Marius, "La campagne arménienne du sultan salğuqide Alp Arslān et la prise d'Ani en 1064," *Revue des Études Arménienne* 2 (1965), 239–59.
Cappel, Andrew J., "The Byzantine Response to the 'Arab (10th–11th Centuries)," *Byzantinische Forschungen* 20 (1994), 113–132.
Carile, Antonio, "Il cesare Niceforo Briennio," *Aevum* 42 (1968), pp. 429–454.
Carile, Antonio, "La Ὕλη Ἱστορίας del cesare Niceforo Briennio," *Aevum* 43 (1969), pp. 56–87, 235–282.
Celâl, Güzel Hasan, Cem, Oğuz C., Osman, Karatay, eds., *The Turks*, 2: *Middle Ages* (Ankara, 2002).
Çetin, Kenan, *Selçuklu Medeniyeti Tarihi* (Istanbul, 2011).
Chalandon, Ferdinand, *Les Comnène: Étude sur l'empire byzantine aux XIe et XIIe siècles*, 1: *Essai sur le règne d'Alexis Ier Comnène (1081–1118)*, 2: *Jean II Comnène (1118–1143) et Manuel Comnène (1143–1180)* (Paris, 1900–1912; repr. New York, n. d.).
Cheynet, Jean-Claude, "Mantzikert : un désastre militaire?," *Byzantion* 50 (1980), 411–438.
Cheynet, Jean-Claude, "Thathoul, Archonte des Archontes," *Revue des Études Byzantines* 48 (1990), 233–242.
Cheynet, Jean-Claude, *Pouvoir et contestations à Byzance (963–1210)*, Byzantina Sorbonensia 9 (Paris, 1996).
Cheynet, Jean-Claude, "La résistance aux Turcs en Asie Mineure entre Mantzikert et la première croisade," in *ΕΥΨΥΧΙΑ, Mélanges offerts à Hélène Ahrweiler*, Byzantina Sorbonensia 16, 2 vols. (Paris, 1998), 1:131–147.

Chrysostomides, Julian, "The Byzantine Empire from the Eleventh to the Fifteenth Century," in *Cambridge History of Turkey*, ed. Fleet, pp. 6–50.

Coureas, Nicos, and Riley-Smith, Jonathan, eds., *Cyprus and the Crusades: Papers given at the International Conference 'Cyprus and the Crusades', Nicosia, 6–9 September, 1994* (Nicosia, 1995).

Cutler, Anthony, "Gifts and Gift Exchange as Aspects of the Byzantine, Arab, and Related Economies," *Dumbarton Oaks Papers* 55 (2001), 247–78.

Dagron, Gilbert, "Minorités ethniques et religieuses dans l'orient byzantin à la fin du Xe et au XIe siècle: l'immigration syrienne," *Travaux et Mémoires* 6 (1976), 177–216.

Decker, Michael, "Settlement and Economy in the Byzantine East," *Dumbarton Oaks Papers* 61 (2007), 217–267.

Dédéyan, Gérard, "Les Arméniens en Cappadoce aux Xe et XIe siècles," in *Le aree omogenee della civiltà rupestre nell'ambito dell'impero bizantino: la Cappadocia, Atti del quinto convegno internazionale di studio sulla civiltà rupestre medioevale nel mezzogiorno d'Italia (Lecce-Nardò, 12-16 ottobre 1979)*, ed. Cosimo Damiano Fonseca (Galatina, 1981), pp. 75–95.

Dédéyan, Gérard, *Les arméniens entre grecs, musulmans et croisés: Étude sur les pouvoirs arméniens dans le Proche-Orient méditerranéen (1068–1150)*, 2 vols. (Lisbon, 2003).

De Gregorio, Giuseppe, and Kresten, Otto, eds., *Documenti medievali Greci e Latini: studi comparative* (Spoleto, 1998).

Demirkent, Işın, *Türkiye Selçuklu Hükümdarı Sultan I. Kılıç Arslan*, Türk Tarih Kurumu Yayınları XXIV. Dizi - Sa. 22 (Ankara, 2006).

Dirimtekin, Feridun, "Selçukluların Anadolu'da Yerleşmelerini ve Gelişmelerini Sağlayan İki Zafer," in *Malazgirt Armağanı*, pp. 231–58.

Divitçioğlu, Sencer, *Oğuz'dan Selçuklu'ya (Boy, Konat ve Devlet)* (Istanbul, 1994).

Dölger, Franz, and Wirth, Peter, *Regesten der Kaiserurkunden des oströmischen Reiches*, 2: *Regesten von 1025–1204*, 2nd revised edition (Munich, 1995).

Donohue, John J., *The Buwayhid Dynasty in Iraq 334 H./945 to 403 H./1012: Shaping Institutions for the Future*, Islamic History and Civilization, Studies and Texts 44 (Leiden, Boston, 2003).

Drews, Wolfram, *Die Karolinger und die Abbasiden von Bagdad: Legitimationsstrategien frühmittelalterlicher Herrscherdynastien im transkulturellen Vergleich* (Berlin, 2009).

Duran, Remzi, "Konya Alâeddin Camisi Kitâbeleri," in *Anadolu Selçukluları ve Beylikler Dönemi* 2, ed. Peker and Bilici, pp. 23–29.

Durand-Guédy, David, "Iranians at War under Turkish Domination: The Example of Pre-Mongol Isfahan," *Iranian Studies* 38 (2005), 587–606.

Durand-Guédy, David, *Iranian Elites and Turkish Rulers: A History of Isfahan in the Saljuq Period*, Routledge Studies in the History of Iran and Turkey (London and New York, 2010).

Durmaz, Sayime, "Haçlılar, Bizans ve Selçuklular," in *Anadolu Selçukluları ve Beylikler Dönemi* 1, ed. Ocak, pp. 37–53.

Durukan, Aynur, "Banîler," in *Anadolu Selçukluları ve Beylikler Dönemi* 2, ed. Peker and Bilici, pp. 137–171.

Eastmond, Antony, ed., *Eastern Approaches to Byzantium: Papers from the Thirty-Third Spring Symposium of Byzantine Studies, University of Warwick, Coventry, March 1999* (Aldershot, 2001).

Eger, A. Asa, "(Re)Mapping Medieval Antioch: Urban Transformations from the Early Islamic to the Middle Byzantine Periods," *Dumbarton Oaks Papers* 67 (2013), 95–134.

Eger, Alexander Asa, *The Islamic-Byzantine Frontier: Interaction and Exchange among Muslim and Christian Communities* (London, 2015).

Eger, Asa, "Ḥiṣn al-Tīnāt on the Islamic-Byzantine Frontier: Synthesis and the 2005–2008 Excavation on the Cilician Plain (Turkey)," *Bulletin of the American School of Oriental Research* 357 (2010), 49–76.

El-Azhari, Taef Kamal, *The Saljūqs of Syria during the Crusades 463–549 A. H./1070–1154 A. D.*, Islamkundliche Untersuchungen 211 (Berlin, 1997).

El Cheikh, Nadia Maria, *Byzantium Viewed by the Arabs*, Harvard Middle Eastern Monographs 36 (Cambridge, MA, 2004).

Elisséeff, Nikita, *Nūr ad-Dīn, un grand prince musulman de Syrie au temps des croisades (511-569 h./1118–1174)*, 3 vols. (Damascus, 1967).

Erkiletlioğlu, Halit, and Güler, Oğuz, *Türkiye Selçuklu Sultanları ve Sikkeleri* (Kayseri, 1996).

Ersan, Mehmet, *Selçuklular Zamanında Anadolu'da Ermeniler*, Türk Tarih Kurumu Yayınları XIX. Dizi, no. 21 (Ankara, 2007).

Eser, Erdal, "Anadolu-Suriye Sanat İlişkileri," in *Anadolu Selçukluları ve Beylikler Dönemi* 2, ed. Peker and Bilici, pp. 67–73.

Farag, W., "The Aleppo Question: A Byzantine-Fatimid Conflict of Interests in Northern Syria in the Later Tenth Century A.D." *Byzantine and Modern Greek Studies* 14 (1990), 44–61.

Felix, Wolfgang, *Byzanz und die islamische Welt im frühen 11. Jahrhundert*, Byzantina Vindobonensia 14 (Vienna, 1981).

Fink, Harold, "The Foundation of the Latin States, 1099–1118," in *History of the Crusades*, ed. Setton and Baldwin, 1:368–409.

Fleet, Kate, ed., *The Cambridge History of Turkey*, 1: *Byzantium to Turkey 1071–1453* (Cambridge, Eng., 2009).

Foss, Clive, "Archaeology and the "Twenty Cities" of Byzantine Asia," *American Journal of Archaeology* 81 (1977), 469–86, reprint in idem, *History and Archaeology of Byzantine Asia Minor*, no. II.

Foss, Clive, "Late Antique and Byzantine Ankara," *Dumbarton Oaks Papers* 31 (1977), 29–87, reprint in idem, *History and Archaeology of Byzantine Asia Minor*, no. VI.

Foss, Clive, *Ephesus after Antiquity: A Late Antique, Byzantine and Turkish City* (Cambridge, 1979).

Foss, Clive, "Late Byzantine Fortifications in Lydia," *Jahrbuch der Österreichischen Byzantinistik* 28 (1979), 297–320, reprint in idem, *Cities, Fortresses and Villages in Byzantine Asia Minor*, no. VI.

Foss, Clive, "The Defenses of Asia Minor against the Turks," *Greek Orthodox Theological Review* 27 (1982), 145–205, reprint in idem, *Cities, Fortresses and Villages in Byzantine Asia Minor*, no. V.

Foss, Clive, "Byzantine Malagina and the Lower Sangarius," *Anatolian Studies* 40 (1990), 161–183, reprint in idem, *Cities, Fortresses and Villages of Byzantine Asia Minor*, no. VII.

Foss, Clive, *History and Archaeology of Byzantine Asia Minor*, Collected Studies Series (Aldershot, 1990).

Foss, Clive, "Lycia in History," in *The Fort of Dereağzi*, ed. J. Morganstern (Tübingen, 1993), pp. 5–25, reprint in idem, *Cities, Fortresses and Villages of Byzantine Asia Minor*, no. I.

Foss, Clive, "The Lycian Coast in the Byzantine Age," *Dumbarton Oaks Papers* 48 (1994), 1–52, reprint in idem, *Cities, Fortresses and Villages of Byzantine Asia Minor*, no. II.

Foss, Clive, *Cities, Fortresses and Villages of Byzantine Asia Minor*, Collected Studies Series (Aldershot, 1996).

Foss, Clive, "The Cities of Pamphylia in the Byzantine Age," in idem, *Cities, Fortresses and Villages in Byzantine Asia Minor*, no. IV.

Foss, Clive, and Winfield, David, *Byzantine Fortifications: An Introduction* (Pretoria, 1986).

Frankopan, Peter, "The Fall of Nicaea and the Towns of Western Asia Minor to the Turks in the Later 11th Century: The Curious Case of Nikephoros Melissenos," *Byzantion* 76 (2006), 153–184.

Frankopan, Peter, *The First Crusade: The Call from the East* (Cambridge, MA., 2012).

Frassetto, Michael, and Blanks, David R., eds., *Western Views of Islam in Medieval and Early Modern Europe: Perceptions of Other* (Houndsmill, 1999).

Garsoïan, Nina G., "The Problem of Armenian Integration into the Byzantine Empire," in *Studies on the Internal Diaspora*, ed. Ahrweiler and Laiou, pp. 53–124.

Gastgeber, Christian, "Das Schreiben Alexios I. Komnenos an Robert I. von Flandern. Sprachliche Untersuchung," in *Documenti medievali Greci e Latini*, ed. de Gregorio and Kresten, pp. 141–185.

Gate, James Lea, "The Crusade of 1101," in *History of the Crusades*, ed. Setton and Baldwin, 1:343–367.

Gibbon, Herbert Adams, *The Foundation of the Ottoman Empire: A History of the Osmanlis up to the Death of Bayezid I (1300–1403)* (New York, 1916).

Goetz, Hans-Werner, *Geschichtsschreibung und Geschichtsbewußtsein im hohen Mittelalter*, Vorstellungswelten des Mittelalters 1 (Berlin, 1999).

Göksu, Erkan, *Türkiye Selçuklularında Ordu*, Türk Tarih Kurumu Yayınları IV/A-2-1.2. Dizi - Sayı 1 (Ankara, 2010).

Golden, Peter, *An Introduction to the History of the Turkic Peoples: Ethnogenesis and State-Foundation in Medieval and Early Modern Eurasia and the Middle East* (Wiesbaden, 1992).

Gouma-Peterson, Thalia, ed., *Anna Komnene and her Times* (New York and London, 2000).

Haldon, John, *Warfare, State and Society in the Byzantine World, 565–1204* (London, 1999).

Haldon, John, *The Palgrave Atlas of Byzantine History* (London, New York, 2005).

Haldon, John, "Approaches to an Alternative Military History of the Period ca. 1025–1071," in *The Empire in Crisis*, ed. Vlyssidou, pp. 45–74.

Haldon, John, Gaffney, Vince, Theodoropoulos, Georgios, Murgatroyd, Phil, "Marching across Anatolia: Medieval Logistics and Modeling the Mantzikert Campaign," *Dumbarton Oaks Papers* 65–66 (2011–2012), 209–235.

Haldon, John F., and Kennedy, Hugh, "The Arab-Byzantine Frontier in the Eighth and Ninth Centuries: Military Organisation and Society in the Borderlands," *Zbornik Radova* 19 (1980), 79–116.

Haldon, John, et al., "The Climate and Environment of Byzantine Anatolia: Integrating Science, History, and Archaeology," *Journal of Interdisciplinary History* 45 (2014), 113–161.

Halm, Heinz, *Die Kalifen von Kairo: Die Fatimiden in Ägypten 973–1074* (Munich, 2003).

Hanne, Eric J., *Putting the Caliph in His Place: Power, Authority, and the Late Abbasid Caliphate* (Madison, Teaneck, 2007).

Harris, Jonathan, *Byzantium and the Crusades* (Hambledon and London, 2003).

Harvey, Alan, *Economic Expansion in the Byzantine Empire 900–1200* (Cambridge, Eng., 1989).

Harvey, Alan, "Competition for Economic Resources: The State, Landowners and Fiscal Privileges," in *Empire in Crisis*, ed. Vlyssidou, pp. 169–177.

Heather, Peter, *Der Untergang des Römischen Weltreichs*, trans. Klaus Kochmann (Stuttgart, 2007).

Heidemann, Stefan, *Die Renaissance der Städte in Nordsyrien und Nordmesopotamien: Städtische Entwicklungen und wirtschaftliche Bedingungen in ar-Raqqa und Harrān in der Zeit der beduinischen Vorherrschaft bis zu den Seldschuken*, Islamic History and Civilization 40 (Leiden, 2002).

Hellenkemper, Hansgerd, and Hild, Friedrich, *Lykien und Pamphylien*, Österreichische Akademie der Wissenschaften, Denkschriften der philosophisch-historischen Klasse 320 = Tabula Imperii Byzantini 8, 3 vols. (Vienna, 2004).

Hild, Friedrich, and Restle, Marcel, *Kappadokien (Kappadokia, Charsianon, Sebasteia und Lykandos)*, Österreichische Akademie der Wissenschaften, Denkschriften der philosophisch-historischen Klasse 149 = Tabula Imperii Byzantini 2 (Vienna, 1981).

Hild, Friedrich, and Hellenkemper, Hansgerd, *Kilikien und Isaurien*, Österreichische Akademie der Wissenschaften, Denkschriften der philosophisch-historischen Klasse 215 = Tabula Imperii Byzantini 5 (Vienna, 1990).

Hillenbrand, Carole, "The Career of Najm al-Dīn İl-Ghāzī," *Der Islam* 58 (1981), 250–292.

Hillenbrand, Carole, "The Establishment of Artuqid Power in Diyār Bakr in the Twelfth Century," *Studia Islamica* 54 (1981), 129–153.

Hillenbrand, Carole, *The Crusades: Islamic Perspectives* (Edinburgh, 1999).

Hillenbrand, Carole, *Turkish Myth and Muslim Symbol: The Battle of Manzikert* (Edinburgh, 2007).

Hillenbrand, Carole, "'Abominable Acts': The Career of Zengi," in *The Second Crusade: Scope and Consequences*, ed. Phillips and Hoch, pp. 111–132.

Holmes, Catherine, *Basil II and the Governance of Empire (976–1025)*, Oxford Studies in Byzantium (Oxford, 2005).

Horst, Heribert, *Die Staatsverwaltung der Grosselǧūqen und Ḫōrazmšāhs (1038–1231): Eine Untersuchung nach Urkundenformularen der Zeit*, Akademie der Wissenschaften und der Literatur, Veröffentlichungen der Orientalischen Kommission 18 (Wiesbaden, 1964).

Hunger, Herbert, *Die hochsprachliche profane Literatur der Byzantiner*, 2 vols., Handbuch der Altertumswissenschaft XII, Byzantinisches Handbuch 5.1–2 (Munich, 1978).

Imber, Colin, "The Ottoman Dynastic Myth," *Turcica* 19 (1987), 7–27.

İnalcık, Halil, "Ottoman Methods of Conquest," *Studia Islamica* 2 (1954), 104–129, reprinted in idem, *Ottoman Empire*, no. I.

İnalcık, Halil, *The Ottoman Empire: Conquest, Organization and Economy: Collected Studies* (London, 1978).

İpekoğlu, Başak, "Birleşik İşlevli Yapılar," in *Anadolu Selçukluları ve Beylikler Dönemi* 2, ed. Peker and Bilici, pp. 111–125.

Irwin, Robert, "The Impact of the Early Crusades on the Muslim World," in *La Primera Cruzada*, ed. Ramos, pp. 137–151, reprint in *The Eastern Mediterranean Frontier of Latin Christendom*, ed. Stuckey, pp. 303–317.

Islam Ansiklopedisi: Islam Alemi Tarih, Coğrafya, Etnoğrafya ve Bioğrafya lügati, ed. Martijn Theodoor Houtsma et al., 13 vols. (Istanbul, 1940–1988).

Jaspert, Nikolas, "Die Wahrnehmung der Muslime im lateinischen Europa der späten Salierzeit," in: *Salisches Kaisertum und neues Europa*, ed. Schneidmüller and Weinfurter, pp. 307–340.

Kaegi, Walter E., "The Contribution of Archery to the Turkish Conquest of Anatolia," *Speculum* 39 (1964), 96–108.

Kafadar, Cemal, *Between Two Worlds: The Construction of the Ottoman State* (Berkeley, 1995).

Kafali Mustafa, "The Conquest and Turkification of Anatolia," in *The Turks*, 2: *Middle Ages*, ed. Celâl, Cem, Osman, pp. 401–417.

Kafesoğlu, İbrahim, *Sultan Melikşah Devrinde Büyük Selçuklu İmparatorluğu*, İstanbul Üniversitesi Edebiyat Fakültesi Yayınlarından 569 (Istanbul, 1953).

Karpozilos, Apostolos, *Βυζαντινοί ιστορικοί και χρονογράφοι*, 3: *(11ος-12ος αι.)* (Athens, 2009).

Kaya, Selim, *I. Gıyâseddin Keyhüsrev ve II. Süleymanşah Dönemi Selçuklu Tarihi (1192–1211)*, Türk Tarih Kurumu Yayınları XIX. Dizi - Sayı 20 (Ankara, 2006).

Kaymaz, Nejat, "Malazgirt Savaşı ile Anadolu'nun Fethi ve Türkleşmesine Dair," in *Malazgirt Armağanı*, pp. 259–68.

Kazhdan, Alexander P., and Epstein, Ann Wharton, *Change in Byzantine Culture in the Eleventh and Twelfth Centuries* (Berkeley, Los Angeles, London, 1985).

Kesik, Muharrem, *Türkiye Selçuklu Devleti Tarihi Sultan I. Mesud Dönemi (1116–1155)*, Türk Tarih Kurumu Yayınları XIX. Dizi - Sa. 19 (Ankara, 2003).

Kesik, Muharrem, "Cenâbî'ye göre Türkiye Selçukluları," *İstanbul Üniversitesi Edebiyat Fakültesi Tarih Dergisi* 36 (2000), 213–259.

Kesik, Muharrem, *At üstünde Selçuklular: Türkiye Selçukluları'nda Ordu ve Savaş* (Istanbul, 2011).

Kesik, Muharrem, *1071 Malazgirt: Zafere Giden Yol* (Istanbul, 2013).

Klausner, Carla L., *The Seljuk Vizierate: A Study of Civil Administration 1055–1194* (Cambridge, MA, 1973).

Koca, Salim, "Türkiye Selçuklu Devleti'nin Kuruluşu ve I. Süleyman-Şâh," in *Anadolu Selçukluları ve Beylikler Dönemi* 1, ed. Ocak, pp. 23–35.

Köprülü, Mehmet Fuad, *Les origines de l'empire ottoman*, Études Orientales publiées par l'Institut français d'archéologie de Stamboul 3 (Paris, 1935).

Köprülü, Mehmet Fuad, *Anadolu Selçukluları Tarihinin Yerli Kaynakları I* (Ankara, 1943).

Korobeinikov, Dimitri A., "Raiders and Neighbours: The Turks (1040–1304)," in *The Cambridge History of the Byzantine Empire*, ed. Shepard, pp. 692–727.

Köymen, Mehmet Altay, *Selçuklu Devri Türk Tarihi*, Ankara Üniversitesi Dil ve Tarih-Coğrafya Fakültesi Yayınları 328, 2nd ed. (Ankara, 1982).

Köymen, Mehmet Altay, *Büyük Selçuklu İmparatorluğu Tarihi*, 1: *Kuruluş Devri*, Türk Tarih Kurumu Yayınları VII. Dizi – Sa. 23a (Ankara, 1989).

Köymen, Mehmet Altay, *Büyük Selçuklu İmparatorluğu Tarihi*, 2: *İkinci İmparatorluk Devri*, Türk Tarih Kurumu Yayınları VII. Dizi – Sa. 23a (Ankara, 1991).

Köymen, Mehmet Altay, *Büyük Selçuklu İmparatorluğu Tarihi*, 3: *Alp Arslan ve Zamanı*, Türk Tarih Kurumu Yayınları VII. Dizi – Sa. 23b (Ankara, 1992).

Krallis, Dimitris, *Michael Attaleiates and the Politics of Imperial Decline in Eleventh Century Byzantium* (Tempe, 2012).

Kreiser, Klaus, *Der osmanische Staat 1300–1922*, Oldenbourg Grundriss der Geschichte 30 (Munich, 2001).

Kreiser, Klaus, and Neumann, Christoph G., *Kleine Geschichte der Türkei*, 2nd ed. (Stuttgart, 2008).

Kuban, Doğan, "Mimarî Tasarım," in *Anadolu Selçukluları ve Beylikler Dönemi* 2, ed. Peker and Bilici, pp. 83–109.

Küçükhüseyin, Şevket, *Selbst- und Fremdwahrnehmung im Prozess kultureller Transformation: Anatolische Quellen über Muslime, Christen und Türken (11.-15. Jahrhundert)*, Österreichische Akademie der Wissenschaften, Sitzungsberichte der philosophisch-historischen Klasse 825 (Vienna, 2011).

Kurat, Akdes Nimet, *Çaka Bey, Izmir ve Civarındaki Adaların İlk Türk Beyi M. S. 1081–1096*, Türk Kültürünü Araştırma Enstitüsü Yayınları 24, Seri 9, no. B2, 3rd ed. (Ankara, 1966).

Lambton, Ann K. S., *Continuity and Change in Medieval Persia: Aspects of Administrative and Social History, 11th–14th century* (London, 1988).

Lambton, Ann K. S., "The Internal Structure of the Saljuq Empire," in *The Cambridge History of Iran*, 5: *The Saljuq and Mongol* Periods, ed. Boyle, pp. 203–302.

Lampakis, Stelios, ed., *Η Βυζαντινή Μικρά Ασία (6ος-12ος αι.)*, Institute for Byzantine Research, International Symposium 6 (Athens, 1998).

Lange, Christian, and Songül, Mecit, eds., *The Seljuqs: Politics, Society and Culture* (Edinburgh, 2011).

Lapina, Elizabeth, "The Problem of Eyewitnesses in the Chronicles of the First Crusade," *Viator* 38 (2007), 117–139.

Laurent, Joseph, *Byzance et les Turcs Seldjoucides dans l'Asie occidentale jusqu'en 1081*, Faculté des Lettres de l'Université de Nancy, Annales de l'Est, 27/1 (Paris, 1913).

Lemerle, Paul, *Cinq études sur le XIe siècle byzantin* (Paris, 1977).

Leppin, Hartmut, *Theodosius der Große: Auf dem Weg zum christlichen Imperium* (Darmstadt, 2003).

Lev, Yacov, "The Fatimids and Byzantium, 10th-12th Centuries," *Graeco-Arabica* 6 (1995), 190–208 and 7–8 (1999–2000), 273–281.

Leveniotis, Georgios A., *Το στασιαστικό κίνημα του Νορμανδού Ουρσελίου (Ursel de Bailleul) στην Μικρά Ασία (1073–1076)*, Εταιρεία Βυζαντινών Ερευνών 19 (Thessalonica, 2004).

Leveniotis, Georgios A., *Η πολιτική κατάρρευση του Βυζαντίου στην Ανατολή: Το ανατολικό σύνορο και η κεντρική Μικρά Ασία κατά το β΄ ήμισυ του 11ου αι.*, 2 vols., Byzantine Texts and Studies, 43/1–2 (Thessalonica, 2007).

Lightfoot, C. S., "The Amorium Project: The 1996 Excavation Season," *Dumbarton Oaks Papers* 52 (1998), 323–336.

Lightfood, C. S., and Ivison, Eric A., "The Amorium Project: The 1995 Excavation Season," *Dumbarton Oaks Papers* 51 (1997), 291–300.

Lightfood, C. S., and Ivison, Eric A., "The Amorium Project: The 1998 Excavation Season," *Dumbarton Oaks Papers* 55 (2001), 371–399.

Lightfood, C. S., et al., "The Amorium Project: The 1997 Study Season," *Dumbarton Oaks Papers* 53 (1999), 333–349.

Lightfood, C. S., Arbel, Y., Böhlendorf-Arslan, B., Roberts, J. A., Witte-Orr, J., "The Amorium Project: Research and Excavation in 2000," *Dumbarton Oaks Papers* 58 (2004), 355–370.

Lightfood, C. S., Arbel, Y., Ivison, E. A., Roberts, J. A., Ioannidou, E., "The Amorium Project: Research and Excavation in 2002," *Dumbarton Oaks Papers* 59 (2005), 231–265.

Lightfood, C. S., Mergen, Y., Olcay, B. Y., Witte-Orr, J., "The Amorium Project: Research and Excavation in 2000," *Dumbarton Oaks Papers* 57 (2003), 279–292.

Lilie, Ralph-Johannes, *Byzantium and the Crusader States 1096–1204*, trans. J. C. Morris and Jean E. Ridings (Oxford, 1993).

Lindner, Rudi Paul, *Nomads and Ottomans in Medieval Anatolia*, Indiana University Uralic and Altaic Series 144 (Indiana University, Bloomington, 1983).

Lounghis, Telemachos C., *Byzantium in the Eastern Mediterranean: Safeguarding East Roman Identity (407–1204)*, Texts and Studies in the History of Cyprus 63 (Nicosia, 2010).

Lowry, Heath W., *The Nature of the Early Ottoman State* (State University of New York, 2003).

MacEvitt, Christopher, "The Chronicle of Matthew of Edessa: Apocalypse, the First Crusade, and the Armenian Diaspora," *Dumbarton Oaks Papers* 61 (2007), 157–181.

Madden, Thomas F., Naus, James L., and Ryan, Vincent, eds., *Crusades: Medieval Worlds in Conflict* (Farnham, 2010).

Magdalino, Paul, "The Pen of the Aunt: Echoes of the Mid-Twelfth Century in the Alexiad," in *Anna Komnene and her Times*, ed. Gouma Peterson, pp. 15–43.

Malamut, Elisabeth, "L'image byzantine des Petchénègues," *Byzantinische Zeitschrift* 88 (1995), 105–147.
Malazgirt Armağanı, Türk Tarih Kurumu Yayınları XIX. Seri – Sa. 4a, 2nd ed. (Ankara, 1993).
Matuz, Josef, *Das osmanische Reich: Grundlinien seiner Geschichte*, 4th ed. (Darmstadt, 2006).
Mayer, Hans Eberhard, *Geschichte der Kreuzzüge*, 9th ed. (Stuttgart, 2000).
Mecit, Songül, *The Rum Seljuqs: Evolution of a Dynasty*, Routledge Studies in the History of Iran and Turkey (London, 2014).
Melville, Charles, "Anatolia under the Mongols," in *C ambridge History of Turkey*, ed. Fleet, pp. 51–101.
Merçil, Erdoğan, *Gazneliler Devleti Tarihi*, Türk Tarih Kurumu Yayınları XXI. Dizi – Sayı 111 (Istanbul, 2007).
Merçil, Erdoğan, *Selçuklular'da Hükümdarlık Alâmetleri*, Türk Tarih Kurumu Yayınları VII. Dizi – Sayı 227 (Ankara, 2007).
Merçil, Erdoğan, *Büyük Selçuklu Devleti, Siyasi Tarih*, 4th ed. (Ankara, 2012).
Merçil, Erdoğan, *Müslüman Türk Devletleri Tarihi*, 8th ed. (Istanbul, 2013).
Metcalf, D. M., *Byzantine Lead Seals from Cyprus*, Texts and Studies of the History of Cyprus 47 (Nicosia, 2004).
Mouton, Jean-Michel, *Damas et sa principauté sous les Saljoukides et les Bourides 468–549/1076–1154, vie politique et religieuse*, Institut Français d'Archéologie Orientale, Textes arabes et études islamiques 33 (Cairo, 1994).
Müller, Andreas, with the collaboration of Beihammer, Alexander, *Regesten der Kaiserurkunden des oströmischen Reiches bearbeitet von Franz Dölger*, 1.2: *Regesten von 867–1025*, 2nd revised ed. (Munich, 2003).
Murray, Alan V., "William of Tyre and the Origin of the Turks: Observations on Possible Sources of the Gesta Orientalium Principum," in *Dei gesta per Francos*, ed. Balard, Kedar, and Riley-Smith, pp. 217–229.
Mutafian, Claude, *L'Arménie du Levant (XIe-XIVe siècle)*, 2 vols. (Paris, 2012).
Noth, Albrecht, *The Early Arabic Historical Tradition: A Source-Critical Study*, second edition in collaboration with Lawrence I. Conrad, trans. from the German by Michael Bonner, Studies in Late Antiquity an Early Islam 3 (Princeton, 1994).
Ocak, Ahmet Yaşar, "Anadolu Selçukluları ve Beylikler Dönemi Uygarlık Tarihi Araştırmalarına Genel Bir Bakış," in *Anadolu Selçukluları ve Beylikler Dönemi* 1, ed. Ocak, pp. 13–19.
Ocak, Ahmet Yaşar, ed., *Anadolu Selçukluları ve Beylikler Dönemi Uygarlığı*, 1: *Sosyal ve Siyasal Hayat* (Ankara, 2006).
Oikonomidès, Nicolas, *Les listes de préséance byzantines des IXe et Xe siècles. Introduction, texte, traduction et commentaire* (Paris, 1972).
Oikonomidès, Nicolas, "L'organisation de la frontière orientale de Byzance aux Xe - XIe siècles et le Taktikon de l'Escorial," in *Actes du XIVe Congrès International des Études Byzantines, Bucarest, 6–12 Septembre, 1971*, ed. M. Berza and E. Stănescu (Bucarest, 1974), pp. 285–302.
Öngül, Ali, *Selçuklular Tarihi*, 1: *Büyük Selçuklular, Irak, Kirman ve Suriye Selçukluları* (Istanbul, 2013).
Öngül, Ali, *Selçuklular Tarihi*, 2: *Anadolu Selçukluları ve Beylikler* (Istanbul, 2013).
Ostrogorsky, Georg, *Geschichte des byzantinischen Staates*, 3rd ed. (Munich, 1963).
Özaydın, Abdülkerim, *Sultan Muhammed Tapar Devri Selçuklu Tarihi (498–511/1105–1118)*, Türk Tarih Kurumu Yayınları XIX. Dizi - Sa. 11 (Ankara, 1990).

Özaydın, Abdülkerim, "Büyük Selçuklu Emîri Kürboğa," *İstanbul Üniversitesi Edebiyat Fakültesi Tarih Dergisi* 36 (2000), 405–421.

Özgüdenli, Osman G., "Yeni Paraların Işığında Kuruluş Devri Selçuklularında Hâkimiyet Münasebetleri Hakkında Bazı Düşünceler," *Belleten* 65 (2001), 547–570.

Özgüdenli, Osman G., *Selçuklular,* 1: *Büyük Selçuklu Devleti Tarihi (1040–1157)* (Istanbul, 2013).

Özme, Adil, "Sikke ve Mühür Sanatı," in *Anadolu Selçukluları ve Beylikler Dönemi* 2, ed. Peker and Bilici, pp. 565–573.

Papadopoullos, Theodoros, ed., *Ιστορία της Κύπρου,* 3: *Βυζαντινή Κύπρος* (Nicosia, 2005).

Papageorgiou, Angeliki, "Οἱ δὲ λύκοι ὡς Πέρσαι: The Image of the 'Turks' in the Reign of John II Komnenos (1118–1143)," *Byzantinoslavica* 69 (2011), 149–161.

Parnell, David Alan, "John II Comnenus and Crusader Antioch," in *Crusades: Medieval Worlds in Conflict,* ed. Madden, Naus, and Ryan, pp. 149–160.

Paul, Jürgen, "The Seljūq Conquest(s) of Nishapur: a Reappraisal," *Iranian Studies* 38 (2005), 575–585.

Paul, Jürgen, ed., *Nomad Aristocrats in a World of Empires* (Wiesbaden, 2013).

Peacock, Andrew C. S., "Nomadic Society and the Seljūq Conquest of Caucasia," *Iran and the Caucasus* 9 (2005), 205–230.

Peacock, Andrew C. S., *Early Seljūq History: A New Interpretation* (London and New York, 2010).

Peacock, Andrew C. S., *The Great Seljuk Empire,* The Edinburgh History of the Islamic Empires (Edinburgh, 2015).

Peacock, Andrew C. S., "From the Balkan-Kuhiyan to the Nawakiya: Nomadic Politics and the Foundations of Seljuq Rule in Anatolia," in *Nomad Aristocrats in a World of Empires,* ed. Paul, pp. 60–85.

Peacock, Andrew C. S., "Seljuq Legitimacy in Islamic History," in *The Seljuqs,* ed. Lange and Mecit, pp. 79–95.

Peacock, Andrew C. S., "The Seljuk Sultanate of Rūm and the Turkmen of the Byzantine Frontier, 1206–1279," *Al-Masāq: Journal of the Medieval Mediterranean* 26 (2014), 267–287.

Peacock, Andrew C. S., and Yildiz, Sara Nur, eds., *The Seljuks of Anatolia: Court and Society in the Medieval Middle East* (London and New York, 2013).

Peker, Ali Uzay, "Anadolu Bazilika Geleneği ve Selçuklu Anıtsal Mimarîsine Etkisi," in *Anadolu Selçukluları ve Beylikler Dönemi* 2, ed. Peker and Bilici, pp. 55–65.

Peker, Ali Uzay, "Evrenin Binası Mimarîde Yazı ve Kozmolojik Anlam," in *Anadolu Selçukluları ve Beylikler Dönemi* 2, ed. Peker and Bilici, pp. 31–40.

Peker, Ali Uzay, and Bilici, Kenan, eds., *Anadolu Selçukluları ve Beylikler Dönemi Uygarlığı,* 2: *Mimarlık ve Sanat* (Ankara, 2006).

Pellegrino, Emmanuel, "Présentation des céramiques issues des fouilles ménées en 1998–1999 sur l'acropole lycienne de Xanthos," *Anatolia Antiqua* 11 (2003), 215–221.

Phillips, Jonathan P., ed., *The First Crusade: Origins and Impact* (Manchester, 1997).

Phillips, Jonathan, *The Second Crusade: Extending the Frontiers of Christendom* (New Haven and London, 2007).

Phillips, Jonathan, and Hoch, Martin, eds., *The Second Crusade: Scope and Consequences* (Manchester and New York, 2001).

Piyadeoğlu, Cihan, *Selçuklular'ın Kuruluş Hikayesi Çağrı Bey* (Istanbul, 2011).

Piyadeoğlu, Cihan, *Güneş Ülkesi Horasan, Büyük Selçuklular Dönemi* (Istanbul, 2012).

Pryor, John H., and Jeffreys, Michael J., "Alexios, Bohemond, and Byzantium's Euphrates Frontier: A Tale of the Two Cretans," *Crusades* 11 (2012), 31–86.

Ramos, Luis García-Guijarr, ed., *La Primera Cruzada, Novecientos Años después: El Concilio de Clermont y los Orígines del Movimiento Cruzado* (Madrid, 1997).

Redford, Scott, "The Alaeddin Mosque in Konya Reconsidered," *Artibus Asiae* 51 (1991), 54–74.

Redford, Scott, "Portable Palaces: On the Circulation of Objects and Ideas about Architecture in Medieval Anatolia and Mesopotamia," *Medieval Encounters* 18 (2012), 382–412.

Redford, Scott, "Mamālik and Mamālīk: Decorative and Epigraphic Programs of Anatolian Seljuk Citadels," in *Cities and Citadels in Turkey: From the Iron Age to the Seljuks*, ed. Scott Redford and Nina Ergin, Ancient Near Eastern Studies, Supplement 40 (Leuven, 2013), pp. 305–346.

Redford, Scott, "Medieval Anatolian Arsenals at Sinop and Alanya," in *Harbors and Harbor Cities in the Eastern Mediterranean*, ed. S. Ladstätter, F. Pirson, and T. Schmidts, BYZAS 19 (Istanbul, 2014), pp. 543–552.

Redford, Scott, and Leiser, Gary, *Victory Inscribed. The Seljuk Fetiḥnāme on the Citadel Walls of Antalya, Turkey/Taşa Yazılan Zafer: Antalya İçkale Surlarındaki Selçuklu Fetihnamesi* (Antalya, 2008).

Ripper, Thomas, *Die Marwāniden von Diyār Bakr: Eine kurdische Dynastie im islamischen Mittelalter*, Mitteilungen zur Sozial- und Kulturgeschichte der islamischen Welt 6, 2nd ed. (Würzburg, 2009).

Runicman, Steven, "The First Crusade: Antioch to Ascalon," in Setton and Baldwin, *A History of the Crusades*, pp. 308–341.

Runciman, Steven, "The First Crusade: Constantinople to Antioch," in Setton and Baldwin, *A History of the Crusades*, pp. 280–307.

Sakaoğlu, Necdet, *Türk Anadolu'da Mengücekoğulları*, 2nd ed. (Istanbul, 2004).

Savvides, Alexis G. C., "The Consolidation of Byzantine Power in Cyprus on the Eve of the First Crusade and the First Decades of the Empire's Relations with the Crusaders," in Coureas and Riley-Smith, *Cyprus and the Crusades*, pp. 3–18.

Savvides, Alexis G. K., "Ο Σελτζούκος εμίρης της Σμύρνης Τζαχάς (Çaka) και οι επιδρομές του στα μικρασιατικά παράλια, τα νησιά του ανατολικού Αιγαίου και την Κωνσταντινούπολη, c. 1081-c. 1106, A': c. 1081–1090, B': 1090-c. 1106," *Chiaka Chronika* 14 (1982), 9–24, 16 (1984), 51–66.

Schneidmüller, Bernd, and Weinfurter, Stefan, eds., *Salisches Kaisertum und neues Europa: Die Zeit Heinrichs IV. und Heinrichs V.* (Darmstadt, 2007).

Schreiner, Peter, "Der Brief des Alexios I. Komnenos and den Grafen Robert von Flandern und das Problem gefälschter byzantinischer Kaiserschreiben in den westlichen Quellen," in *Documenti medievali Greci e Latini*, ed. de Gregorio and Kresten, pp. 111–140.

Schreiner, Peter, "Diplomatische Geschenke zwischen Byzanz und dem Westen ca. 800–1200: Eine Analyse der Texte mit Quellenanhang," *Dumbarton Oaks Papers* 58 (2004), 251–282.

Seibt, Werner, "Vasil Goł - Basileios der "Räuber" - Βασίλειος σεβαστὸς καὶ δούξ," *Jahrbuch der Österreichischen Byzantinistik* 58 (2008), 153–58.

Şeker, Fatih M., *Selçuklu Türklerinin İslâm Tasavvuru* (Istanbul, 2011).

Setton, Kenneth M., and Baldwin, Marshall W., eds., *A History of the Crusades*, 1: *The First Hundred Years* (Madison, Milwaukee, and London, 1969).

Sevim, Ali, *Anadolu'nun Fethi Selçuklular Dönemi (başlangıçtan 1086'ya kadar)*, Türk Tarih Kurumu Yayınları XXIV. Dizi, no. 2 (Ankara, 1988).

Sevim, Ali, *Suriye ve Filistin Selçukluları Tarihi*, Türk Tarih Kurumu Yayınları XIX. Dizi – Sa. 7a, 2nd ed. (Ankara, 1989).

Sevim, Ali, *Anadolu Fatihi Kutalmışoğlu Süleymanşah*, Türk Tarih Kurumu Yayınları XXIV. Dizi, no. 13 (Ankara, 1990).

Sevim, Ali, *Ünlü Selçuklu Komutanları Afşin, Atsız, Artuk ve Aksungur*, Türk Tarih Kurumu Yayınları XXIV. Dizi, no. 14 (Ankara, 1990).

Sevim, Ali, *Anadolu'nun Fethi: Selçuklular Dönemi*, Türk Tarih Kurumu Yayınları XXIV. Dizi - Sayı 23 (Ankara, 2014).

Sevim, Ali, "Malazgirt Meydan Savaşı ve Sonuçları," in *Malazgirt Armağanı*, pp. 219–229.

Sevim Ali, and Merçil, Erdoğan, *Selçuklu Devletleri Tarihi: Siyaset, Teşkilât ve Kültür*, Türk Tarih Kurumu Yayınları XXIV. Dizi - Sayı 19 (Ankara, 2014).

Sevim, Ali, and Yücel, Yaşar, *Türkiye Tarihi: Fetih, Selçuklu ve Beylikler Dönemi*, Türk Tarih Kurumu Yayınları XXIV. Dizi, no. 12 (Ankara, 1989).

Shepard, Jonathan, "Scylitzes on Armenia in the 1040s, and the Role of Catacalon Cecaumenos," *Revue des Études Armeniénnes* n. s. 11 (1975–1976), 269–311.

Shepard, Jonathan, "When Greek meets Greek: Alexius Comnenus and Bohemond in 1097–1098," *Byzantine and Modern Greek Studies* 12 (1988), 185–278.

Shepard, Jonathan, "A Suspected Source of Scylitzes' *Synopsis Historion*: the Great Catacalon Cecaumenos," *Byzantine and Modern Greek Studies* 16 (1992), 171–181.

Shepard, Jonathan, ed., *The Cambridge History of the Byzantine Empire c. 500–1492* (Cambridge, Eng., 2008).

Shepard, Jonathan, "Cross-purposes: Alexius Comnenus and the First Crusade," in *The First Crusade: Origins and Impact*, ed. Phillips, pp. 107–129.

Shukurov, Rustam, "Turkoman and Byzantine Self-identity: Some Reflections on the Logic of the Title-Making in Twelfth- and Thirteenth-Century Anatolia," in *Eastern Approaches*, ed. Eastmond, pp. 259–276.

Simpson, Alicia, *Niketas Choniates: A Historiographical Study*, Oxford Studies in Byzantium (Oxford, 2013).

Sode, Claudia, and Takács, Sarolta, eds., *Novum Millenium: Studies on Byzantine History and Culture Dedicated to Paul Speck* (Aldershot, 2000).

Sönmez, Zeki, "Yapı Faaliyetlerinin Organizasyonu: İşveren, Mimar ve Sanatçılar," in *Anadolu Selçukluları ve Beylikler Dönemi* 2, ed. Peker and Bilici, pp. 127–35.

Strohmeier, Martin, *Seldschukische Geschichte und türkische Geschichtswissenschaft: Die Seldschuken im Urteil moderner türkischer Historiker*, Islamkundliche Untersuchungen 97 (Berlin, 1984).

Stuckey, Jace, ed., *The Eastern Mediterranean Frontier of Latin Christendom*, The Expansion of Latin Europe 1000–1500, 6 (Farnham, 2014).

Sümer, Faruk, *Oğuzlar (Türkmenler), Tarihleri – Boy Teşkilatı – Destanları*, Dil ve Tarih Coğrafya Fakültesi Yayınları 170 (Ankara, 1967).

Sümer, Faruk, and Sevim, Ali, *İslâm Kaynaklarına Göre Malazgirt Savaşı (Metinler ve Çevirileri)*, Türk Tarih Kurumu Yayınları XIX. Dizi – Sa. 3a, 2nd ed. (Ankara, 1988).

Suny, Ronald Grigor, *The Making of the Georgian Nation*, 2nd ed. (Indiana, 1994).

Talbot Rice, Tamara, *The Seljuks in Asia Minor* (New York, 1961).

Tekinalp, V. Macit, "Yerel Geleneğin İzleri," in *Anadolu Selçukluları ve Beylikler Dönemi* 2, ed. Peker and Bilici, pp. 45–53.

Tekinalp, V. Macit, "Palace Churches of the Anatolian Seljuks: Tolerance or Necessity," *Byzantine and Modern Greek Studies* 33 (2009), 148–167.

The Encyclopaedia of Islam: New Edition, 12 vols. (Leiden, 1965–2004).

The Oxford Dictionary of Byzantium, ed. Alexander P. Kazhdan, Alice-Mary Talbot, Anthony Cutler, Timothy E. Gregory, and Nancy Ševčenko, 3 vols. (New York and Oxford, 1991).

Thierry, Jean-Michel, "Données archéologiques sur les principautés arméniennes de Cappadoce orientale au XIe siècle," *Revue des Études Arméniennes* 26 (1996–1997), 119–172.

Thomas, R. D., "Anna Comnena's account of the First Crusade: History and Politics in the Reigns of the Emperors Alexius I and Manuel I Comnenus," *Byzantine and Modern Greek Studies* 15 (1991), 269–312.

Todt, Klaus-Peter, *Region und griechisch-orthodoxes Patriarchat von Antiocheia in mittelbyzantinischer Zeit und im Zeitalter der Kreuzzüge (969–1204)*, unpublished habil. diss. (University of Mainz, 1998).

Tolan, John Victor, "Muslims as Pagan Idolaters in Chronicles of the First Crusade," in: *Western Views of Islam in Medieval and Early Modern Europe: Perceptions of Other*, ed. Frassetto and Blanks, pp. 97–117.

Tor, Deborah G., "Mamlūk Loyalty: Evidence from the Late Seljuq Period," *Journal of the British Institute of Persian Studies* 46 (2008), 213–225.

Tor, Deborah G., "The Islamization of Central Asia in the Sāmānid Era and the Reshaping of the Muslim World," *Bulletin of the School of Oriental and African Studies* 72 (2009), 279–299.

Tor, Deborah G., "A Tale of Two Murders: Power Relations between Caliph and Sultan in the Saljūq Era," *Zeitschrift der Deutschen Morgenländischen Gesellschaft* 159 (2009), 279–297.

Tor, Deborah G., "'Sovereign and Pious': The Religious Life of the Great Seljuq Sultans," in *The Seljuqs*, ed. Lange and Songül, pp. 39–62.

Tülüce, Adem, *Bizans Tarih Yazımında Öteki Selçuklu Kimliği* (Istanbul, 2011).

Turan, Osman, *Selçuklular Tarihi ve Türk-Islâm Medeniyeti*, Türk Kültürünü Araştırma Enstitüsü Yayınları 7 (Istanbul, 1965).

Turan, Osman, *Selçuklular zamanında Türkiye: Siyâsi Tarih Alp Arslan'dan Osman Gazi'ye (1071–1318)*, 3rd ed. (Istanbul, 1993).

Turan, Osman, *Doğu Anadolu Türk Devletleri Tarihi: Saltuklular, Mengücikler, Sökmenliler, Dilmaç Oğulları ve Artuklular'ın siyasî tarih ve medeniyetleri*, 6th ed. (Istanbul, 2001).

Turan, Osman, *Selçuklular ve İslâmiyet*, 6th ed. (Istanbul, 2005).

Tyan, Emile, *Institutions du droit public musulman* (Beirut, 1999).

Tyerman, Christopher, *God's War: A New History of the Crusades* (London, 2007).

Uyumaz, Emine, *Türkiye Selçuklu Devleti'ne Gelen ve Giden Elçiler* (Istanbul, 2011).

Vasiliev, Aleksandr A., *Byzance et les Arabes*, 2.2: *Extraits des sources arabes*, trans. Marius Canard, Corpus Bruxellense Historiae Byzantinae 2.2 (Brussels, 1950).

Vasiliev, Aleksandr A., *Byzance et les Arabes*, 1: *La dynastie d'Amorium (820–867)*, French trans. Henri Grégoire and Marius Canard with the support of C. Nallino and Ernst Honigmann, Corpus Bruxellense Historiae Byzantinae 1 (Brussels, 1954).

Vasiliev, Aleksandr A., *Byzance et les Arabes*, 2.1: *La dynastie macédonienne (867–959)*, French trans. Marius Canard, Corpus Bruxellense Historiae Byzantinae 2.1 (Brussels, 1968).

Väth, Gerhard, *Die Geschichte der artuqidischen Fürstentümer in Syrien und der Ǧazīra'l-Furātīya (496-812/1002-1409)*, Islamkundliche Untersuchungen 212 (Berlin, 1987).

Vionis, Athanasios, Poblome, Jeroen, De Cupere, Bea, and Waelkens, Marc, "A Middle-Byzantine Pottery Assemblage from Sagalassos: Typo-Chronology and Sociocultural Interpretation," *Hesperia: The Journal of the American School of Classical Studies at Athens* 79 (2010), 423–464.

Vlyssidou, Vassiliki N., ed., *The Empire in Crisis (?): Byzantium in the 11th Century (1025–1081)*, Institute for Byzantine Research, International Symposium 11 (Athens, 2003).

Völkl, Martin, *Muslime, Märtyrer, Militia Christi. Identität, Feindbild und Fremdwahrnehmung während der ersten Kreuzzüge*, Wege zur Geschichtswissenschaft (Stuttgart, 2011).

Vryonis, Speros, *The Decline of Medieval Hellenism in Asia Minor and the Process of Islamization from the Eleventh through the Fifteenth Century* (Berkeley, 1971).

Vryonis, Speros, *Byzantine Studies: Essays on the Slavic World and the Eleventh Century* (New Rochelle, 1992).
Vryonis, Speros, "The Decline of Medieval Hellenism in Asia Minor and the Process of Islamization from the Eleventh through the Fifteenth Century. The Book in the Light of Subsequent Scholarship, 1971–98," in *Eastern Approaches*, ed. Eastmond, pp. 1–15.
Vryonis, Speros, "The Eleventh Century: Was There a Crisis in the Empire? The Decline of Quality and Quantity in the Byzantine Armed Forces," in *The Empire in Crisis*, ed. Vlyssidou, pp. 17–43.
Vryonis, Speros, "The Greek and Arabic Sources on the Battle of Mantzikert, A. D. 1071," in idem, *Byzantine Studies*, pp. 125–140.
Vryonis, Speros, "The Greek and the Arabic Sources on the Eight-Day Captivity of the Emperor Romanus IV in the Camp of the Sultan Alp Arslan after the Battle of Mantzikert," in *Novum Millenium*, ed. Sode and Takács, pp. 439–450.
Vryonis, Speros, "A Personal History of the History of the Battle of Mantzikert," in *Η Βυζαντινή Μικρά Ασία (6ος-12ος αι.)*, ed. Lampakis, pp. 225–244.
Weltecke, Dorothea, *Die "Beschreibung der Zeiten" von Mōr Michael dem Großen (1126–1199): Eine Studie zu ihrem historischen und historiographiegeschichtlichen Kontext*, Corpus Scriptorum Christianorum Orientalium, Subsidien 110 (Leuven, 2003).
Wittek, Paul, *The Rise of the Ottoman Empire*, Royal Asiatic Society Monographs 23 (London, 1958).
Yarnley, C. J., "Philaretos Brachamios: Armenian Bandit or Byzantine General," *Revue des Études Arméniennes* 9 (1972), 331–353.
Yıldız, Sara Nur, *Mongol Rule in Thirteenth-Century Seljuk Anatolia: The Politics of Conquest and History Writing, 1243–1282* (Leiden, in print).
Yinanç, Mükrimin Halil, *Türkiye Tarihi, Selçuklular Devri*, 1: *Anadolu'nun Fethi*, Istanbul Üniversitesi Yayınları 240, 2nd ed. (Istanbul, 1944).
Yinanç, Mükrimin Halil, *Türkiye Tarihi, Selçuklular Devri, I. Cilt*, ed. Refet Yinanç, Türk Tarih Kurumu Yayınları IV/A-2-1. Dizi – Sayı 5 (Ankara, 2013).
Yuzbashian, K. N., "L'administration byzantine en Arménie aux Xe-XIe siècles," *Revue des Études Arméniennes* 10 (1973–1974), 139–183.

Index